Introduction to
Learning and Behavior

List of Related Titles

Learning

Sniffy, the Virtual Rat, Pro Version by Tom Alloway, Greg Wilson, Jeff Graham, and Lester Krames.

> Intended for a full course in learning. Contains 40 exercises in operant and classical conditioning.

Sniffy, the Virtual Rat, Lite Version by Tom Alloway, Greg Wilson, Jeff Graham, and Lester Krames.

> Intended as a lighter introduction to learning, for use in introductory psychology and basic courses in learning. Contains 17 exercises in operant and classical conditioning.

For a demo, see http://psychstudy.wadsworth.com/sniffy/

For a demo video of how to incorporate the use of Sniffy in your class, and to listen to students' experiences with Sniffy, call Wadsworth marketing at 1-877-999-2350.

Biological Psychology

Biological Psychology, 7th edition, by James Kalat.

> Includes Active Learner Link, a *free* student CD-ROM with study tools such as quizzes, hands-on activities, video clips, animations, and simulations.

Introduction to Animal Behavior by Roland J. Siiter.

Principles of Neuropsychology by Eric A. Zillmer and Mary V. Spiers.

Introduction to Learning and Behavior

RUSSELL A. POWELL

Grant MacEwan College

DIANE G. SYMBALUK

Grant MacEwan College

SUZANNE E. MACDONALD

York University

Correlations to *Sniffy, the Virtual Rat, Pro Version* supplied by:

MICHAEL R. SNYDER, *University of Alberta*

WADSWORTH

THOMSON LEARNING

Australia • Canada • Mexico • Singapore • Spain • United Kingdom • United States

WADSWORTH

THOMSON LEARNING

Sponsoring Editor: *Marianne Taflinger*
Marketing Team: *Joanne Terhaar, Justine Ferguson, and Tami Strang*
Editorial Assistant: *Stacy Green*
Project Editor: *Mary Anne Shahidi*
Compositor and Production Service: *G&S Typesetters*
Manuscript Editor: *Carolyn Russ*
Permissions Editor: *Sue Ewing*

Interior Design: *Ellen Pettengell*
Cover Design: *Ellen Pettengell*
Cover photos: *Animals Animals* © *Johnny Johnson (main photo); PhotoDisc (inset photo)*
Interior Illustration: *G&S Typesetters*
Print Buyer: *Vena Dyer*
Printing and Binding: *Webcom*

For more information about our products, contact us:
WADSWORTH
10 Davis Drive
Belmont, CA 94002-3098 USA
1-800-423-0563 (Thomson Learning Academic Resource Center)
www.wadsworth.com

Printed in Canada

10 9 8 7 6 5 4 3 2 1

Library of Congress Cataloging-in-Publication Data

Powell, Russell A. [date]
    Introduction to learning and behavior / Russell A. Powell, Diane G. Symbaluk, Suzanne MacDonald.
        p. cm.
    Includes bibliographical references and indexes.
    ISBN 0-534-36585-X (pbk.)
    1. Behaviorism (Psychology) I. Symbaluk, Diane G., 1967– II. MacDonald, Suzanne, 1962– III. Title.
BF199 .P69 2001
150.19′43—dc21   2001035728

To parents, mentors, and students who shaped our behavior so well as to make this book a reality.

Brief Contents

Contents

Preface

"I wouldn't do this to my budgie," a student once muttered following a lecture in which I (the senior author of this text) had discussed the process of reinforcement. She apparently saw the use of reinforcement to alter behavior as manipulative and reprehensible. I can't remember how I responded (probably with something a bit more diplomatic than what follows), but I could have said that she actually does this to her budgie all the time and is simply not aware of it. Moreover, because she's not aware of using reinforcement, she may be using it quite poorly, with the result that she and her budgie are having a less fulfilling relationship than they could be having. Unfortunately, this student's negative reaction to behavioral principles of conditioning is not uncommon, and most instructors who teach such courses can probably recount similar instances. Thus, one goal of this text is to help convince students that conditioning is not some dangerous form of manipulation, but rather a natural process that we do far better to understand and apply wisely than to ignore and apply carelessly.

Another opinion sometimes voiced is that the principles of conditioning, many of which have been derived from research with animals, are largely irrelevant to important aspects of human behavior. After all, how can studies of lever-pressing rats or key-pecking pigeons say anything meaningful about what truly matters to us? This was the very conclusion that I (the senior author again) came to when, as an undergraduate, I first encountered a demonstration of operant conditioning in my introductory psychology class. We were shown a film in which pigeons were taught to peck a little plastic disk (which I later learned is called a "response key") to earn food. The whole endeavor struck me as so completely artificial—not to mention mind-numbingly boring—that I couldn't understand why any psychologist would waste his or her time on it. Little did I know that some years later I would find myself sitting in a pigeon lab, thrilled that I had been given an opportunity to study something so interesting and important! What I had learned in the interim was that (1) you have to be careful what you criticize (fate has a way of making us pay for our arrogance) and (2) many of the principles derived from conditioning experiments with animals are among the most useful principles ever discovered by psychologists. Thus, a second goal of this text is to help convince students that the principles that come out of behavioral research are far from irrelevant, and often have useful and provocative things to say about human behavior.

A third, more immediate reason for writing this text was the authors' continual frustration with finding a text appropriate for the type of course they were teaching and the type of student who enrolled in that course. Most of the available texts emphasized either the application of behavioral principles to human behavior, with little or no discussion of the basic animal research from which those principles were derived, or a discussion of the basic animal research with insufficient mention of how this research may be relevant to humans. Texts that fell into the former category provided students with a wealth of material that obviously pertained to their everyday lives, but too often left them with only a superficial appreciation for behavioral psychology as a discipline. An additional drawback to these texts was that they usually focused on only the most well established principles (such as reinforcement and extinction) and made little mention of less well known but very provocative findings from the animal literature (such activity anorexia, which we discuss in Chapter 11 of this book).

As for those texts that emphasized basic research, students complained that they quickly lost interest when most of the material seemed to have little application to their own lives. Perhaps the real problem, however, was that many of these texts were simply too advanced and/or theoretically oriented for the typical undergraduate who enrolls in an introductory course on learning and behavior. Having had only brief exposure to operant and classical conditioning in a first-year general psychology course, they were still struggling to assimilate the basic principles and soon became lost when exposed to material that moved too rapidly beyond the basics.

The present text was therefore written to provide students with a clear introduction to basic principles of learning and behavior, an introduction that would be both accessible and engaging for those who have had only limited exposure to these principles. Students who later proceed to a higher-level course in the subject matter (one that might utilize, for example, Domjan's *The Principles of Learning and Behavior* or Lieberman's *Learning: Behavior and Cognition* as a text) will then have a solid foundation on which to build. Students who do not proceed to a higher-level course will nevertheless have gained an appreciation for the behavioral perspective and learned much that may be relevant to their everyday lives.

Key Characteristics

The following summarizes some key characteristics of this text:

- *It emphasizes basic principles of learning and behavior rather than theory.* To the extent that theory is discussed, it is either because the theory itself has something meaningful and provocative to say about human behavior (e.g., melioration theory as discussed in Chapter 10) or because a simplified overview of certain theories (e.g., the Rescorla-Wagner theory, as presented in Chapter 5) can help prepare students for a more in-depth discussion of those theories in a higher level course.

- *It attempts to strike an appropriate balance between basic research findings, many of which are derived from animal research, and the application of those findings to important and interesting aspects of human behavior.* Although many texts make this claim, we feel that ours represents a more concerted effort in that direction. Wherever possible, examples from research paradigms with rats or pigeons are juxtaposed with everyday examples with humans. And although some of the applications to humans are highly speculative, they nevertheless represent the type of speculation that behaviorists themselves often engage in and that many students find entertaining and memorable.
- *It is especially innovative in its application of behavioral principles to understanding certain aspects of romantic relationships.* In particular, scattered throughout the text are *Advice for the Lovelorn* columns in which hypothetical students are given behavioral-type advice concerning their relationship difficulties. Personal relationships are, of course, a key concern for many students, and they are often fascinated by the notion that basic principles of behavior may be helpful in understanding and resolving problematic relationships. These columns have thus proven to be an effective way to maintain student interest in the material, enhance their grasp of certain concepts, and provide them with a sense of what it means to think like a behaviorist. (Students are of course given due warning that the advice in these columns is quite speculative and not to be taken too seriously.)
- *It contains numerous pedagogical features designed to facilitate studying and enhance understanding of the material.* These features are described later in the section on learning aids.
- *It contains many interesting and thought-provoking topics not normally found in textbooks on learning and behavior.* Many of these topics are presented in special boxed inserts entitled *And Furthermore*, which are intended to expand on material presented in the preceding section.

Following is a brief overview of the subject matter covered in each chapter, along with a sampling of distinctive material.

Brief Overview and Distinctive Content

Chapter 1

- This chapter presents an overview of the historical antecedents to behaviorism and a description of the five main schools of behaviorism. The intention is to show that behaviorism is not some monolithic entity founded by Watson and propagated by Skinner, but is a rich and varied network of ideas and assumptions, each of which has contributed much to our modern-day understanding of behavior.

- We include biographical information on Watson and Skinner, who, as prototypical behaviorists, have often been subjects of considerable criticism and misinformation. We argue that their approaches are neither as irrational (in the case of Watson) nor as extreme (in the case of Skinner) as many people believe.
- Particularly distinctive is the proposal that Skinner's radical behaviorist perspective is similar to Bandura's notion of reciprocal determinism, the difference being that Skinner strongly emphasizes the environmental determinants of behavior.

Chapter 2

- This chapter outlines various methods and procedures used in behavioral research.
- We describe several types of single-subject designs, to which undergraduates typically have little or no exposure.
- We discuss ethical issues concerning the use of animals in behavioral research, the conclusion being that students need to be fully informed to properly address this issue.
- We present evidence indicating that a moderate level of food deprivation, far from being inhumane, may actually mimic an animal's normal (and healthy) functioning in its natural environment.

Chapter 3

- This chapter introduces the concept of elicited (or reflexive) behavior. We describe simple forms of learning and present a basic outline of classical conditioning.
- We pay particular attention to the opponent process theory of emotion and its relevance for understanding such phenomena as thrill-seeking behavior (of particular interest given the increasing popularity of high-risk activities among young people) and "revictimization" (in which some victims of abusive relationships paradoxically seem to seek out such relationships).

Chapter 4

- We discuss basic processes of classical conditioning along with various extensions of and limitations to conditioning.
- The section on discrimination training includes an overview of Pavlov's experimental neurosis paradigm, how the symptoms produced varied according to the dog's temperament, and how this finding helped pioneer modern-day research into the biological basis of personality.

Chapter 5

- This chapter discusses theories and practical applications of classical conditioning. Considerable space is devoted to outlining the role of classical conditioning in the development and treatment of phobic behavior (which is also touched upon in later chapters).
- We argue that, for several reasons, Little Albert probably recovered quite well following Watson and Raynor's attempt to condition in him a fear of furry animals.
- We list several variables that can affect the development of phobic conditioning, including individual differences in temperament and the processes of US revaluation and incubation.
- The chapter closes with a discussion of how classical conditioning may be implicated in Gulf War Syndrome.

Chapter 6

- We introduce processes of operant conditioning and provide students with a clear description of the three-term contingency and the four types of consequences.
- We give a description of learned industriousness and also discuss the lively debate over the effect of extrinsic rewards on intrinsic motivation. This discussion includes an intriguing anecdote from Skinner's writings on the use of positive reinforcement to instill an appreciation for abstract art.

Chapter 7

- We discuss various schedules of reinforcement along with basic theories of reinforcement.
- We include a description of the beneficial effects of noncontingent reinforcement on reducing the incidence of unwanted behavior. We note that this finding seems to provide empirical support for the effects of what humanistic psychologists have termed "unconditional positive regard."
- This chapter's *Advice for the Lovelorn* column speculates on the relevance of behavioral bliss point theory for understanding why some relationships are less than blissful.

Chapter 8

- The focus in this chapter is on processes of extinction and stimulus control.
- We review evidence concerning the effectiveness of extinction procedures for reducing bedtime tantrums in young children.
- There is also a discussion of the parallelism between behavioral contrast effects and *St. Neots' margin,* an existentialist notion that holds that certain difficulties can sometimes infuse our lives with a sense of meaning.

- We present practical applications of stimulus control, especially as related to improving sleep habits and study behavior (two issues of concern to many students).
- The chapter ends with a description of Guthrie's theory of learning, including some of Guthrie's own advice for improving study habits.

Chapter 9

- This chapter details the effects of aversive stimulation on behavior.
- We include an analysis of the repressed memory/false memory debate from a cognitive-behavioral perspective.
- We also include a description of Stampfl's procedure for producing reliable one-trial avoidance conditioning in rats. His research indicates that effort reduction through early avoidance of the feared stimulus may be a critical variable in the maintenance of phobic behavior.
- We describe Masserman's procedure for inducing experimental neurosis through exposure to unpredictable aversive events, along with the procedure's implications for understanding the development of posttraumatic stress disorder.
- The chapter concludes with a presentation of how behavioral principles may account for the development of dissociative identity disorder, either as an outcome of childhood trauma (that is, as a posttraumatic disorder) or as an "iatrogenic" disorder that has been inadvertently shaped in therapy.

Chapter 10

- We address the issues of choice, matching, and self-control, and include a clear exposition of the basic matching law and deviations from matching.
- We discuss melioration theory, along with the implication that the easy availability of highly reinforcing events can sometimes reduce (not increase) the overall amount of reinforcement in one's life.
- We discuss extensively issues of self-control and impulsiveness, most notably within the framework of the Ainslie–Rachlin model.

Chapter 11

- This chapter outlines the role of biological dispositions in learning.
- We include a description of how processes similar to those involved in sign-tracking may play a role in facilitating the development of drug and alcohol abuse.
- We give a comprehensive description of adjunctive behavior and its relevance to understanding compulsive and addictive behavior patterns in humans. We propose that adjunctive processes might also serve as a type of naturalistic self-control device that helps facilitate the attainment of large delayed rewards.

- The chapter closes with an extensive discussion of activity anorexia in rats, and its implications for understanding, treating, and preventing the development of anorexia nervosa in humans.

Chapter 12

- This chapter covers observational learning, language (especially language training in animals), and rule-governed behavior.
- We include an intriguing description of a personal encounter by one of the authors with Kanzi, considered by many to be the most proficient of the language-trained chimps.
- We analyze the notion of "willpower" as a form of "Say-Do correspondence." We draw supportive examples for this analysis from the writings of William James and the autobiography of Mahatma Gandhi.

Instructor's Manual

The instructor's manual includes a comprehensive test bank containing 80 or more multiple-choice items per chapter (over 1000 total). A large number of these items are conceptual in nature. They are organized by textbook headings and subheadings. A small portion of the test bank items are multiple-choice versions of Quick Quiz and Chapter Test items, thus providing extra incentive for students to work through this material in the text. The instructor's manual also contains answers to all of the study questions found at the end of each chapter (with each answer keyed to the page number within the chapter where this material can be found). Finally, for those instructors who choose to adopt *Sniffy, the Virtual Rat* for their students, the manual contains a set of Sniffy assignments that can be given to students to complete and hand in. (See further discussion of Sniffy on page xxi.)

Computerized Test Bank

To ease the task of creating and generating tests, an electronic version of the test bank is available in either PC or Macintosh configuration. The program is user-friendly and allows instructors to insert their own questions. The test bank also contains a full listing of the end-of-chapter study questions, enabling instructors to easily generate a sample of these items for weekly quizzes or for inclusion as short-answer items on midterm and final exams.

Learning Aids

This text contains many pedagogical features designed to facilitate students' reading and comprehension of the material. These include the following:

- *Quick Quizzes.* Scattered throughout each chapter are numerous fill-in-the-blank quizzes. The purpose of these quizzes is to help students actively work with the material as they read it. Although one early reviewer commented that such frequent quizzing might frustrate students by too often interrupting their reading, actual use of the material in class revealed quite the opposite. Students uniformly commented that the quizzes were extremely beneficial in helping them engage and process the information. They especially appreciated quizzes that were embedded within sections that they perceived as particularly technical, because the quizzes broke the material up into short chunks that they were better able to assimilate. Students therefore demanded more quizzes, not fewer, and the authors duly complied.

- *Study Questions.* A focused set of about 15–20 study questions is listed at the end of each chapter. These study questions cover the most basic concepts discussed in that chapter. Because these questions are quite focused and require a relatively short answer—varying from a sentence to a paragraph in length—students are likely to incorporate them into their studying (as opposed to the standard, comprehensive list of learning objectives, which many students simply ignore). Students can be further motivated to answer the study questions by informing them that some of the questions may appear as short-answer items on exams. A random sample of these questions can also be used for weekly chapter tests.

- *Concept Reviews.* Each chapter is followed by a concept review, which lists all key terms and definitions in the chapter.

- *Chapter Tests.* Each chapter ends with a chapter test, consisting mostly of fill-in-the-blank items. This test provides comprehensive coverage of the material presented in the chapter. It differs from the Quick Quizzes in that more items are of a conceptual, rather than factual, nature, thereby encouraging students to think more deeply about the material. These test items are numbered in random order, which allows students to immediately look up the answer to any particular question without having to worry about inadvertently seeing the answer to the next question.

- *Opening Vignettes.* Each chapter begins with a chapter outline followed by either a quotation or a vignette related to the material presented in that chapter. The vignettes usually consist of a short, fictional scenario that illustrates a particular concept. The exact concept involved is not immediately revealed, however, thus encouraging students to actively ponder how the material they are reading may be related to the scenario. (An explanation of the concept each scenario is intended to illustrate can be found in the instructor's manual.)

Website Materials and Alternative Course Delivery

Accompanying this text is a well-designed website that contains additional information, useful exercises, and interesting links to enhance the students' learning experience. This material will prove especially useful for instructors who are considering offering a learning and behavior course (especially a web-based course) in a nonlecture, alternative delivery format. In fact, this text, with its many pedagogical features (including *Sniffy* exercises), was explicitly designed to function as a student-friendly, independent learning tool, and two of the authors are themselves using it for nonlecture, computer-based course delivery. Materials and procedural information for delivering such courses can be made available to adoptees of this text. (E-mail the senior author for further information.)

Sniffy, The Virtual Rat, Pro Version: An Available Option

Sniffy, the Virtual Rat, Pro Version gives every school the opportunity to provide students with hands-on experience in applying, either at home or in school, the principles of operant and classical conditioning. Sniffy is a computer-generated rat that can be taught to press a lever to earn food, a protocol that is then used to demonstrate many aspects of both operant and classical conditioning. Students purchasing Sniffy receive a laboratory manual with instructions, and a hybrid CD-ROM that operates on Mac OS Version 7.5 or higher and Windows 95 and 98. Over 40 Sniffy exercises teach students about a variety of operant and classical conditioning procedures. The operant phenomena covered include shaping, schedules of reinforcement, generalization, discrimination, extinction, and spontaneous recovery. The classical conditioning phenomena covered include acquisition and extinction, the effects of CS/US intensity, stimulus pre-exposure effects, blocking, overshadowing, and overexpectation effects, among others.

Students enjoy working with Sniffy and report that these exercises greatly enhance their understanding of the basic principles. We do not, of course, propose that Sniffy can fully substitute for the actual experience of working with live animals. Unfortunately, for various reasons, most institutions are no longer able to offer this valuable opportunity to their undergraduates. Sniffy was created precisely to fill this void. Additionally, some schools use Sniffy as a warm-up before allowing students to work with real animals.

Since our reviewers asked that we put Sniffy correlations in the text, we have placed a Sniffy icon and exercise number on each page where appropriate concepts are discussed. At the end of the chapter is a complete listing of these Sniffy exercises as well as any instructions the student may need to successfully complete them. In addition to these correlations, we have also provided a set of hand-in Sniffy assignments in the instructor's manual. Exercises suitable for smaller classes (e.g., 30 students) are included, as well as assignments that can be used effectively with larger classes (e.g., 150 students). Both the correlations and the hand-in assignments were created by Michael Snyder, who uses *Sniffy Pro* with over 160 students a term at the University of Alberta.

More information about *Sniffy, the Virtual Rat, Pro Version* is available on our website at http://psychology.wadsworth.com/sniffy/ or on a 6-minute videotape that can be obtained by calling Wadsworth at 1-877-999-2350. Sniffy's creators discuss on the tape how they use Sniffy in their classes, and students describe their experiences working with Sniffy.

InfoTrac® College Edition: An Available Option

InfoTrac® College Edition is a fully searchable online university library that includes full-text articles from hundreds of scholarly and popular publications. Hot-linked, expertly indexed, and ready to use, InfoTrac College Edition is updated daily and contains articles published within the last four years. Students and faculty have four months' access—24 hours a day, 7 days a week—to this online library if the teacher chooses to package InfoTrac College Edition with this book. Among the large number of publications available to the student are many containing articles relevant to the subject matter in this text. These include: *Psychological Record, American Journal of Psychology, Annual Review of Psychology, British Journal of Psychology, Ecological Monographs, Ecology, Journal of Experimental Education, Journal of General Psychology, Journal of Social Psychology, Quarterly Review of Biology, American Scientist,* and *Science.*

Acknowledgments

We thank Dr. Dee, Ally McBeal, and all the other people (real and fictional) who inspired the *Advice to the Lovelorn* inserts. Beyond these happy folks, we thank Michael Snyder of the University of Alberta, who provided the Sniffy correlations; Sniffy's fathers, Tom Alloway, Jeff Graham, Lester Krames, and Greg Wilson of the University of Toronto–Erindale; and Leslie Krongold, Technology Project Manager, who made sure that Sniffy was student-proof and could not be broken.

We also thank the following reviewers for their helpful comments and suggestions: John Caruso, University of Massachusetts–Dartmouth; David Diamond, University of South Florida; Kendra Jeffcoat, San Diego Mesa College; Nancy Karlin, University of Northern Colorado; Mike Knight, University of Central Oklahoma; Adrienne Lee, New Mexico State University; Dorothea Lerman, Louisiana State University; David Pittenger, The University of Tennessee at Chattanooga; Jeff Rudski, Muhlenberg College; Sherry Serdikoff, James Madison University; Toru Shimizu, University of Southern Florida; James Spencer, West Virginia State College; Catherine Wehlburg, Stephens College; and Cedric Williams, University of Virginia.

In addition, we thank the great people at the Wadsworth Group—including Vicki Knight, Mary Anne Shahidi, Jennifer Wilkinson, Lisa Weber, Sue

Ewing, Stacy Green, and Margaret Parks, as well as Danny Barcinas in the mailroom, who makes it all happen—for their support and hard work. A very special thanks to Marianne Taflinger, acquisitions editor, whose experience and expertise played an invaluable role in seeing this project through to completion. Thanks also to the fine people at G&S Typesetters, especially Cindy Brown and Alison Rainey, who worked so intensely with us down the homestretch.

Last but not least, we owe a debt of gratitude to Monica Hardy, who so strongly encouraged us to undertake this project.

Russ Powell
Diane Symbaluk
Suzanne MacDonald

About the Authors

Russell A. Powell

Russ Powell completed his Ph.D. in psychology under the stimulating supervision of the late Frank Epling and his research partner, David Pierce, at the University of Alberta, and now serves as a senior faculty member in the Department of Social Sciences at Grant MacEwan College, in Edmonton, Alberta. He has a wide range of academic experiences, the influence of which can be seen throughout this text. For many years he has taught a variety of courses, including social psychology, experimental psychology, and theories of personality. More importantly, he has taught learning and behavior for over 15 years using several different textbooks and formats. He was also the first instructor at Grant MacEwan College to develop and offer university-level courses in a nontraditional, alternative delivery format, and now serves as the manager for all social science offerings through "computer-managed learning." In keeping with this diverse teaching background, Russ has also conducted research and published articles on such varied topics as operant conditioning, sleep paralysis nightmares, and Freud criticism. Most recently, he has been involved in the controversy over the nature and causes of dissociative identity disorder, coauthoring articles that have appeared in the *Canadian Journal of Psychiatry* (Powell & Gee, 1999) and *Psychological Bulletin* (Lilienfeld et al., 1999).

Diane G. Symbaluk

Diane Symbaluk received her Ph.D. in sociology from the University of Alberta in 1997, with a specialization in criminology and social psychology. Much of her training, however, was in behavior analysis under the mentorship of David Pierce, Judy Cameron, and the late Frank Epling. She is currently a faculty member in the Department of Social Sciences at Grant MacEwan

College, in Edmonton, Alberta, and serves as chair of the college's research ethics review committee. Diane's student-centered approach to teaching is evident in her many publications, which include five study guides and a teaching resource manual as well as web-course tools and interactive websites. Her research background includes the investigation of self-control and impulsiveness in sex offenders and of activity anorexia in male athletes, and the effect of social modeling and self-efficacy on pain perception and tolerance. Her research publications include articles appearing in *Personality and Social Psychology Bulletin* (Symbaluk et al., 1997) and *Teaching of Psychology* (Symbaluk & Cameron, 1998).

Suzanne E. MacDonald

Suzanne MacDonald launched her academic career in the laboratory, completing her Ph.D. on pigeon memory at the University of Alberta under the supervision of Douglas Grant. After doing postdoctoral work at the University of British Columbia, she moved to Toronto, Ontario, as a professor in the Department of Psychology at York University. Her current research interests focus on animal thinking, especially in primates, and she has published extensively in this area. On any given day, however, she can be found working with rhinos, cheetahs, or elephants at the Toronto Zoo, where she serves as the zoo's resident behaviorist. Suzanne and her graduate students conduct research focused on the reproduction and conservation of endangered species and on environmental enrichment for zoo animals. In addition, Suzanne hosts a regular segment on animal behavior ("Animal Talk") for the Discovery Channel. Suzanne's teaching interests lie in animal learning and behavior and in comparative cognition. She is also an avid experimenter in the use of technology in teaching, and has taught over the Internet for the past five years. This interest has led to her current position as the director of the Office of Technology Enhanced Learning at York University.

Introduction

CHAPTER OUTLINE

A review of Gerald Zuriff's *Behaviorism: A Conceptual Reconstruction* (1985) . . . begins with a story about two behaviorists. They make love and then one of them says, "That was fine for you. How was it for me?" The reviewer, P. N. Johnson-Laird, insists that [this story has a ring of truth about it]. Behaviorists are not supposed to have feelings, or at least to admit that they have them. Of the many ways in which behaviorism has been misunderstood for so many years, that is perhaps the commonest. . . . [In fact] how people feel is often as important as what they do.

B. F. SKINNER, 1989, p. 3

Of all contemporary psychologists, B. F. Skinner is perhaps the most honored and the most maligned, the most widely recognized and the most misrepresented, the most cited and the most misunderstood.

A. CHARLES CATANIA, 1988, p. 3

Imagine that while flipping through a new textbook, you see that it spends a lot of time discussing experiments with rats and pigeons. Pretty boring, huh? But how about if what you learn in that textbook might help you improve your study habits, understand your eating disorder, and overcome your fear of spiders? In fact, what if it even offers you advice on how to improve your romantic relationships or how to be an effective parent? Hmm, perhaps not so boring after all. Well, this book might be just such a book. Let us consider a few of these claims in more detail.

> **Improving study habits.** Many of our behaviors, including study behaviors, are strongly influenced by their consequences. Chapter 6 discusses the basic processes by which consequences influence behavior, while Chapter 10 demonstrates how these processes can be directly applied to the development of self-control.
>
> **Understanding eating disorders.** Contrary to popular belief, eating disorders are not necessarily indicative of a psychological problem. For example, through a simple manipulation of a rat's feeding schedule, the rat can be induced to stop eating and engage in extreme levels of exercise. Chapter 11 discusses how similar processes might account for the development of a clinical disorder in humans known as anorexia nervosa.
>
> **Overcoming fears and phobias.** Whether you fear spiders, snakes, or exams, this textbook will provide you with insight into how these fears develop. You will learn how the principles of classical conditioning and negative reinforcement underlie many fears and anxieties, and how these same principles suggest effective means for treating problematic symptoms.
>
> **Improving relationships with others.** In this text, we often use relationship issues to illustrate basic principles of learning and behavior. As well,

many chapters contain *Advice for the Lovelorn* columns, in which relationship problems are discussed from a behavioral perspective. Although the advice given is necessarily speculative—and as such should not be taken too seriously—these columns highlight the manner in which behavioral principles have the potential to enrich our understanding of human relationships.

Raising children. Our students have sometimes commented that "no one should be allowed to have children until they have taken a course like this." While this is admittedly an exaggeration, it is nevertheless the case that many of the principles discussed in this text are directly applicable to many common parenting problems.

In general, a proper grounding in the basic principles of learning and behavior will help you understand why you behave the way you do and how your behavior can often be changed for the better. This knowledge can make you a better parent; it can make you a better teacher; and it can make you a better friend or partner. In a very real sense, the principles described in this text have the potential to enrich both your life and the lives of others—despite the fact that many of these principles have been derived from research with rats and pigeons!

But let us begin with a brief outline of what this textbook is about. Simply put, *behavior* **is any activity of the organism that can be either directly or indirectly observed**, while *learning* **is a relatively permanent change in behavior that results from some type of experience.** For example, reading this text is a behavior (as are all the blinking, breathing, and salivating that you are doing at the same time), while any lasting change in your behavior as a result of reading this text (e.g., a change in your ability to speak knowledgeably about the subject matter) is an example of learning. Note that the change in behavior does not have to be immediate, and in some circumstances the change might not become evident until long after the experience has occurred.

This text emphasizes two fundamental processes of learning: classical and operant conditioning. Although these will be discussed in more detail later, a brief description of each will be useful at this point. At its most basic level, classical conditioning is the process by which certain inborn, involuntary behaviors, such as sneezing in response to pollen or salivating in response to the taste of food, come to be produced in new situations. A familiar example of classical conditioning, often presented in introductory psychology texts, is that of a dog learning to salivate in response to a bell that has been paired with food. This process can be diagrammed as follows:

Bell: Food → *Salivation*
Bell → *Salivation*

(See "Notation for Conditioning Diagrams" in the And Furthermore box.)

As you will learn in this text, classical conditioning underlies many of our emotional responses and contributes to the development of our likes and

And Furthermore

Notation for Conditioning Diagrams

Throughout this text, you will encounter many diagrams of conditioning procedures. In these diagrams, a colon separating two events indicates that the two events occur in sequence. For example, the term "Bell: Food" means that the sound of a bell is followed by the presentation of food. An arrow between two events also indicates that the two events occur in sequence, but with an emphasis on the fact that the first event *produces or causes* the second. For example, "Food → *Salivation*" means that the presentation of food causes the dog to salivate. Thus, with respect to a standard classical conditioning procedure, the term:

Bell: Food → *Salivation*

means that the bell is presented just before the food, and the food in turn causes salivation. This is followed by:

Bell → *Salivation*

which indicates that the presentation of the bell itself now causes the dog to salivate (because of the bell's previous association with food). Note that, for the sake of clarity, we will usually italicize the behavior that is being conditioned (which is often called the "target behavior"). In writing out your notes, however, you may find it easier to indicate the target behavior by underlining it. For example:

Bell: Food → Salivation
Bell → Salivation

dislikes. It can even lead to the development of debilitating fears and powerful feelings of sexual attraction.

In contrast to classical conditioning, operant conditioning involves the strengthening or weakening of a behavior as a result of its consequences. The behaviors involved are usually those typically regarded as voluntary or goal-directed. A common experimental example is that of a rat that has learned to press a lever to obtain food. This can be diagrammed as follows:

Lever press → **Food pellet**
The effect: **Likelihood of lever pressing increases**

Because the lever press produced a food pellet, the rat is subsequently more likely to press the lever again. In other words, the consequence of the behavior has served to strengthen future occurrences of that behavior. Many of the behaviors that concern us each day are motivated by such consequences: We see a doctor to obtain a prescription, we go to a restaurant for a meal, and we study diligently to achieve a passing grade. Because of its importance for humans, operant conditioning is the type of learning most strongly emphasized in this text.

Although the text concentrates on classical and operant conditioning, other types of behavioral processes will also be discussed. For example, in *observational learning*, observation of a model's behavior facilitates the development of similar behavior in an observer. Certain types of nonlearned, inherited behavior patterns, such as *fixed action patterns*, will also be discussed, as will the effect of inherited dispositions in either facilitating or inhibiting certain types of learning. Let us begin, however, with a brief overview of the historical background to the study of learning and behavior.

Throughout each chapter, you will frequently encounter fill-in-the-blank quizzes such as this. Students report that these quizzes greatly facilitate the task of reading by breaking the material up into manageable chunks and encouraging them to be actively involved with the reading. Note that for many of the items, we have provided helpful hints, usually in the form of the initial letter or two of the word that should be inserted into the blank. But we have not provided an answer key for these quizzes, partly because most of the answers can be easily found in the text and partly because a certain amount of uncertainty can actually facilitate the process of learning (Schmidt & Bjork, 1992).

1. The term _____ refers to any activity of an organism that can be either directly or indirectly _____, while the term _____ refers to a relatively p_____ change in what an organism does as a result of some type of ex _____.

2. In _____ conditioning, behaviors that we typically regard as (voluntary/involuntary) _____ come to be elicited in new situations.

3. In _____ conditioning, a behavior produces some type of consequence, which strengthens or weakens its occurrence. Such behaviors are typically those that we perceive as (voluntary/involuntary) _____ or g_____-directed.

4. Feeling anxious as you enter a dentist's office is an example of a behavior that has most likely been learned through _____ conditioning.

5. Speaking with a loud voice in a noisy environment so that others will be able to hear you is an example of a behavior that has most likely been acquired through _____ conditioning.

6. According to the notational system to be used in this text, the term "A: B" means that event A (produces/is followed by) _____ event B, while the term "X → Y" means that event X (produces/is followed by) _____ event Y.

Historical Background

Just as it is impossible to outline all of the experiences that have made you who you are, it is impossible to outline all of the historical events that have contributed to the modern-day study of learning and behavior. Some particularly important contributions, however, are outlined below.

Aristotle: Empiricism and the Laws of Association

Aristotle was a Greek philosopher who lived between 384 and 322 B.C. Aristotle's teacher, Plato, believed that everything we know is inborn (which he conceived of as "residing in our soul"); thus, learning is simply a process of inner reflection to uncover the knowledge that already exists within. Aristotle, however, disagreed with Plato and argued that knowledge is not inborn but instead is acquired through experience.

Aristotle's disagreement with Plato is an early example of the classic debate of nativism versus empiricism or nature versus nurture. **The *nativist* (*nature*) perspective assumes that a person's characteristics are largely inborn, while the *empiricist* (*nurture*) perspective assumes that a person's characteristics are mostly learned**. Plato is thus an early example of a nativist, while Aristotle is an early example of an empiricist.

Aristotle also suggested that ideas come to be connected or associated with each other via four laws of association (well, actually three, but he also hinted at a fourth that later philosophers expanded upon). These are:

1. **The Law of Similarity.** According to this law, **events that are similar to each other are readily associated.** For example, cars and trucks are readily associated because they are similar in appearance (wheels, doors, headlights, etc.) and function (both are used to carry passengers and materials along roadways). These similarities enable us to learn to view cars and trucks as instances of a larger category of objects known as automobiles.
2. **The Law of Contrast.** Just as events that are similar to each other are readily associated, so too **events that are opposite from each other are readily associated**. For example, on a word association test, the word "black" often brings to mind the word "white" and the word "tall" often brings to mind the word "short." Likewise, the sight of my unwashed car readily reminds me of how nice it would look if I washed it, and an evening of work might remind me of how enjoyable it would be to spend the evening not working.
3. **The Law of Contiguity.** According to this law, **events that occur in close proximity to each other in time or space are readily associated with each other** ("contiguity" means closeness). For example, a child quickly learns to associate thunder and lightning because the sound of thunder often immediately follows the flash of lightning. Thunder and

lightning are also usually perceived as coming from the same direction, meaning that there is a certain degree of spatial proximity between them. Imagine how difficult it would be to associate thunder and lightning if the thunder occurred several minutes after the lightning flash and was perceived to have arrived from an opposite direction.

4. **The Law of Frequency.** In addition to the three preceding laws, Aristotle also mentioned a supplement to the law of contiguity, which holds that **the more frequently two items occur together, the more strongly they are associated**. You will more strongly associate a friend with a certain perfume the more frequently you smell that perfume upon meeting her. Likewise, you will more strongly associate a term (such as the "law of frequency") with its definition the more frequently you practice saying that definition whenever you see the term (as when using flash cards to help memorize basic terminology).

Aristotle's laws of association are not merely of historical interest. As you will read later, the laws of contiguity and frequency are still considered important aspects of learning.

QUICK QUIZ

1. The (empiricist/nativist) _____ position, as exemplified by the Greek philosopher _____, emphasizes the role of heredity over learning.

2. The _____ position, as exemplified by the Greek philosopher _____, emphasizes the role of learning over heredity.

3. Nativist is to (nature/nurture) _____ as empiricist is to (nature/nurture) _____.

4. The law of _____ states that we readily associate events that are opposite to each other, while the law of _____ states that we readily associate events that occur in close proximity to each other.

5. According to the law of _____, we readily associate events that resemble each other. According to the law of _____, the more often two events occur together, the stronger the association.

6. According to the law of _____, animals that have fur, four legs, and a tail and can bark should all quickly be perceived as belonging to the same species.

7. The fact that the words "full" and "empty" are readily associated with each other is an example of the law of _____.

8. According to the law of _____, the more often one practices a particular move in wrestling, the more likely one is to perform that move in a real match.

9. After encountering a snake in her garage, Lisa is now quite nervous each time she enters the garage. This is an example of the law of _____.

René Descartes
(1596–1650)

Descartes: Mind–Body Dualism and the Reflex

René Descartes (1596–1650) is the French philosopher who wrote the famous line "I think, therefore I am." Fortunately for psychology, this was not his only contribution. In Descartes' time, many people assumed that human behavior was governed entirely by free will or "reason." Descartes disputed this notion and proposed a dualistic model of human nature. On the one hand, he claimed, we have a body that functions like a machine and produces involuntary, reflexive behaviors in response to external stimulation (such as sneezing in response to dust). On the other hand, we have a mind that has free will and produces behaviors that we regard as voluntary (such as choosing what to eat for dinner). Thus, Descartes' notion of *mind-body dualism* **holds that some human behaviors are reflexes that are automatically elicited by external stimulation, while other behaviors are freely chosen and controlled by the mind.** Descartes also believed that only humans possess such a self-directing mind, while the behavior of nonhuman animals is entirely reflexive.

Descartes' dualistic view of human nature was a major step in the scientific study of learning and behavior in that it suggested that at least some behaviors—namely, reflexive behaviors—are mechanistic and could therefore be scientifically investigated. It also suggested that the study of animal behavior might yield useful information about the reflexive aspects of human behavior.

The British Empiricists

Although Descartes believed that the human mind has free will, he also assumed, like Plato, that some of the ideas contained within it (e.g., the concepts of time and space) are inborn. This notion was disputed by a group of British philosophers, known as the *British empiricists*, who maintained that almost all knowledge is a function of experience. For example, John Locke (1632–1704) proposed that a newborn's mind is a *blank slate* (in Latin, *tabula rasa*) upon which environmental experiences are written. The British empiricists also believed that the conscious mind is composed of a finite set of basic elements (specific colors, sounds, smells, etc.) that are combined through the principles of association into complex sensations and thought patterns—a sort of psychological version of the notion that all physical matter consists of various combinations of the basic elements.

1. Descartes's dualistic model proposed that human behavior has two aspects: an inv_____ aspect that functions like a machine, and a v_____ aspect governed by f_____ w_____. By contrast, the behavior of animals was believed to be entirely (voluntary/ involuntary) _____.

2. The British _____, such as John _____, maintained that knowledge was largely a function of experience and that the mind of a newborn infant is a (in Latin) t_____ r_____ (which means _____ _____).

3. They also perceived that the mind is composed of a finite set of basic _____ that are then combined through the principles of _____ to form our conscious experiences.

Structuralism: The Experimental Study of Consciousness

The British empiricists did not conduct any experiments to test the notion that the mind consists of various combinations of basic elements; their conclusions were instead based entirely upon logical reasoning and the subjective examination of their own conscious experience. Realizing the deficiencies in this approach, the German philosopher Wilhelm Wundt (1832–1920) proposed using the scientific method to investigate the issue. This approach was strongly promoted by an American student of Wundt, Edward Titchener (1867–1927), and became known as structuralism. ***Structuralism* holds that it is possible to determine the structure of the mind by identifying the basic elements of which it is composed.**

Structuralists made great use of the method of ***introspection,* in which the subject in an experiment attempts to accurately describe his or her conscious thoughts, emotions, and sensory experiences.** To get a feel for how difficult this is, try to describe your conscious experience as you listen to the ticking of a clock (and just saying "I'm bored" does not cut it). One thing you might report is that the ticks seem to have a certain rhythm, with a series of two or three clicks being clustered together. You might also report a slight feeling of tension (is it pleasant or unpleasant?) that builds or decreases during each series of ticks. As you can see, an accurate report of what we introspectively observe can be quite difficult.

Although this approach to psychology died out by the early 1900s (for reasons described below), its emphasis on systematic observation helped establish psychology as a scientific discipline. More importantly, its extreme emphasis on conscious experience as the proper subject matter for psychology laid the groundwork for the later establishment of a more objective approach to psychology known as behaviorism. A partial step in this direction was the school of psychology known as functionalism.

Edward B. Titchener
(1867–1927)

Functionalism: The Study of the Adaptive Mind

William James
(1842–1910)

William James (1842–1910), often regarded as the founder of American psychology, helped establish the approach to psychology known as functionalism. *Functionalism* **holds that the mind evolved to help us adapt to the world around us and that the focus of psychology should be the study of those adaptive processes.** This notion was partially derived from Darwin's theory of evolution, which held that the adaptive characteristics that enable a species to survive and propagate tend to increase in frequency across generations while nonadaptive characteristics tend to die out. Therefore, characteristics that are highly typical of a species, such as the characteristic of consciousness in humans, must have some type of adaptive value.

Thus, rather than study the structure of the mind, functionalists believed that psychologists should study the adaptive significance of the mind. Learning, which is essentially an adaptive process, was therefore a topic of great interest to the functionalists. Additionally, although functionalists still made use of introspection and still emphasized the analysis of conscious experience (in this manner, being similar to the structuralists), they were not averse to the study of animal behavior. They believed, like Darwin, that humans evolved from other animals and that much of what we learn from other animals may be of direct relevance to humans. Not surprisingly, two of the most important figures in the early history of behaviorism, E. B. Thorndike (discussed in Chapter 6) and John B. Watson (discussed below), were both students of functionalist psychologists.

QUICK QUIZ

1. The (functionalist/structuralist) _____ approach held that the goal of psychology should be to identify the basic elements of the mind. The primary research method used for accomplishing this was the method of i_____.

2. Psychologists who adopted the (functionalist/structuralist) _____ approach to psychology emphasized the adaptive processes of the mind and were thus very interested in the study of learning.

3. The functionalist approach was strongly influenced by Darwin's theory of _____. As such, these psychologists viewed animal research as (relevant/irrelevant) _____ to the study of human behavior.

4. The functionalists were quite similar to the structuralists in that they still emphasized the study of c_____ experience. In doing so they often used the method of i_____.

5. William James was a (functionalist/structuralist) _____, while Edward Titchener was a _____.

Behaviorism: The Study of Observable Behavior

In 1913, a flamboyant young psychologist by the name of John B. Watson published a paper entitled *Psychology as the Behaviorist Views It.* In it, he lamented the lack of progress achieved by experimental psychologists up to that time, particularly the lack of findings that had any practical significance. A major difficulty, Watson believed, was the then-current emphasis on the study of conscious experience, especially as promoted by the structuralists. In particular, the method of introspection was proving to be highly unreliable. Researchers frequently failed to replicate each other's findings, which often led to bitter squabbles. Watson mockingly described the types of arguments that often ensued.

John B. Watson
(1878–1958)

> If you fail to reproduce my findings, it is not due to some fault in your apparatus or in the control of your stimulus, but it is due to the fact that your introspection is untrained. . . . If you can't observe 3–9 states of clearness in attention, your introspection is poor. If, on the other hand, a feeling seems reasonably clear to you, your introspection is again faulty. You are seeing too much. Feelings are never clear. (Watson, 1913, p. 163)

The difficulty, of course, is that we are unable to directly observe another person's thoughts and feelings. We therefore have to make an *inference* that the person's verbal reports about those thoughts and feelings are accurate.[1] It is also the case that many of the questions being tackled by the structuralists were essentially unanswerable, such as whether sound has the quality of "extension in space" and whether there is a difference in "texture" between an imagined perception of an object and the actual perception of the object (Watson, 1913, p. 164). In a very real sense, experimental psychology seemed to be drowning in a sea of vaguely perceived images and difficult-to-describe mental events. Moreover, the notion that the proper subject matter of psychology was the study of consciousness was so strongly entrenched that it affected even those who studied animal behavior. As Watson exclaimed,

---

[1] An inference is a supposition or guess that is based on logical deduction rather than observation. For example, if you describe to me a dream that you had last night, your report is based on your direct observation of a subjective experience. But if I accept that description (based on the fact that there seems to be no reason for you to lie about it), I am making an inference that your report is accurate. Now suppose I interpret the dream as indicating that you have some unresolved, unconscious conflict, and you accept that interpretation as true. We are now both making an inference that this unconscious conflict exists, since neither you nor I have directly observed it. Needless to say, inferences about unconscious processes are even more problematic than inferences about conscious processes, since not even the person in whom the unconscious process exists is able to directly observe it.

> On this view, after having determined our animal's ability to learn, the simplicity or complexity of its methods of learning, the effect of past habit upon present response . . . we should still feel that the task is unfinished and that the results are worthless, until we can interpret them by analogy in the light of consciousness. [In other words,] we feel forced to say something about the possible mental processes of the animal. (Watson, 1913, p. 160)

Watson reasoned that the only solution to this dilemma was to make psychology a purely "objective science," a science based solely upon the study of directly observable behavior and the environmental events that surround it. All reference to internal processes, such as thoughts and feelings that could not be objectively measured by an outside observer, were to be stricken from analysis. By objectifying psychology in this manner, Watson hoped that psychology could then join the ranks of the *natural sciences*—biology, chemistry, and physics—that had traditionally emphasized the study of observable phenomena. In Watson's now-classic words,

> Psychology as the behaviorist views it is a purely objective experimental branch of natural science. Its theoretical goal is the prediction and control of behavior. Introspection forms no essential part of its methods, nor is the scientific value of its data dependent upon the readiness with which they lend themselves to interpretation in terms of consciousness. (Watson, 1913, p. 154)

Thus, as originally defined by Watson, **behaviorism is a natural science approach to psychology that emphasizes the study of environmental influences on observable behavior.**

Watson also believed strongly in the value of animal research. In keeping with his functionalist background, he believed that the principles that govern the behavior of nonhuman species might also be relevant to the behavior of humans. Thus, traditional behavioral research is often conducted using nonhuman animals, primarily rats and pigeons. As many of the examples in this text will illustrate, the results obtained from such research are often highly applicable to human behavior.

Behavioral psychology also adheres to the **law of parsimony, which holds that simpler explanations for a phenomenon are generally preferable to more complex explanations.** One version of this law—which strongly influenced Watson—is known as *Morgan's Canon* (canon means "principle"). Conway Lloyd Morgan was a 19th century British physiologist/psychologist who became distressed about the manner in which many scientists of his era were attributing human characteristics to nonhuman animals. Morgan (1894) argued that, whenever possible, one should interpret an animal's behavior in terms of lower, more primitive processes (e.g., reflex or habit) rather than higher, more mentalistic processes (e.g., decision or imagination). Watson essentially took this one step further by arguing that psychologists should avoid interpreting even human behavior in terms of mentalistic processes.

And Furthermore

John B. Watson: Behaviorism's Controversial Founder

John B. Watson was a charismatic and aggressive individual and as such was perhaps ideally suited for lifting psychology out of the mentalistic quagmire in which it had become immersed. Unfortunately, those same traits led to a life of conflict. The most infamous story about Watson concerns the manner in which he was forced to resign from his university position. One commonly told version has it that he and a female student were caught conducting intimate experiments on human sexual responding, and he was forced to resign over the resultant scandal. There is, however, little evidence for this story, and the real events appear to be as follows.

In 1920, at the height of his academic career, Watson began an affair with Rosalie Rayner, a graduate student whose family was both well connected and powerful. Catching wind of the affair, Watson's wife stole into Rosalie's room during a social visit to the Rayners, and stole the love letters that Watson had written to his young lover. Watson's wife then filed for divorce and used the letters to help win a lucrative settlement. Meanwhile, the university told Watson to end his affair with Rosalie. Watson refused and, when given an ultimatum, immediately tendered his resignation. Soon after, news of Watson's divorce and of the affair found its way into the national media, with one of Watson's love letters even appearing in several newspapers. In the space of a few months, his academic career was ruined.

Cast adrift, Watson married Rosalie and obtained a job with a New York advertising firm. In his new position, he promoted the application of conditioning principles to advertising. He also continued to publish books and magazine articles promoting his behavioristic views. In fact, Watson was very much the pop psychologist of his era. Unfortunately, as with pop psychology today, some of his advice was based more on personal opinion than well-established principles. For example, Watson believed that children should be trained to act like adults and even recommended giving them a handshake, rather than a hug or a kiss, when sending them to bed! In fact, the only time he ever showed affection to his own children was when his wife Rosalie died in 1935. Teary eyed, Watson lightly put his arms around his children as he told them that their mother had died, then never again mentioned her name. Not surprisingly, his children retained bitter memories of their upbringing, and one son later committed suicide.

It has been suggested that Watson had an underlying fear of emotions, as though fearful of losing control (Buckley, 1989). Indeed, in his love relationships (and he had numerous affairs throughout his life), he was extremely impulsive and amorous; yet, in a group setting, he would reportedly flee the room when the discussion turned to emotional issues. Thus, although Watson's proposal to banish thoughts and feelings from psychology helped establish it as a more objective science, it may also have reflected some of his personal difficulties.

In his later years, Watson became something of a recluse, living in the country and raising animals. He had always been fond of animals—sometimes claiming that he preferred their company to that of humans—which may account for his early interest in animal research. He died in 1958 at the age of 80. (For an interesting biography of Watson, see Buckley, 1989.)

It is worth noting that Watson was not the first psychologist to recommend a more objective, natural science approach to psychology. He reflected a growing sentiment among many researchers at that time that such a move was necessary. Watson's arguments, however, were the most clearly stated and therefore had a strong effect. Thus, while his 1913 paper (which later became known as the "behaviorist manifesto") did not have an immediate impact, its influence slowly grew until, by the 1920s, the behaviorist revolution was well under way. (For a brief discussion of Watson's personal life, see the And Furthermore box entitled "John B. Watson: Behaviorism's Controversial Founder.")

QUICK QUIZ

1. Watson noted that a major problem with the method of _____ was that the results obtained were often unreliable.

2. A basic problem with relying on someone's report about his or her thoughts and feelings is that we are making a(n) _____ that the report is accurate. This term is defined in the footnote as a supposition or guess based on I_____ d_____ rather than direct _____.

3. The notion that the proper subject matter of psychology was the study of consciousness was so strong that even those who studied _____ behavior felt compelled to make inferences about possible mental processes in their subjects.

4. Watson argued that psychology needed to become a n_____ science (like biology, chemistry, and physics) based solely upon the study of directly o_____ events.

5. According to the law of p_____, the (simpler/more complex) _____ explanation is generally the preferable explanation.

6. One version of the above law, known as _____ _____, holds that it is preferable to interpret animal behavior in terms of lower, more primitive processes, such as reflex or habit, than higher, more mentalistic processes, such as reasoning.

Five Schools of Behaviorism

Many people believe that behaviorism is some monolithic entity, with Watson's views being the same views held by other behaviorists. In fact, there are several schools of behaviorism, each of which is based on a somewhat different set of assumptions about how best to study behavior. In this section, we describe five of these schools, beginning with Watson's original brand of behaviorism, which is sometimes referred to as methodological behaviorism.

Watson's Methodological Behaviorism

One of the most extreme versions of behaviorism is the version originally proposed by Watson. As previously noted, Watson believed that psychologists should study only publicly observable behavior. All reference to internal events—that is, events that can only be subjectively perceived (such as our inner thoughts and feelings) or that are assumed to exist on an unconscious level (e.g., a mother's unconscious hatred of her unwanted child)—were to be stricken from scientific analysis (see Figure 1.1).

Thus, *methodological behaviorism* **asserts that, for methodological reasons, psychologists should study only those behaviors that can be directly observed.** Subjectively perceived activities, such as thinking, are methodologically too difficult to assess to be of much use in a scientific analysis of behavior. Such activities can be included for analysis only if they can, in some way, be directly measured. Watson, for example, hypothesized that thinking involved minute movements of the vocal cords in the larynx—and enjoyed goading his critics by referring to his own thoughts as "laryngeal activity" (Buckley, 1989). If this were true, and if such movements could be precisely measured, then the act of thinking could be subjected to scientific analysis. (As it turns out, laryngeal activity is not a reliable measure of thinking.)

It is important to emphasize that Watson's behavioristic proposal to ignore thoughts and feelings in scientific analysis was not an attempt to dehumanize people or pretend that thoughts and feelings do not exist; rather, it was a logical response to a crisis. If the discipline of psychology was to survive, it would need to break free from the extreme mentalism of the time and adopt a much different perspective. Watson's behavioral call-to-arms, though extreme, accomplished just that.

Nevertheless, it must be conceded that Watson's specific view of learning was rather mechanistic. Drawing from Pavlov's work on classical conditioning, he came to believe that all behavior, both animal and human, is essentially reflexive. He also believed that learning involves the development of a simple connection between an environmental event (the "stimulus") and a specific

FIGURE 1.1 In methodological behaviorism, internal events, such as consciously perceived thoughts and feelings and unconscious drives and motives, are excluded from the analysis of behavior. Instead, one studies the direct relationship between changes in the environment and changes in observable behavior.

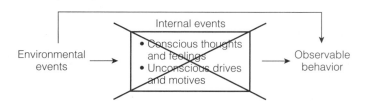

behavior (the "response"). Watson's theory of learning is therefore regarded as a type of *S-R theory*, **in which learning is believed to involve the establishment of a connection between a specific stimulus (S) and a specific response (R)**. Complex behavior is therefore presumed to involve extremely long chains of these S-R connections.

Over time, Watson also became something of an extremist regarding the nature-nurture issue. In his original 1913 article, he had emphasized the influence of *both* heredity and environment on behavior. In fact, he was one of the first individuals to systematically study inborn behavior patterns in animals (he spent several strenuous summers engaged in field research with a type of seabird). Later, however, following extensive observations of human infants, he came to the conclusion that humans inherit only a few fundamental reflexes along with three basic emotions (love, rage, and fear). Everything else, he believed, is learned. This led Watson, in 1930, to make one of his most famous claims.

> Give me a dozen healthy infants, well-formed, and my own specified world to bring them up in and I'll guarantee to take any one at random and train him to become any type of specialist I might select—doctor, lawyer, artist, merchant-chief, and, yes, even beggar-man and thief, regardless of his talents, penchants, tendencies, abilities, vocations, and race of his ancestors. (p. 104)

Unfortunately, many textbooks quote only this passage and omit the very next sentence, which reads "I am going beyond my facts, but so have the advocates of the contrary and they have been doing it for many thousands of years" (p. 104). And this was precisely Watson's point: The supposition that a person's abilities are largely inherited has been strongly promoted throughout history (and has often been used to justify acts of discrimination and racism). Watson was one of the first to issue a strong challenge to this assumption, arguing instead that there is at least as much evidence suggesting that human abilities are mostly learned. For this reason, Watson's behavioral model became quite popular among the reformists of his day who were attempting to combat racism.

As we previously noted, many people mistakenly equate behaviorism with Watson's rather extreme version. In fact, few behaviorists were this extreme; instead, they developed approaches that were considerably more moderate. One of the most influential of these was Hull's neobehaviorism, which we discuss next.[2]

---

[2] While reading about these different schools of behaviorism, one should bear in mind that behavioristic assumptions are just that—assumptions. They do not necessarily reflect some type of absolute truth, nor do they necessarily reflect the private beliefs of the scientist. Thus, one can adopt these assumptions as a useful way for looking at behavior without abandoning other assumptions, such as certain religious beliefs about the existence of free will. After all, even if free will does exist, the environment still has a major impact on our behavior, and it would be foolish for us not to learn the principles by which the environment influences us. In this regard, the first author recalls a seminary student he once taught who could always be seen carrying around his two favorite textbooks—his behavior analysis text and the Bible.

1. Watson's brand of behaviorism is known as _____ behaviorism.

2. According to this type of behaviorism, psychologists should study only those behaviors that can be _____ _____.

3. Watson believed that all reference to _____ events should be eliminated from the study of behavior.

4. Watson's brand of behaviorism is a(n) ___-___ theory in that it hypothesizes that learning involves the formation of a direct connection between a _____ and a _____.

5. In his 1913 article on behaviorism, Watson emphasized the role of both h_____ and e_____ in the development of human behavior. In his later theorizing, however, he downplayed the role of _____.

6. In his later theorizing, Watson proposed that humans inherit (many/few) _____ basic reflexes, along with three basic emotions: _____, _____, and _____.

Hull's Neobehaviorism

One of the first major challenges to methodological behaviorism came from Clark Hull (1884–1952), who claimed that Watson's rejection of unobservable events was scientifically unsound. Hull noted that both physicists and chemists make inferences about events that have never been directly observed but which can nevertheless be *operationalized* (that is, defined in such a way that they can be measured). For example, gravity cannot be directly observed, but its effect on falling objects can be precisely measured. Hull believed that it might likewise be useful for psychologists to infer the existence of internal events that might *mediate* (draw a connection) between the environment and behavior.

The mediating events that Hull incorporated into his theory consisted largely of physiological-type reactions, for example, a "hunger drive" that can be operationalized as number of hours of food deprivation. Such mediating events are formally called *intervening variables*, meaning that they intervene between a cause (such as food deprivation) and an effect (such as speed of running toward food). Thus, Hull's *neobehaviorism* **is a brand of behaviorism that utilizes intervening variables, in the form of hypothesized physiological processes, to help explain behavior** (see Figure 1.2).

It is important to note that Hull's use of intervening variables did not mean that he advocated a return to mentalism. Like Watson, he strongly opposed the use of

Clark L. Hull
(1884–1952)

And Furthermore

Deliberate Practice and Expert Performance

Watson's extreme emphasis on the importance of nurture over nature in determining human behavior is often viewed with a great deal of skepticism. This is especially the case when it comes to behaviors that are indicative of exceptional ability. Most people, including many psychologists (e.g., Gardner, 1993), assume that, unless a person is born with a certain amount of talent, there are limits in how far he or she will be able to progress in a particular endeavor. Indeed, the notion that a Mozart, Babe Ruth, or Albert Einstein is to a large extent born, and not made, is part of the mystique that surrounds these individuals.

But consider the following:

- Expert performers in almost all fields of endeavor, ranging from music to athletics to chess, require a minimum of 10 years of intensive training before achieving a high level of performance. Even Mozart, who started composing at age 4, did not compose world-class music until his late teens. (Mozart's father was also a professional musician who published the first book on violin instruction and provided his children with intensive musical training from an early age.)
- As an experiment, a Hungarian educator, Polgar, set out to systematically train his daughters to become expert chess players. All three daughters have achieved high rankings in international chess, and one daughter, Judit, became the youngest grand master ever at 15 years of age.
- The superlative abilities shown by experts are almost always specific to their field of endeavor. For example, chess experts have the ability to memorize the exact positions of all the chess pieces in a game after only a few seconds' glance at the chessboard. But they perform no better than non–chess players at memorizing chess pieces randomly distributed around the board in a non–game pattern. As well, their performance on standard memory tests is typically no better than that of the average person.
- Almost all of the remarkable feats displayed by *savants*—individuals of low intellectual ability who nevertheless possess some remarkable skill—have been taught to normal individuals. For example, the ability of some savants to name the day of the week for any arbitrary date (e.g., "What day of the week was June 30, 1854?") has been duplicated by ordinary college students after only a few weeks' training.
- Excellent musicians often have perfect pitch, which many people assume is something that a person is born with. Researchers, however, have been able to systematically train this ability in some adults. More importantly, people who display perfect pitch have almost always had considerable exposure to music at an early age. This suggests that, as with language development, there may be a critical period in childhood during which perfect pitch can be more readily acquired.

On the basis of findings such as these, Ericsson, Krampe, and Tesch-Römer (1993; see also Ericsson & Charness, 1994) have argued that the most critical factor in determining expert performance is not innate ability, but deliberate practice. Deliberate practice is practice that is not inherently enjoyable and does not involve mere repetition; it instead involves intense concentration and considerable effort with a view toward improving one's performance. More than any other variable, the accumulated amount of deliberate practice in an activity is strongly predictive of an individual's level of performance.

For example, Ericsson et al. (1993) compared student violinists who were the "best" with those who were merely "good" and with those who were in training to become music teachers. The best students had accumulated about 7400 hours of deliberate practice by the age of 18 compared to 5300 hours for the good students and 3400 hours for the teachers-in-training. Such differences account for why elite performers so often report having begun their training at an early age. An early start allows one to begin accumulating the huge number of practice hours needed to outperform others. Those who begin at a later age are simply unable to catch up.

Because deliberate practice is so effortful, the amount that can be tolerated each day is necessarily limited. For this reason, elite performers often practice about 4 hours per day. Ericsson et al. (1993), for example, found that the best violin students engaged in solitary practice (which was judged to be the most important type of practice) approximately 3.5 hours per day, spread out across 2 to 3 sessions, each session lasting an average of 80 minutes. Note that this did not include time spent receiving instruction, giving performances, or playing for enjoyment. The students also devoted about 3.5 hours a day to rest and recreation, and obtained more than average amounts of sleep.

Top-level performers in intellectual pursuits display similar characteristics. Novelists typically write for about 3 to 4 hours each day, usually in the morning. Eminent scientists likewise write for a few hours each morning—the writing of articles arguably being the most important activity determining their success—and then devote the rest of the day to other duties. Skinner is especially instructive in this regard. In his later life, he would rise at midnight and write for 1 hour, then rise again at 5:00 and write for another 2 hours. The remainder of the morning was devoted to correspondence and other professional tasks, while much of the afternoon was devoted to recreational activities such as tinkering in his workshop and listening to music. He deliberately resisted any urge to engage in serious writing at other times of the day, feeling that this often resulted in poor-quality writing the next morning. The limited amount of writing he did each day was more than compensated for by the consistency with which he wrote, resulting in a steady stream of influential articles and books throughout his career (Bjork, 1993; Skinner, 1987).

Of course, Ericsson et al. (1993) do not completely discount the role of heredity in expert performance. Heredity might well affect the extent to which one becomes interested in an endeavor, as well as one's ability to endure the years of hard work needed to become an elite performer. Nevertheless, the obvious importance of deliberate practice suggests that we should not be too quick to discount our ability to acquire a certain skill. While many of us might not have the desire, time, or resources to become elite athletes, excellent musicians, or famous scientists, this does not rule out the possibility of becoming better tennis players, learning how to play guitar, or significantly improving our math skills. After all, the best evidence available suggests that it is largely a matter of practice.

FIGURE 1.2 In Hull's neobehaviorism, theorists make use of intervening variables, in the form of hypothesized physiological processes, to help explain the relationship between the environment and behavior.

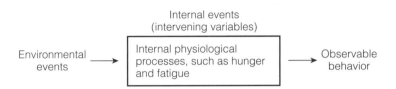

introspection as a scientific tool, believing that subjective experiences are too vague and unreliable to be of much use. Thus, whether the organism actually experienced a feeling of hunger was of no concern to him. What did concern him was whether the *concept of hunger*, as defined in some measurable way (such as number of hours of food deprivation), was scientifically useful and led to testable hypotheses.

Hull's theory was also a pure S-R theory in that it assumed that learning consists of the establishment of connections between specific stimuli and specific responses. Thus, like Watson, he viewed behavior in a very mechanistic fashion. Lest this seem dehumanizing, recognize that it is not far removed from some modern-day cognitive approaches, which view humans as analogous to computers that process bits of information from the environment (input) to produce responses (output). This is actually quite similar to Hull's model of behavior: Specific stimuli (input) yield specific responses (output), with certain internal events mediating the process. In fact, modern-day cognitive psychology can even be considered an outgrowth of Hull's neobehaviorism.[3]

Hull was probably the most influential experimental psychologist of the 1940s and 1950s. Unfortunately, it turned out that major aspects of his theory (which are beyond the scope of this text) were very difficult to test. As well, the theory was highly mathematical and grew increasingly complex as equations were expanded and modified. Many of these modifications were forced upon Hull by his critics, the most famous of whom was Edward C. Tolman. (For a major overview of Hull's theory, as well as to gain a sense of its complexity, see Hull, 1943.)

---

[3] Interestingly, people seem less critical of the cognitive information-processing approach to psychology, which draws an analogy between humans and computers, than they are of the traditional behavioral approach, which draws an analogy between humans and such animals as rats. Perhaps this is because we are impressed by the ability of computers to perform certain human-like tasks (e.g., play chess), and we are insulted by the notion that humans and rats have anything in common. Yet, outside their specialized abilities, computers are quite inferior to rats. Imagine, for example, that a man, a rat, and a computer are washed up on a deserted island. To the extent that the man emulates the rat, he will likely survive; to the extent that he emulates the computer, he will sit on the beach and rot. Rats have a marvelous ability to learn and adapt; present-day computers do not. Fortunately for us, humans are far more rat-like than computer-like.

1. Hull believed that it might be useful to incorporate internal events into one's theorizing so long as they can be op_____ by defining them in such a way that they can be measured.

2. In Hull's approach, the internal events he included were of hypothetical ph_____ processes.

3. Such internal events are called i_____ variables in that they are presumed to m_____ between the environment and behavior.

Tolman's Cognitive Behaviorism

Hull's S-R theory of learning is often categorized as a "molecular" theory because it viewed behavior as consisting of a long chain of specific responses connected to specific stimuli. Edward Tolman (1886–1959) disagreed with this approach and believed that it would be more useful to analyze behavior on a "molar" (i.e., broader) level. For example, he felt that we can understand a rat's behavior in a maze more accurately as a goal-directed attempt to obtain food than as a long chain of discrete stimulus-response connections that, in machine-like fashion, lead to food (e.g., Tolman, 1932). This molar approach to learning is similar to the gestalt approach to perception, from which Tolman drew much of his inspiration. To the gestalt psychologists, perception is not simply the summation of different bits of conscious experience but is instead a "holistic" process resulting in an organized, coherent perceptual experience. We perceive a house as more than just a combination of bricks and boards; it is bricks and boards plus something more. As the famous gestalt saying goes, "The whole is more than the sum of the parts." Similarly, for Tolman, behavior was more than just a chain of discrete responses attached to discrete stimuli. It is instead an overall pattern of behavior directed toward particular outcomes, and it can be properly analyzed only on that level.

Although Tolman disagreed with much of Hull's theorizing, he did agree that intervening variables may be useful in a theory of learning (in fact, it was Tolman who first suggested this). However, while Hull's intervening variables were physiological-type processes like hunger and fatigue, Tolman's were considerably more mentalistic. The Tolmanian rat, as well as the Tolmanian person, was not simply motivated by drives and habits, but also had "expectations" and "hypotheses." Thus, Tolman's *cognitive behaviorism* **(sometimes called "purposive behaviorism") utilizes intervening variables, usually in the form of hypothesized cognitive processes, to help explain behavior** (see Figure 1.3).

Tolman's (1948) most famous intervening variable is the *cognitive map,* **which is a mental representation of one's spatial surroundings**. Tolman and Honzik (1930) obtained evidence for this concept in their "latent learning" experiment. This experiment was conducted in an attempt

Edward C. Tolman
(1886–1959)

FIGURE 1.3 In Tolman's cognitive behaviorism, theorists make use of intervening variables, in the form of hypothesized cognitive processes, to help explain the relationship between environment and behavior.

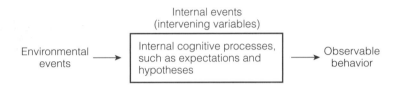

to disprove Hull's notion that behavior must be rewarded in order for learning to take place; that is, in the absence of some type of reward, nothing can be learned. To test this notion, Tolman and Honzik trained three groups of rats on a complex maze task (see Figure 1.4). The rats in a continuous-reward group always found food when they reached the goal box, while the rats in the two other groups found no food when they reached the goal box (they were simply removed from the maze and then fed several hours later). Training proceeded at the rate of one trial per day for 10 consecutive days. As expected, the rewarded group learned to run quickly to the goal box, while the two non-rewarded groups took much longer to do so.

Following this initial phase of training, on day 11 of the study the rats in one of the nonrewarded groups also began receiving food when they reached the goal box. According to Hull, the rats in that group should only then have started to learn their way through the maze, which would have been demonstrated by a gradual improvement in their performance. What Tolman and Honzik found instead was a dramatic improvement in the rats' performance on the very next trial. In fact, on day 12 of the study, the newly rewarded group slightly outperformed the group that had been receiving a reward from the outset (see Figure 1.5).

Tolman interpreted these results as indicating that the initially nonrewarded rats had in fact learned the maze during the first ten trials of the experiment, and that they had learned it at least as well as the group that had been receiving food. In other words, while wandering around the maze, they had developed a "cognitive map" of the maze, which only later became apparent when they were suddenly motivated by the possibility of obtaining food in the goal box. Thus, this experiment is regarded as a classic demonstration of *latent learning*, **in which learning occurs despite the absence of any observable demonstration of learning and only becomes apparent under a different set of conditions.** The experiment also demonstrates the distinction between *learning and performance*, since learning was apparently taking place even when the subjects showed no evidence of such learning in their performance at that time.

Although Tolman believed that it was theoretically useful to incorporate cognitive variables, he remained, in many other ways, a standard behaviorist.

FIGURE 1.4 Maze used by Tolman and Honzik (1930) in their study of latent learning. (Adapted from Tolman, 1948.)

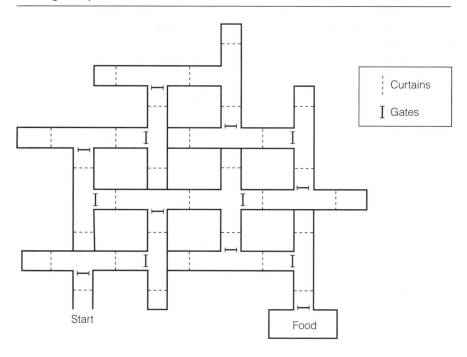

For example, like Hull and Watson, he believed that introspective reports of thoughts and feelings are so unreliable as to be of little scientific value. He maintained that his own theoretical inferences about cognitive processes were based entirely on direct observations of behavior and were thus objectively based. Tolman once even apologized for the "shameful necessity" of having to discuss conscious experience in a text he was writing (Tolman, 1932)—a reflection perhaps of how frustrated psychologists had been by the old introspectionist approach. Like other behaviorists, Tolman also believed strongly in the usefulness of animal research for discovering basic processes of learning, and almost all of his research was conducted with rats.

Much of Tolman's research was directly aimed at refuting Hull's theory of learning. Hull was able, in increasingly complex ways, to modify his theory sufficiently to account for many of Tolman's findings. As a result, Tolman's cognitive approach never achieved the same popularity as Hull's neobehavioral approach. With the advent of the cognitive revolution in psychology, however, many of Tolman's research methods and concepts have been adopted by modern researchers. Cognitive behaviorism is now a flourishing field of study, and the study of cognitive processes in nonhuman animals is specifically known as "animal cognition."

FIGURE 1.5 Errors made by the different groups of rats in Tolman and Honzik's (1930) latent learning experiment. The vertical axis represents the average number of wrong turns the rats in each group made before reaching the goal box. Group NR are those rats that never received a reward for reaching the goal box. Group R are those rats that always received a reward for reaching the goal box. Group NR-R received no reward for the first 10 days of the study, then began receiving a reward on day 11. Note that this group was run for a few days longer than the other two groups to see if there would be any additional change in their performance. (Adapted from Tolman & Honzik, 1930; see also "How to Read Graphs" in the And Furthermore box.)

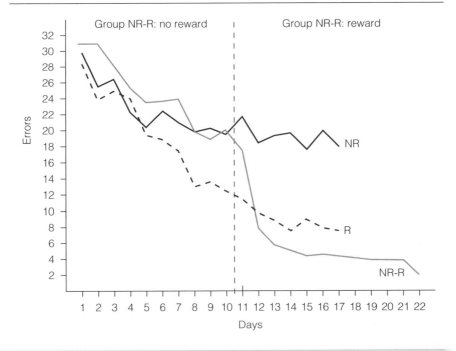

And Furthermore

How to Read Graphs

A graph is a concise way of conveying information. It has two axes: the horizontal or x-axis, which is formally called the abscissa, and the vertical or y-axis, which is formally called the ordinate. The vertical axis is usually a measure of the target behavior in which we are interested, in this case the number of errors the rats made while running through a maze. The horizontal axis usually indicates some aspect of the experimental manipulation, in this case, the days on which the rats were run through the maze. The broken line between days 10 and 11 indicates that there was a change in conditions at this time, which is described by the labels on each side of the broken line (namely, that group NR-R switched from receiving no reward to receiving a reward). The three lines within the graph therefore indicate the average number of errors made by each group of rats for each day of the experiment.

© Ed Arno/*Science* 80

1. Tolman's approach is known as _____ behaviorism because it utilizes mentalistic concepts, such as "expectations," to explain behavior. This approach is also sometimes called p_____ behaviorism.

2. A _____ _____ is an internal representation of one's surroundings.

3. The experiment by Tolman and Honzik (1930) is considered a demonstration of _____ learning, in which learning appears to take place in the absence of any reward. The experiment also demonstrates the distinction between learning and _____.

4. Tolman believed that introspectively observed thoughts and feelings are (useless/useful) _____ in the analysis of behavior. As well, almost all of Tolman's research was conducted using _____ as subjects.

Albert Bandura
(b. 1925)

Bandura's Social Learning Theory

If Tolman's use of cognitive concepts seems to represent a partial return to mentalism, Albert Bandura's social learning theory is an even stronger step in that direction. The roots of social learning theory can be partially traced to Hull's neobehaviorism, in that Bandura had considerable exposure to Hullian theorists during his graduate training. As well, the term "social learning theory" was first used by followers of Hull who were attempting to apply Hullian concepts to human social behavior, particularly the process of imitation (Miller & Dollard, 1941). Bandura was very much interested in imitation, which he referred to as observational learning, and he eventually became the dominant researcher in the field. His most famous investigations concern the influence of observational learning on aggressive behavior (Bandura, 1973).

Although Bandura's interests were partially influenced by Hullian psychologists, his interpretation of the learning process is more closely aligned with that of Tolman. Like Tolman, Bandura focuses upon broad behavior patterns (i.e., he uses a "molar" approach), and emphasizes the distinction between learning and performance. He also gives internal events, such as expectations, a primary role in the learning process. Bandura's approach differs from that of Tolman, however, in that these internal events are viewed as more than just theoretically useful; they are instead viewed as actual events occurring within us that strongly influence our behavior. Additionally, these internal events include *self-referent thoughts* about our abilities and accomplishments, a distinctly human form of cognition that Bandura believes has significant impact on our behavior. This means that, unlike the other behaviorists we have discussed, Bandura does not dismiss the value of introspectively observed, subjective experience in explaining behavior. Thus, **social learning theory is a behavioral approach that strongly emphasizes the importance of observational learning and cognitive variables in explaining human behavior** (Bandura, 1977, 1997).[4]

Social learning theory also has a distinct view of determinism (the notion that each behavior has a cause). More specifically, Bandura has proposed the concept of *reciprocal determinism*, **in which environmental events, observable behavior, and "person variables" (which include thoughts and feelings) are seen as having a reciprocal influence on each other** (see Figure 1.6). Reciprocal determinism can be contrasted with the determinis-

---

[4] Bandura (e.g., 1997) has more recently referred to this approach as "social-cognitive" theory, so as to emphasize the importance of cognitive variables.

FIGURE 1.6 Bandura's model of reciprocal determinism, in which observable behavior, environmental events, and internal events are all viewed as interacting with each other.

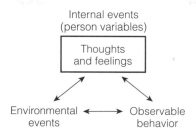

tic models proposed by other behaviorists in which internal events, if they are included, simply mediate between the environment and behavior (Environment → Internal events → Behavior).

As an illustration of reciprocal determinism, imagine that you are out on a date with someone to whom you are very attracted. Trying to impress this individual, you start the evening off by telling a joke (thus, an aspect of your environment—namely, the person you are dating—has affected your behavior). Unfortunately, your off-color sense of humor is not appreciated, and your date reacts to the joke with a look of horror (your behavior has affected your environment). The look of horror in turn elicits feelings of anxiety (your environment has affected your feelings), which then causes you to stammer as you speak (your feelings have affected your behavior). Observing yourself stammer then leads you to conclude that your date must think you are an idiot (your behavior has affected your beliefs), which in turn leads you to interpret your date's smile as a smile of pity (your beliefs have affected the environment—or, more precisely, the environment as you perceive it). Needless to say, the evening turns out to be a complete disaster, with the environment, behavior, and person variables (thoughts and feelings) all interacting to conspire against you. (No wonder life is rough!)

Social learning theory has stimulated a lot of research, particularly in the area of observational learning. It has also stimulated the development of *cognitive-behavior therapy*, in which psychological disorders are treated by altering both environmental variables and cognitive processes. For example, a cognitive-behavioral treatment for an irrational fear of spiders might involve some type of safe exposure to spiders (an environmental manipulation) along with instructions to replace fearful thoughts with certain types of calming thoughts (a cognitive manipulation). Cognitive-behavioral treatments have become very popular in recent years. Social learning theory has thus become a dominant force in behaviorism and is rivaled by only one other school of thought—B. F. Skinner's radical behaviorism.

1. Bandura's _____ _____ theory emphasizes the importance of o_____ learning and c_____ variables.

2. The concept of _____ _____ proposes that three variables: e_____, b_____, and p_____ variables, all interact with each other.

3. Bandura's work has influenced the development of a type of therapy known as _____-_____ therapy, in which an attempt is made to change behavior by altering both environmental and _____ factors.

Skinner's Radical Behaviorism

From Watson to Bandura, we see a steady increase in the use of internal events to help explain behavior. Not everyone has agreed with this trend. Burrhus Frederick Skinner, the most famous behaviorist of the last half of the 20th century, argued for a return to a stricter form of behaviorism. Skinner's version of behaviorism, known as *radical behaviorism*, **emphasizes the influence of the environment on overt behavior, rejects the use of internal events to explain behavior, and views thoughts and feelings as behaviors that themselves need to be explained.** Thus, unlike Watson's methodological behaviorism, radical behaviorism does not completely reject the inclusion of internal events in a science of behavior; it merely rejects the use of these events as explanations for behavior (Skinner, 1953, 1974). We will explain this notion more fully in the following section.

Skinner's View of Internal Events

Burrhus Frederick Skinner
(1904–1990)

Skinner viewed internal events, such as sensing, thinking, and feeling, as "covert" or private behaviors that are subject to the same laws of learning as "overt" or publicly observable behaviors. Thus, internal events can be included in an analysis of behavior, but only as behaviors that themselves need to be explained. For example, whereas a social learning theorist might say that a student studies because she *expects* that studying will result in a high mark, Skinner would say that both the act of studying and any thoughts about achieving a high mark by studying are the result of some experience, such as a history of doing well on exams when the student did study.

Skinner was loath to consider internal events as explanations for behavior for several reasons.

First, he agreed with Watson's concern that, since we do not have direct access to the internal events of others, we must rely on their verbal reports of such events. Our assessments of internal thoughts and feelings thus are often unreliable. Skinner further noted that such unreliability is to be expected, given the manner in which people learn to label their internal events. More specifically, young children need to be taught by their caretakers to describe their internal experiences. Because these caretakers (usually parents) cannot directly observe internal events in their children, they must infer their occurrence from the children's observable behaviors.

Consider, for example, the task of teaching a young boy to correctly label the feeling of pain. The parent must wait until the child is displaying some observable behavior that typically accompanies pain, such as crying in response to a stubbed toe. On the basis of this behavior, the parent then infers that the child is experiencing pain and says something like, "My, your toe must really hurt!" After a few experiences like this, the child will himself begin using the word "hurt" to describe what he is feeling in such circumstances.

Pain is probably one of the easier feelings to teach, given that the observable behaviors accompanying it are usually quite distinct (although even here, there may be considerable variability across individuals in the intensity of sensation required before something is called painful). Consider how much more difficult it is to teach a child to accurately describe subtle emotions such as contentment or discomfort, for which the observable behaviors are often much less distinct. Because the parents have less reliable information on which to base their inferences about such states, the labels they provide to the child are likely to be only crude approximations of the child's actual feelings. This means that the labels adults use for describing their feelings may also be crude approximations of what they actually feel. For this reason, Skinner was uninterested in using a person's description of an internal emotional state as an explanation for behavior; he was, however, quite interested in the means by which people come to label their internal experiences.

A second problem with the use of internal events to explain behavior is that it is often difficult to determine the actual relationship of thoughts and feelings to behavior. Do the thoughts and feelings precede the behavior, follow the behavior, or occur collaterally with (at the same time as) the behavior? Take, for example, the act of providing help in an emergency. Do you provide help because you feel concern for the person involved (Figure 1.7a)? Or do you provide help and feel concerned at the same time, with no necessary link between the two (Figure 1.7b)? After all, people often take action in an emergency quite quickly, without reflecting upon how they feel.

Or do your feelings of concern for someone sometimes arise after you have tried to help them (Figure 1.7c)? Lest this notion seem rather strange to you, consider that people's feelings about an event can often be altered by simply manipulating their behavior toward the event. For example, people can often be induced to change their opinion about a certain issue—for example,

FIGURE 1.7 Three ways in which feelings of concern can be associated with the behavior of helping.

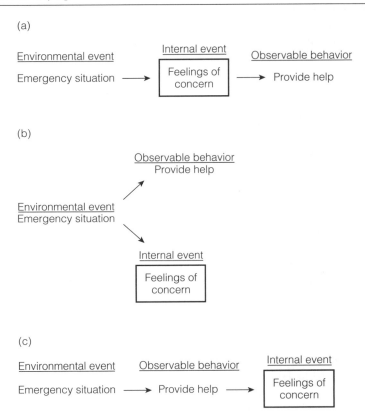

(a)

Environmental event	Internal event	Observable behavior
Emergency situation ⟶	Feelings of concern	⟶ Provide help

(b)

Observable behavior
Provide help

Environmental event
Emergency situation

Internal event

Feelings of concern

(c)

Environmental event	Observable behavior	Internal event
Emergency situation ⟶	Provide help ⟶	Feelings of concern

whether capital punishment should be abolished—by asking them to write an essay promoting a certain point of view. If they do not already hold a strong opinion about that issue and do not feel that they are being forced to write the essay, they may alter their opinion to be consistent with what they have written (Cialdini, 1993). Likewise, the concern you feel for others might sometimes result from, or at least be strengthened by, the act of helping them.

A third difficulty with the use of internal events to explain behavior is that we do not have any means of directly changing these internal events. Our only means of changing both internal events and external behavior is to change some aspect of the environment. For example, if I instruct a client to think calm, relaxing thoughts whenever he or she is in an anxiety-arousing situation and this effectively reduces the anxiety, a radical behaviorist would say that the effective treatment is not the calm, relaxing thoughts, but the instructions I have given the person about thinking calm, relaxing thoughts. And since exposing the client to these instructions is really a manipulation of the client's environment, then it is really a change in the environment that is ultimately responsible for reducing the level of anxiety. Therefore, if changing the environment is the only manner in which behavior can be influenced, then why not emphasize the environment as the ultimate cause of behavior?

A fourth problem with using internal events to explain behavior is that (as with explanations based on instinct) such explanations are sometimes only pseudoexplanations. For example, if I say that I "feel like going to the movies," am I referring to a bodily condition of some sort, or am I simply making a prediction about my future behavior? Perhaps all I am really saying is that I am quite likely to go to the movies under these particular circumstances (which may or may not include a certain bodily state), given that nothing prevents me from doing so. Thus, my "feeling" statement is much more a statement about potential behavior than about a bodily feeling of some sort. For this reason, saying that I am going to the movies because I "feel like going" is really no explanation at all.

For reasons such as these, Skinner rejected internal events as explanations for behavior; instead, he focused on the environment as the ultimate cause of both observable behavior and internal events. But neither did he believe that we are helpless pawns of our environment. He assumed that once we understand the manner in which the environment affects us, we can change the environment so that it will exert a more beneficial influence on our behavior. Skinner referred to this process as ***countercontrol,*** **which is the deliberate manipulation of environmental events so as to alter their impact on our behavior.** Nevertheless, in Skinner's view, even such acts of countercontrol can ultimately be traced to environmental influence. Take, for example, Jamie, who was able to improve her study habits by rearranging her study environment. In making these changes, she altered certain aspects of her environment, which in turn facilitated her studying. On one level of analysis, she is the cause of the improvement in her study habits. On another level of analysis, however, Jamie would not have implemented these changes unless she had first been exposed to some information about the value of doing so. Such information is an environmental influence and is, in Skinner's view, the ultimate cause of the improvement in her study habits.

Thus, Skinner might be seen as agreeing with some aspects of Bandura's notion of reciprocal determinism, in the sense that environmental events, internal events, and observable behavior are seen as capable of interacting with each other. Where Skinner differs, however, is in his assumption that it is the environment that ultimately determines both external behavior and internal events. A diagrammatic depiction of Skinner's approach might therefore look something like that depicted in Figure 1.8. (See Skinner, 1953, 1987, 1989, for a discussion of his perspective on private events; also see Anderson, Hawkins, Freeman, & Scotti, 2000, for the many issues involved in incorporating private events into a science of behavior.)

FIGURE 1.8 A diagrammatic representation of Skinner's view of the relationship between environmental events, internal events, and observable behavior. Although all three components are capable of influencing each other, the emphasis is on environmental events as the ultimate cause of both observable behavior and internal events (as indicated by the solid arrows).

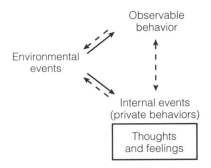

QUICK QUIZ

1. Skinner's _____ behaviorism views both internal and external behaviors as resulting from e_____ influences.

2. Skinner views thoughts and feelings as pr_____ behaviors that themselves need to be explained.

3. In teaching children to label their thoughts and feelings, parents first have to make inf_____ about what the child is feeling.

4. In determining the relationship of thoughts and feelings to behavior, it is sometimes difficult to know if the internal event p_____, f_____, or occurs c_____ with the behavior.

5. Yet another issue with respect to using internal events to explain behavior is that we (can/cannot) _____ directly change such events.

6. Saying that you are feeling "happy" to explain why you are always smiling and laughing is, from Skinner's perspective, an example of using feelings as a ps_____ explanation for your behavior.

7. Altering the environment so as to control our own behavior is referred to as c_____. However, even this type of behavior is ultimately the result of some type of e_____ influence.

Behavior Analysis and Applied Behavior Analysis More so than other behaviorists, Skinner was careful to distinguish between the philosophical aspect of his approach and the experimental science that grew out of that approach. *Radical behaviorism* is actually the philosophical aspect of Skinner's approach. It consists of the set of assumptions, as discussed above, upon which the behavioral science is based. **The science that grew out of radical behaviorism was originally called the *experimental analysis of behavior*** but

ADVICE FOR THE LOVELORN

As noted at the start of this chapter, you will occasionally encounter advice columns such as this, in which basic principles of behavior are applied to relationship problems. Bear in mind that the advice given is often quite speculative and that real relationship difficulties are too complex to be properly assessed and dealt with through simplistic advice columns. Nevertheless, these columns will, in a fun manner, give you a sense for how behavioral principles can offer a unique perspective on important aspects of human behavior.

Dear Dr. Dee,

I have very strong feelings for my new girlfriend, but I can't tell if these are feelings of infatuation or love. My friends tell me I am in love, but my parents tell me I am infatuated. How can I tell the difference?

So Confused

Dear So,

The distinction between love and infatuation is a tough one, and many people find it difficult to differentiate between the two. Interestingly, Skinner (1989) suggested that the more subtle an emotional state (and, presumably, the more subtle the differences between emotional states), the more value there is in analyzing that emotion in terms of the circumstances that surround it. In what circumstance, for example, are we most likely to use the term infatuation? For starters, are we not more likely to use that term when the level of attachment seems to greatly exceed the total rewards available in the relationship? In particular, isn't it the case that we often apply the word infatuation to a relationship that is driven by short-term sexual rewards with few long-term prospects? By contrast, the word love is typically applied to a relationship in which a strong level of attachment seems to properly match the available rewards. The relationship seems to have good long-term prospects and is not driven merely by short-term sexual rewards. Simply put, the word infatuation implies an "unhealthy" relationship that is doomed to failure, while the word love implies a "healthy" relationship that has the potential to prosper.

A little thought will likely reveal other differences between infatuation and love. Nevertheless, our brief analysis suggests that if you wish to determine whether you are "in love" or "merely infatuated," you would do well to ponder the rewards offered by that relationship, and forget about trying to detect minute differences in feelings.

Behaviorally yours,

Dr. Dee

is now more commonly referred to as ***behavior analysis***. Researchers who are committed to behavior analysis are known as behavior analysts. As a group, they have especially concentrated on researching the various principles of operant conditioning, as discussed in Chapters 6 to 10.

Like Watson, Skinner was concerned that the principles discovered through research should have practical application. In this regard, he did not disappoint. His work directly led to the establishment of ***applied behavior analysis,*** **a technology of behavior in which basic principles of behavior are applied to real-world issues**. These applications range from helping people with clinical disorders (such as phobias and schizophrenia), to improving educational practices, to implementing programs that encourage communities to stop polluting and to conserve energy. Applied behavior analysis is particularly well established as the treatment of choice for children with developmental disabilities, including autism, and many graduates from behavior analysis programs find work in this field. (See Miltenberger, 1997, for a more extensive list of areas of application.)

QUICK QUIZ

1. Skinner's philosophy of behaviorism (meaning the set of basic _____ for how best to conduct a science of behavior) is called _____ behaviorism.

2. The science that grew out of that philosophy is called the e_____ a_____ of behavior or, more briefly, _____ _____.

3. The technology that has grown out of that science is known as _____ _____._____

THE LIFE OF B. F. SKINNER

Though quieter, more conservative, and less colorful than Watson, Skinner was nevertheless also the focus of much controversy. As such, it may be worthwhile to briefly describe his life, especially given that he is viewed by many as the classic behaviorist.

Burrhus Frederick Skinner was born in Susquehanna, Pennsylvania, in 1904. Raised in a traditional, Presbyterian household, Skinner's childhood was relatively normal, though not without difficulties. For example, although he was never physically punished as a child (apart from once having his mouth washed out with soap for saying a bad word), he was taught through reprimands and warnings "to fear God, the police, and what people will think" (Skinner, 1967, p. 407). Interestingly, as a behaviorist, he would later conclude that punishment is an ineffective means for managing behavior, often creating more problems than it solves.

One of Skinner's strongest traits, even in childhood, was his love of building and inventing.

> I made sling shots, bows and arrows, blow guns and water pistols from lengths of bamboo, and from a discarded water boiler a steam cannon with which I could shoot plugs of potato and carrot over the houses of our neighbors. . . . I tried again and again to make a glider in which I might fly. (Skinner, 1967, p. 388)

This inventiveness served Skinner well in later years when he was able to build unique devices for studying the behavior of animals, most notably the "Skinner box" (see Chapter 6). In the absence of these inventions, it is conceivable that many of the principles discussed in this text would have remained undiscovered.

Skinner's personality was also characterized by a strange mixture of objectivity and sentimentality (Bjork, 1993). For example, when his younger brother, Ebbie, suddenly died of a cerebral hemorrhage, Skinner observed the death in a surprisingly detached fashion. Nevertheless, he was greatly distressed by the incident and felt pangs of guilt when he later recalled how he had once injured his brother in play. Skinner's objectivity was also apparent in everyday settings. For example, in describing a family friend, he once wrote,

> The doctor and his dog are becoming more than idle amusement. . . . He becomes a fool in the eyes of everyone but me when he attempts to justify the dog's actions. . . . [Pep] comes up to us wagging his tail—"He says 'throw me a stick,'" says the doctor. . . . Lately I've got the habit too. It's quite fun to make up mental processes to fit a dog's every move. (quoted in Bjork, 1993, p. 63)

As a radical behaviorist, Skinner would later argue that mentalistic terms are often mere inferences derived from observable behavior.

Following his graduation from a small liberal arts college, and with some encouragement from the famous poet Robert Frost, Skinner spent a year trying to establish himself as a writer. Although quite disciplined about it, he completed only a few stories and poems and eventually gave up in despair. He sometimes claimed that he had failed as a writer because he had nothing important to say, but he also speculated that his writing was simply too "objective," with too few references to thoughts and feelings, to interest the average reader (Bjork, 1993, p. 56). Years later, Skinner would publish a novel, called *Walden II*, but it was an "objective" novel about a utopian community founded on behavioral principles.

Following his failure at becoming a writer, Skinner came to the conclusion that his real interests lay in the study of behavior. Impressed by the writings of John B. Watson, he entered graduate studies at Harvard in 1928. It was an environment in which he thrived. Much of his graduate and postdoctoral training was, for various reasons, surprisingly unstructured. The result is that he was often left to his own devices to study whatever he wished. In later years, he would write that he had no sense of ever devising a theory or testing a hypothesis; he simply followed his interests. He discounted the notion of science as a formal system of theory building and hypothesis testing, asserting that real science is much less structured than most scientists describe it to be (Skinner, 1956).

Following graduation, Skinner soon became a major figure in behaviorism, in a league with the likes of Tolman and Hull. During the Second World War, he also had an opportunity to apply the principles of conditioning to national defense. While contemplating the widespread destructiveness of bombing attacks, it occurred to him that it might be possible to train pigeons to guide missiles toward specific targets. The basic notion was first to train a pigeon to peck at a moving picture of, say, a ship in order to receive a food reward. The pigeon would then be placed in the nose cone of a missile that was being launched toward a ship. A lens would project the seascape in front of the missile onto a glass screen in front of the pigeon. As the pigeon pecked at the image of the ship, the position of the pecks on the screen would provide feedback to the missile's guidance system. Skinner and his coworkers envisioned squadrons of "kamikaze" pigeons being trained to attack different kinds of targets. After obtaining some funding, they were in fact able to demonstrate that such a device was feasible. Nevertheless, the scientists who viewed the demonstration withdrew their support. The sight of a pigeon tracking a military target across a screen with such accuracy was simply too bizarre, and too amusing, for them to give it serious consideration.

Like Watson before him, Skinner was sometimes the target of false rumors. For example, when Skinner's wife, Eve, did not adjust well to the "joys" of motherhood, Skinner built an "air crib" to ease the burden of raising their youngest daughter, Deborah. The crib was a large enclosed space with an unbreakable glass window. The baby, wearing only a diaper, lay on a woven plastic sheet (the surface of which felt like linen), while the surrounding air was carefully filtered and maintained at a precise temperature. Skinner believed the air crib to be far superior to the jail-like bars, uncertain temperature fluctuations, and loose bedding of the standard crib. It was also much easier to keep clean. Enthused by his invention and by the manner in which Deborah seemed to thrive, Skinner wrote an article on the device for *Ladies' Home Journal* and set out to market it. Unfortunately, a story arose that Skinner was isolating his daughter in an "operant conditioning chamber" and experimenting on her. According to one version of the story—which still makes the rounds today—the daughter eventually went insane and killed herself. The reality is that she had a happy childhood, spent no more time in the air crib than other children do in a regular crib, and grew up to be quite normal. Nevertheless, the damage was done, and relatively few air cribs were ever sold.

In the early 1970s, Skinner was severely criticized by numerous intellectuals and politicians for his book *Beyond Freedom and Dignity*. In the book, Skinner (1971) rejected the concept of free will and argued that we must instead "engineer" society to more effectively control human behavior. He had hoped the book would encourage people to devise better programs for eliminating pollution, preventing crime, and so on, and became quite depressed over the criticism he received. He received a more favorable reaction, however, for his invention of the "teaching machine" and programmed instruction—although in later years, he lamented that this notion too had been largely ignored and never utilized to its full potential. The recent popularity of desktop computers, which are ideally suited for programmed instruction, could well change that.

Throughout his later years, Skinner remained intellectually active, carefully engineering his environment to compensate for the effects of aging. He even wrote a book, *Enjoy Old Age*, offering behavioral advice on self-management for the elderly (Skinner & Vaughan, 1983). His final public presentation was on August 10, 1990, when he was presented with a Lifetime Contribution Award by the American Psychological Association. Terminally ill, but with little fear of death and independent as ever, Skinner used his acceptance speech to lambaste the psychological community for its return to mentalistic explanations for behavior. Eight days later, he passed away from leukemia at the age of 86. (See Bjork, 1993, for a well-written biography of Skinner.)

SUMMARY

This text introduces you to the basic principles of learning and behavior. More specifically, the text emphasizes principles of classical conditioning—in which reflexive behaviors come to be elicited in new situations—and operant conditioning—in which the probability of a behavior is influenced by its consequences.

Individuals of historical significance in the study of learning include Aristotle, who assumed that knowledge is largely gained from experience (as opposed to being inborn) and believed that learning is based upon four laws of association: similarity, contrast, contiguity, and frequency. Descartes proposed that involuntary behaviors, which occur in both humans and animals, are automatically elicited by external stimulation, while voluntary behaviors, which occur only in humans, are controlled by free will. The British empiricists argued that all knowledge is a function of experience, and they strongly emphasized the laws of association in their study of learning. Structuralists, such as Titchener, assumed that the mind is composed of a finite number of basic elements that can be discovered using the method of introspection. This approach was criticized by functionalists, such as William James, who recommended studying the adaptive processes of the mind. Functionalism eventually led to the establishment of behaviorism, with its emphasis on the study of publicly observable behavior and the environmental events that influence it.

There are several schools of behaviorism. Watson's methodological behaviorism rejects all references to internal events, such as thoughts and feelings, that cannot be directly observed. Hull's neobehaviorism includes references to hypothetical internal events, usually of a physiological nature (such as fatigue or hunger), that are presumed to mediate between the environment and behavior. Tolman's cognitive behaviorism differs from Hull's approach in that the hypothesized intervening variables are of a mentalistic nature, such as expectations and cognitive maps. This approach eventually led to Bandura's social learning theory, which emphasizes the importance of observational learning as well as the reciprocal interaction of internal events, environment, and behavior. By contrast, Skinner's radical behaviorism views internal events as private behaviors that are subject to the same laws of learning as publicly observable behaviors. The science that has grown out of radical behaviorism is called the experimental analysis of behavior, or simply behavior analysis. This science has in turn led to a technology of behaviorism, known as applied behavior analysis, in which basic principles of learning are applied to real-world problems. The chapter ends with a brief biography of Skinner, whom many consider to be the classic behaviorist.

STUDY QUESTIONS

Given that many students tend to ignore long lists of broad study questions (or learning objectives) that attempt to cover all of the material in a chapter, these study questions instead focus on the most basic information presented. To determine if you have a grasp of this information, see if you can write out a clear answer to each of these questions. Be aware, however, that obtaining an excellent mark in this course will likely require more than just a simple reiteration of this basic material.

1. Name and briefly describe the two fundamental forms of learning emphasized in this textbook.
2. Describe the nativist versus empiricist approaches to knowledge.
3. Name and briefly describe the four laws of association.
4. Outline Descartes' dualistic model of human behavior.
5. How did the British empiricists view the acquisition of knowledge and the composition of the conscious mind?
6. Describe the structuralist approach to psychology. Name and define the basic method by which the structuralists gathered data.
7. Describe the functionalist approach to psychology. Where did functionalists stand on the issue of animal experimentation, and what was their reasoning behind this?
8. Why, according to Watson, had psychology made such little progress by the start of the 20th century? What did he propose as a solution to this dilemma?
9. Define the Law of Parsimony and Morgan's Canon.
10. Describe Watson's methodological behaviorism. How did Watson's position on the nature-nurture debate change over time?
11. Describe Hull's neobehaviorism.
12. Describe Tolman's cognitive behaviorism.

13. Briefly outline Tolman and Honzik's latent learning experiment, and the results they obtained.
14. Describe Bandura's social learning theory, and his concept of reciprocal determinism.
15. Describe Skinner's radical behaviorism. How does his approach to determinism differ from that of Bandura?
16. What is the distinction between radical behaviorism, behavior analysis, and applied behavior analysis?

CONCEPT REVIEW

applied behavior analysis. A technology of behavior in which basic principles of behavior are applied to real-world issues.

behavior. Any activity of an organism that can be either directly or indirectly observed.

behaviorism. A natural science approach to psychology that traditionally emphasizes the study of environmental influences on observable behavior.

British empiricism. A philosophical school of thought, of which John Locke was a member, that maintained that almost all knowledge is a function of experience.

cognitive behaviorism. A brand of behaviorism that utilizes intervening variables, usually in the form of hypothesized cognitive processes, to help explain behavior. Sometimes called "purposive behaviorism."

cognitive map. The mental representation of one's spatial surroundings.

countercontrol. The deliberate manipulation of environmental events so as to alter their impact on our behavior.

empiricism. The assumption that a person's characteristics are mostly learned or are the result of experience. Also known as the nurture perspective.

experimental analysis of behavior (or behavior analysis). The behavioral science that grew out of the philosophy of radical behaviorism.

functionalism. An approach to psychology that holds that the mind evolved to help us adapt to the world around us, and that the focus of psychology should be the study of those adaptive processes.

introspection. The attempt to accurately describe one's conscious thoughts, emotions, and sensory experiences.

latent learning. Learning that occurs in the absence of any observable demonstration of learning and only becomes apparent under a different set of conditions.

law of contiguity. A law of association holding that events that occur in close proximity to each other in time or space are readily associated with each other.

law of contrast. A law of association holding that events that are opposite from each other are readily associated.

law of frequency. A law of association holding that the more frequently two items occur together, the more strongly they are associated.

law of parsimony. The assumption that simpler explanations for a phenomenon are generally preferable to more complex explanations.

law of similarity. A law of association holding that events that are similar to each other are readily associated.

learning. A relatively permanent change in behavior that results from some type of experience.

methodological behaviorism. A brand of behaviorism that asserts that, for methodological reasons, psychologists should study only those behaviors that can be directly observed.

mind-body dualism. Descartes' philosophical assumption that some human behaviors are bodily reflexes that are automatically elicited by external stimulation, while other behaviors are freely chosen and controlled by the mind.

nativism. The assumption that a person's characteristics are largely inborn. Also known as the nature perspective.

neobehaviorism. A brand of behaviorism that utilizes intervening variables, in the form of hypothesized physiological processes, to help explain behavior.

radical behaviorism. A brand of behaviorism that emphasizes the influence of the environment on overt behavior, rejects the use of internal events to explain behavior, and views thoughts and feelings as behaviors that themselves need to be explained.

reciprocal determinism. The assumption that environmental events, observable behavior, and "person variables" (which include internal events) reciprocally influence each other.

social learning theory. A brand of behaviorism that strongly emphasizes the importance of observational learning and cognitive variables in explaining human behavior. It has more recently been referred to as "social-cognitive theory."

S-R theory. A theory holding that learning involves the establishment of a connection between a specific stimulus (S) and a specific response (R).

structuralism. An approach to psychology holding that it is possible to determine the structure of the mind by identifying the basic elements of which it is composed.

CHAPTER TEST

Chapter tests typically contain fewer hints than quick quizzes—for example, there is usually only a single blank for an answer even though the answer may require more than a single word. Unlike the quick quizzes, however, an answer key has been provided at the end. Note too that the question numbers have been scrambled (e.g., first question below is no. 9). This allows you to immediately look up the answer to a question without having to worry about inadvertently seeing the answer to the next question. Finally, don't worry if you are initially unable to answer some of the items. Fill-in-the blank items can be difficult, and this test is designed to be a learning experience more than a form of self-assessment. You may find it difficult to recall some of the information insofar as it is still relatively unfamiliar to you.

9. When Tara saw the lush green lawn, it reminded her of just how dry the lawn had been the previous year. Among the four laws of association, this is best described as an example of the law of _____.

29. Diane (a coauthor of this textbook) often gets lost when she drives around the city that she lives in. Tolman might say that she has a faulty _____.

17. When Sarah first saw a video of the pop singer Britney Spears, she immediately thought of Paula Abdul, since the two performers seemed to have a common style of performance. Among the four laws of association, this is best described as an example of the law of _____.

1. Steven once became terribly ill while visiting Chicago. As a result, whenever he visits Chicago, he thinks of the illness he suffered at that time. Among the four laws of association, this is best described as an example of the law of _____.

10. After struggling unsuccessfully to completely eliminate his test anxiety, Andres finally accepts that there are some aspects of himself that he can control and some that he cannot. This conclusion is similar to that of the French philosopher _____ and his theory of _____ dualism.

12. In trying to understand her feelings for Juan, Pamela pays close attention to the sensations she feels each time she sees him. This is an example of the method of _____. This was a favorite method of research by psychologists who adhered to the approach known as _____.

27. Hull's theory is a (molar/molecular) _____ type of theory, while Tolman's theory is a _____ type.

7. When Anastasia once visited London, it rained every day for a week. As a result, whenever she is trapped in a rainstorm, it reminds her of her trip to London. Among the four laws of association, this is best described as an example of the law of _____.

20. The law of _____ holds that simpler explanations are usually preferable explanations.

15. "My cat never gets lost. It's like she has a blueprint in her mind of the exact layout of the entire town." This statement fits best with (name the behaviorist) _____'s brand of behaviorism, known as _____.

11. "Babies know nothing," Lana pronounced when her sister commented on how intelligent her new baby seemed to be. Lana obviously believes that

the mind of a newborn is a _____ slate (or, in Latin,
_____), a notion that was promoted by a group
of philosophers known as the _____.

31. Although Roberta just sits there throughout the lecture, she can afterward repeat everything the professor said. This is an example of
_____ learning, which illustrates the distinction between learning and _____.

16. Sue tells her friend Trish that she believes that her husband kept yawning
during their anniversary dinner because he was subconsciously trying to
punish her for having become pregnant. Trish tells Sue to quit being
paranoid and that he was probably just tired. Conway Lloyd Morgan
would likely have leaned toward accepting (Sue/Trish) _____'s explanation as more likely correct.

25. Recall the opening vignette to the chapter where, after making love,
one behaviorist comments, "That was fine for you, how was it for
me?" This joke is most descriptive of which school of behaviorism?
_____

2. Aristotle was a(n) (nativist/empiricist) _____, while Plato was
a(n) _____.

32. Learning is a relatively _____ change in behavior that
results from some type of _____.

22. When I haven't eaten for several hours, I feel a strong sense of hunger and
therefore walk quickly as I head to the cafeteria. This statement fits best
with (name the behaviorist) _____'s brand of behavior-
ism, known as _____.

5. Neal was recently stung by a wasp and is now quite fearful of wasps. This
is best seen as an example of _____ conditioning.

30. John's therapist tells him that, although she cares about what he feels, she
is more interested in what he did and what the circumstances were that affected both his behavior and his feelings. This therapist's approach fits
best with _____'s brand of behaviorism, known as
_____.

23. Shira emphasizes environmental explanations for behavior and believes that thoughts and feelings should be regarded as private behaviors that also need to be explained. As such, she is most likely a
_____ behaviorist. To the extent that Shira also con-
ducts research into basic principles of behavior, she can be called a(n)
_____. To the extent that she applies those principles
to developing better methods for coaching basketball, she can be called
a(n) _____.

19. Descartes believed that the behavior of (animals/humans/both)
_____ is entirely reflexive.

14. Jason found a five-dollar bill when he took out the trash one day. As a result, he often volunteers now to take out the trash. This is an example of
_____ conditioning.

26. A "middleman" in a business transaction is analogous to what Tolman and Hull referred to as a(n) _____.

33. As originally defined by Watson, behaviorism is a _____ approach to psychology that emphasizes the study of _____ influences on directly _____ behavior.

3. After Jasmine saw her sister talk back to the sassy kid next door, she herself did likewise. This is an example of _____ learning.

18. Ally's therapist tells her that he doesn't care what she thinks and feels; he is only concerned about what she did and what the circumstances were that affected her behavior. This therapist's approach fits best with (name the behaviorist) _____'s brand of behaviorism, known as _____.

8. In considering the process of dreaming, a psychologist who adheres to the approach known as _____ would be most concerned with understanding how dreaming facilitates our ability to survive and prosper.

24. Sal claims that the neglect he suffered as a child resulted in low self-esteem, which in turn resulted in his long history of criminal activity. His parole officer tells him that such an explanation is too simplistic, that it ignores the complex manner in which the various facets of life inter-act with each other, and that Sal needs to acknowledge that his own attitude played a role in creating his difficulties. Among the theorists in this chapter, the one who would most appreciate this statement is _____, since it agrees with his concept of _____ determinism.

4. "Great musicians are born, not made" is an example of the (nativist/empiricist) _____ perspective on behavior, while "practice makes perfect" is an example of the _____ perspective.

28. (Hull/Tolman) _____ viewed behavior from a gestalt perspective, while (Hull/Tolman) _____ assumed that behavior consists of a long chain of specific stimulus-response con-nections. This latter approach is known as a(n) _____ theory of behavior.

13. William James was a (structuralist/functionalist) _____, while Titchener was a _____.

6. The defining characteristic of behaviorism, as originally proposed by Watson, is the emphasis on _____.

21. Removing the television set from the room so you won't be distracted while studying each evening is an example of what Skinner called _____.

ANSWERS TO CHAPTER TEST

1. contiguity
2. empiricist; nativist
3. observational
4. nativist (or nature); empiricist (or nurture)
5. classical
6. observable behavior
7. frequency
8. functionalism
9. contrast
10. Descartes; mind-body
11. blank; tabula rasa; British empiricists
12. introspection; structuralism
13. functionalist; structuralist
14. operant
15. Tolman's; cognitive (or purposive) behaviorism
16. Trish's
17. similarity
18. Watson's; methodological behaviorism
19. animals
20. parsimony
21. countercontrol
22. Hull's; neobehaviorism
23. radical; behavior analyst; applied behavior analyst
24. Bandura; reciprocal
25. methodological behaviorism
26. intervening variable
27. molecular; molar
28. Tolman; Hull; S-R
29. cognitive map
30. Skinner's; radical behaviorism
31. latent; performance
32. permanent; experience
33. natural science; environmental; observable

Research Methods

CHAPTER OUTLINE

Mark noticed that he seemed to be suffering a lot of nasal congestion and frequently had to take a decongestant. A friend suggested that he might have an allergy to milk and suggested that he eliminate all milk products for a week to see how he felt. Mark tried that and did feel better, but he wondered if the improvement might have been due instead to a recent change in the weather. He wondered if there might be a more systematic way to conduct an experiment on oneself.

This chapter introduces you to the basic methods of behavioral research. Once a researcher has developed a hypothesis or has decided upon a specific area of interest, such as the effect of reward size on speed of learning, he or she will employ a research method to obtain some behavioral data. Some of the methods for obtaining data include naturalistic observation, case studies, control group designs, and single-subject designs.

The methods used in behavioral research are in many ways similar to those used in other fields of psychology. For example, much behavioral research involves comparisons between "experimental" groups that receive some kind of manipulation (or treatment) and "control" groups that do not receive that manipulation. In some cases, however, the methods are quite distinctive. For example, behavior analysts (as discussed in the previous chapter, these are behaviorists who adhere to Skinner's philosophy of radical behaviorism) have a strong preference for conducting experiments that require only one or, at most, a few subjects. These types of experimental designs, known as *single-subject designs*, have several advantages (as well as disadvantages), which we will discuss. Let us begin, however, with an overview of some basic terms and definitions.

Basic Terms and Definitions

Independent and Dependent Variables

All scientific research involves the manipulation and/or measurement of certain variables. **A *variable* is a characteristic of a person, place, or thing that can change (vary) over time or from one situation to another.** Temperature is an example of a variable since temperature varies from day to day, season to season, and from place to place. Height and weight are also examples of variables in that people come in many different sizes and shapes. Until a person reaches maturity, his or her height will change over a period of time. Weight is even less consistent and can fluctuate endlessly, often in directions we do not particularly like.

Almost anything can be considered a variable. Consider the following singles ad:

Brown-haired, S, M, 25, seeks S, F, aged 20–26, for fun and friendship.

The S in this ad stands for "single" which is one category of the variable *marital status*, which can range from single, to common-law married, to married, to divorced, and even to widowed. The M stands for "male," which is part of the dichotomous (meaning "two categories") variable *gender* (i.e., male and female). *Age, hair color*, and preference for *fun and friendship* are examples of other variables represented in this ad.

Two types of variables are particularly important in setting up an experiment. **The *independent variable* is that aspect of an experiment that systematically varies across the different conditions in the experiment.** In other words, the independent variable is what is *manipulated* in an experiment. For example, we may be interested in whether the size of a reward (or "reinforcer") can affect the efficiency of learning. To test this notion, we might conduct a maze learning experiment with rats. Each rat is given ten trials in which it is placed in a maze and allowed to find its way to the goal box. Depending upon the "experimental condition" to which the rat has been randomly assigned, it receives either one, two, or three pellets of food each time it reaches the goal box. Thus, the independent variable in this experiment is the number of food pellets the rats in each group receive when they reach the goal box.

The *dependent variable* is that aspect of an experiment that is allowed to vary freely to see if it is affected by changes in the independent variable. In other words, the dependent variable is what is measured in an experiment. In a psychology experiment, this is always some type of behavior. Changes in the dependent variable are *dependent upon* changes in the independent variable (which is a useful phrase to remember to help one distinguish between the dependent and independent variable in an experiment). In the experiment above, the dependent variable could be the total number of errors (i.e., number of wrong turns) the rat makes while trying to find its way to the goal box. Alternatively, we might simply look at the speed with which the rat reaches the goal box. Either way, a significant difference between groups on this measure will indicate whether the number of food pellets found in the goal box has an effect on the efficiency with which the rats learn the maze. In turn, this will provide supportive evidence for our more general notion— which is what we are really interested in—that the size of a reinforcer affects the efficiency of learning.

Functional Relationships

In behavioral research, the dependent variable is almost always some behavior, while the independent variable is some environmental event that is presumed to influence the behavior. **The relationship between changes in an independent variable and changes in a dependent variable is known as a *functional relationship*.** Thus, behaviorists are typically interested in discovering functional relationships between environmental events and behavior. A functional relationship can also be thought of as a cause-and-effect relationship, with changes in the independent variable being the cause and changes in the dependent variable being the effect.

QUICK QUIZ

1. A researcher is interested in studying the effects of viewing television violence on aggression in children. She shows one group of participants an extremely violent movie, another group a moderately violent movie, and a third group a nonviolent movie. In this case, the level of movie violence shown to the subjects would be considered the _____ variable, while the children's subsequent level of aggressive behavior would be the _____ variable.

2. A dependent variable is considered to be the (cause/effect) _____ in an experiment, while the independent variable is considered to be the

_____.

3. A _____ relationship is the relationship between a change in an independent variable and an associated change in a dependent variable. Behaviorists are typically concerned with discovering the relationship between changes in e_____ events and changes in b_____.

Stimulus and Response

Two terms used repeatedly throughout this text are *stimulus* and *response*. **A *stimulus* is any event that can potentially influence behavior, while a *response* is a particular instance of a behavior.** For example, food is a stimulus that elicits the response of salivation when presented to a hungry dog. Similarly, loud music (a stimulus) might cause your neighbor to bang on the wall (a response), and a high mark on a test (a stimulus) might cause you to grin with delight (a response). The plural for the word stimulus is "stimuli." Thus, a red light is a stimulus, while a red light and a green light are stimuli.

Note that the response of one organism can act as a stimulus that influences the response of another organism. For example, when one rat bites another, that bite is a stimulus that might elicit a retaliatory response from the other rat. In turn, this retaliatory response might then act as a stimulus that induces the first rat to retreat. Similarly, a smile from Jack is a stimulus that encourages Nav to say hello; Nav's hello is in turn a stimulus that encourages Jack to introduce himself. Thus, social interactions generally consist of a chain of alternating responses, with each response acting as a stimulus for the next response from the other person.

Overt and Covert Behavior

It is also important to distinguish between overt and covert behavior. ***Overt behavior* is behavior that has the potential for being directly observed by an individual other than the one performing the behavior.** In other words, it is behavior that could be publicly observed if others were present. A person's response of saying hello and a rat's response of pressing a lever are both instances of overt behavior. As noted in the previous chapter, behaviorists have traditionally tended to emphasize the study of overt behavior. Skinner, however, maintained that internal events such as thoughts, feelings, and even sensory experiences (e.g., seeing and hearing) should also be classified as behaviors. As noted in the previous chapter, Skinner referred to such behaviors as "private behaviors" or "private events," though they are more commonly referred to as covert behaviors. **Thus, *covert behavior* is behavior that can be perceived only by the person performing the behavior.** In other words, it is behavior that is *subjectively* perceived and is not publicly observable. Dreaming, thinking about your next chess move, visualizing how your date will go on the weekend, and feeling anxiety are all examples of covert behavior. Of course, some covert behaviors have components that could be made publicly observable. A feeling of anxiety, for example, is likely to involve increases in heart rate and muscle tension, both of which could be electronically measured. If such measurements are made, then those particular components of anxiety can be considered overt—which from a behavioral perspective is much preferred over a purely subjective report of anxiety.

Just as the behavior of one person can serve as a stimulus for the behavior of another person, covert and overt behaviors within the same person can act as stimuli for each other. For example, thinking about one's next move in chess (a covert behavior) is a stimulus that influences which chess piece you actually move (an overt behavior), while accidentally moving the wrong chess piece (an overt behavior) is a stimulus that induces you to think unpleasant thoughts about yourself (a covert behavior). As behavior analysts put it, the environment does not stop with the skin: Events both outside the skin and inside the skin can influence our behavior—though behavior analysts will also maintain that the ultimate cause of the behavior is to be found outside the skin. (For example, what might a behavior analyst consider to be the ultimate cause of a person thinking about a certain chess move and then making that move?)

Appetitive and Aversive Stimuli

Many stimuli, both internal and external, can be classified as appetitive or aversive. **An *appetitive stimulus* is an event that an organism will seek out.** Food is an appetitive stimulus when we are hungry; water is an appetitive stimulus when we are thirsty. **An *aversive stimulus* is an event that an organism will avoid.** Electric shock and extreme heat are examples of aversive stimuli. (Note that the word is "aversive" and not "adversive.")

Appetitive and aversive stimuli might also be defined as those events that people usually describe as pleasant or unpleasant. Such descriptions are often quite accurate, but one has to be careful not to place too much reliance upon them. As the Calvin and Hobbes cartoon illustrates, people can vary widely in the types of events they regard as appetitive versus aversive—a point that many parents overlook when they attempt to reinforce or punish a child's behavior. As well, a person may claim that a certain experience is unpleasant, yet work actively to obtain it. For example, someone might describe her pack-a-day smoking habit as "disgusting," yet move heaven and earth to make it to

What is aversive to some can be appetitive to others.

Calvin and Hobbes   by Bill Watterson

the store in time to buy another pack. Despite what she says, tobacco is clearly an appetitive stimulus for her. The moral of the story is that talk is cheap or, as behavior analysts sometimes put it, "just verbal behavior." It may or may not accurately reflect the nonverbal behavior it presumably describes.

1. A(n) _____ is any event that can potentially influence behavior; a(n) _____ is a specific instance of behavior.

2. A tone is a s_____, while a tone and a bell are s_____.

3. One person's response can be another person's _____.

4. Julie dislikes Jake, one of the sales personnel who works in her department. Because Julie avoids Jake like the plague, Jake can be considered an _____ stimulus. For example, Julie closes her office door when Jake is nearby, which is an example of a(n) (overt/covert) _____ behavior.

5. Julie also thinks unkind thoughts about Jake and feels anxious when she sees him in the hallway, both of which are examples of _____ behaviors.

6. Jake is strongly attracted to Julie and often hangs around her office just to get a glimpse of her. Julie is thus an _____ stimulus for Jake.

7. If we think before we act, then our (covert/overt) _____ behavior serves as a stimulus that influences our (covert/overt) _____ behavior. If we act first and regret it later, then our _____ behavior serves as a stimulus that influences our _____ behavior.

Establishing Operations: Deprivation and Satiation

You may have noticed in some of the preceding examples that the appetitiveness or aversiveness of an event depends on a particular state or condition. For example, food is an appetitive stimulus to a hungry rat but might not be an appetitive stimulus to a rat that has just eaten. **A procedure that affects the appetitiveness or aversiveness of a stimulus is called an** *establishing operation.*

Deprivation and satiation are two types of establishing operations. ***Deprivation* is the prolonged absence of an event that tends to increase the appetitiveness of that event.** If the event is being used as a reinforcer (reward) for some behavior—such as food being used as a reinforcer for lever pressing—then we could also define deprivation as a procedure that increases the reinforcing value of an event. Going without food for a long period of time obviously increases the appetitiveness of food, increasing its ability to serve as a reinforcer for some behavior. Less obviously, deprivation of many other events might also increase their appetitiveness. If you have ever gone without television for a while (as did the first author, when he was a poor, starving graduate student), you may have found it quite engrossing when you finally had an opportunity to watch it again. Likewise, lack of social contact for several days (i.e., social deprivation) will usually result in a strong desire for social contact.

In contrast to deprivation, ***satiation* refers to the prolonged exposure to (or consumption of) an event, which tends to decrease the appetitiveness of that event.** Food is much less effective as a reinforcer for lever pressing if a rat has just eaten a large meal and is thus "satiated" on food. Similarly, if you hear a favorite piece of music too often, you may grow tired of hearing it. In fact, you might even become "sick of it," meaning the song has become aversive.

Although the general rule is that deprivation increases the appetitiveness of an event while satiation decreases its appetitiveness, exceptions can occur. For example, people (and rats, as you will read about in a later chapter) who undertake severe diets sometimes acquire a disorder known as anorexia nervosa. In these cases, severe food deprivation seems to decrease the appetitive value of food rather than increase it, in that these individuals begin to eat even less food than the diet allows. People (and rats) who become anorexic also engage in extremely high levels of activity, yet seem to find the activity more, not less, reinforcing—that is, they do not seem to "satiate" on the activity. These processes are discussed more fully in Chapter 11.

Contiguity and Contingency

Two terms that are often confused are contiguity and contingency. Although they sound similar, they actually refer to very different conditions. Contiguity, as mentioned in the opening chapter, means closeness or nearness. Thus, ***temporal contiguity* is the extent to which events occur close together in time**. Thunder and lightning are *temporally contiguous* in that the thunder is heard shortly after the lightning is seen. Temporal contiguity is an important aspect of learning. A rat will more readily learn to press a lever for food if the food immediately follows the lever press than if it appears several seconds later. Likewise, a child will more readily learn to throw a tantrum for candy if the tantrum is immediately followed by the receipt of some candy.

***Spatial contiguity* is the extent to which events are situated close to each other in space.** This type of contiguity also affects learning (though perhaps not as strongly as temporal contiguity). It is easier for a rat to learn to press a lever for food if the food dispenser is close to the lever, as opposed to being several feet away. Likewise, it may take a young child (or a young puppy) somewhat longer to learn that a doorbell, as opposed to a knock, indicates that someone is at the front door. The sound of the knock is *spatially contiguous* with the door (the sound comes from the door), while the sound of the doorbell is not (the sound usually comes from a box located elsewhere in the house).

The term "contingency" has a quite different meaning from contiguity. **A contingency is a dependent relationship between two events, that is, the occurrence of one event is dependent on another.** If a rat receives a food pellet whenever it presses a lever, then a contingency exists between lever pressing and food. We then say that the presentation of food is contingent on lever pressing. Likewise, if a child receives a big balloon every time she goes to the dentist, then a contingency exists between visiting the dentist and receiving the balloon. In other words, receiving the balloon is contingent upon visiting the dentist. As you will see later, contingency is an extremely important aspect of learning.

1*

QUICK QUIZ

1. An e_____ o_____ is a procedure that affects the appetitiveness or aversiveness of a stimulus.

2. Karl has been working out of town and has not seen a movie for over a year. It is likely that the reward value of going to a movie has (increased/ decreased) _____ as a function of (satiation/deprivation) _____.

3. The term _____ means closeness or nearness.

4. Julie says that she once experienced a strong pain in her leg at the precise moment that her son, who was away on a mountain-climbing expedition, broke his leg. Because of the t_____ c_____ between her feeling of pain and her son's injury, Julie now claims that she must have some type of psychic ability.

5. People who live close to each other are more likely to date and fall in love. Thus, s_____ c_____ seems to have a strong effect on the development of romantic relationships.

6. Sasha obtains a high mark on her exams only when she studies diligently. For Sasha, there is a c_____ between studying diligently and doing well on her exams.

7. If a dog receives a dog biscuit only when it begs, then receiving the dog biscuit is c_____ upon the behavior of begging.

---

*Note: From this point forward, the number above Sniffy refers to end-of-chapter notes that reference exercises and material in *Sniffy, the Virtual Rat™: Pro Version* that your instructor may want to assign.

Measurement of Behavior

Behavioral Definitions

When we study the effects of certain variables on a behavior, it is important that we properly define the behavior. Such behavioral definitions should be *objective* in the sense that they refer to some observable aspect of the subject's behavior. For example, yelling and striking are observable aspects of aggressive behavior, while feelings of anger are not. Therefore, it is more precise to define aggression in terms of the physical characteristics of yelling and striking than feelings of anger.

Behavioral definitions should also be clearly defined, that is, *unambiguous*. For example, we might define yelling as a loud vocalization that continues for more than 5 seconds and can be heard outside a closed door. Striking might be defined as a rapid arm or leg movement that results in physical contact. From a scientific perspective, an unambiguous definition will ensure that our measurements of the behavior are relatively consistent over time and across settings. Thus, what counts as an aggressive incident today will also count as an aggressive incident tomorrow. Further, if we are investigating various treatments to reduce the number of aggressive incidents (e.g., by rewarding the child for acting nonaggressively), we can be more certain that any observed change in the aggressive behavior is the result of our treatment as opposed to an unconscious shift in our definition of aggression. Finally, an unambiguous behavioral definition will make it easier for other researchers to replicate our results.

Clear definitions of behavior are also beneficial outside the research setting. Take, for example, the task of child-rearing (the ultimate challenge in behavior management). A major problem faced by many children is that parents often shift their standards as to what constitutes appropriate behavior. For example, a parent might constantly tell a child that eating in the living room is wrong, but then allow eating in the living room when visitors arrive or when the family is watching a movie. A clearer definition of what behaviors are appropriate versus inappropriate would be far less confusing to the child, and reduce the probability of the child violating the rules. One highly effective parent we know of uses a "three-warning" rule for situations that require compliance. For example, if one of the children is asked to get ready to go swimming with her aunt, she must comply before the third warning or else suffer a negative consequence (e.g., she will not be allowed to go swimming that day). Because the rule is so well defined and allows the child a certain amount of time "to get mobilized," negative consequences rarely have to be imposed. And even when the child does not comply and does suffer the consequences, she rarely makes a fuss about it since she was well aware of the contingencies from the outset. (This does not mean that the children in this family are rigidly controlled. In fact, one's first impression upon entering the household is that it is quite chaotic, with children running everywhere, laughing and playing. Within clearly defined limits, the children are allowed a great deal of freedom, which they very much appreciate.)

Recording Methods

Depending on how we define a behavior, there are several ways in which we can go about measuring it. We list several such methods below.

1. Rate of Response   One of the most popular measures in behavioral research is *rate of response,* **which is the frequency with which a response occurs in a certain period of time**. Rate measurements are most appropriate when the response is of brief duration, with a well-defined start and finish (i.e., onset and offset). The number of cigarettes smoked per day (perhaps defined as the number of lit cigarettes), the number of words written in a 1-hour writing session, and the number of body stomps in a half-hour broadcast of professional wrestling are all rate measures of behavior. Certain experimental procedures have been explicitly designed to facilitate measuring behavior in terms of rate. For example, operant conditioning experiments often involve rats pressing levers to earn food. The lever press is a very definable response because once the lever is pressed sufficiently for the microswitch to be activated, a response is electronically recorded. Number of lever presses per session thus provides a very precise measure of the rat's food-directed behavior. Rate is also a very *sensitive* measure of behavior and is thus highly favored by some behaviorists (especially radical behaviorists). The rate at which a rat presses a lever for food will vary closely with the number of hours of food deprivation, the type of food being delivered (preferred or nonpreferred), and the number of responses required for a food pellet to be obtained.

2

A *cumulative recorder* **is a device that measures total number of responses over time and provides a graphic depiction of the rate of behavior.** This instrument consists of a roll of paper that unravels at a slow, constant pace, and a movable pen that makes tracks across it (see Figure 2.1). If there are no responses for a period of time, the pen remains stationary while the paper unrolls beneath it. This results in a flat, horizontal line along the paper, with longer lines indicating longer periods of no responding. When a response occurs (e.g., the rat presses the lever), electronic equipment registers the response and produces a slight upward movement of the pen. Thus, a low rate of response produces a line that slopes upward at a shallow angle (because the pen is slowly moving upward while the paper passes beneath it), while a high rate of response produces a line that slopes upward at a steep angle. *The important thing to remember is that the steeper the line, the higher the rate of response.* A cumulative record thereby provides an easily read, graphic depiction of changes in the organism's rate of response over time.

2. Intensity   Responding can also be measured in terms of intensity. **The intensity of a behavior is the force or magnitude of the behavior.** For example, in Pavlov's classical conditioning procedure with dogs, a tone was associated with food, such that the tone itself eventually came to elicit salivation.

Tone: Food → *Salivation*
Tone → *Salivation*

FIGURE 2.1 Illustration of cumulative recorder. This device consists of a roll of paper that unravels at a slow, constant pace. If no response is made, the pen remains stationary, resulting in a horizontal line. A high rate of response produces a steep line, while a low rate of response produces a shallow line. The short diagonal slashes indicate the points at which reinforcers were delivered, for example, food pellets delivered to a rat for making a certain number of lever presses. (*Source:* Malone, 1990.)

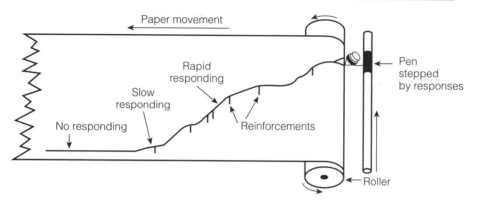

The strength of conditioning was typically measured as the amount (magnitude) of saliva produced whenever the tone was sounded by itself. More saliva indicated stronger conditioning. Another intensity measure of behavior is the force with which a rat presses a lever to obtain food. Likewise, it is intensity that we are concerned with when we teach a child to speak softly and to print firmly.

3. Duration *Duration* **is the length of time that an individual repeatedly or continuously performs a certain behavior.** This measure is appropriate when we are concerned with either increasing or decreasing the length of time the behavior occurs. For example, a student may attempt to increase the amount of time he spends studying each week, as well as decrease the amount of time spent watching television.

4. Speed *Speed* **is the amount of time required to perform a complete episode of a behavior from start to finish.** The length of time it takes for a rat to traverse a maze from the start box to the goal box is a measure of speed. (See Figure 2.2 for examples of the different types of mazes that have been used in psychological research.) We are also concerned with speed when we teach a child to eat more quickly (if he tends to dawdle at the dinner table) or more slowly (if he tends to fling food everywhere in a rush to get finished). Speed measures differ from duration measures in that there is an identifiable end point for the behavioral episode, and the amount of time it takes to reach that end point is the issue of concern. The amount of time it takes us to walk from home to work is a speed measure of behavior, while the total amount of time we spend walking each day is a duration measure of behavior.

FIGURE 2.2 Three types of mazes used in behavioral research. Although the Hampton Court type of maze was often used by researchers at the turn of the century, it was later largely supplanted by the T-maze and straight-alley "maze," which, because of their simplicity, proved more useful for investigating basic principles of behavior. (*Source:* Lieberman, 2000.)

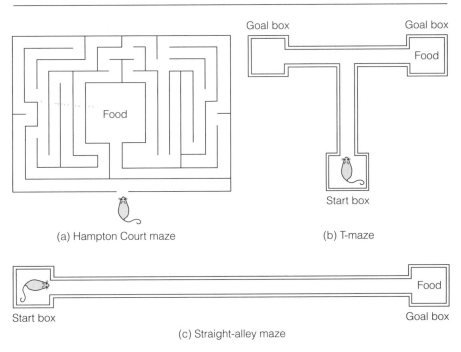

(a) Hampton Court maze

(b) T-maze

(c) Straight-alley maze

5. Latency   The *latency* of a behavior is the length of time required for the behavior to begin. With respect to classical conditioning of salivation, the strength of conditioning can be measured, not in terms of the amount of saliva, but in terms of how soon the dog begins salivating after it hears the tone. Likewise, the amount of time it takes for a student to sit down and begin studying following her evening meal might be a useful measure of the extent to which she finds studying aversive. Quiz shows that require contestants to press buzzers when they believe they have the right answer are using a latency measure of the contestants' performance.

Latency, speed, and duration are often confused because they all involve some type of time measurement. To help distinguish between them, look at the behavior of an athlete who specializes in the 100-meter sprint. The amount of time it takes for her to commence running when she hears the starting pistol—which is only a fraction of a second—is a measure of latency, while the amount of time it takes for her to complete the race is a measure of speed. On the other hand, the amount of time she trains each day is a measure of duration.

6. Interval Recording   A particularly efficient way of measuring behavior, often utilized in applied settings, is *interval recording*: **the measurement of whether or not a behavior occurs within a series of *continuous* intervals.** For example, if we wish to measure the amount of aggressive behavior in a classroom, we might videotape several hours of class time. We would then have observers view the videotape and record whether or not an aggressive incident occurred within each successive 10-minute interval. The proportion of intervals in which an incident occurred would be our measure of aggression.

A major advantage to interval recording is that one does not have to record every single response, which may be difficult if responses occur at a very high rate (e.g., a fistfight that consists of a rapid series of aggressive actions). Interval recording is also useful if it is difficult to determine the point at which the behavior starts and stops. Aggressive incidents are a good example of this in that they sometimes build slowly, and trying to determine the exact moment at which the aggression begins may be difficult.

7. Time Sample Recording   A variant of interval recording is time sample recording. **In *time sample recording*, one measures whether or not a behavior occurs within a series of *discontinuous* intervals (intervals that are spaced apart).** For example, to assess the level of aggression in a classroom, we might have an observer unobtrusively enter the classroom for a 10-minute interval at the start of each hour and record whether or not there was an aggressive incident during that interval. The behavior of the students is thus intermittently sampled, and the proportion of sampled intervals in which an aggressive incident occurred is our measure of aggression. Although we will not catch every act of aggression using such a method, and we may even miss a few whoppers, we will nevertheless have a fairly good overall assessment of the amount of aggression occurring in that setting. As well, this method of recording is very time efficient for our observer, who can spend most of the day working on other tasks.

8. Topography   Sometimes we are concerned with the behavior's *topography*, **which is the exact physical form of the behavior.** For example, rather than record the rate at which a rat presses a lever, we might observe *how* it presses the lever, for example, whether it uses its left paw or right paw. Similarly, it is the topography of the behavior that we are concerned with when we teach a child how to dress appropriately, write neatly, and brush his teeth properly.

9. Number of Errors   Any behavior in which responses can be categorized as right or wrong can be assessed in terms of the number of errors. For example, the number of wrong turns a rat takes before it finds its way through a maze to the goal box is one measure of how well the rat has learned the maze. Likewise, the number of errors a student makes on an exam is a standard method for determining how well the student knows the material.

1. Behavioral definitions should be o_____ and u_____.

2. The force with which a person can squeeze a device that measures grip strength is a measure of i_____.

3. How quickly a musician plays a musical piece from beginning to end is a measure of _____, while the number of hours the musician practices each week is a measure of _____. Conversely, the amount of time it takes the musician to commence playing following the conductor's cue to begin is a measure of _____.

4. The exact manner in which a person lifts a weight is called the t_____ of the behavior.

5. The time it takes before a response begins is a measure of l_____.

6. The number of fish a person catches in a 1-hour period is a measure of r_____.

7. Recording whether Janice hiccups during a continuous series of 5-minute time periods is an example of _____ recording, while measuring whether a hiccup occurs during a 5-minute period at the start of each hour throughout the day is an example of _____-_____ recording.

8. A device commonly used to measure the ongoing rate of a behavior is a c_____ r_____. On this device, a flat line indicates (no/slow/fast) _____ responding, a steep line indicates _____ responding, and a shallow line indicates _____ responding.

Research Designs

Deciding how to measure a behavior is only part of the problem. We must also determine which method to use to assess the impact of certain variables on that behavior. There are several methods available, and they can be divided into one of two general types: descriptive methods and experimental methods.

Descriptive Research

Descriptive methods **of research involve simply describing the behavior and the situation within which it occurs.** Descriptive methods do not involve the manipulation of any variables. Two commonly used descriptive methods are naturalistic observation and case studies.

Naturalistic Observation *Naturalistic observation* **involves the systematic observation and recording of behavior in its natural environment.** Note the word *systematic*. We are not talking here about casual observations, which may be strongly biased by the researcher's preconceptions about behavior. Behavioral scientists have as many preconceptions about behavior as

the average person—perhaps even more, given that it is their job to study behavior—and are therefore quite susceptible to viewing behavior from a biased
perspective. To avoid such biases, researchers attempt to define their variables
objectively and unambiguously and make their observations in a consistent
and uniform manner.

Jane Goodall's systematic study of chimpanzee behavior in the wild is a
classic example of naturalistic observation. Through her detailed observations, we now know that chimpanzees eat meat (they sometimes kill and de-
vour monkeys), use primitive tools (they sometimes dip a twig into a termite
hill to capture termites for food), and engage in warfare (chimpanzees from
one group have been observed stalking, attacking, and killing members of a
neighboring group; see Goodall, 1990).

Naturalistic observation is a commonly used approach in ethology, a
branch of zoology that focuses on the study of inherited behavior patterns
in animals. Such patterns have presumably evolved to help the animal cope
with certain aspects of its natural environment. For this reason, inherited
behavior patterns are usually best studied within the natural environment
(or at least a close approximation to it), because when the animal is removed
from that environment, the behavior may not occur. Displays of dominance
and submission, for example, may not be evident unless an animal is allowed
to freely interact with other members of its own species. And if such displays
do occur in other situations, they may be difficult to identify. For example, a
dog's gesture of rolling over on its back and displaying its underbelly can be
more clearly seen as a submissive gesture when dogs interact with each other
than when they interact with us. One of the authors first realized this when he
witnessed the family dog being attacked by a much larger dog. Following a
brief skirmish, Trixie rolled over on her back and displayed her stomach, the
same behavior she often displayed toward him. What he always took to be a
simple request for a tummy scratch also functioned as an inborn gesture of
subordination.

While naturalistic observation is ideal for studying inherited behavior patterns, it also contributes to our understanding of learning. A famous example
of this is the "cultural adoption" of food-washing behavior among a troop of
macaque monkeys off the coast of Japan. When one monkey acquired the
habit of washing sand off a sweet potato by dipping it in lake water (the researchers had left the potatoes on a sandy beach to attract the monkeys to that
area), other monkeys in the troop soon imitated this behavior. Interestingly,
the oldest monkeys in the troop never adopted this "newfangled way" of
cleaning food (Kawamura, 1963).

The naturalistic approach is excellent for gaining rich, detailed information about a behavior and the circumstances in which it typically occurs. A
problem with this approach is that it often leaves us uncertain as to which variables are most important in determining the behavior. For example, if you
study childhood aggression by observing children interact on a playground,
you might see many displays of aggressive behavior (e.g., grabbing a toy away
from another child, pushing, yelling, etc.). However, it will be difficult to

determine *why* these behaviors are occurring. As a naturalistic observer, you cannot intervene or ask the participants any questions for clarification. It will also be difficult to know if an aggressive child has a long history of aggression, is experiencing considerable frustration that day, or has had frequent exposure to violence in the home. In a sense, the natural environment is a vast sea of variables, and sorting out which variables are responsible for which behavior can be a daunting task. Thus, the naturalistic observation approach is often insufficient for gaining a full understanding of a behavior and the variables that influence it.

Case Studies Another type of descriptive method is **the *case study approach*, which involves the intensive examination of one or a few individuals.** Case studies can be done in natural settings (as a form of naturalistic observation), or they may involve detailed examination in a more structured setting such as a clinician's office. Case studies are especially prevalent in medical research. Individuals who have suffered certain types of neurological damage often provide us with insight into which areas of the brain control which functions. Similarly, examining the lives of highly gifted individuals, such as Albert Einstein and Judit Polgar (the famous young chess player described in the previous chapter), can sometimes yield important information as to how exceptional skills can be acquired.

The case study approach is frequently employed in some areas of clinical psychology. Especially with respect to relatively rare disorders—for example, *fugue states*, in which a person suddenly moves away from home and assumes a different identity—the few case studies available constitute our only source of information. Some clinical case studies have become quite famous. Consider, for example, the case of Anna O., which was reported by Sigmund Freud and his colleague Joseph Breuer (1896). Anna O. is the pseudonym given to a young woman Breuer treated for symptoms of hysteria—a common psychiatric disorder in the latter part of the 19th century. A major characteristic of the disorder was various neurological symptoms, such as limb paralysis, that seemed to have no actual neurological basis, though psychological symptoms, such as "dual" personality and hallucinations, were also common. Breuer and Freud reported that most of Anna O.'s symptoms disappeared when she was encouraged to talk about upsetting events that had occurred to her and that seemed to be related to the onset of her symptoms. This case is generally regarded as the first clear demonstration of the therapeutic effectiveness of *catharsis* (that is, the release of tension that is assumed to automatically result from expressing pent-up thoughts and emotions).

As with naturalistic observations, it is important to ensure that case studies are based on systematic observation and that researcher bias has been reduced to a minimum. Unfortunately, these criteria are sometimes lacking. For example, scholars have recently discovered that the case of Anna O. actually had a far different outcome than that reported by Breuer and Freud. Following her "successful" treatment, Anna O. quickly relapsed and needed to be institutionalized. It was in fact several years before she finally recovered from her hysterical illness, a fact that Breuer and Freud were aware of but never publicly acknowledged. Nevertheless, Breuer and Freud's false report of Anna O.'s recovery helped establish psychoanalysis as the dominant school of psychotherapy in the first half of the 20th century.[1] (For these and other examples of how Freud may have misled people with his reported case studies — which has evolved into quite a controversy — see Esterson, 1993; Powell & Boer, 1994, 1995; and Webster, 1995.)

In addition to the problem of researcher bias, case studies are also limited in the extent to which the results can be generalized to other people, places, and times. For example, Anna O.'s case history, even if it had been accurate, may not have been at all representative of how most cases of hysteria at that time could best be treated. Because case studies often involve only one person, we have no way of knowing if the case being described is the norm or the exception. Additionally, as with naturalistic observation, it is often difficult to specify which variables are responsible for which behavior. Despite the limitations, however, the case study method of research, as with the naturalistic observation method, often provides a valuable starting point for further investigations.

1. Two common descriptive methods are n_____ _____ and c_____ _____.

2. Both approaches are susceptible to the problem of researcher b_____ in which the opinions and beliefs of the researcher can unduly influence his or her observations.

3. In both approaches, it is often (easy/difficult) _____ to specify which variables influence which behavior.

4. Because the case study approach often involves only one subject, the results may be limited in the extent to which they can be g_____ to other people, places, and times.

QUICK QUIZ

Experimental Research

Although descriptive research methods such as naturalistic observations and case studies often provide detailed information about behavior, they usually do not allow us to draw firm conclusions about the causes of a behavior. If, for example, we observe that children who read a lot tend to have higher marks in school, is it the case that reading leads to higher marks, or do "bright"

---

[1] By contrast, behavioral methods of therapy are usually subjected to rigorous experimentation before being widely adopted by practitioners (although informative case studies are also published). Thus, it is not surprising that in a recent list of "empirically validated therapies" — that is, therapies for which there is good research evidence demonstrating their effectiveness — a large majority of the therapies listed were either behavioral or cognitive-behavioral in orientation (Task Force on Promotion and Dissemination of Psychological Procedures, 1995; see also Wilson, 1997).

children simply like to read? To answer this question, it is necessary to conduct an experiment. In general, behavioral researchers, in their quest to discover cause-and-effect relationships (that is, functional relationships) between environmental events and behavior, have a strong preference for the experimental approach to research.

In an experiment, one or more independent variables are systematically varied in order to determine their effect on a dependent variable (the behavior you suspect will change as a result of changes in the independent variable). Any differences in behavior across the different conditions of the experiment are presumed to be caused by the differences in the independent variable.

Behavioral researchers use two main types of experimental designs: control group designs and single-subject designs. As will be seen, each type of design has its advantages and disadvantages, and the decision to employ one method or the other largely has to do with the nature of the particular issue being investigated.

Control Group Designs   The most common type of experimental design is the *control group design.* In its simplest form, subjects are randomly assigned to either an experimental (or treatment) group or a control group; subjects assigned to the experimental group are exposed to a certain manipulation or treatment while those assigned to the control group are not. Imagine, for example, that 20 rats are randomly assigned to either an experimental group or a control group. Rats in the experimental group are individually placed in an experimental chamber for 30 minutes during which time they receive a free food pellet every minute. The rats in the control group are treated exactly the same except they receive no food during the 30-minute session. They are simply allowed to snoop around the chamber. The rats in each group receive one session per day for 10 consecutive days. On day 11, a mechanical lever is placed in each chamber that the rats must learn to press in order to obtain food. The question of interest is whether the rats that previously received free food will learn to press the lever more readily or less readily than the rats that did not receive free food. Thus, the *independent variable* in this experiment is the presence versus absence of free food during the initial phase of the experiment, while the *dependent variable* is the average amount of time it takes for the rats in each group to learn to press the lever for food. (By the way, research has shown that animals that receive free food subsequently have more difficulty learning how to respond for food [Welker, 1976; Wheatley, Welker, & Miles, 1977]. This suggests that exposure to free reinforcers can sometimes impair an organism's ability to learn how to respond for reinforcers.)

Control group designs are often considerably more complicated than the simple experiment described above. For example, we might wonder if the damaging effects of free food on ability to learn are dependent on age. Thus, we might rerun this experiment with groups of old rats, middle-aged rats, and young rats. This would yield what is known as a 2×3 *factorial design*, in which there are two independent variables (food and age), the first of which has two levels (free food versus no food) and the second of which has three levels (old age versus middle age versus young age). This would result in a total of six groups (old with free food, old with no food, middle-aged with free food, middle-aged with no food, young with free food, and young with no food; see Table 2.1). If free food affects learning ability only in rats of a certain age, then we say that there is an *interaction* between the effects of free food and age. Such interaction effects obviously give us a much finer understanding of the variables in which we are interested, and a lot of research is designed to search for such effects.

Control group designs are excellent for assessing the general effects of certain variables. Cause-and-effect statements are possible due to the strict control over the environment that allows the experimenter to rule out alternative explanations. Because all subjects receive identical experiences except for the independent variable that is being manipulated, we can be fairly confident that differences between groups in performance are the result of differences in the independent variable. Random assignment of the subjects to each condition also ensures that various characteristics of the subjects in each group are likely to be evenly distributed across the experimental and control conditions. Thus, the two groups will be pretty much alike at the onset of the experiment, and any differences found at the end of the experiment can therefore be attributed to our manipulation of the independent variable.

Control group designs, however, are not without their drawbacks. To begin with, this type of design usually requires a large number of subjects (often ten or more per group). In fact, for statistical reasons, the larger the number of subjects in a group, the more trustworthy the results. But what if you wished to conduct research on the effectiveness of a behavioral treatment for one individual? It would be impractical to conduct an experiment with a large number of subjects just to determine if a certain treatment might be effective for one person. Control group designs are therefore not well suited for investigating the effect of a certain treatment on a particular individual.

A second difficulty with control group designs is that they typically focus on the *average* performance of subjects in each group. This means that little attention is given to the performance of individual subjects, even if some subjects differ markedly from the average. For example, going back to our rat study, suppose that two out of the ten rats previously given free food learned to press the lever almost immediately, while the others took much longer. Even if, on average, the rats in this free-food group learned more slowly than

TABLE 2.1 Six experimental conditions (groups of subjects) in a 2/3 factorial experiment involving 2 levels of a "food" variable and 3 levels of an "age" variable.

	AGE		
Food	Young (Y)	Middle–aged (M)	Old (O)
No food (NF)	NFY	NFM	NFO
Free food (FF)	FFY	FFM	FFO

the rats in the no-food group, what about the two quick learners? Should we regard them as mere aberrations ("I guess some rats are just brighter than others"), or is it the case that exposure to free food actually facilitates subsequent learning in some individuals? By ignoring individual data, we might never ask such questions.

A third limitation of control group designs is that the results are often analyzed and interpreted only at the end of the experiment rather than during the experiment. In some situations, this may be undesirable. If, for example, we are treating a child for self-injurious behavior, we need to be aware throughout whether our treatment is having a positive effect. If the effect is positive, we can maintain the treatment; if the effect is negative, we should immediately halt our treatment and try something different. By contrast, control group designs that measure effects only at the end of the study usually do not provide us with this type of flexibility.

In conclusion, control group designs are excellent for assessing general relationships between independent and dependent variables. There are drawbacks, however, in that these designs are inefficient when we are interested in relating the findings to a particular individual, when the focus upon average effects results in the neglect of unusual effects displayed by certain individuals, and when there is a need to monitor the individual's progress throughout the study. Alternative designs that do not suffer from these limitations—but have their own limitations—are single-subject designs.

1. In an experiment, a(n) _____ variable is systematically varied (manipulated) to determine its effects upon the _____ variable.

2. In the simplest form of a control group design, subjects are r_____ assigned to either an e_____ (or tr_____) group and a _____ group.

3. Briefly stated, three problems with control group designs are the following:

1. _____
_____
_____

2. _____
_____
_____

3. _____
_____
_____

Single-Subject Designs Unlike control group designs, *single-subject designs* are research designs that require only one or a few subjects to conduct an entire experiment. There are several types of single-subject designs, four of which are described below.

1. Simple-Comparison (AB) Design. In a ***simple-comparison design***, **behavior in a baseline condition is compared to behavior in a treatment condition.** Suppose, for example, that Jack wishes to cut down on smoking (as a first step toward quitting), and wonders if he might be able to do so by punishing himself. In a *self-punishment* procedure, people apply an aversive consequence to themselves each time they engage in an unwanted target behavior. Self-punishment of smoking might therefore consist of Jack giving his buddy 25 cents for each cigarette he smokes. (Another way of looking at this is that Jack has implemented a fine or tax upon himself to try to reduce the amount he smokes.)

The first step in the program would be for Jack to take a baseline measure of the number of cigarettes he typically smokes each day. **The *baseline* is the normal frequency of the behavior prior to some intervention.** Jack could, for example, keep an index card tucked inside the flap of his cigarette pack and make a check mark on it for each cigarette he smokes.

The baseline period should last several days to provide a good assessment of the typical frequency of Jack's smoking. If it appears that there is a gradual upward or downward trend in the amount smoked during baseline (sometimes the mere act of closely monitoring a behavior can result in some improvement, a process known as *reactivity*), Jack should continue the baseline period until the behavior stabilizes. Following the baseline, he should then institute the self-punishment procedure for several days. If the treatment is effective, the frequency of smoking during the treatment period should be consistently lower than it was during the baseline period (see Figure 2.3).

FIGURE 2.3 Simple Comparison (AB) Design. Hypothetical results using a simple comparison design to assess the effectiveness of a treatment (self-punishment) on number of cigarettes smoked. The dashed vertical line divides the baseline condition from the treatment condition. Results are consistent with, but do not provide strong evidence for, the notion that the treatment was effective.

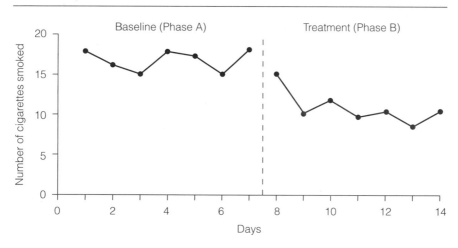

In this type of study, the baseline period is often called the A phase, while the treatment period is called the B phase. Thus, this design is sometimes referred to as an AB design. (Note that students sometimes think the baseline phase is the B phase, since the word baseline starts with a B. Do not think this way. The *baseline phase is the A phase* because that is the phase we start with, and the treatment phase is the B phase because it follows the A phase. The letters A and B simply indicate the order in which the conditions occur.)

A major problem with the simple-comparison design is that it does not control for the possibility that some other event occurred at the same time that the treatment was implemented, and it was this other event that caused the change in the behavior. For example, perhaps Jack caught a cold at the same time that he began self-punishment, and it is actually the cold that accounts for the reduction in smoking. The simple-comparison design does not allow us to assess this possibility and thus constitutes a poor experimental design. In other words, it does not clearly demonstrate a functional relationship between the independent variable (self-punishment) and the dependent variable (smoking). At best, it provides only suggestive evidence that the treatment is effective. On the other hand, if one has limited resources and time for investigating a treatment effect and is simply interested in seeing whether there is some type of improvement, then a simple-comparison design may be sufficient.

2. Reversal (ABAB) Design. A much better design is the reversal, or ABAB, design. **The *reversal design* is a type of single-subject design that involves repeated alternations between a baseline period and a treatment period.** If the behavior systematically changes each time the treatment is instituted and later withdrawn, then a functional relationship has been demonstrated between the treatment and the behavior. In Jack's case, he would begin with the baseline phase, then institute a self-punishment phase, then revert back to baseline, and then back to the self-punishment procedure. If the results are something like those depicted in Figure 2.4, with smoking decreasing each time the treatment is implemented and increasing each time the treatment is withdrawn, then we have obtained fairly strong evidence that the treatment is the cause of the improvement. It is extremely unlikely that some other event, such as illness, coincided precisely with each application of the treatment to produce such systematic changes in behavior.

The reversal design has many strengths. Unlike the control group design, an entire experiment can be conducted with a single subject. As such, the reversal design is often ideal for determining the effectiveness of a behavioral intervention for one person. As well, some behaviorists argue that statistical tests are not needed to determine if the changes in behavior are significant (Sidman, 1960). One can simply "eyeball" the graph to see if the treatment is working. The underlying logic is that if the results are not clear enough to be judged significant by visual inspection alone, then the treatment should be altered to produce a stronger effect. This forces the investigator to attain precise control over the variables influencing the target behavior, and to strive for powerful treatments that can produce large effects.

FIGURE 2.4 Reversal (ABAB) Design. Hypothetical results using a reversal design to assess the effectiveness of a treatment (self-punishment) on number of cigarettes smoked. The systematic change in smoking across the alternating conditions provides *strong evidence* that the treatment is the cause of the improvement.

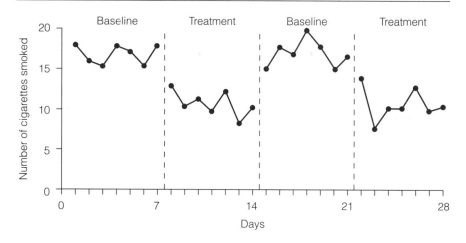

You might want to ask whether results from a reversal design can be generalized to other subjects, since we have demonstrated the effect with only one subject. This is an important question, since in science we are concerned with finding effects that have generality. With single-subject designs, generality is established by rerunning the study with additional subjects. Since each subject in the study constitutes an entire experiment, each additional subject constitutes a replication of that experiment. If we find the same pattern of results for all of the subjects submitted to these procedures, the findings are likely to have good generality. For example, if we tried the self-punishment treatment with three additional individuals and they too showed consistent decreases in smoking, then it is quite likely that this treatment will be effective for many individuals (although the nature of the punishing consequence might have to be tailored to each individual; what is punishing for one person might not be punishing for another). Thus, results that have been obtained with only four or so individuals often have good generality.

While reversal designs have some advantages, they also have some disadvantages. The main disadvantage is that the behavior must revert to its original baseline frequency when the treatment is withdrawn; otherwise, it will be impossible to determine if the treatment has had an effect. If, for example, the results for Jack's study looked something like those depicted in Figure 2.5, in which smoking does not return to its pretreatment level during the reversal to baseline, we would be in no better situation than if we had run a simple-comparison design. Although the rate of smoking dropped when Jack first instituted the self-punishment procedure, it did not climb back up when the procedure was halted; therefore, we cannot be sure that self-punishment was the actual cause of the initial decrease. Although we may be pleased that Jack is

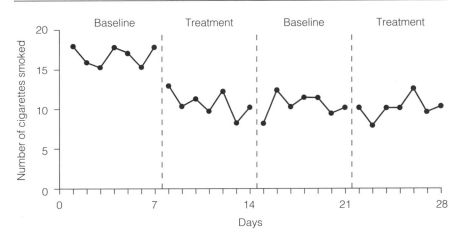

FIGURE 2.5 Reversal (ABAB) Design. Hypothetical results in which a reversal design was used to assess the effectiveness of a self-punishment treatment on smoking. In this case, the behavior did not revert to its baseline level when the treatment was withdrawn. Thus, although it is possible that the treatment was the cause of the improvement, these results do *not* provide strong evidence in this regard.

now smoking less than he used to, from a scientific perspective of demonstrating the effectiveness of self-punishment, these results are less than ideal.

We must also bear in mind that some treatments are intended to produce long-lasting effects. For example, a student who is exposed to a new method of teaching math will hopefully experience a permanent increase in his or her math ability. A reversal design would not be appropriate for assessing the effect of such an intervention, since the improvement should remain evident long after the intervention has ended.

A final difficulty with a reversal design is that it may be ethically inappropriate to remove a treatment once some improvement has been obtained. If, for example, the implementation of a treatment results in the elimination of a person's severe drug addiction, is it reasonable for us to temporarily withdraw the treatment in the hope that the addictive behavior will reappear? Although from a scientific perspective withdrawing the treatment would help confirm its effectiveness, withdrawal would not be ethical. We must instead look for another method of demonstrating a functional relationship between the implementation of the treatment and the improvement in behavior. One alternative is to use a multiple-baseline design.

1. In a simple-comparison design, behavior in a b_____ condition is compared to behavior in a t_____ condition.

2. A simple-comparison design (does/does not) _____ allow us to determine if there is a f_____ relationship between the independent and dependent variables.

3. A reversal design (also called an _____ design) involves repeated alternations between a _____ period and a _____
period.

4. What type of result do we need to see during the second B phase in order to
determine if our treatment is the cause of the change in the behavior?

_____

_____.

5. A reversal design is inappropriate for an experiment in which the treatment produces a (temporary/permanent) _____ change in the behavior.

6. A reversal design is also inappropriate when the act of withdrawing the treatment
during the second B phase would lead to e_____ problems.

3. Multiple-Baseline Design. **In a *multiple-baseline design*, a treatment is
instituted at successive points in time for two or more persons, settings,
or behaviors.** As an example of a *multiple-baseline-across-persons* design, imagine that we have three people who wish to try a self-punishment program for
smoking. We begin by taking a baseline measurement of smoking for each
person. At the end of the first week, we have one person begin the treatment,
while the other two carry on with the baseline. At the end of the second week,
we have a second person begin the treatment while the third person carries on
with the baseline. Finally, at the end of the third week, the third person also
begins the treatment. Thus, across the three individuals, the treatment is implemented at different points in time. If for each person, the improvement in
smoking coincides with the implementation of the treatment, then a functional relationship between the treatment and the improvement in behavior
has been demonstrated (see Figure 2.6).

As an example of a *multiple-baseline-across-settings* design, imagine that the
three graphs in Figure 2.6 represent Jack's rate of smoking in three different
settings: at work, at home, and at the coffee shop. After a week of baseline, Jack
begins self-punishing his smoking, but only at work. After the second week,
he begins self-punishing smoking at home, while continuing to punish it at
work. Finally, after the third week, he also starts punishing his smoking behavior at the coffee shop. If his rate of smoking in each setting drops only at
the point when the self-punishment procedure is implemented, then the procedure is highly likely to be the cause of the improvement.

As an example of a *multiple-baseline-across-behaviors* design, imagine that the
three graphs in Figure 2.6 represent three of Jack's problem behaviors—for
example, smoking, swearing, and nail-biting. In this case, we implement the
treatment at different points in time for each behavior. If each behavior shows
improvement only when the treatment is implemented, then we have again
demonstrated a functional relationship between the treatment and behavior.

The multiple-baseline design is a good alternative to the reversal design in
that we do not have to worry about withdrawing the treatment to determine
that it is effective. This design is therefore appropriate for situations in which
the treatment is likely to produce a permanent change in behavior, or in which

FIGURE 2.6 Multiple Baseline Design. Hypothetical results using a multiple-baseline-across-persons design to assess the effectiveness of a treatment (self-punishment) on number of cigarettes smoked. The three graphs represent the data for three different persons. For each person, the improvement in behavior coincides with the point at which the treatment was implemented. This shows that there is a functional relationship between the treatment and the improvement in behavior.

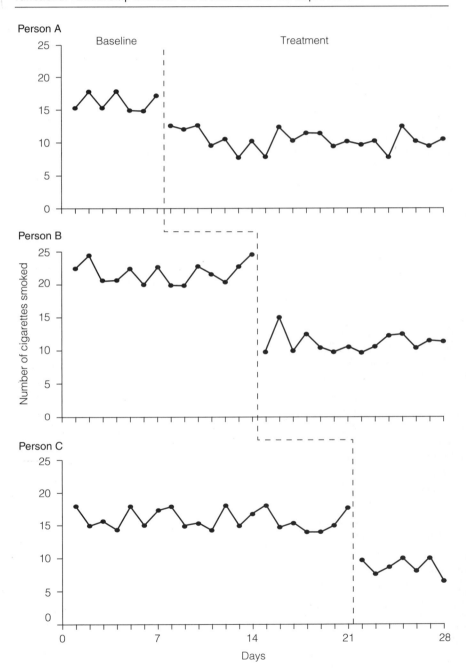

it may be unethical to withdraw the treatment once some improvement has been achieved. Nevertheless, this design is limited in that we need to have more than one person, setting, or behavior to which the treatment can be applied.

QUICK QUIZ

1. With a multiple-baseline design, the treatment is instituted at different points in t_____ for _____ or more p_____, s_____, or b_____.

2. A key advantage of the multiple-baseline design is that we do not have to w_____ the treatment to determine if it is effective.

3. It is therefore a preferable design for situations in which the treatment has resulted in a (temporary/permanent) _____ change in behavior, or it might be une_____ to withdraw the treatment.

4. Changing-Criterion Design. In some circumstances, the treatment is not intended to produce a large, immediate change in behavior, but rather a gradual change over time. A useful design for measuring such changes is a **changing-criterion design.** In this type of design, the effect of the treatment is demonstrated by the extent to which the behavior matches a criterion that is systematically altered.

Imagine, for example, that Jack decides to use self-punishment to gradually reduce his smoking behavior. Following a baseline period, he sets a certain criterion for an allowable number of cigarettes that is only slightly less than the average number of cigarettes he smoked during the baseline. If he successfully meets this criterion for 3 consecutive days, he reduces the allowable limit by two cigarettes. If he meets that criterion for 3 successive days, he reduces the limit by two more cigarettes. He repeats this process until the eventual goal of no smoking has been achieved. The self-punishment procedure consists of tearing up a dollar bill for every cigarette that is smoked over the allowable limit (see Axelrod, Hall, Weiss, & Rohrer, 1974, for a case report of such a procedure).

Hypothetical results for this program are displayed in Figure 2.7. Jack was generally successful in meeting each criterion, with number of cigarettes smoked per day either matching or falling below the criterion for that day. The one exception occurred on day 33, at which point the criterion was zero cigarettes per day. Because Jack exceeded the criterion on this day, he would have implemented the self-punishment contingency of tearing up a dollar bill.

As noted above, the changing-criterion design is especially appropriate for situations in which the behavior is intended to change gradually in accord with some changing criterion for performance. Thus, it would be an appropriate design for such programs as, say, gradually increasing the amount of time one studies each day or decreasing the amount of time spent playing computer games. It is important, however, that the behavior closely match the criteria; otherwise, it will be difficult to determine if the change in behavior is the result of the treatment or some other, extraneous factor.

FIGURE 2.7   Hypothetical data illustrating use of a changing-criterion design to assess the effect of a self-punishment procedure to gradually reduce smoking. The dashed horizontal lines indicate the changing criterion for maximum allowable number of cigarettes smoked per day.

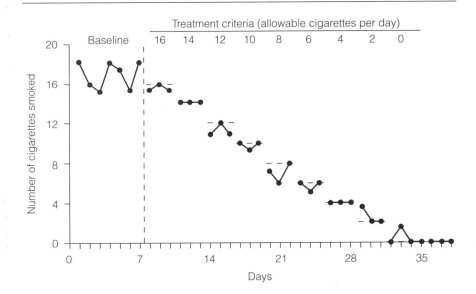

The reversal design and multiple-baseline design are the most basic single-subject designs, with the changing-criterion design less often utilized. Other types of single-subject designs have also been devised, each of which has its advantages and disadvantages (see Barlow & Hersen, 1984; Kazdin, 1994). Most of these have been developed for use in applied settings. In experimental research, the reversal design (or some variation of it) is often employed in studies of operant conditioning. By contrast, studies of classical conditioning most often use some type of control group design, and single-subject designs are rarely employed.

Taken together, the strength of any experimental design is that it enables us to make causal statements about the effects of independent variables on dependent variables. Control over the environment enables the researcher to isolate the effects of the independent variables while controlling for extraneous influences. Despite this advantage, experimental methods also have a major disadvantage. Because of the need to strictly control the environment, experimental settings are sometimes quite artificial, with the result that the findings may have limited applicability to the real world. However, the precise control over the environment that can be obtained with experimental research lends itself to replication, and with each replication across new subjects and new settings, we gain confidence that our findings do have generality.

ADVICE FOR THE LOVELORN

Dear Dr. Dee,

I am suspicious that my boyfriend is having an affair with his old girlfriend. Whenever she is in town, he phones me significantly less often. For example, between May and August, when I know for a fact that she was in town, he phoned me an average of 5.8 times per week, while between September and December, when she was out of town, he phoned an average of 6.4 times per week. I worked it out, and sure enough, this is a statistically significant difference! But when I confronted him with this hard evidence of his unfaithfulness, he denied it, and said that I am being paranoid.

Am-I Being-paranoid?

Dear Am-I,

Given the evidence that you have presented, I would have to say yes, you are being paranoid. But worse than that, you are being a poor scientist. For example, you have neglected to consider other factors that might account for the observed difference. Quite apart from his old girlfriend being in town, your boyfriend may be calling less between May and August for several other reasons, such as spending more time in outdoor activities, visiting with relatives, and so on. These other possibilities need to be assessed before you can draw any conclusions about your boyfriend's unfaithfulness.

You also need to recognize that statistically significant differences do not provide hard evidence of anything. What they provide is *supportive* evidence for a certain *possibility*. Thus, even with a highly significant difference between two sets of scores, there is still a slight possibility that the difference is actually due to chance variation. As well, you need to consider that a difference that is *statistically* significant may not be *meaningfully* significant. The difference you have described seems quite small. I bet that if you chart the number of phone calls week by week, as in a simple-comparison design, you will have a hard time spotting much of any difference between the May–August period and the September–December period. And in this particular case, if you cannot see much of a difference by eyeballing the data, then maybe there is not much of a difference.

Behaviorally yours,

Dr. Dee

1. In a changing-criterion design, the question of interest is whether the changes in behavior match changes in a c_____ for the behavior that is being systematically a_____.

2. A changing-criterion design is most appropriate for assessing the effect of programs designed to produce a (sudden/gradual) _____ change in behavior.

3. In using this type of design, it is important that the level of behavior closely _____ the changes in the criterion for that behavior.

Use of Animals in Behavioral Research

Animal research has greatly contributed to our understanding and treatment of serious diseases and illnesses, as well as our understanding of basic physiological processes. Similarly, many of the basic principles of behavior have been discovered through research with animals, especially rats and pigeons. But if the ultimate goal of such research is to discover principles of behavior that are applicable to humans, why use animals at all? In the following section, we outline some of the arguments for and against animal research that will help inform your opinion in this highly controversial debate.

A major advantage of using animals in research is the ability to control both their genetic makeup and learning history. Knowledge of an animal's genetic makeup helps us eliminate, or assess, the effects of inherited differences on learning and behavior. Rats, for example, can be bred so that an entire batch of research subjects has virtually identical genes. It is possible to control for genetic differences in humans by studying identical twins, but the number of people we can obtain for such research is necessarily quite limited. Similarly, animals bred for research have had somewhat identical experiences during their upbringing, along with a fairly limited learning history. It is virtually impossible to control for the learning histories of humans who volunteer for psychological research. If we are conducting experiments designed to assess basic principles of learning, then the learning histories of one's subjects could critically influence the outcome of the experiment.

A second advantage to using animals as subjects is that researchers are often able to more strictly control the experimental environment for animals than for humans. This is especially important in behavioral research, in which we are attempting to isolate and manipulate certain aspects of the environment to determine their effect on behavior. For example, if we are interested in the effect of food deprivation on activity level in rats (as discussed in Chapter 11), then it is highly advantageous to strictly control the rat's feeding schedule—to a degree that would be impossible in humans. Human subjects participating in ongoing research also have a tendency to discuss the project with their friends when they go home each day, even when they are asked not to do so. These conversations can easily lead to a significant change in the person's behavior during the next experimental session. By contrast, rats and mice tend not to give each other suggestions while lounging about in their home cages following a hard day of maze running. Their behavior therefore tends to be more consistent from day to day. In general, because animals are more easily insulated from extraneous influences during the course of the experiment, their behavior is more likely to reflect the true influence of the independent variable.

A third reason for using animals in behavioral research has to do with the fact that some research cannot ethically be conducted with humans. This is particularly the case with experimental manipulations that are potentially aversive or harmful. For example, rats have been used to investigate the manner in which classical conditioning might account for unusual instances of drug overdose (this finding is discussed in Chapter 5). Such research has the potential to save lives but would be impossible to conduct with human subjects.

In reaction to these claimed benefits of animal research, critics have offered several counterarguments. One criticism is that because animals are not humans, the findings from animal research necessarily have limited applicability to humans. The physiological processes, genetic tendencies, and learning histories of animals are simply too different for research with animals to be of much relevance to humans. In this text we hope to convince you of the opposite, but the argument should not be dismissed out of hand. Despite the demonstrated benefits of animal research, some research with animals almost certainly does have little applicability to humans. Unfortunately, determining ahead of time which research findings are likely to be applicable to humans is a difficult task. It could well be that some of the most applicable findings from animal research, such as basic research on schedules of reinforcement (discussed in Chapter 7), would have initially struck some people as trivial and unimportant. (In fact, some people still regard them as trivial and unimportant.)

Perhaps the most fundamental criticism of animal research is that it is morally wrong and that animals have rights similar to humans. Animal rights activists therefore oppose "inhumane" research practices, such as confining animals to cages, subjecting them to electric shock, depriving them of food, **4** and so on. From this perspective, even the reported benefits of animal research for saving lives and improving the human condition are insufficient to justify submitting animals to such morally reprehensible practices.

Beginning in the 1800s, researchers have reacted to such criticism by developing guidelines that weigh the benefits of research against the injurious or aversive nature of the procedures. The first guidelines were formulated in 1876, with the introduction of the British Cruelty to Animals Act. It was in the 1960s, however, that animal care committees and review boards became strongly established. Today, researchers in most professional organizations, including the American Psychological Association, are regulated by ethical standards that provide strict guidelines for the care and use of animals.

It is also worth noting that animal researchers are themselves concerned about the welfare of their animals. Skinner, for example, disliked shocking rats

And Furthermore

Enhanced Motivation or Cruel Starvation: The Ethics of Food Deprivation

In many of the animal studies described in this text, food is used as a reward (reinforcer) for performing certain behaviors. As such, the animals are typically food deprived to ensure that they are well motivated to work for food. Pigeons, for example, are typically placed on a diet until their weight is about 80–85% of their free-feeding weight (that is, the amount they weigh when food is constantly available). Some people regard such food deprivation procedures as inhumane. But is this really the case?

First, we have to remember that the 80–85% level is calculated based on the pigeon's free-feeding weight. Free food is an unnatural state of affairs for a pigeon, which in its natural environment has to constantly forage for food. The result is that the weight of a pigeon on free food is well beyond its natural weight. Poling, Nickel, and Alling (1990), for example, found that wild pigeons placed on free food for 42 days experienced an average weight increase of 17%, with some pigeons gaining as much as 30%. (This latter figure is equivalent to a 160-pound individual who, with little to do but eat, balloons up to 208 pounds!) Thus, the weight of a pigeon at 80% of its free-feeding weight is quite close to what it would be if it were foraging for food in its natural environment.

A second point to bear in mind is that a certain amount of food restriction can be quite healthy. In fact, calorie restriction is the most reliable means known for slowing the aging process. Virtually all species tested, ranging from spiders to monkeys, have shown significant increases in both health status and life span when raised on diets that provide 30% to 50% fewer calories than normal (Weindruch, 1996). (Of course, the animals growing up on these diets are also significantly smaller than normal.) This effect has yet to be confirmed in humans, and sometimes the diet produces negative results when it is suddenly imposed later in life. Nevertheless, enough evidence exists to suggest that a moderate level of calorie restriction—given that one eats adequate amounts of highly nutritious foods— might be a healthy regimen for both people and pigeons.

and therefore conducted few studies of punishment (Bjork, 1993). Many researchers also acknowledge that the animal rights movement has served a valuable purpose by ensuring the development of strict standards of ethical conduct. They likewise recognize that the extent to which animal research is justified is a difficult question that individuals must answer for themselves. The important thing, however, is to make it an informed decision. (For a discussion of these issues, see Mukerjee, 1997.)

1. A key advantage to using animals for behavioral research is that one can more strictly control an animal's g_____ make-up and l_____ history.

2. A second advantage to using animals is that the e_____ environment can more easily be controlled for animals than humans.

3. A third advantage to using animals for research is that it would be un_____ to conduct certain types of studies with humans, such as examining the effects of brain lesions on learning ability.

4. Two arguments against the use of animals in research are the following:

(1)

_____

(2)

_____

SUMMARY

Behavioral research involves the manipulation and measurement of variables. The independent variable is that aspect of an experiment that is systematically varied across conditions in an experiment and is believed to affect the dependent variable, which is the behavior being measured. Appetitive stimuli are events that are sought out by an organism, while aversive stimuli are events that are avoided. Establishing operations are conditions that affect the appetitiveness or aversiveness of an event. Deprivation is one such condition, which tends to increase the appetitiveness of an event, while satiation tends to decrease the appetitiveness of an event. A contingency exists if there is a conditional (or dependent) relationship between two events. This is often the case in experimental research where changes in an independent variable produce changes in a dependent variable.

Behavioral researchers strive to employ objective, unambiguous definitions of behavior. Depending on the research question, there are several ways to measure behavior. Rate of response indicates the frequency with which a response occurs in a certain period of time, while intensity is the force or magnitude of a behavior. Duration is the length of time an ongoing behavior is performed, speed is the time required to perform a complete episode of behavior, and latency is the amount of time it takes for the behavior to commence. Interval recording measures whether a behavior occurs within each of a series of continuous intervals, while time sample recording measures whether a behavior occurs within a series of discontinuous intervals. Other behavioral measures include topography (the physical form of a behavior) and number of errors.

In addition to selecting a measure of behavior, researchers need to determine the most appropriate method for conducting research. Research methods can be classified as descriptive or experimental. Two descriptive methods are naturalistic observation and the case study approach. Descriptive methods provide rich, detailed information but do not demonstrate causal relationships. Experimental methods do demonstrate causal relationships and generally take the form of control group or single-subject designs. Control group designs involve the random assignment of subjects to experimental and nonexperimental (control) conditions. However, control group designs have certain drawbacks, such as requiring large numbers of subjects.

In contrast, single-subject designs can be used to demonstrate cause-and-effect relationships using only one or a few subjects. Types of single-subject designs include the simple-comparison design, reversal design, multiple-baseline design, and changing-criterion design, each of which has its strengths and weaknesses.

Advantages of using animals as subjects in behavioral research include enhanced control over learning history, genetic background, and experimental environment relative to human participants. Also, animals can be used in studies that cannot ethically be conducted on humans. Disadvantages of using animals are the possibility that findings may have limited application to humans, and the notion that animals have the same rights as humans. Ethics committees have been established to weigh the costs and benefits of proposed research involving animals.

STUDY QUESTIONS

1. Distinguish between independent and dependent variables.
2. What is a functional relationship?
3. Define stimulus and response. Differentiate between the terms stimulus and stimuli.
4. Distinguish between overt and covert behavior.
5. Distinguish between appetitive and aversive stimuli.
6. Define establishing operation. Name and describe two types of establishing operations.
7. Distinguish between contiguity and contingency. Name and define two types of contiguity.
8. Define rate of response. Why is rate of response a favored measure of behavior among radical behaviorists?
9. How does one distinguish a high rate of response versus a low rate of response versus a period of no response on a cumulative record?
10. Distinguish between speed, duration, and latency measures of behavior.
11. Distinguish between the intensity and topography of a behavior.
12. Distinguish between interval recording and time sample recording.
13. Name and describe two types of descriptive research methods used by researchers. What is a major limitation of descriptive research methods?
14. Describe the simplest form of a control group design. How are subjects assigned to the different conditions and why is this done?
15. What are three limitations of control group designs?
16. What are single-subject designs? Describe a simple-comparison design. In what sense is it a "flawed" design?
17. Describe a reversal design. What are the drawbacks to this type of design?
18. Describe a multiple-baseline design. What is a limitation of this type of design?
19. Describe a changing-criterion design. For what types of situations is this design appropriate?

20. List three advantages and two disadvantages of using animals as subjects in behavioral research.

CONCEPT REVIEW

appetitive stimulus. An event that an organism will seek out.

aversive stimulus. An event that an organism will avoid.

baseline. The normal frequency of a behavior prior to some intervention.

case study approach. A descriptive research approach that involves intensive examination of one or a few individuals.

changing-criterion design. A type of single-subject design in which the effect of the treatment is demonstrated by the extent to which the behavior matches a criterion that is systematically altered.

contingency. A dependent relationship between two events—that is, the occurrence of one event is dependent on the occurrence of another.

control group design. A type of experiment in which, at its simplest, subjects are randomly assigned to either an experimental (or treatment) group and a control group; subjects assigned to the experimental group are exposed to a certain manipulation or treatment while those assigned to the control group are not.

covert behavior. Behavior that can be perceived only by the person performing the behavior. Thoughts and feelings are covert behaviors.

cumulative recorder. A device that measures total number of responses over time and provides a graphic depiction of the rate of behavior.

dependent variable. That aspect of an experiment that is allowed to freely vary to determine if it is affected by changes in the independent variable.

deprivation. The prolonged absence of an event that tends to increase the appetitiveness of that event.

descriptive research. Research that focuses on describing the behavior and the situation within which it occurs.

duration. The length of time that an individual repeatedly or continuously performs a certain behavior.

establishing operation. A procedure that affects the appetitiveness or aversiveness of a stimulus.

functional relationship. The relationship between changes in an independent variable and changes in a dependent variable; a cause-and-effect relationship.

independent variable. That aspect of an experiment that systematically varies across the different conditions in an experiment.

intensity. The force or magnitude of a behavior.

interval recording. The measurement of whether a behavior occurs within a series of continuous intervals.

latency. The length of time required for a behavior to begin.

multiple-baseline design. A type of single-subject design in which a treatment is instituted at successive points in time for two or more persons, settings, or behaviors.

naturalistic observation. A descriptive research approach that involves the systematic observation and recording of behavior in its natural environment.

overt behavior. Behavior that has the potential for being directly observed by an individual other than the one performing the behavior.

rate of response. The frequency with which a response occurs in a certain period of time.

response. A particular instance of a behavior.

reversal design. A type of single-subject design that involves repeated alternations between a baseline period and a treatment period.

satiation. The prolonged exposure to (or consumption of) an event that tends to decrease the appetitiveness of that event.

simple-comparison design. A type of single-subject design in which behavior in a baseline condition is compared to behavior in a treatment condition.

single-subject design. A research design that requires only one or a few subjects in order to conduct an entire experiment.

spatial contiguity. The extent to which events are situated close to each other in space.

speed. The amount of time required to perform a complete episode of a behavior from start to finish.

stimulus. Any event that can potentially influence behavior.

temporal contiguity. The extent to which events occur close together in time.

time sample recording. The measurement of whether a behavior occurs within a series of discontinuous intervals.

topography. The physical form of a behavior.

variable. A characteristic of a person, place, or thing that can change (vary) over time or from one situation to another.

CHAPTER TEST

12. Using a(n) _____ recording procedure, we find that during a 10-minute task, Erik chewed his nails during each of the first 2 minutes, as well as during the fourth, sixth, and tenth minutes.

27. Being quite addicted to computer games, Jules decides to implement a program to gradually reduce the amount of time that he spends playing these games. A useful design for determining if his program is successful would be a _____ design.

18. The reversal design is also known as a(n) _____ design.

3. Each time it rains, I see an increased number of umbrellas being carried. There appears to be a _____ relationship between the weather and the appearance of umbrellas.

8. You have eaten nothing but pizza for 4 months. It is likely that the reward value of eating a pizza has (increased/decreased) _____ as a function of (which type of establishing operation) _____.

23. The amount of time it takes Zak to read a chapter is a _____ measure of behavior, while the amount of time it took him to begin reading the chapter is a _____ measure of behavior. By contrast, the total amount of time he spends reading each day is a _____ measure of behavior.

15. In a _____ design, subjects are randomly assigned to a treatment or nontreatment condition.

11. Number of cigarettes smoked each week is a _____ measure of smoking.

19. Animals are often used in behavioral research because this practice allows for greater _____ over learning history, genetic influences, and experimental environment than is possible with humans. As well, animals are often used when the use of humans would be _____ questionable.

10. The force with which a boxer delivers a blow is a(n) _____ measure of behavior.

26. I wish to test a new drug that I believe will permanently remove the symptoms of a rare neurological disorder. Unfortunately, only three patients who suffer from the disorder have volunteered to take the drug. What would be a useful type of design to demonstrate the effectiveness of this drug? _____.

16. An experiment that utilizes a type of _____ design requires only one or a few subjects.

4. A flash of light is a _____, while two flashes of light are _____. A specific eyeblink that is elicited by a flash of light is a _____.

20. After Trish told Jennifer that Lorne was the most popular guy in school, Jennifer became extremely interested in him. Trish's statement about Lorne apparently functioned as an _____ that increased Lorne's value as an _____ stimulus.

7. You have not had a pizza in 4 months. It is likely that the reward value of eating a pizza has (increased/decreased) _____ as a function of (which type of establishing operation) _____.

24. When people feel confident, they tend to stand straight. In this case, we are using a _____ measure of behavior as an index of confidence.

1. Any characteristic of a person, place, or thing that can change can be called a _____.

9. Robbie is afraid of spiders while Naseem finds them interesting. A spider is a(n) _____ stimulus to Robbie, and a(n) _____ stimulus to Naseem.

6. A knife and spoon are placed side by side in a dinner setting creating spatial (contiguity/contingency) _____ between the two utensils.

13. Using a(n) _____ recording procedure, a school psychologist drops into a classroom for a 20-minute period four times each

day and notes whether some type of disruption occurs during the time that he is there.

17. The _____ approach is a descriptive method of research often used by psychiatrists who encounter a very unusual case.

2. In a classical conditioning experiment, one group of dogs first hears a tone and then receives food, while another group of dogs receives food and then hears a tone. Following this, the researcher measures how much the dogs in each group salivate when they simply hear the tone. In this experiment, the order in which tone and food are presented is the _____ variable, while the amount of salivation to the tone is the _____ variable.

22. On a cumulative recorder, a gradually sloping line indicates a _____ rate of response while a steep line indicates a _____ rate of response. By contrast, a _____ line indicates no response.

14. Two main approaches to behavioral research are the _____ approach and the _____ approach.

5. Blinking is a(n) _____ behavior, while thinking about blinking is a(n) _____ behavior.

25. Dr. Roberts studies the effects of schizoid personality disorder by sitting in the park each day and observing the behavior of street derelicts who are known to be suffering from the disorder. Dr. Roberts is using a descriptive research method known as _____.

21. To determine whether drinking coffee in the evening keeps me awake at night, I observe my sleep patterns for a 2-week period in which I drink coffee each evening, followed by a 2-week period in which I do not drink coffee in the evening. I am using a _____ design to conduct this study, which will likely give me (strong/questionable) _____ evidence concerning how coffee affects my sleep patterns.

ANSWERS TO CHAPTER TESTS

1. variable
2. independent; dependent
3. functional
4. stimulus; stimuli; response
5. overt; covert
6. contiguity
7. increased; deprivation
8. decreased; satiation
9. aversive; appetitive
10. intensity
11. rate
12. interval
13. time sample
14. descriptive; experimental
15. control group
16. single-subject
17. case study
18. ABAB
19. control; ethically
20. establishing operation; appetitive
21. simple comparison; questionable
22. low; high; flat
23. speed; latency; duration
24. topography
25. naturalistic observation
26. multiple-baseline (across persons)
27. changing-criterion

Put Learning into Action with Sniffy, the Virtual Rat

The following material refers to *Sniffy, the Virtual Rat™: Pro Version*, a separate Wadsworth product that consists of a manual and a CD-ROM.

1. This would be a good point at which to read Chapter 1 (pp. 1–6) in *Sniffy, the Virtual Rat™* (i.e., *Sniffy Pro*). (Henceforth, page numbers and exercises in these endnotes will refer to pages and exercises in *Sniffy, the Virtual Rat™*; page references from the textbook will be identified as such.)
2. Note: the Sniffy exercises use a cumulative recorder to give a measure of the rat's behavior.
3. Note: Sniffy uses a somewhat different technique to measure the intensity of behavior. As you can probably imagine, measuring salivation in a rat is more difficult than in a dog. Instead, classical conditioning studies with Sniffy measure behavioral intensity with a suppression ratio, using a technique called conditioned emotional response (CER). If you want to know more about suppression ratios and CER, you can skip ahead to pp. 84–86 in *Sniffy Pro* and pp. 106–108 in the textbook.
4. Note: As indicated on p. 2, the *Sniffy Pro* software developers filmed real rats engaging in various behaviors, then digitized these images to animate Sniffy. However, for ethical reasons the rats were not actually given shocks. To read about how Sniffy was animated to represent a rat receiving a shock, see p. 86.
5. This would be a good place at which to start working with the *Sniffy Pro* software. Read the Preface (pp. xi–xv) for instructions on how to load the program software onto your computer. Once the software is loaded, begin to train Sniffy to press the lever in his operant chamber using a process called "shaping." The features of Sniffy's operant chamber are explained on pp. 11–12. Read and follow the instructions for exercises 1–3 (pp. 17–31) to train Sniffy to press the lever in his operant chamber for a food reward.

CHAPTER 3

Elicited Behaviors and Classical Conditioning

CHAPTER OUTLINE

*Put Learning into Action
with Sniffy, the Virtual Rat*

At a friend's party, Uma witnessed her boyfriend flagrantly flirting with another woman. She was initially quite angry, but when he later apologized for his actions and was very attentive to her, she experienced unusually strong feelings of attraction toward him. Still, she somehow felt manipulated by the whole affair. After all, her friends had warned her that he had a terrible reputation for playing "mind games."

Elicited Behaviors

The word elicit means to draw out or bring forth. Thus, an elicited behavior is one that is automatically drawn out by a certain stimulus. (Note that the word is *elicit*, not *illicit*, which refers to something illegal, such as an illicit drug.) A sneeze produced by a particle of dust and a startle reaction to the sound of a gunshot are examples of elicited behaviors. They are elicited in the sense that they are automatically drawn out by the stimuli that produce them. In this sense, such behaviors can also be thought of as involuntary. For example, you do not choose to be startled by a gunshot; your startle reaction is an involuntary response to the gunshot. Similarly, you do not choose to salivate when you bite into a lemon; salivating is an involuntary response to the lemon.

In this chapter, we begin by describing different types of elicited behaviors as well as some simple mechanisms by which they can be modified. This will include a discussion of the opponent-process theory of emotion, an intriguing theory that explains a wide variety of emotional phenomena ranging from symptoms of drug withdrawal to the sense of loss you feel following the breakup of a relationship. The remainder of the chapter will then be devoted to introducing the concept of classical conditioning, the first major type of learning to be discussed in this text.

Reflexes

Reflexes are the most basic form of elicited behavior. **A *reflex* is a relatively simple, involuntary response to a stimulus.** (It can also be defined as the *relationship* between such a response and the stimulus that elicits it.) Some reflexes involve only one gland or set of muscles, such as when you salivate in response to a drop of lemon juice or blink in response to a puff of air. Other reflexes are more general in scope, involving the coordinated action of several body parts. For example, the *startle response*—**a defensive reaction to a sudden, unexpected stimulus**—involves the automatic tightening of skeletal muscles as well as various hormonal and visceral (internal organ) changes. Similarly, the *orienting response*—**in which we automatically position ourselves to facilitate attending to a stimulus**—can involve a relatively major body movement, such as when we automatically turn in response to an unfamiliar noise behind us.

Many reflexes are closely tied to survival. For example, food consumption involves a chain of reflexes including salivation, peristalsis (wave-like actions that push food down the esophagus and through the digestive system), and secretion of digestive juices in the stomach. Conversely, the vomiting reflex serves a protective function by expelling potentially poisonous substances from the digestive system. Other protective reflexes include the *flexion response,* **in which we automatically jerk our hand or foot away from a hot or sharp object that we have inadvertently contacted,** and the aforementioned startle reaction—designed to ready us for fight or flight if the unexpected stimulus should prove dangerous.

Newborns come "prepackaged" with a host of reflexes that facilitate their survival. For example, if you touch a baby's cheek with your finger, the baby will automatically turn his or her head in that direction. This reflex action is designed to facilitate taking a nipple into the mouth. Once the nipple is in the mouth, the baby's sucking reflex is activated (which in turn elicits a "milk letdown" reflex in the mother). Many of these reflexes disappear within a few years (e.g., the sucking reflex) while others, such as salivating and vomiting, remain with us throughout life.

Many of the simpler reflexes are activated through a reflex arc. **A *reflex arc* is a neural structure that underlies many reflexes and consists of a sensory neuron, an interneuron, and a motor neuron.** Take, for example, a flexion response in which we quickly jerk our hand away from an open flame. Upon touching the flame, receptors in the hand stimulate sensory neurons that carry a danger message (in the form of a burst of nerve impulses) toward the spinal cord. Within the spinal cord, interneurons receive this message and immediately pass it on to the motor neurons. These motor neurons then activate the muscles in the arm that pull the hand away from the flame. Simultaneous with this process, pain messages are also sent up the spinal cord to the brain, but by the time they are received and the person consciously feels the pain, the hand is already being withdrawn from the flame. Thus, we do not withdraw our hand from the flame because of the pain; we actually begin withdrawing our hand prior to feeling any pain. Because the flexion response utilizes a simple reflex arc through the spinal cord, we are able to withdraw our hand from the flame much quicker than if the message had to be routed all the way through the brain and then back down to the arm muscles (see Figure 3.1).

QUICK QUIZ

1. A simple, involuntary response to a stimulus is called a _____.

2. Reflexes are e_____ in the sense that they are drawn out by stimuli that precede their occurrence.

3. A s_____ reaction is an automatic defensive response to a sudden, unexpected stimulus; the o_____ response consists of movements designed to facilitate attending to a stimulus.

4. Many simple reflexes are activated through a r_____ a_____ that consists of a(n) _____ neuron, a(n) _____ neuron, and a(n) _____ neuron (in that order).

5. Quickly jerking your hand or foot away from contact with an open flame or sharp object is a reflexive action known as a fl_____ response. In such cases, the perception of pain generally (precedes/follows) _____ the initiation of the response.

FIGURE 3.1 The reflex arc underlying a flexion response. Upon touching the flame, receptors in the finger stimulate sensory neurons that carry the message via nerve impulses toward the spinal cord. Interneurons within the spinal cord receive the message and pass it directly to motor neurons. The motor neurons in turn activate muscles in the arm that pull the finger away from the flame. At the same time that this is occurring, a pain message is sent to the brain. (*Source:* Nairne, 2000.)

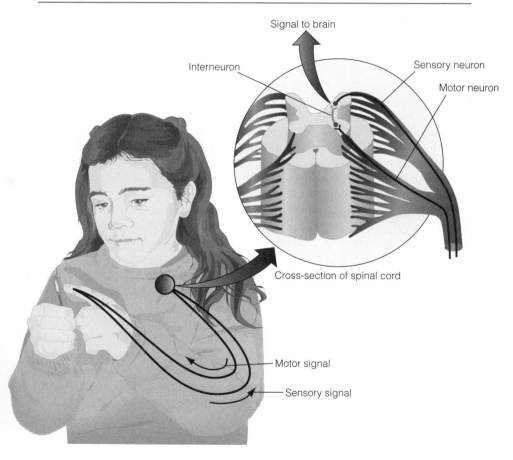

Fixed Action Patterns

Some types of elicited behaviors are more complex than simple reflexes. **A** *fixed action pattern* **is a fixed sequence of responses elicited by a specific stimulus.** Fixed action patterns are also sometimes called "modal action patterns" (Domjan, 1998). Examples include web building by spiders, V-shaped formation flying by ducks, and nut burying by some species of squirrels. Dogs and cats display numerous fixed action patterns. Cats compulsively scratch the ground to cover up urine and feces (effective in a litter box but completely ineffective on your carpet) and rub up against the legs of visitors to "mark" them as belonging to their territory. Dogs indicate their desire to play by wagging their tails, stretching out their front legs, and lowering their heads to the ground (see Figure 3.2). In fact, by adopting this posture (and looking completely foolish in front of any visitors), you can effectively ask your dog if it wishes to play (which of course it will not, given that it now has you looking like an idiot).

A specific stimulus that elicits a fixed action pattern is called a *sign stimulus* or *releaser*. For example, a male *Betta splendens*, better known as a Siamese fighting fish, immediately takes an aggressive posture at the sight of another male (the releaser), with both fish then spreading out their brilliant red or blue fins and gills. If introduced into the same tank, the two fish will attack each other, sometimes even resulting in death. Similarly, during mating season, a male stickleback fish displays a fixed sequence of aggressive actions when another male enters its territory (Tinbergen, 1951). Interestingly, the sign stimulus for the stickleback's aggressive actions is not the presence of the other male but the sight of its red underbelly. If the red belly is covered up or painted a different color, the intruder will not be attacked. On the other hand, if a pie-shaped or cigar-shaped piece of wood with a red patch on the bottom is introduced into the tank, it will be attacked.

Fixed action patterns tend to be unique to certain species and are therefore sometimes called *species-specific behaviors.* They used to be called instincts, but this term has been largely abandoned because it implies that the behavior is more rigid and inflexible than is actually the case. For example, if two rats are subjected to a painful stimulus, such as an electric shock, they will automatically aggress toward each other (Ulrich & Azrin, 1962). Such aggression often takes the form of a fixed action pattern in which the two combatants rear up on their hind legs and essentially box by striking out at each other with their front paws (see Figure 3.3). Sometimes, however, the two rats will forgo such "niceties" and start biting each other. Additionally, both boxing and biting are more likely to occur in rats that have been trained to be aggressive than in those that have not been trained to be aggressive (Baeninger & Ulm, 1969). Thus, the rats' fixed action pattern of aggression is actually quite variable and can be significantly modified by experience.

Fixed action patterns are highly adaptive responses that have evolved to help animals cope with consistent aspects of their environment. The difficulty

FIGURE 3.2 Fixed action pattern for play. A dog will indicate its desire for play by stretching out its front legs and lowering its head to the ground. (*Source:* Reprinted with permission of The Free Press, a Division of Simon & Schuster, Inc., from *The Intelligence of Dogs: Canine Consciousness and Capabilities,* by Stanley Coren, p. 113. Copyright © 1994 Stanley Coren.)

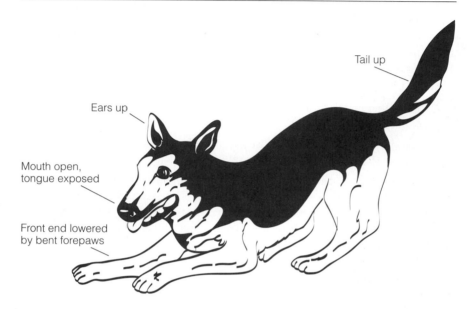

FIGURE 3.3 Stereotyped fighting posture displayed by rats. Although this is a fixed action pattern, it can nevertheless be modified through experience.

with such inherited behavior patterns is that a sudden, large-scale change in the environment may render the pattern useless or even harmful. For example, deer have an inborn tendency to run a zigzag pattern when being pursued by a predator. This action, which confuses the predator, greatly increases the deer's chances of survival in the wild; however, this same action greatly reduces its chances of survival when it is being pursued down the highway by an automobile. The inborn tendency to zigzag is an extremely maladaptive way of responding to the modern threat of automobiles. By comparison, an animal that can modify its behavior patterns through learning can better adapt to a changing environment.

1. A fixed action pattern is a fixed _____ of responses that occurs in reaction to a specific stimulus.

2. The specific stimulus that elicits a fixed action pattern is called a s_____ stimulus or r_____.

3. Different species of spiders spin different kinds of webs. Web spinning of this sort can thus be considered a s_____-s_____ behavior. Such behaviors used to be called i_____, but this term has now been largely abandoned because it implies that the behavior is more inflexible than is actually the case.

Simple Mechanisms of Learning

Habituation and Sensitization

The repeated presentation of an eliciting stimulus can alter the strength of the elicited behavior. *Habituation* **is a decrease in the strength of an elicited behavior following repeated presentations of the eliciting stimulus.** For example, we quickly stop attending to low-intensity background noises such as the ticking of a clock or the distant noise of traffic. Similarly, a sudden, unexpected tap on the shoulder may elicit a startle response, while further taps have no such effect. Through habituation to such stimuli, we can selectively focus on other, more important aspects of the environment.

By contrast, *sensitization* **is an increase in the strength of an elicited behavior following repeated presentations of the eliciting stimulus.** For example, soldiers under attack generally do not habituate to the sound of artillery shells exploding nearby. Instead, their startle reaction grows stronger. Needless to say, this greatly contributes to the stress they experience and the inevitable breakdown virtually all soldiers suffer after repeated exposure to battle conditions (though Hollywood would often have you think otherwise).

Why does repeated exposure to certain stimuli sometimes result in habituation and sometimes in sensitization? One factor is the intensity of the eliciting stimulus. A low-intensity stimulus, such as the ticking of a clock, generally results in habituation. A high-intensity stimulus, such as exploding artillery shells, generally results in sensitization. And a stimulus of intermediate intensity often results in an initial period of sensitization followed by habituation. For example, at a shooting range, the first few shots you hear might produce an increasingly strong startle reaction. But you then begin to habituate to the shots, and after a while they are hardly noticed.

The effects of habituation and sensitization usually dissipate when the stimulus is not presented for a period of time. For example, you might habituate to the sound of a neighbor's stereo one evening, only to be once more bothered by it when she first turns it on the next evening. Nevertheless, some forms of habituation last for long periods of time. For example, if you move into an apartment in which you hear the sound of a train each morning, your reaction to the noise will probably be most intense on the first day and then decrease slowly thereafter. This type of habituation is known as *long-term habituation*, as opposed to *short-term habituation*, which dissipates fairly quickly.

Note that sensitization often generalizes to other stimuli. A shell-shocked soldier is likely to jump not only in response to artillery explosions but also to any sudden stimulus. By contrast, habituation is quite stimulus-specific, such that any change in the stimulus is likely to result in the reappearance of the habituated response. Thus, many people suddenly become aware of the sound of their car when the motor sounds a bit different or when the car has a slightly different feel to it as they are driving along. Only a slight change is needed to alert the driver that something is potentially wrong (and hopefully inexpensive to fix). One version of this process is known as the *Coolidge effect*, based on an old joke about former U.S. president Calvin Coolidge. The story has it that he and his wife were once being separately escorted around a chicken farm. When Mrs. Coolidge was informed that the resident rooster was capable of mating several times a day, she replied, "You should tell that to the president." Informed about this, the president asked whether the repeated matings occurred with the same chicken or different chickens. When told that it was different chickens, he replied, "You should tell that to my wife." The Coolidge effect therefore is the enhanced sexual arousal displayed by the males of some species when presented with different sexual partners as opposed to the same sexual partner to whom it has habituated.

Habituated responses can also reappear following the presentation of a seemingly irrelevant novel stimulus, a phenomenon called *dishabituation.* For example, Cheryl might quickly habituate to the sound of gunshots at a shooting range. If, however, a handsome stranger approaches and stands nearby, she might again be startled when the next shot is fired. Likewise, couples can sometimes rekindle their romance by traveling to a new and different environment—or even just treating themselves to a night in a hotel room rather than staying at home.

1. An (increase/decrease) _____ in the strength of a behavior following repeated presentations of the eliciting stimulus is called habituation.

2. An (increase/decrease) _____ in the strength of a behavior following repeated presentations of the eliciting stimulus is called sensitization.

3. One factor that influences whether we habituate or become sensitized to a particular stimulus is the _____ of the eliciting stimulus.

4. In general, repeated presentations of a low-intensity stimulus result in _____, while repeated presentations of a high-intensity stimulus result in _____.

5. A stimulus of intermediate intensity will initially result in a period of _____, which is then followed by _____.

6. Learning to ignore the sound of dripping water is an example of _____; becoming increasingly aware of the sound of a jackhammer on the street below your apartment is an example of _____.

7. The fact that it has been several months since you noticed the sound of the fan in your home computer is an example of l_____-t_____h_____.

8. In general, sensitization (is/is not) _____ stimulus specific, while habituation (is/is not) _____ stimulus specific.

9. The presentation of a novel stimulus during a period of habituation can sometimes result in dis_____, in which the habituated response (reappears/disappears) _____.

Opponent–Process Theory of Emotion

Habituation and sensitization represent two opposing tendencies: weaker reactivity to a stimulus versus stronger reactivity. Solomon (1980; see also Solomon & Corbit, 1974) has proposed an intriguing theory of emotion that involves a similar dual mechanism. Known as the opponent-process theory, it is particularly good at explaining the aftereffects of strong emotional responses. Consider, for example, the following anecdote quoted by Solomon:

> [M]y neighbor's son was struck by lightning as he was returning from a golf course. He was thrown to the ground. His shorts were torn to shreds and he was burned across his thighs. When his companion sat him up, he screamed "I'm dead, I'm dead." His legs were numb and blue and he could not move. By the time he reached the nearest hospital he was *euphoric* [italics added]. (Taussig, 1969, p. 306, quoted in Solomon, 1980, p. 691)

In one sense, the boy's euphoria is logical in that he was lucky to be alive. But in another sense, it is illogical in that he was injured and decidedly worse off than before the incident. Should he not have remained at least somewhat distressed about the incident?

Consider too the following scenario. Suppose you purchase a lottery ticket during a visit home. Next weekend, your mom phones to tell you the winning numbers, and lo and behold you discover that you have won 50,000 dollars! Wow!! You are absolutely elated. Unfortunately, an hour later you receive another call from your mom informing you that she made a mistake on the numbers. It turns out that you *only* won 50 dollars. You are now extremely disappointed, despite the fact that you are still 50 dollars better off than when you climbed out of bed that morning. Within a day, however, your disappointment wears off and you carry on with your impoverished lifestyle as usual.

Now consider an experiment in which a dog is exposed to electric shock (e.g., Katcher, Solomon, Turner, LoLordo, Overmier, & Rescorla, 1969). During the shock, the dog's heart rate quickly rises to a peak, decreases slightly, and then stabilizes at a relatively high level. Now guess what happens when the shock is turned off. Does the dog's heart rate return to normal? No, it does not. When the shock is removed, the dog's heart rate plunges to *below* normal and then after a few minutes moves back up to normal (see Figure 3.4). In fact, the pattern of changes in heart rate during and after the shock—an index of the dog's emotional response to shock—is very similar to the emotional pattern displayed in the preceding lottery scenario. In both cases, an event elicits a strong emotional response, but when the event is withdrawn, an

FIGURE 3.4   Heart rate changes accompanying the application and withdrawal of shock. Our emotional responses often follow a similar pattern, with the onset of the emotional event followed by one type of response and the offset of the event followed by an opposite response.

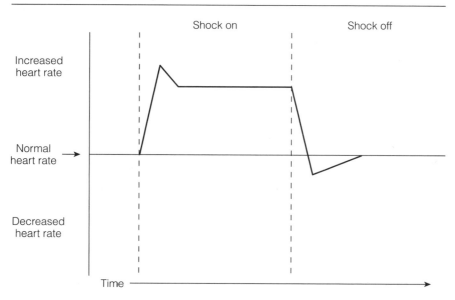

opposite response is elicited and then gradually disappears. In fact, this pattern of emotional changes is relatively common.

An explanation for these emotional changes is provided by the opponent-process theory of emotion. **The *opponent-process theory* proposes that an emotional event elicits two competing processes: (1) an *a-process* (or *primary process*) that is directly elicited by the event, and (2) a *b-process* (or *opponent process*) that is elicited by the a-process and serves to counteract the a-process.** For example, the presentation of shock directly elicits a tendency for the dog's heart rate to increase, which is the a-process. This increase in heart rate in turn elicits a compensatory reaction that tries to decrease heart rate, which is the b-process. The purpose of this compensatory b-process is to counter the sudden increase in heart rate, thereby maintaining a state of internal balance (known as *homeostasis*). In other words, the b-process tries to prevent the increase in heart rate from becoming too extreme, which could be damaging or even fatal. The actual heart rate elicited by shock is therefore the net result of the tendency for heart rate to increase in the presence of shock (the a-process), minus the compensatory tendency for heart rate to decrease (the b-process) (see Figure 3.5). Similarly, in the lottery example, the feeling of elation you experience when you think you have won the lottery is the amount of elation directly elicited by winning the money (the a-process) minus the compensatory reaction to this elation (the b-process), which is trying to keep your elation from becoming too extreme.

QUICK QUIZ

1. The opponent-process theory of emotion accounts for why a strong emotional response is often followed by a(n) (similar/opposite) _____ emotional response.

2. The ___-_____ is directly elicited by the emotional event; this in turn elicits the ___-_____, the purpose of which is to maintain a relatively balanced internal state known as h_____.

3. The a-process is also known as the pr_____ process, while the b-process is also known as the o_____ process.

The a- and b-processes have some important characteristics:

1. *The a-process correlates closely with the presence of the emotional event.* As shown in Figure 3.5, the tendency for heart rate to increase in response to shock is directly tied to the presence of the shock. When the shock is removed, the tendency for heart rate to increase immediately disappears. Similarly, your sense of elation immediately appears when you think you have won the lottery and immediately disappears when you discover that you have not.

2. *The b-process is slow to increase and slow to decrease.* The slow buildup in the b-process accounts for why our emotional response to an event is often strongest at the outset. If you look again at Figure 3.5, you can see that when the shock is first turned on, the dog's heart rate quickly peaks and

FIGURE 3.5 Opponent-process mechanisms that underlie changes in heart rate due to the onset and offset of shock. During the shock, as the b-process acquires strength, it pulls heart rate down from its initial peak and stabilizes it at a moderately high level. Following shock, when the a-process is no longer active, the b-process pulls heart rate to below normal, then gradually dissipates, allowing heart rate to return to normal.

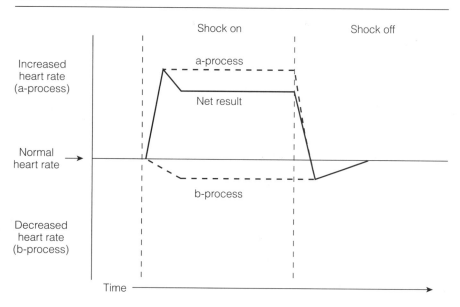

then declines slightly before stabilizing. The immediate peak happens because, during the early moments of shock, the b-process has not yet attained sufficient strength to counteract the a-process, thereby allowing the a-process free rein to increase heart rate. After a few moments, though, the b-process becomes strong enough to moderate the a-process, causing a slight decrease in heart rate before stabilizing. On the other hand, when the shock is removed, the a-process immediately disappears while the b-process only slowly declines. For this reason, when the shock is turned off, the dog's heart rate plunges to well below normal, because all that remains is the b-process that has been trying to pull heart rate down. (It is as though, in a tug-of-war, the other team suddenly let go of the rope, with the result that your team goes flying backwards in the direction they were pulling.) Similarly, when you discover that you have not won the lottery, you immediately feel depressed because the counterreaction to the elation you have been feeling is all that remains. As the b-process gradually weakens, however, your emotional response slowly returns to normal, just as the dog's heart rate slowly returns to normal.

3. *With repeated presentations of the emotional event, the b-process increases in both strength and duration.* This is the most interesting part of the theory. For example, what happens to the dog's heart rate if it is repeatedly shocked?

As it turns out, the increase in heart rate during each shock becomes less and less extreme. Additionally, each time the shock is turned off, the dog's heart rate plunges more and more deeply and takes increasingly longer to return to normal (see Figure 3.6).

The dog's overt emotional responses match these changes in heart rate. Whereas in the early sessions, the dogs show considerable distress in response to the shock, in later sessions they appear more annoyed than distressed. More surprising, though, is the change in their emotional responses following the shock. Whereas in the early sessions, the dogs appear somewhat relieved when the shock is turned off, in the later sessions they show signs of extreme pleasure and euphoria, jumping about and greeting the experimenter with enthusiasm.

Similar emotional patterns have been found in humans. For example, Epstein (1967) found that military parachutists became less and less terrified with repeated jumps and also became more and more elated following each jump. This sense of elation can last several hours among veteran jumpers and probably accounts, at least partially, for the strong attraction some people feel toward parachuting and other high-risk activities.[1]

The opponent-process theory can account for several other emotional phenomena. For example, it seems to explain some aspects of drug addiction. The physiological and psychological reactions directly elicited by the drug are the a-process, while the compensatory reactions to the drug are the b-process. The actual effect of the drug is the net effect of the a-process minus the b-process. In keeping with opponent-process theory, repeated experiences with the drug usually result in less and less of a drug-induced high, while the symptoms of withdrawal (the b-process) become increasingly strong and more persistent. These withdrawal symptoms may become so strong and so persistent that the person is strongly tempted to escape from them by redosing with the drug. At that point, the person is essentially addicted to the drug, because the drug is now being taken mostly to avoid the symptoms of withdrawal.

The opponent-process theory of emotion also has implications for a phenomenon known as revictimization (van der Kolk, 1989). Some people become repeatedly involved in abusive relationships or have great difficulty leaving such relationships. A contributing factor in some cases may be that the person has become hooked on the powerful feelings of pleasure that occur during the "honeymoon period" of forgiveness that often follows an intense episode of abuse. This intense pleasure is the compensatory after-reaction (the b-process) that has become greatly strengthened during the repeated ep-

---

[1] Note, however, that emotional changes during skydiving can be a bit more complex than this. Veteran skydivers experience a peak of anxiety just prior to leaving the plane, followed by a strong sense of elation during the free fall, another peak of anxiety when the chute is being deployed (a high-risk moment), and then a sense of elation after they land. The strong sense of elation that occurs during free fall may be a contributing factor to accidents as veteran jumpers may be tempted to delay deploying the chute until the last possible moment (Delk, 1980).

FIGURE 3.6 Effects of repeated stimulus presentations on primary and opponent process. With repeated stimulation, the b-process becomes stronger and takes longer to dissipate. The result is that heart rate rises only slightly above normal during the shock, then drops considerably below normal following the shock and takes a relatively long time to return to normal.

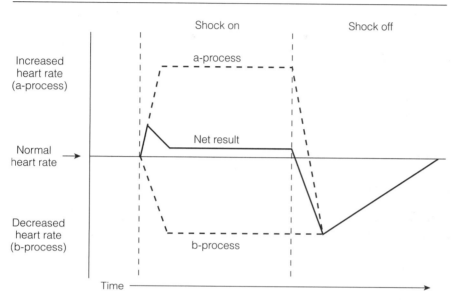

isodes of abuse. As suggested in the opening vignette to this chapter, a weaker version of this honeymoon effect might even occur in relationships in which one is exposed to a period of emotional distress rather than actual abuse.

It must be remembered that the opponent-process theory, however intriguing, is still a theory, with some of the research failing to support the theory (e.g., Fanselow, DeCola, & Young, 1993). Furthermore, as you will see in Chapter 5, classical conditioning might often play an important role in the elicitation of opponent processes. Nevertheless, opponent-process theory has stimulated a considerable amount of research and has proven extremely useful for enhancing our understanding of emotional responses.

1. With repeated presentations of the emotional event, the b-process (increases/decreases) _____ in both strength and duration.

2. The ____-_____ is directly tied to the presence of the emotional event, while the ____-_____ is (slow/quick) _____ to increase and (slow/quick) _____ to decrease.

3. Feeling elated while talking on the phone to someone with whom you are in love is an example of the ____-_____. Feeling lovesick after you finally hang up for the night is an example of the ____-_____.

QUICK QUIZ

ADVICE FOR THE LOVELORN

Dear Dr. Dee,

Several months ago, I broke up with my boyfriend when he took a job in another city. We were together 5 years, and it had turned into a pretty monotonous relationship by the time it ended. But it sure is taking me a long time to get over it. My friend tells me that I must have some kind of "unresolved dependency issue" for me to be this depressed. She recently broke up with her boyfriend—she went out with him for only a month but claims that she was madly in love—and got over it in a week. Is there something wrong with me, or is my friend just superficial?

Still Depressed

Dear Still,

There can be several reasons why some people take longer than others to recover from a breakup. The opponent-process theory, however, might be particularly applicable in your case. Remember that our primary emotional response to an event typically weakens with repeated exposure, while the emotional after-reaction typically strengthens. Solomon (1980) suggested that these processes are as applicable to love relationships as they are to other emotional events. Couples that have been together for only a short time usually have much stronger feelings of affection for each other than do couples that have been to-gether for a long time. In other words, the emotional response of affection generally de-creases over time. When relationships end, however, couples that have been together for a long time experience a much deeper and longer-lasting sense of loss than do couples that have been together for only a short time. According to opponent-process theory, this sense of loss is the compensatory reaction to the relationship, which should be much stronger in those couples that have been together longer. For this reason, it will naturally take more time for you to get over your long-term "monotonous" relationship than for your friend to get over her brief "madly-in-love" relationship.

Behaviorally yours,

Dr. Dee

Classical Conditioning

We have so far discussed those situations in which a certain stimulus (e.g., lemon juice) elicits a particular response (e.g., salivation). We have also noted that repeated presentations of a stimulus can sometimes change the nature of the response, either strengthening it (sensitization), weakening it (habituation), or eliciting a compensatory reaction (the opponent process). But these are relatively simple means of adaptation. The world is a complex place filled with a vast array of stimuli. As such, we often need to anticipate whether an event is about to occur and to recognize whether certain events are meaningfully related to other events. For example, when we are first stung by a wasp, it is adaptive for us to associate the pain with the sight and sound of the wasp. It is also adaptive for us to be wary of insects that resemble wasps since many of these (e.g., honeybees and hornets) also sting. Thus, the ability to relate events to each other allows us to better anticipate the future, thereby greatly facilitating our chances of surviving.

Classical conditioning **is a process in which one stimulus that does not elicit a response is associated with a second stimulus that does; as a result, the first stimulus also comes to elicit a response.** Classical conditioning is also known as *Pavlovian conditioning*, after Pavlov, who discovered many of the basic principles of classical conditioning. It is also sometimes called *respondent conditioning*, in which case the elicited behaviors are called *respondent behaviors* or simply *respondents*.

Pavlov's Discovery of Classical Conditioning

Ivan P. Pavlov (1849–1936), a Russian physiologist, is generally credited with the first systematic investigations into classical conditioning.[2] Beginning in the late 1800s, Pavlov conducted important research on digestive secretions as well as the neural mechanisms that control them. He is, in fact, responsible for much of what we now know about digestion and eventually won the Nobel Prize for his discoveries.

As part of this research enterprise, Pavlov also investigated salivation, the initial step in the digestive process. By this time, Pavlov was well

Ivan P. Pavlov
(1849–1936)

---

[2] At about the same time, an American graduate student by the name of E. B. Twitmyer also conducted experiments on this type of conditioning and even reported his results at the 1904 conference of the American Psychological Association. However, his report generated little interest, and he abandoned the topic, which is fortunate because the term "Twitmyerian conditioning" is a mouthful. (See Hothersall, 1984).

Pavlov with his research team. If the dog seems more relaxed than most of the assistants, this is not surprising. Pavlov was very demanding of his assistants, but quite concerned about the welfare of his dogs.

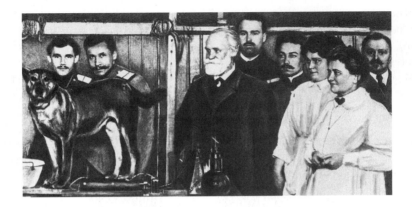

aware that salivation could be initiated by psychic factors such as the sight of food (visual perception being regarded as a psychic, meaning psychological, process). He was nevertheless surprised at the amount of control exerted by these factors. For instance, he noted that different substances affected both the quantity and quality of saliva produced. For example, a moist, edible substance, such as meat, elicited a small amount of slimy saliva, while a dry, inedible substance, such as sand, elicited a large amount of watery saliva (to facilitate spitting it out). These differences existed both when the substances were actually placed in the dogs' mouths and, later, when the dogs were merely shown these substances. Subsequent research confirmed that these psychic secretions exhibited a great deal of regularity and lawfulness, and Pavlov began to devote more and more resources to their investigation. By 1907, classical conditioning, as it would come to be known, had become the sole focus of his research efforts.

In the decades that followed, Pavlov discovered most of the basic principles of classical conditioning and explored their application in such diverse areas as personality, hypnosis, sleep, and psychopathology. The epitome of the devoted scientist, Pavlov could be a tough taskmaster with students and assistants (once refusing to accept an assistant's excuse that he was late because he had to avoid the revolutionary battles going on in the streets). Yet, in other ways, he was a devoted humanitarian. When the Soviet regime took control—fortunately, the regime continued to support his research endeavors—he was openly critical of its denial of basic rights and religious freedoms. Pavlov also showed great concern for the welfare of his dogs. He invested considerable effort in devising surgical procedures that, while allowing for the accurate observation of internal mechanisms of digestion, also minimized the animals' discomfort and ensured a full post-operative recovery.

Basic Procedure and Definitions

To illustrate the process of classical conditioning, we will use one of Pavlov's basic procedures in which a dog is trained to salivate to the sound of a metronome.

During these experiments, the dog was restrained in a harness, while a tube was inserted into an incision that had been made in its cheek. Whenever the dog salivated, the saliva would run down the tube into a container where it could be precisely measured (see Figure 3.7). Although the apparatus appears uncomfortable, the dogs in fact grew quite accustomed to it.

Pavlov's basic procedure worked as follows. Prior to conditioning, the dogs would automatically salivate in response to the taste of food. Because salivation to food occurs naturally and does not require prior training (conditioning), it is called an *unconditioned response* (UR), while the food is called an *unconditioned stimulus* (US). The sound of a metronome, however, does not elicit salivation and is therefore said to be a *neutral stimulus* (NS) with respect to salivation. During conditioning, the sound of the metronome is presented just prior to the food, which of course continues to elicit salivation. After

FIGURE 3.7 Pavlov's conditioning apparatus. In some of Pavlov's early experiments, a dog was trained to salivate to the sound of a metronome. The dog was restrained in a harness, while a tube was inserted into an incision in its cheek. Whenever the dog salivated, the tube carried the saliva to a container that activated a recording device. (*Source:* Coon, 2001.)

conditioning, as a result of having been paired with the food, the metronome itself now elicits salivation. Because salivating to the metronome requires prior training (conditioning), it is called a *conditioned response* (CR) while the sound of the metronome is called a *conditioned stimulus* (CS).[3] (See Figure 3.8.)

This procedure can be schematically diagrammed as follows.

Prior to conditioning:
Food → *Salivation*
  US   UR
Metronome → **No salivation**
    NS   —
During conditioning:
Metronome: Food → *Salivation*
  NS (or CS) US   UR

(During conditioning, the metronome can be labeled either an NS or a CS, because during this phase it begins as an NS and then becomes a CS.)

After conditioning:
Metronome → *Salivation*
    CS   CR

Each pairing of the NS and US during conditioning is called a *conditioning trial*.[4] Several conditioning trials are often needed before the NS becomes established as a CS. Measuring the level of conditioning can be done in various ways. The most common procedure is to intersperse the conditioning trials with an occasional *test trial* in which the NS is presented by itself. For example, every once in a while, the metronome can be presented alone to see if it elicits salivation. Alternatively, one can continue to pair the metronome with the food and simply observe whether salivation occurs in the short interval between the start of the metronome and the presentation of food.

As an everyday example of classical conditioning, let us suppose that a child is bitten by a dog and subsequently develops a fear of dogs. This process can be diagrammed as follows (omitting the "before conditioning" phase):

Dog: Bite → *Fear*
 NS US   UR
Dog → *Fear*
 CS   CR

---

[3] Note that the Russian terms used by Pavlov were originally translated as "conditioned" and "unconditioned." They are, however, more precisely translated as "conditional" and "unconditional." We will continue to use the former terms as they have been in standard use for longer.

[4] It is also sometimes referred to as a *reinforcement trial*, but in this text we will reserve the term reinforcement for certain operant conditioning procedures, as discussed in the last half of this text.

FIGURE 3.8 Classical conditioning of salivation. Prior to conditioning, the dog automatically salivates to the taste of food. During conditioning, the sound of a metronome is presented just prior to the presentation of food. After conditioning, the metronome itself now elicits salivation. (*Source:* Nairne, 2000.)

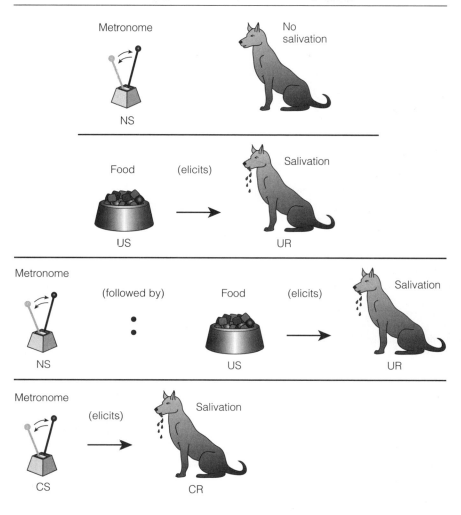

The bite can be considered an unconditioned stimulus that elicits an unconditioned response of fear (actually more pain than fear, but we will simplify matters a bit). As a result of the bite, the sight of the dog becomes a conditioned stimulus that elicits a conditioned response of fear.

Let us now look more closely at each component of the classical conditioning procedure. **The *unconditioned stimulus* (US) is a stimulus that naturally elicits a response,** while **the *unconditioned response* (UR) is the**

Fortunately, Pavlov realized that the value of such experiments lay in their ability to reveal basic principles of behavior, not in their ability to simply make a dog salivate.

"PERHAPS, DR. PAVLOV, HE COULD BE TAUGHT TO SEAL ENVELOPES."

response that is naturally elicited by the US. When we say that the response is naturally elicited by the US, we mean that it is an *unlearned* or *innate* reaction to that stimulus. For example, food naturally elicits the response of salivation, and a bite naturally elicits the response of fear (and pain).

The *conditioned stimulus* **(CS) is any stimulus that, although initially neutral, comes to elicit a response because it has been associated with an unconditioned stimulus.** The metronome is initially neutral with respect to salivation in that it does not naturally elicit salivation.[5] When the metronome has been associated with food, however, it does elicit salivation. **The** *conditioned response* **(CR) is the response, often similar to the UR, that is elicited by the CS.** Note that the conditioned response is at most only *similar* to the unconditioned response. It is never identical (a fact that is overlooked in many introductory psychology textbooks). Even when the UR and CR appear identical, as in the case of salivation elicited by the food (US) and by the metronome (CS), there are always some differences. For example, the CR is usually weaker or less intense than the UR. Thus, the dog will salivate

---

[5] Although the metronome is neutral with respect to salivation, it may not be neutral with respect to other types of responses. For example, it is likely a US for an orienting response (turn on the metronome and the dog will prick up his ears and turn toward it).

less to the metronome than it will to the food. The CR is also sometimes quite different from the UR. For example, as noted earlier, the unconditioned response elicited by a bite is actually somewhat different from the conditioned response elicited by the sight of the dog that bit us. For the sake of simplicity, we labeled both responses as fear responses. Nevertheless, the response to the bite is mostly what we would describe as a pain reaction ("Yeow!"), while the subsequent response to the dog is most likely to be one that is clearly identified as fear (e.g., freezing). The extent to which the CR can differ from the UR will be more fully discussed in a later chapter.

1. Classical conditioning is also known as P_____ conditioning or r_____ conditioning.

2. In the latter case, the behaviors themselves are called _____ behaviors or simply _____.

3. In the metronome example, the metronome is initially a(n) _____ stimulus because it (does/does not) _____ elicit salivation. The food, however, is a(n) _____ stimulus that elicits a(n) _____ response of salivation.

4. During conditioning, the metronome can be labeled as either a(n) _____ stimulus or a(n) _____ stimulus.

5. Following conditioning, the metronome is a(n) _____ stimulus, while the salivation elicited by the metronome is a(n) _____ response.

6. Each pairing of the metronome and the food is called a c_____ tr_____.

7. Write out the term indicated by each of the following abbreviations:
CS: _____ _____ ;
UR: _____ _____ ;
NS: _____ _____ ;
CR: _____ _____ ;
US: _____ _____ .

8. In the basic classical conditioning procedure, a (CS/US/NS) _____ is paired with a (CS/US/NS) _____, which in turn elicits a (CR/UR) _____. As a result, the first stimulus becomes a (CS/US/NS) _____, which elicits a (CR/UR) _____.

9. Using the appropriate abbreviations, label each component in the following classical conditioning procedure:

Wasp: Painful sting → *Fear*

Wasp → *Fear*

10. Using the above format, diagram a classical conditioning procedure involving the stimuli of "nurse" and "painful injection," and the response of "anxiety." Label each component using the appropriate abbreviations.

11. The CR is (often/always) _____ (similar/identical) _____ to the UR.

12. A CR that appears identical to the UR is almost always (less/more) _____ intense.

13. Define each of the following terms (do not worry if at this point you find that you still have to go back and look at the definitions above).

Unconditioned stimulus:

Unconditioned response:

Conditioned stimulus:

Conditioned response:

Appetitive and Aversive Conditioning

Most classical conditioning procedures can be divided into two categories, based on whether the US is pleasant or unpleasant. **In *appetitive conditioning*, the US is an event that is usually considered pleasant and that an organism seeks out.** Examples include food (if the organism is hungry), water (if the organism is thirsty), or addictive drugs (especially if the organism is a drug addict). Sexual stimuli too are regarded as appetitive stimuli, and there is good evidence that sexual responses can be classically conditioned. For example, Rachman and Hodgson (1968) took seven male volunteers and presented them with conditioning trials in which a picture of black, knee-length boots was followed by a picture of a nude woman. After about 30 trials, five of the males became sexually aroused by the sight of the boots. (Don't worry. The researchers later eliminated the conditioning by repeatedly presenting the picture of the boots without the picture of the nude—a process known as *extinction*, which is discussed later.)

In *aversive conditioning*, the US is an event that is usually considered unpleasant and that an organism usually avoids. Examples of aversive USs include an electric shock, a painful bite, and an unpleasant odor. Aversive conditioning often occurs more rapidly than appetitive conditioning, sometimes requiring only one or two pairings of the NS and the US. This reflects the close relationship between aversive conditioning and survival; to survive, we must quickly learn to dislike those events that cause pain or illness.

Given the ease with which aversive conditioning can occur, it is not surprising that this type of conditioning probably accounts for many of our fears and anxieties. When the fear is appropriate—as in learning to fear an angry dog that has bitten us—such conditioning is beneficial. When the fear is inappropriate—as when we begin to fear all dogs—such conditioning can be problematic. Therefore, a great deal of effort has gone into the study of fear conditioning, as well as into how such fears can be eliminated. This has yielded important information on how real-world fears and anxieties can best be treated, a topic that will be more fully discussed later.

When conducting research on fear conditioning in animals, measuring the level of fear can be problematic. Changes in certain physiological responses, such as heart rate, that might be indicative of fear are difficult to record, especially in small experimental animals such as rats. An ingenious solution to this problem was developed by Estes and Skinner (1941); it is known as the *conditioned suppression or conditioned emotional response (CER) paradigm.* In this para- **3** digm, the rat is first trained to engage in some ongoing behavior, such as lever pressing to obtain food. When a steady rate of lever pressing has been established, a fear conditioning procedure is introduced. For example,

Tone: Shock → *Fear*
  NS   US   UR
Tone → *Fear*
  CS   CR

In the initial phase, the rat will become emotionally upset (fearful) whenever it receives a shock and will stop pressing the lever. As conditioning proceeds, the tone too will come to elicit fear, and the rat will stop pressing the lever when it hears the tone. Thus, the degree to which lever pressing for food is suppressed in the presence of the tone can be used as an indirect measure of the extent to which the tone elicits fear. Think of the procedure as similar to a gunfighter walking in and out of a saloon. The extent to which the saloon patrons fear the gunfighter can be accurately measured by the extent to which they stop talking to each other when he is in the saloon (you can hear a pin drop!), and resume talking when he leaves the saloon. Similarly, the rat's level of fear can be assessed by the extent to which it stops lever pressing when the tone is sounding and resumes lever pressing when the tone is not sounding. The CER paradigm has proven to be a useful method for investigating fear conditioning in animals (but has yet to be systematically applied to the study of saloon patrons). (Be especially careful to note that the CR in this type of procedure is the covert response of fear; the CR is *not* the reduction in lever pressing, which serves as the indirect measure of the covert response of fear.)

Note that classical conditioning can transform a normally aversive stimulus into an appetitive stimulus. Pavlov found that if a dog received a shock to one of its paws that was followed by food, the dog would eventually begin to salivate in response to the shock. The dog's overt reactions to the shock, such as tail wagging, provided further indication that the shock had lost its aversiveness. Interestingly, if the shock was then applied to a different paw, the dog would not salivate but would react with discomfort. The perception of shock as pleasurable appeared to be quite specific to the body part involved in the conditioning.

As you may have already guessed, this same process might partially account for the development of masochistic tendencies (the tendency to perceive painful stimulation as pleasurable) in humans. The painful stimulation from, say, being whipped has for some people become associated with feelings of sexual arousal, as a result of which the painful stimulation itself can elicit arousal. Interestingly, as with Pavlov's dogs, people who are masochistic do not perceive all pain as pleasurable; rather, it is only the type of pain that is connected with their erotic experiences (e.g., being whipped) that is perceived as pleasurable. The pain they feel from accidentally stubbing a toe or banging a shin is as aversive for them as it is for anyone else (Rathus, Nevid, & Fichner-Rathus, 2000).

QUICK QUIZ

1. In _____ conditioning, the US is an event that is usually considered unpleasant and that the organism avoids.

2. In _____ conditioning, the US is an event that is usually considered pleasant and that the organism seeks out.

3. Learning to associate the corner bar with the happy times you experience in that bar is an example of _____ conditioning.

4. Learning to associate your refrigerator with the nauseating smell of spoiled food is an example of _____ conditioning.

5. In a c_____ e_____ response (CER) paradigm, the level of fear elicited by a CS is indicated by the degree to which the rat's rate of lever pressing for food (decreases/increases) _____ in the presence of that stimulus.

6. The CER paradigm is also known as a c_____ s_____ paradigm.

Excitatory and Inhibitory Conditioning

In all of the examples above, the NS is associated with the presentation of a US. The metronome is associated with the presentation of food, the dog is associated with a painful bite, and the tone is associated with shock. **Conditioning in which the NS is associated with the presentation of a US is known as *excitatory conditioning*.** The result of excitatory conditioning is that the CS comes to elicit a certain response, such as salivation or fear.

But what if a stimulus is associated with the absence of the US rather than its presentation? What if, for example, a vicious dog always bites you except

And Furthermore

Classical Conditioning and Interpersonal Attraction

Classical conditioning may play an important role in interpersonal attraction. According to the reinforcement-affect model of attraction (Byrne & Clore, 1970; see also Baron & Byrne, 1997), the extent to which we are attracted to someone can be significantly affected by the degree to which the person is associated with events that elicit positive emotions. It is for this reason that we are generally attracted to people who say and do the kinds of things that make us feel good. Eventually, we feel good just being around such people.

Interestingly, the model also predicts that we can become attracted to a person who is only incidentally associated with positive events. Experiments have revealed that events as innocuous as pleasant background music or a positive news story on the radio can heighten the extent to which a person we are meeting is perceived as attractive. Of course, this means that associating ourselves with pleasant stimuli—pleasant music, attractive clothing, and even a clean car—during an initial date can greatly facilitate the possibility of a second date.

The reinforcement-affect model also suggests that we are less attracted to someone who is associated with aversive events. Thus, dressing like a slob or drinking to the point of vomiting during a first date is probably not a good idea. On the other hand, there may be times when you *want* to be perceived as less attractive. A letter once appeared in a newspaper advice column in which a woman described how she finally managed to dissuade a persistent acquaintance from continually asking her out. She agreed to a date and then ate plenty of garlic beforehand! Her suitor was apparently not a big garlic fan, and she had no further difficulties with him.

when its owner is present? The owner then is a sort of safety signal that indicates the absence of a painful bite. **Conditioning in which the NS is associated with the absence or removal of a US is known as *inhibitory conditioning*.** The result of inhibitory conditioning is that the CS comes to inhibit the occurrence of a certain response—that is, the response is less likely to occur when that stimulus is present. Thus, although the dog is an excitatory CS for fear, the owner is an inhibitory CS for fear, and your fear of the dog will be suppressed when the owner is present. Similarly, if a rat is consistently shocked when a tone is presented, the tone will become an excitatory stimulus for fear. But if the rat is never shocked when a tone and a light are presented, the light will become an inhibitory CS for fear because it explicitly signals the absence of shock. In such procedures, the excitatory CS is usually labeled a CS+, while the inhibitory CS is labeled a CS−.

4

Traditionally, researchers have focused on the study of excitatory conditioning, and most of the basic principles of classical conditioning have been established using excitatory procedures. For this reason, most of the examples

5 in this text are examples of excitatory conditioning. In recent years, however, the study of inhibitory conditioning has begun to attract a good deal of interest (Domjan, 1998).

1. Conditioning associated with the removal of a US is known as _____ conditioning, while conditioning associated with the presentation of a US is known as _____ conditioning.

2. Your grandmother always cooks great meals except when your vegetarian sister is present. As a result, you usually salivate a great deal when sitting at your grandmother's table for a meal, but not when your sister is present. Your grandmother's table is an _____ CS for salivation, while your vegetarian sister is an _____ CS for salivation.

3. Most of the basic principles of classical conditioning have been established using procedures that involve _____ conditioning.

4. A conditioned excitatory stimulus (an excitatory CS) is one that is associated with the (presentation/removal) _____ of a US; a conditioned inhibitory stimulus (an inhibitory CS) is one that is associated with the (presentation/removal) _____ of a US.

5. An excitatory CS for fear is one that will (elicit/suppress) _____ a fear response; an inhibitory CS for fear is one that will (elicit/suppress) _____ a fear response.

6. For the residents of Berlin and London during World War II, an air-raid siren would have been a (CS+/CS−) _____ for anxiety, while the all-clear siren would have been a (CS+/CS−) _____ for anxiety.

Temporal Arrangement of Stimuli

In the classical conditioning examples discussed to this point, the NS was always presented prior to the US. This temporal arrangement, though, is only one of several ways in which the NS and US can be arranged. In the following section, we will outline four such arrangements and note the effectiveness of each for producing a conditioned response.

1. **Delayed Conditioning.** In *delayed conditioning,* **the onset of the NS precedes the onset of the US,** *and* **the two stimuli overlap.** For example, if we want a rat to associate a tone with a brief shock, we first present the tone and then, while the tone is still on, present a shock. As shown in Figure 3.9a, the onset of the tone precedes the onset of the shock and the tone is still on when the shock is presented. (Note that it is the point at which the two stimuli are turned on, rather than turned off, that is critical.) A delayed conditioning procedure is often the best arrangement for conditioning, especially if the time between the onset of the NS and the onset of the US (known as the *interstimulus interval* or *ISI*) is relatively short. When conditioning certain autonomic responses (responses that are

FIGURE 3.9 Four ways in which presentation of the NS and US can be temporally arranged.

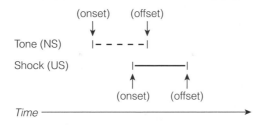

(a) Delayed conditioning procedure

(onset)   (offset)

Tone (NS) |– – – – –|

Shock (US) |————|

(onset)   (offset)

Time

(b) Trace conditioning procedure

Tone (NS) |– – – – –|

Shock (US) |————|
Time

(c) Simultaneous conditioning procedure

Tone (NS) |– – – – –|

Shock (US) |————|
Time

(d) Backward conditioning procedure

Tone (NS) |– – – – –|

Shock (US) |————|
Time

controlled by the autonomic nervous system), such as salivation, the optimal ISI is generally in the range of a few seconds. When conditioning skeletal responses (responses that are controlled by skeletal muscles), such as the eyeblink reflex, the optimal ISI is about a half second. Conditioning works best if the onset of the NS immediately precedes the onset of the US; this fact is consistent with the notion that the NS generally serves as a predictor of the US, a notion that will be further discussed in Chapter 5. Nevertheless, some forms of classical conditioning do not require a close temporal pairing between the NS and US. One such form, known as taste aversion conditioning, is described in Chapter 11.

2. **Trace Conditioning. In** *trace conditioning,* **the onset and offset of the NS precede the onset of the US.** In other words, the NS occurs before

the US, and the two stimuli do not overlap. For example, a tone is turned on and then off, and this is then followed by the presentation of a shock (see Figure 3.9b). The time between the offset of the NS and the onset of the US (e.g., between the point at which the tone was turned *off* and the shock was turned *on*) is called the *trace interval*. Because the tone is no longer present when the shock occurs, you might say that the organism has to "remember" the occurrence of the tone (or have some "memory trace" of it) to be able to associate the two. Trace conditioning can be almost as effective as delayed conditioning if the trace interval is relatively short (no more than a few seconds). If the trace interval is longer than that, conditioning is unlikely to occur.

3. **Simultaneous Conditioning.** In *simultaneous conditioning,* **the onset of the NS and the onset of the US are simultaneous.** For example, a tone and a shock are turned on at the same time (see Figure 3.9c). Although simultaneous conditioning involves the closest possible contiguity between the NS and the US, this procedure often results in poor conditioning. One reason for this is that if the NS occurs at the same time as the US, the NS is no longer a good predictor of the US.

4. **Backward Conditioning.** In *backward conditioning,* **the onset of the NS follows the onset of the US.** In other words, the US is presented first and the NS is presented later. For example, the rat receives a shock and then hears a tone (see Figure 3.9d). Backward conditioning usually results in little or no conditioning. This is especially true for conditioning of an excitatory response like fear. Nevertheless, under some circumstances, backward excitatory conditioning can be achieved, such as when the NS is a "biologically relevant" stimulus for fear (Keith-Lucas & Guttman, 1975). For example, if instead of using a tone as the NS for shock, we use the sight of a snake, then backward conditioning might occur (see Figure 3.10).

Why does backward conditioning work with the snake but not the tone? It is assumed that most animals have an innate predisposition to fear certain types of events. Because poisonous snakes have constituted a significant threat throughout the rat's evolutionary history, rats may have an inherited predisposition to fear snakes. This predisposition is so strong that even if the snake is presented after the shock, the fear elicited by the shock still becomes associated with the snake.

FIGURE 3.10 A potentially effective backward conditioning procedure in which the NS is a biologically relevant stimulus for a conditioned fear response.

Backward conditioning can also result in inhibitory conditioning. For example, if a tone sounds just as a shock is being terminated, then the tone essentially predicts the absence of shock. The tone in this case may become a safety signal (CS–) that inhibits the occurrence of fear. Similarly, if a child is often bullied by other children at recess, but the bullying stops the moment a teacher approaches, the presence of the teacher will become a safety signal that effectively inhibits the child's response of fear. Whenever this teacher is nearby, the child will feel especially safe and comfortable.

QUICK QUIZ

1. The most successful temporal arrangement for conditioning is delayed conditioning, in which the onset of the NS (precedes/follows) _____ the onset of the US, and the two stimuli (overlap/do not overlap) _____.

2. In delayed conditioning, the time between the onset of the NS and the onset of the US is called the _____ interval (abbreviated _____).

3. In trace conditioning, the _____ and _____ of the NS precedes the _____ of the US. The time between the _____ of the NS and the _____ of the US is called the _____ interval. Trace conditioning can be effective if this interval is relatively (long/short) _____.

4. In simultaneous conditioning, the _____ of the NS occurs at the same time as the _____ of the US. Simultaneous conditioning usually results in (good/poor) _____ conditioning.

5. In backward conditioning, the (US/NS) _____ is presented first and the (US/NS) _____ is presented later. Backward conditioning is generally considered to result in (good/poor) _____ conditioning.

6. Backward conditioning can result in excitatory conditioning of fear when the NS is a b_____ relevant stimulus. Backward conditioning can also result in inhibitory conditioning when the NS signals the (presentation/removal) _____ of the US.

7. Suppose that we attempt to condition a reflex response of sneezing using a flower as the NS and pollen as the US. Name each of the four NS-US arrangements below.

A. _____ conditioning: **Flower** |----|
   Pollen |—|

B. _____ conditioning: **Flower** |----------|
   Pollen |—|

C. _____ conditioning: **Flower** |------|
   Pollen |————|

D. _____ conditioning: **Flower** |-------|
   Pollen |——|

SUMMARY

In general, elicited behaviors are involuntary reactions to specific stimuli. Examples of elicited behaviors include reflexes and fixed action patterns. Repeated presentations of the same stimulus may decrease the strength of a behavior (known as habituation) or increase the strength of a behavior (known as sensitization) depending on the intensity of the eliciting stimulus. A similar dual mechanism is evident in the opponent-process theory of emotion in which an emotionally arousing event elicits an emotional response (the a-process) that in turn elicits a compensatory response (the b-process).

In classical conditioning, a neutral stimulus is associated with some other stimulus that naturally elicits a response, and as a result the neutral stimulus also comes to elicit a response. In Pavlov's basic procedure, the unconditioned stimulus (US) is the stimulus that naturally elicits a response, while the unconditioned response (UR) is the response that is naturally elicited by the US. The conditioned stimulus (CS) is the stimulus that, although initially a neutral stimulus (NS), comes to elicit a response because it has been associated with the US. The conditioned response (CR) is the response that is elicited by the CS.

There can be various temporal arrangements of the NS and US in classical conditioning. In delayed conditioning, the onset of the NS precedes the onset of the US and overlaps with it. In trace conditioning, the onset and offset of the NS precede the onset of the US. In simultaneous conditioning, the NS and US are presented at the same time. Finally, in backward conditioning, the onset of the NS follows the onset of the US. Delayed conditioning and trace conditioning are usually the most effective procedures, with backward conditioning being the least effective. However, backward conditioning can occur under some circumstances, such as when the NS is a biologically relevant stimulus for fear and the US is an aversive stimulus.

STUDY QUESTIONS

1. What is a reflex?
2. Describe the startle response, orienting response, and flexion response.
3. Describe, or diagram, the sequence of events in a reflex arc.
4. Define fixed action pattern. What is a sign stimulus or releaser?
5. Define habituation and sensitization.
6. What is the effect of high versus low versus moderate stimulus intensity on habituation and sensitization?
7. Distinguish between long-term and short-term habituation.
8. Describe the phenomenon of dishabituation.
9. Define the opponent-process theory of emotion.
10. List three main characteristics of opponent processes.
11. Define classical conditioning.

12. Diagram an example of a classical conditioning procedure, using the appropriate abbreviations to label each component.
13. Define the terms unconditioned stimulus and unconditioned response.
14. Define the terms conditioned stimulus and conditioned response.
15. Distinguish between appetitive and aversive conditioning.
16. Describe the conditioned suppression (or CER) procedure.
17. Distinguish between excitatory and inhibitory conditioning.
18. Name and diagram four temporal arrangements of the NS and US.
19. Which two temporal arrangements of the NS and US are likely to be most effective? Under what conditions is backward conditioning likely to be effective?

CONCEPT REVIEW

appetitive conditioning. Conditioning procedure in which the US is an event that is usually considered pleasant and that an organism seeks out.

aversive conditioning. Conditioning procedure in which the US is an event that is usually considered unpleasant and that an organism avoids.

backward conditioning. Conditioning procedure in which the onset of the NS follows the onset of the US.

classical conditioning. A process whereby one stimulus that does not elicit a certain response is associated with a second stimulus that does; as a result, the first stimulus also comes to elicit a response.

conditioned response (CR). The response, often similar to the unconditioned response, that is elicited by the conditioned stimulus.

conditioned stimulus (CS). Any stimulus that, although initially neutral, comes to elicit a response because it has been associated with an unconditioned stimulus.

delayed conditioning. Conditioning procedure in which the onset of the NS precedes the onset of the US, and the two stimuli overlap.

dishabituation. The reappearance of a habituated response following the presentation of a seemingly irrelevant novel stimulus.

excitatory conditioning. Conditioning procedure in which the NS is associated with the *presentation* of a US.

fixed action pattern. A fixed sequence of responses elicited by a specific stimulus.

flexion response. The automatic response of jerking one's hand or foot away from a hot or sharp object.

habituation. A decrease in the strength of an elicited behavior following repeated presentations of the eliciting stimulus.

inhibitory conditioning. Conditioning procedure in which the NS is associated with the *absence or removal* of a US.

opponent-process theory. A theory that proposes that an emotional event elicits two competing processes: (1) an a-process (or primary process) directly elicited by the event, and (2) a b-process (or opponent process) that is elicited by the a-process and serves to counteract the a-process.

orienting response. The automatic positioning of oneself to facilitate attending to a stimulus.

reflex arc. A neural structure that underlies many reflexes and consists of a sensory neuron, an interneuron, and a motor neuron.

reflex. A relatively simple, involuntary response to a stimulus.

sensitization. An increase in the strength of an elicited behavior following repeated presentations of the eliciting stimulus.

sign stimulus (or releaser). A specific stimulus that elicits a fixed action pattern.

simultaneous conditioning. Conditioning procedure in which the onset of the NS and the onset of the US are simultaneous.

startle response. A defensive reaction to a sudden, unexpected stimulus, which involves automatic tightening of skeletal muscles and various hormonal and visceral changes.

trace conditioning. Conditioning procedure in which the onset and offset of the NS precede the onset of the US.

unconditioned response (UR). The response that is naturally elicited by the unconditioned stimulus.

unconditioned stimulus (US). A stimulus that naturally elicits a response.

CHAPTER TEST

4. A sudden loud noise is likely to elicit a(n) _____ reaction, which is a reflexive defensive response to a sudden stimulus.

13. With repeated presentations of the emotional event, the b-process (increases/decreases) _____ in both _____ and _____.

23. Seeing a wasp land on your arm and then watching it as it stings you is an example of a _____ conditioning procedure, while noticing the wasp at the same moment that you feel the sting is an example of a _____ conditioning procedure.

6. When a subordinate dog submits to a threatening display from a dominant dog, it will often roll over on its back and display its stomach. This sequence of actions is called a _____, while the threatening display from the dominant dog is called the _____ stimulus or _____ for these actions.

14. Classical conditioning is also known as P_____ conditioning or _____ conditioning. In the latter case, the elicited behaviors are referred to as _____.

9. The faint sound of a jackhammer several blocks away will likely result in _____, while the extremely loud sound of a jackhammer right outside your window will likely result in _____.

On the other hand, the moderately loud sound of a jackhammer half a block away may result in a period of ———————————————— followed by ————————————————.

26. In general, aversive conditioning occurs (more/less) ———————— readily than appetitive conditioning.

2. The most basic type of elicited behavior is the ————————————, which is a simple, involuntary response to a stimulus.

12. According to the opponent-process theory of emotion, b-processes are (slow/quick) ———————— to increase and (slow/quick) ———————— to decrease.

18. Imagine an eyeblink conditioning procedure in which the sound of a click is paired with a puff of air to the eye. Each pairing of the click and air puff during conditioning is referred to as a(n) ————————————————.

11. In the opening scenario, Uma witnessed her boyfriend flirting with another woman. First, she experienced intense anger. Later, however, when he apologized for his actions and was very attentive to her, she experienced unusually strong feelings of attraction toward him. An explanation for this pattern of emotional changes is provided by the ———————————————— ———————————————— theory of emotion. In this case, Uma's feelings of anger are an example of the ———————————— process, while her feelings of affection following his apology are an example of the ———————————— process.

1. Behaviors that are automatically drawn out by the stimuli that precede them are referred to as ———————————— behaviors.

20. When you opened the refrigerator last evening, the putrid smell of rotten eggs made you feel extremely nauseous. Today, when you are about to open the refrigerator again, you find yourself experiencing a slight twinge of nausea, even though the refrigerator has been thoroughly cleaned. In classical conditioning terms, the refrigerator has become a(n) ———————————— stimulus that now elicits a(n) ———————————— response of nausea. In this case, the nausea produced by the sight of the refrigerator is likely to be (less/more) ———————————— severe than the nausea produced by the smell of rotten eggs.

5. The reflexive action of pulling your hand away from a hot pot handle is activated through a ————————————————: a neural structure underlying simple reflexes that consists of a (in correct order) ————————————————————————————————————— —————————————————————————————————————.

25. Feeling a sting and then seeing the wasp on your arm is an example of a ———————————— conditioning procedure, which in this case may be (effective/ineffective) ———————————————— because the CS is a ———————————————————————— for a fear response.

10. You finally habituate to the faint sound of a jackhammer half a block away, such that you cease to notice it. The lights in your house then flicker, at which point you again notice the sound of the jackhammer. This is an example of the process of ————————————————.

15. Imagine an eyeblink conditioning procedure in which the sound of a click is paired with a puff of air to the eye. The puff of air is called the _____ stimulus (abbreviated _____) while the eyeblink that it elicits is called the _____ response (abbreviated _____).

19. When you opened the refrigerator one evening, the putrid smell of rotten eggs made you feel extremely nauseous. In classical conditioning terms, the putrid smell is a(n) _____ stimulus that elicits a(n) _____ response of nausea.

28. Inadvertently touching a hot object is likely to elicit a(n) _____ response; the sound of a gunshot is likely to elicit a(n) _____ response; the sound of someone talking behind us may elicit a(n) _____ response.

7. Fixed action patterns are sometimes called _____ behaviors because they are often unique to a certain species.

3. The reflexive action of a dog pricking up its ears in response to a sound is an example of a(n) _____ response, which consists of movements designed to facilitate _____.

17. Imagine an eyeblink conditioning procedure in which the sound of a click is paired with a puff of air to the eye. After conditioning, the click becomes a(n) _____ stimulus (abbreviated _____) since it now elicits an eyeblink. The eyeblink elicited by the click is called the _____ response (abbreviated _____).

27. Dana always feels very relaxed when she takes her large dog for a walk even though it is a relatively dangerous neighborhood. This appears to be an example of _____ conditioning, with the dog functioning as an _____ CS (abbreviated _____).

21. When you opened the refrigerator one evening, the putrid smell of rotten eggs made you feel extremely nauseous. The subsequent response of nausea to the sight of the refrigerator is an example of (aversive/appetitive) _____ conditioning as well as (excitatory/inhibitory) _____ conditioning.

16. Imagine an eyeblink conditioning procedure in which the sound of a click is paired with a puff of air to the eye. Prior to conditioning, the sound of the click does not elicit an eyeblink. At this point, the click is considered to be a(n) _____ stimulus.

24. In an experiment involving the conditioning of an eyeblink response to the sound of a click, hearing the click and then a second later feeling the puff of air in your eye is an example of a _____ conditioning procedure. Conversely, feeling the puff of air and then hearing the click is an example of a _____ conditioning procedure. In general, the (former/latter) _____ procedure is likely to produce more effective conditioning.

8. In a restaurant, the parents of a very noisy child hardly notice the commotion. This is an example of _____. On the

other hand, the customers at neighboring tables are becoming increasingly annoyed by the child. This is an example of _____.
22. Bert is allergic to bee stings. He eats and drinks heartily when he is inside the restaurant, but not when he is seated on the outdoor patio surrounded by flowers. This circumstance is similar to the _____ paradigm, which is also known as the _____ (CER) procedure.

ANSWERS TO CHAPTER TEST

1. elicited
2. reflex
3. orienting; attending to a stimulus
4. startle
5. reflex arc; sensory neuron; interneuron; motor neuron
6. fixed action pattern; sign; releaser
7. species-specific
8. habituation; sensitization
9. habituation; sensitization; sensitization; habituation
10. dishabituation
11. opponent-process; primary (or a-) process; opponent (or b-) process
12. slow; slow
13. increases; strength; duration
14. Pavlovian; respondent; respondents
15. unconditioned stimulus (US); unconditioned response (UR)
16. neutral
17. conditioned; CS; conditioned; CR
18. conditioning trial
19. unconditioned; unconditioned
20. conditioned; conditioned; less
21. aversive; excitatory
22. conditioned suppression; conditioned emotional response
23. delayed; simultaneous
24. trace; backward; former
25. backward; effective; biologically relevant stimulus
26. more
27. inhibitory; inhibitory; CS−
28. flexion; startle; orienting

Put Learning into Action with Sniffy, the Virtual Rat

 The following material refers to *Sniffy, the Virtual Rat*™: *Pro Version*, a separate Wadsworth product that consists of a manual and a CD-ROM.

1. There is a Sniffy exercise, number 38 (pp. 187–194), that deals with habituation. However, at this point you probably have not learned enough about operating the *Sniffy Pro* software to complete this exercise easily. We will return to this exercise later.

2. Note: Remember that classical conditioning studies with Sniffy use conditioned suppression (also called the *conditioned emotional response*), rather than salivation, to measure the amount of learning.

3. See pp. 84–86 for more information on CER.

4. See pp. 143–144 for additional information on excitatory and inhibitory conditioning.

5. Read Chapter 6 (pp. 83–101) in *Sniffy Pro*. This chapter explains the mechanics of running and interpreting conditioning studies with Sniffy. If you have not already done so, follow the instructions in the Preface (pp. xi–xv) to install the *Sniffy Pro* software on your computer. Pages 11–12 explain the features of Sniffy's operant chamber. You should also work through exercises 1–3 (pp. 17–31) to train Sniffy to press the lever.

6. Note: The classical conditioning studies in *Sniffy Pro* used delay conditioning protocols.

CHAPTER 4

Classical Conditioning: Basic Phenomena and Various Complexities

CHAPTER OUTLINE

Jana enjoys being wildly unpredictable in her relationships, believing that most men find unpredictable women quite exciting. She cancels dates at the last minute, shows up on the guy's doorstep at odd hours of the day or night, and tries as much as possible to be completely spontaneous. Unfortunately, many of the guys she goes out with seem to be rather stressed out and neurotic, though it usually takes a while before this becomes apparent. She is starting to wonder if there are any good men around these days.

Some Basic Conditioning Phenomena

Acquisition

In classical conditioning, *acquisition* **is the process of developing and strengthening a conditioned response through repeated pairings of an NS with a US.** In general, acquisition proceeds rapidly during early conditioning trials, then gradually levels off. The maximum amount of conditioning that can take place in a particular situation is known as the *asymptote* of conditioning (see Figure 4.1).

The asymptote of conditioning, as well as the speed of conditioning, is dependent on several factors. In general, *more intense USs produce stronger and more rapid conditioning than less intense USs.* For example, we can obtain stronger conditioning of a salivary response when the US consists of a large amount of food or a highly preferred food than if it consists of a small amount or less preferred food. Likewise, a severe bite from a dog will result in a stronger conditioned fear response than a minor bite. In a similar fashion, *more intense NSs result in stronger and more rapid conditioning than less intense NSs.* For example, a loud metronome that has been paired with food produces a stronger response of salivation than a faint metronome that has been paired with food. And, not surprisingly, conditioned fear responses to dogs are more readily acquired if the person is bitten by a large dog as opposed to a small dog.

1

1. The process of strengthening a conditioned response through repeated pairings of an NS with a US is known as _____.

2. In general, conditioning proceeds more (rapidly/slowly) _____ during the early trials of a conditioning procedure.

3. The maximum amount of learning that can take place in a given situation is known as the _____ of learning.

4. In general, a (more/less) _____ intense US produces better conditioning.

5. In general, a (more/less) _____ intense NS produces better conditioning.

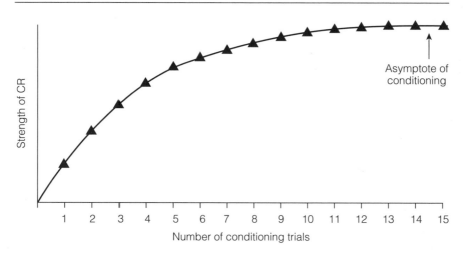

FIGURE 4.1 A typical acquisition curve in which strength of conditioning increases rapidly during the first few trials and then gradually levels off over subsequent trials.

Extinction, Spontaneous Recovery, and Disinhibition

Given that a certain stimulus now elicits a conditioned response, is there any way to eliminate the response? In a *process* known as ***extinction,* a conditioned response can be weakened or eliminated when the CS is repeatedly presented in the absence of the US.** The term extinction also applies to the *procedure* whereby this happens, namely, **the repeated presentation of the CS in the absence of the US.**

Suppose, for example, that a metronome has been paired with food such that it now elicits a conditioned response of salivation:

Metronome: Food → *Salivation*
  NS   US   UR
Metronome → *Salivation*
  CS   CR

If we now continue to present the metronome by itself and never again pair it with food (each presentation of the metronome being known as an "extinction trial"), the conditioned response of salivation will eventually die out—that is, the CR of salivation will have been *extinguished.*

Metronome → No salivation
  NS   —

The process of extinction is the decrease in the strength of the CR, while the procedure of extinction is the means by which this was carried out, namely, the repeated presentation of the metronome without the food.

In a similar manner, if a dog that once bit me never again bites me, my fear response to the dog should eventually extinguish. Unfortunately, some people who were once bitten by a dog continue to fear that dog as well as other dogs, in which case we might say that they have a "phobia" about dogs. But if the person has never again been bitten by the dog, why is their fear so persistent? One reason is that people who fear dogs tend to avoid them, and to the extent that they avoid them, their fear response cannot extinguish. As you will see in later chapters, this tendency to avoid a feared event is a major factor in the development and maintenance of a phobia, and treatment procedures for phobias are often based on preventing this avoidance response from occurring.

Once a CR has been extinguished, one should not assume that the effects of conditioning have been completely eliminated. For one thing, *a response that has been extinguished can be reacquired quite rapidly when the CS (or NS) is again paired with the US.* If we again pair the metronome with food following an extinction procedure, it may take only a few pairings before we achieve a fairly strong level of conditioning. Likewise, if I somehow manage to overcome my phobia of dogs, I might rapidly reacquire that phobia if I again have a frightening experience with dogs.

Further evidence that extinction does not completely eliminate the effects of conditioning is the fact that an extinguished response can reappear even in the absence of further pairings between the CS and US. Suppose, for example, that we do extinguish a dog's conditioned salivary response to a metronome by repeatedly presenting the metronome without food. By the end of the extinction session, the metronome no longer elicits salivation. However, if we come back the next morning and sound the metronome, the dog will very likely salivate. It seems as though the dog has forgotten that the metronome no longer predicts food. As a result, we are forced to conduct another series of extinction trials, repeatedly sounding the metronome without the food. After several trials, the response again extinguishes. The next day, however, the dog again starts salivating when we present the metronome. At this point, we might be tempted to conclude that we have an awfully dumb dog on our hands. The dog, however, is simply displaying a phenomenon known as spontaneous recovery.

Spontaneous recovery is the reappearance of a conditioned response following a rest period after extinction. Fortunately, spontaneous recovery does not last forever. Each time the response recovers, it is usually somewhat weaker and extinguishes more quickly than before (see Figure 4.2). Therefore, after several extinction sessions, we should be able to sound the metronome at the start of the session and find little or no salivation.

The phenomenon of spontaneous recovery is particularly important to remember when attempting to extinguish a conditioned fear response. For example, we might arrange for a dog-phobic child to spend several hours with a dog. At the end of that time, the child's fear of the dog might seem to have been totally eliminated. Nevertheless, we should expect that the fear will at least partially recover the next time the child is confronted with a dog, and that several sessions of extinction may be needed before the fear is completely

FIGURE 4.2 Hypothetical results illustrating a decline in spontaneous recovery across repeated sessions of extinction.

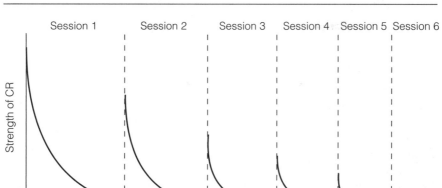

eliminated. Similarly, if with a new date, you feel terribly anxious at the start of the evening but more at ease after a couple of hours, do not be disappointed if you again find yourself becoming quite anxious at the start of your next date. It may take several dates with that person before you feel comfortable right from the outset. Furthermore, following a breakup, it may take a while before your feelings of attraction to the other person finally extinguish, and even then, they may intermittently reappear for a considerable period of time.

To Pavlov (1927), the phenomenon of spontaneous recovery indicated that extinction is not simply a process of unlearning the conditioning that has taken place. Rather, extinction involves learning something new, namely, to inhibit the occurrence of the CR in the presence of CS. For example, rather than unlearning the response of salivation to the metronome during extinction, the dog learns to inhibit the response of salivation to the metronome, with the connection between metronome and salivation still remaining intact on some underlying level. Spontaneous recovery may therefore represent the partial dissipation of this inhibition during the rest period between extinction sessions.

Support for the notion that extinction involves a buildup of inhibition is also provided by a phenomenon known as disinhibition. **Disinhibition is the sudden recovery of a response during an extinction procedure when a novel stimulus is introduced.** For example, if we are in the process of extinguishing conditioning to a metronome but then present a novel humming noise in the background, the sound of the metronome may again elicit a considerable amount of salivation.

Metronome: Food → *Salivation*
     NS   **US**   **UR**
Metronome → *Salivation*
     CS   **CR**

Following repeated presentations of metronome:

Metronome → *Weak salivation*   **(Partial extinction)**
    CS   **CR (weak)**

(Presentation of novel humming noise in background)

Novel humming noise { Metronome → *Salivation*
                                CS   **CR**

Similarly, if while giving a speech in class, your anxiety gradually fades, you may find that it suddenly recovers when a noisy ceiling fan starts up or someone walks in late. (Note that the phenomenon of disinhibition is similar to dishabituation, discussed in Chapter 3, in which the presentation of a novel stimulus results in the reappearance of a habituated response. To distinguish these concepts, it will help to remember that dis*habituation* involves the reappearance of a *habituated* response, while dis*inhibition* involves the recovery of a response that has become partially *inhibited* due to extinction.)

1. In the *process* of extinction, a conditioned response grows weaker because
_____
_____.

2. The *procedure* of extinction involves _____
_____
_____.

3. Once a CR has been extinguished, reacquisition of that response tends to occur (more/less) _____ rapidly than the original conditioning.

4. The sudden recovery of an extinguished response following some delay after extinction is known as s_____ r_____.

5. With repeated sessions of extinction, each time a response recovers, it is usually somewhat (weaker/stronger) _____ and extinguishes more (slowly/quickly) _____.

6. Pavlov believed that this phenomenon indicates that extinction involves the (inhibition/unlearning) _____ of a conditioned response.

7. The sudden recovery of a response during an extinction procedure when a novel stimulus is introduced is called _____.

Stimulus Generalization and Discrimination

Classical conditioning would not be very useful if it only enabled us to learn about relationships between particular stimuli. For example, if we are bitten by a spider, it would not be very helpful for us to fear only that particular spider (which, in any case, we probably obliterated the moment it bit us). It would be far more adaptive to learn to fear other spiders as well, particularly those spiders that look similar to the one that bit us. Fortunately, this is precisely what happens, through a process known as stimulus generalization.

In classical conditioning, *stimulus generalization* **is the tendency for a CR to occur in the presence of a stimulus that is similar to the CS.** In general, the more similar the stimulus is to the original CS, the stronger the response. For example, if a dog is conditioned to salivate to a tone that has a pitch of 2000 Hz, it will salivate to similar tones as well. But it will salivate more strongly to a 1900 Hz tone or a 2100 Hz tone than it will to a 1000 Hz tone or a 3000 Hz tone. In other words, tones that are most similar to the original CS will elicit the strongest response. Similarly, after being bitten by a dog, a child will probably fear not only that particular dog, but other dogs as well. And the child is particularly likely to fear dogs that most closely resemble the dog that bit him.

The process of generalization is most readily apparent when the stimuli involved are physically similar and vary along a continuum. Tones of varying pitch or loudness and lights of varying color or brightness are examples of such stimuli. However, generalization can also occur across nonphysical dimensions, particularly in humans who use language. *Semantic generalization* **is the generalization of a conditioned response to verbal stimuli that are similar in** *meaning* **to the CS.** For example, if human subjects are exposed to a conditioning procedure in which the sight of the word "car" is paired with shock, that word eventually becomes a CS that elicits a fear response. When subjects are shown other words, generalization of the fear response is more likely to occur to those words that are similar in meaning to "car," such as "automobile" or "truck," than to words that look similar, such as "bar" or "tar." Thus, the meaning of the word is the critical factor in semantic generalization. For this reason, words that have similar meaning for an individual—for example, "Madonna" and "Material Girl"—are likely to generate the same conditioned emotional response.

The opposite of stimulus generalization is *stimulus discrimination:* **the tendency for a response to be elicited by one stimulus and not another.** For example, if the dog salivates in the presence of the 2000 Hz tone, but not in the presence of a 1900 Hz tone, then we say that it is able to *discriminate*, or has *formed a discrimination*, between the two stimuli. Such discriminations can be deliberately trained through a procedure known as *discrimination training*. For example, we could repeatedly present the dog with one type of trial in which a 2000 Hz tone is always followed by food and another type of trial in which a 1900 Hz tone is never followed by food. The dog will soon learn to salivate in the presence of the 2000 Hz tone and not in the presence of the 1900 Hz tone.

Conditioning Phase (with the two types of trials presented several times in *random order*)

2000 Hz tone: Food → *Salivation*
     NS   **US**   **UR**
1900 Hz tone: No food
     NS   —

Test Phase:

2000 Hz tone	→	*Salivation*
CS+		CR
1900 Hz tone	→	No salivation
CS−		—

As a result of training, the 2000 Hz tone has become an excitatory CS (CS+) because it predicts the presentation of food, while the 1900 Hz tone has become an inhibitory CS (CS−) because it predicts the absence of food. The discrimination training has, in effect, countered the tendency for gener-

alization to occur. (Note that the two types of trials were presented in random order during the conditioning phase. If they were instead presented in alternating order, the dog might associate the presentation of food with every second tone, rather than with the tone that has a pitch of 2000 Hz.)

As you have probably already guessed, discrimination training is a useful means for determining the sensory capacities of animals. For example, by presenting an animal with a CS+ tone and a CS− tone that are successively more and more similar, we can determine the animal's ability to discriminate be-

tween tones of different pitch. If it salivates to a CS+ of 2000 Hz and does not salivate to a CS− of 1950 Hz, then it has shown us that it can distinguish between the two. But if it salivates to both a CS+ of 2000 Hz and a CS− of 1950 Hz, then it cannot distinguish between the two.

Generalization and discrimination play an important role in many aspects of human behavior. Phobias, for example, involve not only the classical conditioning of a fear response but also an overgeneralization of that fear response to inappropriate stimuli. For example, a woman who has been through an abusive relationship may develop feelings of anxiety and apprehensiveness toward all men. Eventually, however, through repeated interactions with men, this tendency will dissipate and she will begin to adaptively discriminate between men who are potentially abusive and those who are not. Unfortunately, such discriminations are not always easily made, and further bad experiences could greatly strengthen her fear. Moreover, if the woman begins to avoid all men, then the tendency to overgeneralize may remain, thereby significantly impairing her social life. As noted earlier, if we avoid that which we are afraid of, it is difficult for us to overcome our fears.

QUICK QUIZ

1. Stimulus generalization is the tendency for a (CR/UR) _____ to occur in the presence of stimuli that are similar to the original (CS/US) _____. In general, the more (similar/different) _____ the stimulus, the stronger the response.

2. The generalization of a conditioned response to stimuli that are similar in meaning to a verbal CS is called s_____ generalization.

3. The opposite of stimulus generalization is stimulus _____. This can be defined as _____
_____
_____
_____.

4. Feeling "icky" around all objects that look like a snake is an example of stimulus _____, while feeling icky only around snakes is an example of stimulus _____.

5. Suppose that Cary disliked his physics instructor and, as a result, came to dislike all science instructors. This example illustrates the process of over-_____.

Discrimination Training and Experimental Neurosis

Overgeneralization is not the only way in which processes of discrimination versus generalization influence the development of psychological disorders. For example, Pavlov (1927, 1928) reported an interesting discovery made by a colleague, Shenger-Krestovnikova, that arose during a discrimination training procedure.

In this experiment, an image of a circle signaled the presentation of food while an ellipse signaled no food (see Figure 4.3).

In keeping with normal processes of discrimination, the dog dutifully learned to salivate when it saw the circle (a CS+) and not to salivate when it saw the ellipse (a CS−). Following this, the ellipse was gradually made more circular, such that it became more difficult for the dog to determine when food was about to appear. When the ellipse was almost completely circular, the dog was able to make only a weak discrimination, salivating slightly more in the presence of the circle than in the presence of the ellipse. Interestingly, continued training with these stimuli did not result in any improvement. In fact, after several weeks, the discrimination was lost. More interestingly, however, the hitherto well-behaved dog became extremely agitated during each session—squealing, wriggling about, and biting at the equipment. It acted as though it was suffering a nervous breakdown.

Pavlov called this phenomenon *experimental neurosis:* **an experimentally produced disorder in which animals exposed to unpredictable events develop neurotic-like symptoms.** Pavlov hypothesized that human neuroses might develop in a similar manner. Situations of extreme uncertainty can be stressful, and prolonged exposure to such uncertainty might result in the development of neurotic symptoms. Thus, in the opening vignette to this chapter, it is not surprising that Jana's boyfriends often display increasing

FIGURE 4.3 Discrimination training procedure used by Shenger-Krestovnikova in which the picture of a circle functioned as the CS+ and the picture of the ellipse functioned as the CS−.

symptoms of neuroticism as the relationship progresses. While a little uncertainty in one's romantic relationships can be exciting, extreme uncertainty can eventually become aversive.

In carrying out their studies of experimental neurosis, Pavlov and his assistants also discovered that different dogs displayed different patterns of symptoms. Some dogs displayed symptoms of anxiety when exposed to the procedure, while others became catatonic (rigid) and acted almost hypnotized. Additionally, some dogs displayed few if any symptoms and did not have a nervous breakdown. Pavlov speculated that such differences reflected underlying differences in temperament. This was an extension of one of Pavlov's earlier observations, that some dogs condition more easily than others. Shy, withdrawn dogs seem to make the best subjects, conditioning easily, while active, outgoing dogs are more difficult to condition (which is quite the opposite of what Pavlov had originally expected).

On the basis of results such as these, Pavlov formulated a theory of personality in which inherited differences in temperament interact with classical conditioning to produce certain patterns of behavior. This work served to initiate the study of the biological basis of personality (Gray, 1999). For example, Eysenck (1957) later utilized certain aspects of Pavlov's work in formulating his own theory of personality. A major aspect of Eysenck's theory is the distinction between introversion and extroversion. In very general terms, introverts are individuals who are highly reactive to external stimulation (hence, cannot tolerate large amounts of stimulation and tend to withdraw from such stimulation), condition easily, and develop anxiety-type symptoms in reaction to stress. By contrast, extroverts are less reactive to external stimulation (hence, can tolerate, and will even seek out, large amounts of stimulation), condition less easily, and develop physical-type symptoms in reaction to stress. Eysenck's theory also proposes that psychopaths, individuals who engage in antisocial behavior, are extreme extroverts who condition very poorly. As a result, they experience little or no conditioned anxiety when harming or taking advantage of others, such anxiety being the underlying basis of a conscience.

Both Pavlov's and Eysenck's theories of personality are considerably more complicated than presented here, involving additional dimensions of personality and finer distinctions between different types of conditioning, especially excitatory and inhibitory conditioning. Thus, extroverts do not always condition more poorly than introverts, and additional factors are presumed to influence the development of neurotic symptoms (Clark, Watson, & Mineka, 1994; Eysenck, 1967; Monte, 1999). Nevertheless, processes of classical conditioning interacting with inherited differences in temperament could well be major factors in determining one's personality. The experimental neurosis

6 paradigm also suggests that prolonged exposure to unpredictable events can sometimes have serious effects on our well-being. We will further explore this topic in Chapter 9, where the focus will be on exposure to unpredictable *aversive* events.

1. In Shenger-Krestovnikova's experiment, the animal suffered a nervous breakdown when exposed to a CS+ and a CS− that were made progressively (more/less) _____ similar.

2. Pavlov referred to this nervous breakdown as e_____ _____: an experimentally produced disorder in which animals exposed to unp_____ events develop n_____-like symptoms.

3. Pavlov and his assistants noted that the dogs displayed two general patterns of symptoms. These were _____.
_____

As well, (all/not all) _____ dogs developed symptoms.

4. Pavlov believed that these differences between dogs reflected (learned/inherited) _____ differences in t_____.

5. In Eysenck's theory, introverts are (more/less) _____ reactive to external stimulation than extroverts and therefore (can/cannot) _____ tolerate large doses of stimulation.

6. Introverts also condition (more/less) _____ easily than extroverts.

7. Introverts seem to develop _____-type symptoms in reaction to stress, while extroverts develop _____-type symptoms.

8. Psychopaths are extreme (introverts/extroverts) _____ who condition (very easily/very poorly) _____. They therefore feel little or no conditioned _____ when harming or manipulating others.

Two Extensions to Classical Conditioning

The normal classical conditioning procedure involves associating a single neutral stimulus with a US. But stimuli rarely exist in isolation. For example, a neighborhood bully does not exist as an isolated element in a child's world. The bully is associated with a variety of other stimuli, such as the house he lives in, the route he takes to school, and the kids he hangs around with. If a child is assaulted by the bully and learns to fear him, will he also fear the various objects, places, and people with which the bully is associated? In more technical terms, can classical conditioning of a CS also result in the development of a conditioned response to various stimuli that have been, or will be, associated with the CS? The processes of higher-order conditioning and sensory preconditioning indicate that it can.

Higher-Order Conditioning

Suppose you are stung by a wasp while out for a run one day and, as a result, develop a terrible fear of wasps. Imagine too that following the development of this fear, you notice a lot of wasps hanging around the trash bin outside your apartment building. Could the trash bin also come to elicit a certain amount of fear, or at least a feeling of edginess or discomfort? In a process known as ***higher-order conditioning,* a stimulus that is associated with a CS can also become a CS.** Thus, the trash bin could very well come to elicit a fear response through its association with the wasps. This process can be diagrammed as follows:

(**Step 1:** Basic conditioning of a fear response to wasps. As part of a higher-order conditioning procedure, this first step is called *first-order conditioning,* and the original NS and CS are respectively labeled NS_1 and CS_1.)

> **Wasp: Sting** $\rightarrow$ *Fear*
> NS_1 US   UR
> **Wasp** $\rightarrow$ *Fear*
> CS_1 CR

(**Step 2:** Higher-order conditioning of the trash bin through its association with wasps. This second step is sometimes also called *second-order conditioning,* and the new NS and CS are labeled NS_2 and CS_2.)

> **Trash bin: Wasp** $\rightarrow$ *Fear*
> NS_2 CS_1 CR
> **Trash bin** $\rightarrow$ *Fear*
> CS_2 CR

Note that the CS_2 generally elicits a weaker response than the CS_1 (which, as noted in the last chapter, generally elicits a weaker response than the US). Thus, the fear response produced by the trash bin is likely to be much weaker than the fear response produced by the wasps. This is not surprising given that the trash bin is only *indirectly* associated with the unconditioned stimulus (i.e., the wasp sting) upon which the fear response is actually based.

An experiment on higher-order conditioning might involve pairing a metronome with food so that the metronome becomes a CS_1 for salivation, and then pairing a light with the metronome so that the light becomes a CS_2 for salivation (see Figure 4.4). In diagram form:

(**Step 1:** First-order conditioning)

> **Metronome: Food** $\rightarrow$ *Salivation*
> NS_1 US   UR
> **Metronome** $\rightarrow$ *Salivation*
> CS_1 CR

(**Step 2:** Second-order, or higher-order, conditioning)

> **Light: Metronome** $\rightarrow$ *Salivation*
> NS_2 CS_1 CR
> **Light** $\rightarrow$ *Salivation*
> CS_2 CR

The light now elicits salivation although it has never been directly paired with food.

FIGURE 4.4 In this example of higher-order conditioning, a metronome is paired with food and becomes a CS_1 for salivation, following which a light paired with the metronome becomes a CS_2 for salivation. (*Source:* Nairne, 2000.)

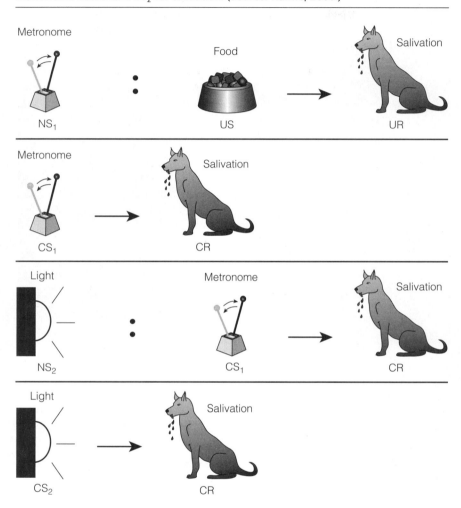

We could also attempt *third-order conditioning* by pairing yet another stimulus, say, the sound of a tone, with the light. However, third-order conditioning is difficult to obtain, and when it is obtained the conditioned response to a third-order conditioned stimulus (the CS_3) is likely to be very weak.

Higher-order conditioning is commonly used in advertising. Advertisements often pair a company name or product with objects, events, or people (usually attractive people) that have been conditioned to elicit positive emotional responses. For example, the advertisement in Figure 4.5 presents an attractive woman in conjunction with a certain product. The assumption is that the positive emotional response elicited by the sight of the woman will be

FIGURE 4.5 An example of higher-order conditioning in advertising. The advertiser assumes that the positive emotional response elicited by the sight of the model will be associated with the clothes, increasing the probability that some readers of the ad (presumably female) will purchase the clothes.

8 associated with the product, thereby increasing the probability that male readers of the ad will wish to purchase that product. (Of course, readers who are concerned about sexism in advertising would likely find the advertisement offensive, in which case they might be less likely to purchase that product.)

1. In _____-_____ conditioning, an already established CS is used to condition a new CS.

2. In general, the CS_2 elicits a (weaker/stronger) _____ response than the CS_1.

3. In higher-order conditioning, conditioning of the CS_1 is often called _____-order conditioning, while conditioning of the CS_2 is called _____-order conditioning.

4. In a higher-order conditioning procedure in which a car is associated with an attractive model, the attractive model is the (CS_1/CS_2) _____ while the car is the (CS_1/CS_2) _____.

Sensory Preconditioning

We have seen that an event that is *subsequently* associated with wasps, such as trash bins, can become a CS for fear. What about an event that was *previously* associated with wasps, such as a toolshed that has had a wasps' nest hanging in it? Will walking near the shed now also elicit feelings of anxiety?

In *sensory preconditioning,* **when one stimulus is conditioned as a CS, another stimulus with which it was previously associated can also become a CS.** If you previously associated the toolshed with wasps and then acquired a fear of wasps as a result of being stung, you might also feel anxious when walking near the toolshed. This process can be diagrammed as follows:

(**Step 1:** Preconditioning phase in which the toolshed is associated with wasps)

> **Toolshed: Wasps**
> NS_2 NS_1

(**Step 2:** Conditioning of wasps as a CS_1)

> **Wasp: Sting** → *Fear*
> NS_1 US   UR
> **Wasp** → *Fear*
> CS_1 CR

(**Step 3:** Presentation of the toolshed)

> **Toolshed** → *Fear*
> CS_2 CR

The toolshed now elicits a fear response, although it was never directly associated with a wasp sting.

An experiment on sensory preconditioning might involve first presenting a dog with several pairings of two neutral stimuli such as a light and a metronome. The metronome is then paired with food to become a CS for salivation. As a result of this, the light, which has never been directly paired with the food but has been associated with the metronome, also comes to elicit salivation (see Figure 4.6). This process can be diagrammed as follows:

(**Step 1:** Preconditioning phase, in which the light is repeatedly associated with the metronome)

> **Light: Metronome** (200 presentations of light followed by metronome)
> NS_2 NS_1

(**Step 2:** Conditioning of the metronome as a CS_1)

> **Metronome: Food** → *Salivation*
> NS_1 US   UR
> **Metronome** → *Salivation*
> CS_1 CR

(**Step 3:** Presentation of the light)

> **Light** → *Salivation*
> CS_2 CR

A simple way to think of what is happening here is that it involves a chain of predictions. The light predicts the metronome and the metronome predicts the food; the dog therefore salivates not only to the metronome but also to the

9

light. As with higher-order conditioning, the response elicited by the light (CS₂) is likely to be much weaker than the response elicited by the metronome (CS₁). Likewise, the fear response elicited by the toolshed (CS₂) is likely to be much weaker than the fear response elicited by wasps (CS₁).

Sensory preconditioning is significant in that it demonstrates that stimuli can become associated with each other in the absence of any identifiable response (other than an orienting response). In this sense, sensory precondi-

FIGURE 4.6 In this example of sensory preconditioning, a dog is presented with several pairings of a light and a metronome. The metronome is then paired with food and becomes a conditioned stimulus for salivation. As a result, the light that was previously paired with the metronome also becomes a conditioned stimulus for salivation. (*Source:* Nairne, 2000.)

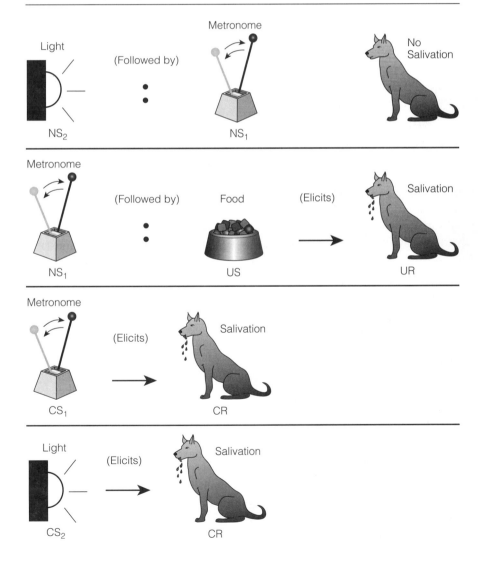

tioning is a form of *latent learning*, which was first discussed in Chapter 1. Just as Tolman's rats learned to find their way around a maze even when it seemed like there were no significant consequences for doing so (i.e., food had not yet been introduced into the goal box), animals will associate stimuli with each other even when those stimuli seem to have little significance for them.

Suppose you suddenly developed a strong fear of dogs after being severely bitten. You are now reluctant to go rollerblading because, on several occasions in the past, you witnessed people walking their dogs on the rollerblade paths.

1. This example illustrates the phenomenon of _____ _____.

2. The rollerblade paths are a (CS_1/CS_2) _____, while the dogs are a (CS_1/CS_2) _____.

3. Rollerblade paths will probably elicit a (stronger/weaker) _____ fear response than will the sight of the dogs.

Is this scenario most likely an example of higher-order conditioning or sensory preconditioning? (You will find the answer when you complete the end-of-chapter test.)

"HE'S BEEN AT IT TOO LONG. NOW, WHEN THE BELL RINGS, DR. PAVLOV SALIVATES."

Three Limitations to Classical Conditioning

In the preceding section, we examined two ways in which the classical conditioning process can be extended to conditioning of additional CSs. In this section, we discuss three procedures—overshadowing, blocking, and latent inhibition—in which little or no conditioning occurs despite close pairing of a neutral stimulus with a US. Two of these procedures (overshadowing and blocking) involve the presentation of what is known as a compound stimulus. **A *compound stimulus* consists of the simultaneous presentation of two or more individual stimuli** (e.g., the sound of a metronome is presented at the same time as a light).

11

Overshadowing

If you were stung by a wasp during a walk in the woods, would it make sense to develop a conditioned fear response to every stimulus associated with that event (e.g., the trees surrounding you, the butterfly fluttering by, and the cloud formation in the sky)? No, it would not. Rather, it would make more sense to develop a fear of those stimuli that are most salient (that really stand out) at the time of being stung, such as the sight of the wasp.

In *overshadowing*, **the most salient member of a compound stimulus is more readily conditioned as a CS and thereby interferes with conditioning of the less salient member.** In the wasp example, you are likely to develop a conditioned fear response to the most distinctive stimuli associated with that event, such as the sight of the wasp and perhaps the buzzing sound it makes.

An experimental example of overshadowing might involve first pairing a compound stimulus, such as a bright light and a faint-sounding metronome, with food. After several pairings, the compound stimulus becomes a CS that elicits salivation. However, when each member of the compound is tested separately, the bright light elicits salivation while the faint metronome elicits no salivation (or very little salivation). In diagram form:

(**Step 1:** Conditioning of a compound stimulus as a CS. Note that the compound stimulus consists of the simultaneous presentation of the two bracketed stimuli.)

    [Bright light + Faint metronome]: Food → *Salivation*
               NS   US   UR
    [Bright light + Faint metronome] → *Salivation*
               CS   CR

(**Step 2:** Presentation of each member of the compound separately)

    Bright light → *Salivation*
        CS   CR
    Faint metronome → No salivation
        NS   —

Because of the presence of the bright light during the conditioning trials, no conditioning occurred to the faint metronome. This is not because the faint metronome is unnoticeable. If it had been paired with the food by itself, it could easily have become an effective CS. Only in the presence of a more salient stimulus does the less salient stimulus come to elicit little or no response (see Figure 4.7).

Top managers make use of the overshadowing effect when they assign an assistant to announce an unpopular decision. Although the employees might

FIGURE 4.7   In this example of overshadowing, a bright light and a faint-sounding metronome are simultaneously presented as a compound stimulus and paired with food. After several pairings, the compound stimulus becomes a CS that elicits salivation. However, when each member of the compound is tested separately, the bright light elicits salivation while the faint-sounding metronome does not. (*Source:* Nairne, 2000.)

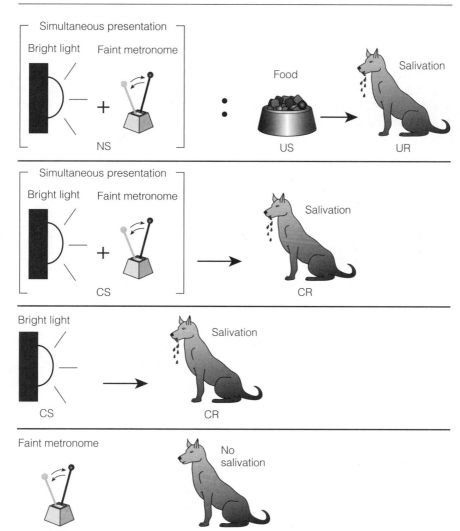

recognize that the top manager is mostly responsible, the assistant is the most salient stimulus and will, as a result, bear the brunt of the blame. It is thus the assistant who is likely to become most disliked by the employees. On the other hand, head managers often make a point of personally announcing popular decisions, thereby attracting most of the positive associations to themselves, even if they have been only minimally involved in those decisions. Similarly, the positive feelings generated by the music of a rock band will be most strongly associated with the most salient member of that band (e.g., the lead singer)—a fact that often leads to problems when other band members conclude that they are not receiving their fair share of the accolades.

12

Blocking

The phenomenon of overshadowing demonstrates that, in some circumstances, mere contiguity between a neutral stimulus and a US is insufficient for conditioning to occur. An even clearer demonstration of this fact is provided by a phenomenon known as blocking (Kamin, 1969). **In *blocking*, the presence of an established CS interferes with conditioning of a new CS.** Blocking is similar to overshadowing, except that the compound consists of a neutral stimulus and a CS rather than two neutral stimuli that differ in salience. For example, suppose that a light is first conditioned as a CS for salivation. If the light is then combined with a metronome to form a compound, and this compound is then paired with food, little or no conditioning occurs to the metronome. In diagram form:

(**Step 1:** Conditioning of the light as a CS)

    Light: Food → *Salivation*
      NS   US   UR
    Light → *Salivation*
      CS   CR

(**Step 2:** Several pairings of compound stimulus with the US)

    [Light + Metronome]: Food → *Salivation*
        CS + NS   US   UR

(**Step 3:** Presentation of each member of the compound separately. The question at this point is whether conditioning occurred to the metronome.)

    Light → *Salivation*
      CS   CR
    Metronome → *No salivation*
        NS   —

In step 2, the presence of the light blocked conditioning to the metronome. An easy way of thinking about what is happening here is that the light already predicts the food, so the dog only pays attention to the light. As a result, the metronome does not become an effective CS despite being paired with the food (see Figure 4.8).

13

FIGURE 4.8 In this example of blocking, a light is first conditioned as a CS for salivation. When the light is then combined with a metronome to form a compound stimulus, and this compound stimulus is paired with food, the metronome does not become a conditioned stimulus. The presence of the already established CS blocks conditioning to the metronome. (*Source:* Nairne, 2000.)

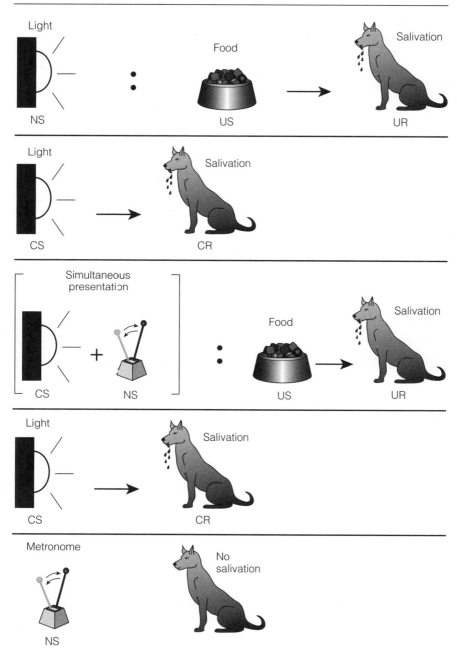

Latent Inhibition

Do we condition more readily to stimuli that are familiar or unfamiliar? You might think that familiar stimuli are more readily conditioned, since if we already know something about a topic, it seems easier to learn more about it. In fact, in what is known as *latent inhibition*, **a familiar stimulus is more difficult to condition as a CS than an unfamiliar (novel) stimulus.**[1] Or, stated the other way around, *an unfamiliar stimulus is more readily conditioned than a familiar stimulus*. For example, if, on many occasions, a dog has heard the sound of a metronome prior to conditioning, then a standard number of conditioning trials might result in little or no conditioning to the metronome.

(**Step 1:** Stimulus preexposure phase in which a neutral stimulus is repeatedly presented)

    Metronome (say, 40 presentations)
        NS

(**Step 2:** Conditioning trials in which the preexposed neutral stimulus is now paired with a US)

    Metronome: Food → *Salivation* (say, 10 trials)
        NS   US   UR

(**Step 3:** Test trial to determine if conditioning has occurred to the metronome)

    Metronome → *No salivation*
        NS   —

If the dog had not been preexposed to the metronome and it had been a novel stimulus when first paired with food, then the ten conditioning trials would have resulted in significant conditioning to the metronome. Because of the preexposure, however, no conditioning occurred (see Figure 4.9). It will take many more pairings of metronome and food before the metronome will reliably elicit salivation.

Latent inhibition prevents the development of conditioned associations to redundant stimuli in the environment. Such stimuli are likely to be relatively inconsequential with respect to the conditioning event. For example, if a rabbit in a grassy field is attacked by a coyote and then escapes, it will be much more adaptive for the rabbit to associate the attack with the novel scent of the coyote than with the familiar scent of grass. The scent of the coyote is a good predictor of a possible attack, and a conditioned fear response to that scent

---

[1] Latent inhibition is also known as the *CS preexposure effect*. A related phenomenon, known as the *US preexposure effect*, holds that conditioning is slower with familiar, as opposed to unfamiliar, USs.

FIGURE 4.9 In latent inhibition, familiar stimuli are more difficult to condition as CSs than novel stimuli. If a dog has, on many occasions, heard the sound of a metronome prior to conditioning, then it will be difficult to obtain conditioning to the metronome using a standard number of conditioning trials. (*Source:* Nairne, 2000.)

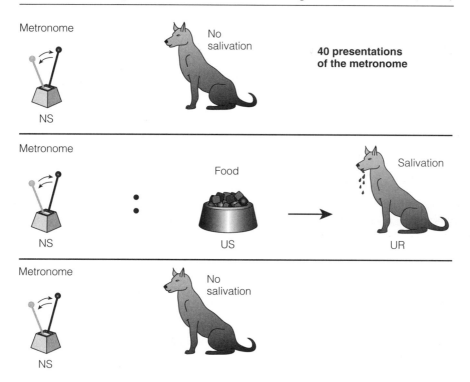

will help the rabbit avoid such attacks in the future. A conditioned fear response to grass, however, will be completely maladaptive since the rabbit is surrounded by grass day in and day out and may even feed upon it. Thus, it is the novel stimuli that precede the presentation of a US that are most likely to be meaningfully related to it.

Problems concerning latent inhibition are evident in people who have schizophrenia (Lubow & Gewirtz, 1995). These individuals often have great difficulty attending to relevant stimuli in their environment and are instead distracted by irrelevant stimuli, such as various background noises or people passing nearby. Experiments have revealed that people with schizophrenia display less latent inhibition than is normal—that is, they condition more easily to familiar stimuli—indicating that the disorder partly involves an inability to screen out redundant stimuli. Experiments have also revealed that drugs used to treat schizophrenia tend to increase levels of latent inhibition, thereby normalizing the person's attentional processes.

ADVICE FOR THE LOVELORN

Dear Dr. Dee,

My friend is involved with someone who has recently started acting quite aggressively toward her. I am worried for her safety, yet she keeps saying that he is not that frightening. To the rest of us, it is obvious that the guy is dangerous. Is she blinded by love?

Deeply Concerned

Dear Deeply,

On the one hand, your friend is more familiar with this person than you are, so it may be that her judgment is indeed more accurate. On the other hand, this increased familiarity with him might also mean that it will take longer for her to develop a fear of him. This is in keeping with the process of latent inhibition, in which we condition less readily to familiar stimuli than unfamiliar stimuli. This is yet another factor that might contribute to people remaining in an abusive relationship, when the people around them clearly recognize the danger signals. So it may be that she is blinded by latent inhibition, not love.

Behaviorally yours,

QUICK QUIZ

1. A compound stimulus consists of the (simultaneous/successive) _____ presentation of two or more separate stimuli.

2. In _____, the most salient member of a compound stimulus is more readily conditioned as a CS and thereby interferes with conditioning of the less salient member.

3. In _____, the presence of an established CS interferes with conditioning of another stimulus.

4. In _____ _____, a familiar stimulus is more difficult to condition as a CS than an unfamiliar stimulus.

5. In a(n) _____ procedure, the compound stimulus consists of a neutral stimulus and a CS, while in a(n) _____ procedure, the compound stimulus consists of two neutral stimuli.

6. Latent inhibition (prevents/promotes) _____ the development of conditioned associations to redundant stimuli.

7. Because Jason has a history of getting into trouble, he often catches most of the blame when something goes wrong, even when others are at least as responsible for what happened. This is similar to the phenomenon of _____.

Additional Phenomena

In this section, we will briefly cover some additional ways in which the process of classical conditioning can be affected by modifications in the typical conditioning procedure.

Temporal Conditioning

In all of the preceding examples, the CS is a distinctive, external stimulus of some sort, such as a light, a metronome, or a dog. But this need not always be the case. *Temporal conditioning* **is a form of classical conditioning in which the CS is the passage of time.** For example, if a dog is given a bite of food every 10 minutes, it will eventually salivate more strongly toward the end of each 10-minute interval than at the start of the interval. The end of the 10-minute interval is the effective CS for salivation. Similarly, residents of a city who experience a bombing attack each night at 2:00 A.M. for several nights in a row will likely start feeling anxious as 2:00 A.M. approaches, even in the absence of any clock indicating the time. The various cues that we use to estimate time, some of which are internal, are sufficient to elicit the feelings of anxiety.

Occasion Setting

In higher-order conditioning, we saw that an NS that predicted the occurrence of a CS could itself become a CS. For example:

Metronome: Food → *Salivation*
Metronome → *Salivation*
Light: Metronome → *Salivation*
Light → *Salivation*

But what if the situation were altered somewhat, so that the light not only predicted the metronome, but also predicted whether the metronome would be followed by food? For example, what if we presented the dog with the following types of trials:

(**Step 1:** Presentation of light-metronome and metronome-alone trials in random order)

Light: Metronome: Food → *Salivation*
  NS   NS   US   UR
Metronome: No food
     NS   —

In this circumstance, we are likely to find that the metronome comes to elicit salivation only when it is preceded by the light and not when it is presented by itself.

(**Step 2:** Test trials)

    Light: Metronome → *Salivation*
      OS   **CS**   **CR**
    Metronome → **No salivation**
        NS   —

The light in this instance is referred to as an *occasion setter* (which we will abbreviate as OS), because it predicts the occasions on which the metronome is followed by food. Its presence therefore comes to control the extent to which the metronome serves as CS for salivation. Thus, in classical conditioning, *occasion setting* **is a procedure in which a stimulus (known as an *occasion setter*) signals that a CS is likely to be followed by the US with which it is associated.** The presence of this stimulus then facilitates the occurrence of the CR in response to the CS.

An occasion setter can be associated with not only the presentation of a US, but also a change in the intensity of the US. Imagine for example that an abused child receives the worst beatings from his parents whenever they are drinking alcohol. Thus:

> *When alcohol is not present:*
> **Parents: Mild abuse** → *Mild anxiety*

> *When alcohol is present:*
> **Alcohol: Parents: Severe abuse** → **Strong anxiety**

The result is that although the child typically feels a certain amount of anxiety around his parents, the sight of a bottle of alcohol on the table greatly increases his anxiety. Thus:

> *Presence of parents:*
> **Parents** → *Mild anxiety*

> *Presence of alcohol and parents:*
> **Alcohol: Parents** → **Strong anxiety**

The conditioned response of anxiety to the parents is greatly facilitated by the presence of alcohol. The alcohol is therefore an occasion setter that heightens the child's anxiety in the presence of the parents.

Insofar as the real world consists of a complex mixture of stimuli, occasion setting is an important factor in many instances of classical conditioning. Women are typically more anxious about being harassed while walking by a construction worker at a construction site than while walking by a construction worker in an office complex. And hikers are more anxious about bears with cubs than they are about bears without cubs. The additional stimuli present in these circumstances (construction site and bear cubs) indicate a higher probability of certain events (harassment and bear attack).

1. In temporal conditioning, the (NS/US) _____ is presented at regular intervals, with the result that the end of each interval becomes a (CS/US) _____ that elicits a (CR/UR) _____.

2. In classical conditioning, o_____ s_____ is a procedure in which a stimulus signals that a CS is likely to be followed by the _____. This stimulus is called a(n) _____ _____, and serves to (facilitate/retard) _____ the occurrence of the (UR/CR) _____.

3. Kaz became very accustomed to having a snack at about 4:00 each afternoon. As a result, he now finds that he automatically starts thinking about food at about 4:00 each afternoon, even before he notices the time. These automatic thoughts of food seem to represent an example of _____ conditioning.

4. Brandon notices that the doctor gives him an injection only when a nurse is present in the examining room. As a result, he feels more anxious about the medical exam when the nurse is present than when the nurse is absent. In this case, the nurse functions as an o_____ s_____ for his conditioned feelings of anxiety in the examining room.

US Revaluation

At the start of this chapter, we mentioned how more-intense stimuli produce stronger conditioning than less-intense stimuli. For example, a strong shock will produce stronger fear conditioning than a weak shock. But what would happen if we conducted our conditioning trials with one level of shock and then presented a different level of shock on a subsequent nonconditioning trial? In other words, would changing the intensity or value of the US subsequent to the conditioning of a CS also change the strength of response to the CS?

Imagine, for example, that the sound of a metronome is followed by a small amount of food, with the result that the metronome comes to elicit a small amount of saliva.

> **Metronome: Small amount of food** → *Weak salivation*
>   NS   US   UR
> **Metronome** → *Weak salivation*
>   CS   CR

Once this conditioning has been established, we now present the dog with a large amount of food, which elicits a large amount of saliva.

> **Large amount of food** → *Strong salivation*
>   US   UR

What type of response will now be elicited by the metronome? As it turns out, the dog is likely to react to the metronome as though it is predictive of a large amount of food rather than a small amount of food.

> **Metronome** → *Strong salivation*
>   CS   CR

Note that the metronome was never directly paired with the large amount of food; the intervening experience with the large amount of food by itself produced the stronger level of conditioned salivation. Thus, *US revaluation* **involves the post-conditioning presentation of the US at a different level of intensity, thereby altering the strength of response to the previously conditioned CS.**

Pseudoconditioning

Hopefully, you are now pretty familiar with the basic classical conditioning procedure and some of the phenomena associated with it. Be aware, however, that determining whether classical conditioning has occurred is not always as straightforward as it might seem. A phenomenon known as *pseudoconditioning* poses a particular problem. **In *pseudoconditioning*, an elicited response that appears to be a CR is actually the result of sensitization rather than conditioning.** Suppose, for example, that we try to condition a leg withdrawal reflex (leg flexion) in a dog by presenting a light flash followed by a slight shock to its foot.

Light flash: Shock → *Leg flexion*

After a few pairings of the light with the shock, we now find that the flexion response occurs immediately when the light is flashed.

Light flash → *Leg flexion*

On the surface, it seems that the light flash has become a CS and that we have successfully conditioned a flexion response. But have we? What if instead of flashing a light, we sound a beep and find that, lo and behold, it too elicits a response?

Beep → *Leg flexion*

What is going on here?

Remember the process of sensitization in which the repeated presentation of an eliciting stimulus can sometimes increase the strength of the elicited response? Well, sensitization can also result in the response being elicited by other stimuli as well. For example, soldiers with war trauma exhibit an enhanced startle response, not just to the sound of exploding artillery shells, but to all kinds of other stimuli as well, including doors slamming, cars backfiring, or even an unexpected tap on the shoulder. Similarly, if a dog has been shocked in the paw a couple of times, it would not be at all surprising if any sudden stimulus in that setting could make the dog quickly jerk its leg up. Therefore, although we thought we had established a CR—which is the result of a CS having been associated with a US—in reality we have simply produced a hypersensitive dog that automatically reacts to almost any sudden stimulus.

Pseudoconditioning is a potential problem whenever the US is some type of emotionally arousing stimulus. Fortunately, there are ways of determining the extent to which a response is the result of pseudoconditioning rather than real conditioning. One alternative is to employ a control condition in which the NS and US are presented separately. For example, while subjects in the experimental group receive several pairings of the light flash and the shock, subjects in the control group receive light flashes and shocks that are well separated in time.

Experimental group	*Control group*
Light flash: Shock → *Leg flexion*	**Light flash / / Shock** → *Leg flexion*

(where the symbol / / for the control group means that the light flash and the shock are *not* paired and are instead presented separately in random order) When the animals in each group are then exposed to the light flash presented on its own, we find the following:

Experimental group	*Control group*
Light flash → *Strong leg flexion*	**Light flash** → *Weak leg flexion*

The level of responding shown by the control group is presumed to reflect the amount of sensitization (pseudoconditioning) due to the use of an upsetting stimulus like shock. However, because the response shown by the experimental group is stronger than that shown by the control group, conditioning is assumed to have occurred, with the difference between the two groups indicating the strength of conditioning. Classical conditioning experiments typically utilize one or more control groups like this to assess how much actual conditioning has taken place versus how much the subject's responses are the result of nonconditioning factors like sensitization.

1. The _____ r_____ procedure involves the (pre-/post-) _____ conditioning presentation of the (CS/US) _____ at a different level of intensity.

2. Cynthia feels all excited when she sees her father arrive home each evening because he always brings her some licorice. One day, however, her mother bought her a lot of licorice earlier in the day, such that she had no desire for licorice when evening came around. As a result, she was not as excited when her father came home that evening. In this example, her father is a (CS/US) _____ through his association with licorice. Satiating on licorice therefore reduced the value of the (CS/US)_____ that typically followed her father's arrival home. As a result, her (CR/UR) _____ of excitement on seeing her father was greatly reduced.

3. When an elicited response that appears to be a CR is actually the result of sensitization, we say that _____ has taken place.

4. The above phenomenon is a potential problem whenever the US produces a strong e_____ response.

5. An appropriate control procedure to test for this phenomenon involves presenting a control group of subjects with the NS and US (close together/quite separate) _____. Whatever responding is later elicited by the NS in this group is assumed to be the result of s_____ rather than real conditioning.

Notice

In this chapter, you have been exposed to a considerable number of conditioning procedures, some of which are quite similar (such as overshadowing and blocking). Be sure to *overlearn* these procedures, as many students often confuse them, especially under the stress of examination conditions.

SUMMARY

Strengthening a conditioned response by pairing a CS (NS) with a US is known as acquisition. In general, early conditioning trials produce more rapid acquisition than later trials. Weakening a conditioned response by repeatedly presenting the CS by itself is known as extinction. Spontaneous recovery is the reappearance of a previously extinguished response after a rest period, while disinhibition is the sudden recovery of an extinguished response following introduction of a novel stimulus.

In stimulus generalization, we learn to respond similarly to stimuli that resemble an original stimulus. One version of stimulus generalization, known as semantic generalization, involves generalization of a response to verbal stimuli that are similar in meaning to the original stimulus. In stimulus discrimination, we respond to one stimulus and not another, a process that is established through discrimination training. Pavlov discovered that dogs that were exposed to a difficult discrimination problem often suffered from nervous breakdowns, a phenomenon that he called experimental neurosis.

In higher-order conditioning, a previously conditioned stimulus (CS_1) is used to condition a new stimulus (CS_2). The CS_2 elicits a weaker response than the CS_1 since there is only an indirect association between the CS_2 and the US. In sensory preconditioning, when one stimulus is conditioned as a CS, another stimulus with which it was previously associated also becomes a CS.

Certain situations can also interfere with the process of conditioning. For example, overshadowing occurs when the most salient member of a compound stimulus is more readily conditioned as a CS and thereby interferes with the conditioning of a less salient member. Blocking occurs when the presence of an established CS during conditioning interferes with conditioning of a new CS. Familiar stimuli are also more difficult to condition than unfamiliar stimuli, a phenomenon known as latent inhibition.

In temporal conditioning, the effective CS is the passage of time between USs that are presented at regular intervals. In occasion setting, an additional stimulus (an occasion setter) indicates whether a CS will be followed by a US; the CS therefore elicits a CR only in the presence of the occasion setter. US revaluation involves exposure to a stronger or weaker US follow-ing conditioning, which then alters the strength of response to the previously conditioned CS. Pseudoconditioning is a false form of conditioning in which the response is actually the result of sensitization rather than classical conditioning.

STUDY QUESTIONS

1. Define acquisition. Draw a graph of a typical acquisition curve, and indicate the asymptote of conditioning.
2. Define the processes of extinction and spontaneous recovery.
3. Define disinhibition. How does it differ from dishabituation?
4. Describe stimulus generalization and semantic generalization.
5. What is stimulus discrimination? Outline an example of a discrimination training procedure.
6. Define experimental neurosis, and describe Shenger-Krestovnikova's procedure for producing it.
7. Define higher-order conditioning, and diagram an example.
8. Define sensory preconditioning, and diagram an example.
9. Define overshadowing, and diagram an example.
10. Define blocking, and diagram an example.
11. Define latent inhibition, and diagram an example.
12. What is temporal conditioning? Describe an example.
13. Define occasion setting, and diagram an example.
14. Define US revaluation and diagram an example.
15. How does pseudoconditioning differ from classical conditioning? How can one experimentally determine whether a response is the result of classical conditioning or pseudoconditioning?

CONCEPT REVIEW

acquisition. The process of developing and strengthening a conditioned response through repeated pairings of an NS (or CS) with a US.
blocking. The phenomenon whereby the presence of an established CS interferes with conditioning of a new CS.
compound stimulus. A complex stimulus that consists of the simultaneous presentation of two or more individual stimuli.
disinhibition. The sudden recovery of a response during an extinction procedure when a novel stimulus is introduced.
experimental neurosis. An experimentally produced disorder in which animals exposed to unpredictable events develop neurotic-like symptoms.
extinction. The process whereby a conditioned response can be weakened or eliminated when the CS is repeatedly presented in the absence of the US;

also, the procedure whereby this happens, namely, the repeated presentation of the CS in the absence of the US.

higher-order conditioning. The process whereby a stimulus that is associated with a CS can also become a CS.

latent inhibition. The phenomenon whereby a familiar stimulus is more difficult to condition as a CS than an unfamiliar (novel) stimulus.

occasion setting. A procedure in which a stimulus (known as an *occasion setter*) signals that a CS is likely to be followed by the US with which it is associated.

overshadowing. The phenomenon whereby the most salient member of a compound stimulus is more readily conditioned as a CS and thereby interferes with conditioning of the less salient member.

pseudoconditioning. A situation in which an elicited response that appears to be a CR is actually the result of sensitization rather than conditioning.

semantic generalization. The generalization of a conditioned response to verbal stimuli that are similar in meaning to the CS.

sensory preconditioning. In this phenomenon, when one stimulus is conditioned as a CS, another stimulus with which it was previously associated can also become a CS.

spontaneous recovery. The reappearance of a conditioned response following a rest period after extinction.

stimulus discrimination. The tendency for a response to be elicited by one stimulus and not another.

stimulus generalization. The tendency for a CR to occur in the presence of a stimulus that is similar to the CS.

temporal conditioning. A form of classical conditioning in which the CS is the passage of time.

US revaluation. A process that involves the post-conditioning presentation of the US at a different level of intensity, thereby altering the strength of response to the previously conditioned CS.

CHAPTER TEST

12. In higher-order conditioning, the CS_2 generally elicits a (stronger/weaker) _____ response than the CS_1.

5. The fact that you learned to fear wasps and hornets, as well as bees, after being stung by a bee is an example of the process of _____.

8. During an eyeblink conditioning procedure, you not only blinked in response to the sound of the click but also when someone tapped you on the shoulder. Your response to the tap on the shoulder may be indicative of _____ conditioning, which means that the elicited response is likely the result of _____ rather than classical conditioning.

18. While playing tennis one day, you suffer a minor ankle sprain. Two weeks later you severely twist your ankle while stepping off a curb. The next

time you play tennis, you find yourself surprisingly worried about spraining your ankle. This is an example of _____.

23. According to Eysenck, psychopaths tend to be extreme (extroverts/introverts) _____ who condition (easily/poorly) _____.

20. Charlene feels anxious whenever the manager walks into the store accompanied by the owner, because the manager always finds fault with the employees when the owner is there. This is best seen as an example of _____ with the owner functioning as the _____.

14. Two limitations to conditioning, known as _____ and _____, both involve pairing a compound stimulus with a US.

2. Following an experience in which you were stung by a bee and subsequently developed a fear of bees, you are hired for a 1-day job with a biologist in which your task is to catch bees. During the day, you never once get stung by a bee. As a result, your fear of bees will likely (decrease/increase) _____, a process known as _____.

10. The researcher feels that you have done such a fine job catching bees that she hires you for another day. At the start of the next day, you will likely find that your fear of bees has (completely disappeared/partially returned) _____, a phenomenon known as _____.

22. By the end of the second day, your fear of bees has mostly disappeared. However, you then hear thunder in the distance and become a bit worried about whether you should immediately head back to the lab. You decide first to catch one more bee, but find that your fear of bees is now somewhat stronger. The sudden recovery of your fear response is an example of a process known as _____.

15. Marty once played in an all-star game alongside Bobby Orr (a famous and talented hockey player). Marty scored two goals and an assist, as did Orr. Orr was later voted the game's most valuable player, while Marty's name was barely mentioned. This situation seems analogous to the _____ effect in classical conditioning.

25. Remember the cartoon of Pavlov learning to salivate to the bell after watching the dogs being conditioned? Of the two types of extensions to classical conditioning, this is most similar to _____. This situation might have arisen during conditioning if the dogs were being fed bites of juicy steak, the *sight* of which for most humans is probably a (CS_1/CS_2) _____ for salivation. The bell would then become a (CS_1/CS_2) _____ through its association with the sight of the steak.

19. Jared's parents always start arguing at about midnight each night. As a result, he wakes up feeling anxious each night just prior to midnight. This seems to be an example of _____ conditioning.

3. Consider the following example:

(Step 1)

John: Rude behavior → *Anger*
John → *Anger*

(Step 2)

Bill: John → *Anger*
Bill → *Anger*
This is an example of _____
conditioning.

11. In higher-order conditioning, conditioning of the CS_1 is sometimes called _____ conditioning, while conditioning of the CS_2 is called _____ conditioning.

6. The *procedure* of extinction involves the _____
_____
_____.

24. The gradual strengthening of a classically conditioned fear response by repeated pairings of a tone with shock is an example of the process of _____. During this process, early pairings of tone and shock are likely to produce (larger/smaller) _____ increments in conditioning compared to later pairings.

1. The maximum amount of conditioning that can take place in a particular situation is known as the _____ of conditioning.

9. Consider the following example:

(Step 1: Repeated experiences in restaurant)
Restaurant: Bob

(Step 2: Not in restaurant)
Bob: Argument → *Tension*
Bob → *Tension*

(Step 3)
Restaurant → *Tension*

This process is best seen as an example of _____.

4. Based partially on Pavlov's work on experimental neurosis, Eysenck concluded that (introverts/extroverts) _____ tend to be highly reactive to external stimulation, condition easily, and develop anxiety-type symptoms in reaction to stress. By contrast, _____ are less reactive, condition less easily, and develop physical-type symptoms in reaction to stress.

17. You once played in an all-star game alongside Joe, an unknown basketball player just like you. Joe, however, has a very flamboyant manner on the court. Although you both played equally well, almost all the credit for the win went to _____, which seems analogous to the _____ effect in classical conditioning.

13. If the scent of ammonia and the ticking of a clock are combined to form a compound stimulus, then the two stimuli are being presented (simultaneously/successively) _____.
21. Johanne had never experienced a more difficult multiple-choice test. Virtually every alternative for every question looked equally correct. By the end of the exam, he felt extremely anxious. Johanne's experience is somewhat analogous to a phenomenon discovered by Pavlov's associates, which they called _____.
16. A student has great difficulty focusing on the relevant material being discussed in class and is easily distracted. This student might also display (stronger/weaker) _____ evidence of _____ inhibition compared to the average student.
7. A person who fears dogs also feels anxious when he hears the word "canine." This is an example of _____.

ANSWERS TO CHAPTER TEST

1. asymptote
2. decrease; extinction
3. higher-order conditioning
4. introverts; extroverts
5. stimulus generalization
6. repeated presentation of the CS without the US
7. semantic generalization
8. pseudo; sensitization
9. sensory preconditioning
10. partially returned; spontaneous recovery
11. first-order conditioning; second-order conditioning
12. weaker
13. simultaneously
14. blocking; overshadowing
15. blocking (with Orr functioning as an established CS)
16. weaker; latent
17. Joe; overshadowing
18. US revaluation
19. temporal
20. occasion setting; occasion setter
21. experimental neurosis
22. disinhibition
23. extroverts; poorly
24. acquisition; larger
25. higher-order conditioning; CS_1; CS_2

Put Learning into Action with Sniffy, the Virtual Rat

The following material refers to *Sniffy, the Virtual Rat™: Pro Version*, a separate Wadsworth product that consists of a manual and a CD-ROM.

1. Read pp. 103–108 and follow the instructions in exercise 20. Once you have done this, Sniffy will have learned, through classical conditioning, a basic CS–US association. That is, the CS (here, a tone) predicts the occurrence of a US (a shock). You may find it helpful to read pp. 45–50, which explain the details of the variable-ratio 25 (VR 25) schedule that you will use in exercise 20. After completing exercise 20, move ahead to exercise 23 (pp. 112–119). This exercise demonstrates the effect of the CS's intensity on learning. Similarly, exercise 24 (pp. 120–122) effectively demonstrates how the intensity of the US can influence learning in classical conditioning.

2. Follow the instructions in exercise 21 (pp. 108–110) to extinguish the conditioned response that you established in exercise 20.

3. Follow the instructions in exercise 22 (pp. 110–112) to observe the spontaneous recovery of the CR you extinguished in exercise 21.

4. Read pp. 143–144 for additional information on inhibitory conditioned stimuli.

5. (Optional) Complete exercise 29 (pp. 144–148), which is a demonstration of how a CS− can affect learning about a CS+. Read p. 124 for an explanation of the notation used on p. 144.

6. (Optional) Complete exercise 30 (pp. 149–152), which demonstrates the power of a CS− to influence behavioral responses. As this exercise shows, a CS− can inhibit response not only to the initial CS+ with which it was conditioned, but also to a CS+ with which the CS− has not previously been paired. Read p. 124 for an explanation of the notation used in the chart on p. 149.

7. Read pp. 153–154 for additional information on higher-order conditioning.

8. Run exercise 32 (pp. 160–163) to train Sniffy to respond to a CS_2.

9. If you have not already done so, read pp. 153–154 for additional information on sensory preconditioning.

10. Run exercise 31 (pp. 154–160). The background information for this exercise makes reference to stimulus-response (S-R) and stimulus-stimulus (S-S) associations. For now, do not worry too much about this distinction, but *do* make sure that you select the S-S association option, as specified in step 3 (p. 156) of this exercise. S-S and S-R learning will be covered in chapter 5 of the textbook.

11. Complete exercise 25 (pp. 123–130). In this exercise you will use the principles of compound conditioning to form an association between two CSs—a light and a tone. The exercise is divided into two parts. The first part involves the initial compound conditioning of the two CSs. In the

second part, you will carry out a control procedure (see Chapter 2 in the textbook for a discussion of the importance of controls in experimental designs) in which you use a separate-pairing protocol to determine whether or not presenting the two CSs in various ways will produce different degrees of conditioning to the CSs.

12. Complete exercise 27 (pp. 135–138) to test how important the salience is of each CS of a compound stimulus.
13. Complete exercise 26 (pp. 130–135) to investigate blocking in classical conditioning.
14. Complete exercise 39 (pp. 194–197), which demonstrates latent inhibition (the CS preexposure effect). You should also work through exercise 40 (pp. 197–199), which shows a related phenomenon, the US preexposure effect. You can compare the influence of these two preexposure effects by importing the data from exercises 39 and 40 into a spreadsheet or statistical program to produce a graph of your results (see pp. 115–119 for some guidance on how to graph data from *Sniffy Pro* studies). By now you have enough knowledge of the *Sniffy Pro* software to complete exercise 38 (pp. 189–194) on habituation. You may want to try this exercise now. It might be helpful first to read through the appropriate section of Chapter 2 in the textbook to review the principles of habituation.

CHAPTER 5

Classical Conditioning: Underlying Processes and Practical Applications

CHAPTER OUTLINE

Evelyn thought Jason looked a bit tipsy as he left the picnic to drive home. She wondered if she should tell him that the supposedly nonalcoholic punch he had been drinking was actually spiked with vodka. On the other hand, he had only had a single glass. He surely couldn't be drunk.

Underlying Processes in Classical Conditioning

By now, you probably realize that classical conditioning is not as simple a process as it first seems. It is a complex phenomenon that is only slowly yielding its secrets to researchers. The following sections discuss major theoretical notions concerning the underlying processes of classical conditioning. As you will learn, some of these theories have resulted in findings with great practical importance.

S-S versus S-R Learning

There are two basic ways to conceptualize the type of learning that occurs in classical conditioning. One way is to view classical conditioning as a process of directly attaching a reflex response to a new stimulus. According to this ***S-R (stimulus-response) model* of conditioning, the NS becomes directly associated with the UR and therefore comes to elicit the same response as the UR.** For example, when bitten by a dog, a child directly associates the dog with the pain and fear that were elicited by the bite and therefore experiences fear when he next encounters the dog. Similarly, if I can somehow cause you to salivate in the presence of a tone (such as by presenting food immediately after the tone), then the response of salivation will become connected to the tone, and you will subsequently salivate whenever you hear the tone. In each case, the purpose of the US is simply to elicit the UR so that it occurs in close proximity to the NS, thereby allowing a connection to be created between the NS and the UR (see Figure 5.1).

Another way of conceptualizing classical conditioning is the ***S-S (stimulus-stimulus) model* of conditioning, in which the NS becomes directly associated with the US and, because of this association, comes to elicit a response that is related to the US.** Thus, a child who is bitten by a dog associates the dog with the bite, and as a result of that association the child comes to fear the dog. Likewise, pairing a tone with food results in the tone being associated with food, as a result of which the tone comes to elicit salivation. A mentalistic way of thinking about it is that the tone makes the dog think of the food, and because it is thinking of food, it now salivates (see Figure 5.2). Although the S-R and S-S models might seem mutually exclusive (i.e., it seems as though both cannot be correct) and have often been pitted against each other by theorists, many researchers now believe that both types of processes may be involved in conditioning. Many basic conditioning

FIGURE 5.1 According to the S-R model of conditioning, the NS is directly associated with the UR.

Tone: Food ⟶ *Salivate*
  NS   US   UR

FIGURE 5.2 According to the S-S model of conditioning, the NS is directly associated with the US.

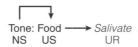

Tone: Food ⟶ *Salivate*
  NS   US   UR

procedures do result in the development of an association between the NS and the US (an S-S association); some instances of conditioning, however, seem to involve the establishment of an S-R association (see Domjan, 1998, for further details). Nevertheless, modern theories of conditioning have generally emphasized the establishment of S-S associations. In particular, they have attempted to specify the manner in which the NS and US become associated during the conditioning process, a problem with which Pavlov himself grappled.

1. In the _____-_____ model of classical conditioning, conditioning is viewed as a process of directly attaching a reflex response to a new stimulus.

2. In the _____-_____ model of classical conditioning, conditioning involves establishing a direct connection between an NS and a US.

3. Jason was once bitten by Rover, the neighbor's dog, and as a result he developed a strong fear of the dog. However, when he heard that Rover had to have all his teeth removed, Jason's fear of the dog completely disappeared. This suggests that Jason's fear response was based on an _____-_____ association. (Think: Was Jason's fear based on associating Rover with the response of fear or with the stimulus of being bitten?)

Stimulus–Substitution versus Preparatory–Response Theory

An early S-S theory of conditioning was introduced by Pavlov (1927). According to Pavlov's ***stimulus-substitution theory*, the CS acts as a substitute for the US.** For example, pairing a tone with food results in the tone becoming a substitute for the food, eliciting salivation just as the food does.

Pavlov was a physiologist who believed that classical conditioning was an effective, though indirect, way of studying neurological processes in the brain.

Thus, he often made inferences about the kinds of neurological processes that are activated during conditioning. He claimed that presentation of a US, like food, activated an area of the cerebral cortex (the outermost layer of the brain) that was responsible for sensing the occurrence of that event. Activation of this "food center" in the brain in turn activated another part of the cortex (the "salivation center") that produced the unconditioned response of salivation.

Food → *Activates food center in cortex* → *Activates salivation center in cortex* → **Salivation**

Pavlov also believed that the presentation of a neutral stimulus, like a light, activated another area of the cortex responsible for detecting that type of stimulus. According to Pavlov, when the light is presented just prior to the food during conditioning, a connection is formed between the area of the cortex activated by the light and the area activated by the food. As a result, activation of the light center of the cortex also activates the food center of the cortex, resulting in salivation. In other words, Pavlov believed that the presentation of the light set in motion the following sequence of events:

Light → *Activates light center in cortex* → *Activates food center in cortex* → *Activates salivation center in cortex* → **Salivation**

Pavlov's notions about the kinds of neurological processes underlying classical conditioning are now considered to be incorrect. These processes are known to be considerably more complex than he presumed. Nevertheless, this does not negate all aspects of Pavlov's theory. For example, consider the notion that the CS is somehow a direct substitute for the US. In at least some cases, it seems as though animals do react to the CS as if it were the US. The dog salivates to the tone just as it does to food. More importantly, the dog may even approach the light and start to lick it, as though pairing the light with the food resulted in the light being perceived as edible (Pavlov, 1941). This sort of phenomenon, now known as *sign tracking*, will be discussed more fully in Chapter 11.

However, if the CS is merely a substitute for the US, then the CR and UR *should always be identical or at least highly similar*. As it turns out, this is not the case. Although the CR and UR are often similar, there are sometimes substantial differences between them. For example, a rat that receives foot shock (the US) will probably jump (the UR). However, if it sees a light (CS) that has been paired with foot shock, it will freeze (the CR). Why would the rat jump in one instance and freeze in the other? Examination of the rat's natural response to danger gives us a clue. If a rat is attacked by a snake, jumping straight up (and rats can really jump!) may cause the snake to miss. On the other hand, if a rat detects a snake in the vicinity, tensing its muscles and freezing will minimize the possibility of being detected or, if the rat is attacked, will enable it to jump quickly. This suggests that the purpose of the CR, rather than merely being a version of the UR, is to ready the organism for the occurrence of the US.

Thus, according to *preparatory-response theory*, **the purpose of the CR is to prepare the organism for the presentation of the US** (Kimble, 1961, 1967). The dog salivates to the tone to get ready for food. Similarly, the rat freezes in response to the light to get ready for the shock. Note that in one case, the preparatory response is highly similar to the UR, while in the other case it is quite different. Thus, unlike stimulus-substitution theory, preparatory-response theory allows for situations in which the CR and UR are different. In some cases, the CR may even be the opposite of the UR. We will examine this possibility in the next section, in which we discuss a version of preparatory-response theory known as the compensatory-response model.

2

1. According to _____ _____ theory, the CS acts as a substitute for the US.

2. According to _____ _____ theory, the purpose of the CR is to prepare the organism for the occurrence of the US.

3. According to _____ _____ theory, the CR and UR should be highly similar.

Compensatory-Response Model

Perhaps the strongest evidence against Pavlov's stimulus-substitution theory are cases in which a conditioned response is the exact opposite of the unconditioned response. For example, the unconditioned response to shock is usually an increase in heart rate. Yet the conditioned response to a tone that has been paired with shock is, in many cases, a decrease in heart rate (Obrist, Sutterer, & Howard, 1972).

> **Shock** → *Increased heart rate*
>   US   UR
> **Tone: Shock** → *Increased heart rate*
>   NS   US   UR
> **Tone** → *Decreased heart rate*
>   CS   CR

How can this be? Remember the *opponent-process theory* of emotion that we learned about in Chapter 3. Recall how certain stimuli, such as shock or drugs (which can be considered USs) elicit both a primary response (the a-process) and a compensatory after-reaction (the b-process). According to the *compensatory-response model* of classical conditioning, the compensatory after-reactions to a US may come to be elicited by a CS. In the above example, the shock (US) elicits the primary reaction of an increase in heart rate (UR), while the tone (CS) elicits the compensatory after-reaction of a decrease in heart rate (CR).

Remember too that in the opponent-process theory, the compensatory re-actions to a US serve to maintain a state of homeostasis (internal balance) in the body. If these compensatory reactions started occurring *prior* to the presentation of the US, they would be even more effective in minimizing the disturbance produced by the US. For example, suppose that a certain drug produces an immediate increase in blood pressure. If the compensatory reaction to that drug (a decrease in blood pressure) could be elicited just prior to injection of the drug, then the immediate physical reaction (change in blood pressure) to the drug would be effectively moderated. In this sense, the conditioned response allows the body to prepare itself ahead of time for the onslaught of the drug.

This theory has some important implications for drug tolerance (Siegel, 1983). For example, if you have a habit of always drinking in a particular setting, then the various cues in that setting—people greeting you as you walk in the front door of the bar ("Norm"), the stool upon which you always sit—become CSs for the ingestion of alcohol. The presence of these CSs will initiate physiological reactions that compensate for the alcohol you are about to consume. As a result, in the presence of these CSs, you should have greater tolerance for alcohol than you would in their absence.

Research has confirmed this prediction. In a study by McCusker and Brown (1990), participants consumed alcohol in either an "alcohol expected" environment (i.e., alcohol was consumed in a simulated lounge during the evening with pub noises playing in the background) or an "alcohol unexpected" environment (i.e., alcohol was consumed during the day in an office environment). Those who consumed alcohol in the expected environment performed significantly better on various measures of cognitive and motor functioning compared to those who consumed alcohol in the unexpected environment. They also showed smaller increases in pulse rate. This suggests that the alcohol-related cues in the expected condition (evening, lounge setting) elicited compensatory reactions that partially compensated for the effects of the alcohol.

These findings have serious implications for one's drinking habits. If you consume alcohol in an environment in which you typically do not drink (e.g., a business luncheon), the alcohol could have a much stronger effect on you than if it had been consumed in an environment in which you typically do drink (e.g., a bar). This means that your ability to drive safely could be significantly more impaired following a noontime drink during lunch than an evening drink at a bar. Worse yet, even if you do consume alcohol in an alcohol-related setting such as a bar, consider what happens when you leave that setting. Your compensatory reactions might significantly be reduced because you have now removed yourself from the alcohol-related cues that elicit those reactions. As a result, you may become more intoxicated during the drive home from the bar than you were in the bar (Linnoila, Stapleton, Lister, Guthrie, & Eckhardt, 1986)! This means that the amount of alcohol you consume is not, by itself, a reliable gauge for determining the extent to which you are intoxicated. (Thus, going back to the opening vignette for this chapter, why should Evelyn be especially concerned about Jason's ability to drive?)[1]

The compensatory-response model has also been applied to incidents of drug overdose. Many "overdose" fatalities do not, in fact, involve an unusually large amount of the drug. For example, heroin addicts often die after injecting a dosage that has been well tolerated on previous occasions. A critical factor appears to be the setting within which the drug is administered. If a heroin addict typically administers the drug in the presence of certain cues, those cues become CSs that elicit compensatory reactions to the drug. An addict's tolerance to heroin therefore is much greater in the presence of those cues than in their absence.

Anecdotal evidence supports this possibility. Siegel (1984) interviewed ten survivors of heroin overdose, seven of whom reported that the overdose had been preceded by an unusual change in the setting or drug administration procedure. For example, one woman reported that she overdosed after hitting a vein on the first try at injecting the drug, whereas she usually required several tries. Further evidence comes from studies with rats that had become addicted to heroin. When the cues usually associated with heroin were absent, the rats' ability to tolerate a large dose was markedly reduced to the point that many of the rats died. Thus, heroin-tolerant rats who were administered a very strong dose of heroin in a novel setting were more likely to die than those who received the dose in the setting previously associated with the drug (Siegel, Hinson, Krank, & McCully, 1982).

Conditioning of compensatory responses also has some implications for managing the symptoms of drug withdrawal. As noted in the previous chapter, withdrawal symptoms are the compensatory reactions to a drug. According to the compensatory-response model, these withdrawal symptoms are elicited by CSs associated with drug use. This suggests that removing those CSs should weaken the withdrawal symptoms and make it easier to remain abstinent. This possibility too is supported by anecdotal evidence. A large number of American soldiers became heroin users during their tour of duty in Vietnam, leading to fears that they would remain addicted when they returned home. These fears, however, did not materialize (Robins, 1974). One explanation for this is that the change in environment when they returned home removed many of the cues associated with heroin use, thereby alleviating the symptoms of withdrawal and making it easier for them to remain heroin-free. Similarly, when one of the authors of this textbook quit smoking, she found that avoiding friends who smoke and staying out of lounges and

---

[1] The type of alcohol consumed can also have an effect. People become significantly more intoxicated following consumption of an unusual drink (such as a strange liqueur) than a familiar drink (such as beer). The familiar drink can be seen as a CS for alcohol that elicits compensatory reactions to the alcohol (Remington, Roberts, & Glautier, 1997).

coffee shops for a couple of months significantly reduced her cravings for cigarettes.

Finally, it should be noted that there are exceptions to the typical compensatory reactions to a CS. Stimuli associated with drug use sometimes elicit *druglike* reactions rather than drug-compensatory reactions. For example, in one study, rats became *more* sensitive to cocaine when it was administered in the usual cocaine administration environment than in a different one (Hinson & Poulos, 1981). The CSs for cocaine administration apparently elicited reactions that *mimicked* the drug, thereby strengthening its effect. There is also evidence that stimuli associated with drug use sometimes elicit *both* drug-compensatory responses in one system of the body and druglike responses in another (Lang, Ross, & Glover, 1967). Thus, the circumstances in which conditioning results in druglike reactions versus drug-compensatory reactions are complex and not entirely understood (Siegel, 1989).

QUICK QUIZ

1. According to the _____ _____ model of conditioning, the after-reactions to an emotional event come to be elicited by a (US/CS) _____ that is associated with that event.

2. A person who drinks a glass of wine in a fine restaurant is likely to be (more/less) _____ affected than if she had drunk the same amount of wine in a courtroom.

3. Suppose a heroin user always injects the drug in her bedroom at home, but one time she stays overnight at a friend's house and decides to take an injection there. The heroin user will likely experience a(n) (increased/decreased) _____ reaction to the drug at her friend's house.

4. The compensatory-response model suggests that withdrawal symptoms can be significantly (alleviated/strengthened) _____ by avoiding cues associated with drug use. This is because the withdrawal symptoms are actually (unconditioned/conditioned) _____ responses that are elicited by those cues.

Rescorla–Wagner Theory

One of the most influential theories of classical conditioning was proposed by Rescorla and Wagner (1972). Their theory attempted to explain the effect of each conditioning trial on the strength, or what might be called the "associative value," of the CS in its relationship to the US. **The *Rescorla-Wagner theory* proposes that a given US can support only so much conditioning, and this amount of conditioning must be distributed among the various CSs available.** Another way of saying this is that there is only so much associative value to be distributed among the various cues associated with the US.

One assumption of this theory is that *stronger USs support more conditioning than weaker USs.* For example, the use of a highly preferred food as the US produces a stronger conditioned response of salivation than a less preferred

And Furthermore

Conditioned Compensatory Responses and Drug Overdose: Two Anecdotes

Siegel (1989) describes two cases that clearly illustrate the dangers of drug overdose resulting from conditioning effects.

> The respondent (E. C.) was a heavy user of heroin for three years. She usually self-administered her first, daily dose of heroin in the bathroom of her apartment, where she lived with her mother. Typically, E. C. would awake earlier than her mother, turn on the water in the bathroom (pretending to take a shower), and self-inject without arousing suspicion. However, on the occasion of the overdose, her mother was already awake when E. C. started her injection ritual, and knocked loudly on the bathroom door telling E. C. to hurry. When E. C. then injected the heroin, she immediately found that she could not breathe. She was unable to call her mother for help (her mother eventually broke down the bathroom door and rushed E. C. to the hospital, where she was successfully treated for heroin overdose). (pp. 155–156)

Siegel goes on to explain that the mother knocking on the bathroom door was an unusual cue that may have disrupted the environmental CSs that would normally have elicited compensatory reactions to the heroin.

The second example described by Siegel involves administration of a drug to a patient to alleviate the pain of pancreatic cancer.

> The patient's [17-year old] son, N. E., regularly administered the [morphine] in accordance with the procedures and dosage level specified by the patient's physician. . . . The patient's condition was such that he stayed in his bedroom which was dimly lit and contained much hospital-type apparatus necessary for his care. The morphine had always been injected in this environment. For some reason, on the day that the overdose occurred, the patient dragged himself out of the bedroom to the living room. The living room was brightly lit and different in many ways from the bedroom/sickroom. The patient, discovered in the living room by N. E., appeared to be in considerable pain. Inasmuch as it was time for his father's scheduled morphine injection, N. E. injected the drug while his father was in the living room. N. E. noticed that his father's reaction to this injection was atypical; his pupils became unusually small, and his breathing shallow. . . . The father died some hours later. (pp. 156–157)

Two years later, N. E. took a class in which conditioning effects on drug tolerance were discussed, at which point he realized the implications of these effects for his own experience.

food. Imagine, for example, that a tone paired with a highly preferred food (say, steak) elicits a maximum of 10 drops of saliva, while a tone paired with a much less preferred food (say, dog food) elicits only 5 drops of saliva. If we regard each drop of saliva as a unit of associative value, then we could say that the highly preferred food supports a maximum associative value of 10 units, while the less preferred food supports a maximum associative value of 5 units.

We can use the following format to diagram changes in associative value (we will assume the highly preferred food is the US):

Tone (V = 0): **Food** (*Max = 10*) → *Salivation*
Tone (V = 10) → *Salivation*

The letter "V" will stand for the associative value of the CS (which at the start of conditioning is zero). The term "Max" will stand for the maximum associative value that can be supported by the US once conditioning is complete. In our example, imagine V as the number of drops of saliva the tone elicits — zero drops to begin with and 10 drops once the tone is fully associated with the food — and Max as the maximum number of drops of saliva that the tone elicits if it is fully associated with the food. (If this is starting to look a bit mathematical to you, you are correct. In fact, the model can be expressed in the form of an equation. For our purposes, however, the equation is unnecessary.)

Now suppose that a compound stimulus consisting of a tone and a light are repeatedly paired with the food, to the point that the compound stimulus obtains the maximum associative value.

[Tone + Light] (V = 0): **Food** (*Max = 10*) → *Salivation*
[Tone + Light] (V = 10) → *Salivation*

This associative value, however, must somehow be distributed between the two component members of the compound. For example, if the tone is a bit more salient than the light, then the tone might have picked up 6 units of associative value while the light picked up only 4 units. In other words, when tested separately, the tone elicits 6 drops of saliva while the light elicits 4.

Tone (V = 6) → *Salivation*
Light (V = 4) → *Salivation*

If the tone was even more salient than the light — for example, it was a very loud tone and a very faint light — then *overshadowing* might occur, with the tone picking up 9 units of associative value and the light only 1 unit:

[Loud tone + Faint light] (V = 0): **Food** (*Max = 10*) → *Salivation*
Loud tone (V = 9) → *Salivation*
Faint light (V = 1) → *Salivation*

The loud tone now elicits 9 drops of saliva (a strong CR) while the faint light elicits only 1 drop of saliva (a weak CR). Thus, the Rescorla-Wagner explanation for the overshadowing effect is that there is only so much associative value available (if you will, only so much spit available for conditioning), and if the more salient stimulus in the compound picks up most of the associative value, then there is little associative value left over for the less salient stimulus.

As can be seen, the Rescorla-Wagner theory readily explains conditioning situations involving compound stimuli. Take, for example, a *blocking* procedure. One stimulus is first conditioned to its maximum associative value:

Tone (V = 0): **Food** (*Max = 10*) → *Salivation*
Tone (V =10) → *Salivation*

This stimulus is then combined with another stimulus for further conditioning trials:

[Tone + Light] (V = 10 + 0 = 10): **Food** (*Max = 10*) → *Salivation*

But note that the food only supports a maximum associative value of 10 units, and the tone has already acquired that much value. The light can therefore acquire no associative value because all of the associative value has already been assigned to the tone. Thus, when the two stimuli are later tested for conditioning, the following occurs:

Tone (V = 10) → *Salivation*
Light (V = 0) → **No salivation**

So far we have described the Rescorla-Wagner theory in terms of changes in associative value. The theory can also be interpreted in more cognitive terms. To say that a CS has high associative value is similar to saying that it is a strong predictor of the US or that the subject strongly "expects" the US whenever it encounters the CS. For example, to say that the tone has high associative value means that it is a good predictor of food such that the dog "expects" food whenever it hears the tone. In the case of blocking, however, the tone is such a good predictor of food that the light with which it is later paired becomes redundant, and the presence of the light does not affect the subject's expectations about food. As a result, no conditioning occurs to the light. In general, then, conditioning can be viewed as a matter of building the subject's expectations that one event will follow another.

The Rescorla-Wagner theory also leads to some counterintuitive predictions. Consider what happens if you first condition two CSs to their maximum associative value and then combine them into a compound stimulus for further conditioning. For example, suppose we condition a tone to its maximum associative value, as follows:

Tone (V = 0): **Food** (*Max = 10*) → *Salivation*
Tone (V = 10) → *Salivation*

and then do the same for the light:

Light (V = 0): **Food** (*Max = 10*) → *Salivation*
Light (V = 10) → *Salivation*

We now combine the tone and the light into a compound stimulus and conduct further conditioning trials:

[Tone + Light] (V = 10 + 10 = 20): **Food** (*Max = 10*) → *Salivation*

Note that the tone and the light together have 20 units of associative value (10 for the tone and 10 for the light). However, the maximum associative value that can be supported by the food at any one moment is only 10 units. This means that the associative value of the compound stimulus must decrease to match the maximum value that can be supported by the US. Thus, according to the Rescorla-Wagner theory, after several pairings of the compound stimulus with food, the total associative value to the compound stimulus will be reduced to 10:

[Tone + Light] (V = 10) → *Salivation*

This in turn means that when each member in the compound is tested separately, its value also will have decreased. For example:

Tone (V = 5) → *Salivation*
Light (V = 5) → *Salivation*

Thus, even though the tone and light were subjected to further pairings with the food, the associative value of each decreased (i.e., each stimulus elicited less salivation than it originally did when it had been conditioned individually).

The effect we have just described is known as the *overexpectation effect*. It is as though presenting the two CSs together leads to an "overexpectation" about what will follow. When this expectation is not fulfilled, the subject's expectations are modified downward. As a result, each CS in the compound loses some of its associative value.

Although the Rescorla-Wagner model has been a source of inspiration for researchers, not all of its predictions have been confirmed. As a result, revisions to the model have been proposed along with alternative models. Some behaviorists have also criticized the common practice of interpreting the Rescorla-Wagner model in cognitive terms, arguing that the concept of associative value, which can be objectively measured by the strength of the CR, makes such inferences about mentalistic processes unnecessary (e.g., Pierce & Epling, 1995). Despite these criticisms, however, few models have been as productive in furthering our understanding about the underlying processes of classical conditioning.

1. The Rescorla-Wagner theory proposes that a given _____ can support only so much conditioning, and this amount of conditioning must be distributed among the various _____s available.

2. In general, stronger USs support (more/less) _____ conditioning than weaker USs.

3. According to the Rescorla-Wagner theory, overshadowing occurs because the more salient CS picks up (most/little) _____ of the associative value available in that setting.

4. According to the Rescorla-Wagner theory, blocking occurs because the (conditioned stimulus/neutral stimulus) _____
in the compound has already picked up all of the available associative value.

5. Suppose a compound stimulus has an associative value of 25 following conditioning. According to the Rescorla-Wagner theory, if one CS has acquired 15 units of associate value, the other CS must have acquired _____ units of associative value.

6. Suppose a tone and a light are each conditioned with food to a maximum associative value of 8 units. If the tone and light are combined into a compound stimulus for further conditioning trials, the associative value of each stimulus must necessarily (decrease/increase) _____. This is known as the o_____ effect.

QUICK QUIZ

ADVICE FOR THE LOVELORN

Dear Dr. Dee,

My friend says that if you are deeply and madly in love with someone, then you will necessarily be much less interested in anyone else. I think my friend is wrong. There is no reason why someone can't be deeply in love with more than one person at a time. So who is right?

The Wanderer

Dear Wanderer,

I honestly do not know who is right. But your friend's hypothesis seems somewhat consistent with the Rescorla-Wagner theory. If feelings of love are to some extent classically conditioned emotional responses, then the more love you feel for one person (meaning that he or she is a distinctive CS that has strong associative value), the less love you should feel for alternative partners who are simultaneously available (because there is little associative value left over for those other CSs). In other words, there is only so much love (so much associative value) to go around, and strong romantic feelings for one person will likely result in weak romantic feelings for others. It is the case, however, that some people are strongly attracted to many different partners, though perhaps what is attracting them in such cases is some quality that those partners have in common, such as a high degree of physical attractiveness. But would we then define such attraction as love?

Behaviorally yours,

Practical Applications of Classical Conditioning

Understanding Phobias

A particularly salient way in which classical conditioning affects our lives is through its involvement in the development of fears and anxieties. As already noted, a conditioned fear response can be elicited by a previously neutral stimulus that has been associated with an aversive stimulus. In most cases, this sort of fear conditioning is a highly adaptive process, in that it motivates the individual to avoid a dangerous situation. A person who is bitten by a dog and learns to fear dogs is less likely to be bitten in the future, simply because he will tend to avoid dogs.

This process, however, occasionally gets exaggerated, with the result that we become very fearful of events that are not at all dangerous or only minimally dangerous. Such extreme, irrational fear reactions are known as phobias. In many cases, these phobias seem to represent a process of *overgeneralization*, in which a conditioned fear response to one event has become overgeneralized to other harmless events. Thus, while it may be rational to fear a mean-looking dog that once bit you, it is irrational to fear a friendly-looking dog that has never bitten you.

Watson and Rayner's "Little Albert" The importance of classical conditioning and overgeneralization in the development of phobias was first noted by John B. Watson and his student (and wife-to-be), Rosalie Rayner. In 1920, Watson and Rayner published a now-famous article in which they described their attempt to condition a fear response in an 11-month-old infant named Albert. Albert was a very healthy, well-developed child, whose mother worked as a wet nurse in the hospital in which the tests were conducted. Albert was described as "stolid and unemotional," almost never cried, and had never been seen to display rage or fear. In fact, he seemed to display an unusual level of emotional stability.

The researchers began the experiment by testing Albert's reactions to a variety of objects. These included a white rat, a rabbit, a dog, some cotton wool, and even a burning newspaper. None of the objects elicited any fear, and in fact Albert often attempted to handle them. He was, however, startled when the experimenters made a loud noise by banging a steel bar with a hammer. The experimenters thus concluded that the loud noise was an unconditioned stimulus that elicited a fear response (or, more specifically, a startle reaction), while the other objects, such as the rat, were neutral stimuli with respect to fear:

Loud noise → *Fear (as indicated by startle reaction)*
    US   UR
Rat → **No fear**
 NS   —

In the next part of the experiment, Watson and Rayner paired the loud noise (US) with the white rat (NS). The rat was presented to Albert, and just as his hand touched it, the steel bar was struck with the hammer. In this first conditioning trial, Albert "jumped violently and fell forward, burying his face in the mattress. He did not cry, however" (p. 4). He reacted similarly when the trial was repeated, except that this time he began to whimper. The conditioning session was ended at that point.

The next session was held a week later. At the start of the session, the rat was handed to Albert to test his reaction to it. He tentatively reached for the rat, but he quickly withdrew his hand after touching it. Since, by comparison, he showed no fear of some toy blocks that were handed to him, it seemed that a slight amount of fear conditioning to the rat had occurred during the previous week's session. Albert was then subjected to further pairings of the rat with the noise, during which he became more and more fearful. Finally, at one point, when the rat was presented without the noise, Albert "began to crawl so rapidly that he was caught with difficulty before reaching the edge of the table" (p. 5). Albert's strong avoidance reaction suggested that the rat had indeed become a conditioned fear stimulus as a result of its association with the noise. This process can be diagrammed as follows:

Rat: Loud noise → *Fear*
NS   US   UR
Rat → *Fear (as indicated by crying and crawling away from the rat)*
CS   CR

In subsequent sessions (during which Albert occasionally received further pairings of the rat with the noise to "freshen" the conditioning), Albert showed not only a fear of the rat but also of objects that were in some way similar to the rat, such as a rabbit, a fur coat, a dog, and even a Santa Claus mask. In other words, Albert's fear response had generalized to objects that were similar to the original CS. His conditioned fear to the rat, and his generalized fear of similar objects, persisted even following a 30-day break, although the intensity of his reactions was somewhat diminished. At that point, Albert's mother moved away, taking Albert with her, so further tests could not be conducted. Watson and Rayner were therefore unable to carry out their stated plan of using behavioral procedures to eliminate Albert's newly acquired fear response.

Watson and Rayner with Little Albert. (The white rat is beside Albert's left arm.)

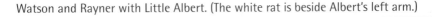
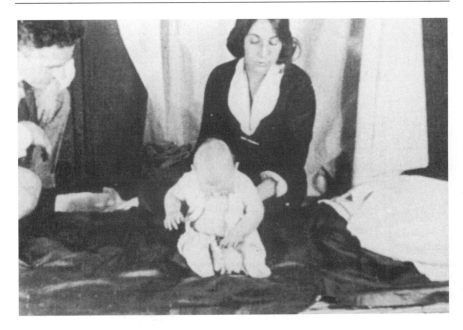

Although the Little Albert experiment is often depicted as a convincing demonstration of phobic conditioning in a young infant, it is actually quite limited in this regard. For example, it took several pairings of the loud noise with the rat before the rat reliably elicited a strong fear reaction; additionally, although Albert's fear reaction remained evident following a 30-day rest period, it had also started to diminish by that time. By contrast, real-life phobias usually require only one pairing of the US with the CS to become established, and they often grow stronger over time. Watson and Rayner also noted that Albert displayed no fear so long as he was able to suck his thumb, and the experimenters had to repeatedly remove his thumb from his mouth during the sessions to enable a fear reaction to be elicited. This suggests that Albert's fear response was relatively weak since it was easily countered by the pleasure derived from thumb sucking.

Thus, although Watson and Rayner speculated about the possibility of Albert growing up to be a neurotic individual with a strange fear of furry objects, it is quite likely that he did not develop a true phobia and soon got over any aversion to furry objects. In fact, more recent evidence suggests that additional factors are often involved in the development of a true phobia. Some of these factors are discussed in the next section.

1. A phobia is an extreme, irrational fear reaction to a particular event. From a classical conditioning perspective, it seems to represent a process of over-_____.

2. In the Little Albert experiment, the rat was originally a(n) _____ stimulus, while the loud noise was a(n) _____ stimulus.

3. Albert's startle response to the noise was a(n)_____ response, while his crying in response to the rat was a(n) _____ response.

4. One difference between Albert's fear conditioning and conditioning of real-life phobias is that the latter often require (only one/more than one) _____ conditioning trial.

5. Unlike real-life phobias, Albert's fear of the rat seemed to grow (stronger/weaker) _____ following a 30-day break.

6. Albert's fear response was (present/absent) _____ whenever he was sucking his thumb, which suggests that the fear conditioning was actually relatively (strong/weak) _____.

QUICK QUIZ

Additional Factors in Phobic Conditioning   Not all phobias are acquired through a direct process of classical conditioning. Indeed, many people with phobias are unable to recall any particular conditioning event prior to the development of their symptoms (Marks, 1969). Additionally, most people exposed to extremely frightening events do not develop phobias. For example, the vast majority of people exposed to air raids during the Second World War endured them rather well, developing only short-term fear reactions that

And Furthermore

The Ethics of the Little Albert Experiment

By today's standards, the Little Albert study is highly unethical, and many people are astounded that such an experiment could ever have taken place. The lack of established ethical guidelines for psychological research at that time no doubt played a role. But it is also interesting to note that the Little Albert study hardly raised an eyebrow at the time it was published. In fact, Watson received far more criticism for his research with rats (from animal rights activists) than he ever did for his research with Albert (Buckley, 1989). This might seem strange to us, living as we do in an era in which people are quite sensitive to issues of child abuse and maltreatment. But in Watson's era, such issues, though not ignored, were certainly given less attention. Nevertheless, Watson and Rayner were not completely oblivious to the possible harm their procedures might evoke. For example, they deliberately chose Albert as a subject because of his strong emotional stability, which to them implied that they could do him "relatively little harm by carrying out such experiments. . . ." (Watson & Rayner, 1920, p. 3). They also "comforted themselves" with the notion that the experiences Albert would receive during the experiment were probably not much different from what he would naturally encounter when he left "the sheltered environment of the nursery for the rough and tumble of the home" (p. 3). Unfortunately, Watson and Rayner's cautious concerns seemed to disappear later in the article when they joked about the possibility of Albert's fear response remaining with him when he grew into adulthood:

> The Freudians twenty years from now, unless their hypotheses change, when they come to analyze Albert's fear of a seal skin coat . . . will probably tease from him the recital of a dream which upon their analysis will show that Albert at three years of age attempted to play with the pubic hair of the mother and was scolded violently for it. (Watson & Rayner, 1920, p. 14)

One can only hope that this statement was more an example of Watson's showmanship and an attempt to convince others of the superiority of his behavioral approach than any belief that he and Rayner had induced a permanent phobia in Albert. In any event, the Little Albert experiment certainly illustrates the need for stringent ethical standards regarding the use of humans (especially children) in experimental research.

quickly dissipated (Rachman, 1977). Researchers have therefore suggested several additional variables that, singly or in combination, may be involved in the development of phobic symptoms. These include the following:

1. Observational Learning. Many phobias are acquired through observation of fearful reactions in others. For example, in World War II, a major predictor of whether children developed a fear of air raids was whether their mothers displayed such fears. As well, airmen who became phobic of combat often developed their symptoms after witnessing fear reactions in a crewmate (Rachman, 1977).

This tendency to acquire conditioned fear reactions through observation may be inherited (Mineka, 1987). If so, a display of fear by another person may be conceptualized as an unconditioned stimulus that elicits an unconditioned fear response in oneself:

Display of fear by others → *Fear (in oneself)*
       US   **UR**

A neutral stimulus that is associated with this display might then becomes a conditioned stimulus for fear:

Snake: Display of fear by others → *Fear*
  NS   **US**   **UR**
Snake → *Fear*
  CS   **CR**

The result is that a person who has had no direct confrontation with snakes may indirectly acquire a conditioned fear of snakes.

2. Temperament. **Temperament is an organism's base level of emotionality and reactivity to stimulation, which, to a large extent, is genetically determined.** Temperament seems to affect the ease with which a conditioned response can be acquired. As noted in Chapter 4, Pavlov found that dogs that were shy and withdrawn conditioned more readily than dogs that were active and outgoing. Similarly, individuals with certain temperaments may be more genetically susceptible than others to the development of conditioned fears (Clark, Watson, & Mineka, 1994).

Even Watson, who made a career out of downplaying the role of genetic influences in human behavior, acknowledged the possible influence of temperament. Watson and Rayner (1920) deliberately chose Albert as a subject under the assumption that his emotional stability would grant him a good deal of immunity against the harmful effects of their procedures. They also noted that "had he been emotionally unstable probably both the directly conditioned response [to the rat] and those transferred [to similar stimuli] would have persisted throughout the month unchanged in form" (p. 12), when in fact his fears had somewhat diminished following the 30-day break. Thus, they believed that Albert did not have the sort of temperament that would facilitate the acquisition of a conditioned fear response.

3. Preparedness. **The concept of *preparedness* holds that many species are genetically prepared to learn certain kinds of associations more easily than others** (Seligman, 1971). Thus, we may have an inherited predisposition to develop certain types of fears. This notion was initially proposed by Valentine (1930), who attempted to replicate Watson and Rayner's experiment with his 1-year-old daughter by blowing a loud whistle whenever she touched certain objects. When the object she touched was a pair of opera glasses, she displayed no fear, even to the sound of the whistle. When the object was a caterpillar, however, some fear was elicited. By contrast, Valentine observed a 2-year-old who became fearful of dogs "at slight provocation." He concluded that people may have an innate tendency to fear certain kinds of events (such as insects and certain other animals), and that Watson had been able to successfully condition Albert to fear rats because of this tendency.

Recent evidence for the role of preparedness in fear conditioning includes a study by Cook and Mineka (1989). They exposed laboratory-raised rhesus monkeys to videotapes edited to show another monkey reacting either fearfully or nonfearfully to either a fear-relevant stimulus (toy snake or toy crocodile) or fear-irrelevant stimulus (flowers or toy rabbit). Only those monkeys who observed the model reacting fearfully to the fear-relevant stimulus acquired a conditioned fear reaction to that stimulus. Similarly, Soares and Öhman (1993) found that human subjects displayed physiological signs of anxiety in reaction to certain subliminal stimuli—pictures presented so briefly that subjects were consciously unaware of the content—that had been paired with uncomfortable levels of electric shock. This reaction occurred when the pictures were of fear-relevant stimuli (snakes and spiders) as opposed to fear-irrelevant stimuli (flowers and mushrooms). This result supports the notion that humans too may be predisposed to learn certain types of fears more readily than others. (The concept of preparedness will be more fully discussed in Chapter 11.)

QUICK QUIZ

1. From a conditioning perspective, viewing a display of fear in others can be conceptualized as a(n) _____ stimulus that elicits a(n) _____ response of fear in oneself. The event to which the other person is reacting might then become a(n) _____ stimulus that elicits a(n) _____ response of fear in oneself.

2. The term _____ refers to an individual's genetically determined level of emotionality and reactivity to stimulation. It (does/does not) _____ seem to affect the extent to which responses can be classically conditioned.

3. The concept of p_____ holds that we are genetically programmed to acquire certain kinds of fears, such as fear of snakes and spiders, more readily than other kinds.

4. Jason rolled his pickup truck, yet he had no qualms about driving home afterwards; Michael was in a minor fender bender last week and remained petrified of driving for several days afterward. These different outcomes may reflect inherited differences in t_____ between the two individuals.

5. The fact that many people are more petrified of encountering snakes than they are of being electrocuted by their toaster, even though the latter is a far more relevant danger in the world in which they live, reflects differences in _____ for acquiring certain kinds of fears.

4. History of Control. Another factor that may influence susceptibility to fear conditioning is a history of being able to control important events in one's environment. For example, in one study, young monkeys who had a history of controlling the delivery of food, water, and treats (such as by pulling a chain) were considerably less fearful of a mechanical toy monster than were monkeys who had simply been given these items regardless of their behavior (Mineka, Gunnar, & Champoux, 1986). Living in an environment in which they had some degree of control over important events seemed to effectively immunize them against the traumatic effects of encountering a strange and frightening object. Presumably, these monkeys would also have been less susceptible to classical conditioning of fear responses, although this prediction was not directly tested. The harmful effects of prolonged exposure to uncontrollable events, and the beneficial effects of prior exposure to controllable events, will be further examined in later chapters under the topic of *learned helplessness*.

5. *Incubation.* When a phobia develops through a direct process of classical conditioning, an important question must be asked: Why does the conditioned fear not extinguish with subsequent exposures to the CS? To some extent, extinction does not occur because the person tends to avoid the feared stimulus (the CS), which means that repeated exposure to the CS in the absence of the US does not take place. Additionally, however, because of this tendency to move away from the feared stimulus, any exposures that do occur are likely to be very brief. Such brief exposures may result in a phenomenon known as "incubation" (Eysenck, 1968). *Incubation* **is the strengthening of a conditioned fear response as a result of brief exposures to the aversive CS.** For example, a child who is bitten by a dog and then runs away each time he encounters a dog may find that his fear of dogs grows worse despite the fact that he is never again bitten. As a result, what may have started off as a moderate fear of dogs may evolve over time into a severe fear. In fact, this process might even result in a conditioned fear that is actually stronger than the unconditioned fear that was originally elicited when the child was bitten. Thus, the CR would be stronger than the UR, which contradicts the general rule that a CR is weaker than the UR.

6. *US revaluation.* As noted in Chapter 4, exposure to a US of a different intensity (a different value) than that used during conditioning can alter the strength of the response to a previously conditioned CS. This process could play a major role in human phobias (Davey, 1992). Consider, for example, a skateboarder who experiences a minor injury as a result of a fall:

Skateboarding: Minor injury → *Slight anxiety*
Skateboarding → *Slight anxiety*

Because the injury was relatively minor, skateboarding elicits only a slight amount of conditioned anxiety, most of which will likely extinguish as the skateboarder continues the activity. But imagine that this person later is in a car accident and suffers a severe injury:

Severe injury → *Strong anxiety*

(Or imagine that he witnesses such a severe injury in another person, which would be an instance of observational learning.) What might happen is that he might now display a strong degree of anxiety to skateboarding:

Skateboarding → *Strong anxiety*

It is as though the skateboarder finally realizes just how painful an injury can be. And given that skateboarding is associated with being injured, it now elicits strong feelings of anxiety.

7. *Selective sensitization.* Yet another process that could influence the development of a phobia is *selective sensitization,* **which is an increase in one's reactivity to a potentially fearful stimulus following exposure to an unrelated stressful event.** For example, people with *agoraphobia* (fear of being alone in a public place) often report that the initial onset of the disorder occurred during a period in which they were emotionally upset or suffering from some type of physical illness (Rachman, 1977). Similarly, an individual going through a stressful divorce might find that her previously minor anxiety about driving in heavy traffic suddenly develops into severe anxiety. The stressful circumstance surrounding the divorce affects her reactions not only to the divorce but to other potentially aversive events as well. Therefore, during turbulent times in one's life, minor fears and anxieties may become exacerbated into major fears and anxieties (Barlow, 1988).

QUICK QUIZ

1. We will probably be (more/less) _____ susceptible to acquiring a conditioned fear response if we grow up in a world in which our every need is taken care of.

2. Brief exposures to a feared CS in the absence of the US may result in a phenomenon known as _____ in which the conditioned fear response grows (stronger/weaker) _____. This runs counter to the general principle that presentation of the CS without the US usually results in ext_____.

3. According to the concept of _____ revaluation, phobic behavior might sometimes develop when the person encounters a (more/less) _____ intense version of the (CS/US) _____ than was used in the original conditioning.

4. The process of s_____ s_____ refers to an increase in one's reactivity to a potentially fearful stimulus following exposure to a stressful event. This stressful event is (related/unrelated) _____ to the feared stimulus.

Treating Phobias

Perhaps more than any other disorder, phobias are highly susceptible to treatments based on behavioral principles of conditioning. In this section, we will discuss the two basic types of treatment: systematic desensitization and flooding.

Systematic Desensitization   Recall how Watson and Rayner had intended to use behavioral procedures to eliminate Albert's fears but were unable to do so because his mother suddenly moved away. A few years later, Mary Cover Jones (1924) did carry out such a treatment (under Watson's supervision) with

Peter, a 2-year-old boy who had an extreme fear of rabbits. Jones's treatment strategy consisted of first feeding Peter cookies while presenting a rabbit at a considerable distance. It was assumed that the positive emotional response elicited by the cookies would overcome the mild anxiety elicited by the distant rabbit. Over successive sessions, the rabbit was gradually brought closer to Peter as he continued to eat cookies. Within a few months, Peter was holding the rabbit in his lap while munching on cookies. As a result of this gradual conditioning procedure, Peter's fear of the rabbit was eliminated.

Although Jones's treatment procedure, carried out in 1924, had effectively eliminated a phobia, it languished in obscurity until Joseph Wolpe (1958) essentially rediscovered it 30 years later. As a graduate student, Wolpe conducted research on experimental neurosis in cats exposed to electric shocks. The cats displayed a strong fear of both the experimental chamber in which they had been shocked and the room containing the chamber. A major indication of this fear was the cats' refusal to eat while in the room (an example of conditioned suppression). Wolpe then devised a treatment plan to eliminate this fear. He began by feeding the cats in a room that was quite dissimilar from the original "shock" room. Then, over a period of days, the cats were fed in rooms that were made progressively more similar to the shock room. Eventually they were able to eat in the original room and even in the experimental cage in which they had been shocked. This procedure effectively eliminated the conditioned fear response in all 12 cats that Wolpe studied.

Wolpe interpreted the cats' improvements to be the result of ***counterconditioning,*** **in which a CS that elicits one type of response is associated with an event that elicits an incompatible response.** In Wolpe's study, the experimental room originally elicited a fear response because of its association with shock. Later, it elicited a positive emotional reaction after it had become associated with food. Wolpe proposed that the underlying process in counterconditioning is ***reciprocal inhibition*** **in which certain responses are incompatible with each other, and the occurrence of one response necessarily inhibits the other.** Thus, the positive emotional response elicited by food inhibited the cats' anxiety because the two responses countered each other.

As a result of his success, Wolpe began to ponder ways in which this treatment procedure might be applied to human phobias. Although both he and Jones had successfully used food to counter feelings of anxiety, Wolpe felt that this would be impractical for most treatment situations involving humans. He toyed with other types of responses that might counter anxiety, such as anger and assertiveness (i.e., the client was taught to act angry or assertive in situations that were normally associated with fear), but then he finally hit upon the use of deep muscle relaxation. Deep muscle relaxation is largely incompatible with the experience of anxiety (Jacobson, 1938), making it ideal from Wolpe's perspective as a tool for counterconditioning.

Wolpe also realized that real-life exposure to a phobic stimulus was often impractical in some treatment scenarios. For example, it would be extremely difficult to expose a person with a fear of thunderstorms to a succession of storms that are made progressively more frightening. To solve this dilemma, Wolpe decided to have the patient simply visualize the feared stimulus. A series of visualized scenarios could then be constructed that would represent varying intensities of the feared event. For example, the person could imagine a storm some distance away that had only a mild amount of thunder and lightening, then a storm that was somewhat closer with a bit more thunder and lightening, and so on. One drawback to this procedure is that the counterconditioning occurs only to the visualized event, and it will then have to generalize to the real event. Nevertheless, if the visualization is fairly vivid, then the amount of generalization to the real world should be considerable.

Thus, three basic aspects of Wolpe's treatment procedure, which is generally known as *systematic desensitization*, are as follows:

1. *Training in relaxation.* An abbreviated version of Jacobson's (1938) deep muscle relaxation procedure is commonly employed for inducing relaxation, but other methods such as meditation or hypnosis have also been used.
2. *Creation of a hierarchy of imaginary scenes that elicit progressively more intense levels of fear.* Experience has shown that about 10–15 scenes are sufficient, starting with a scene that elicits only a minor degree of fear (e.g., for a dog-phobic individual, it might be visualizing a friendly poodle tied to a tree at a distance of several yards) and finishing with a scene that elicits a tremendous amount of anxiety (e.g., visualizing standing beside a large dog that is barking).
3. *Pairing of each item in the hierarchy with relaxation.* Starting with the least fearful scene in the hierarchy, the person is asked to visualize the scene for about 10–30 seconds and then engage in a short period of relaxation. This process is repeated until the first scene no longer elicits anxiety, at which point the process is carried out using the next scene. By the time the top item in the hierarchy is reached, most of the person's conditioned fear will have been eliminated, resulting in only a residual amount of fear to what was once an intensely fearful scene. The fear response to this final scene is also eliminated, at which point it is quite likely that the person will now feel significantly less anxious when confronted with the phobic stimulus in real life.

Thus, **systematic desensitization is a behavioral treatment for phobias that involves pairing relaxation with a succession of stimuli that elicit increasing levels of fear.** Although Wolpe emphasized, mostly for convenience, the use of imaginary stimuli (the procedure then being referred to as *imaginal desensitization*), the treatment can also be carried out with real phobic stimuli. This version of desensitization is sometimes referred to as *in vivo desensitization*. Mary Cover Jones's treatment of Peter's rabbit phobia is an example of in vivo desensitization. As with imaginal desensitization, in vivo desensitization usually makes use of relaxation to counter the person's fear response. For example, a dog-phobic client might move gradually closer to a real dog, pausing after each step and relaxing for several seconds. Additionally, the process might first be carried out with a very small dog and then gradually progress to a very large dog. In vivo desensitization has an obvious advantage in that one does not have to worry about whether the treatment effect will generalize to a real-life stimulus, since one is already working with a real-life stimulus. As previously noted, however, it is often difficult or impossible to arrange such systematic real-life exposures. Additionally, in severely phobic clients, the real stimulus might elicit a tremendous amount of anxiety. In such cases, it might be wiser to first use imaginal desensitization to eliminate much of the fear, and then switch to in vivo desensitization to complete the process. More detailed information on systematic desensitization can be found in behavior modification texts such as Miltenberger (1997) and Spiegler & Guevremont (1998).

Considerable research has been carried out on systematic desensitization. The procedure has proven to be highly effective in certain circumstances. For example, systematic desensitization tends to be quite effective with patients who have relatively few phobias that are quite specific in nature (e.g., a fear of dogs and spiders). By contrast, people who suffer from social phobias tend to experience a general fear of many different social situations and do not respond as well to this form of treatment. Additionally, when using imaginal desensitization, the client must be able to clearly visualize the feared event and experience anxiety while doing so. Unfortunately, some individuals are unable to visualize clearly, or they feel no anxiety even with clear visualization. In these cases, in vivo desensitization is the better alternative.

Wolpe assumed that systematic desensitization is a counterconditioning procedure that works through the process of reciprocal inhibition. Not everyone agrees. Some researchers (e.g., Eysenck, 1976) have claimed that systematic desensitization is really just a simple matter of extinction, in which a CS is repeatedly presented in the absence of the US. From this perspective, systematic desensitization for a dog-phobic individual works because it involves repeated presentations of dogs (or images of dogs) in the absence of anything bad happening. Evidence for the extinction explanation comes from the fact that relaxation is not always needed for the treatment to be effective; gradual exposure to the feared stimulus is by itself often sufficient. On the other hand, in support of the counterconditioning explanation, severe phobias respond better to treatment when relaxation is included (Wolpe, 1995). The exact mechanism by which systematic desensitization produces its effects is, however, still unknown, and it could well be that *both* extinction and counterconditioning are involved.

1. Associating a stimulus that already elicits one type of response with an event that elicits an incompatible response is called _____.
Wolpe believed that the underlying process is r_____
i_____ in which certain types of responses are (compatible/incompatible) _____ with each other, and the occurrence of one type of response necessarily i_____ the other.

QUICK QUIZ

2. Mary Cover Jones used the stimulus of _____ to counter Peter's feelings of anxiety, while Wolpe, in his s_____ d_____ procedure, used _____.

3. The three basic components of Wolpe's procedure are:

(1)

_____ ,

(2)

_____

(3)

_____ .

4. A version of Wolpe's procedure that uses real-life rather than imaginary stimuli is called _____ _____. A major advantage of this procedure is that one does not have to worry about whether the treatment effect will g_____ to the real world.

5. Wolpe's procedure is very effective with people who have (few/many) _____ phobias that are highly (general/specific) _____. Thus, this procedure (does/does not) _____ work well with people who have a social phobia.

6. One bit of evidence against the counterconditioning explanation for this type of treatment is that relaxation (is/is not) _____ always necessary for the treatment to be effective. On the other hand, in keeping with the counterconditioning explanation, relaxation does seem to facilitate treatment when the phobia is (nonspecific/severe) _____.

Flooding Consider a rat that continues to avoid a goal box in which it was once shocked, despite the fact that no further shocks will ever be delivered. One way to eliminate this phobic behavior is to place the rat in the goal box and insert a barrier that prevents it from leaving. Forced to remain in the box, the rat will initially show considerable distress, but this distress will disappear as time passes and no shock is delivered. By simply preventing the avoidance response from occurring, we can eliminate the rat's irrational fear.

The treatment procedure that makes use of this response-prevention principle is *flooding therapy:* **a behavioral treatment that involves prolonged exposure to a feared stimulus, thereby providing maximal opportunity for the conditioned fear response to extinguish** (Spiegler & Guevremont, 1998). This method can be contrasted with systematic desensitization, in which exposure to the feared stimulus occurs gradually, and which also involves pairing the feared event with a response that will counteract the fear (such as relaxation).

As with systematic desensitization, there are two basic types of flooding procedures. In *imaginal flooding*, the client is asked to visualize, as clearly as possible, a scenario involving the feared event. For example, an individual who is spider phobic might imagine waking up at night to find a large hairy spider on the pillow beside her. A person with a fear of heights might imagine having to climb down a fire escape from a 10th floor apartment. The greater the level of fear induced by the visualized scenario, the better.

The client first visualizes the scenario in the therapist's office and then practices visualizing it at home. Although the level of fear during visualization may initially increase, it should eventually begin to decrease and finally extinguish. Once the fear response to one scenario has been extinguished, the fear response to other scenarios (e.g., having to remove a spider from the kitchen) can be similarly extinguished. After extinction has occurred to several scenarios, it is likely that the client will experience considerably less fear when encountering the feared event in the real world.

In vivo flooding is an alternative to imaginal flooding. In vivo flooding consists of prolonged exposure to the actual feared event. Consider, for example, a woman who is extremely fearful of balloons (perhaps because someone once burst a balloon in her face when she was a young child). An in vivo flooding procedure might involve filling a room with balloons, then having the woman enter the room, close the door, and remain inside for an hour or more. After a few sessions of this, her fear of balloons might well be eliminated.

Of course, flooding is something that people have been intuitively aware of for centuries. The famous German poet and philosopher, Goethe, described how, as a young man, he had cured himself of a fear of heights by climbing the tower of the local cathedral and standing on the ledge. He repeated this procedure until his fear was greatly alleviated (Lewes, 1965). As with in vivo desensitization, in vivo flooding is advantageous in that it does not require the treatment effect to generalize from an imagined encounter to a real encounter. It is also not dependent on a person's visualization ability. Unfortunately, in vivo flooding can be highly aversive. It is also not a realistic alternative with some types of feared events, such as house fires, which are impossible to replicate in the therapy setting.

One concern with any type of flooding therapy is that the stress involved may result in medical complications. One must be particularly cautious about using flooding to treat clients suffering from post-traumatic stress disorder (a severe stress reaction produced by a traumatic event such as an accident or wartime experience). It is also important that the duration of each exposure, whether in vivo or imaginal, be sufficiently long (at least 30–45 minutes), otherwise the fear may not extinguish or, worse yet, may grow more intense. As well, clients who have a history of other psychiatric disorders may experience an exacerbation of their fears as a result of this type of treatment. In this sense, it is a riskier procedure than systematic desensitization (Spiegler & Guevremont, 1998).

THE FAR SIDE   By GARY LARSON

Professor Gallagher and his controversial technique of simultaneously confronting the fear of heights, snakes and the dark.

1. In flooding therapy, the avoidance response is (blocked/facilitated) _____, thereby providing maximal opportunity for the conditioned fear to _____.

2. Two types of flooding therapy are _____ flooding in which one visualizes the feared stimulus, and _____ flooding in which one encounters a real example of the feared stimulus.

3. For flooding therapy to be effective, the exposure period must be of relatively (long/short) _____ duration.

Aversion Therapy for Eliminating Problem Behaviors

Some behavior problems stem from events being overly enticing rather than overly aversive. For example, nicotine and alcohol can be highly pleasurable, with the result that many people become addicted to these substances. Similarly, pedophiles have inappropriate feelings of sexual attraction to young

And Furthermore

Single-Session Treatment of Phobic Behavior

Systematic desensitization and flooding are basic behavioral approaches to the treatment of phobic behavior. Several variations of these approaches have since been devised, all of which retain, as a fundamental aspect of treatment, some type of exposure to the feared object. Such approaches are therefore generally known as *exposure-based treatments* or *exposure therapies* and are now considered the treatment of choice for phobic disorders (Spiegler & Guevremont, 1998).

For example, Öst (1989) described a method for rapidly eliminating specific phobias, such as fear of injections or spiders, in a single session. The major component of the treatment package was an *in vivo exposure* procedure in which clients were encouraged to approach the feared object as closely as possible, remain there until the anxiety faded away, then approach the object even more closely. This process continued until the client had approached the object closely and her reported level of fear toward the object had been reduced by 50% or more. Note that the exposure procedure is similar to both systematic desensitization in that it is somewhat gradual, and flooding in that the client is encouraged to endure a fairly intense level of anxiety each step of the way.

Öst's treatment package included several additional components. For example, throughout the procedure, most clients were accompanied by a person (the therapist) who acted as a model to demonstrate to the client how to interact with the feared object (such as how to use a jar to capture a spider). The model also helped the client physically contact the feared object, say, by first touching the object while the client touched the model's hand, then touching the object while the client also touched the object, and then gradually removing his hand while the patient continued touching the object. The therapeutic use of modeling in this manner is called *participant modeling, contact desensitization,* or *guided participation,* and has been shown to greatly facilitate fear reduction (Bandura, 1975; Bandura, Blanchard, & Ritter, 1969).

Öst reported that out of 20 female patients who had been treated with this method (interestingly, men rarely volunteer for such treatment), 19 showed considerable improvement following an average session length of only 2.1 hours. As well, 18 of the clients remained either much improved or completely recovered at long-term follow-up (follow-up information was gathered an average of 4 years after treatment). Needless to say, these results are quite encouraging, especially in view of the fact that most of the clients had suffered from their phobia for several years prior to treatment.

Question: Although the results are encouraging, what is a major weakness of this study in terms of its methodology (which the author himself readily acknowledged)?

children. Obviously, one way to counter these problem behaviors is to directly reduce the attractiveness of the relevant stimuli.

Aversion therapy **reduces the attractiveness of a desired event by associating it with an aversive stimulus** (Spiegler & Guevremont, 1998). An ancient version of this treatment was suggested by the Roman writer Pliny the Elder, who suggested treating overindulgence in wine by secretly slipping the putrid body of a large spider into the bottom of the wine drinker's glass. The intention was that the feelings of revulsion elicited by a mouthful of spider would become associated with the wine, thereby significantly reducing the person's desire for drinking (Franks, 1963). More recent versions of this therapy are no less dramatic. For example, the taste of alcohol has sometimes been paired with painful electric shocks. An alternative version—which is more similar to Pliny's treatment in that it makes use of stimuli associated with ingestion—involves pairing the taste of alcohol with nausea. In this case, the client is first given an *emetic*, that is, a drug that produces nausea. As the nausea develops, the client takes a mouthful of alcohol. This procedure is repeated several times; as well, the type of alcohol is varied across trials to ensure generalization. Research has shown that such nausea-based treatments are more effective than shock-based treatments, presumably because we have a biological tendency to quickly associate nausea with substances that we ingest (Baker & Cannon, 1979; Masters, Burish, Hollon, & Rimm, 1987). This tendency, known as taste aversion conditioning, is discussed more fully in Chapter 11.

Aversion therapy has also been used with smoking, with similar results. Early attempts to pair smoking and electric shock were relatively ineffective, possibly because physical pain is not a biologically relevant response to smoking. A more effective procedure has been to pair smoking with nicotine-induced nausea. This procedure, known as "rapid smoking," involves having the client smoke continuously, inhaling every 6–10 seconds (Danaher, 1977). Within a few minutes, extreme feelings of nausea are elicited and the person will become unable to continue. One session is usually sufficient to produce at least temporary abstinence. This is especially the case with smokers who do not yet have a strong physical addiction to smoking and who smoke more for the pleasure of smoking—which the aversive conditioning counteracts—than for the avoidance of withdrawal symptoms (Zelman, Brandon, Jorenby, & Baker, 1992). Long-term abstinence is much less certain but can be facilitated through the use of additional treatment procedures (such as *relapse prevention training*, in which the person learns to identify and cope with situations in which there is a high risk of resuming the problematic behavior [Marlatt & Gordon, 1985]). Rapid smoking is, however, very stressful, usually resulting in extreme increases in heart rate. Thus, this type of treatment must be employed cautiously, particularly if the client has a history of medical difficulties (Lichtenstein & Glasgow, 1977). (In other words, do not try this at home!)

Aversion therapy has also been used to treat sex offenders (Hall, Shondrick, & Hirschman, 1993). In the case of pedophiles, photographic images of unclothed children may be paired with drug-induced nausea or a powerfully unpleasant scent, such as ammonia. As part of a comprehensive treatment package, such procedures help reduce the risk that the individual will reoffend following release from prison.

Aversion therapy is sometimes carried out with the use of imaginal stimuli rather than real stimuli. This version of the treatment is usually called *covert sensitization*. For example, a person addicted to smoking might imagine experiencing extreme illness and vomiting (as well as social disapproval from others) each time she tries to smoke. Alternatively, she might visualize being forced to smoke cigarettes that have been smeared with feces. As with imaginal desensitization, the effectiveness of this procedure is dependent on the client's ability to visualize images clearly and to experience strong feelings of revulsion in response to these images. The treatment effect also has to generalize from the visualized event to the real event, which, as in imaginal versus in vivo desensitization and flooding, is likely to result in some loss of effectiveness. Thus, covert sensitization may be somewhat less effective than aversion therapy, which utilizes exposure to the actual stimulus.

1. In _____ therapy, one attempts to reduce the attractiveness of an event by associating that event with an unpleasant stimulus.

2. A standard treatment for alcoholism is to associate the taste of alcohol with feelings of n_____ that have been induced by consumption of an e_____.

3. A highly effective procedure for reducing cigarette consumption, at least temporarily, is r_____ s_____.

4. In general, aversion therapy is (more/less) _____ effective when the unpleasant response that is elicited is biologically relevant to the problematic behavior.

5. Aversion therapy is sometimes carried out using _____ stimuli rather than real stimuli. This type of treatment procedure is known as _____ sensitization.

Medical Applications

There is a growing body of evidence indicating that processes of classical conditioning have significant medical implications. For example, Russell et al. (1984) were able to condition guinea pigs to become allergic to certain odors by pairing those odors with an allergy-inducing protein. People who have allergies may suffer from a similar process, since their allergic reaction is elicited not only by the substance that originally caused the allergy, but also by stimuli associated with that substance. Thus, for a person who is allergic to pollen, even the mere sight of flowers might elicit an allergic reaction.

Flowers: Pollen → *Allergic reaction*
  NS   US   UR
Flowers → *Allergic reaction*
  CS   CR

Other studies have shown that various aspects of the immune system can be classically conditioned. For example, Ader and Cohen (1975) exposed rats to an immunosuppressive drug paired with saccharin-flavored water. These rats were then given an injection of foreign cells, followed by a drink of either saccharin-flavored water or plain water. The rats that drank the saccharin-flavored water produced fewer antibodies in reaction to the foreign cells than did the rats that drank the plain water. The flavored water had apparently become a CS for immunosuppression.

In a real-world extension of this study, Bovbjerg et al. (1990) found that women who received chemotherapy in a hospital setting displayed evidence of immunosuppression when they later returned to the hospital. The hospital environment had become associated with the immunosuppressive effect of the chemotherapy and was now a CS for a conditioned immunosuppressive response, thus:

> **Hospital: Chemotherapy** → *Immunosuppression*
>   **NS**   **US**   **UR**
> **Hospital** → *Immunosuppression*
>   **CS**   **CR**

Other studies have shown that classical conditioning can be used to *strengthen* immune system functioning. For example, one team of researchers gave human subjects a taste of sweet sherbet followed by shots of adrenaline (Buske-Kirschbaum, Kirschbaum, Stierle, Jabaij, & Hellhammer, 1994). Adrenaline tends to increase the activity of natural killer cells, which are an important component of the body's immune system. After pairing the sweet sherbet with the adrenaline, the sweet sherbet itself elicited an increase in natural killer cell activity. Hence:

> **Sweet sherbet: Adrenaline** → *Increased natural killer cell activity*
>   **NS**   **US**   **UR**
> **Sweet sherbet** → *Increased natural killer cell activity*
>   **CS**   **CR**

(See also Solvason, Ghanata, & Hiramoto, 1988).

The medical implications of such findings are enormous. Obviously, many patients would benefit considerably from enhanced immune functioning during the course of their illness. Other patients, however—namely those who suffer from autoimmune diseases, such as arthritis, in which the immune system seems to be overactive—would benefit from a procedure that could reliably weaken their immune system. (See Exton et al., 2000, for a review of research into this issue.)

1. When Christopher entered his friend's house, he noticed a dog dish beside the door. He soon began experiencing symptoms of asthma and assumed that the house was filled with dog dander (particles of fur or skin), to which he is allergic. Only later did he discover that his friend's children had placed the dish by the door in anticipation of soon owning a dog. In fact, no dog had yet been in the house. Assuming that Christopher's reaction is an example of higher-order conditioning, diagram the

And Furthermore

Classical Conditioning and Gulf War Syndrome

Processes of classical conditioning may be implicated in the controversial disorder known as Gulf War Syndrome. Many veterans returning home from that war began suffering from a wide array of symptoms—such as nausea, headaches, sleep problems, and rashes—which they attributed to their experiences in the war. Explanations for these symptoms have ranged from exposure to various chemical agents to the notion that they are psychological in origin. Ferguson and Cassaday (1999), however, have proposed that the cluster of symptoms displayed by these veterans is virtually identical to that induced by interleukin-1, a small protein produced by the immune system during periods of stress or illness that produces inflammatory reactions in the body. Ferguson and Cassaday suggest that the chronic stresses and chemical agents to which the veterans were exposed during the war produced an increase in interleukin-1 production and its resultant symptoms. These symptoms then became associated with the sights, sounds, and smells of the war zone. At home, these symptoms were again elicited when the veterans encountered stimuli that were similar to those encountered in the war zone.

For example, one veteran reported that he experienced a headache any time he smelled petroleum, which had been a particularly prevalent smell in the war zone at that time. According to the Ferguson and Cassaday model, this veteran had presumably been exposed to toxic levels of petroleum fumes, which elicited an increase in interleukin-1 and its perceived symptoms, such as a headache. Through the process of conditioning, the smell of petroleum became a conditioned stimulus that by itself elicited interleukin-1 symptoms:

Petroleum smell: Toxic petroleum fumes → *Interleukin-1 symptoms*
      NS   US   UR
Petroleum smell → *Interleukin-1 symptoms*
      CS   CR

If this conditioning explanation of Gulf War Syndrome is accurate, it suggests two possible treatment strategies for the syndrome: (1) administration of drugs to block the effect of interleukin-1 and (2) delivery of cognitive-behavioral treatments designed to eliminate the conditioned associations.

conditioning process that resulted in Christopher's allergic reaction. Label each component using the appropriate abbreviations.

2. Diagram the classical conditioning process in Ader and Cohen's (1975) study of immunosuppression. Label each component using the appropriate abbreviations.

QUICK QUIZ

SUMMARY

According to the S-S approach to classical conditioning, conditioning involves the formation of an association between the NS and US. In contrast, the S-R approach claims that conditioning involves the formation of an association between the NS and a reflex response. Pavlov's stimulus-substitution theory was an early S-S approach in which the CS is presumed to act as a substitute for the US. The fact that the CR is sometimes different from the UR does not support this theory; rather, it seems like the CR response often serves to prepare the organism for the onset of the US (the preparatory-response theory of conditioning). In one version of preparatory-response theory, known as the compensatory-response model, the CS is viewed as eliciting opponent processes that counteract the effect of the US. This approach has significant application to understanding addiction. The Rescorla-Wagner theory accounts for certain conditioning phenomena (e.g., blocking) by proposing that a given US can support only so much conditioning, which must be distributed among the various CSs available.

The principles of classical conditioning are useful in understanding and treating phobias. This was first demonstrated by Watson and Rayner, who conditioned an 11-month old infant named Albert to fear a rat by associating presentations of the rat with a loud noise. True phobic conditioning, however, may involve several additional factors, including observational learning, temperament, preparedness, history of control, incubation, US revaluation, and selective sensitization.

One treatment procedure for phobias is systematic desensitization. This is a counterconditioning procedure in which a CS that elicits one type of response is associated with a stimulus that elicits a different response. Counterconditioning works through the process of reciprocal inhibition, in which the occurrence of one type of response can inhibit another incompatible response. The three components of systematic desensitization are (1) training in deep muscle relaxation, (2) creation of a hierarchy of imaginary scenes that elicit progressively more intense levels of fear, and (3) pairing each item in the hierarchy with relaxation. In one variant of this procedure, known as in vivo desensitization, the imaginary scenes are replaced by a hierarchy of real-life encounters with the feared stimulus. An alternative treatment procedure for phobias is flooding, which involves prolonged exposure to a feared stimulus, thus allowing the conditioned fear response to extinguish. As with desensitization, this procedure can be carried out either imaginally or in vivo.

Aversion therapy attempts to reduce the attractiveness of a desired event by associating it with an aversive stimulus. Examples include associating nausea with alcohol ingestion or cigarette smoking and, in pedophiles, associating the smell of ammonia with the sight of young children. In a technique known as covert sensitization, aversion therapy is carried out with the use of imaginal stimuli rather than real stimuli.

Classical conditioning has been shown to have medical implications. For example, neutral stimuli that have been associated with an allergy-inducing substance can become CSs that elicit a conditioned allergic response. Research has also revealed that stimuli that have been paired with a drug that alters immune-system functioning can become CSs that likewise alter immune-system functioning.

STUDY QUESTIONS

1. Distinguish between S-R and S-S models of conditioning.
2. Describe stimulus-substitution theory. What is the major weakness of this theory?
3. Describe the preparatory-response theory of conditioning.
4. Describe the compensatory-response model of conditioning.
5. Explain why the amount we drink might not be a reliable gauge for determining whether we are intoxicated.
6. How does the compensatory-response model account for drug overdoses that occur when an addict seems to have injected only a normal amount of the drug?
7. Describe the Rescorla-Wagner theory. According to this theory, how does the strength of the US affect conditioning?
8. Describe how the Rescorla-Wagner theory accounts for overshadowing and blocking.
9. Describe the overexpectation effect and how the Rescorla-Wagner theory accounts for it.
10. Briefly describe the Watson and Rayner experiment with Little Albert and the results obtained.
11. Describe how observational learning, temperament, and preparedness can affect the acquisition of a phobia.
12. Describe how history of control and incubation can affect the acquisition of a phobia.
13. Describe how US revaluation and selective sensitization can affect the acquisition of a phobia.
14. What is counterconditioning? Name and define the underlying process.
15. Define systematic desensitization and outline its three components.
16. Define flooding. Be sure to mention the underlying process by which it is believed to operate. Also, what is the distinction between imaginal and in vivo versions of flooding (and desensitization)?
17. Define aversion therapy. What is covert sensitization?
18. Describe some of the evidence demonstrating how classical conditioning may be involved in allergic reactions and in immune-system functioning.

CONCEPT REVIEW

aversion therapy. A form of behavior therapy that attempts to reduce the attractiveness of a desired event by associating it with an aversive stimulus.

compensatory-response model. A model of classical conditioning that holds that the compensatory after-reactions to a US may come to be elicited by a CS.

counterconditioning. The procedure whereby a CS that elicits one type of response is associated with an event that elicits an incompatible response.

flooding therapy. A behavioral treatment for phobias that involves prolonged exposure to a feared stimulus, thereby providing maximal opportunity for the conditioned fear response to extinguish.

incubation. The strengthening of a conditioned fear response as a result of brief exposures to the aversive CS.

preparatory-response theory. A theory of classical conditioning that holds that the purpose of the CR is to prepare the organism for the presentation of the US.

preparedness. The notion that some species are genetically prepared to learn certain kinds of associations more easily than others.

reciprocal inhibition. The process whereby certain responses are incompatible with each other, and the occurrence of one response necessarily inhibits the other.

Rescorla-Wagner theory. A theory of classical conditioning that proposes that a given US can support only so much conditioning, and this amount of conditioning must be distributed among the various CSs available.

selective sensitization. An increase in one's reactivity to a potentially fearful stimulus following exposure to an unrelated stressful event.

S-R (stimulus-response) model. As applied to classical conditioning, a model that assumes that the NS becomes directly associated with the UR and therefore comes to elicit the same response as the UR.

S-S (stimulus-stimulus) model. A model of classical conditioning that assumes that the NS becomes directly associated with the US, and because of this association, it comes to elicit a response that is related to that US.

stimulus-substitution theory. A theory of classical conditioning that holds that the CS acts as a substitute for the US.

systematic desensitization. A behavioral treatment for phobias that involves pairing relaxation with a succession of stimuli that elicit increasing levels of fear.

temperament. An organism's base level of emotionality and reactivity to stimulation that, to a large extent, is genetically determined.

CHAPTER TEST

8. The three steps in systematic desensitization are (1) training in _____, (2) creation of a _____ of feared stimuli, and (3) pairing _____ with each item in the _____.

21. In the Little Albert study, the loud noise was the (CS/US) _____, while the white rat was the (CS/US) _____. Little

Albert's fear of other furry objects illustrates the process of stimulus
_____.

3. Lothar's job has recently become quite stressful. Interestingly, he is also developing a fear of driving through rush hour traffic. This is best described as an example of _____.

13. The _____ approach holds that classical conditioning involves establishing a direct connection between an NS and a US.

7. The procedure of pairing the sight of a hornet with an appetitive stimulus such as candy is an example of _____. This type of procedure is effective because of the process of _____.

20. When Uncle Bob and Aunt Shirley were separated, they each gave Little Billy great Xmas presents, with the result that he developed strong positive feelings for both. They then resolved their difficulties and moved back together. They now give Little Billy one great present from the two of them. The Rescorla-Wagner theory predicts that Little Billy's positive feelings for each will now be (stronger/weaker/unaffected) _____. This is known as the _____ effect.

9. Desensitization and flooding procedures that utilize thoughts about the feared stimulus are known as _____ procedures, while procedures that involve exposure to the real stimulus are known as _____ procedures.

2. While playing with a spider, Suyen was frightened by the sound of a firecracker. As a result, she acquired a lasting fear of spiders, but not of firecrackers. This is an illustration of the concept of _____.

17. According to the Rescorla-Wagner theory, overshadowing occurs because the _____ stimulus picks up most of the associative value.

14. Whenever I see Attila, the neighbor's dog, I am reminded that he once bit me, which makes me quite nervous. This sequence of events fits best with an (S-R/S-S) _____ approach to classical conditioning.

10. In _____ therapy, one attempts to (decrease/increase) _____ the attractiveness of a *desired* event by pairing it with an (appetitive/aversive) _____ stimulus. An imagery-based form of this therapy is called _____.

6. Traditional advice has it that if you fall off a horse, you should immediately get back on and keep riding until your fear has disappeared. This approach is similar to the therapeutic technique known as _____. Furthermore, getting back on immediately allows no opportunity for brief exposures to the feared stimulus that could result in _____ of the conditioned fear response.

12. The _____ approach to learning views classical conditioning as a process of directly attaching a reflex response to a new stimulus.

18. According to the Rescorla-Wagner theory, _____ occurs because the (CS/NS) _____ in the compound has already picked up most of the available associative value.

4. Bo's friend Emmet contracted a life-threatening bout of pneumonia. Bo now becomes quite anxious each time he catches a cold. This is best described as an example of (selective sensitization/US revaluation/incubation) _____.

15. A cat salivates to the sound of your alarm clock in anticipation of a breakfast feeding. It also freezes at the sight of another cat in anticipation of an attack. These examples best illustrate the _____ theory of conditioning.

1. The ease with which an individual can acquire a conditioned fear response may be influenced by that person's base level of emotionality and reactivity to stimulation, which is known as t_____. This may, to a large extent, be (genetically/environmentally) _____ determined.

11. Warren begins wheezing whenever people even talk about dogs. In the terminology of classical conditioning, the talk about dogs appears to be a (use the abbreviation) _____ while the wheezing is a _____.

19. According to the _____ effect, if two fully conditioned stimuli are combined into a compound stimulus that is then subjected to further pairings with the US, the amount of associative value to each member of the compound will (increase/decrease) _____.

5. Gina's parents are extremely concerned about her well-being, and as a result they do almost everything for her. By contrast, Sarah's parents make sure that she does a lot of things on her own. Between the two of them, _____ may be less susceptible to the development of a phobia, insofar as a history of being able to _____ important events in one's environment may (reduce/increase) _____ one's susceptibility to acquiring a phobia.

16. According to the _____ model, withdrawal symptoms evoked by the sight of the desired drug are actually _____ reactions to the drug that have come to be elicited by stimuli associated with that drug.

ANSWERS TO CHAPTER TEST

1. temperament; genetically
2. preparedness
3. selective sensitization
4. US revaluation
5. Sarah; control; reduce
6. flooding; incubation
7. counterconditioning; reciprocal inhibition
8. relaxation; hierarchy; relaxation; hierarchy
9. imaginal; in vivo
10. aversion; decrease; aversive; covert sensitization
11. CS; CR

12. S-R
13. S-S
14. S-S
15. preparatory-response
16. compensatory-response; compensatory
17. more salient
18. blocking; CS
19. overexpectation; decrease
20. weaker; overexpectation
21. US; CS; generalization

Put Learning into Action with Sniffy, the Virtual Rat

The following material refers to *Sniffy, the Virtual Rat™: Pro Version*, a separate Wadsworth product that consists of a manual and a CD-ROM.

1. Read pp. 165–168 for additional information on S-S and S-R models of conditioning, and also for details on how the *Sniffy Pro* software can be configured to test these two models.
2. At this point you may want to begin working through the five exercises (33–37) in Chapter 11 (pp. 165–186). These exercises will give you a greater appreciation for the theoretical issues associated with the S-S and S-R models of learning. Assuming that you have been working through the exercises in *Sniffy Pro* in the order suggested in these endnotes, by this point you have sufficient experience to complete, and learn from, the exercises in Chapter 11.
3. Complete exercise 28 (pp. 138–141) for a demonstration of the overexpectation effect. Try to interpret the results of the suppression ratio and CS response strength in terms of the Rescorla-Wagner model.

CHAPTER 6

Operant Conditioning: Introduction

CHAPTER OUTLINE

"Hurry up," Joe growled as Sally carefully searched the selection of videos.

"Oh, don't be so grumpy," she said sweetly, hooking her arm into his.

"Just pick one, damn it!"

She quickly picked out a video, then gave him a hug as they walked to the checkout counter. (Based on a real incident observed in a video store.)

In the last few chapters, we focused upon elicited behavior and the type of learning known as classical conditioning. Elicited behavior is controlled by the stimuli that precede it. Recall how in Pavlov's classic experiment food elicited salivation and how, after a tone had been paired with food, it too elicited salivation:

Food → *Salivation*
Tone: Food → *Salivation*
Tone → *Salivation*

Note how the target response in this type of learning always occurs at the end of the sequence. The preceding stimulus, by itself, is sufficient to elicit the response. In this sense, the process is very reflexive: Present the stimulus and the response automatically follows.

But is everything we do this reflexive? Does the sight of this text, for example, automatically elicit the response of reading? Obviously it does not (though students who tend to procrastinate might sometimes wish that it did). Rather, if you had to explain why you are reading this text, you are likely to say you are reading it in order to achieve something—such as an understanding of the subject matter or a high grade in a course. Reading the text is oriented toward some goal, a consequence, and this consequence is the reason for the behavior. Indeed, most behaviors that concern us each day are motivated by some consequence. For example, we go to a restaurant for a meal, we turn on a radio to hear music, and we ask someone out on a date hoping he or she will accept. When we fail to achieve the desired outcome, we are unlikely to continue the behavior. How long would you persist in asking someone out on a date if that person never accepted?

Behaviors that are influenced by their consequences are called *operant behaviors*, and the effects of those consequences upon behavior are called *operant conditioning*. They are called operant conditioning because the response *operates on the environment* to produce a consequence. This type of learning is also called *instrumental conditioning* because the response is *instrumental* in producing the consequence.

1. Operant behaviors are behaviors that are influenced by their _____.

2. Elicited behavior is behavior that is controlled by what (precedes/follows) _____ it; operant behavior is behavior that is controlled by what (precedes/follows) _____ it.

3. Another name for operant conditioning is _____ conditioning.

QUICK QUIZ

Historical Background

Although people have used operant conditioning for thousands of years (e.g., in raising children, training animals, etc.), this kind of learning was not subjected to scientific analysis until the late 1800s when Edwin L. Thorndike investigated the learning ability of animals.

Thorndike's Law of Effect

Edwin L. Thorndike
(1874–1949)

The first experimental studies of operant conditioning were undertaken by Edwin L. Thorndike in the 1890s. As a graduate student, Thorndike was interested in animal intelligence. Many people at that time were speculating that animals were capable of higher forms of reasoning. Particularly impressive were stories about lost dogs and cats finding their way home over long distances. As Thorndike (1898) noted, however, "Dogs get lost hundreds of times and no one ever notices it or sends an account of it to a scientific magazine, but let one find his way from Brooklyn to Yonkers and the fact immediately becomes a circulating anecdote" (p. 4). Thorndike's skepticism was driven by a belief that the intellectual ability of animals could be properly assessed only through *systematic investigation.*

Thorndike conducted numerous experiments with animals, the most famous of which involved cats. In a typical experiment, a hungry cat was enclosed in a puzzle box, and a dish of food was placed outside. In order to reach the food, the cat had to learn how to escape from the box, such as by stepping on a treadle that opened a gate. The first time the cat was placed in the puzzle box, several minutes passed before it accidentally stepped on the treadle and opened the gate. Over repeated trials, it learned to escape the box more quickly. There was, however, no sudden improvement in

A convincing example of animal intelligence.

DILBERT reprinted by permission of United Feature Syndicate, Inc.

FIGURE 6.1 Thorndike's puzzle box. In a typical experiment, a hungry cat was enclosed in a puzzle box and a dish of food was placed outside the box. In order to reach the food, the cat had to learn how to escape from the box by stepping on a treadle that opened the gate. The graph illustrates the general decrease across trials in the amount of time it took the cat to escape. (*Source:* Nairne, 2000; Weiten, 1995.)

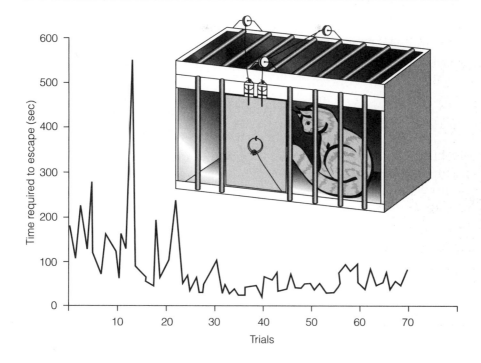

performance as would be expected if the cat had experienced a "flash of insight" about how to solve the problem. Rather, it seemed as though the response that worked (stepping on the treadle) was gradually strengthened, while responses that did not work (e.g., clawing at the gate, chewing on the cage) were gradually weakened (see Figure 6.1). Thorndike suspected that a similar process governed all learning, and on this basis he formulated his famous law of effect.

The *law of effect* states that behaviors leading to a satisfactory state of affairs are strengthened or "stamped in," while behaviors leading to an unsatisfactory or annoying state of affairs are weakened or "stamped out." In other words, the *consequences* of a behavior determine whether that behavior will be repeated. Thorndike's law of effect is a hallmark in the history of psychology. However, it was another young scientist by the name of Burrhus Frederick Skinner who fully realized the implications of this principle for understanding and changing behavior.

Skinner's Learning by Consequences

Skinner came upon the study of operant conditioning by a somewhat different route. As a graduate student in the late 1920s, he was well aware of Thorndike's law of effect. However, like many psychologists of the time, he believed that behavior could best be analyzed as though it were a reflex. He also realized, like Pavlov, that a scientific analysis of behavior required finding a procedure that yielded regular patterns of behavior. In the absence of such regularity, which could only be achieved in a well-controlled environment, it would be difficult to discover the underlying principles of behavior.

In this context, Skinner set out to devise his own procedure for the study of behavior, eventually producing one of the best-known apparatuses in experimental psychology: the operant conditioning chamber or "Skinner box." In a standard Skinner box for rats, the rat is able to earn food pellets by pressing a response lever or bar (see Figure 6.2).

Skinner's procedure is known as the "free operant" procedure because the rat freely controls the rate at which it responds for food. This contrasts with other procedures for studying animal learning, such as maze learning, in which the experimenter must initiate each trial by placing the rat in the start box.[1]

FIGURE 6.2 Operant conditioning chamber for rats. When the rat presses the lever (or bar), a food pellet drops into the food tray. Aversive stimuli can also be presented by delivering electric shock through the floor grids. (*Source:* Lieberman, 1993.)

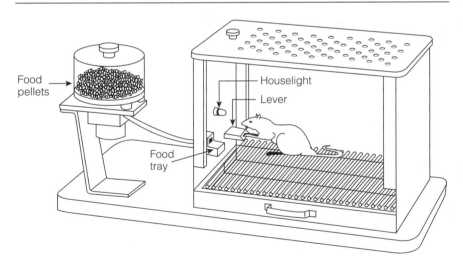

---

[1] Although the terms *operant conditioning* and *instrumental conditioning* are often used interchangeably, the term *instrumental conditioning* is sometimes reserved for procedures that involve distinct learning trials, such as maze learning experiments, as opposed to Skinner's free operant procedure.

Because an animal in an operant chamber controls the rate at which it earns food, rate is the primary measure of behavior in such experiments. Later, Skinner invented a variant of the operant chamber for pigeons, in which the pigeon pecks an illuminated plastic disc called a response key (named after the telegraph key) to earn a few seconds of access to food (see Figure 6.3). Many of the principles of operant conditioning, particularly those concerning schedules of reinforcement (discussed in Chapter 7), were discovered with the use of this key-pecking procedure.

With the evolution of the Skinner box, Skinner's beliefs about the nature of behavior also changed. He abandoned the notion that all behavior could be analyzed in terms of reflexes and, along with other learning theorists, came to believe that behaviors can be conveniently divided into two categories. One category consists of involuntary, reflexive-type behaviors, which as Pavlov had demonstrated can often be classically conditioned to occur in new situations. Skinner referred to such behavior as *respondent behavior*. The other category, which Skinner called *operant behavior*, consists of behaviors that seem more voluntary in nature and are controlled by their consequences rather than by the stimuli that precede them. It was this type of behavior that Thorndike had studied in his puzzle box experiments and upon which he had based his law of effect. It was this type of behavior that most interested Skinner as well. He spent the rest of his life investigating the basic principles of operant conditioning and applying those principles to important aspects of human behavior.

FIGURE 6.3 Operant conditioning chamber for pigeons. When the pigeon pecks the response key (a translucent plastic disc that can be illuminated with different colored lights), grain is presented in the food cup for a period of a few seconds. (*Source:* Domjan, 2000.)

Pecking key

Food cup

1. Thorndike's cats learned to solve the puzzle box problem (gradually/suddenly) _____.

2. On the basis of his research with cats, Thorndike formulated his famous _____ of _____, which states that behaviors that lead to a(n) _____ state of affairs are strengthened, while behaviors that lead to a(n) _____ state of affairs are weakened.

3. According to Thorndike, behaviors that worked were s_____ i_____, while behaviors that did not work were s_____ o_____.

4. The Skinner box evolved out of Skinner's quest for a procedure that would, among other things, yield (regular/irregular) _____ patterns of behavior.

5. In the original version of the Skinner box, rats earn food by _____ a _____; in a later version, pigeons earn a few seconds of access to food by _____ at an illuminated plastic disc known as a _____ _____.

6. Skinner's procedures are also known as fr_____ o_____ procedures in that the animal controls the rate at which it earns food.

7. Skinner originally thought all behavior could be explained in terms of _____, but he eventually decided that this type of behavior could be distinguished from another, more voluntary type of behavior known as _____ behavior.

Operant Conditioning

Operant conditioning **is a type of learning in which the future probability of a behavior is affected by its consequences.** Note that this is essentially a restatement of Thorndike's law of effect. Skinner, however, was dissatisfied with Thorndike's mentalistic description of consequences as being either satisfying or annoying. Satisfaction and annoyance are internal states inferred from the animal's behavior. Skinner avoided any speculation about what the animal (or person) might be thinking or feeling and simply emphasized the effect of the consequence on the future *probability* of the response.

Note that Skinner's principle of operant conditioning bears a striking resemblance to Darwin's principle of natural selection (which forms the basis of the theory of evolution). According to the principle of natural selection, members of a species who inherit certain adaptive characteristics are more likely to survive and propagate, thereby passing that characteristic on to offspring. Thus, over many generations, the frequency of those adaptive characteristics within the population will increase and become well established. Similarly, according to the principle of operant conditioning, behaviors that lead to favorable outcomes are more likely to be repeated than those that do not lead to favorable outcomes. Thus, operant conditioning is sort of a mini-evolution of an organism's behaviors, in which behaviors that are adaptive (lead to favorable outcomes) become more frequent while behaviors that are nonadaptive (do not lead to favorable outcomes) become less frequent.

The operant conditioning process can be conceptualized as involving three components: (1) a response that produces a certain consequence (e.g., lever pressing produces a food pellet), (2) the consequence that serves to either increase or decrease the probability of the response that preceded it (e.g., the consequence of a food pellet increases the rat's tendency to again press the lever), and (3) a discriminative stimulus that precedes the response and signals that a certain consequence is now available (e.g., a tone signals that a lever press will now produce food). These components are examined in more detail below.

Operant Behavior

An *operant behavior* is a class of emitted responses that result in certain consequences; these consequences, in turn, affect the future probability or strength of those responses. Operant responses are sometimes simply called *operants*. Suppose, for example, that a rat presses a lever and receives a food pellet, with a result that it is more likely to press the lever in the future.

Lever press → **Food pellet**
The effect: The future probability of lever pressing increases.

Or Jonathan might tell a joke and receive a frown from the person he tells it to. He is now less likely to tell that person a joke in the future.

Tell a joke → **Person frowns**
The effect: The future probability of telling a joke decreases.

In each case, the behavior in question (the lever pressing or the joke telling) is an operant response (or an "operant") because its occurrence results in the delivery of a certain consequence, *and* that consequence affects the future probability of the response.

In contrast to classically conditioned behaviors, which are said to be *elicited by stimuli* (e.g., food elicits salivation), operant behaviors are technically said to be *emitted by the organism* (e.g., the rat emits lever presses or the person emits the behavior of telling jokes). This wording is used to indicate that operant behavior generally has a more voluntary, flexible quality to it compared to elicited behavior, which is generally more reflexive and automatic.

Note too that operant behavior is usually defined as a *class of responses*, with all of the responses in that class capable of producing the consequence. For example, there are many ways a rat can press a lever for food: hard or soft, quick or slow, right paw or left paw. All of these responses are effective in depressing the lever and producing food, and therefore they all belong to the same class of responses known as "lever presses." Similarly, Jonathan could tell many different jokes, and he could even tell the same joke in many different ways, all of which might result in a laugh. Defining operants in terms of classes has proven fruitful in that it is easier to predict the occurrence of a class of responses than it is to predict the *exact* response that will be emitted at a particular point in time. For example, it is easier to predict that a hungry rat will press a lever to obtain food than it is to predict exactly how it will press the lever on any particular occasion.

QUICK QUIZ

1. Skinner's definition of operant conditioning differs from Thorndike's law of effect in that it views consequences in terms of their effect upon the strength of behavior rather than whether they are s_____ing or a_____ing.

2. Operant conditioning is similar to the principle of natural selection in that behaviors that are (adaptive/nonadaptive) _____ tend to increase in frequency, while behaviors that are _____ tend to decrease in frequency.

3. The process of operant conditioning involves the following three components:
   (1) a r_____ that produces a certain _____,
   (2) a c_____ that serves to either increase or decrease the likelihood of the _____ that preceded it, and (3) a d_____ stimulus that precedes the _____ and signals that a certain _____ is now available.

4. Classically conditioned behaviors are said to be e_____ by the stimulus, while operant behaviors are said to be e_____ by the organism.

5. Operant responses are also simply called _____.

6. Operant behavior is usually defined as a(n) _____ of responses rather than a specific response.

Operant Consequences: Reinforcers and Punishers

The second component of an operant conditioning procedure is the consequence that either increases (strengthens) or decreases (weakens) the frequency of a behavior. Consequences that strengthen a behavior are called reinforcers, while consequences that weaken a behavior are called punishers. More specifically, **an event is a *reinforcer* if (1) it follows a behavior, and (2) the future probability of that behavior *increases*.** Conversely, **an event is a *punisher* if (1) it follows a behavior, and (2) the future probability of that behavior *decreases*.**

Diagrams of operant conditioning procedures generally use the following symbols. Reinforcers are usually given the symbol S^R (which stands for *reinforcing stimulus*), and punishers are given the symbol S^P (which stands for *punishing stimulus*). The operant response is given the symbol R. Using these abbreviations, a diagram of a procedure in which a lever press is reinforced by the delivery of a food pellet looks like this:

$$\textit{Lever press} \rightarrow \textbf{Food pellet}$$
$$\textbf{R} \qquad\qquad S^R$$

The food pellet is a reinforcer because it follows the lever press *and* increases the future probability of lever pressing. A diagram of Jonathan's failed attempt at humor, in which a frown punished his behavior of telling jokes, looks like this:

$$\textit{Tell a joke} \rightarrow \textbf{Person frowns}$$
$$R \qquad\qquad S^P$$

The frown is a punisher because it follows the joke *and* the future probability of joke telling decreases.

Note that, from an operant conditioning perspective, we do NOT say that the person or animal has been reinforced or punished; rather, it is the behavior that has been reinforced or punished. Only the behavior increases or decreases in frequency. (There is actually a lesson in this. If you want a child to stop doing something, should you tell her that her behavior displeases you or that she displeases you? Similarly, when someone does something that bothers you, will it be more constructive to tell him that his behavior disturbs you or that he disturbs you? Is it easier for people to change their behavior or to change who they are?)

It is also important to differentiate the terms *reinforcer* and *punisher* from *reinforcement* and *punishment*. *Reinforcer* and *punisher* both refer to the specific *consequences* used to strengthen or weaken a behavior. In the above examples, the food pellet is a reinforcer for lever pressing, and the frown is a punisher for joke telling. In contrast, the terms *reinforcement* and *punishment* usually refer to the *process* or *procedure* by which a certain consequence changes the strength of a behavior. Thus, the use of food to increase the strength of lever pressing is an example of reinforcement, while the food itself is a reinforcer. Similarly, the process of frowning to encourage Jonathan to stop telling jokes is an example of punishment, while the frown itself is a punisher. In summary, the terms *reinforcer* and *punisher* refer to the actual consequences of the behavior; the terms *reinforcement* and *punishment* refer to the process or procedure of strengthening or weakening a behavior by instituting those consequences.

Note too that reinforcers and punishers are defined entirely by their effect on behavior. For example, a laugh is a reinforcer for the behavior of joke telling only to the extent that joke telling then increases. If, for some reason, joke telling decreased as a result of the laugh (maybe the person telling the joke delights in disgusting his listeners and does not want them to find his joke funny), the laugh would by definition be a punisher. It is important to remember this, because events that on the surface seem like reinforcers or punishers do not always function in that manner. We encountered this notion earlier, in Chapter 2, in our discussion of the distinction between appetitive and aversive events (and particularly in the cartoon depiction of Calvin ravenously eating what he believes to be a bowl of maggot soup). In similar fashion, teachers sometimes yell at their students for being disruptive, and as a result, the students become MORE (not less) disruptive. Although the teacher is clearly trying to punish the disruptive behavior, the yelling is actually having the opposite effect. By definition, therefore, the yelling is a reinforcer because it is causing the disruptive behavior to increase in frequency (perhaps because disruptive students find that other students admire them if they upset the teacher).

Thus, the safest bet is to define consequences as reinforcers or punishers in terms of their effect on behavior and not in terms of how pleasant or unpleasant they seem. It is for this reason that many behaviorists prefer the term *reinforcer* rather than *reward*, the latter term being too strongly associated with events that are seemingly pleasant (e.g., affection, food, money). For example, the teacher's yelling is hardly what anyone would call a reward, but technically speaking it is a reinforcer for the students' disruptive behavior. Not all behaviorists are this strict in their terminology, however, and the terms *reward* and *reinforcer* are sometimes used interchangeably (e.g., Bandura, 1997; Herrnstein, 1997).[2] Moreover, because students often find it helpful to think of consequences in terms of whether they are pleasant or unpleasant, we will sometimes make use of such terms in our discussion of consequences. In other words, to help you gain an initial grasp of this material, we will sometimes be rather informal in the terminology we use. (Note, however, that such informality may not be acceptable in an examination on this material.)

3

QUICK QUIZ

1. Simply put, reinforcers are those consequences that s_____ a behavior, while punishers are those consequences that w_____ a behavior.

2. More specifically, a reinforcer is a consequence that (precedes/follows) _____ a behavior and (increases/decreases) _____ the probability of that behavior. A punisher is a consequence that (precedes/follows) _____ a behavior and (increases/decreases) _____ the probability of that behavior.

3. The terms *reinforcement* and *punishment* refer to the pr_____ or pr_____ whereby a behavior is strengthened or weakened by its consequences.

4. Strengthening a child's tendency toward cleanliness by praising her when she washes her hands is an example of _____, while the praise itself is a _____.

5. Eliminating a dog's tendency to jump up on visitors by scolding her when she does so is an example of _____, while the scolding itself is a _____.

_____

[2] Furthermore, some behaviorists use the term *reward* to refer to the effect of the consequence on the animal as opposed to the behavior (Rachlin, 1991). For example, a dog biscuit can be both a reinforcer for the dog's *behavior* of begging and a reward to the *dog* for having carried out such a behavior. Thus, reinforcers strengthen behavior, while rewards make us happy.

6. Reinforcers and punishers are defined entirely by their _____ on behavior. For this reason, the term *reinforcer* is often preferred to the term _____ because the latter is too closely associated with events that are commonly regarded as pleasant or desirable.

7. When Moe stuck his finger in a light socket, he received an electric shock. As a result, he now sticks his finger in the light socket as often as possible. By definition, the electric shock was a _____ because the behavior it followed has (increased/decreased) _____ in frequency.

8. Each time Edna talked out in class, her teacher immediately came over and gave her a hug. As a result, Edna no longer talks out in class. By definition, the hug is a(n) _____ because the behavior it follows has (increased/decreased) _____ in frequency.

9. When labeling an operant conditioning procedure, punishing consequences (punishers) are given the symbol _____ (which stands for _____ _____), while reinforcing consequences (reinforcers) are given the symbol _____ (which stands for _____ _____). The operant response is given the symbol _____.

10. When we give a dog a treat for fetching a toy, we are attempting to reinforce (the behavior of fetching the toy/the dog that fetched the toy) _____.

11. When we chastise a child for being rude, we are attempting to punish (the child who was rude/the child's rude behavior) _____.

Operant Antecedents: Discriminative Stimuli

The operant response and its consequence are the most essential components of the operant conditioning procedure. In most circumstances, however, a third component can also be identified. When a behavior is consistently reinforced or punished in the presence of certain stimuli, those stimuli will begin to influence the occurrence of the behavior. For example, if lever pressing produces food only when a tone is sounding, the rat soon learns to press the lever only when it hears the tone. This situation can be diagrammed as follows:

Tone: *Press lever* → Food pellet
S^D R S^R

This sequence can be read as follows: In the presence of the tone, if the rat presses the lever, it will receive food. The tone is called a discriminative stimulus (usually given the symbol S^D [pronounced "es-dee"]). **A *discriminative stimulus* (S^D) is a stimulus in the presence of which responses are reinforced and in the absence of which they are not reinforced.** In other words, a discriminative stimulus is a signal that indicates that a response will be followed by a reinforcer.

Another example: If Susan always laughs at Jonathan's jokes, then he is more likely to tell her a joke. Susan is an S^D for Jonathan's behavior of telling jokes. This can be diagrammed as follows:

Susan: *Tell her a joke* → She laughs
    S^D R S^R

Discriminative stimuli are said to "set the occasion for" the behavior, meaning that the behavior is more likely to occur in the presence of those stimuli. Discriminative stimuli do not elicit behavior in the manner of a CS or US in classical conditioning. For example, the tone does not automatically elicit a lever press; it merely increases the probability that a lever press will occur. Whether or not lever pressing occurs is still a function of its consequence (food), and the S^D simply indicates that this consequence is now available. Similarly, the presence of Susan does not automatically elicit the behavior of joke telling in Jonathan; rather, he is simply more likely to tell a joke in her presence. Therefore, rather than saying that the S^D elicits the behavior, we say that the person or animal emits the behavior in the presence of the S^D. (Remember, it is only in classical conditioning where we say that the stimulus *elicits* the behavior. In operant conditioning, we say that the organism *emits* the behavior.)

The discriminative stimulus, the operant behavior, and the reinforcer or punisher constitute what is known as the *three-term contingency*. The three-term contingency can also be viewed as consisting of an *antecedent event* (an antecedent event is a *preceding* event), a *behavior*, and a *consequence* (which can be remembered by the initials *ABC*).

Antecedent	*Behavior*		*Consequence*
Susan:	*Tell joke*	→	She laughs
S^D	R		S^R
Tone:	*Press lever*	→	Food pellet
S^D	R		S^R

Another way of thinking about this sequence is that you notice something (Susan), do something (tell a joke), and get something (Susan laughs). Similarly, you notice that it is 7:00 P.M., you turn on the TV, and you get to see your favorite sitcom. Or maybe your dog notices that you have popcorn, begs persistently, and gets some of the popcorn. Many students find this easy to remember: Notice something, do something, get something. (As you will see later, however, the consequence in some cases involves losing or avoiding something rather than getting something.)

So far, we have dealt only with stimuli that are associated with reinforcement. Stimuli can also be associated with punishment. **A stimulus that signals that a response will be punished is called a** *discriminative stimulus for punishment.* For example, if a water bottle signals that meowing will result in being sprayed with water (rather than being fed), a cat will quickly learn to stop meowing whenever it sees the water bottle.

Water bottle: *Meow* → **Get sprayed**
    S^D R S^P

Similarly, a motorist who once received a fine for speeding no longer speeds in the presence of a police car.

Police car: *Speed* → **Receive fine**
    S^D R S^P

For the speeding motorist, the presence of a police car is a discriminative stimulus for punishment.

Finally, you should be aware that processes of operant and classical conditioning often overlap, such that a particular stimulus can simultaneously act as both a discriminative stimulus and a conditioned stimulus. For example, consider a tone that serves as an S^D for the operant behavior of lever pressing:

Tone: *Lever press* → **Food**
   S^D R S^R

The tone is closely associated with food, and food of course elicits salivation. This means that during the course of our operant conditioning procedure, the tone will also become a CS that elicits salivation as a CR. Thus, if we ignore the lever pressing and concentrate just on the salivation, then what is happening is this:

Tone: Food → *Salivation*
  NS   US   UR
Tone → *Salivation*
  CS   CR

Whether the tone should be considered an S^D or a CS depends on the response to which one is referring. It is an S^D with respect to the operant response of lever pressing, and a CS with respect to the classically conditioned response of salivation.

1. The operant conditioning procedure usually consists of three components:
(1) a d_____ s_____, (2) an o_____ behavior, and (3) a c_____.

2. A discriminative stimulus is usually indicated by the symbol _____.

3. A discriminative stimulus is said to "_____ for the behavior," meaning that its presence makes the response (more/less) _____ likely to occur.

4. A discriminative stimuli (does/does not) _____ elicit behavior in the same manner as a CS.

5. Using the appropriate symbols, label each component in the following three-term contingency (assume that the behavior will be strengthened):
Phone rings: *Answer phone* → Conversation with friend

_____   _____   _____

QUICK QUIZ

6. The three-term contingency can also be thought of as an ABC sequence, where A stands for _____ event, B stands for _____, and C stands for _____.

7. Another way of thinking about the three-term contingency is that you _____ something, _____ something, and _____ something.

8. A stimulus in the presence of which a response is punished is called a _____ _____ for _____.

9. A bell that signals the start of a round and therefore serves as an S^D for the operant response of beginning to box may also serve as a(n) (S^D/CS) _____ for a fear response. This is an example of how the two processes of _____ conditioning and _____ conditioning often overlap.

Four Types of Contingencies

We have seen that there are two main types of consequences in operant conditioning: reinforcers and punishers. If the response is followed by a reinforcer, then we say that a *contingency of reinforcement* exists (meaning that the delivery of the reinforcer is contingent upon the response), while if the response is followed by a punisher, then a *contingency of punishment* exists. However, contingencies of reinforcement and punishment can be further divided into two subtypes: positive and negative. This results in four basic types of contingencies (response-consequence relationships): positive reinforcement, negative reinforcement, positive punishment, and negative punishment. Because these are sometimes confusing to students, they will be described in some detail below.

As we learned previously, reinforcement is a procedure that strengthens a behavior, while punishment is a procedure that weakens a behavior. That part is pretty straightforward, but this next part can be tricky. When combined with the word *reinforcement* or *punishment*, the word *positive* means only that the behavior is followed by the *presentation* or addition of something (think of a + [positive] sign, which means add). Thus, the word *positive*, when combined with the term *reinforcement* or *punishment*, does NOT mean good or pleasant; it means only that the response has resulted in something being added or presented. The event that is presented could either be pleasant (receiving a compliment) or unpleasant (getting yelled at).

Similarly, the word *negative*, when combined with the word *reinforcement* or *punishment*, means only that the behavior is followed by the *removal* of something; that is, something is subtracted from the situation (think of a − [negative] sign, which means subtract). The word *negative*, therefore, in this context, does NOT mean bad or unpleasant; it means only that the response results in the removal of something. The something that is removed could be an event that is either pleasant (your dessert is taken away) or unpleasant (the person stops yelling at you).

To summarize, in the case of positive reinforcement and positive punishment, the word *positive* means only that the behavior has resulted in something being presented or added. In negative reinforcement and negative punishment, the word *negative* means only that the behavior has resulted in something being removed or subtracted. The word *reinforcement*, of course, means that the behavior will increase in strength, and the word *punishment* means that the behavior will decrease in strength. Keep these points in mind, and you should have no problem sorting out the four types of contingencies described below.

1. The word *positive*, when combined with the word *reinforcement* or *punishment*, means only that the behavior is followed by the _____ of something. The word *negative*, when combined with the word *reinforcement* or *punishment*, means only that the behavior is followed by the _____ of something.

2. The word *positive*, when combined with the word *reinforcement* or *punishment*, (does/does not) _____ mean that the consequence is good or pleasant. Similarly, the term *negative*, when combined with the word *reinforcement* or *punishment*, (does/does not) _____ mean that the consequence is bad or unpleasant.

3. Within the context of reinforcement and punishment, positive refers to the (addition/subtraction) _____ of something, while negative refers to the (addition/subtraction) _____ of something.

4. Reinforcement is related to a(n) (increase/decrease) _____ in behavior, while punishment is related to a(n) (increase/decrease) _____ in behavior.

Positive Reinforcement

Positive reinforcement **consists of the** *presentation* **of a stimulus (one that is usually considered pleasant or rewarding) following a response, which then leads to an** *increase* **in the future strength of that response.** Loosely speaking, the behavior results in the delivery of something the recipient likes, so the person or animal is more likely to behave that way in the future. Some of the examples stated earlier have been examples of positive reinforcement. The standard rat procedure in which lever pressing produces food is an example of positive reinforcement, because the consequence of food leads to an increase in lever pressing. It is reinforcement because the behavior increases in frequency, and it is positive reinforcement because the consequence involves the presentation of something, namely, food (which we would call a

QUICK QUIZ

positive reinforcer). Some additional examples of positive reinforcement are listed below:

Turn on TV → **See the show**
    R S^R

Smile at person → **The person smiles at you**
    R S^R

Order coffee → **Receive coffee**
    R S^R

Study diligently for quiz → **Obtain an excellent mark**
    R S^R

Compliment partner → **Receive a kiss**
    R S^R

Negative Reinforcement

Negative reinforcement **is the** *removal* **of a stimulus (one that is usually considered unpleasant or aversive) following a response that then leads to an** *increase* **in the future strength of that response.** Loosely speaking, the behavior results in the prevention or removal of something the person or animal hates, so they are more likely to behave that way in the future. For example, if by pressing a lever, a rat terminates an electric shock that it is receiving, it will become more likely to press the lever the next time it receives an electric shock. This is an example of reinforcement because the behavior increases in strength; it is negative reinforcement because the consequence consists of taking something away. Some additional examples are listed below.

Open umbrella → **Escape rain**
    R S^R

Claim illness → **Avoid writing an exam**
    R S^R

Take aspirin → **Eliminate headache**
    R S^R

Turn on the heater → **Escape the cold**
    R S^R

The last example is interesting in that it illustrates how it is sometimes a matter of interpretation as to whether something is an example of negative reinforcement or positive reinforcement. Does the person turn on the heater to escape the cold (negative reinforcement) or to obtain warmth (positive reinforcement)? Either interpretation would be correct.

Negative reinforcement involves two types of behavior: escape and avoidance. *Escape behavior* **results in the termination (stopping) of an aversive stimulus.** In the first example above, the person is getting rained on, and by opening the umbrella, the person stops this from happening. Likewise, taking aspirin removes a headache, and turning on the heater allows one to escape the cold. Avoidance is similar to escape except that ***avoidance behavior occurs before the aversive stimulus is presented and therefore prevents its delivery.*** For example, if the umbrella were opened prior to stepping out into the rain, the person would avoid getting rained on. And by pretending to be ill, a student avoids having to write an exam. Escape and avoidance are discussed in more detail in Chapter 9.

1. When you reached to take the dog's toy away from him, he nipped at your hand. You quickly pulled your hand back and let him keep the toy. As a result, he now nips at your hand whenever you try to take something away from him. The consequence for *the dog's behavior of nipping* consisted of the (presentation/removal) _____ of a stimulus (namely, your hand), and his behavior of nipping subsequently (increased/decreased) _____ in frequency; therefore, this is an example of _____ reinforcement.

2. When the dog sat at your feet and whined during breakfast one morning, you fed him. As a result, he sat at your feet and whined during breakfast the next morning. The consequence for the dog's whining consisted of the (presentation/removal) _____ of a stimulus, and his behavior of whining subsequently (increased/decreased) _____ in frequency; therefore, this is an example of _____ reinforcement.

3. Karen cries while saying to her boyfriend, "John, I don't feel as though you love me." John gives Karen a big hug saying, "That's not true, dear, I love you very much." If John's hug is a reinforcer, Karen is (more/less) _____ likely to cry the next time she feels insecure about her relationship. More specifically, this is an example of _____ reinforcement of Karen's crying behavior.

4. With respect to escape and avoidance, an _____ response is one that *terminates* an aversive stimulus, while an _____ response is one that *prevents* an aversive stimulus from occurring. Escape and avoidance responses are two classes of behavior that are maintained by (positive/negative) _____ reinforcement.

5. Turning down the heat because you are too hot is an example of an (escape/avoidance) _____ response; turning it down before you become too hot is an example of an (escape/avoidance) _____ response.

Positive Punishment

***Positive punishment* consists of the *presentation* of a stimulus (one that is usually considered unpleasant or aversive) following a response, which then leads to a *decrease* in the future strength of that response.** Loosely speaking, the behavior results in the delivery of something the person or animal hates, so they are less likely to behave that way in the future. For example, if a rat received a shock when it pressed a lever, it would stop pressing the lever. This is an example of punishment because the behavior decreases in strength, and it is positive punishment because the consequence involves the presentation of something (i.e., shock). Consider some further examples of positive punishment:

> *Talk back to the boss* → **Get reprimanded**
>   **R**   **S**^{P}
> *Swat at the wasp* → **Get stung**
>   **R**   **S**^{P}
> *Meow constantly* → **Get sprayed with water**
>   **R**   **S**^{P}

In each case, the behavior is followed by the presentation of an aversive stimulus, with the result that there is a decrease in the future probability of the behavior.

People frequently confuse positive punishment with negative reinforcement. One reason for this is the fact that many behaviorists, including Skinner, use the term *negative reinforcer* to refer to an aversive (unpleasant) stimulus and the term *positive reinforcer* to refer to an appetitive (pleasant) stimulus. Unfortunately, people with less knowledge of the field have then assumed that the presentation of a negative reinforcer is an instance of negative reinforcement, which it is not. It is instead an instance of positive punishment.

Negative Punishment

Negative punishment **consists of the *removal* of a stimulus (one that is usually considered pleasant or rewarding) following a response, which then leads to a *decrease* in the future strength of that response.** Loosely speaking, the behavior results in the removal of something the person or animal likes, so they are less likely to behave that way in the future. Some examples of negative punishment:

> *Stay out past curfew* → **Lose car privileges**
>   **R**   **S**^{P}
> *Argue with boss* → **Lose job**
>   **R**   **S**^{P}
> *Play with food* → **Lose dessert**
>   **R**   **S**^{P}
> *Tease sister* → **Sent to room (loss of social contact)**
>   **R**   **S**^{P}

In each case, it is punishment because the behavior decreases in strength, and it is negative punishment because the consequence consists of the removal of something. The last example above is known as "time-out" and is employed by many parents as a replacement for spanking. Removal of social contact is usually one consequence of such a procedure; more generally, however, the child loses the opportunity to receive any type of positive reinforcer during the time-out interval. Children find such situations to be quite unpleasant, with the result that even very brief time-outs can be quite effective.

Consider another example of negative punishment: Jonathan's girlfriend, who is quite jealous, completely ignored him (withdrew her attention from him) when she observed him having a conversation with another woman at a party. As a result, he stopped talking to the other women at the party.

Jonathan talks to other women → His girlfriend ignores him
$$\text{R} \qquad\qquad\qquad\qquad \text{S}^\text{P}$$

Jonathan's behavior of talking to other women at parties has been negatively punished. It is punishment in that the frequency with which he talked to other women at the party declined, and it is negative punishment because the consequence consisted of the withdrawal of his girlfriend's attention.

Question: In the above scenario, Jonathan's behavior has been negatively punished. But what contingencies are operating on the girlfriend's behavior? When she ignored him, he stopped talking to other women at the party. Given that this occurred, she might ignore him at future parties if she again sees him talking to other women. If so, her behavior has been negatively reinforced by the fact that it was effective in getting him to stop doing something that she disliked. If we diagram this interaction from the perspective of each, we get the following:

For Jonathan:
I talk to other women → My girlfriend ignores me
$$\text{R} \qquad\qquad\qquad\quad \text{S}^\text{P}$$

For his girlfriend:
I ignore Jonathan → He stops talking to other women
$$\text{R} \qquad\qquad\qquad\quad \text{S}^\text{R}$$

As you can see, a reduction in one person's behavior as a result of punishment can reinforce the behavior of the person who implemented the punishment. This is why punishment is so seductive: It is often successful in getting a person to stop behaving in ways that we dislike. This success then reinforces our tendency to use punishment in the future, which of course can create major problems in the long run. We discuss the uses and abuses of punishment more fully in Chapter 9.[3]

---

[3] Note that the labels for the two types of punishment are not standardized. For example, positive and negative punishment are sometimes called _Type 1_ and _Type 2 punishment_ (e.g., Chance, 1994) or _punishment by contingent application_ and _punishment by contingent withdrawal_ (e.g., Miller, 1997).

Some students mistakenly equate behaviorism with the use of punishment. It is important to recognize that behaviorists actually emphasize the use of positive reinforcement. Indeed, Skinner (1953) believed that many societal problems can be traced to the overuse of punishment as well as negative reinforcement. For example, teachers too often control their students by attempting to punish maladaptive behavior rather than by reinforcing adaptive behavior. Moreover, the educational system in general is designed in such a way that students too often study to avoid failure (a negative reinforcer) rather than to obtain knowledge (a positive reinforcer). As a result, schooling is often more onerous and less effective than it could be.

Similarly, in interpersonal relationships, people too often attempt to change each other's behavior through the use of aversive consequences, such as complaining, when positive reinforcement for appropriate behavior might work just as well or better. Marsha, for example, says that Roger forgets to call whenever he is going to be late, despite the fact that she often complains about it. Perhaps a more effective approach would be for her to express her appreciation when he does call.

Furthermore, although many people believe that the key to a great relationship is open communication, research has shown that a much more important element is the ratio of positive (pleasant) interactions to negative (aversive) interactions. In fact, one of the best predictors of a successful marriage is when the positives outweigh the negatives by a ratio of about five to one (Gottman, 1994). Even volatile relationships, in which there seems to be an enormous amount of bickering, can thrive if the number of positive exchanges (teasing, hugging, and praising) greatly outweigh the negative exchanges.

A summary of the four types of contingencies—positive reinforcement, negative reinforcement, positive punishment, and negative punishment—are depicted in Table 6.1.

TABLE 6.1 Four types of contingencies. The words *positive* and *negative* within this context refer only to whether the consequence involves the addition (presentation) of something or the subtraction (removal) of something.

	CONSEQUENCE (WHAT FOLLOWS THE BEHAVIOR)	
EFFECT ON BEHAVIOR	POSITIVE (SOMETHING ADDED: +)	NEGATIVE (SOMETHING SUBTRACTED: −)
Reinforcement Behavior increases: ⇑	Positive Reinforcement	Negative Reinforcement
Punishment Behavior decreases: ⇓	Positive Punishment	Negative Punishment

1. When Sasha was teasing the dog, it bit her. As a result, she no longer teases the dog. The consequence for *Sasha's behavior* of teasing the dog was the (presentation/removal) _____ of a stimulus, and the teasing behavior subsequently (increased/decreased) _____ in frequency; therefore, this is an example of _____ _____.

2. Whenever Sasha pulled the dog's tail, the dog left and went into another room. As a result, Sasha now pulls the dog's tail less often when it is around. The consequence for pulling the dog's tail was the (presentation/removal) _____ of a stimulus, and the behavior of pulling the dog's tail subsequently (increased/decreased) _____ in frequency; therefore, this is an example of _____ _____.

3. When Alex burped in public during his date with Stephanie, she got angry with him. Alex now burps quite often when he is out on a date with Stephanie. The consequence for burping was the _____ of a stimulus, and the behavior of belching subsequently _____ in frequency; therefore, this is an example of _____ _____.

4. When Alex held the car door open for Stephanie, she made a big fuss over what a gentleman he was becoming. Alex no longer holds the car door open for her. The consequence for holding open the door was the _____ of a stimulus, and the behavior of holding open the door subsequently _____ in frequency; therefore, this is an example of _____ _____.

5. When Tenzing shared his toys with his brother, his mother stopped criticizing him. Tenzing now shares his toys with his brother quite often. The consequence for sharing the toys was the _____ of a stimulus, and the behavior of sharing the toys subsequently _____ in frequency; therefore, this is an example of _____ _____.

Positive Reinforcement: Further Distinctions

Because positive reinforcement is so strongly emphasized by behaviorists, let us have a closer look at this type of contingency. More specifically, we will examine various categories of positive reinforcement.

Immediate versus Delayed Reinforcement

A reinforcer can be presented either immediately after a behavior occurs or following some delay. In general, *the more immediate the reinforcer, the stronger its effect upon the behavior.* Suppose, for example, you wish to reinforce a child for playing quietly by giving him a treat. The treat should ideally be given while the quiet period is still in progress. If instead you deliver the treat several minutes later, while he is engaged in some other behavior (e.g., banging a stick on his toy box), you might inadvertently reinforce this other behavior rather than the one you wish to reinforce.

The weak effect of delayed reinforcers on behavior accounts for some major difficulties in life. Do you find it tough to stick to a diet or exercise regime? This is because the benefits of exercise and proper eating are delayed and therefore weak, while the enjoyable effects of alternative activities, such as watching television and drinking a soda, are immediate and therefore powerful. Similarly, have you ever promised yourself that you would study all weekend, only to find that you completely wasted the time reading novels, watching television, and going out with friends? The immediate reinforcement associated with these recreational activities effectively outweighed the delayed reinforcement associated with studying. Of course, what we are talking about here is the issue of self-control, a topic that will be more fully discussed in Chapter 10.

QUICK QUIZ

1. In general, the more _____ the reinforcer, the stronger its effect upon behavior.

2. It is sometimes difficult for students to study, in that the reinforcers for studying are _____ and therefore _____, while the reinforcers for alternative activities are _____ and therefore _____.

Primary and Secondary Reinforcers

A *primary reinforcer* (also called an *unconditioned reinforcer*) is an event that is innately reinforcing. Loosely speaking, primary reinforcers are those things we are born to like rather than learn to like and that therefore naturally reinforce our behavior. Examples of primary reinforcers are food, water, proper temperature (neither too hot nor too cold), and sexual contact.

Many primary reinforcers are associated with basic physiological needs, and their effectiveness is closely tied to a state of deprivation. For example, food is a highly effective reinforcer when we are food deprived and hungry but not when we are satiated. Some primary reinforcers, however, do not seem to be associated with a physiological state of deprivation. An animal (or person) cooped up in a boring environment will likely find access to a more stimulating environment highly reinforcing and will perform a response such as lever pressing (or driving to the mall) to gain such access. In cases such as this, the deprivation seems more psychological than physiological.

A *secondary reinforcer* (also called a *conditioned reinforcer*) is an event that is reinforcing because it has been associated with some other reinforcer. Loosely speaking, secondary reinforcers are those events that we have learned to like because they have become associated with other things that we like. Much of our behavior is directed toward obtaining secondary reinforcers, such as good marks, fine clothes, and a nice car. Because of past experiences with these events, they can function as effective reinforcers for our behavior. Thus, if good marks in school are consistently associated with praise, then the good marks themselves can serve as reinforcers for behaviors such as studying. And a high school teacher who provided you with lots of praise can become an effective reinforcer for the behavior of visiting her after you have graduated.

Conditioned stimuli that have been associated with appetitive USs can also function as secondary reinforcers. For example, the sound of a metronome that has been paired with food to produce a classically conditioned response of salivation:

Metronome: Food $\rightarrow$ *Salivation*
    NS   US   UR
Metronome $\rightarrow$ *Salivation*
    CS   CR

can then be used as a secondary reinforcer for an operant response such as lever pressing:

Lever pressing $\rightarrow$ **Metronome**
    R S^R

Because the metronome has been closely associated with food, it can now serve as a reinforcer for the operant response of lever pressing.

Discriminative stimuli associated with positive reinforcers can likewise function as secondary reinforcers. A tone that has served as an S^D signaling the availability of food for lever pressing:

Tone: *Press lever* $\rightarrow$ **Food**
  S^D R S^R

can then function as a secondary reinforcer for some other behavior, such as running in a wheel:

Run in wheel $\rightarrow$ **Tone**
    R S^R

An important type of secondary reinforcer is known as a generalized secondary reinforcer (or generalized reinforcer). **A *generalized secondary reinforcer* is a type of secondary reinforcer that has been associated with several other reinforcers.** For example, money is a powerful generalized secondary reinforcer for humans because it is associated with an almost unlimited array of other reinforcers including food, clothing, furnishings, entertainment, and even dates (insofar as money will likely increase our attractiveness to others). In fact, money can become such a powerful reinforcer that some people would rather just have the money than the things it can buy. Social attention too is a highly effective generalized reinforcer, especially for young children (though some aspects of it, such as touching, are probably also primary reinforcers). Attention from caretakers is usually associated with a host of good things such as food and play and comfort, with the result that attention by itself can become a powerful reinforcer. It is so powerful that some children will even misbehave in order to get someone to pay attention to them.

Note also that an event can function as both a primary reinforcer and a secondary reinforcer. A Thanksgiving dinner, for example, can be both a primary reinforcer, in the sense of providing food, and a secondary reinforcer due to its association with, say, a beloved grandmother who prepared many similar dinners in your childhood.

Finally, just as stimuli that are associated with reinforcement can become secondary reinforcers, so also can the *behaviors* that are associated with reinforcement. For example, children who are consistently praised for helping others might eventually find the behavior of helping others to be reinforcing in and of itself. They will then help others, not to receive praise, but because they "like to help." We might then describe such children as having an altruistic nature. By a similar mechanism, even hard work can sometimes become a secondary reinforcer (see the And Furthermore box entitled "Learned Industriousness").

4

QUICK QUIZ

1. Events that are innately reinforcing are called _____ reinforcers. They are sometimes also called un_____ reinforcers.

2. Events that become reinforcers through their association with other reinforcers are called _____ reinforcers. They are sometimes also called _____ reinforcers.

3. Honey is an example of a _____ reinforcer, while a coupon that is used to purchase the honey is an example of a _____ reinforcer.

4. A (CS/US) _____ that has been associated with an appetitive (CS/US) _____ can serve as a secondary reinforcer for an operant response. A stimulus that is a(n) _____ for an operant response can also serve as a secondary reinforcer for some other response.

5. A generalized secondary reinforcer (or generalized reinforcer) is a secondary reinforcer that has been associated with _____.

6. Two generalized secondary reinforcers that have strong effects on human behavior are _____.

Intrinsic and Extrinsic Reinforcement

In the preceding discussion, we noted that operant behavior itself can sometimes be reinforcing. Such a behavior is said to be intrinsically reinforcing or motivating. Thus, *intrinsic reinforcement* **is reinforcement provided by**

And Furthermore

Learned Industriousness

Some people seem to enjoy hard work while others do not. Why is this? According to *learned industriousness theory,* if working hard (displaying high effort) on a task has been consistently associated with reinforcement, then working hard might itself become a secondary reinforcer (Eisenberger, 1992). This can result in a generalized tendency to work hard. Experiments with both humans and animals have confirmed this possibility. For example, rats that have been reinforced for emitting forceful lever presses will then run faster down an alleyway to obtain food (Eisenberger, Carlson, Guile, & Shapiro, 1979). Similarly, students who have been reinforced for solving complex math problems will later write essays of higher quality (Eisenberger, Masterson, & McDermitt, 1982). Experiments have also confirmed the opposite: Rats and humans that have been reinforced for displaying low effort on a task will show a generalized tendency to be lazy. (Something to think about if you have a strong tendency to take the easy way out.)

the mere act of performing the behavior. We rollerblade because it is invigorating, we party with friends because we like their company, and we work hard at something partly because hard work has, through experience, become enjoyable (though you are probably still not convinced about that one). Animals too sometimes engage in activities for their own sake. In some of the earliest research on intrinsic motivation, it was found that monkeys repeatedly solved mechanical puzzles in the absence of any additional incentive (Harlow, Harlow, & Meyer, 1950).

Unfortunately, many activities are not intrinsically reinforcing and instead require additional incentives to ensure their performance. ***Extrinsic reinforcement* is the reinforcement provided by some consequence that is external to the behavior (i.e., an "extrinsic reinforcer").** For example, perhaps you are reading this text solely because of an upcoming exam. Passing the exam is the extrinsic consequence that is motivating your behavior. Other examples of extrinsically motivated behaviors are driving to get somewhere, working for money, and dating an attractive individual merely to enhance your prestige.

Question: What happens if you are given an extrinsic reinforcer for an activity that is already intrinsically reinforcing? What if, for example, you love rollerblading and are fortunate enough to be hired one weekend to blade around an amusement park displaying a new line of sportswear? Will the experience of receiving payment for rollerblading increase, decrease, or have no effect on your subsequent enjoyment of the activity?

Although you might think that it would increase your enjoyment of rollerblading (since the activity is not only enjoyable but also associated with

And Furthermore

Positive Reinforcement of Artistic Appreciation

B. F. Skinner (1983) once described how two students used positive reinforcement to instill in their new roommate an appreciation of modern art. These students had several items of modern art in their apartment, but the roommate had shown little interest in them and was instead proceeding to "change the character" of the space. As a counterploy, the students first decided to pay attention to the roommate only when they saw him looking at one of the works of art. Next, they threw a party and arranged for an attractive young woman to engage him in a discussion about the art. They also arranged for him to receive announcements from local art galleries about upcoming art shows. After about a month, the roommate himself suggested attending a local art museum. Interestingly, while there, he just "happened" to find a five-dollar bill lying at his feet while he was looking at a painting. According to Skinner, "It was not long before [the two students] came again in great excitement—to show me his first painting" (p. 48).

money), many researchers claim that experiences like this can *decrease* intrinsic interest. For example, Lepper, Green, and Nisbett (1973) found that children who enjoyed drawing with Magic Markers became less interested following a session in which they had been promised, and then received, a "good player" award for drawing with the markers. In contrast, children who did not receive an award or who received the award unexpectedly after playing with the markers did not show a loss of interest. Similar results have been reported by other investigators (e.g., Deci & Ryan, 1985). However, some researchers have found that extrinsic rewards have no effect on intrinsic interest (e.g., Amabile, Hennessey, & Grossman, 1986) or actually produce an *increase* in intrinsic interest (e.g., Harackiewicz, Manderlink, & Sansone, 1984). Unfortunately, despite these mixed findings, it is the damaging effects of extrinsic rewards on intrinsic motivation that are often emphasized in discussions of this literature (e.g., Kohn, 1993). But is this a fair assessment of the evidence? Are the harmful effects of reinforcement the rule or the exception?

Cameron and Pierce (1994) attempted to answer this question by conducting a meta-analysis of 96 well-controlled experiments that examined the effects of extrinsic rewards on intrinsic motivation. (A meta-analysis is a statistical procedure that combines the results of several separate studies, thereby producing a more reliable, overall assessment of the variable being studied.) The meta-analysis by Cameron and Pierce indicates that extrinsic rewards usually have little or no effect on intrinsic motivation. External rewards can occasionally undermine intrinsic motivation, but only when *the reward is expected* (i.e., the person has been instructed beforehand that she will receive a reward), *the reward is tangible* (e.g., it consists of money rather than praise), and *the reward is given for simply performing the activity* (and not for how well it is performed). It also turns out that verbal rewards, such as praise, often produce an increase in intrinsic motivation, as do tangible rewards given for high-quality performance (see Deci & Ryan, 1985). Cameron and Pierce conclude that extrinsic rewards can be safely applied in most circumstances and that the limited circumstances in which they decrease intrinsic motivation are easily avoided. Bandura (1997) likewise has argued that the dangers of extrinsic rewards on intrinsic motivation have been greatly overstated. (See Deci, Koestner, & Ryan, in press, and Cameron, in press, for further contributions to this debate.)

1. An _____ motivated activity is one in which the activity is itself reinforcing; an _____ motivated activity is one in which the reinforcer for the activity consists of some type of additional consequence that is not inherent to the activity.

2. Running to lose weight is an example of an _____ motivated activity; running because it "feels good" is an example of an _____ motivated activity.

3. In their meta-analysis of relevant research, Cameron and Pierce (1994) found that extrinsic rewards decrease intrinsic motivation only when they are (expected/unexpected) _____, (tangible/verbal) _____, and given for (performing well/merely engaging in the behavior) _____.

4. They also found that extrinsic rewards generally increased intrinsic motivation when the rewards were (tangible/verbal) _____, and that tangible rewards increased intrinsic motivation when they were delivered contingent upon (high/low) _____ quality performance.

Shaping

What if the behavior that we wish to reinforce never occurs? For example, what if you want to reinforce a rat for pressing a lever but are unable to do so because the rat never presses the lever? What can you do? The solution is to use a procedure called shaping.

Shaping **is the gradual creation of new operant behavior through reinforcement of successive approximations to that behavior.** With our rat, we could begin by delivering food whenever it stands near the lever. As a result, it begins standing near the lever more often. We then deliver food only when it is facing the lever, at which point it starts engaging in that behavior more often. In similar manner, through this step-by-step process, we reinforce touching the lever, then placing a paw on the lever, and then pressing down on the lever. When the rat finally presses down on the lever with enough force, it will close the microswitch and activate the food magazine. The rat has now earned a reinforcer on its own. After a few more experiences like this, the rat will reliably press the lever whenever it is hungry. By reinforcing successive approximations to the target behavior, we have managed to teach the rat an entirely new behavior.

Another example: How do you teach a dog to catch a Frisbee? Many people simply throw the Frisbee at the dog, at which point the dog probably wonders what on earth has gotten into its owner as the Frisbee sails over its head. Or possibly the dog runs after the Frisbee, picks it up after it falls on the ground, and then makes the owner chase after him to get back the Frisbee. Karen Pryor (1999), a professional animal trainer, recommends the following procedure. First, reinforce the dog's behavior of taking the Frisbee from your hand and immediately returning it. Next, raise the criterion by holding the Frisbee in the air to make the dog jump for it. When this is well established, toss the Frisbee slightly so the dog jumps and catches it in midair. Then toss it a couple of feet so he has to run after it to catch it. Now gradually throw it further and further so the dog has to run farther and farther to get it. Remember to provide lots of praise each time the dog catches the Frisbee and returns it.

Shaping is a basic method for training animals to perform tricks. During such training, the trainers often use a sound, such as a click from a handheld clicker, to reinforce the behavior. The sound has been repeatedly paired with food so that it has become a secondary reinforcer. The benefit of using a sound as a reinforcer is that it can be presented immediately upon the occurrence of the behavior, even if the animal is some distance away. Also, if food were presented each time the correct behavior occurred, the animal would quickly satiate, at which point the food would become ineffective as a reinforcer. By using a secondary reinforcer such as a click, with food delivered only intermittently, satiation will take longer to occur, thereby allowing for longer training sessions.

Most of our behaviors have, to some extent, been learned or modified through shaping. For example, when children first learn to eat with a knife and fork, parents might praise even very poor attempts. Over time, though, they expect better and better performance before offering praise. In a similar manner, with children, we gradually shape the behavior of dressing appropriately, speaking politely, and writing legibly. And shaping is not confined merely to childhood. All of us are in the position of receiving constant feedback about our performance—be it ironing clothes, cooking a meal, or slam-dunking a basketball—thus allowing us to continually modify our behaviors and improve our skills. In such circumstances, it is usually the natural consequences of the behavior—the extent to which we are successful or unsuccessful—that provide the necessary reinforcement for gradual modifications of the behav-

Shaping is the basic method for teaching animals to display unusual patterns of behavior.

ior. For further information on shaping as applied to both animals and humans, you might wish to obtain a copy of Karen Pryor's highly readable book, *Don't Shoot the Dog*. Pryor also has a website on "clicker training" (shaping through the use of clicks as secondary reinforcers) that can be accessed via the Internet (just search for "clicker training"). Clicker training has become increasingly popular with dog owners and is being used to shape behavior in everything from budgies to horses and even llamas and elephants. Interestingly, Pryor observes that many animals greatly enjoy the "game" of clicker training.

1. Shaping is the creation of _____ operant behavior through the reinforcement of s_____ a_____ to that behavior.

2. In clicker training with dogs, the click is a s_____ reinforcer that has been established by first pairing it with f_____.

3. The advantages of using the click as a reinforcer is that it can be delivered i_____. It also prevents the animal from becoming s_____.

QUICK QUIZ

ADVICE FOR THE LOVELORN

Dear Dr. Dee,

My boyfriend has a terrible tendency to boss me around. I have tried to counter this tendency by being especially nice to him, but the problem seems to be getting worse. He also refuses to discuss it or see a counselor. He says I am too sensitive and that I am making a mountain out a molehill. What should I do?

Just-about Had-enough

Dear Just-about,

You should first recognize that some people have a long history of being reinforced for being dominant or aggressive, and that it can sometimes be difficult to alter such tendencies. In fact, you might eventually have to bail out of this relationship, particularly in view of the fact that he refuses to discuss what seems to be an obvious problem.

Nevertheless, you might also wish to consider the possibility that you are inadvertently reinforcing his aggressiveness. Remember how, in the opening vignette to this chapter, the young woman reacted to her partner's angry demands by a show of affection. While this might reduce his anger in the short run, it might also reinforce his tendency to be aggressive. After all, not only was his anger effective in getting her to hurry up, it also resulted in a hug. The next time he wants her to hurry up and/or desires affection, what better way than to get angry?

As a first step, you might wish to take careful note of the situations in which your boyfriend becomes bossy. If it appears that you might be reinforcing his bossiness by being particularly nice to him when he acts that way, you could try offering him little or no attention when he behaves like that and lots of attention when he behaves more appropriately. Can this work? In her book *Don't Shoot the Dog*, Karen Pryor (1999) relates the following story about a woman who implemented just such a program:

> A young woman married a man who turned out to be very bossy and demanding. Worse yet, his father, who lived with them, was equally given to ordering his daughter-in-law about. It was the girl's mother who told me this story. On her first visit she was horrified at what her daughter was going through. "Don't worry, Mother," the daughter said. "Wait and see." The daughter formed the practice of responding minimally to commands and harsh remarks, while reinforcing with approval and affection any tendency by either man to be pleasant and thoughtful. In a year, she had turned them into decent human beings. Now they greet her with smiles when she comes home and leap up—both of them—to help with the groceries. (p. 30)

By reinforcing successive approximations toward decent behavior and not reinforcing bossy behavior (yet still responding minimally to their requests), this woman was apparently able to shape more appropriate behavior in her husband and father-in-law. Remember, though, such problems are often difficult to manage and may require professional help.

Behaviorally yours,

Dr. Dee

SUMMARY

In contrast to elicited behaviors that are automatically evoked by the stimuli that precede them, operant behaviors are controlled by their consequences. Thus, in operant (or instrumental) conditioning, the future probability of a response is affected by its consequence. Reinforcers are consequences that increase the probability of (or strengthen) a response, while punishers decrease the probability of (or weaken) a response. In positive reinforcement and positive punishment, the consequence involves the presentation of a stimulus, while in negative reinforcement and negative punishment, the consequence involves the removal of a stimulus.

When a behavior has been consistently reinforced or punished in the presence of certain stimuli, those stimuli will begin to influence the occurrence of the behavior. A discriminative stimulus is a stimulus in the presence of which a response has been reinforced and in the absence of which it has not been reinforced.

Immediate reinforcers have a much stronger effect on behavior than delayed reinforcers. Primary reinforcers are events that are innately reinforcing, while secondary reinforcers are events that become reinforcing because they have been associated with other reinforcers. A generalized secondary reinforcer is a secondary reinforcer that has been associated with many other reinforcers. Intrinsic reinforcement occurs when performing a behavior is inherently reinforcing; extrinsic reinforcement occurs when the effective reinforcer is some consequence that is external to the behavior.

Shaping is the creation of novel behavior through the reinforcement of gradual approximations to that behavior. Effective shaping is often carried out with the use of a secondary reinforcer, such as the sound of a whistle or click, that can be delivered immediately following the occurrence of the appropriate behavior.

STUDY QUESTIONS

1. State Thorndike's law of effect.
2. Define operant conditioning. Name the three components of an operant conditioning procedure.
3. Explain why operant behaviors are said to be emitted and why they are defined as a "class" of responses.
4. Define the terms *reinforcer* and *punisher*.
5. What is the difference between the terms *reinforcement* and *reinforcer?*
6. What is a discriminative stimulus? Define the three-term contingency and diagram an example.
7. Define positive reinforcement and diagram an example (include the appropriate symbols).

8. Define negative reinforcement and diagram an example (include the appropriate symbols).
9. Define positive punishment and diagram an example (include the appropriate symbols).
10. Define negative punishment and diagram an example (include the appropriate symbols).
11. How does negative reinforcement differ from positive punishment?
12. How does immediacy affect the strength of a reinforcer? How does this often lead to difficulties for students in their academic studies?
13. Distinguish between primary and secondary reinforcers.
14. What is a generalized secondary reinforcer? What are two examples of such reinforcers?
15. Define intrinsic and extrinsic reinforcement and provide an example of each.
16. Under what three conditions does extrinsic reinforcement undermine intrinsic interest?
17. Under what two conditions does extrinsic reinforcement enhance intrinsic interest?
18. Define shaping. What are two advantages of using a secondary reinforcer, such as a sound, as an aid to shaping?

CONCEPT REVIEW

avoidance behavior. Behavior that occurs before the aversive stimulus is presented and therefore prevents its delivery.

discriminative stimulus (S^D). A stimulus in the presence of which responses are reinforced and in the absence of which they are not reinforced.

discriminative stimulus for punishment. A stimulus that signals that a response will be punished.

escape behavior. A behavior that results in the termination of an aversive stimulus.

extrinsic reinforcement. The reinforcement provided by a consequence that is external to the behavior, that is, an extrinsic reinforcer.

generalized secondary reinforcer. A type of secondary reinforcer that has been associated with several other reinforcers.

intrinsic reinforcement. Reinforcement provided by the mere act of performing the behavior; the performance of the behavior is inherently reinforcing.

law of effect. As stated by Thorndike, the proposition that behaviors that lead to a satisfactory state of affairs are strengthened or "stamped in," while behaviors that lead to an unsatisfactory or annoying state of affairs are weakened or "stamped out."

negative punishment. The removal of a stimulus (one that is usually considered pleasant or rewarding) following a response, which then leads to a decrease in the future strength of that response.

negative reinforcement. The removal of a stimulus (one that is usually considered unpleasant or aversive) following a response, which then leads to an increase in the future strength of that response.

operant behavior. A class of emitted responses that result in certain consequences; these consequences, in turn, affect the future probability or strength of those responses.

operant conditioning. A type of learning in which the future probability of a behavior is affected by its consequences.

positive punishment. The presentation of a stimulus (one that is usually considered unpleasant or aversive) following a response, which then leads to a decrease in the future strength of that response.

positive reinforcement. The presentation of a stimulus (one that is usually considered pleasant or rewarding) following a response, which then leads to an increase in the future strength of that response.

primary reinforcer (or unconditioned reinforcer). An event that is innately reinforcing.

punisher. An event that (1) follows a behavior and (2) decreases the future probability of that behavior.

reinforcer. An event that (1) follows a behavior and (2) increases the future probability of that behavior.

secondary reinforcer (or conditioned reinforcer). An event that is reinforcing because it has been associated with some other reinforcer.

shaping. The gradual creation of new operant behavior through reinforcement of successive approximations to that behavior.

three-term contingency. The relationship between a discriminative stimulus, an operant behavior, and a reinforcer or punisher.

CHAPTER TEST

31. Shaping is (A) the reinforcement of a new operant behavior, (B) the gradual reinforcement of a new operant behavior, (C) the reinforcement of gradual approximations to a new operant behavior, (D) the creation of new operant behavior through successive approximations to reinforcement, (E) none of the preceding. _____

20. A positive reinforcer is a stimulus, (A) the presentation of which increases the strength of a response, (B) the presentation of which follows a response and increases the strength of that response, (C) the presentation of which decreases the strength of a response, (D) the presentation of which follows a response and decreases the strength of that response. _____

2. Elicited behaviors are controlled by the events that (precede/follow) _____ their occurrence, while operant behaviors are controlled by the events that (precede/follow) _____ their occurrence.

14. An easy way to remember the three-term contingency is that you _____ something, _____ something, and _____ something.

25. Behaviors that are performed for their own sake are said to be _____ motivated; behaviors that are performed in order to achieve some additional incentive are said to be _____ motivated.

11. Reinforcers and punishers are defined entirely by their _____ on behavior.

8. An event is a punisher if it _____ a behavior and the future probability of that behavior _____.

23. Money and praise are common examples of _____ _____ reinforcers.

12. If the rat does not press the lever, then it does not receive a shock. As a result, the rat is more likely not to press the lever. This is an example of (A) negative reinforcement, (B) negative punishment, (C) positive reinforcement, (D) positive punishment. _____ (*Think carefully about this question.*)

28. At the zoo one day, you notice that a zookeeper is leading a rhinoceros into a pen by simply whistling at it. It is probably the case that the whistle has been paired with _____ and is now functioning as a _____ _____.

1. Compared to elicited behaviors, operant behaviors seem (more/less) _____ automatic and reflexive.

15. The three-term contingency can be thought of as an ABC sequence in which A stands for _____, B stands for _____, and C stands for _____.

27. The gradual development of new operant behavior through reinforcement of _____ to that behavior is called _____.

6. Operant responses are sometimes simply called _____.

21. Each time a student studies at home, she is praised by her parents. As a result, she no longer studies at home. This is an example of what type of contingency? _____

17. When combined with the word *reinforcement* or *punishment*, the word *negative* indicates that the consequence consists of something being _____, while the word *positive* indicates that the consequence consists of something being _____.

10. The term *reinforcer* or *punisher* refers to the specific _____ that follows a behavior, while the term *reinforcement* or *punishment* refers to

the _____ or _____ whereby the probability of a behavior is altered by its consequences.

24. Sach very much enjoys hard work and often volunteers for projects that are quite demanding. According to _____ theory, it is likely the case that, for Sach, the act of expending a lot of effort has often been _____.

3. According to Thorndike's _____, behaviors that lead to a _____ state of affairs are strengthened, while behaviors that lead to an _____ state of affairs are weakened.

30. A generalized secondary reinforcer is one that has become a reinforcer because it has been associated with (A) a primary reinforcer, (B) a secondary reinforcer, (C) several secondary reinforcers, (D) several primary reinforcers, or (E) several reinforcers (either primary or secondary). _____

19. When Beth tried to take the bone away from her dog, Jack, Jack bared his teeth and growled threateningly. Beth quickly pulled her hand back. Jack growled even more threateningly the next time Beth reached for the bone, and she again pulled her hand away. Eventually, Beth gave up and she now lets Jack chew on bones for as long as he wants. Jack's behavior of baring his teeth and growling served to (positively/negatively) _____ (punish/reinforce) _____ Beth's behavior of trying to take the bone away from him. Beth's behavior of pulling her hand away served to _____ Jack's behavior of growling.

5. Operant behaviors are usually defined as a _____ of responses, all of which are capable of producing a certain _____.

16. A stimulus that signals that a response will be punished is called a _____ for punishment.

22. Events that are innately reinforcing are called _____ reinforcers; events that become reinforcers through experience are called _____ reinforcers.

9. A reinforcer is usually given the symbol _____, while a punisher is usually given the symbol _____. The operant response is given the symbol _____, while a discriminative stimulus is given the symbol _____.

26. Steven has fond memories of his mother reading fairy tales to him when he was a child, and as a result he now enjoys reading fairy tales as an adult. For Steven, the act of reading fairy tales is functioning as what type of reinforcer? (A) primary, (B) secondary, (C) intrinsic, (D) extrinsic, (E) both B and C. _____

4. Classically conditioned behaviors are said to be _____ by stimuli; operant behaviors are said to be _____ by the organism.

18. Referring to the opening vignette for this chapter, among the four types of contingencies described in this chapter, Sally's actions toward Joe probably best illustrate the process of _____.
In other words, Joe's abusive behavior will likely (increase/decrease) _____ in the future as a result of Sally's actions.

7. An event is a reinforcer if it _____ a behavior and the future probability of that behavior _____.

29. Major advantages of using the sound of a click for shaping are that the click can be delivered _____ and the animal is unlikely to _____ upon it.

13. A discriminative stimulus is a stimulus that signals that a _____ is available. It is said to "_____" for the behavior.

ANSWERS TO CHAPTER TEST

1. less
2. precede; follow
3. law of effect; satisfactory; unsatisfactory
4. elicited; emitted
5. class; consequence
6. operants
7. follows; increases
8. follows; decreases
9. S^R; S^P; R; S^D
10. consequence (event); process; procedure
11. effect
12. D (because "*lever press* → shock" is the effective contingency)
13. reinforcer; set the occasion
14. notice; do; get
15. antecedent; behavior; consequence
16. discriminative stimulus
17. removed (or subtracted); presented (or added)
18. positive reinforcement; increase
19. positively; punish; negatively reinforce
20. B
21. positive punishment
22. primary; secondary
23. generalized secondary (or generalized)
24. learned industriousness; positively reinforced
25. intrinsically; extrinsically
26. E
27. successive (or gradual) approximations; shaping
28. food; secondary reinforcer
29. immediately; satiate
30. E
31. C

Put Learning into Action with Sniffy, the Virtual Rat

The following material refers to *Sniffy, the Virtual Rat™: Pro Version*, a separate Wadsworth product that consists of a manual and a CD-ROM.

1. Read pp. 7–8 for more information on Thorndike and the Law of Effect.
2. Read pp. 8–11 for more information on B. F. Skinner and operant conditioning.
3. Read pp. 13–15 for more information on reinforcement and punishment.
4. Read pp. 31–34 (exercise 4) for more information on primary and secondary reinforcers. If you have a pet dog or cat, you may want to try training it to perform a trick using the principles outlined in exercise 4.
5. By now you should have already worked through exercise 2 (pp. 23–26), in which you shaped Sniffy to press a lever. However, you may want to reread the material in *Sniffy Pro* that deals with shaping and compare it to the information in the textbook.

CHAPTER 7

Operant Conditioning: Schedules and Theories of Reinforcement

CHAPTER OUTLINE

*Put Learning into Action
with Sniffy, the Virtual Rat*

"I don't understand why Alvin is so distant," Mandy commented. "He was great when we first started going out. Now it's like pulling teeth to get him to pay attention to me."

"So why do you put up with it?" her sister asked.

"I guess I'm in love with him. Why else would I be so persistent?"

Schedules of Reinforcement

In this section, we discuss schedules of reinforcement. **A *schedule of reinforcement* is the response requirement that must be met in order to obtain reinforcement.** In other words, a schedule indicates what exactly has to be done for the reinforcer to be delivered. For example, does each lever press by the rat result in a food pellet or are several lever presses required? Did your mom give you a cookie each time you asked for one or only some of the time? And just how persistent does Mandy have to be before Alvin will pay attention to her? As you will discover in this section, different response requirements can have dramatically different effects on behavior. And although many of these effects (known as *schedule effects*) were first observed in experiments with pigeons (Ferster & Skinner, 1957), they also help to explain some puzzling aspects of human behavior, aspects that are often attributed to internal traits or desires.

Continuous versus Intermittent Schedules

A *continuous reinforcement schedule* is one in which each specified response is reinforced. For example, each time a rat presses the lever, it obtains a food pellet; each time the dog rolls over on command, it gets a treat; and each time Karen turns the ignition in her car, the motor starts. Continuous reinforcement (abbreviated CRF) is very useful when a behavior is first being shaped or strengthened. For example, when shaping a rat to press a lever, reinforcement should be delivered for each approximation to the target behavior. Similarly, if we wish to encourage a child to always brush her teeth before bed, we would do well to initially praise her each time she does so.

An *intermittent (or partial) reinforcement schedule* is one in which only some responses are reinforced. For example, perhaps only some of the rat's lever presses result in a food pellet, and perhaps only occasionally did your mother give you a cookie when you asked for one. Intermittent reinforcement obviously characterizes much of everyday life. Not all concerts we attend are enjoyable, not every person we invite out on a date accepts, and not every date that we go out on leads to an enjoyable evening. And although we might initially praise a child each time she properly completes her homework, we might soon praise her only occasionally, in the belief that such behavior should persist in the absence of praise.

There are four basic types of intermittent schedules: fixed ratio, variable ratio, fixed interval, and variable interval. These are described below, along with the characteristic response pattern produced by each. Note that this characteristic response pattern is the stable pattern that emerges once the organism has had considerable exposure to the schedule. Such stable patterns are known as *steady-state behaviors*, in contrast to the more variable patterns of behavior that are evident when an organism is first exposed to a schedule.

1

1. A s_____ of reinforcement is the r_____ requirement that must be met in order to obtain reinforcement.

2. On a c_____ reinforcement schedule (abbreviated _____), each response is reinforced, while on an i_____ reinforcement schedule, only some responses are reinforced. The latter is also called a p_____ reinforcement schedule.

3. Each time you flick the light switch, the light comes on. The behavior of flicking the light switch is on a(n) _____ schedule of reinforcement.

4. When the weather is very cold, you are sometimes unable to start your car. The behavior of starting your car in very cold weather is on a(n) _____ schedule of reinforcement.

5. S_____ e_____ are the different effects on behavior produced by different schedules of reinforcement. These are the stable patterns of behavior that emerge once the organism has had sufficient exposure to the schedule. Such stable patterns are known as st_____-st_____ behaviors.

Four Basic Intermittent Schedules

Fixed Ratio Schedules   On a fixed ratio schedule, reinforcement is contingent upon a fixed, predictable number of responses. For example, on a fixed ratio 5 schedule (abbreviated FR 5), a rat has to press the lever 5 times to obtain a food pellet. On an FR 50 schedule, it has to press the lever 50 times to obtain a food pellet. Similarly, earning a dollar for every 10 carburetors assembled on an assembly line is an example of an FR 10 schedule, while earning a dollar for each carburetor assembled is an example of an FR 1 schedule. Note that an FR 1 schedule is the same as a CRF (continuous reinforcement) schedule in which each response is reinforced (thus, such a schedule can be correctly labeled as either an FR 1 or a CRF).

FR schedules generally produce a high rate of response along with a short pause following the attainment of each reinforcer (see Figure 7.1). This short pause is known as a *post-reinforcement pause*. For example, a rat on an FR 25 schedule will rapidly emit 25 lever presses, munch down the food pellet it receives, and then snoop around the chamber for a few seconds before rapidly emitting another 25 lever presses. In other words, it will take a short break following each reinforcer, just as you might take a short break after reading each chapter in a

FIGURE 7.1 Response patterns for FR, VR, FI, and VI schedules. This figure shows the characteristic pattern of responding on the four basic schedules. Note how there is a high response rate on the fixed and variable-ratio schedules, a moderate response rate on the variable-interval schedule, and a scalloped response pattern on the fixed interval schedule. Also, both the fixed ratio and fixed interval schedules are accompanied by post-reinforcement pauses. (*Source:* Modified from Nairne, 2000.)

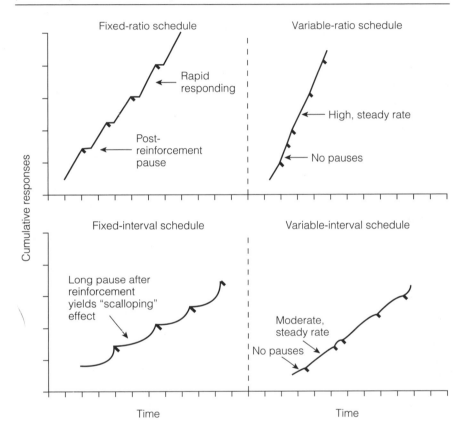

textbook or completing a particular assignment. Note too that each pause is followed by a quick return to a high rate of response. Thus, the typical FR pattern is described as a "break-and-run" pattern—a short break followed by a steady run of responses. Similarly, students sometimes find that when they finally sit down to start work on the next chapter or assignment, they quickly become involved in it. (Perhaps this is why just starting a task is often the most important step in overcoming procrastination; once you start, the work often flows naturally. For this reason, it is sometimes helpful to use certain tricks to get started, such as beginning with a short, easy task before progressing to a more difficult task. Alternatively, you might promise yourself that you will work for only 5 or 10 minutes and then quit for the evening if you really do not feel like carrying on. What often happens is that once the promised time period has passed, it is actually quite easy to carry on.)

In general, higher ratio requirements produce longer post-reinforcement pauses. This means that you will probably take a longer break after completing a long assignment than after completing a short one. Similarly, a rat will show longer pauses on an FR 100 schedule than on an FR 30 schedule. With very low ratios, such as FR 1 (CRF) or FR 2, there may be little or no pausing other than the time it takes for the rat to munch down the food pellet. In such cases, the next reinforcer is so close—only a few lever presses away—that the rat is tempted to immediately go back to work. (If only the reinforcers for studying were so immediate!)

Schedules in which the reinforcer is easily obtained are said to be very "dense" or "rich," while schedules in which the reinforcer is difficult to obtain are said to be very "lean." Thus, an FR 5 schedule is considered a very dense schedule of reinforcement compared to an FR 100. During a 1-hour session, a rat can earn many more food pellets on an FR 5 schedule than it can on an FR 100. Similarly, an assembly line worker who earns a dollar for each carburetor assembled (a CRF schedule) can earn considerably more during an 8-hour shift than a worker who earns a dollar for every 10 carburetors assembled (an FR 10 schedule).

In general, "stretching the ratio"—moving from a low ratio requirement (a dense schedule) to a high ratio requirement (a lean schedule)—should be done gradually. For example, once lever pressing is well established on a CRF schedule, the requirement can be gradually increased to FR 2, FR 5, FR 10, and so on. If the requirement is increased too quickly—for example, CRF to FR 2 and then a sudden jump to FR 20—the rat's behavior may become erratic and even die out altogether. Likewise, if you try to raise the requirement too high, say, to FR 2000, there may be a similar breakdown in the rat's behavior. Such breakdowns in behavior are technically known as *ratio strain*: **a disruption in responding due to an overly demanding response requirement.**

Ratio strain is what most people would refer to as burnout, and it can be a big problem for students faced with a heavy workload. Some students, especially those who have a history of getting by with minimal work, may find it increasingly difficult to study under such circumstances and may even choose to drop out of college. If they had instead experienced a gradual increase in workload over a period of several months or years, they might have been able to put forth the needed effort to succeed.

1. On a(n) _____ _____ schedule, reinforcement is contingent upon a fixed number of responses.

2. A schedule in which 15 responses are required for each reinforcer is abbreviated _____.

3. A mother finds that she always has to make the same request three times before her child complies. The mother's behavior of making requests is on an _____ schedule of reinforcement.

4. An FR 1 schedule of reinforcement can also be called a _____ schedule.

5. A fixed ratio schedule tends to produce a (high/low) _____ rate of response, along with a p_____-r_____ p_____.

6. An FR 200 schedule of reinforcement will result in a (longer/shorter) _____ pause than an FR 50 schedule.

7. The typical FR pattern is sometimes called a b_____-and-r_____ pattern, with a _____-_____ pause that is followed immediately by a (high/low) _____ rate of response.

8. An FR 12 schedule of reinforcement is more (dense/lean) _____ than an FR 100 schedule.

9. A very dense schedule of reinforcement can also be referred to as a very r_____ schedule.

10. Over a period of a few months, Billy changed from complying with each of his mother's requests to complying with every other request, then with every third request, and so on. The mother's behavior of making requests has been subjected to a procedure known as "s_____ the r_____."

11. Graduate students often have to complete an enormous amount of work in the initial year of their program. For some students, the workload involved is far beyond anything they have previously encountered. As a result, their study behavior may become increasingly (disrupted/stereotyped) _____ throughout the year, a process known as r_____ s_____.

Variable Ratio Schedules   On a *variable ratio schedule,* reinforcement is contingent upon a varying, unpredictable number of responses. For example, on a variable ratio 5 (VR 5) schedule, a rat has to emit an *average* of 5 lever presses for each food pellet, with the number of lever responses on any particular trial varying between, say, 1 and 10. Thus, the number of required lever presses might be 3 for the first pellet, 6 for the second pellet, 1 for the third pellet, 7 for the fourth pellet, and so on, with the overall average being 5 lever presses for each reinforcer. Similarly, on a VR 50 schedule, the number of required lever presses may vary between 1 and 100, with the average being 50.

VR schedules generally produce a high and steady rate of response with little or no post-reinforcement pause (see Figure 7.1). The lack of a post-reinforcement pause is understandable if you consider that each response on a VR schedule has the potential of resulting in a reinforcer. For example, on a VR 50 schedule in which the response requirement for each reinforcer varies between 1 and 100, it is possible that the very next lever press will produce another food pellet, even if the rat has just obtained a food pellet.

The real world is filled with examples of VR schedules. Some predatory behaviors, such as that shown by cheetahs, are on VR schedules in that only some attempts at chasing down prey are successful. In humans, only some acts

3

of politeness receive an acknowledgment, only some residents who are called upon by canvassers will make a contribution, and only some CDs that we buy are enjoyable. Many sports activities, such as shooting baskets in basketball and shots on goal in hockey, are also reinforced largely on a VR schedule. A colleague just stopped by and joked that his golf drive is probably on a VR 200 schedule. In other words, he figures that an average of about one in every 200 drives is a good one. I (Russ Powell) replied that my own drives are probably on a much leaner schedule with the result that ratio strain has set in, which is fancy behaviorist talk for "I so rarely hit the ball straight that I have just about given up playing."

Variable ratio schedules help to account for the persistence with which some people display certain maladaptive behaviors. Gambling is a prime example in this regard: The unpredictable nature of these activities results in a very high rate of behavior. In fact, the behavior of a gambler playing a slot machine is the classic example of a VR schedule in humans. Certain forms of aberrant social behavior may also be accounted for by VR schedules. For example, why do some men persist in using cute, flippant remarks to introduce themselves to women when the vast majority of women view such remarks negatively? One reason is that a small minority of women actually responds favorably, thereby intermittently reinforcing the use of such remarks. For example, Kleinke, Meeker, and Staneske (1986) found that although 84% of women surveyed rated the opening line "I'm easy. Are you?" as poor to terrible, 14% rated it as either very good or excellent!

Variable ratio schedules of reinforcement may also facilitate the development of an abusive relationship. At the start of a relationship, the individuals involved typically provide each other with an enormous amount of positive reinforcement (a very dense schedule). This strengthens the relationship and increases each partner's attraction to the other. As the relationship progresses, such reinforcement naturally becomes somewhat more intermittent. In some situations, however, this process becomes malignant, with one person (let us call this person the victimizer) providing reinforcement on an extremely intermittent basis, and the other person (the victim) working incredibly hard to obtain that reinforcement. Because the process evolves gradually (a process of slowly "stretching the ratio"), the victim may have little awareness of what is happening until the abusive pattern is well established. What would motivate such an unbalanced process? One source of motivation is that the less often the victimizer reinforces the victim, the more attention (reinforcement) he or she receives from the victim. In other words, the victim works so hard to get the partner's attention that he or she actually reinforces the very process of being largely ignored by that partner. Of course, it does not necessarily have to be a one-way process, and there may be relationships in which the partners alternate the role of victim and victimizer. The result may be a volatile relationship that both partners find exciting, but which is constantly on the verge of collapse due to frequent periods in which each partner experiences "ratio strain."

1. On a variable ratio schedule, reinforcement is contingent upon a _____ un_____ _____ of responses.

2. A variable ratio schedule typically produces a (high/low) _____ rate of behavior (with/without) _____ a post-reinforcement pause.

3. About one in ten people approached by a panhandler actually gives him money. His behavior of panhandling is on a _____ schedule of reinforcement.

4. As with an FR schedule, an extremely lean VR schedule can result in r_____ s_____.

Fixed Interval Schedules   On a *fixed interval schedule,* **reinforcement is contingent upon the first response after a fixed, predictable period of time.** For a rat on a fixed interval 30-second (FI 30-sec) schedule, the first lever press *after* a 30-second interval has elapsed results in a food pellet. Following that, another 30 seconds must elapse before a lever press will again produce a food pellet. Any lever pressing that occurs during the interval, before the 30-second period has elapsed, is ineffective. Similarly, trying to phone a friend who is due to arrive home in exactly 30 minutes will be effective only after the 30 minutes have elapsed, with any phone calls prior to that being ineffective.

FI schedules often produce a "scalloped" (upwardly curved) pattern of responding, consisting of a post-reinforcement pause followed by a gradually increasing rate of response as the interval draws to a close (see Figure 7.1). For example, a rat on an FI 30-sec schedule will likely emit no lever presses at the start of the 30-second interval. This will be followed by a few tentative lever presses, say, midway through the interval, with a gradually increasing rate of response thereafter. By the time the interval draws to a close and the reinforcer is imminent, the rat will be emitting a high rate of response, with the result that the reinforcer will be attained as soon as it becomes available.

Would the behavior of trying to phone someone who is due to arrive home in 30 minutes also follow a scalloped pattern? If we have a watch available, it probably would not. We would simply look at our watch to determine when the 30 minutes have elapsed and then make our phone call. The indicated time would be a discriminative stimulus (S^D) for when the reinforcer is available (i.e., the person is home), and we would wait until the appropriate time before phoning. But what about the behavior of looking at your watch during the 30 minutes (the reinforcer for which would be noticing that the interval has elapsed)? You are unlikely to spend much time looking at your watch at the start of the interval. As time progresses, however, you will begin looking at it more and more frequently. In other words, your behavior will follow the typical scalloped pattern of responding.

The distribution of study sessions throughout the term can also show characteristics of an FI scallop. At the start of a course, many students engage in little or no studying. This is followed by a gradual increase in studying as the first exam approaches. The completion of the exam is again followed by little or no studying until the next exam approaches. Unfortunately, these post-reinforcement pauses are often too long, with the result that many students obtain much poorer marks than they would have if they had studied at a steadier pace throughout. (Note, however, that studying for exams is not a pure example of an FI schedule insofar as a certain amount of work must be accomplished during the interval in order to obtain the reinforcer of a good mark. On a pure FI schedule, any responding that happens during the interval is essentially irrelevant.)

1. On a fixed interval schedule, reinforcement is contingent upon the _____ response following a _____, pr_____ period of _____.

2. If I have just missed the bus when I get to the bus stop, I know that I have to wait 15 minutes for the next one to come along. Given that it is absolutely freezing out, I snuggle into my parka as best I can and grimly wait out the interval. Every once in a while, though, I emerge from my cocoon to take a quick glance down the street to see if the bus is coming. My behavior of looking for the bus is on a(n) _____ (use the abbreviation) schedule of reinforcement.

3. In the above example, I will probably engage in (few/frequent) _____ glances at the start of the interval followed by a gradually (increasing/decreasing) _____ rate of glancing as time passes.

4. Responding on an FI schedule is often characterized by a sc_____ pattern of responding.

5. On a pure FI schedule, any response that occurs (during/following) _____ the interval is irrelevant.

Variable Interval Schedules On a *variable interval schedule*, reinforcement is contingent upon the first response after a varying, unpredictable period of time. For a rat on a variable interval 30-second (VI 30-sec) schedule, the first lever press after an *average* interval of 30 seconds will result in a food pellet, with the actual interval on any particular trial varying between, say, 1 and 60 seconds. Thus, the number of seconds that must pass before a lever press will produce a food pellet could be 8 seconds for the first food pellet, 55 seconds for the second pellet, 24 seconds for the third, and so on, the average of which is 30 seconds. Similarly, if each day you are waiting for a bus and have no idea when it will arrive, then looking down the street for the bus will be reinforced after a varying, unpredictable period of time, for example, 2 minutes the first day, 12 minutes the next day, 9 minutes the third day, and so on, with an average interval of, say, 10 minutes (VI 10-min).

VI schedules usually produce a moderate, steady rate of response with little or no post-reinforcement pause (see Figure 7.1). By responding at a relatively steady rate throughout the interval, the rat on a VI 30-sec schedule will attain the reinforcer almost as soon as it becomes available. Similarly, if you need to contact a friend about some emergency and know that she always arrives home sometime between 6:00 P.M. and 6:30 P.M., a good strategy would be to phone every few minutes throughout that time period. By doing so, you will almost certainly contact her within a few minutes of her arrival.

Because VI schedules produce such a steady pattern of behavior, they are often used to investigate other aspects of operant conditioning, such as those involving matters of choice between alternative sources of reinforcement. You will encounter examples of this when we discuss choice behavior in Chapter 10.

1. On a variable interval schedule, reinforcement is contingent upon the _____ response following a _____, un_____, period of _____.

2. You find that by frequently switching stations on your radio, you are able to hear your favorite song being played about once every 20 minutes. Your behavior of switching stations is thus being reinforced on a _____ schedule.

3. In general, variable interval schedules produce a (low/moderate/high) _____, (steady/fluctuating) _____ rate of response with little or no _____-_____ _____.

Comparing the Four Basic Schedules As you can see, the four basic schedules produce quite different patterns of behavior, which vary in both the rate of response and in the presence or absence of a post-reinforcement pause. These characteristics are summarized in Table 7.1.

As can be seen, ratio schedules (FR and VR) produce higher rates of response than interval schedules (FI and VI). This makes sense in that the reinforcer in such schedules is entirely "response contingent," that is, entirely dependent on the number of responses emitted. For this reason, a rat on a VR 100 schedule can double the number of food pellets earned in a 1-hour session by doubling its rate of lever pressing. Similarly, a door-to-door salesman can double the number of sales he makes during a day by doubling the

TABLE 7.1 Characteristic response rates and post-reinforcement pauses for each of the four basic intermittent schedules. Note that these are only general characteristics, which are not found under all circumstances. For example, an FR schedule with a very low response requirement, such as FR 2, is unlikely to produce a post-reinforcement pause. By contrast, an FR schedule with a very high response requirement, such as FR 2000, may result in ratio strain and a complete cessation of responding.

	FR	VR	FI	VI
Response Rate	High	High	Increasing	Moderate
Post-reinforcement Pause	Yes	No	Yes	No

number of customers he calls upon (given that he continues to give an adequate sales pitch to each customer). Compare this to an interval schedule in which reinforcement is mostly time contingent. For example, on an FI 1-min schedule, no more than 50 reinforcers can be earned in a 50-minute session. Under such circumstances, responding at a high rate throughout each interval does not pay off and is essentially a waste of energy. Instead, it makes more sense to respond in a way that will maximize the possibility of attaining the reinforcer soon after it becomes available. On an FI schedule, this means responding at a gradually increasing rate as the interval draws to a close; on a VI schedule, this means responding at a moderate, steady pace throughout the interval.

It can also be seen that fixed schedules (FR and FI) tend to produce post-reinforcement pauses, while variable schedules (VR and VI) do not. On a variable schedule, there is always the possibility of a relatively immediate reinforcer, even if one has just attained a reinforcer, which tempts the organism to continue responding. By comparison, on a fixed schedule, the attainment of one reinforcer means that the next reinforcer is necessarily some distance away. On an FR schedule, this results in a short post-reinforcement pause before grinding out another set of responses; on an FI schedule, the post-reinforcement pause is followed by a gradually increasing rate of response as the interval draws to a close and the reinforcer becomes imminent.

6

QUICK QUIZ

1. In general, (ratio/interval) _____ schedules tend to produce a high rate of response. This is because the reinforcer in such schedules is entirely r_____ contingent, meaning that the rapidity with which responses are emitted (does/does not) _____ greatly affect how soon the reinforcer is obtained.

2. On _____ schedules, the reinforcer is largely time contingent, meaning that the rapidity with which responses are emitted has (little/considerable) _____ effect upon the speed with which the reinforcer is obtained.

3. In general, (variable/fixed) _____ schedules produce little or no post-reinforcement pausing. This is because such schedules provide the possibility of relatively i_____ reinforcement, even if one has just obtained a reinforcer.

4. In general, _____ schedules produce post-reinforcement pauses. This is because obtaining one reinforcer means that the next reinforcer is necessarily quite (distant/close) _____.

Other Simple Schedules of Reinforcement

Response–Rate Schedules   As we have seen, different types of intermittent schedules produce different rates of response. These different rates are essentially by-products of the schedule. However, in a ***response-rate schedule,*** re-

Which of these workers is on a pure ratio schedule of reinforcement?

DILBERT reprinted by permission of United Feature Syndicate, Inc.

inforcement is directly contingent upon the organism's rate of response. Below, we examine three types of response-rate schedules.

In *differential reinforcement of high rates* (DRH), reinforcement is contingent upon emitting *at least* a certain number of responses in a certain period of time—or, more generally, reinforcement is provided for responding at a fast rate. The term *differential reinforcement* means simply that one type of response is reinforced while another is not. In a DRH schedule, reinforcement is provided for a high rate of response and not a low rate. For example, a rat might receive a food pellet only if it emits at least 30 lever presses within a period of a minute. Similarly, a worker on an assembly line may be told that she can keep her job only if she assembles a minimum of 20 carburetors per hour. By requiring so many responses in a short period of time, DRH schedules ensure a high rate of responding. Athletic events such as running and swimming are prime examples of DRH schedules in that winning is directly contingent on a very rapid series of responses.

In *differential reinforcement of low rates* (DRL), a minimum amount of time must pass between each response before the reinforcer will be delivered—or, more generally, reinforcement is provided for responding at a slow rate. For example, a rat might receive a food pellet only if it waits at least 10 seconds between lever presses. So how is this different from an FI 10-sec schedule? Remember that on an FI schedule, responses that occur during the interval have no effect; on a DRL schedule, however, responses that occur during the interval do have an effect—an adverse effect in that they *prevent* reinforcement from occurring. In other words, responding during the interval must *not* occur in order for a response following the interval to produce a reinforcer.

Human examples of DRL schedules consist of situations in which a person is required to perform some action slowly. For example, a parent might praise a child for brushing her teeth slowly or completing her homework slowly, given that going too fast generally results in sloppy performance. Once the quality of performance improves, reinforcement can then be made contingent on responding at a normal speed.

In *differential reinforcement of paced responding* (DRP), reinforcement is contingent upon emitting a series of responses at a set rate—or, more generally, reinforcement is provided for responding neither too fast nor too slow. For example, a rat might receive a food pellet if it emits 10 consecutive responses, with each response separated by an interval of no less than 1.5 and no more than 2.5 seconds. Similarly, musical activities, such as playing in a band or dancing to music, require that the relevant actions be performed at a specific pace. People who are very good at this are said to have a good sense of timing or rhythm. Further examples of DRP schedules can be found in noncompetitive swimming or running. People often perform these activities at a pace that is fast enough to ensure benefits to health and a feeling of well-being, yet not so fast as to result in overexhaustion and possible injury. In fact, even competitive swimmers and runners, especially athletes who compete over long distances, will often set a specific pace throughout much of the race. This will ensure that they have sufficient energy at the end for a last-minute sprint (DRH) to the finish line, thereby maximizing their chances of clocking a good time.

QUICK QUIZ

1. In practicing the slow-motion form of exercise known as tai chi, Yang noticed that the more slowly he moved, the more thoroughly his muscles relaxed. This is an example of d_____ reinforcement of _____ behavior (abbreviated _____).

2. On a video game, the faster you destroy all the targets, the more bonus points you obtain. This is an example of _____ reinforcement of _____ _____ behavior (abbreviated _____).

3. Frank discovers that his golf shots are much more accurate when he swings the club with a nice, even rhythm that is neither too fast nor too slow. This is an example of _____ reinforcement of _____ behavior (abbreviated _____).

Noncontingent Schedules On a *noncontingent schedule of reinforcement,* the reinforcer is delivered *independently* of any response. In other words, a response is not required for the reinforcer to be obtained. Such schedules are also called *response-independent schedules.* There are two types of noncontingent schedules: fixed time and variable time.

On a *fixed time schedule,* the reinforcer is delivered following a fixed period of time, regardless of the organism's behavior. For example, on a fixed time 30-second (FT 30-sec) schedule, a pigeon receives access to food every 30 seconds regardless of its behavior. Likewise, many people receive Christmas gifts each year, independently of whether they have been naughty or nice—an FT 1-year schedule. FT schedules therefore involve the delivery of a "free" reinforcer following a predictable period of time.

On a *variable time schedule,* the reinforcer is delivered following a varying period of time, regardless of the organism's behavior. For example, on a variable time 30-second (VT 30-sec) schedule, a pigeon receives access to food after an average interval of 30 seconds, with the actual interval on any particular trial ranging from, say, 1 second to 60 seconds. Similarly, you may coincidentally run into an old high school chum about every 3 months on average (a VT 3-month schedule). VT schedules therefore involve the delivery of a free reinforcer following an unpredictable period of time. (Question: How do FT and VT schedules differ from FI and VI schedules?)

1. On a non_____ schedule of reinforcement, a response is not required to obtain a reinforcer. Such a schedule is also called a response i_____ schedule of reinforcement.

2. Every morning at 7:00 A.M., a robin perches outside Marilyn's bedroom window and begins singing. Given that Marilyn very much enjoys the robin's song, this is an example of a _____ _____ 24-hour schedule of reinforcement (abbreviated _____).

3. For farmers, rainfall is an example of a noncontingent reinforcer that is typically delivered on a _____ _____ schedule (abbreviated _____).

Noncontingent reinforcement may account for some forms of superstitious behavior. In the first investigation of this possibility, Skinner (1948b) presented pigeons with food every 15 seconds (FT 15-sec) regardless of their behavior. Although you might think that such free reinforcers would have little effect on the pigeons' behavior (other than encouraging them to stay close to the feeder), quite the opposite occurred. Six of the eight pigeons began to display ritualistic patterns of behavior. For example, one bird began turning counterclockwise circles, while another repeatedly thrust its head into an upper corner of the chamber. Two other pigeons displayed a swaying pendulum motion of the head and body. Skinner believed these behaviors evolved because they had been accidentally reinforced by the coincidental presentation of food. For example, if a pigeon just happened to turn a counterclockwise circle prior to food delivery, that behavior would be accidentally reinforced and increase in frequency. This would increase the likelihood of the same behavior occurring the next time food was delivered, which would further strengthen it. The eventual result would be a well-established pattern of turning circles, as though turning circles somehow caused the food to appear.

Subsequent research has shown that Skinner's evidence for superstitious behavior in the pigeon may not be as clear-cut as he believed. At least some of the ritualistic behaviors he observed may have consisted of innate tendencies, almost like fidgeting behaviors, that are often elicited during a period of waiting (Staddon & Simmelhag, 1971). These tendencies, which are discussed in Chapter 11, are known as *adjunctive behaviors*. Nevertheless, other experiments have replicated the effect of noncontingent reinforcement on the development of superstitious behavior. Ono (1987), for example, placed students in a booth that contained three levers and a counter. The students were told that "if you do something, you may get points on the counter" (p. 263). They were also told to get as many points as possible. In reality, the points were delivered on either an FT or VT schedule, so the students' behavior actually had no effect on point delivery. Nevertheless, most students developed at least temporary patterns of superstitious lever pulling, that is, they pulled the lever as though it were effective in producing points. Interestingly, one student started with lever pulling but then coincidentally received a point after simply touching the counter. This led to a superstitious pattern of climbing on the counter and touching different parts of the apparatus, apparently in the belief that this action produced the points. She then jumped off the apparatus at just the time that she received another point, which led to a superstitious pattern of repeatedly jumping in the air and touching the ceiling! After several minutes of this, she finally quit, apparently as a result of fatigue.

Professional athletes and gamblers are particularly prone to the development of superstitions, some of which may evolve in the manner that Skinner suggests. Under constant threat of losing their position to an eager newcomer, professional athletes are constantly on the lookout for anything that might enhance their performance. As a result, unusual events that precede a fine performance, such as humming a certain tune or wearing an unusual article of clothing, may be quickly identified and then deliberately reproduced in the hopes of reproducing that performance. Gamblers display even stronger tendencies toward the development of superstitions, probably because the activity in which they are engaged is even more uncertain in its outcome. Bingo players, for example, commonly carry lucky pendants, stuffed animals, or pieces of jewelry to each game, and they are often adamant (almost pathologically so) about obtaining cards that contain certain patterns or are drawn from the top or bottom of the stack. Many of these rituals probably evolved because they were at one time associated with a big win.

Herrnstein (1966) noted that superstitious behaviors can sometimes develop as byproducts of contingent reinforcement for some other behavior. For example, a businessman might believe that it is important to impress customers with a firm handshake, when in fact it is merely the handshake, and not the firmness of the handshake, that is the critical factor. (Unfortunately, such a superstition could have serious consequences if the businessman then attempts to branch out into the Asian market, since a firm handshake is regarded by many Asians as a sign of disrespect.) Similarly, some managers might come to believe that "pushing the panic button" is an effective way to deal with crises, simply because it is usually followed by a successful outcome. What they fail to realize is that a low-key approach might have been equally if not more effective—and certainly a lot less stressful.

QUICK QUIZ

1. When noncontingent reinforcement happens to follow a particular behavior, that behavior may (increase/decrease) _____ in strength. Such behavior is referred to as s_____ behavior.

2. Herrnstein (1966) noted that superstitious behaviors can sometimes develop as a by-product of c_____ reinforcement for some other behavior.

What happens if a noncontingent schedule of reinforcement is superimposed on a regular, contingent schedule of reinforcement? What if, for example, a pigeon responding on a VI schedule of food reinforcement also receives extra reinforcers for free. Will the pigeon's rate of response on the VI schedule increase or decrease? In fact, the pigeon's rate of response on the response-dependent schedule will decrease (Rachlin & Baum, 1972). Just as people on welfare sometimes become less inclined to look for work, the pigeon that receives free reinforcers will work less vigorously for the contingent reinforcers. Evidence of this can also be found among professional athletes. One study, conducted several years ago, found that major-league pitchers who had signed long-term contracts showed a significant decline in number of innings pitched relative to pitchers who only signed a one-year contract (O'Brien, Figlerski, Howard, & Caggiano, 1981; see Figure 7.2). Insofar as a long-term contract virtually guarantees a hefty salary regardless of performance, these results suggest that athletic performance may suffer when the money earned is no longer contingent on performance. (Question: Can you think of some alternative explanations for this finding?)

FIGURE 7.2 Average number of innings pitched by major league pitchers in the years before and after signing long-term contracts. (*Source:* Coon, 1998. Data from O'Brien et al., 1981.)

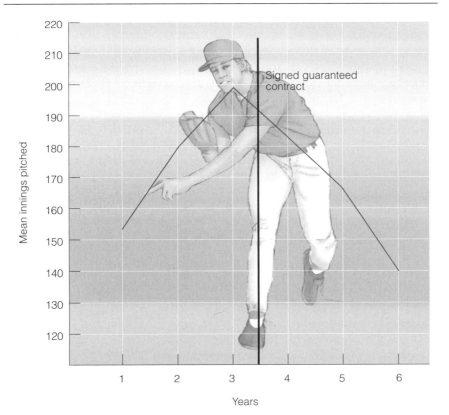

Years

At this point, you might be thinking that noncontingent reinforcement is all bad, given that it leads to superstitious behavior in some situations and to poor performance in others. In fact, noncontingent reinforcement is sometimes quite beneficial. More specifically, it can be an effective means of reducing the frequency of maladaptive behaviors. For example, children who act out often do so to obtain attention. If, however, they are given a sufficient amount of attention on a noncontingent basis, they will no longer have to act out to obtain it. Noncontingent reinforcement has even been shown to reduce the frequency of self-injurious behavior. Such behavior, which can consist of head banging or biting chunks of flesh out of one's arm, is sometimes displayed by people who suffer from retardation or autism; it can be notoriously difficult to treat. In many cases, the behavior appears to be maintained by the attention it elicits from caretakers. Research has shown, however, that if the caretakers provide the individual with plenty of attention on a noncontingent basis, then the frequency of their self-injurious behavior may be greatly reduced (e.g., Hagopian, Fisher, & Legacy, 1994). In a sense, such individuals no longer have to injure themselves to receive attention, because they are now receiving lots of attention for free.

Interestingly, the beneficial effects of noncontingent reinforcement can be seen as providing empirical support for the value of what Carl Rogers (1959), the famous humanistic psychologist, called "unconditional positive regard." Unconditional positive regard refers to the love, respect, and acceptance that one receives from significant others, regardless of one's behavior. Rogers assumed that such regard is a necessary precondition for the development of a healthy personality. From a behavioral perspective, unconditional positive regard can be viewed as a form of noncontingent social reinforcement, which can indeed have beneficial effects. In fact, it seems likely that proper child-rearing requires healthy doses of both noncontingent reinforcement, thereby giving the child a secure base from which to explore the world and take risks, and contingent reinforcement, which helps to shape the child's behavior in appropriate ways, maximize skill development, and prevent the development of passivity. Thus, Abraham Maslow (1971), another famous humanistic psychologist, argued that child-rearing should be neither too restrictive nor too lenient, which in behavioral terms can be taken to imply that the social reinforcement children receive should be neither excessively contingent nor excessively noncontingent.

1. During the time that a rat is responding for food on a VR 100 schedule, we begin delivering additional food on a VT 60-sec schedule. As a result, rate of response on the VR schedule is likely to (increase/decrease/remain unchanged) _____.

2. In modern-day boxing matches, boxers typically receive a guaranteed purse, regardless of the outcome. Compared to the old days in which more money was paid to the winner of the match, we would expect modern-day boxers to fight (more/less) _____ intensively to win.

3. A child who is often hugged during the course of the day, regardless of what he is doing, is in humanistic terms receiving unconditional positive regard. In behavioral terms, he is receiving a form of non_____ social reinforcement. As a result, this child may be (more/less) _____ likely to act out in order to receive attention.

Chained Schedules

A *chained schedule* **consists of a sequence of two or more simple schedules, each of which has its own S^D and the last of which results in a terminal reinforcer.** In other words, the person or animal must work through a series of component schedules to obtain the sought-after reinforcer. Chained schedules can involve two types of chains: homogeneous chains and heterogeneous chains.

In a *homogeneous chain,* **the same type of response is required in each component of the chain.** For example, a pigeon in a standard operant conditioning chamber might first be presented with a VR 20 schedule on a green key, followed by an FI 10-sec schedule on a red key, which then leads to the terminal reinforcer of food. Thus, an average of 20 responses on the green key will result in a change in key color to red, following which the first response on the red key after a 10-second interval will be reinforced by food. The food is the terminal reinforcer that supports the entire chain. This chain can be diagrammed as follows:

$$\begin{array}{ccc} \textbf{VR 20} & & \textbf{FI 10-sec} \\ \textbf{Green key: } \textit{Peck} & \rightarrow \textbf{Red key: } \textit{Peck} & \rightarrow \textbf{Food} \\ \text{S}^D \quad\quad \text{R} & \text{S}^R/\text{S}^D \quad\quad \text{R} & \text{S}^R \end{array}$$

Note that the presentation of the red key is both a secondary reinforcer for completing the preceding VR 20 schedule and an S^D for responding on the subsequent FI 10-sec schedule. Note too that this is an example of a *two-link chain,* with the VR 20 schedule constituting the first, or initial, link and the FI 10-sec schedule constituting the second, or terminal, link. By adding yet another schedule to the start of the chain, we can create a three-link chain, for example:

$$\begin{array}{cccc} \textbf{VI 30-sec} & & \textbf{VR 20} & & \textbf{FI 10-sec} \\ \textbf{White key: } \textit{Peck} & \rightarrow \textbf{Green key: } \textit{Peck} & \rightarrow \textbf{Red key: } \textit{Peck} & \rightarrow \textbf{Food} \\ \text{S}^D \quad\quad \text{R} & \text{S}^R/\text{S}^D \quad\quad \text{R} & \text{S}^R/\text{S}^D \quad\quad \text{R} & \text{S}^R \end{array}$$

In this case, both the green and red keys function as secondary reinforcers that help maintain behavior throughout the chain.

1. A chained schedule consists of a sequence of two or more simple schedules, each of which has its own _____ and the last of which results in a t_____ r_____.

2. A rat pressing a lever on a series of different schedules in order to obtain a terminal reinforcer of food is an example of a(n) _____ chain.

3. Within a chain, completion of each of the early links ends in a(n) _____ reinforcer, which also functions as the _____ for the next link of the chain.

Once pigeons learn which schedule is associated with which key, they generally show the appropriate response patterns for those schedules. In the preceding example, this would be a moderate, steady rate of response on the white key, a high rate of response on the green key, and a scalloped pattern of responding on the red key. Nevertheless, responding tends to be somewhat weaker in the earlier links of a chain than in the later links. This can be seen most clearly when each link consists of the same schedule. For example, Kelleher and Fry (1962) presented pigeons with a three-link chained schedule with each link consisting of an FI 60-sec schedule:

$$\begin{array}{ccccc}
\textbf{FI 60-sec} & & \textbf{FI 60-sec} & & \textbf{FI 60-sec} \\
\textbf{White key: } Peck & \rightarrow & \textbf{Green key: } Peck & \rightarrow & \textbf{Red key: } Peck & \rightarrow & \textbf{Food} \\
S^D \quad R & & S^R/S^D \quad R & & S^R/S^D \quad R & & S^R
\end{array}$$

The pigeons displayed very long pauses and a slow rate of response on the white key compared to the other two keys. The greatest amount of responding occurred on the red key.

Why would the earlier links of the chain be associated with weaker responding? One way of looking at it is that in the later links, the terminal reinforcer is more immediate and hence more influential, while in the early links, the terminal reinforcer is more distant and hence less influential (remember that delayed reinforcement is less effective than immediate reinforcement). Another way of looking at it is that the secondary reinforcers that support behavior in the early links are less directly associated with food and are therefore relatively weak (e.g., the green key is associated with food only indirectly through its association with the red key). From this perspective, a chained schedule can be seen as the operant equivalent of higher-order classical conditioning, in which, for example, a tone (CS_1) associated with food (US) elicits less salivation than the food, and a light (CS_2) associated with the tone elicits less salivation than the tone. Similarly, in the above chained schedule, the red key associated with the food is a less powerful reinforcer than the food, and the green key associated with the red key is a less powerful reinforcer than the red key. (If you find that you can no longer remember higher-order classical conditioning, you should go back and review it.)

The difference in response strength between the early and later links in a chain is representative of a more general behavioral principle known as the goal gradient effect. **The *goal gradient effect* is an increase in the strength and/or efficiency of responding as one draws near to the goal.** For example, rats running through a maze to obtain food tend to run faster and make fewer wrong turns as they near the goal box (Hull, 1932). Similarly, a student writing an essay is likely to take shorter breaks and work more intensely as she nears the end. (Perhaps the most profound example of a goal gradient, however, is that shown by people who desperately need to urinate and become speed demons as they near the washroom.)

An efficient way to establish responding on a chained schedule is to train the final link first and the initial link last, a process known as *backward chain-*

ing. In the above example, the pigeon would first be trained to respond on the red key to obtain food. This will establish the red key as a secondary reinforcer through its association with food. As a result, the presentation of the red key can then be used to reinforce responding on the green key. Once this is established, the presentation of the green key can be used to reinforce responding on the white key.

Although homogeneous chains are of considerable interest to researchers, they are not a common aspect of everyday life. More common in everyday life is a heterogeneous chain. **In a *heterogeneous chain*, a different type of response is required in each component of the chain.** For example, a rat might have to climb over a barrier and then run through a tunnel to obtain food. This can be diagrammed as follows:

$$\text{CRF} \qquad\qquad\qquad \text{CRF}$$
Barrier: *Climb over barrier* $\rightarrow$ **Tunnel:** *Run through tunnel* $\rightarrow$ **Food**
$$S^D \qquad\qquad R \qquad\qquad S^R/S^D \qquad\qquad R \qquad\qquad S^R$$

Note that the sight of the tunnel is both a secondary reinforcer for climbing over the barrier and a discriminative stimulus for then running through the tunnel. Also, in this particular example, each behavior has to be emitted only once and is thus on a CRF schedule of reinforcement.

As with homogeneous chains, backward chaining is often the best way to train a heterogeneous chain. In the above example, the rat would first be trained to run through the tunnel for food. Once this is established, it would be taught to climb over the barrier to get to the tunnel, with the sight of the tunnel acting as a secondary reinforcer for this action. In this manner, very long chains of behavior can be established. In one reported example, a rat was trained to go up a ladder, cross a platform, climb a rope, cross a bridge, get into a little elevator box, release the pulley holding the box, lower the box "paw over paw" to the floor, and then press a button to obtain the food (Pryor, 1975). Of course, each of these behaviors also had to be shaped (through reinforcement of successive approximations to the target behavior). Shaping and chaining are thus the basic means by which circus and marine animals are trained to perform some remarkable feats (see Figure 7.3).

Most human endeavors involve response chains, some of which are very long. The act of reading this chapter, for example, consists of reading section after section, until the terminal reinforcer of completing the entire chapter has been attained. The completion of each section serves as both a secondary reinforcer for having read that section as well as an S^D for reading the next section. Reading the chapter is in turn part of a much larger chain of behaviors that includes attending lectures, taking notes, and studying, the terminal reinforcer for which is passing the course. Fortunately, backward chaining is not required for the development of such chains, since language enables us to describe to one another the required sequence of behaviors (as in a course syllabus). In other words, for humans, response chains are often established through instructions.

FIGURE 7.3 Through shaping and chaining, animals can be taught to display some remarkable behaviors.

Unfortunately, in the case of very long chains, such as completing a course, the terminal reinforcer is often extremely distant, with the result that behavior is often easily disrupted during the early part of the chain (remember the goal gradient principle). It is much easier to be a diligent student the night before the midterm than during the first week of the semester. Can anything be done to alleviate this problem? One possibility is to make the completion of each link in the chain more salient (i.e., more noticeable), thereby enhancing its value as a secondary reinforcer. Novelists, for example, need to write hundreds, or even thousands, of pages before the terminal reinforcer of a completed book is attained. To keep themselves on track, some novelists keep detailed records of their progress, such as charting the number of words written each day as well as the exact dates on which chapters were started and completed (Wallace & Pear, 1977). These records outline their achievements, thereby providing a much-needed source of secondary reinforcement throughout the process. Similarly, students sometimes keep detailed records of the number of hours studied or pages read. They might also compile a "to do" list of assignments and then cross off each item as it is completed. Crossing off an item not only provides a clear record that the task has been accomplished, but the action may also function as a secondary reinforcer that helps maintain behavior (Lakein, 1973).

A chained schedule is a type of *complex schedule,* **which is a schedule that consists of a combination of two or more simple schedules.** There can be a wide variety of complex schedules. Two other types of complex schedules—multiple schedules and concurrent schedules—will be discussed in later chapters.

1. Responding tends to be weaker in the (earlier/later) _____ links of a chain. This is an example of the g_____ g_____ effect in which the strength and/or efficiency of responding (increases/decreases) _____ as the organism approaches the goal.

2. An efficient way to train a complex chain, especially in animals, is through b_____ chaining, in which the (first/last) _____ link of the chain is trained _____. However, this type of procedure usually is not required with verbally proficient humans, with whom behavior chains can be quickly established through the use of i_____.

3. One suggestion for enhancing our behavior in the early part of a long response chain is to make the completion of each link more s_____, thereby enhancing its value as a _____ reinforcer.

4. A complex schedule is one that consists of _____ _____.

Theories of Reinforcement

In this section, we will briefly discuss some major theories of reinforcement. We will begin with Clark Hull's early drive reduction view of reinforcement. This will be followed by a brief description of a highly influential approach known as the Premack principle. This principle is not only of immense practical importance, it has also helped revolutionize the manner in which the process of reinforcement is now conceptualized. In fact, the two other theoretical approaches that we will discuss, the response deprivation hypothesis and the bliss point approach, can be viewed as direct outgrowths of the Premack principle.

Drive Reduction Theory

An early approach to understanding reinforcement, and one that was strongly championed by Hull (1943), is *drive reduction theory*. According to this theory, **an event is reinforcing to the extent that it is associated with a reduction in some type of physiological drive.** Thus, food deprivation produces a "hunger drive," which then propels the animal to seek out food. When food is obtained, the hunger drive is reduced. At the same time, the behavior that preceded this drive reduction, and which led to the food, is automatically strengthened. In very simple terms (in actuality, the theory is more complex than this), if a hungry rat in a maze turns right just before it finds food in the goal box, the act of turning right in the maze will be automatically strengthened by the subsequent reduction in hunger.

We touched upon this theory in the previous chapter when we noted that primary reinforcers are often those events that seem to reduce a physiological need. From this perspective, secondary reinforcers are events that have become reinforcers because they have been indirectly associated with a primary reinforcer and, hence, with some type of drive reduction. Thus, a person enjoys collecting cookbooks because cooking is associated with eating food, which in turn has been associated with a reduction in hunger. Thus, according to Hull, all reinforcers are associated, either directly or indirectly, with some type of drive reduction.

In the previous chapter, we also noted that a major problem with this physiological view of reinforcement is that some reinforcers do not seem to be associated with any type of drive reduction. A rat will press a lever to obtain access to a running wheel, a chimpanzee will press a button so that it can obtain a peek into another room, and teenagers will spend considerable amounts of money to be exposed to ear-splitting, and potentially damaging, levels of rock music. It is difficult to see how such events are associated with a reduction in some type of physiological need. Instead, it seems as though the motivation for such behavior exists more in the reinforcing stimulus than in some type of internal state.

Motivation that is derived from some property of the reinforcer, as opposed to an internal drive state, is referred to as *incentive motivation.* Thus, playing a video game for the fun of it or attending a concert because you enjoy the music are examples of behavior that is motivated by incentive factors. Even events that seem to be clearly associated with drive reduction can be strongly affected by incentive factors. For example, going to a restaurant for a meal might be largely driven by hunger; however, the fact, that you prefer a restaurant that serves hot, spicy food is an example of incentive motivation. The spiciness of the food plays no role in the reduction of hunger; it is simply a form of sensory stimulation that you find highly reinforcing.

In conclusion, most theorists no longer believe that drive reduction theory can offer a comprehensive account of reinforcement, and this approach has now been largely abandoned. Some recent approaches have instead emphasized observable behavior patterns as opposed to hypothetical internal processes in their explanation of the reinforcement process. A major step in this direction was the Premack principle.

QUICK QUIZ

1. According to drive reduction theory, an event is reinforcing if it is associated with a reduction in some type of p_____ drive.

2. According to this theory, a secondary reinforcer is one that has been (indirectly/directly) _____ associated with _____ _____.

3. A major problem with drive reduction theory is that _____ _____.

4. The motivation that is derived from some property of the reinforcer is called _____ motivation.

5. Research has shown that hungry rats will perform more effectively in a T-maze when the reinforcer for a correct response (right turn versus left turn) consists of several small pellets as opposed to one large pellet (Capaldi, Miller, & Alptekin, 1989). Chickens will also run faster down a runway to obtain a popcorn kernel presented in four pieces than in one whole piece (Wolfe & Kaplon, 1941). The fact that several small bites of food is a more effective reinforcer than one large bite is consistent with the notion of (drive reduction/incentive motivation) _____.

The Premack Principle

Remember how we earlier noted that Skinner defined reinforcers (and punishers) by their effect on behavior. This unfortunately presents us with a problem. In the real world, it would be nice to know ahead of time whether a certain event can function as a reinforcer. One way to do this, of course, would be to take something the person or animal seems to like and use that as a reinforcer. But it is not always easy to determine what a person or animal likes. Moreover, events that we might believe should be liked might not actually function as reinforcers. To a 5-year-old boy, a kiss from his mother is great if he needs comforting, but not when he is trying to show off to his friends. Fortunately, the Premack principle provides a more objective way to determine if something can be used as a reinforcer (Premack, 1965).

The Premack principle is based on the notion that reinforcers can often be viewed as behaviors rather than stimuli. For example, rather than saying that lever pressing was reinforced by *food* (a stimulus), we could say that lever pressing was reinforced by the act of *eating food* (a behavior). Similarly, rather than saying that playing appropriately was reinforced by *television*, we could instead say that it was reinforced by *watching television*. When we view reinforcers in this manner—as behaviors rather than stimuli—then the process of reinforcement can be conceptualized as a sequence of two behaviors: (1) the behavior that is being reinforced, followed by (2) the behavior that is the reinforcer. Moreover, according to Premack, by comparing the frequency of various behaviors, we can determine if one can be used as a reinforcer for the other.

More specifically, **the *Premack principle* states that a high-probability behavior can be used to reinforce a low-probability behavior.** For example, when a rat is hungry, eating food has a higher likelihood of occurrence than running in a wheel. This means that eating food (the high-probability behavior [HPB]), can be used to reinforce the target behavior of running in a wheel (the low-probability behavior [LPB]). In other words, the rat will run in the wheel in order to obtain access to the food, thus:

Target behavior	Consequence
Running in a wheel (LPB) →	**Eating food** (HPB)
R	S^R

On the other hand, if the rat is not hungry, then eating food is less likely to occur than running in a wheel. In this case, running in a wheel can be used as a reinforcer for the target behavior of eating food. In other words, the rat will eat in order to obtain access to the wheel.

Target behavior   **Consequence**
Eating food (LPB) → **Running in a wheel** (HPB)
        R S^R

By focusing on the relative probabilities of behaviors, the Premack principle allows us to quickly identify potential reinforcers in the real world. If Sandra spends only a few minutes each morning doing chores, but at least an hour reading comic books, then the opportunity to read comic books (a higher-probability behavior) can be used to reinforce doing chores (a lower-probability behavior).

Do chores → **Read comic books**
      R S^R

In fact, if you want an easy way to remember the Premack principle, just think of Grandma's rule: First you work (a low-probability behavior), then you play (a high-probability behavior).

The Premack principle has proven to be very useful in applied settings. For example, a person with autism who spends many hours each day rocking back and forth might be very unresponsive to consequences that are normally reinforcing for others, such as receiving praise. The Premack principle, however, suggests that the opportunity to rock back and forth can be used as an effective reinforcer for whatever behavior we might wish to strengthen, such as interacting with others. (Then, once an appropriate level of interaction has been attained, we might find that the natural contingencies associated with the interaction take over such that social interaction will come to replace rocking as a major reinforcer in the person's life.) Thus, the Premack principle is a handy principle to keep in mind when confronted by a situation in which normal reinforcers seem to have little effect.

QUICK QUIZ

1. The Premack principle holds that reinforcers can often be viewed as _____ rather than stimuli. For example, rather than saying that the rat's lever pressing was reinforced with food, we could say that it was reinforced with _____ food.

2. The Premack principle states that a _____ _____ behavior can be used as a reinforcer for a _____ _____ behavior.

3. If you crack your knuckles 3 times per hour and burp 20 times per hour, then the opportunity to _____ can probably be used as a reinforcer for _____.

4. If you drink five soda pops each day and only one glass of orange juice, then the opportunity to drink _____ can likely be used as a reinforcer for drinking _____.

5. If the following is a diagram of a reinforcement procedure based on the Premack principle:

Chew bubble gum → Play video games

then chewing bubble gum must be a (lower/higher) _____ probability behavior than playing video games.

6. What is Grandma's rule and how does it relate to the Premack principle? _____
_____
_____
_____.

Response Deprivation Hypothesis

The Premack principle requires us to know the relative probabilities of two behaviors before we can judge whether one will be an effective reinforcer for the other. But what if we have information on only one behavior? Is there any way that we could still tell if that behavior can function as a reinforcer prior to actually trying it out?

The *response deprivation hypothesis* **states that a behavior can serve as a reinforcer when (1) access to the behavior is restricted and (2) its frequency thereby falls below its preferred level of occurrence** (Timberlake & Allison, 1974). The preferred level of an activity is its baseline level of occurrence when the animal can freely engage in that activity. For example, imagine that a rat typically runs for 1 hour a day whenever it has free access to a running wheel. This 1 hour per day is the rat's preferred level of running. If the rat is then allowed free access to the wheel for only 15 minutes per day, it will necessarily be unable to reach this preferred level and will be in a state of deprivation with regard to running. According to the response deprivation hypothesis, the rat will now be willing to work (e.g., press a lever) to obtain additional time on the wheel.

Lever press → **Running in a wheel**
　　R　　　　　　　　S^R

The response deprivation approach also provides a general explanation for why contingencies of reinforcement are effective. Contingencies of reinforcement are effective to the extent that they create a condition in which the organism is confronted with the possibility of a certain response falling below its baseline level. Take Sandra, who enjoys reading comic books each day. If we establish a contingency in which she has to do her chores before reading comic books, her baseline level of free comic book reading will drop to zero. She will therefore be willing to do chores to gain back her comic book time.

Do chores → **Read comic books**
　　R　　　　　　　S^R

You will notice that the diagram given here is the same as that given for the Premack principle. In this case, however, reading comic books is a reinforcer because the contingency pushes free comic book reading to below its preferred rate of occurrence. The relative probabilities of the two behaviors is irrelevant, meaning that it does not matter if the probability of reading comic books is higher or lower than the probability of doing chores. The only thing that matters is whether comic book reading is now in danger of falling below its preferred level. Thus, the response deprivation hypothesis is applicable to a wider range of conditions than the Premack principle. (Question 4 below will help clarify this.)

1. According to the response deprivation hypothesis, a response can serve as a reinforcer if free access to the response is (provided/restricted) _____ and its frequency then falls (above/below) _____ its baseline level of occurrence.

2. If a child normally watches 4 hours of television per night, we can make television watching a reinforcer if we restrict free access to the television to (more/less) _____ than 4 hours per night.

3. The response deprivation hypothesis differs from the Premack principle in that we need only know the baseline frequency of the (reinforced/reinforcing) _____ behavior.

4. Sandra typically watches television for 4 hours per day and reads comic books for 1 hour per day. You then set up a contingency whereby Sandra must watch 5 hours of television each day in order to have access to her comic books. According to the Premack principle, this will likely be an (effective/ineffective) _____ contingency. According to the response deprivation hypothesis, this will likely be an (effective/ineffective) _____ contingency.

Behavioral Bliss Point Approach

The response deprivation hypothesis assumes that there is an optimal level of behavior that an organism strives to maintain. This same assumption can be made for the manner in which an organism distributes its behavior between two or more activities. According to the *behavioral bliss point approach,* **an organism that has free access to alternative activities will distribute its behavior in such a way as to maximize overall reinforcement** (Allison, 1983). For example, a rat that can freely choose between running in a wheel and exploring a maze might spend 1 hour per day running in the wheel and 2 hours exploring the maze. This distribution of behavior represents the optimal reinforcement available from those two activities—that is, the behavioral bliss point—for that particular rat.

Note that this optimal distribution of behavior is based on the notion that each activity is freely available. When activities are not freely available—as when the two activities are intertwined in a contingency of reinforcement—

then the optimal distribution may become unattainable. Imagine, for example, that a contingency is created in which the rat now has to run in the wheel for 60 seconds to obtain 30 seconds of access to the maze:

Wheel running (60 seconds) → **Maze exploration (30 seconds)**
$\quad\quad$ R $\quad\quad\quad\quad\quad\quad\quad\quad\quad\quad$ S^{R}

It will now be impossible for the rat to reach its behavioral bliss point for these two activities. When freely available, the rat prefers twice as much maze exploration (2 hours) as wheel running (1 hour). But our contingency forces the rat to engage in twice as much wheel running as maze exploration. To obtain the preferred 2 hours of maze exploration, the rat would have to engage in 4 hours of running, which is far beyond its preferred level for that activity. Thus, it will be impossible for the rat to attain its behavioral bliss point for those activities.

A reasonable assumption as to what will happen in such circumstances is that the rat will compromise by distributing its activities in such a way as to draw as near as possible to its behavioral bliss point. For instance, it might choose to run a total of 2 hours per day to obtain 1 hour of maze exploration. This is not as enjoyable as the preferred distribution of 1 hour of running and 2 hours of maze exploration, but, given the contingencies, it will have to do. Likewise, most of us are forced to spend several more hours working and several fewer hours enjoying the finer things in life than we would if we were independently wealthy and could freely do whatever we wanted. The behavioral bliss point for our varied activities is essentially unattainable. Instead, faced with certain contingencies that must be met in order to survive, we distribute our activities in such a way as to draw as near to the bliss point as possible.

Note that the behavioral bliss point approach assumes that organisms attempt to distribute their behavior so as to maximize overall reinforcement. This of course is a very rational way to behave. In Chapter 10, you will encounter an alternative theory, known as melioration theory, which maintains that organisms, including people, are not that rational, and that various processes often entice the organism away from maximization.

1. According to the behavioral _____ _____ approach, an organism that (is forced to/can freely) _____ engage in alternative activities will distribute its behavior in such a way as to (optimize/balance) _____ the available reinforcement.

2. Contingencies of reinforcement often (disrupt/enhance) _____ the distribution of behavior such that it is (easy/impossible) _____ to obtain the optimal amount of reinforcement.

3. Given this state of affairs, how is the organism likely to distribute its activities? _____ _____ _____.

QUICK QUIZ

ADVICE FOR THE LOVELORN

Dear Dr. Dee,

I recently began dating a classmate. We get along really well at school, so it seemed like we would be a perfect match. Unfortunately, once we started dating, our relationship seemed to lose a lot of its energy, and our lives seemed a lot less satisfying. Someone suggested that we must each have an unconscious fear of commitment. What do you think?

Less Than Blissful

Dear Less,

I suppose it is possible that you have an unconscious fear of commitment—if there is such a thing as an unconscious fear of commitment. On the other hand, it may be that the amount of time you spend interacting with one another at school is actually the optimal amount of time, given the various reinforcers available in your relationship. Spending additional time together (which also means spending less time on alternative activities) has for each of you resulted in a distribution of behavior that is further removed from your behavioral bliss point. Obviously, a good relationship should move you toward your bliss point, not away from it. Try being just friends-at-school again, and see if that restores some of the satisfaction in your relationship.

Behaviorally yours,

Dr. Dee

SUMMARY

A schedule of reinforcement is the response requirement that must be met in order to obtain a reinforcer. Different types of schedules produce different patterns of responding, which are known as schedule effects.

In a continuous schedule of reinforcement, each response is reinforced. In an intermittent schedule of reinforcement, only some responses are reinforced. There are four basic intermittent schedules. On a fixed ratio schedule, a fixed number of responses is required for reinforcement, while on a variable ratio schedule, a varying number of responses is required. Both schedules produce a high rate of response, with the fixed ratio schedule also producing a post-reinforcement pause. On a fixed interval schedule, the first response after a fixed period of time is reinforced, while on a variable interval schedule, the first response after a varying period of time is reinforced. The former produces a scalloped pattern of responding, while the latter produces a moderate, steady rate of response.

Response-rate schedules specifically reinforce the organism's rate of response. For example, on a DRH schedule, reinforcement is contingent on a high rate of response, while on a DRL schedule, it is contingent on a low rate of response. On a DRP schedule, reinforcement is contingent on a particular rate of response, neither too fast nor too slow. By contrast, on a noncontingent schedule of reinforcement, the reinforcer is delivered following a certain period of time regardless of the organism's behavior. The time period can either be fixed (a fixed time schedule) or it can vary (a variable time schedule). Noncontingent schedules sometimes result in the development of superstitious behavior.

On a chained schedule, reinforcement is contingent upon meeting the requirements of two or more successive schedules, each with its own discriminative stimulus. In a homogeneous chain, the same type of behavior is required in each link of the chain, while in a heterogeneous chain, a different type of behavior is required. Responding tends to become stronger and/or more efficient toward the end of the chain, which is an instance of the goal gradient effect. Behavior chains are often best established by training the last link first and the first link last. Chained schedules are an example of a complex schedule that consists of two or more simple schedules.

According to drive reduction theory, an event is reinforcing if it is associated with a reduction in some type of internal physiological drive. However, some behaviors seem motivated more by the external consequence (known as incentive motivation) than an internal drive state. The Premack principle assumes that high-probability behaviors can be used as reinforcers for low-probability behaviors. The response deprivation hypothesis states that a behavior can be used as a reinforcer if access to the behavior is restricted so that its frequency falls below its baseline rate of occurrence. The behavioral bliss point approach assumes that organisms distribute their behavior in such a manner as to maximize their overall reinforcement.

STUDY QUESTIONS

1. What is a schedule of reinforcement?
2. Distinguish between continuous versus intermittent schedules of reinforcement.
3. Define fixed ratio schedule. Describe the typical pattern of responding produced by this schedule.
4. Define variable ratio schedule. Describe the typical pattern of responding produced by this schedule.
5. Define fixed interval schedule. Describe the typical pattern of responding produced by this schedule.
6. Define variable interval schedule. Describe the typical pattern of responding produced by this schedule.

7. Name three types of response rate schedules and provide an example of each.
8. Name and define the two types of noncontingent schedules.
9. What is a chained schedule? How does a homogeneous chain differ from a heterogeneous chain?
10. What type of reinforcement serves to maintain behavior throughout the early links in a chain? What is the best way to establish responding on a chained schedule in animals?
11. Define the goal gradient effect and give an example.
12. Describe the drive reduction theory of reinforcement. What is a major difficulty with this theory? What is incentive motivation?
13. Outline the Premack principle and give an example.
14. Outline the response deprivation hypothesis and give an example.
15. Describe the behavioral bliss point approach to reinforcement.

CONCEPT REVIEW

behavioral bliss point approach. The theory that an organism that has free access to alternative activities will distribute its behavior in such a way as to maximize overall reinforcement.

chained schedule. A schedule that consists of a sequence of two or more simple schedules, each of which has its own S^D and the last of which results in a terminal reinforcer.

complex schedule. A schedule that consists of a combination of two or more simple schedules.

continuous reinforcement schedule. A schedule in which each specified response is reinforced.

differential reinforcement of high rates (DRH). A schedule in which reinforcement is contingent upon emitting at least a certain number of responses in a certain period of time—or, more generally, reinforcement is provided for responding at a fast rate.

differential reinforcement of low rates (DRL). A schedule in which a minimum amount of time must pass between each response before the reinforcer will be delivered—or, more generally, reinforcement is provided for responding at a slow rate.

differential reinforcement of paced responding (DRP). A schedule in which reinforcement is contingent upon emitting a series of responses at a set rate—or, more generally, reinforcement is provided for responding neither too fast nor too slow.

drive reduction theory. According to this theory, an event is reinforcing to the extent that it is associated with a reduction in some type of physiological drive.

fixed interval schedule. A schedule in which reinforcement is contingent upon the first response after a fixed, predictable period of time.

fixed ratio schedule. A schedule in which reinforcement is contingent upon a fixed, predictable number of responses.

fixed time schedule. A schedule in which the reinforcer is delivered following a fixed period of time, regardless of the organism's behavior.

goal gradient effect. An increase in the strength and/or efficiency of responding as one draws near to the goal.

heterogeneous chain. A behavior chain in which a different type of response is required in each component of the chain.

homogeneous chain. A behavior chain in which the same type of response is required in each component of the chain.

incentive motivation. Motivation that is derived from some property of the reinforcer, as opposed to an internal drive state.

intermittent (or partial) reinforcement schedule. A schedule in which only some responses are reinforced.

noncontingent schedule of reinforcement. A schedule in which the reinforcer is delivered independently of any response.

Premack principle. The notion that a high-probability behavior can be used to reinforce a low-probability behavior.

ratio strain. A disruption in responding due to an overly demanding response requirement.

response deprivation hypothesis. The notion that a behavior can serve as a reinforcer when (1) access to the behavior is restricted and (2) its frequency thereby falls below its preferred level of occurrence.

response-rate schedule. A schedule in which reinforcement is directly contingent upon the organism's rate of response.

schedule of reinforcement. The response requirement that must be met in order to obtain reinforcement.

variable interval schedule. A schedule in which reinforcement is contingent upon the first response after a varying, unpredictable period of time.

variable ratio schedule. A schedule in which reinforcement is contingent upon a varying, unpredictable number of responses.

variable time schedule. A schedule in which the reinforcer is delivered following a varying period of time, regardless of the organism's behavior.

CHAPTER TEST

21. On a _____ schedule, reinforcement is contingent upon the first response *during* a varying period of time. (A) fixed interval, (B) variable time, (C) fixed time, (D) variable interval, (E) none of the preceding.

6. On a _____ schedule (abbreviated _____), reinforcement is contingent upon a fixed, predictable number of responses. This produces a _____ rate of response often accompanied by a _____.

17. On a (use the abbreviation) _____ schedule, a minimum amount of time must pass between each response before the reinforcer will be delivered. On a _____ schedule, reinforcement is contingent upon emitting at least a certain number of responses in a certain period of time. On a _____ schedule, reinforcement is contingent on emitting a series of responses at a specific rate.

10. If Jason is extremely persistent in asking Neem out for a date, she will occasionally accept his invitation. Of the four basic schedules, Jason's behavior of asking Neem for a date is most likely on a _____ _____ schedule of reinforcement.

8. On a _____ schedule, a response *must not occur* until 20 seconds have elapsed since the last reinforcer. (A) VI 20-sec, (B) VT 20-sec, (C) FT 20-sec, (D) FI 20-sec, (E) none of the preceding.

28. Post-reinforcement pauses are most likely to occur on which two types of simple intermittent schedules? _____

16. On _____ schedules, reinforcement is contingent upon the rate of response.

31. Shawna often goes for a walk through the woods, but she rarely does yard work. According to the _____, walking through the woods could be used as a _____ for yard work.

5. On a _____ schedule (abbreviated _____), reinforcement is contingent upon the first response after a fixed period of time. This produces a _____ pattern of responding.

13. A _____ schedule generally produces a high rate of response with a short pause following the attainment of each reinforcer. In general, the higher the requirement, the (longer/shorter) _____ the pause.

29. On a _____ schedule, a response cannot be reinforced until 20 seconds have elapsed since the last reinforcer. (A) VI 20-sec, (B) VT 20-sec, (C) FT 20-sec, (D) FI 20-sec, (E) none of the preceding.

3. If a dog receives a treat each time it begs for one, its begging is being maintained on a(n) _____ schedule of reinforcement. If it only sometimes receives a treat when it begs for one, its begging is being maintained on a(n) _____ schedule of reinforcement.

27. Dersu often carried a lucky charm with him when he went out hunting. This is because the appearance of game was often on a (use the abbreviation) _____ schedule of reinforcement.

32. Gina often goes for a walk through the woods, and even more often she does yard work. According to the _____, walking through the woods could still be used as a reinforcer for yard work given that one restricts the frequency of walking to _____ its _____ level.

26. On a fixed interval schedule, reinforcement is contingent upon the first response _____ a fixed period of time. (A) during, (B) prior to, (C) following, (D) none of the preceding.

9. Neem accepts Jason's invitation for a date only when she has "nothing better to do." Of the four basic intermittent schedules, Jason's behavior of asking Neem for a date is best described as being on a _____ schedule of reinforcement.

30. Drinking a soda to quench your thirst is an example of _____ reduction; drinking a soda because you love its tangy sweetness is an example of _____ motivation.

4. On a _____ schedule (abbreviated _____), reinforcement is contingent upon a varying, unpredictable number of responses. This produces a _____ rate of response.

24. A pigeon pecks a green key on a VI 60-sec schedule, which results in the insertion of a treadle into the chamber. The pigeon then steps on the treadle ten times following which it receives food. This is an example of a _____ chain.

11. Neem accepts Jason's invitation for a date only when he has just been paid his monthly salary. Of the four simple schedules, Jason's behavior of asking Neem for a date is on a _____ schedule of reinforcement.

25. Dagoni works for longer and longer periods of time and takes fewer and fewer breaks as his project nears completion. This is an example of the _____ effect.

18. On a _____ schedule of reinforcement, the reinforcer is delivered independently of any response.

7. On a _____ schedule (abbreviated _____), reinforcement is contingent upon the first response after a varying interval of time. This produces a _____ rate of response.

15. Gambling is often maintained by a _____ schedule of reinforcement.

20. On a _____ schedule (abbreviated _____), the reinforcer is delivered following a varying period of time. It differs from a VI schedule in that a response (is/is not) _____ required in order to obtain the reinforcer.

33. Anna ideally likes to exercise for 1 hour each morning, followed by a 30-minute sauna, in turn followed by a half hour of drinking coffee and reading the newspaper. Unfortunately, due to other commitments, she actually spends 45 minutes exercising, followed by a 15-minute sauna, and a half hour drinking coffee and reading the paper. According to the _____ approach, Anna's ideal schedule provides the _____ amount of overall reinforcement that can be obtained from those activities. Her actual distribution of behavior represents her attempt to draw as near to the _____ point as possible for these activities.

1. A _____ is the response requirement that must be met in order to obtain reinforcement.

22. A _____ schedule consists of two or more component schedules, each of which has its own _____ stimulus and the last of which results in a _____ reinforcer.

34. The abbreviation DRL refers to _____ reinforcement of _____ rate behavior.

14. As noted in the opening scenario to this chapter, Mandy found that she had to work harder and harder to entice Alvin to pay attention to her. It is quite likely that her behavior was on a _____ schedule of reinforcement. As a result, she began experiencing periods of time where she simply gave up and stopped trying. Eventually, she stopped seeing him altogether. When her sister asked why, Mandy, having just read this chapter, replied, "_____ _____."

2. Different response requirements have different effects on behavior. These effects are known as _____.

23. A pigeon pecks a green key on a VR 9 schedule, then a red key on an FI 20-sec, following which it receives food. This is an example of a _____ chain. The reinforcer for pecking the green key is the presentation of the _____, which is a _____ reinforcer.

12. Edy finds that he has to thump his television set twice before the picture will clear up. His behavior of thumping the television set is on a (be specific and use the abbreviation) _____ schedule of reinforcement.

19. On a _____ schedule (abbreviated _____), the reinforcer is delivered following a fixed interval of time, regardless of the organism's behavior.

ANSWERS TO CHAPTER TEST

1. schedule of reinforcement (reinforcement schedule)
2. schedule effects
3. continuous; intermittent
4. variable ratio; VR; high, steady
5. fixed interval; FI; scalloped
6. fixed ratio; FR; high; post-reinforcement pause
7. variable interval; VI; moderate, steady
8. E
9. variable interval
10. variable ratio
11. fixed interval
12. FR 2
13. fixed ratio; longer
14. variable ratio; ratio strain
15. variable ratio
16. response rate
17. DRL; DRH; DRP

18. noncontingent
19. fixed time; FT
20. variable time; VT; is not
21. E
22. chained; discriminative; terminal
23. homogeneous chain; red key; secondary
24. heterogeneous
25. goal gradient
26. C
27. VT
28. fixed interval and fixed ratio
29. D
30. drive; incentive
31. Premack principle; reinforcer
32. response deprivation hypothesis; below; baseline
33. behavioral bliss point; optimal (maximum); bliss
34. differential; low

Put Learning into Action with Sniffy, the Virtual Rat

The following material refers to *Sniffy, the Virtual Rat™: Pro Version*, a separate Wadsworth product that consists of a manual and a CD-ROM.

1. Read pp. 45–48 for more information on continuous (CRF) and partial reinforcement (FR, VR, FI, and VI) schedules.
2. See p. 50 for additional material on FR schedules, as well as a graphical representation of response rates on high and low ratio schedules.
3. See pp. 49–50 for more information on VR schedules.
4. See pp. 50–51 for more information on FI schedules.
5. If you have not already done so, read pp. 49–50 for more information on VI schedules.
6. Now that you have learned about the four different reinforcement schedules, it is time to test your knowledge with Sniffy. Make sure to read the section entitled "Setting Up a Schedule in the Design Operant Experiment Dialogue Box" (pp. 51–52) carefully, then work your way through exercises 8–12 (pp. 52–58).

   When shaping Sniffy from a lower to a higher schedule (e.g., from VR 10 to VR 25), make sure that Sniffy's rate of lever pressing on the lower schedule has stabilized before shifting to the higher schedule. You can tell if Sniffy's response rate has stabilized by examining the slope of the line on the cumulative record (see p. 28). If the slope looks the same across about 300 responses (note: responses, *not* delivered reinforcers) then you can assume that Sniffy's response rate has stabilized and you can move on to a higher schedule.

Examining the Bar-Sound graph in the Operant Association mind window is another way to see if you can safely progress to a higher schedule. After shifting to a higher schedule, the Bar-Sound level will decrease due to extinction, then gradually increase again to approach the maximum strength level. (For more information on extinction in operant conditioning, take a look at exercise 5 [pp. 34–38] or Chapter 8 in the textbook.) When the Bar-Sound graph has returned to a level close to the maximum, you can move on to a higher schedule.

In working through exercises 9–12, keep in mind the advice offered in exercise 9, step 8a–b (pp. 55–56); if you want to increase a reinforcement schedule from a low to a high value, you should do so in small increments, lest you extinguish Sniffy's lever pressing altogether.

Extinction and Stimulus Control

Poppea gained access to Nero, and established her ascendancy. First she used flirta-

tious wiles, pretending to be unable to resist her passion for Nero's looks. Then,

as the emperor fell in love with her, she became haughty, and if he kept her for

more than two nights she insisted that she was married and could not give up her

marriage.

TACITUS, *The Annals of Imperial Rome*

Extinction

In the past few chapters, we have concentrated on the strengthening of operant behavior through the process of reinforcement. However, a behavior that
has been strengthened through reinforcement can also be weakened through
extinction. **Extinction is the nonreinforcement of a previously reinforced
response, the result of which is a decrease in the strength of that response.** As with classical conditioning, the term extinction refers to both a
procedure and a process. The *procedure* of extinction is the nonreinforcement
of a previously reinforced response; the *process* of extinction is the resultant decrease in response strength.

Take, for example, a situation in which a rat has learned to press a lever
for food:

$$\underset{\text{R}}{\textit{Lever press}} \rightarrow \underset{\text{S}^{\text{R}}}{\textbf{Food}}$$

If lever pressing is no longer followed by food:

$$\underset{\text{R}}{\textit{Lever press}} \rightarrow \underset{\text{---}}{\textbf{No food}}$$

then the frequency of lever pressing will decline. The act of withholding food
delivery following a lever press is the procedure of extinction, while the resultant decline in responding is the process of extinction. If lever pressing
ceases entirely, the response is said to have been *extinguished;* if it has not yet
ceased entirely, then the response has been only *partially extinguished.*

Similarly, consider a child who has learned to whine to obtain candy:

$$\underset{\text{R}}{\textit{Whining}} \rightarrow \underset{\text{S}^{\text{R}}}{\textbf{Candy}}$$

If whining no longer produces candy:

$$\underset{\text{R}}{\textit{Whining}} \rightarrow \underset{\text{---}}{\textbf{No candy}}$$

the frequency of whining will decline. The procedure of extinction is the non-
delivery of candy following the behavior, while the process of extinction is the
resultant decline in the behavior. If the whining is completely eliminated, then
it has been extinguished. If whining still occurs, but at lower frequency, then
it has been partially extinguished.

An important, but often neglected, aspect of applying an extinction procedure is to ensure that the consequence being withheld is in fact the reinforcer that is maintaining the behavior. You might believe that the consequence of a candy is reinforcing a child's tendency to whine, when in fact it is the accompanying attention from the parent. If this is the case, and the parent continues to provide attention for whining (for example, by arguing with the child each time he or she whines), then withholding the candy might have little or no effect on the behavior. Of course, another possibility is that the whining is being maintained by both candy and attention, in which case withholding the candy might only partially extinguish the behavior. Thus, determining the effective reinforcer that is maintaining a behavior is a critical first step in extinguishing a behavior.

1. Extinction is the _____ of a previously _____ response, the result of which is a(n) _____ in the strength of that response.

2. Whenever Jana's friend, Karla, phoned late in the evening, she would invariably begin complaining about her coworkers. In the beginning, Jana listened attentively and provided emotional support. Unfortunately, Karla started phoning more and more often, with each call lasting longer and longer. Jana began to wonder if she was reinforcing Karla's behavior of phoning and complaining, so she decided to screen her late-evening calls and not answer any such calls from Karla. Eventually, Karla stopped phoning at that time, and they resumed a normal friendship that excluded lengthy complaints over the phone. Jana used the (procedure/process) _____ of extinction when she stopped answering Karla's late-evening calls, while the _____ of extinction is the eventual cessation of such calls.

3. In carrying out an extinction procedure, an important first step is to ensure that the consequence being withdrawn is in fact _____.

Side Effects of Extinction

When an extinction procedure is implemented, it is often accompanied by certain side effects. It is important to be aware of these side effects since they can mislead one into believing that an extinction procedure is not having an effect when in fact it is.

1. **Extinction Burst.** The implementation of an extinction procedure does not always result in an immediate decrease in responding. Instead, one often finds an *extinction burst:* **a temporary increase in the frequency and intensity of responding when extinction is first implemented.** Suppose, for example, that we reinforce every fourth lever press by a rat (an FR 4 schedule of reinforcement). When extinction is implemented, the rat will initially react by pressing the lever both more rapidly and more forcefully. The rat's behavior is analogous to our behavior when we

plug money into a candy machine, press the button, and receive nothing in return. We do not just give up and walk away. Instead, we press the button several times in a row, often with increasing amounts of force. Our behavior toward the machine shows the same increase in frequency and intensity that characterizes an extinction burst.

2. **Increase in Variability.** An extinction procedure can also result in an increase in the variability of a behavior (Antonitis, 1951). For example, a rat whose lever pressing no longer produces food might vary the manner in which the lever is pressed. If the rat typically pressed the lever with its right paw, it might now try pressing it with its left paw. As well, if the rat usually pressed the lever in the center, it might now press it more to one side or the other. Similarly, confronted by a candy machine that has just stolen our money, we will likely vary the manner in which we push the button, such as holding it down for a second before releasing it. And we will almost certainly try pressing other buttons on the machine to see if we can at least obtain a different selection.

3. **Emotional Behavior.** Extinction is often accompanied by emotional behavior (Zeiler, 1971). The hungry pigeon that suddenly finds that key pecking no longer produces food soon becomes agitated (as evidenced, for example, by quick jerky movements and wing flapping). Likewise, people often become upset when confronted by a candy machine that does not deliver the goods. Such emotional responses are what we typically refer to as *frustration*.

4. **Aggression.** One type of emotional behavior that is particularly common during an extinction procedure is aggression. In fact, extinction procedures have been used to study aggressive behavior in animals. For example, research has shown that a pigeon whose key pecking is placed on extinction will reliably attack another pigeon (or model of a pigeon) that happens to be nearby (Azrin, Hutchinson, & Hake, 1966). Extinction-induced aggression (also called frustration-induced aggression) is also common in humans. People often become angry with those who block them from obtaining an important goal. For that matter, even uncooperative vending machines are sometimes attacked.

5. **Resurgence.** A rather unusual side effect of extinction is ***resurgence: the reappearance during extinction of other behaviors that had once been effective in obtaining reinforcement*** (Epstein, 1985). Hull (1934), for example, trained rats to first run a 20-foot pattern through a maze to obtain food, then a 40-foot pattern. When all running was then placed on extinction, the rats initially persisted with the 40-foot pattern, then returned to the 20-foot pattern before quitting. It was as though they were attempting to make the food reappear by repeating a pattern that had earlier been effective. Resurgence resembles the psychoanalytic concept of *regression*, which is the reappearance of immature behavior in reaction to frustration or conflict. Thus, a husband faced with a wife who largely ignores him might begin spending increasing amounts of time at his parents' house. Faced with the lack of reinforcement in his marriage, he returns to a setting that once provided a rich source of reinforcement.

6. **Depression.** Extinction can also lead to depressive-like symptoms. For example, Klinger, Barta, and Kemble (1974) had rats run down an alleyway for food and then immediately followed this with an assessment of the rats' activity level in an open field test. Thus, each session consisted of two phases: (1) running down an alleyway for food, followed by (2) placement in an open area that the rats could freely explore. When extinction was implemented on the alleyway task, activity in the open field test first increased to above normal, then decreased to below normal, followed by a return to normal (see Figure 8.1).

Klinger, Barta, and Kemble (1974) also noted that low activity is a common symptom of depression, and depression is often associated with loss of reinforcement (Lewinsohn, 1974). For example, if someone dies, the people for whom that individual was a major source of reinforcement are essentially experiencing extinction, and they will likely become depressed for a period of time. And one symptom of such depression is a low level of activity. The fact that a similar process occurs in rats suggests that a temporary period of depression (accompanied by a decrease in activity) following the loss of a major reinforcer should be regarded as a normal aspect of disengagement from that reinforcer (Klinger, 1975).

FIGURE 8.1 Changes in rats' activity level in an open field test as a function of extinction on a preceding straight-alley maze task. (*Source:* Adapted from "Cyclic activity changes during extinction in rats: A potential model of depression," by E. Klinger, S. G. Barta, & E. D. Kemble, 1974, *Animal Learning and Behavior, 2,* pp. 313–316. Copyright © 1974 by the Psychomonic Society. Adapted with permission.)

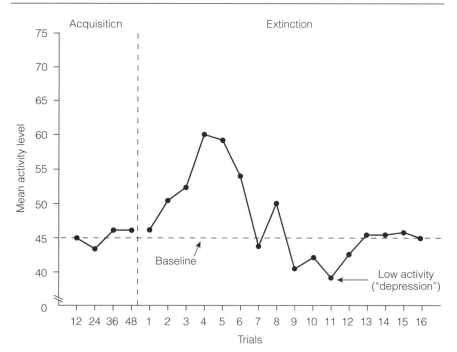

ADVICE FOR THE LOVELORN

Dear Dr. Dee,

Why is it that I act so weird whenever I break up with a guy? One day I am intent on reestablishing the relationship, the next day I am so angry I don't ever want to see him again. Then I usually get all depressed and lie around in bed for days on end.

What-a Rollercoaster

Dear What-a,

Sounds like extinction to me. The loss of a relationship is the loss of a major reinforcer in your life. You therefore go through many of the side effects that accompany extinction. You experience an extinction burst ("intent on reestablishing the relationship"), become angry ("don't ever want to see the guy again"), and eventually get depressed.

Solution: Extinction effects are a normal part of life, so don't expect that you shouldn't feel something. But you might be able to moderate your feelings a bit so they are not quite so painful. In particular, stay active as much as possible and seek out alternative sources of reinforcement. And try to avoid lying in bed for days on end, as this will only further reduce the reinforcement in your life. In fact, lying in bed for days on end will make just about anyone depressed, regardless of his or her relationship status!

Behaviorally yours,

QUICK QUIZ

1. Krissy asked her father to buy her a toy, as he usually did, when they were out shopping. Unfortunately, Krissy's father had spent all of his money on building supplies and told her that he had nothing left for a toy. The first thing that might happen is that Krissy will (increase/decrease) ＿＿＿＿＿＿＿＿＿ the frequency with which she asks for a toy and ask for a toy with a (louder/softer) ＿＿＿＿＿＿ voice. This process is known as an e＿＿＿＿＿＿ b＿＿＿＿＿＿＿.

2. Krissy is also likely to ask for the toy in many different ways, since extinction often results in an increase in the v＿＿＿＿＿＿＿ of a behavior.

3. Krissy might also begin showing a lot of e＿＿＿＿＿＿ behavior, including a＿＿＿＿＿＿.

4. When her father still refuses to buy her a toy, Krissy suddenly asks her dad to pick her up and carry her, something she has not asked for since she was much smaller. This could be an example of r＿＿＿＿＿＿, or what psychoanalysts call r＿＿＿＿＿＿.

5. On the trip home, Krissy, who never did get a toy, sat silently and stared out the window. This is not surprising since extinction is sometimes followed by a temporary period of d_____.

Resistance to Extinction

Resistance to extinction **is the extent to which responding persists after an extinction procedure has been implemented.** A response that is very persistent is said to have high resistance to extinction, while a response that disappears quickly is said to have low resistance to extinction (see Figure 8.2). For example, a dog that continues to beg for food at the dinner table for 20 minutes after everyone has stopped feeding it is displaying much higher resistance to extinction than a dog that stops begging after 5 minutes.

FIGURE 8.2 Two hypothetical extinction curves. Following an initial period of reinforcement at the start of the session, the extinction procedure is implemented. This results in a brief extinction burst, followed by a decline in responding. The decline is more gradual in the top example than in the bottom example, and hence illustrates greater resistance to extinction.

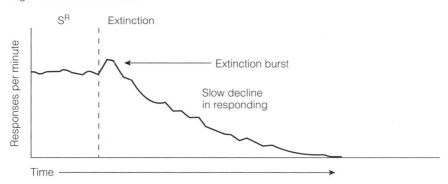

High resistance to extinction

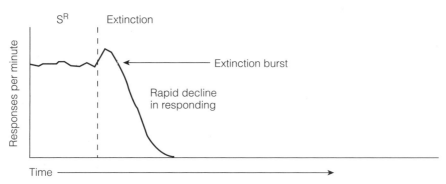

Low resistance to extinction

Resistance to extinction can be affected by a number of factors. These include the following:

1. **Schedule of Reinforcement.** The schedule of reinforcement is the most important factor influencing resistance to extinction. According to the *partial reinforcement effect*, **behavior that has been maintained on an intermittent (partial) schedule of reinforcement will extinguish more slowly than behavior that has been maintained on a continuous schedule.** Thus, lever pressing that has been reinforced on an FR 10 schedule will take longer to extinguish than lever pressing that has been reinforced on a CRF (FR 1) schedule. Similarly, lever pressing that has been reinforced on an FR 100 schedule will take longer to extinguish than lever pressing that has been reinforced on an FR 10 schedule. Resistance to extinction is particularly strong when behavior has been maintained on a variable ratio schedule (Reynolds, 1975); thus, a VR 20 schedule will produce greater resistance to extinction than an FR 20 schedule.

   One way of thinking about the partial reinforcement effect is that the less frequent the reinforcer, the longer it takes the animal to discover that reinforcement is no longer available (Mowrer & Jones, 1945). It obviously takes much longer for an animal to discover that reinforcement is no longer available when it has been receiving reinforcement on, say, a VR 100 schedule than on a CRF schedule. Yet another way of thinking about it is that there is a much greater contrast between a CRF schedule and extinction than between a VR 100 schedule and extinction. On a VR 100 schedule, the animal has learned to emit many responses in the absence of reinforcement; hence, it is more persistent in its responding when an extinction procedure is implemented (Capaldi, 1966).

   The partial reinforcement effect helps account for certain types of annoying or maladaptive behaviors that are difficult to eliminate. Dogs that beg for food are often extremely persistent. Paradoxically, this is sometimes the result of previously unsuccessful attempts at extinction. Imagine, for example, that all family members agree to stop feeding the dog at the dinner table. If one person nevertheless slips the dog a morsel when it is making a particularly big fuss, the begging will become both more intense and more persistent. This means that the next attempt at extinction will be even more difficult. Of course, the partial reinforcement effect also suggests a possible solution to this problem. If behavior that has been continuously reinforced is less resistant to extinction, then it might help to first spend several days reinforcing each instance of begging. Then, when extinction is implemented, the dog's tendency to beg might extinguish more rapidly (Lerman & Iwata, 1996).

2. **History of Reinforcement.** In general, the more reinforcers an individual has received for a behavior, the greater the resistance to extinction. Lever pressing will extinguish more rapidly if a rat has previously earned only 10 reinforcers for lever pressing than if it has earned 100 reinforcers. Likewise, a child who has only recently picked up the habit of whining for

candy should stop relatively quickly when the behavior is placed on extinction, as opposed to a child who has been at it for several weeks. From a practical perspective, this means that it is much easier to extinguish an unwanted behavior, such as whining for candy, when it first becomes evident (hence the saying, "nip it in the bud"). There is, however, a limit in the extent to which further reinforcers will produce increased resistance to extinction. Furomoto (1971), for example, found that resistance reached its maximum after about 1000 reinforcers.

3. **Magnitude of the Reinforcer.** The magnitude of the reinforcer can also affect resistance to extinction. For example, large-magnitude reinforcers sometimes result in greater resistance to extinction than small-magnitude reinforcers. Thus, lever pressing might take longer to extinguish following a training period in which each reinforcer consisted of a large pellet of food than if the reinforcer were a small pellet of food. Lever pressing might also take longer to extinguish if the reinforcer was a highly preferred food item than if it were a less preferred food item. From a practical perspective, this means that a dog's behavior of begging at the dinner table might extinguish more easily if you first spend several days feeding it small bites of less preferred morsels (Lerman & Iwata, 1996). Unfortunately, one problem with this strategy is that the effect of reinforcer magnitude on resistance to extinction is not entirely consistent. In fact, researchers sometimes find that smaller reinforcers result in greater resistance to extinction (e.g., Ellis, 1962).

4. **Degree of Deprivation.** Not surprisingly, the degree to which an organism is deprived of a reinforcer also affects resistance to extinction. In general, the greater the level of deprivation, the greater the resistance to extinction (Perin, 1942). A rat that is only slightly hungry will cease lever pressing more quickly than a rat that is very hungry. This suggests yet another strategy for extinguishing a dog's tendency to beg at the table: Feed the dog prior to the meal.

5. **Previous Experience with Extinction.** When sessions of extinction are alternated with sessions of reinforcement, the greater the number of prior exposures to extinction, the quicker the behavior will extinguish during subsequent exposures (Bullock & Smith, 1953). For example, if a rat experiences several sessions of extinction randomly interspersed with several sessions of reinforcement, it will eventually learn to stop lever pressing soon after the start of an extinction session. The rat has learned that if it has not received reinforcement soon after the start of a session, then it is likely that no reinforcement will be forthcoming for the remainder of the session. Similarly, a child might learn that if he does not receive candy within the first 10 minutes of whining during a trip to the supermarket, he might as well give up for the day.

6. **Distinctive Signal for Extinction.** Extinction is greatly facilitated when there is a distinctive stimulus that signals the onset of extinction. Such a stimulus is called a *discriminative stimulus for extinction* and is more fully discussed later in this chapter.

1. R_____ to _____ is the extent to which responding persists after an extinction procedure is implemented.

2. According to the p_____ r_____ effect. responses that have
bee   /less) _____
resi: rced on a continuous
sch(

3. Am(breviation) _____
sch(extinction.

4. In g   kely to be (much eas-
ier/r

5. Resi   r that is being extin-
guis   _____-magnitude re-
info

6. In g   _____ relationship
betv   deprivation for the
reinf

7. Prev   ignal for extinction,
tend   _____ in resistance to
extir

Spontaneous Recovery

Although extinction is a reliable process for weakening a behavior, it would be
a mistake to assume that once a response has been extinguished, it has been
permanently eliminated. As with extinction of a classically conditioned response, extinction of an operant response is likely to be followed by spontaneous recovery (Skinner, 1938). As you will recall, *spontaneous recovery* **is
the reappearance of an extinguished response following a rest period
after extinction.** Suppose, for example, that we extinguish a rat's behavior of
lever pressing. The next day, when we place the rat back in the experimental
chamber, it will probably commence lever pressing again. It seems as though
it has forgotten that lever pressing no longer produces food. Nevertheless, the
behavior will likely be weaker than it was at the start of the extinction phase
the day before, and will extinguish more quickly given that we continue to
withhold reinforcement. Similarly, on the third day, we might again find some
recovery of lever pressing, but it will be even weaker than the day before and
will extinguish even more quickly. This process might repeat itself several
times, with each recovery being weaker and more readily extinguished than
the previous one. Following several extinction sessions, we will eventually
reach the point at which spontaneous recovery does not occur (apart from a
few tentative lever presses every once in a while), and the behavior will have
essentially been eliminated (see Figure 8.3). Likewise, a child's tendency to
throw tantrums in the supermarket to obtain candy might require several visits to the supermarket in which a tantrum does not produce candy before the

FIGURE 8.3 Graph of hypothetical data illustrating spontaneous recovery across repeated sessions of extinction.

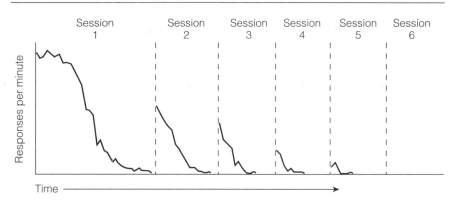

behavior is fully eliminated. In short, when applying an extinction procedure, you have to be persistent.

Skinner (1950) proposed that spontaneous recovery is a function of discriminative stimuli (S^Ds) associated with the start of the session. For an experimental rat, the experience of being taken from the home cage, weighed, and placed in an operant chamber is itself a signal for the availability of food. ("Oh, goody, I'm being weighed. That means I'll soon be able to earn some food by lever pressing.") Only after repeated exposure to these events without receiving food does the rat at last fail to show the learned behavior. Similarly, for the child who has learned to throw tantrums in the supermarket to receive candy, entering the supermarket is itself an S^D for the availability of candy. The child will require repeated exposure to the sequence of entering the supermarket, throwing a tantrum, and not receiving candy before this cue becomes ineffective.

1. S_____ _____ is the reappearance of an extinguished response at a later point in time.

2. In general, each time this occurs, the behavior is (weaker/stronger) _____ than before and extinguishes (more/less) _____ readily.

3. Skinner believed that this phenomenon is a function of _____ that are uniquely associated with the start of the session.

Differential Reinforcement of Other Behavior

The process of extinction can be greatly facilitated by both extinguishing the target behavior *and* reinforcing the occurrence of a replacement behavior. This procedure is known as ***differential reinforcement of other behavior (DRO): reinforcement of any behavior other than the target behavior***

And Furthermore

Extinction of Bedtime Tantrums in Young Children

A common difficulty faced by many parents is training children to go to bed at night without fussing or throwing a tantrum. The problem often arises from the fact that parents pay attention to a child who is throwing a tantrum and getting out of bed, thereby inadvertently reinforcing the very behavior that is annoying them. Of course, the obvious solution to this problem is for the parents to place the child's tantrums on extinction by leaving the child alone in his or her room until he or she finally falls asleep. Research has in fact shown this to be a highly effective procedure. Rickert and Johnson (1988), for example, randomly assigned children to either a systematic ignoring condition (extinction), scheduled awakenings throughout the night (to comfort the child), or a control condition in which parents carried on as normal. In the systematic ignoring condition, the parents were told to initially check on their child's safety when the child made a fuss and then ignore all further cries. Results revealed that children who underwent the extinction procedure experienced considerably greater improvement in their sleep patterns than the children in the other two conditions.

Thus, extinction seems to be an effective treatment for this type of problem. Unfortunately, it suffers from a major drawback. Many parents find it impossible to totally ignore their children's persistent heartfelt pleas during the night, especially during the initial stages of treatment when such pleas are likely to be magnified in both intensity and duration (the typical extinction burst). As a result, "graduated extinction procedures" have been devised that are more acceptable to parents and less upsetting to the child. Adams and Rickert (1989), for example, instructed parents to wait for a predetermined period of time, based on what they felt was an acceptable duration, before responding to the child's calls. The parents were also instructed to comfort the child for only 15 seconds or less. Combined with a consistent bedtime routine, this less stringent procedure was quite effective in helping many parents, and children, finally to get a good night's sleep (see Mindell, 1999, for a review).

that is being extinguished. One variant of this procedure, known as *differential reinforcement of incompatible behavior (DRI)*, involves reinforcing a behavior that is specifically incompatible with the target behavior. Paying attention to a child only if he is doing something other than fighting with his little sister is a DRO procedure; paying attention to him only when he is interacting in a friendly manner with his little sister is a DRI procedure.

DRO and DRI procedures tend to be more effective than simple extinction procedures. This is because the target behavior is weakened both by the lack of reinforcement for that behavior and by the reinforcement of alternative behaviors that come to replace it. Hence, it is easier to extinguish a child's habit of whining for candy at a supermarket if you not only withdraw the reinforcement for whining but also explicitly reinforce well-mannered behaviors. Note that the reinforcement for well-mannered behavior can include the very candy for which the child has been whining. He can therefore still obtain candy, but only if he exhibits a proper pattern of behavior. (The candy, of course, can then be gradually phased out—or replaced by a healthier treat— as the appropriate behavior becomes firmly established.) In this manner, DRO and DRI procedures can reduce many of the unwanted side effects of extinction, such as frustration and aggression. As a general rule, therefore, whenever one attempts to extinguish an unwanted behavior, one should also provide plenty of reinforcement for more appropriate behavior (Miltenberger, 1997).

1. The procedure of reinforcing all behaviors except the particular target behavior that you wish to extinguish is known as d_____ r_____ of o_____ behavior (abbreviated _____).

2. The procedure of reinforcing only those behaviors that are specifically incompatible with the target behavior that you wish to extinguish is known as _____ _____ _____ of _____ behavior (abbreviated _____).

3. Giving a dog a treat whenever it does something other than jump up on visitors as they enter the house is an example of a (use the abbreviation) _____ procedure. Giving a dog a treat for sitting quietly when visitors enter the house is an example of a _____ procedure.

4. DRO and DRI procedures are useful in that they tend to reduce many of the side effects associated with an _____ procedure.

Stimulus Control

As previously noted, when a behavior has been consistently reinforced in the presence of a certain stimulus, that stimulus will begin to affect the probability of the behavior. This stimulus, known as a discriminative stimulus (S^D), does not automatically elicit the behavior in the manner of a CS eliciting a reflex; it merely signals the availability of reinforcement, thereby increasing the probability that the behavior will occur. Such behavior is then said to be under *stimulus control,* **meaning that the presence of a discriminative stimulus reliably affects the probability of the behavior.**

For example, if a 2000 Hz tone signals that lever pressing will lead to food:

2000 Hz Tone: *Lever press* $\rightarrow$ Food
  S^D **R** S^R

and the rat thus learns to press the lever only in the presence of the tone, the behavior of lever pressing is said to be under stimulus control. Similarly, the sound of a ringing telephone has strong stimulus control over whether people will pick it up and say hello. People never answer phones that are not ringing and almost always answer phones that are ringing. Following are other examples of stimulus control (with the S^D italicized):

- At *red lights*, we stop; at *green lights*, we proceed.
- If *someone smiles at us*, we smile at them.
- In an *elevator*, we stand facing the front rather than the back.
- When we hear an *ambulance siren behind us*, we pull our car over to the side of the road and slow down or stop.
- When the *professor begins lecturing*, students cease talking among themselves (hint, hint).

In this section, we will look more closely at discriminative stimuli and their effects on behavior. Note that some of the principles discussed, such as stimulus generalization, represent operant versions of principles discussed in earlier chapters on classical conditioning.

Stimulus Generalization and Discrimination

In our discussion of classical conditioning, we noted that stimuli that are similar to a CS can also elicit a CR, a process known as stimulus generalization. A similar process occurs in operant conditioning. In operant conditioning, *stimulus generalization* **is the tendency for an operant response to be emitted in the presence of a stimulus that is similar to an S^D.** In general, the more similar the stimulus, the stronger the response. Take, for example, a rat that has learned to lever press for food whenever it hears a 2000 Hz tone. If we then present the rat with a series of tones that vary in pitch, we will find that it also presses the lever in the presence of these other tones, particularly in the presence of a tone that is similar to the original S^D. Thus, the rat will display a higher rate of lever pressing in the presence of a 1800 Hz or 2200 Hz tone, which are more similar to the original S^D, than a 1200 Hz or a 2800 Hz tone, which are less similar.

This tendency to generalize across different stimuli can be depicted in a *generalization gradient*, **which is a graphic description of the strength of responding in the presence of stimuli that are similar to the S^D and which vary along a continuum.** As shown in Figure 8.4, gradients can vary in their degree of steepness.

A relatively steep gradient indicates that rate of responding drops sharply as the stimuli become increasingly different from the S^D, while a relatively flat gradient indicates that responding drops gradually as the stimuli become increasingly different from the S^D. In other words, a flat gradient indicates more generalization, while a steep gradient indicates less generalization.[1]

---

[1] Generalization gradients are also used to indicate the extent of stimulus generalization in classical conditioning. Imagine, for example, that the 2000 Hz tone in Figure 8.4 is a CS that has been associated with food and now elicits a conditioned salivary response. The steep generalization gradient would indicate weak generalization of the CR across tones, while a flat gradient would indicate strong generalization of the CR across tones.

FIGURE 8.4 Two hypothetical generalization gradients depicting rate of lever pressing in the presence of tones that vary in pitch between 1200 and 2800 Hz ("Hertz" is the number of sound waves per second generated by a sound source). In both examples, tones that are more similar to the original S^D (a 2000 Hz tone) are associated with stronger responding. However, generalization is much greater in the bottom gradient, which is relatively flat, than in the top gradient, which is relatively steep.

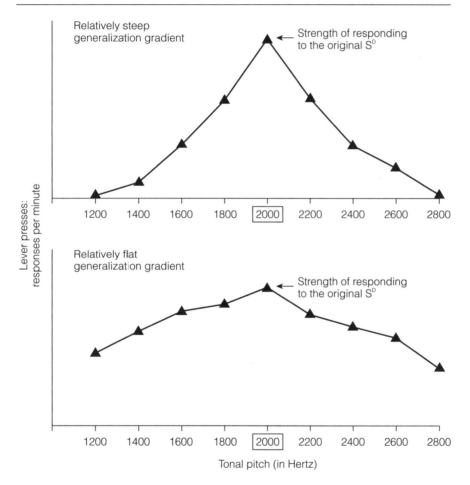

As in classical conditioning, the opposite of stimulus generalization in operant conditioning is *stimulus discrimination:* **the tendency for an operant response to be emitted more in the presence of one stimulus than another.** More generalization means less discrimination, and less generalization means more discrimination. Thus, a steep gradient indicates weak generalization and strong discrimination, while a flat gradient indicates strong generalization and weak discrimination.

1. A behavior is said to be under s_____ c_____ when it is highly likely to occur in the presence of a certain stimulus.

2. In operant conditioning, the term s_____ g_____ refers to the tendency for a response to be emitted in the presence of stimuli that are similar to the original _____. The opposite process, called s_____ d_____, refers to the tendency for the response to be emitted more in the presence of one stimulus than another.

3. In general, stimuli that are (more/less) _____ similar produce stronger generalization.

4. A g_____ g_____ indicates the strength of responding to stimuli that vary along a continuum.

5. In a graph that depicts a g_____ g_____, a relatively flat line indicates more _____ and less _____. A relatively steep line indicates more _____ and less _____.

6. When John looked at his watch and noticed that it was 12:30 P.M., he decided that it was time for lunch. John's eating behavior appears to be under strong s_____ c_____, with the time of 12:30 being the effective _____ for this behavior.

7. John always goes for lunch around 12:30, with the range being somewhere between 12:25 and 12:35 P.M. The generalization gradient for this behavior across various points in time would therefore be much (steeper/flatter) _____ than if the range was between 12:00 and 1:00. This indicates a pattern of strong (discrimination/generalization) _____ and weak _____ for John's lunch-going behavior across different points in time.

Discrimination training, as applied to operant conditioning, involves reinforcement of responding in the presence of one stimulus (the S^D) and not another stimulus. The latter is called a *discriminative stimulus for extinction,* which is a stimulus that signals the absence of reinforcement. A discriminative stimulus for extinction is typically given the symbol S^Δ (pronounced "es-delta"). For example, if we wish to train a rat to strongly discriminate between, say, a 2000 Hz tone and a 1200 Hz tone, we would present the two tones in random order. Whenever the 2000 Hz tone sounds, a lever press produces food; whenever the 1200 Hz tone sounds, a lever press does *not* produce food.

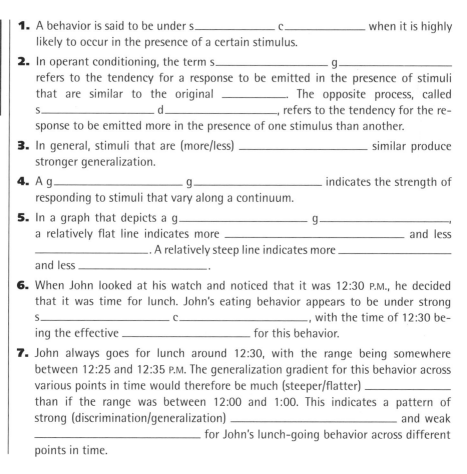

2000 Hz Tone: *Lever press* → Food
$\quad S^D \qquad\qquad R \qquad\quad S^R$
1200 Hz Tone: *Lever press* → No food
$\quad S^\Delta \qquad\qquad R \qquad\quad$ —

After repeated exposure to these contingencies, the rat will soon learn to press the lever in the presence of the 2000 Hz tone and not in the presence of the

1200 Hz tone. We can then say that the rat's behavior of lever pressing is under strong stimulus control.

In similar fashion, if the manager where you work complies with your requests for a day off only when he appears to be in a good mood and does not comply when he appears to be in a bad mood, you learn to make requests only when he is in a good mood. The manager's appearance exerts strong stimulus control over the probability of your making a request. In this sense, one characteristic of people who have good social skills is that they can make fine discriminations between social cues—such as facial expression and body posture—which enables them to maximize the amount of social reinforcement (and minimize the amount of social punishment) obtained during their exchanges with others.

1. In a discrimination training procedure, responses that occur in the presence of the (use the symbols) _____ are reinforced, while those that occur in the presence of the _____ are not reinforced. This latter stimulus is called a d_____ s_____ for e_____.

2. An "Open for Business" sign is an _____ for entering the store and making a purchase, while a "Closed for Business" sign is an _____ for entering the store and making a purchase.

The Peak Shift Effect

An unusual effect often produced by discrimination training is the peak shift effect. According to the *peak shift effect,* **the peak of a generalization gradient following discrimination training will shift from the S^D to a stimulus that is further removed from the S^Δ** (Hanson, 1959). This constitutes an exception to the general principle that the strongest response in a generalization gradient occurs in the presence of the original S^D.

Suppose, for example, that we first train a rat to press a lever in the presence of a 2000 Hz tone. We then conduct a test for generalization across a range of tones varying in pitch between 1200 and 2800 Hz, and we find a generalization gradient like that shown in the top panel of Figure 8.5. We then submit the rat to a discrimination training procedure in which we reinforce lever pressing in the presence of a 2000 Hz tone (S^D) and not in the presence of a 1200 Hz tone (S^Δ). When this has been successfully accomplished (the rat responds only in the presence of the 2000 Hz tone and not in the presence of the 1200 Hz tone), we again test for generalization across a range of tones. What we are likely to find with this rat is a generalization gradient something like that depicted in the bottom panel of Figure 8.5. Look carefully at this gradient. How does it differ from the gradient in the top portion of the figure, which represents generalization in the absence of discrimination training?

One obvious difference is that, with discrimination training, the gradient drops off more sharply on the side toward the S^Δ, which simply means that this rat strongly discriminates between the S^Δ and the S^D. But what is the other

FIGURE 8.5 Illustration of a peak shift effect following discrimination training. Prior to discrimination training (top panel), the gradient is relatively flat. Following discrimination training (bottom panel), in which a 1200 Hz tone has been established as an S$^\Delta$, the strongest response occurs not in the presence of the S^D (the 2000 Hz tone), but in the presence of a stimulus further removed from the S$^\Delta$. The gradient in the bottom panel therefore illustrates the peak shift effect.

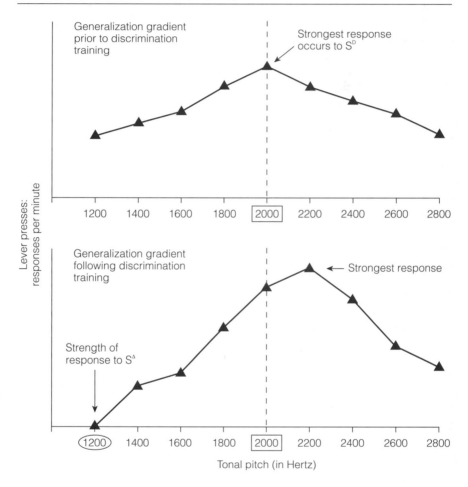

difference between the two graphs? Prior to discrimination training (the top panel), the strongest response occurs to the S^D (the 2000 Hz tone). Following discrimination training (the bottom panel), the strongest response shifts away from the S^D to a stimulus that lies in a direction opposite to the S$^\Delta$ (in this case, it shifts to a 2200 Hz tone). This shift in the peak of the generalization gradient is the peak shift effect.

Perhaps a fanciful example will help clarify the peak shift effect. Suppose that Mr. Shallow identifies women entirely on the basis of hair color. Jackie, with whom he had a very boring relationship, had light brown hair (an S$^\Delta$), while Dana, with whom he had a wonderfully exciting relationship, had dark brown hair (an S^D). He then moves to a new city and begins touring the singles bars seeking a new mate. According to the peak shift effect, he will likely seek out a woman whose hair color is even darker than Dana's.

One explanation for the peak shift effect is that during discrimination training, subjects respond in terms of the relative, rather than the absolute values, of stimuli (Kohler, 1918/1939). Thus, according to this interpretation, the rat does not learn merely that a 2000 Hz tone indicates food and a 1200 Hz tone indicates no food; rather, it learns that a higher-pitched tone indicates food and a lower-pitched tone indicates no food. Given a choice, the rat therefore emits the strongest response in the presence of a tone that has an even higher pitch than the original S^D. Likewise, Mr. Shallow chooses a woman who has even darker hair than Dana because in his mind darker hair color means a better relationship.

Another explanation for the peak shift effect is that, despite discrimination training, the S^D is still somewhat similar to the S$^\Delta$ and has acquired some of its inhibitory properties (Spence, 1937). From this perspective, the 2000 Hz tone (the S^D) is somewhat similar to the 1200 Hz tone (the S$^\Delta$), making the 2000 Hz tone slightly less attractive than it would have been if the S$^\Delta$ had never been trained. Thus, a tone that has a slightly higher pitch than 2000 Hz, and is thereby less similar to the 1200 Hz tone, will result in the highest rate of responding. Likewise, Mr. Shallow seeks a woman with very dark hair color because he is attempting to find a woman who is even more dissimilar from Jackie with whom he had such a poor relationship.[2]

6

1. In the peak shift effect, the peak of a generalization gradient, following d_____ t_____, shifts away from the _____ to a stimulus that is further removed from the _____.

2. If an orange key light is trained as an S^D in a key-pecking task with pigeons, and the pigeons are then exposed to other key colors ranging from yellow on one end of the continuum to red on the other (with orange in the middle), then the peak of the generalization gradient will likely be to a (yellowish-orange/orange/orange-reddish) _____ key light.

3. If a pigeon undergoes discrimination training in which a yellow key light is explicitly established as an S$^\Delta$ and an orange key light is explicitly established as the S^D, the strongest response in the generalization gradient will likely be to a (yellowish-orange/orange/orange-reddish) _____ key light. This effect is known as the _____ _____ effect.

---

[2] The peak shift effect is also found in classical conditioning following discrimination training between a CS+ and a CS−. For example, if the CS+ was a 2000 Hz tone and the CS− was a 1200 Hz tone, what would the peak shift effect consist of?

Multiple Schedules and Behavioral Contrast

Stimulus control is often studied using a type of complex schedule known as a multiple schedule. **A *multiple schedule* consists of two or more independent schedules presented in sequence, each resulting in reinforcement and each having a distinctive S^D.** For example, a pigeon might first be presented with a red key that signals an FI 30-sec schedule, completion of which results in food. The key light then changes to green, which signals a VI 30-sec schedule, completion of which also results in food. These two schedules can be presented in either random or alternating order, or for set periods of time (such as 2 minutes on the red FI 30-sec schedule followed by 2 minutes on the green VI 30-sec schedule followed by another 2 minutes on the red FI 30-sec schedule, etc.). The following schematic shows the two schedules presented in alternating order:

FI 30-sec   **VI 30-sec**

Red key: *Key peck* $\longrightarrow$ **Food / Green key:** *Key peck* $\longrightarrow$ **Food / etc.**

Note that a multiple schedule differs from a chained schedule in that a chained schedule requires that all of the component schedules be completed before the sought-after reinforcer is delivered. For example, on a Chain FI 30-sec VI 30-sec schedule, both the FI and VI components must be completed to obtain food. On a Multiple FI 30-sec VI 30-sec, however, completion of each component schedule results in food.

On a multiple schedule, stimulus control is demonstrated when the subject responds differently in the presence of the S^{D}s associated with the different schedules. For example, with sufficient experience on a Multiple FI 30-sec VI 30-sec schedule, a pigeon will likely show a scalloped pattern of responding on the red key signaling the FI component, and a moderate, steady pattern of responding on the green key signaling the VI component. The pigeon's response pattern on each key color will be the appropriate pattern for the schedule of reinforcement that is in effect on that key.

QUICK QUIZ

1. On a _____ schedule, two or more schedules are presented (sequentially/simultaneously) _____, with each resulting in a r_____ and having its own distinctive _____.

2. This type of schedule differs from a chained schedule in that a _____ is provided after each component schedule is completed.

3. On a Multiple FR 50 VR 50 schedule, we are likely to find a high rate of response on the (FR/VR/both) _____ component(s) along with a p_____ r_____ pause on the (FR/VR/both) _____ component(s).

An interesting phenomenon that can be investigated using multiple schedules is behavioral contrast. ***Behavioral contrast* occurs when a change in the** *rate of reinforcement* on one component of a multiple schedule produces an opposite change in the *rate of response* on another component (Reynolds, 1961). In other words, as the rate of reinforcement on one component changes in one direction, the rate of response on the other component changes in the other direction.

There are two basic contrast effects: positive and negative. In a *negative contrast effect,* **an increase in the rate of reinforcement on one component produces a decrease in the rate of response on the other component.** Suppose, for example, that a pigeon first receives several sessions of exposure to a Multiple VI 60-sec VI 60-sec schedule:

VI 60-sec   **VI 60-sec**
Red key: *Key peck* ⟶ **Food / Green key:** *Key peck* ⟶ **Food / etc.**

Because both schedules are the same, the pigeon responds equally on both the red key and the green key. Following this, the VI 60-sec component on the red key is changed to VI 30-sec, which provides a higher rate of reinforcement (on average, two reinforcers per minute as opposed to one reinforcer per minute):

VI 30-sec   **VI 60-sec**
Red key: *Key peck* ⟶ **Food / Green key:** *Key peck* ⟶ **Food / etc.**

With more reinforcement now available on the red key, the pigeon will decrease its rate of response on the green key, which is associated with the unchanged VI 60-sec component. Simply put, because the first component in the sequence is now more attractive, the second component seems relatively less attractive. The situation is analogous to a woman whose husband has suddenly become much more affectionate and caring at home; as a result, she spends less time flirting with other men at work. The men at work seem relatively less attractive compared to her Romeo at home.

In *positive behavioral contrast,* **a decrease in rate of reinforcement on one component results in an increase in rate of response on the other component.** If, for example, on a Multiple VI 60-sec VI 60-sec schedule:

VI 60-sec   **VI 60-sec**
Red key: *Key peck* ⟶ **Food / Green key:** *Key peck* ⟶ **Food / etc.**

the first VI 60-sec component is suddenly changed to VI 120-sec:

VI 120-sec   **VI 60-sec**
Red key: *Key peck* ⟶ **Food / Green key:** *Key peck* ⟶ **Food / etc.**

the pigeon will increase its rate of response on the unchanged VI 60-sec component. As one component becomes less attractive (changing from VI 60-sec to VI 120-sec), the unchanged component becomes relatively more attractive. The situation is analogous to the woman whose husband has become less caring and affectionate at home; as a result, she spends more time flirting with other men at work. The men at work seem relatively more attractive compared to the dud she has at home.

Positive contrast effects are also evident when the change in one component of the multiple schedule involves not a decrease in the amount of reinforcement, but the implementation of a punisher, such as a mild electric shock. As the one alternative suddenly becomes punishing, the remaining alternative, which is still reinforcing, is viewed as even more attractive (Brethower & Reynolds, 1962). This might explain what happens in some volatile relationships in which couples report strong overall feelings of affection for each other (Gottman, 1994). The intermittent periods of aversiveness seem to heighten the couple's appreciation of each other during periods of affection. Such relationships can therefore thrive, *given* that the positive aspects of the relationship significantly outweigh the negative aspects.[3]

1. In _____ behavioral contrast, an increase in reinforcement on one alternative results in a(n) (increase/decrease) _____ in (responding/reinforcement)_____ on the other alternative.

2. In _____ behavioral contrast, a decrease in reinforcement on one alternative results in a(n) _____ in _____ on the other alternative.

3. A pigeon that experiences a shift from a Multiple FR 10 VI 60-sec schedule to a Multiple FR 100 VI 60-sec schedule will likely (increase/decrease) _____ its rate of response on the VI 60-sec component.

4. When Levin (a lonely bachelor in Tolstoy's novel *Anna Karenina*) proposed to the beautiful young Kitty, she rejected him. Levin was devastated and decided to devote the rest of his life to his work. Kitty in turn was subsequently rejected by the handsome young military officer, Vronsky, whom she had mistakenly assumed was intent on marrying her. Kitty was devastated and deeply regretted having turned down Levin, whom she now perceived to be a fine man. A year later, they encountered each other at a social gathering. Relative to individuals who have not experienced such hardships in establishing a relationship, we would expect their affection for each other to be much (deeper/shallower) _____ than normal. This can be seen as an example of (positive/negative) _____ behavioral contrast.

An additional type of contrast effect is ***anticipatory contrast, in which the rate of response varies inversely with an upcoming ("anticipated") change in the rate of reinforcement*** (Williams, 1981). For example, Pliskoff (1963) found that pigeons increased their rate of responding for reinforcement when they were presented with a stimulus that signaled that

---

[3] Similar contrast effects occur when there is a shift in the magnitude of a reinforcer (Crespi, 1942). For example, rats that experience a sudden switch from receiving a small amount of food for running down an alleyway to receiving a large amount of food for running down the same alleyway will run faster for the large amount (a positive contrast effect) than if they had always received the large amount.

extinction was imminent. In other words, faced with the impending loss of re-inforcement, the pigeons responded all the more vigorously for reinforce-ment while it was still available.

Anticipatory contrast seems analogous to what many of us have experi-enced—that things we are about to lose often seem to increase in value. For example, Sue views her relationship with Bert as rather dull and uninteresting until she learns that Bert might be romantically interested in another woman. Faced with the possibility that she might lose him, she now becomes intensely interested in him. Unfortunately, some people may use anticipatory contrast as a deliberate tactic to strengthen a partner's feelings of attachment. Read again the anecdote at the start of this chapter about Poppea's relationship with the Roman emperor Nero. In behavioral terms, Poppea first established her-self as an effective reinforcer for Nero, then, to further increase her value, in-termittently threatened to withdraw herself from Nero's company. In antici-pation of possibly losing her, Nero became even more attached.

The occurrence of these contrast effects indicates that behaviors should not be viewed in isolation. Consequences for behavior in one setting can greatly affect the strength of behavior in another setting. Consider, for example, a young girl who is increasingly neglected at home, perhaps because her parents are going through a divorce. She might try to compensate for this circum-stance by seeking more attention at school (a positive contrast effect), perhaps to the point of misbehaving. Although the parents might blame the school for her misbehavior, she is in fact reacting to the lack of reinforcement at home. Thus, to borrow a concept from humanistic psychology, behavior needs to be viewed in a holistic manner, with the recognition that behavior can be in-fluenced by contingencies operating in multiple settings.

1. An increase in the rate of responding for an available reinforcer when faced with the possibility of losing it in the near future is known as _____ contrast.

2. If Jackie hears her mother say that it is getting close to her bedtime, she is likely to become (more/less) _____ involved in the computer game she is playing.

3. Vronsky (another character in Tolstoy's *Anna Karenina*) falls deeply in love with Anna, who is the wife of another man. For several months, they carry on a pas-sionate affair. When Anna, however, finally leaves her husband to be with him, Vronsky finds that he soon becomes bored with their relationship. The fact that his feelings for Anna were much stronger when their relationship was more precarious is in keeping with the principle of _____ contrast.

QUICK QUIZ

Fading and Errorless Discrimination Learning

While discrimination training is an effective way for establishing stimulus control, it has its limitations. For example, during the process of learning to discriminate an S^D from an S$^\Delta$, the subject will initially make several "mistakes"

And Furthermore

St. Neots' Margin

The anticipatory contrast effect described by Pliskoff (1963) reflects the pigeon's reaction to a potential difficulty, namely, the impending loss of a reinforcer. According to British writer Colin Wilson (1972), such difficulties may provide our lives with a sense of meaning when more pleasant stimuli have failed. Wilson's description of how he discovered this concept provides an interesting illustration.

> In 1954, I was hitch-hiking to Peterborough on a hot Saturday afternoon. I felt listless, bored and resentful: I didn't want to go to Peterborough—it was a kind of business trip—and I didn't particularly long to be back in London either. There was hardly any traffic on the road, but eventually I got a lift. Within ten minutes, there was an odd noise in the engine of the lorry. The driver said: 'I'm afraid something's gone wrong—I'll have to drop you off at the next garage.' I was too listless to care. I walked on, and eventually a second lorry stopped for me. Then occurred the absurd coincidence. After ten minutes or so, there was a knocking noise from *his* gearbox. When he said: 'It sounds as if something's gone wrong,' I thought: 'Oh *no!*' and then caught myself thinking it, and thought: 'That's the first definite reaction I've experienced today.' We drove on slowly—he was anxious to get to Peterborough, *and by this time, so was I.* He found that if he dropped speed to just under twenty miles an hour, the knocking noise stopped; as soon as he exceeded it, it started again. We both listened intently for any resumption of the trouble. Finally, as we were passing through a town called St. Neots, he said: 'Well, I think if we stay at this speed, we should make it.' And I felt a surge of delight. Then I thought: 'This is absurd. My situation hasn't *improved* since I got into the lorry—in fact, it has got worse, since he is now crawling along. All that has happened is that an inconvenience has been threatened and then the threat withdrawn. And suddenly, my boredom and indifference have vanished.' I formulated then the notion that there is a borderland or threshold of the mind that can be stimulated by pain or inconvenience, but not pleasure. (p. 27)

Wilson labeled the concept *St. Neots' margin* after the town they were driving through at the time. He proposes that such difficulties create "meaning" by forcing us to concentrate, and that the absence of such concentration makes life dull and uninteresting. But we can also view these difficulties as a type of contrast effect in which we are in danger of losing a reinforcer. As a result, we respond more vigorously for the reinforcer and value it more highly.

Contrast effects may therefore provide our lives with a sense of meaning that might otherwise be missing. Wilson describes, for example, how the writer Sartre claimed that he never felt so free as during the war when, as a member of the French Resistance, he was in constant danger of being arrested. In danger of losing his freedom, he truly appreciated his freedom. Consider too Balderston's (1924) play, *A Morality Play for the Leisured Class,* which recounts the story of a man who dies and finds himself in the afterlife. When a shining presence tells him that he can have any pleasure he desires by merely wishing it, he is overjoyed and fully indulges himself. He soon discovers, however, that things quickly lose their value when they are so easily attained. Facing an eternity of profound boredom (in which contrast effects are completely absent), he finally exclaims that he would rather be in hell—at which point the presence asks: "And wherever do you think you *are,* sir?"

by responding in the presence of the S$^\Delta$. Because such responses do not result in reinforcement, the subject is likely to become frustrated and display a great deal of emotional behavior. It would be helpful, therefore, if there were a method of discrimination training that minimized these effects.

Errorless discrimination training **is a procedure that minimizes the number of errors (i.e., nonreinforced responses to the S$^\Delta$) and reduces many of the adverse effects associated with discrimination training.** It involves two aspects: (1) The S$^\Delta$ is introduced early in training, soon after the animal has learned to respond appropriately to the S^D; and (2) the S$^\Delta$ is presented in weak form to begin with and then gradually strengthened. **This process of gradually altering the intensity of a stimulus is known as** *fading.* (For example, one can *fade in* music by presenting it faintly to begin with and gradually turning up the volume, or *fade out* music by presenting it loudly to begin with and gradually turning down the volume.)

Terrace (1963a) used errorless discrimination training to establish a red-green discrimination in pigeons. The pigeons were first trained to peck a red key on a VI 60-sec schedule of reinforcement. As soon as this behavior was established, occasional 5-second periods of extinction were presented in which the key light was switched off. Since pigeons tend not to peck a dark key, the dark key was easily established as an effective S$^\Delta$ for not responding. The VI period and the extinction period were then gradually lengthened until they each lasted 3 minutes. Following this, the dark key was illuminated with a faint greenish hue that was slowly intensified. As the green key color was faded in (as an S$^\Delta$) and gradually replaced the dark key, the pigeons emitted almost no responses toward it, that is, they made almost no errors. By comparison, pigeons that were exposed to standard discrimination training, in which the dark key was suddenly replaced by a brightly lit green key, made numerous responses on it before finally discriminating it from the red S^D. The pigeons exposed to the errorless procedure also showed few of the adverse side effects of discrimination training, such as emotional behavior.

Errorless procedures can also be used to transfer control from one type of stimulus to another. For example, Terrace (1963b) first trained pigeons to discriminate between a red key as the S^D and a green key as the S$^\Delta$. He then gradually faded in a vertical line (the new S^D) on the red key and a horizontal line (the new S$^\Delta$) on the green key, while at the same time fading out the colors. Eventually, the pigeons were pecking a colorless key that had a vertical line and not pecking a colorless key that had a horizontal line. With virtually no errors, stimulus control for pecking had been transferred from key color (red versus green) to line orientation (vertical versus horizontal).

Errorless discrimination training may have practical applications. For example, Haupt, Van Kirk, and Terraciano (1975) used an errorless procedure to enhance the learning of basic arithmetic skills. In their study, a 9-year-old girl who had a history of difficulties in basic arithmetic was given a series of addition problems using a standard drill procedure and a series of subtraction problems using an errorless procedure. The standard drill procedure for the addition problems consisted of presenting the problems on flash cards in which the answers were initially covered. If the child did not know the answer, the answer was uncovered and shown to her. The errorless procedure for the subtraction problems was similar except that the answer on each flash card was initially left exposed to view and then, over successive presentations, gradually blocked out by adding successive sheets of cellophane. The correct answer was thus initially available as a prompt for the correct answer and then gradually faded out. During a subsequent test, the girl made significantly fewer errors on the subtraction problems for which the errorless procedure had been used, than on the addition problems for which the standard drill procedure had been used.

Although errorless discrimination training might seem like the perfect answer to many unresolved problems in education, it has some serious drawbacks. Discriminations that have been established through errorless training are more difficult to modify at a later point in time. For example, Marsh and Johnson (1968) taught pigeons to discriminate between two key colors in which one color was the S^D and the other the S$^\Delta$. Pigeons who had been taught to discriminate using an errorless procedure experienced extreme difficulty learning a new discrimination in which the meaning of the key colors was reversed (i.e., the color that had previously been the S^D now became the S$^\Delta$, and vice versa). In contrast, pigeons that had learned the original discrimination in the normal error-filled way handled the reversal quite handily. Thus, although normal discrimination training has more adverse side effects compared to errorless discrimination training, it also results in greater flexibility when what is learned has to be modified later. For this reason, errorless procedures may be most useful in rote learning of basic facts, such as arithmetic and spelling, in which the substance of what is learned is unlikely to change. With material that requires greater flexibility, however, such as that which is typically found in most college-level courses, errorless learning might be a significant impediment (Pierce & Epling, 1999).[4]

1. In e_____ discrimination training, the S$^\Delta$ must be presented (early/later) _____ in the training procedure, and at very (weak/strong) _____ intensity to begin with.

2. This type of discrimination training is likely to produce (more/less) _____ emotional behavior compared to the standard form of discrimination training.

3. This type of discrimination training is also likely to produce behavior patterns that are (easy/difficult) _____ to modify at a later point in time.

4. Gradually altering the intensity of a stimulus is called f_____.

[4]This accords with the more general finding, briefly mentioned in Chapter 1, that experiencing a certain amount of difficulty during the learning process can enhance long-term retention and understanding (Schmidt & Bjork, 1992).

Stimulus Control: Additional Applications

There are many ways in which stimulus control can be used to manage behavior. Perhaps the most impressive use of stimulus control is by animal trainers, especially those who train animals for public performance. Dolphin trainers, for example, use a mere whistle or gesture to set off a dazzling array of leaps and twirls. Indeed, the control is so precise that the dolphins often seem like robots, an impression that probably contributes to the growing opposition to such shows. Not only has the animal been removed from its natural environment, it now appears to be a slave to the trainer's every whim. (Karen Pryor, 1999, however, contends that the reality is quite different, with such training—especially training through positive reinforcement—being much more a two-way process of communication than brute force control.)

A particularly useful form of stimulus control for animal management is *targeting*. Targeting involves shaping an animal to approach and touch a particular object, for example, shaping a dog to touch the end of a stick with its nose. Targeting is a key aspect of training dolphins to make their impressive leaps. The dolphin is first shaped to touch a target stick with its nose, following which the stick is raised higher and higher, enticing the dolphin to leap higher and higher to touch it. Targeting is commonly used to manage animals in zoos. By simply moving the target stick, zookeepers can lead the animals from one cage to another or position them precisely for medical examinations. Animals can also be taught to target a point of light from a laser beam, which then allows the handler to send the animal to a spot some distance away. This can be a useful procedure for directing search-and-rescue dogs in disaster areas that are difficult for the handler to traverse (Pryor, 1999).

Stimulus control can also be used to eliminate certain types of problem behaviors. Pryor (1999), for example, describes how she once experienced considerable difficulty in training a dolphin to wear suction cups over its eyes (as part of a demonstration of the dolphin's ability to swim solely by sonar). Although the cups did not hurt, the dolphin refused to wear them and would cleverly sink to the bottom of the pool for several minutes whenever it saw Pryor approaching with the cups. Initially stumped, Pryor finally hit on the idea of reinforcing the behavior of sinking by giving the dolphin a fish whenever it did so (which, she reports, seemed to greatly surprise the dolphin). Soon, the dolphin was sinking at high frequency to earn fish, at which point Pryor began to reinforce the behavior only after a cue had been presented. In short order, the dolphin was sinking only on cue, meaning that the behavior was now under strong stimulus control. Pryor found that she was then able to reintroduce the suction cups and place them on the dolphin without difficulty. In the absence of the cue for sinking, the dolphin no longer had a tendency to sink to avoid the cups. In similar fashion, a dog that has been trained to bark on cue may be less likely to bark at other times. In short, by putting a behavior "on cue," the behavior is less likely to occur in the absence of the cue.

Stimulus control is obviously an important aspect of human behavior, though we sometimes overlook it as a simple means for facilitating certain aspects of our own behavior. Consider Stephanie, who promises herself that she will take vitamins each evening but so often forgets to do so that she eventually gives up. All she really needs to do is create a salient cue for taking vitamins, such as placing the vitamin bottle beside the alarm clock that she sets each evening. Likewise, the person who remembers to take his umbrella in the morning is the person who sets it beside the door the night before when he hears that it will likely rain the next day.

Stimulus control is also useful for creating an effective study environment. Too often students attempt to study in settings that contain strong cues for nonstudy behaviors, such as interacting with others or watching television. Far better to study in a setting where such cues are kept to a minimum. For example, Heffernan and Richards (1981) found that students who, on their own, isolated themselves from interpersonal distractions in order to improve their study habits reported a major improvement. Likewise, Skinner (1987) recommends establishing a particular setting, such as a certain desk, that is used only for studying. Over time, the desk will become so strongly associated with the act of studying that just sitting at the desk will facilitate one's ability to study. Of course, this kind of stimulus control cannot be established overnight. Sitting at a desk for 3 hours at a time trying to study but daydreaming instead will only associate the desk with the act of daydreaming. Better to begin with short, high-quality study periods and then gradually progress to longer study periods (although, as the Calvin and Hobbes cartoon suggests, not too gradually).

An example of a procedure to improve study habits was reported by Fox (1962). The program began by first examining each student's schedule and finding a 1-hour period each day that was always available for studying. The students were instructed to spend at least part of that hour studying their most difficult subject matter. They were also told to conduct that studying only in a particular setting (such as a certain room in the library), to have only their study materials with them when they were in that setting, and not to be in that setting on other occasions. Most importantly, if they became bored or started

Calvin and Hobbes   by Bill Watterson

CALVIN AND HOBBES © Watterson. Reprinted with permission of Universal Press Syndicate. All rights reserved.

to daydream, they were to complete just a bit more studying (such as reading one page) and then leave the setting. Finally, any studying done outside the special 1-hour period had to be done elsewhere. Initially, none of the students could study throughout the 1-hour period, but over time they gradually built up the ability to do so. A similar procedure was then carried out for each of their other courses. Soon, the students were studying each of their courses for 1 hour per day, with a good level of concentration. The students were also given instruction in other academic skills, such as how to read a textbook and take lecture notes. The result was that all of the students experienced considerable improvement in their grades.

Stimulus control procedures are also the treatment of choice for sleep-onset insomnia, in which people have difficulty falling asleep. For example, Bootzin, Epstein, and Wood (1991) recommend the following procedure:

1. Go to bed only when you are sleepy.
2. Use the bed only for sleeping (or sex). Do not lie in bed to read, study, or watch television.
3. If you cannot fall asleep within 10 to 20 minutes, get out of bed and go to another room. Go back to bed only when you feel sleepy.
4. Repeat the above rule as often as necessary. This rule should also be applied if you are unable to fall asleep after a middle-of-the-night awakening.
5. Use your alarm to get up at the same time each morning, regardless of how you slept the night before.
6. Do not take naps during the day.

The obvious goal of the program is to make lying in bed a strong cue for sleeping. Research has shown this to be a very effective program, with many people reporting considerable improvement in their sleep habits both immediately following the program and at long-term follow-up (Lichstein & Riedel, 1994).

QUICK QUIZ

1. Shaping a rhinoceros to touch the end of a stick with its nose is an example of a useful behavior management technique called t_____.

2. Jaclyn's cat has a terrible habit of jumping up on the kitchen counter whenever Jaclyn is preparing food. How might Jaclyn use a stimulus control procedure to eliminate this behavior? _____
_____.

3. Briefly put, six rules for overcoming sleep-onset insomnia through the use of stimulus control are (chances are that you will have to check back to fill these out):

(1) _____
(2) _____
(3) _____
(4) _____
(5) _____
(6) _____

And Furthermore

Edwin Guthrie: Stimulus Control for the Practical Person

Edwin Guthrie (1886–1959) was a famous learning theorist who strongly emphasized the role of stimulus control because, from his perspective, all learning is a function of one basic principle: If a behavior occurs in the presence of certain stimuli, that behavior becomes automatically attached to those stimuli (Guthrie, 1952). Repeat those stimuli, and the person or animal must necessarily repeat the behavior.

Guthrie's theory makes a startlingly blunt prediction about behavior. Whatever you did the last time you were in a certain setting is exactly what you will do the next time you are in that setting. Suppose, for example, that the last time you walked down a certain hallway, you entered the first doorway to the right. Guthrie's theory predicts that the next time you walk down that hallway, you will again enter the first doorway to the right, *given that all the stimuli are the same as when you last walked down that hallway.* Of course, this last part is the catch. The stimuli that precede a behavior—and this can include both internal and external stimuli—are never exactly the same from one occasion to the next. Instead, they are only more or less the same, with the result that a behavior is only more or less likely to be repeated. But note that the consequences of the behavior—for example, perhaps you entered the first doorway to the right because it leads to the cafeteria where you bought coffee—do not enter into the equation. Guthrie viewed consequences as having only an indirect effect on behavior, though his explanation for how this works is too complex to delve into here.

Guthrie himself did little research, and the research that was done provided only equivocal support for his theory. As a result, it receives relatively little attention from modern-day researchers. Nonetheless, Guthrie's approach still has its adherents and is still considered a major theory of learning (Hergenhahn, 1988). Perhaps one reason for its enduring attraction is the simplicity of the theory (scientists often find a parsimonious explanation quite attractive, possibly because they so often have to deal with complexities). Another reason is the engaging practicality of the theory. Guthrie by nature was a pragmatic individual and often used homey, practical examples for illustration.

SUMMARY

Extinction is the nonreinforcement of a previously reinforced response, the result of which is a decrease in the strength of that response. Implementation of an extinction procedure is often followed by an extinction burst, which is a temporary increase in the rate and intensity of a behavior. Extinction is also followed by an increase in the variability of behavior and in emotional behavior, especially aggression. Extinction can also be accompanied by resurgence—the sudden appearance of a different behavior that had once been reinforced—and depression.

Resistance to extinction is the extent to which responding persists during extinction. According to the partial reinforcement effect, an intermittent

One of Guthrie's most cited examples is that of a young girl who each day threw her coat on the floor when she arrived home and was each day scolded by her mother (Guthrie, 1952). On the surface, we might speculate that the girl repeated the behavior because it was reinforced by the attention she received from her mother. From Guthrie's perspective, however, the mother's reaction had little effect on the behavior. Rather, the stimuli that the girl encountered when she entered the house had become so strongly connected to the response of throwing the coat on the floor that this response automatically occurred each time she entered. To finally solve the problem, the mother began to insist that the child pick up her coat, go back outside, and then practice the behavior of entering the house and hanging up the coat. The stimuli present when the girl entered the house then became associated with the act of hanging up the coat rather than throwing it on the floor, and the new behavior supplanted the old. Thus, from Guthrie's perspective, problem behaviors in a certain setting can often be rectified by deliberately practicing appropriate behaviors in that setting.

Another example is that of a student who was having difficulty studying because she was continually distracted by the sound of a neighbor's radio (Guthrie, 1952). Instead of trying to force herself to study, the student read mystery stories. The stories were so interesting that she was able to read them without being distracted by the sound of the radio. Within a week, the behavior of concentrating while reading had become so firmly established in that setting that she was then able to switch back to her study materials and concentrate well despite the radio.

This last example implies that students who have difficulty concentrating might sometimes do well to study something interesting before they study something boring. Starting with interesting material might establish a strong level of concentration that will then carry over to the less interesting material. This, of course, seems to contradict Grandma's rule—or the Premack principle, if you will—which contends that you should work before you play (applied to studying, this means that you should start with less interesting material and finish off with more interesting material). Guthrie, by contrast, seems to suggest that it might sometimes be useful to play before you work.

schedule of reinforcement, especially a VR schedule, produces greater resistance to extinction than a continuous schedule. Resistance also varies directly with the number of times the behavior has been reinforced, the magnitude of the reinforcers that have been used, and the extent to which the animal has been deprived of the reinforcer. Previous experience with extinction tends to lower resistance to extinction, as does the presence of a discriminative stimulus for extinction (known as an S^{Δ}).

Spontaneous recovery is the reappearance of an extinguished response following a rest period after extinction. With repeated sessions of extinction, however, the amount of recovery gradually diminishes. The process of extinction can be facilitated through differential reinforcement of other behaviors (especially incompatible behaviors).

A behavior is said to be under stimulus control when the presence of an S^D reliably affects the likelihood of a behavior. The tendency to respond to stimuli similar to the S^D is called stimulus generalization; the tendency to not respond to such stimuli is stimulus discrimination. A graph that indicates the degree of generalization to similar stimuli is a generalization gradient. A flat gradient indicates strong generalization; a steep gradient indicates weak generalization. The peak shift effect is the tendency, following discrimination training, for the peak of a generalization gradient to shift to one side of the S^D, to a point that is further removed from the S$^\Delta$.

A multiple schedule consists of two or more schedules presented in sequence, each resulting in reinforcement and each having a distinctive S^D. Multiple schedules are used to study contrast effects. In a negative contrast effect, an increase in reinforcement on one component of a multiple schedule produces a decrease in responding on the other component. In a positive contrast effect, a decrease in the reinforcement on one component produces an increase in responding on the other component. In anticipatory contrast, the rate of response varies inversely with an upcoming ("anticipated") change in the rate of reinforcement.

Errorless discrimination training is a procedure that minimizes the number of errors and reduces many of the side effects associated with discrimination training. It involves presenting the S$^\Delta$ early in training, beginning in weak form, then gradually strengthening it (known as a fading procedure). A drawback to errorless discrimination training is that behavior that has been acquired in this fashion is later more difficult to modify.

Stimulus control procedures have been applied to a number of behavior problems, ranging from moving animals about in zoos, to facilitating the act of studying, to treating insomnia.

STUDY QUESTIONS

1. Define extinction as it applies to operant conditioning. Be sure to distinguish between the process of extinction and the procedure of extinction.
2. What is an extinction burst? What is resurgence?
3. What are four side effects of extinction, other than extinction burst and resurgence?
4. What is resistance to extinction? Be sure to distinguish between low resistance and high resistance to extinction.
5. Define the partial reinforcement effect. Of the four basic intermittent schedules, which produces the strongest resistance to extinction?
6. How is resistance to extinction affected by history of reinforcement, magnitude of reinforcement, degree of deprivation, and previous experience with extinction?
7. What is spontaneous recovery and how is it affected by successive sessions of extinction?
8. Define a DRO procedure. How does it differ from a DRI procedure?

9. Why is a DRO procedure more effective in eliminating a behavior than a straight extinction procedure?

10. Define stimulus control. What would be an example of stimulus control of behavior at a hockey game and at a church service?

11. Define stimulus generalization and stimulus discrimination as they occur in operant conditioning.

12. What is an S^Δ? Describe the process of discrimination training.

13. What is a generalization gradient? How does the shape of the gradient reflect the degree of generalization?

14. Define the peak shift effect. Illustrate your answer with a graph of a generalization gradient.

15. Define a multiple schedule. Diagram (and label) an experimental example involving the response of lever pressing for food on an FR 20 and VI 30-sec schedule, and the stimuli of tone and light.

16. What is behavioral contrast? Define positive and negative contrast effects.

17. Define anticipatory contrast and give an example.

18. Describe errorless discrimination training and the two basic aspects of this procedure. What is a major drawback of such training?

19. How might a bird owner use stimulus control to eliminate a parrot's tendency to squawk for long periods of time? How might a novelist use stimulus control to facilitate the act of writing?

CONCEPT REVIEW

anticipatory contrast. The process whereby the rate of response varies inversely with an upcoming ("anticipated") change in the rate of reinforcement.

behavioral contrast. A change in the rate of reinforcement on one component of a multiple schedule produces an opposite change in the rate of response on another component.

differential reinforcement of other behavior (DRO). Reinforcement of any behavior other than a target behavior that is being extinguished. One variant of this is called differential reinforcement of incompatible behavior (DRI), in which the behavior that is being reinforced is specifically incompatible with the behavior being extinguished.

discrimination training. As applied to operant conditioning, the differential reinforcement of responding in the presence of one stimulus (the S^D) and not another.

discriminative stimulus for extinction (S^Δ). A stimulus that signals the absence of reinforcement.

errorless discrimination training. A discrimination training procedure that minimizes the number of errors (i.e., nonreinforced responses to the S^Δ), and reduces many of the adverse effects associated with discrimination training.

extinction burst. A temporary increase in the frequency and intensity of responding when extinction is first implemented.

extinction. The nonreinforcement of a previously reinforced response, the result of which is a decrease in the strength of that response.

fading. The process of gradually altering the intensity of a stimulus.

generalization gradient. A graphic description of the strength of responding in the presence of stimuli that are similar to the S^D and vary along a continuum.

multiple schedule. A complex schedule that consists of two or more independent schedules presented in sequence, each resulting in reinforcement and each having a distinctive S^D.

negative contrast effect. The process whereby an increase in the rate of reinforcement on one component of a multiple schedule produces a decrease in the rate of response on the other component.

partial reinforcement effect. The process whereby behavior that has been maintained on an intermittent (partial) schedule of reinforcement extinguishes more slowly than behavior that has been maintained on a continuous schedule.

peak shift effect. Following discrimination training, the peak of a generalization gradient will shift from the S^D to a stimulus that is further removed from the S^Δ.

positive behavioral contrast. The process whereby a decrease in rate of reinforcement on one component of a multiple schedule produces an increase in the rate of response on the other component.

resistance to extinction. The extent to which responding persists after an extinction procedure has been implemented.

resurgence. The reappearance during extinction of other behaviors that had once been effective in obtaining reinforcement.

spontaneous recovery. The reappearance of an extinguished response following a rest period after extinction.

stimulus control. A situation in which the presence of a discriminative stimulus reliably affects the probability of a behavior.

stimulus discrimination. The tendency for an operant response to be emitted more in the presence of one stimulus than another.

stimulus generalization. The tendency for an operant response to be emitted in the presence of a stimulus that is similar to an S^D.

CHAPTER TEST

16. When Asha's parents won the lottery and bought her lots of neat playthings, she became (less/more) _____ interested in school. This is an example of a _____ contrast effect.

4. When Erin was babysitting Lulu, it took hours before Lulu would stop pestering her for a treat (Erin had been instructed not to give her any treats). The next time Erin baby-sits Lulu, Lulu will (probably/probably

not) _____ resume asking for a treat. This can be considered an example of an extinction effect known as _____. This may be occurring in this case because the entry of a babysitter into the house is, for Lulu, a _____ stimulus indicating that a treat will soon become available.

10. Lulu is ecstatic when Tore is her baby-sitter, and completely indifferent when Natasha is her baby-sitter. This is because Tore tends to give her treats, while Natasha does not. Thus, Tore is an (give the abbreviation) _____ for the availability of treats, while Natasha is an _____.

27. More persistent is to less persistent as (high/low) _____ resistance to extinction is to _____ resistance to extinction.

15. When Trish's friend, Laura, spread some nasty rumors about her, Trish stopped talking to her. Laura did not understand the reason for Trish's silence and initially (increased/decreased) _____ the frequency with which she attempted to talk to Laura. From the perspective of this being an extinction process, Laura's behavior can be seen as an example of a(n) _____.

9. Right after Gina was stung by a hornet, she was as likely to run away from houseflies as from hornets, which is an example of stimulus _____. One year later, we find that Gina runs away from hornets but not houseflies, which is an example of stimulus _____.

19. Lana finds that the children in her class are extremely unruly. To solve this problem, she announces that whenever she is holding up a flag, the children can run around and do whatever they want. Then, periodically throughout the day, she holds up the flag for a few minutes and lets the children run around like crazy. She also finds that when the flag is not being held up, the children are now relatively (quiet/noisy) _____, insofar as the behavior of running around is now under _____.

5. When Erin was baby-sitting Lulu, it took hours before Lulu would stop pestering her for a treat. Erin could likely have speeded up this process through the use of a (give the abbreviation) _____ procedure.

11. When Megan lived in Vancouver, she dated Mike, who was quite uneducated, and David, who was moderately educated. She had a boring time with Mike and a great time with David. She then moved to Dallas and set her sights on meeting someone new. According to the _____ effect, we would expect her to be most interested in meeting someone (as educated as/more educated than) _____ David.

21. In behavioral _____, a change in the rate of _____ on one component of a multiple schedule is followed by a(n) (similar/opposite) _____ change in the rate of _____ on the other component.

7. On a generalization gradient, the strongest response typically occurs to the _____.

13. The nonreinforcement of a previously reinforced response defines the _____ of extinction, while the resultant decrease in the strength of that response defines the _____ of extinction.

3. A dog whose begging for food has been reinforced 200 times is likely to show greater _____ than a dog whose begging has been reinforced only 10 times.

17. Yan lives in a very crowded city, so he teaches his little boy to stay in close contact with his right hand whenever they are walking in a crowd. This is similar to a behavior management technique known as _____ that is used to guide animals.

6. When the commander yells "Charge!" all of his troops climb out of the trench and start running toward the enemy. The behavior of these troops is obviously under strong _____ control.

25. While teaching his daughter the letters of the alphabet, Vern would say each letter as he showed it to her and then encourage her to repeat what he said. He then began to say the letters more and more softly, with the result that she eventually said them on her own without any prompt from him. This can be seen as an example of _____ discrimination learning. One problem with this type of method is that the learning that results from this procedure tends to be (inflexible/too flexible) _____.

22. When Trish's friend Laura spread some nasty rumors about her, Trish stopped talking to her. Laura tried very hard to get Trish to talk to her. She also became emotionally (upset/distant) _____, which included becoming quite _____ with Trish.

2. When visiting a foreign resort last summer, you frequently encountered a group of children in the street who were trying to sell souvenirs. Although you always rejected their sales pitches, they were incredibly persistent. Chances are that this persistence results from the fact that their behavior of selling merchandise is on a(n) _____ schedule of reinforcement. Another factor would be the fact that the children seemed quite poor; hence, they were relatively _____ of the sought-after reinforcer.

8. A _____ indicates the strength of responding in the presence of stimuli that are similar to the _____ and that vary along a _____.

23. When Tamara first moved to the city, she went out each evening and had a great time. One night, however, she had a frightening experience at a nightclub, which really turned her off the club scene. Interestingly, she subsequently became (more/less) _____ interested in other activities, including her job. This may be an example of a(n) _____ contrast effect.

14. The first step in carrying out an extinction procedure is to identify the _____ that is maintaining the behavior.

18. When Trish's friend Laura spread some nasty rumors about her, Trish stopped talking to her. Laura tried very hard to get Trish to talk to her

but quickly gave up. Laura's behavior of trying to interact with Trish seems to have (low/high) _____ resistance to extinction.

24. Sven found school only slightly interesting. Unfortunately, his lack of studying led to some very poor marks one semester, with the result that he faced the real threat of being forced to withdraw for a year. Throughout the remainder of the semester, Sven was probably (more/less) _____ interested in his schoolwork. This can be seen as an example of _____ contrast.

12. A _____ schedule consists of two or more independent schedules presented (simultaneously/sequentially) _____, each resulting in a _____ and each having a distinctive _____.

1. When Trish's friend Laura spread some nasty rumors about her, Trish stopped talking to her. Laura tried hard to get Trish to talk to her. She even asked Trish if she would like to go to the local video arcade, which had been a favorite activity of theirs when they first became friends. This may be an example of an extinction effect known as _____.

20. When Trish's friend Laura spread some nasty rumors about her, Trish stopped talking to her. Laura tried hard to get Trish to talk to her, phoning her, emailing, writing letters, and sending messages through mutual friends. The many ways in which Laura attempted to interact with Trish are indicative of an effect that often accompanies extinction, which is an increase in the _____ of a behavior.

26. When Trish's best friend Laura spread some nasty rumors about her, Trish stopped talking to her. Laura tried very hard to get Trish to talk to her. When Trish refused, Laura eventually became _____, one symptom of which was a relatively (low/high) _____ level of activity.

ANSWERS TO CHAPTER TEST

1. resurgence
2. intermittent (VR); deprived
3. resistance to extinction
4. probably; spontaneous recovery; discriminative
5. DRO (or DRI)
6. stimulus
7. S^D
8. generalization gradient; S^D; continuum
9. generalization; discrimination
10. S^D; S$^\Delta$
11. peak shift; more educated than
12. multiple; sequentially; reinforcer; S^D
13. procedure; process
14. reinforcer
15. increased; extinction burst

16. less; negative
17. targeting
18. low
19. quiet; stimulus control
20. variability
21. contrast; reinforcement; opposite; response
22. upset; angry
23. more; positive
24. more; anticipatory
25. errorless; inflexible
26. depressed; low
27. high; low

Put Learning into Action with Sniffy, the Virtual Rat

The following material refers to *Sniffy, the Virtual Rat*™: *Pro Version*, a separate Wadsworth product that consists of a manual and a CD-ROM.

1. Complete exercise 5 (pp. 34–38) for a demonstration of the extinction of Sniffy's lever pressing behavior after he had been trained on a CRF (i.e., an FR 1) schedule. Take note of the extinction burst on the cumulative record.

   At this point you might also want to complete exercise 6 (pp. 38–39) on the role of secondary reinforcement in extinction. (Consider re-reading the relevant section of Chapter 6 in the textbook to refresh your memory of the use of secondary reinforcement in operant conditioning.)

2. Exercise 13 (pp. 58–59) will allow you to investigate Sniffy's resistance to extinction when he has been trained on partial reinforcement schedules.

3. Complete exercise 7 (pp. 40–42) for a demonstration of spontaneous recovery with Sniffy.

4. Read pp. 61–67 for additional background information on stimulus generalization and discrimination, and to understand how the *Sniffy Pro* software models these operant conditioning processes. Next, carefully read the information and instructions on pp. 67–73, which you will need to successfully complete exercises 14–19. Finally, follow the instructions to run exercises 14–16 (pp. 73–77). (Note that Sniffy uses the symbol S+ rather than S^D and S− rather than S^Δ.)

5. See pp. 81–82 for additional information on the peak shift effect.

6. Complete exercises 17–19 (pp. 77–80). When you have finished, try to generate a graph showing the peak shift effect, similar to the one illustrated on p. 81.

Escape, Avoidance, and Punishment

Jim informed Misha, his new girlfriend, that he was once married to a woman who had been diagnosed with depression. He explained that she had stopped working, moped around the house all day, and would often break down and start crying. Despite his best efforts to be supportive, they finally got a divorce. Misha felt a lot of sympathy for Jim, who was obviously a very caring fellow. After several months, though, she noticed that she herself was becoming depressed. Although Jim was often quite affectionate, he would also become angry with her or, worse yet, grow coldly silent for no apparent reason. He also had a tendency to contradict her whenever she offered her opinion on some matter, and he took special pains to point out her mistakes (because, he said, he loved her so much that he wanted to be honest with her). Misha then learned that Jim's former wife had made a remarkable recovery soon after their divorce.

   This chapter explores the effects of aversive consequences on behavior. We will begin by examining the role of negative reinforcement in the development of escape and avoidance behaviors. As you will see, this process plays a critical role in the development and maintenance of phobic and obsessive-compulsive disorders in humans. We will follow this with a discussion of punishment, in which the presentation or withdrawal of consequences serves to suppress a behavior. The discussion will include a listing of some undesirable side effects of punishment, as well as some of the ways in which punishment can be effective. The chapter will then close with a discussion of the harmful effects of noncontingent punishment, in which the punishing stimulus is delivered independently of the individual's behavior.

Escape and Avoidance

As you will recall from Chapter 6, negative reinforcement consists of the removal of an aversive stimulus following a response, which then leads to an increase in the strength of that response. For example, if we wave our hands at a bothersome wasp and the wasp flies away, we will likely repeat that action with the next wasp that annoys us. Negative reinforcement is associated with two types of behavior: (1) *escape behavior*, in which performance of the behavior terminates the aversive stimulus, and (2) *avoidance behavior*, in which performance of the behavior prevents the aversive stimulus from occurring. Thus, we escape from the rain when we run indoors after it has started; we avoid the rain when we head indoors before it has started.
   Typically, one first learns to escape from an aversive stimulus and then to avoid it. This process can be demonstrated using a *shuttle avoidance procedure*, in which an animal has to shuttle back and forth in a box in order to avoid an aversive stimulus. In one version of this procedure, a rat is placed in a cham-

ber divided by a low barrier. A stimulus of some sort, such as a light, is presented for, say, 10 seconds, followed by a mild electric shock. The rat can escape the shock by climbing over the barrier to the other side of the compartment, as it will quickly learn to do whenever it feels a shock (see top panel of Figure 9.1). Technically speaking, at this early point in the process, the presence of shock is a discriminative stimulus that sets the occasion for the escape behavior of crossing the barrier. Crossing the barrier is then negatively reinforced by the removal of shock:

Shock: *Cross barrier* → **Removal of shock**
S^D **R** S^R

Now, remember that the shock is preceded by the presentation of a light, which is in essence a warning signal that a shock is about to occur. As the rat learns to associate the light with the shock, it will begin crossing the barrier whenever the light is presented and before the shock begins (see bottom panel of Figure 9.1). The light is now the effective discriminative stimulus for the avoidance response of crossing the barrier.

Light: *Cross barrier* → **Avoidance of shock**
S^D **R** S^R

In similar fashion, we might first learn to escape from an upsetting conversation with a racist acquaintance by inventing an excuse for leaving. After

FIGURE 9.1 Escape and avoidance in a shuttle avoidance task. As shown in the top panel, the animal first learns to escape from the shock by climbing over the barrier whenever a shock occurs. Later, as it learns that the light predicts the occurrence of shock, it climbs over the barrier whenever the light appears, thereby avoiding the shock (as shown in the bottom panel). (*Source:* Nairne, 2000.)

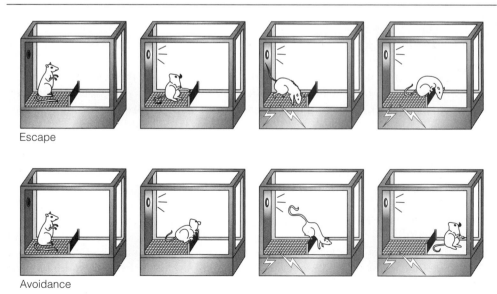

Escape

Avoidance

a few experiences, however, we might begin actively avoiding that individual prior to any encounter. By doing so, we avoid having to endure any exposure to that person's racist views.

1. Behavior that terminates an aversive stimulus is called _____ behavior, while behavior that prevents an aversive stimulus from occurring is called _____ behavior.

2. Typically, one first learns to _____ from an aversive stimulus, and then to _____ it.

3. Roman initially takes vitamin C whenever he has a cold, in the hope that it will shorten the duration of his symptoms. Feeling that this is effective, he begins taking it daily in the hope that it will keep him from contracting a cold. Roman initially took the vitamin C in order to (avoid/escape) _____ the symptoms of a cold; he later took it in order to _____ the symptoms of a cold.

4. In the shuttle avoidance procedure described above, the rat first learns to _____ from the shock, with the _____ acting as the S^D for the behavior. The rat later learns to _____ the shock, with the _____ acting as the S^D for the behavior.

Two-Process Theory of Avoidance

Researchers have generally shown more interest in studying avoidance behavior than escape behavior. This is because, from a theoretical perspective, escape behavior is relatively easy to understand. For example, when escaping from shock by climbing over a barrier, the rat moves from a clearly aversive situation to a nonaversive situation. But the motivation underlying avoidance behavior is less apparent. When climbing over a barrier to avoid shock, the rat seems to be moving from one nonaversive situation (no shock) to another nonaversive situation (no shock). How can a lack of change function as a reinforcer?

An early attempt to explain avoidance behavior was the *two-process theory of avoidance* (also known as the *two-factor theory of avoidance*) proposed by Mowrer (1947, 1960). According to this theory, two processes are involved in learning an avoidance response. The first process is classical conditioning of a fear response to a CS. For example, in the shuttle avoidance procedure described above, the light that precedes the shock becomes a CS that elicits a conditioned fear reaction:

Light: Shock → *Fear*
  NS   US   UR
Light → *Fear*
  CS   CR

Once this conditioned fear has been established, it then forms the basis of an operant conditioning procedure. If the CS generates a conditioned fear response, then moving away from the CS should result in a reduction of fear. This reduction of fear should in turn serve as a negative reinforcer for the response that produced it. In our experimental example, the presentation of the light elicits a conditioned fear response, while climbing over the barrier produces a reduction in fear that serves as a negative reinforcer for climbing over the barrier.

Light: *Climb over barrier* → **Reduction in fear**
$\quad$ S^D $\qquad\qquad$ R $\qquad\qquad\qquad$ S^R

Thus, Mowrer's *two-process theory of avoidance* proposes that avoidance behavior is the result of two distinct processes: (1) classical conditioning in which a fear response comes to be elicited by a CS, and (2) operant conditioning in which moving away from the CS is negatively reinforced by a reduction in fear.

1. It is relatively easy to understand the process underlying (escape/avoidance) _____ conditioning because the organism moves from an _____ situation to a non_____ situation. By contrast, it is more difficult to understand _____ conditioning because the organism moves from a(n) _____ situation to another _____ situation.

2. According to Mowrer, avoidance is the result of two distinct processes: (1) _____ conditioning of a _____ response, and (2) _____ conditioning in which an avoidance response is n_____ r_____ by a reduction in _____.

Mowrer's two-process theory became the focus of a considerable amount of research, with the result that researchers soon discovered a number of apparent difficulties with it. One problem was that avoidance responses are often extremely persistent. Solomon, Kamin, and Wynn (1953), for example, found that dogs would continue to jump a barrier to avoid shock for hundreds of trials even though the shock apparatus had been disconnected and avoidance was no longer necessary. One dog, for example, made over 600 avoidance responses before the experimenters finally gave up and put a stop to the session.

On the surface, it seems as though two-process theory cannot account for such persistence. If the animal repeatedly encounters the CS in the absence of the US, then fear of the CS should eventually extinguish—meaning that the animal should eventually stop jumping over the barrier. But it seemed as though the behavior would not extinguish. Why not?

A possible answer to this question is provided by a modification of two-process theory known as the *anxiety conservation hypothesis* (Solomon & Wynne, 1954). According to this approach, avoidance responses usually occur so quickly that there is insufficient exposure to the CS for the conditioned fear to fully extinguish—that is, a good deal of the conditioned fear is conserved because exposures to the CS are too brief for extinction to take place.[1] For this reason, avoidance responses can be extremely persistent. In addition, supporters of two-process theory have pointed out that avoidance responses are not as persistent as sometimes claimed (Levis, 1989). If one persists in exposing the animal to the aversive CS, extinction will eventually occur given that there are no further pairings of the CS with the US. Thus, the fact that avoidance responses are extremely persistent might not be as damaging a criticism of two-process theory as was first assumed.

Researchers, however, also discovered a second, more serious difficulty with two-process theory. They found that, after repeated avoidance trials, animals appeared to show no evidence of fear but continued to make the avoidance response anyway (Solomon & Wynn, 1953). In other words, once the animals had become adept at making the avoidance response, they seemed to become almost nonchalant and relaxed while carrying it out. This constituted a major problem for two-process theory, since if the animals were no longer afraid of the CS, how could avoidance of the CS have been negatively reinforced by a reduction in fear?

This was a pretty damaging criticism, and for a while it looked as though two-process theory was pretty much on the ropes. Levis (1989), however, has recently argued that although animals in avoidance experiments may become significantly *less* fearful with experience, there is no evidence that they become completely nonfearful. In fact, evidence suggests that if an animal completely loses its fear of the aversive CS, then, just as two-process theory predicts, the avoidance response ceases to occur. But as long as some fear remains, the avoidance response continues, suggesting that fear reduction is still functioning as a negative reinforcer for the behavior (Levis & Boyd, 1979).

Various other theories have been proposed to account for avoidance behavior. According to *one-process theory*, for example, the act of avoidance is negatively reinforced simply by the lower rate of aversive stimulation with which it is associated (Herrnstein, 1969; Herrnstein & Hineline, 1966). Thus, the rat in a shuttle avoidance task persistently climbs over the barrier when the light comes on because this action results in a decreased rate of shock, and not because it results in decreased feelings of fear. The attractive aspect of this theory is that it does away with any reference to an internal state of fear, the existence of which has to be inferred. The overall reduction in aversive stimulation that accompanies avoidance is regarded as a sufficient explanation for the behavior. By contrast, Bolles's (1970) *species-specific defense reaction theory* contends that many avoidance behaviors are actually elicited behaviors rather than operant behaviors. (This theory will be described in Chapter 11.) Evi-

---

[1] It is also possible, according to Eysenck's (1968) theory of incubation (discussed in Chapter 5), that such brief exposures might sometimes strengthen a conditioned fear response, which would further counteract the process of extinction.

dence exists both for and against each of these theories. (See Domjan, 1998, for an overview of these and other theories of avoidance.)

The debate over the processes underlying avoidance behavior will likely continue for some time, and it could well be that several processes are involved. At the very least, avoidance behavior is turning out to be more complicated than researchers originally suspected. Fortunately, the knowledge gained from all this theorizing and research is proving to have practical application, particularly in the analysis and treatment of anxiety disorders—a topic to which we turn next.

1. One apparent problem with two-process theory is that, even after hundreds of trials, the avoidance response does not seem to e_____.

2. However, according to the a_____ c_____ hypothesis, avoidance responses usually occur so (quickly/slowly) _____ that exposures to the (CS/US) _____ are too (long/brief) _____ for _____ to take place.

3. A second problem with Mowrer's theory is that after sufficient experience with avoiding the aversive CS, the animals no longer show any _____, yet continue to make the avoidance response. Levis (1989), however, contends that such animals are nevertheless still (slightly/strongly) _____ fearful, otherwise the avoidance response would extinguish.

4. According to the one-process theory of avoidance, the avoidance response is negatively reinforced by a reduction in overall rate of _____ _____, as opposed to a reduction in _____.

5. According to species-specific defense reaction theory, avoidance responses are often (learned/innate) _____ reactions to aversive stimulation that are automatically (emitted/elicited) _____ in dangerous situations.

Avoidance Conditioning and Phobias

In Chapter 5, we noted that the basis of many phobias is the development of a classically conditioned fear response, which then fails to extinguish because the individual avoids the feared stimulus. At that time, we focused upon the classical conditioning aspect of a phobia. Let us now examine the role of avoidance learning in phobic development.

As noted, avoidance learning appears to be a fundamental process in the development and maintenance of phobic behavior. This is no doubt one reason for the intense interest researchers have shown in studying avoidance. Indeed, demonstrations of avoidance learning in laboratory rats have often been regarded as applicable to phobic conditioning in humans. But is avoidance conditioning in the laboratory a true analogue of human phobic conditioning? Does a rat avoid shock in a shuttle avoidance procedure in the same

And Furthermore

Repression: Avoidance of Distressing Thoughts?

Repression is one of the most contentious concepts in present-day psychology. Simply defined (and ignoring some of the complexities), repression refers to the removal of anxiety-provoking thoughts from conscious awareness. Beginning in the 1980s, many therapists became intensely interested in this concept. In particular, they discovered that many clients were able to uncover seemingly forgotten memories of childhood abuse when encouraged to do so, and these memories seemed to be related to their symptoms (Herman, 1992). A controversy arose, however, when some memory researchers warned that such "recovered memories" might often be false memories of traumatic incidents that never occurred (e.g., Loftus, 1993).

Can the principles of conditioning give us any insight into this controversy? As it turns out, repression can be viewed as a type of avoidance response. More specifically, the process of repression might be a covert form of avoidance conditioning in which the event being avoided is not an external event, such as a phobic object, but an internal thought. The memory of a childhood trauma is therefore an aversive stimulus that generates anxiety, which in turn motivates one to escape from the anxiety by thinking of something else. With practice, one eventually learns to think of something else before the memory even arises, thereby avoiding the memory (e.g., Levis, 1995; see also Skinner, 1953). To the extent that the memory is consistently avoided, never entering consciousness, then it meets the definition of being repressed.

The process of repression is therefore consistent with some basic principles of conditioning. Principles of conditioning, however, also suggest that it may be possible to generate false memories of abuse. If covert behavior is governed by many of the same principles as overt behavior, then it is conceivable that a therapist might inadvertently shape an individual to produce novel patterns of thought that depict a history of abuse and then reinforce the individual for labeling such thoughts as memories. Consistent with this notion of shap-

manner that a person avoids dogs after being bitten? In fact, some have argued that there are considerable differences between avoidance conditioning in an experimental setting and human phobic conditioning.

Mineka (1985), for example, has claimed that there are two limitations in applying models of experimental avoidance to human phobias. The first limitation concerns the nature of what is being avoided. *In experimental avoidance conditioning, the animal avoids the aversive US.* For example, in the shuttle avoidance procedure discussed earlier, the rat avoids the shock (US) by climbing over the barrier whenever it sees the light (CS). *In human phobias, however, people avoid the CS.* A person who has been attacked by a dog and now has a severe phobia of dogs not only avoids being attacked by a dog, but also avoids the possibility of even encountering a dog. A person who has a fear of eleva-

ing, some therapists admit that the process of uncovering repressed memories is often gradual, with the memories first appearing as fragmented images that are then strengthened and clarified by repeatedly thinking about them. As well, some therapists warn clients to discuss their recovered memories only with other survivors of abuse, who will reinforce the clients for believing that these memories are real. The overall result is that clients may become increasingly proficient at generating mental images of childhood trauma, which are believed to be genuine memories (Pendergrast, 1995).

Of course, the possibility that reinforcement and shaping may be involved in the generation of recovered memories does not prove that recovered memories are mostly false. It could be that by first uncovering and confirming a fragmented memory of abuse, a sort of desensitization occurs which then allows a more complete memory to emerge (Levis, 1995). On the other side of the coin, however, the fact that the process of repression is explainable in terms of avoidance conditioning does not constitute strong evidence that repression actually occurs and that recovered memories are often real. Thus, if our behavioristic analysis of recovered memories offers any insight into this controversy, it is simply that there are no easy answers. One would therefore do well to approach this issue with caution.

Finally, in an interesting aside to the controversy over recovered memories, Newman and Baumeister (1996) have recently proposed a cognitive-behavioral explanation for why some individuals become strongly committed to apparently false memories of UFO abductions. They point out that abduction memories share many of the characteristics of masochistic experiences (in which erotic pleasure is derived from pain and humiliation). In particular, stories of UFO abductions, like masochistic experiences, typically involve feelings of complete helplessness and the loss of one's normal identity. Newman and Baumeister also note that abduction accounts, like masochistic tendencies, are more common among individuals who are relatively successful, yet stressed out by their responsibilities. The act of "remembering" an alien abduction might therefore be a form of masochism that allows the "abductee" to temporarily escape from a stressful lifestyle, thereby negatively reinforcing the production of such memories.

tors because he was once trapped in an elevator does not simply avoid being trapped in an elevator; he avoids elevators altogether, planning his day well ahead of time so that riding an elevator will not ever become an issue.

A second limitation of avoidance-conditioning experiments is that they typically require at least a few pairings of the CS and US (e.g., light and shock) before avoidance has been reliably established. Even then, the avoidance response is usually less than 100% certain, with the animal occasionally reencountering the aversive US. For example, in a shuttle avoidance task, the rat will occasionally be tardy in climbing over the barrier, with the result that it sometimes receives a shock. By contrast, *human phobias often require only a single, brief conditioning trial to produce an avoidance response that is very strong and persistent.* For example, a very persistent dog phobia may develop following a single attack.

1. According to Mineka (1985), one limitation in applying experimental models of avoidance to human phobias is that the animals are usually avoiding the aversive (CS/US) _____ while human phobics are avoiding the aversive _____.

2. According to Mineka, a second limitation of applying experimental models of avoidance to phobic conditioning is that avoidance experiments with animals usually require (one/a few) _____ conditioning trial(s), while phobic conditioning usually requires _____ conditioning trial(s).

In response to Mineka's (1985) concerns about the applicability of experimental avoidance conditioning to human phobias, Stampfl (1987) proposed that an adequate experimental analogue of a human phobia would require (1) the reliable establishment of a fear response with only a single, brief pairing of the CS and US, (2) subsequent avoidance of the CS as well as the US, and (3) the occurrence of successful avoidance on 100% of trials. Stampfl acknowledged that, using these criteria, the typical avoidance-conditioning procedure is an inadequate analogue of human phobic conditioning. He then devised an experimental procedure that produced avoidance conditioning that met all three criteria.

Stampfl's procedure focuses on the fact that human phobics typically make the avoidance response early in the chain of events leading up to the feared stimulus. For example, a person with an elevator phobia will plan his day well ahead of time so that he will not be faced with any pressure to take an elevator. He may, for example, arrange an appointment with a dentist whose office is on the main floor of an office building. This type of planning is important because not doing so could result in a direct encounter with a phobic stimulus, which in turn could greatly increase the cost involved in avoiding it (such as by having to climb the stairs to get to a dentist's office on the 23rd floor). Thus, the phobic individual learns to make the avoidance response early on so as to minimize the effort of avoiding.

The opportunity to make an early avoidance response is typically absent from most avoidance-conditioning procedures. Stampfl, however, designed an apparatus that provided just such an opportunity. As depicted in Figure 9.2, the apparatus consisted of an alleyway that was 5 feet in length and contained a dark compartment at one end. Each rat was first allowed to explore the alleyway at its leisure, during which time it came to strongly prefer the black compartment (rats generally prefer the dark). The rat was then given foot shock while in the black compartment, at which point it fled to the far end of the alleyway. Three minutes later, a conveyor belt was turned on which began to slowly carry the rat toward the dark compartment. During this first trial, most rats waited until they reached the black sidewall area of the apparatus before running back to the far end. When they did run back to the far end, they broke a photobeam that temporarily stopped the conveyor belt for a 3-minute period. The conveyor belt then started up again and the procedure was repeated. This initial session lasted 2 hours. During the second session, the re-

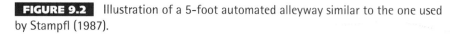

FIGURE 9.2 Illustration of a 5-foot automated alleyway similar to the one used by Stampfl (1987).

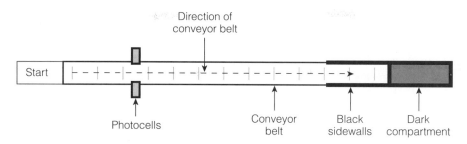

sponse requirement for stopping the conveyor belt was increased from FR 1 to FR 10 (that is, the rat had to run back and cross the photobeam ten times before the conveyor belt would stop).

Stampfl found that the rats soon learned to run back to the safe area immediately after the conveyor belt started up. In other words, rather than waiting until they reached the black sidewalls before running back, they began running back after traveling only a short distance. In this manner, they were able to minimize the effort involved in breaking the photobeam and stopping the belt. Moreover, under these circumstances, the rats completely avoided entering the black compartment on more than 1000 consecutive trials, thereby consistently avoiding the aversive CS that was associated with shock. Furthermore, this persistent avoidance response resulted from only a single brief exposure to shock.

In summary, Stampfl's results confirm that a critical factor in the maintenance of phobic behavior is that the avoidance response occurs early in the sequence of events leading up to the phobic stimulus, thereby minimizing the effort involved in making the response. Such early responding greatly reduces the extent to which the avoidance response can extinguish since the individual experiences little or no exposure to the aversive CS. In terms of the anxiety conservation hypothesis discussed earlier, exposure to the aversive stimulus is so minimal that the avoidance response is extremely resistant to extinction. It is therefore not surprising that phobic behaviors are often extremely persistent.

1. A critical aspect of Stampfl's experimental analogue of phobic conditioning is that the avoidance response can occur (early/late) _____ in the sequence of events leading up to the feared CS, thereby (maximizing/minimizing) _____ the amount of effort involved in making the response.

2. This results in (little/considerable) _____ exposure to the feared CS thereby greatly (increasing/reducing) _____ the likelihood that the fear response will e_____.

QUICK QUIZ

Avoidance Conditioning and Obsessive–Compulsive Disorder

Phobia is one type of disorder in which avoidance conditioning plays a critical role. Another is *obsessive-compulsive disorder (OCD)*: a disorder characterized by persistent thoughts, impulses, or images (called obsessions), and repetitive, stereotyped actions (called compulsions) that are carried out in response to the obsessions. For example, a person might have an obsessive worry about contacting germs; this leads to a compulsive tendency to take a shower and clean the house many times each day. Or a person might have an obsessive worry about whether she locked her apartment door when she left that morning, which leads to a compulsive pattern of returning to the apartment several times a day to check it. Note that the person recognizes that the compulsive behavior is clearly excessive, but nevertheless feels compelled to perform the action. (Interestingly, cleaning and checking are the two most common forms of compulsive behavior.)

OCD was once considered a particularly difficult disorder to treat. This changed when clinicians began analyzing OCD in terms of avoidance conditioning, especially Mowrer's two-process theory of avoidance conditioning (Rachman & Hodgson, 1980). The applicability of this theory to OCD lies in the fact that obsessions and compulsions have opposite effects on anxiety. In general, obsessions are associated with an increase in anxiety, while compulsions are associated with a decrease in anxiety. For example, a person who has

"I THINK I WAS BETTER OFF WHEN I WAS OBSESSIVE-COMPULSIVE."

a contamination fear and is a compulsive cleaner usually experiences an increase in anxiety after exposure to situations in which "contamination" might have occurred, such as when taking out the garbage. Garbage elicits such a strong anxiety response that any part of the body that has been exposed to garbage also elicits an anxiety response. Taking a shower, however, results in the removal of this anxiety. From the perspective of two-process theory, the feeling of anxiety is a classically conditioned response elicited by contact with the garbage, while showering is an operant response that is negatively reinforced by a reduction in anxiety.

Note that the role of avoidance in OCD is virtually the same as in phobic behavior, with the exception that OCD involves an active avoidance response while phobic behavior involves a passive avoidance response. More specifically, a person with OCD will generally *do* something to reduce anxiety (such as showering), while a person with a phobia will generally *not do* something to reduce anxiety (such as not going near a dog). Nevertheless, individuals with OCD might also utilize passive avoidance responses (e.g., by avoiding garbage whenever possible), such that some of their behavior patterns can also be characterized as phobic.

Two-process theory not only helped clarify our understanding of OCD, it also led to the development of the first effective treatment for the disorder. If a compulsive behavior pattern (such as excessive washing) is maintained by avoidance of an anxiety-arousing event (such as contact with germs), then preventing the avoidance response from occurring should result in the eventual extinction of anxiety. This treatment method is known as *exposure and response prevention (ERP):* **a method of treating OCD that involves prolonged exposure to the anxiety-arousing event while not engaging in the compulsive behavior pattern that reduces the anxiety** (e.g., Steketee & Foa, 1985).

As with exposure-based treatments for phobic behavior (especially as described in an And Furthermore box in Chapter 5), ERP combines the graduated exposure of systematic desensitization with the prolonged exposure of flooding therapy. For example, a compulsive cleaner might be required to first touch objects associated with slight anxiety (such as door handles and hand rails), then objects associated with moderate anxiety (such as garbage cans and dogs), and finally objects associated with intense anxiety (such as dead birds and dog excrement). These graduated exposures are first carried out imaginally—given that the person has good imagery ability—and then in vivo— given that live exposure to the anxiety-arousing event is practical. The exposures are also relatively long, often 90 minutes or more, which ensures sufficient time for the anxiety to begin to extinguish. In addition to scheduled treatment sessions, the client is told to practice exposures at home. The client is also told not to perform any compulsive behavior patterns; for example, a compulsive washer might be instructed to avoid all nonessential showers except for one 10-minute shower every 5 days! Once the obsessive-compulsive pattern has been successfully eliminated, normal patterns of behavior are then reestablished (Steketee & Foa, 1985).

Mowrer's two-process theory has therefore proven quite useful in enhancing our understanding and treatment of OCD. Nevertheless, two-process theory does not provide an entirely adequate explanation for OCD (Steketee & Foa, 1985). For example, people with OCD are usually unable to recall any particular conditioning event that could account for the obsessional anxiety response. People who have a contamination fear, for example, typically do not recall, say, falling into a cesspool prior to the onset of the fear. On the other hand, onset of OCD does often coincide with a period of stress. One possibility, therefore, is that stress sensitizes certain individuals in such a way that normal concerns, say, about cleanliness and safety, become greatly exaggerated. Thus, just as the process of selective sensitization might lead to the development of a phobia (as discussed in Chapter 5), so too it might lead to the development of OCD. Furthermore, just as genetic factors may predispose some people to develop a phobia (also discussed in Chapter 5), so too some people might have a genetic predisposition toward the development of OCD (Billet, Richter, & Kennedy, 1998).

On a more cognitive level, people with OCD often hold the irrational belief that they should be in complete control of their thoughts—failing to realize that intrusive thoughts are not uncommon and that most people simply ignore them. In other words, they fail to realize that some thoughts are essentially respondents (reflexes) that are automatically elicited by certain stimuli, and that it is futile to try to control such thoughts (as though they were operants). People with OCD also have a tendency to feel personally responsible for events that are highly improbable. They therefore carry out various safety actions, such as rechecking doors and stoves, that other people would not bother with (Salkovskis, 1998). Given these cognitive factors in OCD, attempts have been made to combine ERP with cognitive therapy on the assumption that modifying these false belief systems might enhance treatment. There is, however, little evidence as yet that such cognitive manipulations are effective; thus, ERP by itself remains the treatment of choice for OCD (Foa, Franklin, & Kozak, 1998).

QUICK QUIZ

1. Janice continually worries that her alarm clock may not be set, and that she will wake up late and be late for class. She therefore checks the alarm clock about 20 times each night before finally falling asleep. The persistent thoughts about the alarm clock not being set are classified as a(n) (compulsion/obsession) _____ while the frequent checking of the clock is classified as a(n) _____.

2. In general, (compulsions/obsessions) _____ are associated with an increase in anxiety, while _____ are associated with a decrease in anxiety.

3. From the perspective of two-process theory, this decrease in anxiety likely functions as a n_____ r_____ for the compulsive behavior.

4. Exposure and response prevention (ERP) therapy for OCD involves prolonged exposure to anxiety-arousing events while (engaging/not engaging) _____ in the (obsessive/compulsive) _____ behavior that serves to reduce the anxiety.

5. ERP is similar to systematic desensitization in that exposure to the anxiety-provoking event is usually (gradual/sudden) _____. It is similar to flooding therapy in that exposure to the anxiety-provoking event is (brief/prolonged) _____.

6. People with OCD are usually (able/unable) _____ to recall a particular conditioning event that was the cause of the obsessional anxiety response. The disorder often arises, however, during times of st_____. This suggests that a process of s_____ s_____ may exacerbate normal concerns about cleanliness and safety.

7. People with OCD fail to realize that intrusive thoughts are (common/uncommon) _____ and that such thoughts are often (controllable/uncontrollable) _____. They also (take/fail to take) _____ responsibility for highly (probable/improbable) _____ events.

8. Combined with ERP, cognitive interventions for OCD have been found to provide (much/little) _____ additional benefit.

Punishment

Escape and avoidance conditioning involves the strengthening of a behavior through the removal of an aversive stimulus. By contrast, punishment involves the weakening of a behavior through the application of an aversive stimulus or the removal of an appetitive stimulus. In this section, we discuss various types of punishment, as well as issues to be concerned with in the application of punishment. We will also briefly describe various theories of punishment.

Types of Punishment

Let us begin by reviewing the basic distinction between positive and negative punishment. *Positive punishment* consists of the presentation of a certain event following a response, which then leads to a decrease in the future strength of that response. In simple terms, the behavior results in the delivery of something the person or animal hates, so they are less likely to behave that way in the future. Receiving a spanking for swearing and being reprimanded for talking back to the boss are both examples of positive punishment (given that these consequences result in a subsequent decrease in the frequency of these behaviors).

By contrast, *negative punishment* consists of the removal of a certain event following a response, which then leads to a decrease in the future strength of that response. Simply put, the behavior results in the removal of something the person or animal likes, so they are less likely to continue that behavior in the future. A loss of employment for being obnoxious and a loss of dessert for complaining at the dinner table are both examples of negative punishment (again, given that the consequence results in a subsequent decrease in behavior). Note that the events being removed are the types of pleasant events that can also serve as positive reinforcers; thus, negative punishment can also be defined as the loss of a positive reinforcer (a pleasant event) following a response.

There are two basic types of negative punishment: time-out and response cost. *Time-out* **involves the loss of access to positive reinforcers for a brief period of time following the occurrence of a problem behavior.** Time-out has become popular with modern-day parents, who frequently attempt to punish a child's misbehavior by sending her to the bedroom or by making her sit in a corner for several minutes. Unfortunately, time-out procedures are often poorly applied, with the result that they have little effect on the problem behavior. For example, time-out is likely to be ineffective if the time-out setting is actually more reinforcing than the setting from which the child was removed. In fact, sending a child to his room for acting out at the dinner table might reinforce rather than punish the behavior of acting out if the child dislikes sitting at the dinner table. Another problem is that parents often use time-outs that are too long. The purpose of time-out is not to get the child "out of your hair" for a period of time, but to facilitate the development of more appropriate behaviors. Those appropriate behaviors need to be reinforced, which cannot be done if the child is sitting in his room for hours on end. Time-out periods should therefore be quite brief, especially for young children. In fact, a time-out period as short as a minute may be all that is required to effectively suppress the unwanted behavior, especially if one immediately sets out to reinforce more appropriate behaviors as soon as the child is returned to the normal setting (Miltenberger, 1997).

The other type of negative punishment is *response cost,* **which is the removal of a specific reinforcer following the occurrence of a problem behavior.** Receiving a fine (which leads to loss of money) for speeding or taking a child's toys away for playing too roughly are examples of response cost. One advantage of response cost over time-out is that one can easily adjust the severity of the punishment to suit the behavior being punished. Slight aggression with a younger sibling could result in the loss of dessert, while more severe aggression could result in the loss of dessert and the opportunity to watch television that evening. A drawback to response cost, however, is that you must clearly identify a reinforcer that, if removed, will have an impact on behavior. It therefore requires a more careful analysis of the situation than a time-out procedure. (See Miltenberger, 1997, for a more complete discussion of time-out and response cost procedures.)

Note that negative punishment is quite different from extinction, even though both involve the removal of reinforcers and both result in a decrease in the strength of a behavior. In the case of extinction, a behavior that used to produce a reinforcer no longer does, and the person therefore stops performing the behavior. If Jason used to receive cookies as a result of whining, but he no longer receives cookies by whining, then he will eventually stop whining.

In the case of negative punishment, however, performing the behavior results in the loss of a reinforcer that the person would otherwise possess. Imagine, for example, that Jason has already received some cookies but then starts whining for a soda pop. If, each time he whines, one of his cookies is taken away, then he is likely to stop whining. Thus, to distinguish between extinction and negative punishment, ask yourself whether the behavior grows weaker because *performing the behavior no longer leads to something* (in which case, the process is extinction), or because *performing the behavior leads to the removal of something that you otherwise possess* (in which case, the process is negative punishment).

1. When the cat sat at your feet and meowed annoyingly during breakfast one morning, you sprayed it with water. As a result, the cat did not come near the table or meow the next time you sat down for a meal. The consequence for the cat's begging consisted of the (presentation/removal) _____ of a stimulus, and the cat's behavior subsequently (decreased/increased) _____ in frequency. Therefore, this is an example of _____ _____.

2. Negative punishment involves the (presentation/removal) _____ of a stimulus following a response that subsequently results in a (increase/decrease) _____ in the likelihood of that response occurring again.

3. When Bobbi threw a temper tantrum, her mother turned off the television program that Bobbi was watching. Bobbi's mother is attempting to apply a (response cost/time-out) _____ procedure.

4. When Bobbi threw a temper tantrum, Bobbi's mother made her sit in the corner for a minute. Bobbi's mother is attempting to apply a (response cost/time-out) _____ procedure.

5. A(n) (advantage/disadvantage) _____ of a time-out procedure is that one (does/does not) _____ have to clearly identify a specific reinforcer prior to implementing the procedure. An (advantage/disadvantage) _____ of a response cost procedure is that one (can/cannot) _____ easily modify the severity of the punishment to suit the behavior.

6. When Val began whining, her mother immediately stopped playing with her and left the room. Val quickly stopped whining. This is an example of (extinction/negative punishment) _____.

7. Val's mother used to play with Val whenever she whined but then stopped doing so. As a result, Val's whining soon ceased. This is an example of (extinction/negative punishment) _____.

8. If the frequency of a behavior decreases because performing the behavior no longer leads to something, the process involved is (extinction/negative punishment) _____. If the frequency of a behavior decreases because performing the behavior leads to the removal of something, the process involved is _____.

Punishment can also be differentiated in other ways. For example, just as one can distinguish between intrinsic and extrinsic reinforcement, one can also distinguish between intrinsic and extrinsic punishment. ***Intrinsic punishment* is punishment that is an inherent aspect of the behavior that is being punished.** In other words, the activity itself is punishing, such that the person performing the behavior is now less likely to repeat it. Watching an upsetting television show is intrinsically punishing if you stop watching such shows in the future because of their upsetting nature. ***Extrinsic punishment* is punishment that is not an inherent aspect of the behavior being punished, but simply follows the behavior.** In other words, the activity is followed by a separate event that serves to punish the activity. Being chastised after lighting up a cigarette ("Are you still indulging in that filthy habit?") is extrinsically punishing if it subsequently reduces the frequency with which you smoke.

One can also distinguish between primary and secondary punishers. **A *primary (or unconditioned) punisher* is an event that is naturally punishing.** Loosely speaking, these are events that we are born to dislike. Electric shock, intense heat, and loud noise are examples of primary punishers. **A *secondary (or conditioned)* punisher is an event that has become punishing because it has in the past been associated with some other punisher.** For example, if shock is an effective punisher, then a tone that has been paired with shock in a classical conditioning procedure

$$\underset{\text{NS}}{\text{Tone:}} \ \underset{\text{US}}{\text{Shock}} \ \rightarrow \underset{\text{UR}}{\textit{Fear}}$$

$$\underset{\text{CS}}{\text{Tone}} \ \rightarrow \underset{\text{CR}}{\textit{Fear}}$$

will become a conditioned aversive stimulus that can then be used as a secondary punisher. For example, presentation of the tone could now be used to punish wheel running:

$$\underset{\text{R}}{\textit{Running in a wheel}} \ \rightarrow \underset{\text{S}^{\text{P}}}{\text{Tone}}$$

Human behavior is often under the control of secondary punishers. A traffic ticket might effectively punish our tendency to speed, and an icy stare from our partner might effectively punish our tendency to drink too much at a party. Both the fine and the stare are punishing because they have been associated with other types of aversive events: loss of money in the one case and heated arguments in the other.

A special type of secondary punisher is a ***generalized secondary (or generalized conditioned) punisher*, which is an event that has become punishing because it has in the past been associated with many other punishers.** The icy stare mentioned above is probably best categorized as a generalized secondary punisher because it has no doubt been associated with numerous unpleasant events such as reprimands as a child, marital arguments as an adult, and disciplinary action during one's stint in the army.

1. Exercising to the point of exhaustion is for many people likely to be an (extrinsically/intrinsically) _____ punishing event.

2. Bad-tasting food can be classified as a (primary/secondary) _____ punisher, while a restaurant that commonly serves such food may become a _____ punisher.

3. Looking at an old photo album reminds you of your loneliness as a child, the loss of a favorite pet, and a childhood friend who died. As a result, you tend not to look at it. The old photo album can be classified as a g_____ s_____ punisher. Looking at it is also (intrinsically/extrinsically) _____ punishing.

Problems with the Use of Punishment

Although some students are of the opinion that behaviorists promote the use of punishment, behaviorists in fact have a general bias against it. This bias results from several problems that are associated with punishment (e.g., Newsom, Favell, & Rincover, 1983). These include the following:

1. *Punishment of an inappropriate behavior does not directly strengthen the occurrence of appropriate behavior. It may even result in a general suppression of behavior.* A child who has been punished for playing aggressively will not necessarily begin playing more cooperatively, which is really the intended goal. She might instead simply stop playing with other children, which is not at all desirable.

2. *The person delivering the punishment could become an S^D for punishment, with the result that the unwanted behavior is suppressed only when he or she is present.* The child, for example, might come to view the father as a discriminative stimulus for punishment and therefore continue to misbehave when the father is absent. The child has thus learned to not get caught for misbehaving, rather than to not misbehave.

3. *Punishment might simply teach the individual to avoid the person who delivered the punishment.* A child who is severely punished by his father might begin minimizing the time spent with his father. This would obviously be less than ideal, especially if the father has much to offer the child.

4. *Punishment is likely to elicit a strong emotional response.* This is especially the case with the use of positive punishment, such as spanking or yelling, which is likely to result in crying or other displays of distress. These strong emotional responses are not only unpleasant but will also interfere with any subsequent attempt to teach the child more appropriate behavior. A child who is crying uncontrollably is not in an ideal state for learning anything new, such as how to play appropriately.

5. *Punishment can sometimes elicit an aggressive reaction.* Earlier in this text, we mentioned how a painful stimulus, such as electric shock, can elicit attack behavior in rats. Humans can also react with anger when subjected to aversive stimulation. This anger can be directed toward the individual responsible for the aversive event, or, if there are inhibitions about doing so,

can be directed toward a substitute target. Thus, a child who is severely punished for being noisy might not aggress toward the parent who spanked her but will instead aggress toward her younger sibling.

6. *The use of punishment, through the process of modeling, could teach the person that punishment is an acceptable means of controlling behavior.* The child whose behavior is being punished might come to believe that punishment is an appropriate method for controlling others. For this reason, children who are abused will sometimes (but not always) begin to abuse others.

7. *Because punishment often has an immediate effect in stopping an unwanted behavior, the use of punishment is often strongly reinforced.* If hitting one's children has the immediate effect of getting them to stop making noise (an immediate negative reinforcer), then the behavior of hitting them has been strongly reinforced. The use of punishment can therefore be quite seductive, enticing the parent to use it more and more frequently, possibly to the point of being clearly abusive.

QUICK QUIZ

1. Punishment, especially (positive/negative) _____ punishment, can often elicit a strong e_____ reaction. This reaction might include a_____ that, if not directed directly toward the punisher, might be directed toward a substitute target.

2. Punishment of an inappropriate behavior (will/will not) _____ directly strengthen the occurrence of an appropriate behavior. It might even result in a general s_____ of behavior.

3. The use of punishment could, through the process of m_____, teach the recipient that punishment is an acceptable means for modifying a person's behavior.

4. Punishing your dog for chewing your slippers might teach the dog to avoid _____ rather than the slippers.

5. Punishing your dog for chewing your slippers might also teach your dog not to chew the slippers only when _____.

6. If punishment has an i_____ effect in getting someone to stop annoying us, this result can then act as a strong n_____ r_____ for using punishment in the future.

Effective Use of Punishment

For the reasons outlined above, most behaviorists tend to avoid or minimize the use of punishment, especially positive punishment. Nevertheless, there may be some circumstances in which punishment is judged appropriate, such as in suppressing potentially dangerous behavior patterns in a young child (for example, to stop a child from poking at another child's face with a sharpened pencil). This is especially the case given that alternative interventions, such as extinction and reinforcement of other behaviors, often take time to have an effect. If punishment is used, then the following requirements should be met to ensure that it is effective.

1. *As much as possible, punishment should be immediate rather than delayed.* Unfortunately, in the real world, delayed punishment is often the rule rather than the exception. A child's misbehavior is frequently discovered only several minutes or hours after its occurrence, and the delivery of a reprimand following such a long delay may have little effect. This is particularly the case with very young children and animals who, because they are unable to understand explanations, are unlikely to associate the punishment with the unwanted behavior. For example, punishing a dog for making a mess on the carpet several hours after the incident has occurred will probably only upset the animal and do little to prevent future mishaps.

2. *At least at the outset, punishment should consistently follow each occurrence of the unwanted behavior.* Punishment tends to be less effective in suppressing a behavior when only some instances of the unwanted behavior are punished. In other words, unlike intermittent reinforcement, which has a strong effect on behavior, intermittent punishment tends to have a relatively weak effect on behavior. Nevertheless, once the behavior has been effectively suppressed, then intermittent punishment may be sufficient to maintain the suppression (Clark, Rowbury, Baer, & Baer, 1973).

3. *Punishment should be intense enough from the outset to suppress the target behavior* (though—and this is the tricky part—not so intense as to be unnecessarily abusive). If one begins with a very mild punisher that is ineffective, and then gradually increases the intensity, it might require a very intense punisher to eventually suppress the unwanted behavior. For example, Miller (1960) presented rats with a very mild shock whenever they entered an alleyway, and he then gradually increased the intensity of the shock until it effectively punished the rats' behavior. What he found was that these rats ceased responding only upon very high levels of shock, far beyond what would normally have been required to suppress such a behavior. Likewise, a father who initially uses a very mild reprimand to try to get his daughter to stop teasing the dog and then gradually increases the severity of the reprimand, might eventually have to deliver a very severe reprimand or worse before she will comply. But if the father had started with a moderately severe reprimand, the daughter might have immediately complied, thereby saving the two of them (as well as the dog) a lot of grief. By starting with such a mild intervention and then gradually increasing its severity, the father essentially allowed the daughter to adapt to the punishing stimulus.

4. *With individuals who have language capacity, punishment is more effective when accompanied by an explanation.* A possible reason for this is that an explanation will help clarify the exact behavior that is being punished, thereby making it easier for the child to avoid punishment in the future. This accords with the more general recommendation that children should be given frequent feedback about their behavior, both good and

bad, since this will greatly facilitate the child's attempts to learn appropriate behavior (Craig, Kermis, & Digdon, 1998).

5. *Punishment of inappropriate behavior should be combined with positive reinforcement for appropriate behavior.* This is perhaps the most important rule. As with extinction, punishment of unwanted behavior will be more effective if it is combined with differential reinforcement for other behavior, especially behavior that is incompatible with the target behavior. As the appropriate behavior is strengthened, it will come to supplant the inappropriate behavior. Thus, to simply apply a time-out period to a child for playing inappropriately might have little effect if the child has been inadequately reinforced for playing appropriately. Time-out periods should therefore be accompanied by abundant reinforcement of appropriate behavior. In fact, positive reinforcement for appropriate behavior should always be considered the primary tool for eliminating unwanted behaviors. (For a complete discussion of issues involved in the punishment of human behavior, see Axelrod & Apsche, 1983.)

QUICK QUIZ

1. With verbally proficient humans, punishment tends to be more effective when it is accompanied by an e_____.

2. In general, when implementing a punishment procedure, one should begin with a punisher of sufficient i_____ to s_____ the behavior.

3. Unlike reinforcement, punishment tends to have a stronger impact on behavior if delivered (consistently/intermittently) _____.

4. In general, when attempting to punish a maladaptive behavior, one should also attempt to _____ more adaptive behavior.

5. If punishment is to be used, it should be i_____, since d_____ punishment tends to be relatively ineffective.

Theories of Punishment

Although a good deal of research has gone into investigating the effectiveness of punishment, less attention has been paid to developing and testing various theories of punishment. We will nevertheless briefly consider three theoretical approaches to punishment.

Conditioned Suppression Theory This theory is based on early work by Skinner (1938). He found that although punishment can quickly suppress a behavior, the behavior often quickly recovers to pre-punishment levels when the punishment is withdrawn. What Skinner (1953) assumed was happening was that punishment generates a conditioned emotional response (the classically conditioned fear response that we previously discussed in Chapter 3) that tends to suppress any ongoing appetitive behavior. Crudely put, when the rat is shocked for pressing a lever that produces food, it becomes so upset at the possibility of receiving a shock that it loses interest in the food and therefore does not press the lever to obtain it. If, however, the shock is withdrawn, the rat resumes lever pressing as soon as it calms down enough for its interest in food to be revived. Thus, *conditioned suppression theory* **assumes that punishment does not weaken a behavior but instead produces an emotional response that interferes with the occurrence of the behavior.**

The temporary effect that Skinner (1938) found when he attempted to punish a rat's behavior therefore led him to conclude that punishment is an ineffective means of producing a lasting change in behavior. Skinner's experiment, however, utilized a relatively weak form of punishment: a device that slapped the rat on the paw when it attempted to press a lever. Subsequent research revealed that more intense forms of punishment, such as strong electric shocks, are capable of suppressing behavior for much longer periods of time (Azrin & Holz, 1966).

Avoidance Theory of Punishment   The *avoidance theory of punishment* **holds that punishment actually involves a type of avoidance conditioning, in which the avoidance response consists of any behavior other than the behavior being punished** (e.g., Dinsmoor, 1954). In other words, just as the behavior of jumping over a barrier is strengthened by shock avoidance in a shuttle avoidance situation, so too the behavior of doing "anything other than lever pressing" is reinforced by shock avoidance in a punishment-of-lever-pressing situation. Thus, in carrying out the following punishment procedure:

$$Lever\ press \rightarrow \textbf{Shock}$$
$$\textbf{R} \qquad\qquad \textbf{S}^\textbf{P}$$

one is actually carrying out the following avoidance conditioning procedure:

$$Any\ behavior\ other\ than\ lever\ pressing \rightarrow \textbf{No shock}$$
$$\textbf{R} \qquad\qquad\qquad\qquad\qquad \textbf{S}^\textbf{R}$$

in which a behavior other than lever pressing is negatively reinforced by the absence of shock (e.g., Dinsmoor, 1954).

As with conditioned suppression theory, the avoidance theory of punishment assumes that punishment does not directly weaken a behavior. It simply replaces the punished behavior with an avoidance response of some sort. A disadvantage of this theory, however, is that it carries with it all of the theoretical difficulties associated with avoidance conditioning, some of which we discussed earlier in this chapter.

The Premack Approach to Punishment   As you will recall from Chapter 5, the Premack principle holds that a high-probability behavior (HPB) can be used to reinforce a low-probability behavior (LPB). As it turns out, the opposite can be applied to punishment. According to the *Premack principle of* *punishment,* **a low-probability behavior (LPB) can be used to punish a high-probability behavior (HPB)** (Premack, 1971).

Take, for example, a rat that is both hungry and tuckered out from exercising. The rat in this condition is much more likely to eat food (an HPB) than to run in a wheel (an LPB). In terms of the Premack principle of reinforcement, this means that the behavior of eating can be used as a reinforcer for the behavior of running in a wheel:

$$\text{\textit{Running in a wheel} (LPB)} \rightarrow \text{\textbf{Eating food (HPB)}}$$
$$\text{\textbf{R}} \qquad\qquad\qquad \text{S}^\text{R}$$

According to the Premack principle of punishment, however, one can also use running in a wheel to punish the response of eating:

$$\text{\textit{Eating food} (HPB)} \rightarrow \text{\textbf{Running in a wheel (LPB)}}$$
$$\text{\textbf{R}} \qquad\qquad\qquad \text{S}^\text{P}$$

If eating food is followed by the consequence of being forced to run in a wheel, the rat will be less likely to eat than if this consequence did not exist. To bring this point home, imagine how much easier it would be for a person who hates exercising to stick to a diet if she were forced to run a mile each time she ate something not on the diet.

Note that this approach implicitly assumes that punishment is the converse of reinforcement: If reinforcement strengthens behavior, then punishment weakens behavior. In this sense, it differs from the previous two theories in that it views punishment as the mirror opposite of reinforcement. (See Domjan, 1998, for an extended discussion concerning theories of punishment.)

QUICK QUIZ

1. According to the conditioned suppression theory of punishment, the application of punishment does not directly w_____ a behavior; instead, it produces an em_____ reaction that tends to interfere with ongoing behavior.

2. This theory was based on evidence that punishment tends to produce only a (temporary/permanent) _____ effect. This effect, however, generally results from using relatively (strong/weak) _____ forms of punishment.

3. According to the a_____ theory of punishment, a rat stops lever pressing when lever pressing is followed by shock because the occurrence of any behavior other than lever pressing is n_____ r_____ by the nonoccurrence of shock.

4. According to the punishment version of the Premack principle, the occurrence of a _____ _____ behavior can be used to punish the occurrence of a _____ _____ behavior. This means that if Sally rarely washes dishes and often chews her nails, then the behavior of _____ _____ can be used to punish the occurrence of _____ _____.

Effects of Noncontingent Punishment

In the typical escape/avoidance procedure, the aversive stimulus is control-lable in the sense that the animal is able to make a response that significantly reduces its effect. Likewise, in a punishment procedure, the animal has some semblance of control in that if it does not make the response, then it will not be punished. In both cases, some type of contingency exists. But what if such a contingency were absent? What if the aversive event was essentially uncon-trollable (and even unpredictable), such that whatever you do, you are unable to influence your exposure to that event? In the same manner that noncon-tingent reinforcement has some unique effects on behavior (as discussed in Chapter 7), so too does noncontingent punishment. Let us therefore spend the remainder of this chapter examining some of these effects.

Learned Helplessness

Consider the following experiment by Seligman and Maier (1967). The ex-periment began with an initial phase in which dogs were suspended in a har-ness and exposed to one of three conditions. In an *inescapable-shock condition*, the dogs received a series of shocks but were unable to do anything about them. In an *escapable-shock condition*, the dogs received shocks but were able to terminate each shock by pressing a panel with their snout. Each dog in this condition was also *yoked to* (paired up with) a dog in the first condition, such that when it turned off the shock for itself, it also turned off the shock for its partner dog in the other condition. Thus, the only difference between these two dogs was that the dog in the escapable-shock condition had control over the shocks while the dog in the inescapable-shock condition did not. Finally, some dogs were in a *no-shock control condition:* These dogs were never shocked and simply waited out the session suspended in the harness.

In the next phase of the experiment, all of the dogs were exposed to a shut-tle avoidance procedure in which the task was to learn to avoid shock by jump-ing over a barrier, each shock being preceded by a 10-second period of dark-ness. The dogs exposed to the no-shock control condition in the initial phase of the experiment soon learned to avoid the shock by jumping over the bar-rier during the period of darkness that preceded the shock. The dogs exposed to the escapable-shock condition also learned the avoidance task quickly. The dogs from the inescapable-shock condition, however, behaved quite differ-ently. When shocked, many of them initially ran around in great distress but then lay on the floor and whimpered. They made no effort to escape the shock. Even stranger, the few dogs that did by chance jump over the barrier, successfully escaping the shock, seemed unable to learn from this experience and failed to repeat it on the next trial. In summary, the prior exposure to in-escapable shock seemed to impair the dogs' ability to learn to escape shock when escape later became possible. This phenomenon is known as ***learned helplessness:* a decrement in learning ability that results from repeated exposure to uncontrollable aversive events.**

Seligman and Maier (1967) theorized that the dogs became helpless because they had learned during exposure to inescapable shock that any attempt to escape was useless—in other words, that there was a *lack of contingency* between making a response and achieving a certain outcome. As a result, when confronted with shock in a new situation, they simply gave up. Other researchers, however, have proposed alternative explanations. For example, one theory suggests that animals exposed to inescapable aversive stimulation are distressed, and because of this distress they have difficulty attending to the relationship between behavior and its outcomes. Evidence for this theory includes the fact that if animals are given a very salient feedback stimulus whenever they make a successful escape response, such as by sounding a loud bell, the learned helplessness effect disappears and the animals can once more learn such tasks effectively (Maier, Jackson, & Tomie, 1987).

Learned helplessness may account for certain difficulties experienced by humans. For example, Dweck and Reppucci (1973) found that children who attempted to answer unsolvable problems later had considerable difficulty answering solvable problems. This suggests that children who have difficulty passing math exams in school, possibly because of poor teaching, might grow up to become "math-anxious" individuals who quickly give up when confronted by any sort of math problem. Learned helplessness has also been related to certain forms of depression (Seligman, 1975). People who suffer a series of uncontrollable aversive events—loss of a job, physical illness, divorce, and so on—may become extremely passive and despondent. Like animals exposed to inescapable shock, they show little interest in improving their lot in life. (See also the opening vignette to this chapter.)

Fortunately, researchers have discovered a way to eliminate learned helplessness. The helpless animal will eventually recover its ability to escape on its own if it is repeatedly forced to escape the aversive stimulus—for example, if it is repeatedly dragged from the shock side of the chamber to the no-shock side (Seligman & Maier, 1967; Seligman, Rosellini, & Kozak, 1975). In similar fashion, behavioral treatments for depression often involve encouraging the patient to accomplish a graded series of tasks, starting with relatively minor tasks, such as writing a letter, and progressing to more difficult tasks, such as seeking a new job (Seligman, 1975).

Research has also suggested a means for preventing the development of learned helplessness. Experiments have revealed that prior exposure to escapable shock often immunizes an animal against becoming helpless when it is later exposed to inescapable shock (Seligman et al., 1975); the animal will persist in trying to escape the shock rather than give up. This suggests that a history of successfully overcoming minor adversities might immunize a person against depression when the person is later confronted by more serious difficulties. As a tree is strengthened by exposure to winds strong enough to bend but not break its limbs, so too individuals seem to be strengthened by exposure to manageable amounts of misfortune.

1. The original experiments on learned _____ revealed that dogs that had first been exposed to inescapable shock had (no difficulty/difficulty) _____ learning an escape response when later exposed to (escapable/inescapable) _____ shock.

2. It seemed as though these dogs had learned that there is a (strong/lack of) _____ contingency between their behavior and the offset of shock.

3. This effect can be overcome by (forcing/enticing) _____ the dogs to make an escape response. As well, dogs that have had previous exposure to escapable shock are (more/less) _____ susceptible to becoming helpless when later exposed to inescapable shock.

4. Learned helplessness may account for various difficulties in humans, including the clinical disorder known as d_____.

Masserman's Experimental Neurosis

As you may recall, *experimental neurosis is an experimentally produced disorder in which animals exposed to unpredictable events develop neurotic-like symptoms.* We first encountered this phenomenon in our discussion of Pavlov's work on discrimination training in dogs (in Chapter 4). He and his colleagues discovered that dogs that had difficulty discriminating which cues predicted the delivery of food seemed to experience a nervous breakdown. Pavlov hypothesized that human neuroses might likewise develop as a result of exposure to unpredictable events.

A variation on Pavlov's procedure, involving the use of aversive rather than appetitive stimuli, was developed by Masserman (1943). He found that cats that experienced unpredictable electric shocks or blasts of air while eating often developed a pattern of neurotic-like symptoms. For example, normally quiet cats became restless and agitated, while normally active cats became withdrawn and passive—sometimes even to the point of becoming rigidly immobile (a symptom known as catalepsy). The cats also developed phobic responses to cues associated with feeding (since feeding had become associated with shock), as well as unusual "counterphobic" responses (for example, a cat might run to the goal box, stick its head inside the box, and then simply stare at the experimenter but not eat). It generally took only two or three presentations of the aversive stimulus to elicit these symptoms, which might then last several months.

More recent work (but with rats, not cats) has shown that many of these symptoms are similar to those found in post-traumatic stress disorder in humans (PTSD; e.g., Foa, Zinbarg, & Rothbaum, 1992). PTSD is a disorder that results from exposure to unpredictable life-threatening events, such as tornadoes, physical and sexual assaults, and battlefield experiences. Symptoms include sleep difficulties, exaggerated startle response, and intrusive recollections about the trauma. As well, victims often demonstrate fear and avoidance

ADVICE FOR THE LOVELORN

Dear Dr. Dee,

I am in a relationship that is starting to depress me, though most of what is happening is quite subtle. For example, when I am really excited about something, my partner will usually act quite disinterested. Similarly, when I suggest doing something that I believe will be fun, she usually turns it down and suggests something else. She also gets snippy with me (or worse yet, gives me the silent treatment) at the most unexpected moments.

I have tried talking to her about it, but she says that I am overreacting and then points to how affectionate she is (which is true). So am I . . .

Overreacting?

Dear Over,

Sounds like you are in a relationship where much of your behavior is being subtly punished, some of it on a noncontingent basis. Thus, you are starting to perceive that whatever you do makes little difference. So it is not surprising that you are becoming depressed. You need to calmly point out to your partner the damaging effects of what she is doing, and the extent to which it is making you depressed.

First, however, you might wish to examine your own behavior to see if you are doing something to reinforce this pattern of behavior in your partner. Relationship problems are usually a two-way street, with neither party solely responsible for the difficulty. For example, perhaps you acquiesce to your partner's wishes so often that you are essentially reinforcing her for behaving this way. If that is the case, you may need to become a bit more assertive about your wishes. In fact, it could well be that she would be much happier if you were more assertive and your relationship with each other was more balanced.

Behaviorally yours,

Dr. Dee

of trauma-associated stimuli, as well as a general numbing of responsiveness (for example, a restricted range of emotions). Although the subjective symptoms of PTSD, such as intrusive recollections, are impossible to replicate in animals (we have no idea what animals are actually thinking), many of the overt symptoms, such as phobic behavior, agitation, and passivity, are similar to those shown by animals subjected to noncontingent, unpredictable aversive stimulation.

Experimental neurosis is therefore proving to be a useful means for investigating the development of traumatic symptoms. For instance, as a general rule, traumatic symptoms are more easily induced in animals when the aversive stimulus is delivered in an environment that the animal has long associated with safety or some type of appetitive event. For example, unpredictable shocks delivered in a setting in which the animal typically eats food are especially likely to induce neurotic symptoms (Masserman, 1943). In similar fashion, symptoms of PTSD may be more likely to arise when a person is unexpectedly attacked in the safety of their own home as opposed to a strange or dangerous area of town. The person who is attacked in his or her own home generalizes the experience and perceives that the world at large is a dangerous, unpredictable place to live in, with the result that the person thereafter remains constantly vigilant (Foa et al., 1992).

You may be wondering how Masserman's experimental neurosis procedure differs from learned helplessness. The basic difference is that the typical learned helplessness procedure involves repeated exposure to aversive events that are predictable but uncontrollable. It is equivalent to being beaten every day at 8:00 A.M. At first you try to escape from the beating, but eventually you give up any hope of escape. Masserman's experimental neurosis, on the other hand, involves infrequent but unpredictable exposure to aversive events. It is analogous to being unexpectedly dragged out of bed every once in a while and beaten. The result is constant hypervigilance and an array of psychological and behavioral symptoms. But note that unpredictability also implies uncontrollability, so there is a considerable degree of overlap between the symptoms produced by learned helplessness and those produced by Masserman's experimental neurosis procedure (Foa et al., 1992).

1. Experimental neurosis occurs when animals exposed to unp⎽⎽⎽⎽⎽⎽⎽⎽⎽⎽⎽⎽⎽⎽⎽ events develop neurotic-like symptoms.

2. Masserman (1943) found that normally quiet cats exposed to unpredictable shocks or blasts of air became (restless and agitated/withdrawn and passive) ⎽⎽⎽⎽⎽⎽⎽⎽⎽⎽⎽⎽⎽⎽⎽⎽⎽⎽⎽⎽⎽⎽⎽⎽⎽⎽⎽⎽⎽, while normally active cats became (restless and agitated/withdrawn and passive) ⎽⎽⎽⎽⎽⎽⎽⎽⎽⎽⎽⎽⎽⎽⎽⎽⎽⎽⎽.

3. When food was paired with unpredictable shock, the cats also developed p⎽⎽⎽⎽⎽⎽⎽⎽⎽⎽⎽⎽ and counter⎽⎽⎽⎽⎽⎽⎽⎽⎽⎽⎽⎽⎽⎽⎽⎽ responses to the food.

4. Evidence suggests that neurotic symptoms are more likely to develop when the traumatic event occurs in an environment that the animal (or person) generally regards as (safe/dangerous) ⎽⎽⎽⎽⎽⎽⎽⎽⎽⎽⎽⎽⎽⎽⎽⎽⎽⎽.

5. Learned helplessness can be viewed as resulting from repeated exposure to aversive events that are p⎽⎽⎽⎽⎽⎽⎽⎽⎽⎽⎽⎽⎽⎽ but unc⎽⎽⎽⎽⎽⎽⎽⎽⎽⎽⎽⎽⎽; experimental neurosis can be viewed as resulting from exposure to events that are unp⎽⎽⎽⎽⎽⎽⎽⎽⎽⎽⎽.

And Furthermore

Dissociative Identity Disorder: A Behavioral Perspective

Some clinicians believe that the most severe disorder produced by exposure to traumatic events is dissociative identity disorder (DID; formerly called multiple personality disorder). The essential characteristic of this disorder is two or more personality states (or alter personalities) that repeatedly take control of behavior. Patients also suffer from extensive amnesia, with some personalities often unaware of the existence of other personalities. In the classic case of Eve White, for example (portrayed in the 1957 movie *The Three Faces of Eve*), the original personality of Eve White was reportedly unaware of an alter personality named Eve Black. Eve Black, however, was fully aware of Eve White and enjoyed making life difficult for her (Thigpen & Cleckley, 1957). This type of amnesia bears some similarity to repression, and in fact many clinicians prefer to conceptualize hidden memories of abuse as dissociated memories rather than repressed memories. Unfortunately, as with the concept of repression, the concept of DID is extremely controversial.

Behaviorists have traditionally viewed multiple personalities as distinct patterns of behavior (both overt and covert) that have arisen in response to distinctly different contingencies of reinforcement (Skinner, 1953). This reasoning has been carried a step further in the *post-traumatic model* of DID, which holds that DID usually results from childhood trauma (e.g., Ross, 1997). According to this model, an abused child can more easily cope with everyday life by usually forgetting about the abusive incidents and by pretending that the abuse is happening to someone else. In behavioral terms, this self-deception can be conceptualized as a type of covert avoidance response—"Nothing bad is happening to me"— which is negatively reinforced by a reduction in anxiety. As a result, the child learns to compartmentalize the distressing experience into a separate personality pattern that has its own dispositions and memories (Kohlenberg & Tsai, 1991; Phelps, 2000). This style of coping may become so habitual that it eventually results in the formation of dozens, or even hundreds, of separate personality states.

Others, however, have argued that DID is usually not the result of trauma but instead the result of suggestive influence (Spanos, 1996; Lilienfeld et al., 1999). According to this *sociocognitive model* (which can also be conceptualized as a cognitive-behavioral model), the patient's displays of alter personalities have been inadvertently shaped through processes of social reinforcement and observational learning. Supportive evidence for this model includes the following:

SUMMARY

Negative reinforcement plays an important role in the development of escape and avoidance behaviors. A typical procedure for studying escape and avoidance is a shuttle avoidance task. In it, the rat first learns to escape shock by climbing over a barrier whenever it feels a shock; it then learns to avoid shock by climbing over the barrier in the presence of a cue that predicts shock delivery.

- The first clear observations of alter personalities are often obtained following exposure to a therapist who communicates to the patient that displays of alter personalities will be considered appropriate (and hence socially reinforced)—such as by asking the patient "if there is another thought process, part of the mind, part, person or force" (Braun, 1980, p. 213).
- The number of alter personalities displayed by patients usually increases as therapy progresses, as does the patients' ability to quickly switch from one alter to another (Ross, 1997). This suggests that a process of shaping may be involved.
- The number of DID cases rose sharply following dramatic presentations of the disorder to the public during the 1970s and 1980s, such as the case of Sybil, which became a best-selling book (Schreiber, 1973) and a popular movie. This suggests that observational learning may have played a role in the increased prevalence of the disorder.
- Many (though not all) of the patients' memories of childhood trauma are memories that were recovered during therapy (Kluft, 1998). As noted in our previous discussion of repression, such recovered memories might sometimes be false.

Direct evidence for the role of behavioral processes in DID was reported by Kohlenberg (1973). He found that by manipulating the amount of reinforcement a patient received for displaying one of three alter personalities, he was able to change the amount of time that a particular personality was displayed. He then devised a successful treatment program that included reinforcing displays of the personality that acted most normally and ignoring displays of other personalities.

Supporters of the post-traumatic model (e.g., Gleaves, 1996; Ross, 1997; Ross & Norton, 1989) and the sociocognitive model (e.g., Lilienfeld et al., 1999; Powell & Gee, 1999; Spanos, 1994, 1996) have each presented a series of arguments and counterarguments in support of their positions. The result has been some movement toward a middle ground. Ross (1997), for example, now acknowledges that at least some cases of DID have been artificially induced in therapy, while Lilienfeld et al. (1999) have acknowledged that a tendency toward developing DID-type symptoms might sometimes be the result of trauma. Likewise, Phelps (2000) has presented a behavioral account of DID, arguing that, although alter personalities could conceivably arise from a history of childhood trauma, therapists might also inadvertently strengthen displays of alter personalities through processes of social reinforcement.

According to Mowrer's two-process theory, avoidance behavior results from (1) classical conditioning in which a fear response comes to be elicited by a CS, and (2) operant conditioning in which moving away from the CS is negatively reinforced by a reduction in fear. One criticism of this theory is that the avoidance response is extremely persistent, even when the aversive US is no longer presented. According to the anxiety conservation hypothesis, however, avoidance occurs so quickly that there is insufficient exposure to the CS for extinction of the fear response to take place. A second criticism of two-process theory is that once the animals become accustomed to making the avoidance response, they no longer seem fearful of the CS—hence, it seems that reduction in fear cannot serve as a negative reinforcer for avoidance. One answer to this criticism is that, although the animals may be significantly less fearful, they are not completely nonfearful.

Mineka pointed out that experimental avoidance conditioning in animals differs in several ways from phobic conditioning in humans. More specifically, the animals avoid the aversive US while phobic humans avoid the CS, and phobic conditioning in humans often requires only a single trial to produce extremely persistent avoidance. Stampfl, however, showed that phobic-like avoidance could be achieved in rats by providing them with the opportunity to make the avoidance response early in the chain of events leading up to the CS.

Avoidance conditioning plays a role in obsessive-compulsive disorders. Obsessions produce an increase in anxiety that is then reduced by carrying out the compulsive behavior pattern. Treatment procedures have been developed involving prolonged exposure to the anxiety-arousing event without engagement in the compulsive behavior pattern, thereby allowing the anxiety to extinguish.

Positive punishment involves the presentation of an aversive stimulus, while negative punishment involves the removal of an appetitive stimulus. Two common forms of negative punishment are time-out, which involves the removal of access to all reinforcers, and response cost, which involves the removal of a specific reinforcer. Intrinsic punishment is punishment that is an inherent aspect of the behavior being punished, while extrinsic punishment is punishment that is not an inherent aspect of the behavior being punished. A primary punisher is one that is naturally punishing, and a secondary punisher is an event that is punishing because it has been associated with some other punisher. A generalized secondary punisher has been associated with many other punishers.

There are several problems with the use of punishment including a general suppression of behavior (rather than a strengthening of appropriate behavior), avoidance of the person carrying out the punishment, elicitation of strong emotional responses, and an increase in aggressive behavior. Punishment is more effective if delivered immediately, consistently, and at sufficient intensity to suppress the behavior. It also helps if punishment is accompanied by an explanation and if it is combined with positive reinforcement for appropriate behavior.

According to the conditioned suppression theory of punishment, punishment suppresses a behavior because it produces an emotional response that interferes with the behavior. According to the avoidance theory of punishment, punishment is a type of avoidance conditioning in which the avoidance response consists of doing anything other than the behavior that is being punished. The Premack principle, as applied to punishment, holds that low-probability behaviors can be used as punishers for high-probability behaviors.

Learned helplessness is a decrement in learning ability following exposure to inescapable aversive stimulation. Learned helplessness can be overcome by repeatedly forcing the animal to make the avoidance response. It can be prevented by providing an animal with prior exposure to escapable aversive stimulation. In Masserman's experimental neurosis procedure, animals are exposed to unpredictable aversive stimulation. This produces symptoms that are similar to those experienced by people who have developed post-traumatic stress disorder.

STUDY QUESTIONS

1. Distinguish between escape and avoidance behavior.
2. Describe the evolution of avoidance behavior in a shuttle avoidance procedure.
3. Describe Mowrer's two-process theory of avoidance behavior.
4. Outline two criticisms of two-process theory.
5. What is the anxiety conservation hypothesis? Outline Levis's answer to the problem of the "nonchalant" rat.
6. In what ways is experimental avoidance conditioning different from human phobic conditioning?
7. According to Stampfl, what is a critical factor in the development and maintenance of phobic behavior?
8. How can two-process theory account for obsessive-compulsive disorder?
9. Distinguish between time-out and response cost procedures.
10. What is the distinction between extrinsic punishment and intrinsic punishment?
11. What is the distinction between a primary punisher and a secondary punisher? What is a generalized secondary punisher?
12. Briefly outline the various problems listed concerning the use of punishment.
13. Outline the five characteristics of effective punishment.
14. Describe the conditioned suppression theory of punishment.
15. Describe the avoidance theory of punishment.
16. Describe the Premack approach to punishment.
17. Describe the basic procedure that was first used to demonstrate learned helplessness in dogs.
18. How can dogs be inoculated against the development of learned helplessness? How can learned helplessness in dogs be eliminated?
19. Describe Masserman's procedure for inducing experimental neurosis, and some of the symptoms he observed.

CONCEPT REVIEW

avoidance theory of punishment. Punishment involving a type of avoidance conditioning, in which the avoidance response consists of any behavior other than the behavior being punished.

conditioned suppression theory of punishment. The assumption that punishment does not weaken a behavior but instead produces an emotional response that interferes with the occurrence of the behavior.

exposure and response prevention (ERP). A method of treating obsessive-compulsive behavior (and phobic behavior) that involves prolonged exposure to anxiety-arousing events while not engaging in the compulsive (or phobic) behavior pattern that reduces the anxiety.

extrinsic punishment. Punishment that is not an inherent aspect of the behavior being punished, but simply follows the behavior.

generalized secondary (or generalized conditioned) punisher. An event that has become punishing because it has in the past been associated with many other punishers.

intrinsic punishment. Punishment that is an inherent aspect of the behavior that is being punished.

learned helplessness. A decrement in learning ability that results from repeated exposure to uncontrollable aversive events.

Premack principle of punishment. A low-probability behavior (LPB) can be used to punish a high-probability behavior (HPB).

primary (or unconditioned) punisher. Any event that is naturally punishing.

response cost. A form of negative punishment involving the removal of a specific reinforcer following the occurrence of a behavior.

secondary (or conditioned) punisher. An event that has become punishing because it has in the past been associated with some other punisher.

time-out. A form of negative punishment involving the loss of access to positive reinforcers for a brief period of time following the occurrence of a problem behavior.

two-process theory of avoidance. The theory that avoidance behavior is the result of two distinct processes: (1) classical conditioning in which a fear response comes to be elicited by a CS, and (2) operant conditioning in which moving away from the CS is negatively reinforced by a reduction in fear.

CHAPTER TEST

11. According to Mowrer, the two processes that underlie avoidance behavior are (1) _____ conditioning in which a _____ response comes to be elicited by a CS, and (2) _____ conditioning in which moving away from the CS is _____ reinforced by a reduction in _____.

3. According to the _____ theory of punishment, if a rat is shocked for pressing a lever, then any behavior other than _____ will be _____ reinforced by the nonoccurrence of shock.

27. If a father punishes his son for being aggressive with his playmates, the son may learn not to be aggressive only when the father is _____.

8. Otto woke up one night to find an intruder standing over him in his bedroom. When the intruder saw that Otto was awake, he stabbed him and fled. Boyd was walking through a strange part of town one night when he too was stabbed. In keeping with certain research findings on experimental _____, the person most likely to suffer symptoms of PTSD is _____.

14. One criticism of Mowrer's two-process theory is that animals continue to make the avoidance response even though they no longer seem to be _____ of the CS. One reply to this criticism is that although the animals may become significantly less _____ of the CS, they do not in fact become completely _____.

20. A person who checks her apartment door dozens of times each night to make sure that it is locked probably experiences a(n) _____ in anxiety when she thinks about whether the door is locked and a(n) _____ in anxiety when she checks it. This then acts as a _____ reinforcer for the behavior of checking.

15. According to the _____ theory of avoidance, I avoid bees simply because I am then less likely to be stung and not because I feel a reduction in fear.

9. Obert did not want to go to school one morning and so pretended that he was ill. Sure enough, his mother fell for the trick and let him stay home that day. Thereafter, Obert often pretended that he was ill so that he did not have to go to school. Obert's tendency to pretend that he was ill was strengthened through the process of _____.

28. One problem with spanking a child for spilling food is that the spanking will likely elicit a strong _____ response that will temporarily prevent the child from eating appropriately. The child may also become _____ as a result of the spanking, which might later be directed to his little brother or sister. He might also learn that an effective means of controlling others is through the use of _____.

2. Skinner (1938, 1953) concluded that punishment generates a conditioned _____ reaction that then suppresses any appetitive behavior, and that the appetitive behavior (will/will not) _____ quickly recover once the punishment is withdrawn. Later research showed that this may be because Skinner had used a relatively (strong/weak) _____ form of punishment in his research.

19. Mowrer's two-process theory seems highly applicable to obsessive-compulsive disorder in that the occurrence of an obsessive thought is associated with a(n) _____ anxiety, while performance of a compulsive behavior is associated with a(n) _____ in anxiety.

13. One criticism of Mowrer's two-process theory is that an avoidance response often does not seem to _____, even after hundreds of trials. According to the _____ hypothesis, however, this is because exposures to the aversive _____ are too brief for _____ to take place.

4. According to the Premack principle, if Rick loves to paint and hates to vacuum, then _____ can serve as an effective punisher for _____.

22. Losing your wallet by being careless is an example of a (negative/positive) _____ punisher, while getting a shock by being careless is an example of a _____ punisher (assuming in each case that the behavior _____ in frequency).

12. According to Mowrer, I go out of my way to avoid bees because behaving this way has been (positively/negatively) _____ (reinforced/punished) _____ by a _____.

29. One problem with spanking a child for being noisy while playing is that this will likely have an _____ effect in suppressing the behavior, which then serves as a strong reinforcer for the use of spanking on future occasions.

25. If you punish a dog for making a mess on the carpet, the dog might learn to avoid _____ rather than avoid making a mess on the carpet.

10. The theoretical difficulty with avoidance behavior, as opposed to escape behavior, is that the individual is moving from one (aversive/nonaversive) _____ situation to another, and it is difficult to see how a lack of change serves as a reinforcer.

21. One difference between OCD and a phobia is that a phobia requires a(n) (passive/active) _____ avoidance response, while OCD requires a(n) _____ avoidance response.

7. Pietro is having great difficulty sleeping, is easily startled, and has developed various phobias. Pietro's symptoms are similar to those shown by Masserman's cats that were exposed to _____ aversive stimulation. This set of symptoms in experimental animals is known as experimental _____; in humans, it is known as _____ stress disorder.

16. According to Mineka, there are limitations in the extent to which experimental demonstrations of avoidance are analogous to human phobias. For example, in an experimental demonstration of avoidance that involves a tone and an aversive air blast, the rat avoids the _____, which is a (CS/US) _____. By comparison, the bee-phobic person

who was once stung avoids _____, which is a (CS/US) _____.

1. For children who are old enough to understand language, punishment should always be combined with an _____.

23. Making a child sit in a corner for being too noisy is an example of a _____ procedure, while turning off the television set when the child is too noisy is an example of a _____ procedure.

5. When Renee was in elementary school, she was cruelly teased by a classmate each recess. The teachers ignored her pleas for help, as did her other classmates. Seligman would predict that, as time passes, Renee is likely to (decrease/increase)_____ her efforts to stop the teasing. In other words, she will begin to suffer from learned _____. She may also become clinically _____.

17. According to Mineka, there are limitations in the extent to which experimental demonstrations of avoidance are analogous to human phobias. For example, in an experimental demonstration of avoidance that involves a tone and an aversive air blast, the rat will likely require (one/more than one) _____ conditioning trial. By comparison, a bee phobia may be acquired after _____ conditioning trial(s). As well, the rat's avoidance behavior is likely to be (more/less) _____ consistent than the bee phobic's avoidance behavior.

26. One problem with punishing a child for being noisy while playing is that he might not only stop being noisy but also stop _____.

30. A parent who wishes to punish her little girl for playing too roughly with the cat would do well to impose the punishing consequence _____ after the occurrence of the unwanted behavior and, at least initially, on a(n) (consistent/unpredictable) _____ basis. The parent should also _____ the child for playing appropriately with the cat.

6. According to learned helplessness research, Clint is (more/less) _____ likely to become depressed following a bitter divorce if his own parents divorced when he was a child and he later recovered from the experience.

24. Hugh got injured at work while goofing around, and as a result he became less likely to goof around in that way. Eduardo got reprimanded by the boss for goofing around, and he also became less likely to goof around. Getting injured is a (primary/secondary) _____ punisher for the behavior of goofing around, while getting reprimanded is a _____ punisher.

18. Stampfl demonstrated that a critical factor in phobic conditioning is the possibility of making an (early/late) _____ avoidance response, thereby minimizing the amount of _____ involved in making the response.

ANSWERS TO CHAPTER TEST

1. explanation
2. emotional; will; weak
3. avoidance; lever pressing; negatively
4. vacuuming; painting
5. decrease; helplessness; depressed
6. less
7. unpredictable; neurosis; post-traumatic
8. neurosis; Otto
9. negative reinforcement
10. nonaversive
11. classical; fear; operant; negatively; fear
12. negatively; reinforced; reduction in fear
13. extinguish; anxiety conservation; CS; extinction
14. afraid; fearful; nonfearful
15. one-process
16. air blast; US; bees; CS
17. more than one; one; less
18. early; effort
19. increase; decrease
20. increase; decrease; negative
21. passive; active
22. negative; positive; decreases
23. time-out; response cost
24. primary; secondary
25. you
26. playing
27. present (or nearby)
28. emotional; aggressive; punishment.
29. immediate
30. immediately; consistent; positively reinforce

CHAPTER 10

Choice, Matching, and Self-Control

CHAPTER OUTLINE

Mark was becoming quite frustrated by Jan's insistence that they were spending too much time together. He told her that if two people truly love each other, then they should want to spend as much time together as possible. Jan countered that she did love him, but that spending too much time together was making their relationship dull and boring.

Operant conditioning in the real world is rarely a matter of being offered only one source of reinforcement. Instead, individuals typically choose between alternative sources of reinforcement. In this chapter, we examine some of the principles by which such choices are made—especially the principle of matching, which stipulates that the amount of behavior directed toward an alternative is proportional to the amount of reinforcement we receive from that alternative. We also examine the types of choices involved when people attempt to exert "self-control" over their own behavior.

Choice and Matching

Concurrent Schedules

In operant conditioning experiments, investigations of choice behavior often make use of a type of complex schedule known as a concurrent schedule. **A concurrent schedule of reinforcement consists of the simultaneous presentation of two or more independent schedules, each of which leads to a reinforcer.** The organism is thus allowed a choice between responding on one schedule versus the other.

For example, a pigeon may be given a choice between responding on a red key that is associated with a VR 20 schedule of reinforcement and a green key that is associated with a VR 50 schedule of reinforcement (see Figure 10.1). We can diagram this situation as follows:

Which alternative would you choose? If you think of this situation as analogous to choosing between two slot machines, one of which pays off after an average of 20 quarters are plugged in and the other of which pays off after an average of 50 quarters are plugged in, the choice becomes easy. You would pick the better paying machine, that is, the one that requires an average of only 20 quarters to produce a win (if you can fight off everyone else who wants

FIGURE 10.1   Illustration of a two-key operant procedure in which two schedules of reinforcement are simultaneously available, in this case, a VR 20 schedule on
the red key and a VR 50 schedule on the green key. The two schedules thus form the
two components of a *Concurrent VR 20 VR 50* schedule of reinforcement. (*Source:*
Domjan, 1998.)

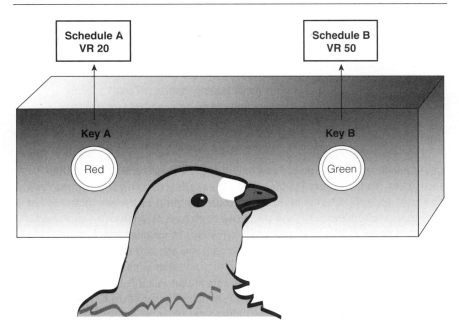

that machine). Similarly, the pigeon will come to develop an exclusive preference for the VR 20 alternative (Herrnstein & Loveland, 1975).

Choice between concurrent VR schedules is easy because an exclusive preference for the richer alternative clearly provides the better payoff. But what
about concurrent VI schedules? What if, for example, a pigeon is presented
with a Concurrent VI 30-sec VI 60-sec schedule?

Remember that on VI schedules, reinforcers become available at unpredictable points in time (and any responses prior to that point will not result in
reinforcement). Given this unpredictability, will the bird just randomly distribute its responses between the two alternatives, hoping to catch the reinforcers on each alternative as they become available (just as in trying to phone

two friends, you might repeatedly dial each number in random order hoping to catch each person soon after he or she arrives home)? Herrnstein (1961) carried out just such an experiment using various schedule values and found that the pigeon's behavior under such circumstances is actually quite systematic. It is so systematic in fact that it led to the formulation of what is known as the matching law.

1. Many behaviors are reinforced on a c_____ schedule in which two or more ind_____ schedules of reinforcement are s_____ available.

2. If a VR 25 and VR 75 schedule of reinforcement are simultaneously available, your best strategy would be to choose the _____ schedule (100/50/25) _____% of the time.

The Matching Law

The *matching law* holds that the proportion of responses emitted on a particular schedule matches the proportion of reinforcers obtained on that schedule. Thus, a pigeon will emit approximately twice as many responses on the VI 30-sec schedule as on the VI 60-sec schedule, because the rate of reinforcement on the former will be twice as great as on the latter (an average of two reinforcers per minute on the VI 30-sec schedule versus one reinforcer per minute on the VI 60-sec schedule). Similarly, a pigeon will emit three times as many responses on a VI 10-sec schedule as it will on a VI 30-sec schedule because the VI 10-sec schedule provides three times the rate of reinforcement (an average of six reinforcers per minute on the VI 10-sec schedule versus two per minute on the VI 30-sec schedule). *The matching law therefore predicts a consistent relationship between the proportion of reinforcers obtained on a certain alternative and the proportion of responses emitted on that alternative.* If a pigeon earns 10% of its reinforcers on a particular alternative, then it will emit 10% of its responses on that alternative; if it earns 60% of its reinforcers on an alternative, then it will emit 60% of its responses on it.

The matching law can also be expressed in the form of an equation:

$$\frac{R_A}{R_A + R_B} = \frac{S^R{}_A}{S^R{}_A + S^R{}_B}$$

where R is the number of responses emitted, S^R is the number of reinforcers earned, and the subscripts A and B refer to the two schedules of reinforcement. Thus, R_A is the number of responses emitted on schedule A, R_B is the number of responses emitted on schedule B, $S^R{}_A$ is the number of reinforcers earned on schedule A, and $S^R{}_B$ is the number of reinforcers earned on schedule B. Therefore, the term to the left of the equal sign:

$$\frac{R_A}{R_A + R_B}$$

indicates the proportion of responses emitted on schedule A. It is the number of responses emitted on schedule A divided by the total number emitted on both schedules. The term to the right of the equal sign:

$$\frac{S^R_A}{S^R_A + S^R_B}$$

indicates the proportion of reinforcers earned on schedule A. It is the number of reinforcers earned on schedule A divided by the total number earned on both schedules.

As an illustration of how the equation works, let us look at some hypothetical data from an experiment involving a choice between a VI 30-sec and a VI 60-sec schedule. If the pigeon picks up most or all of the reinforcers available on each alternative in a 1-hour session, it should obtain about twice as many reinforcers on the VI 30-sec schedule as on the VI 60-sec. Imagine that this is essentially what happens: Our hypothetical pigeon obtains 119 reinforcers on the VI 30-sec schedule and 58 on the VI 60-sec schedule. Plugging these values into the right-hand term of the equation, we get

$$\frac{S^R_{VI\,30}}{S^R_{VI\,30} + S^R_{VI\,60}} = \frac{119}{119 + 58} = \frac{119}{177} = .67$$

which means that the proportion of reinforcers obtained from the VI 30-sec schedule is .67. In other words, 67% of the reinforcers acquired during the session are obtained from the VI 30-sec schedule (and 33% are obtained from the VI 60-sec schedule). As for responses, imagine that our hypothetical pigeon emits 2800 responses on the VI 30-sec schedule and 1450 responses on the VI 60-sec schedule. Plugging these values into the left-hand term of the equation, we get

$$\frac{R_{VI\,30}}{R_{VI\,30} + R_{VI\,60}} = \frac{2800}{2800 + 1450} = \frac{2800}{4250} = .66$$

Thus, the proportion of responses emitted on the VI 30-sec schedule is .66. In other words, 66% of the responses are emitted on the VI 30-sec schedule (and 34% are emitted on the VI 60-sec schedule). In keeping with the matching law, this figure closely matches the proportion of reinforcement obtained on that schedule (.67). In other words, the proportion of responses emitted on the VI 30-sec schedule approximately matches the proportion of reinforcers earned on that schedule. (For results from Herrnstein's [1961] original matching experiment in which pigeons chose between several different combinations of schedules, see Figure 10.2).

Matching appears to be a basic principle of choice behavior, applicable to a variety of situations and species. For example, Houston (1986) investigated the extent to which the pied wagtail, an insectivorous bird in Britain, distributed its foraging behavior between two separate patches of food: (1) a stretch of territory along the banks of the Thames River, which the territorial owner defended from other wagtails (and only some birds owned territories), and

FIGURE 10.2 Experimental results depicting the proportion of responses emitted by two pigeons on key A. Different combinations of schedules were offered on key A versus key B across the different conditions of the experiment, with the schedule values ranging from VI 90-sec to VI 540-sec to extinction (no reinforcers available). As the schedule combinations changed and the proportion of reinforcers earned on key A increased from approximately .1 to 1.0, the proportion of responses emitted on key A increased in similar fashion. (*Source:* Adapted from "Relative and absolute strength of response as a function of frequency of reinforcement," by R. J. Herrnstein, 1961, *Journal of Experimental Analysis of Behavior, 4,* pp. 267–272. Copyright © 1961 by the Society for the Experimental Analysis of Behavior, Inc. Reprinted with permission.

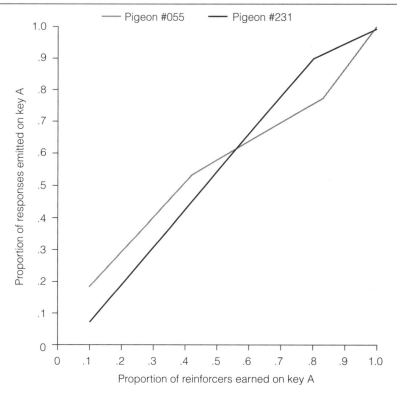

(2) an open meadow that any wagtail could visit and feed upon as part of the flock. Those birds that owned territories tended to walk circular routes within their territories feeding off insects that were regularly washed up by the river. If, however, food along the river was scarce, the owner could fly over to the meadow and feed with the flock. (In a sense, finding nothing to eat at home, the bird had the option of eating out at the corner restaurant.) Houston found that the proportion of time a bird spent in one food patch versus the other (its own territory versus the public meadow) approximately matched the proportion of food it obtained in that patch.

Matching is also applicable to human social behavior. For example, in a group situation, we must choose between directing our conversation to one person or another, each of whom provides a different rate of reinforcement (in the form of comments or acknowledgments). In one investigation, Conger and Killeen (1974) asked student volunteers to participate with three other students in a discussion session on drug abuse. Each volunteer was unaware that the other members of the group were actually confederates of the experimenter. During the discussion session, while the volunteer was talking, the two confederates sat on either side and intermittently expressed approval in response to whatever the volunteer happened to be saying at that time. The experimenters systematically varied the frequency of verbal approvals delivered by each of the confederates. They found that the relative amount of time the volunteer looked at each confederate matched the relative frequency of verbal approval delivered by that confederate. If one confederate delivered twice as many approvals as the other confederate, then that confederate was looked at twice as often.

QUICK QUIZ

1. According to the matching law, the _____ of _____ matches the _____ of _____ obtained on an alternative.

2. On a concurrent VI 60-sec VI 120-sec schedule, the pigeon should emit about (half/twice) _____ as many responses on the VI 60-sec alternative as opposed to the VI 120-sec alternative.

3. If a pigeon emits 1100 responses on key A and 3100 responses on key B, then the proportion of responses on key A is _____. If the pigeon also earned 32 reinforcers on key A and 85 reinforcers on key B, then the proportion of reinforcers earned on key A is _____. This pigeon (did/did not) _____ approximately match pr_____ of r_____ to pr_____ of r_____.

Deviations from Matching

Although matching provides a good description of behavior in many choice situations, a variety of exceptions have been noted. In general, there are three types of exceptions, or deviations, from matching (Baum, 1974, 1979). The first deviation, which is quite common, is called undermatching. **In *undermatching*, the proportion of responses on the richer alternative versus the poorer alternative is less different than would be predicted by matching** (to remember this, think of *under*matching as *less* different). For example, if the matching law predicts that the proportion of responses should be .67 on the richer schedule (say, a VI 30-sec schedule) and .33 on the poorer schedule (say, a VI 60-sec schedule), but we instead find proportions of .60 and .40 respectively, then undermatching has occurred. There is less of a difference in responding between the richer and poorer schedules than would be predicted by matching.

Undermatching can occur when there is little cost for switching from one alternative to another. For example, in our previous description of a hypothetical matching experiment, we actually left out an important aspect of the procedure. Whenever the pigeon switches from one key to another, the act of

And Furthermore

Basketball and the Matching Law

In an interesting application of the matching law to sports activities, Vollmer and Bourret (2000) examined the allocation of 2- versus 3-point shots made by male and female basketball players at a major university. The question of interest was whether the players would match the proportion of shots taken from the 3-point range to the proportion of reinforcers (baskets) they obtained from that range. The researchers found that such matching did indeed occur (particularly when the matching equation was altered somewhat to account for the greater value of 3-point shots). In other words, if a certain player obtained about 35% of his or her points from the 3-point range, then about 35% of his or her shots tended to occur from that range. The authors speculated that this ability to match the proportion of shots attempted from a certain range to the proportion of points obtained from that range may be a distinguishing characteristic of player excellence. One author, for example, described how he casually observed a local street game in which 3-point shots were frequently attempted despite the fact that they were almost never successful. In other words, these less skillful players did not display the same tendency to match that the university players had displayed (this was a top-ranked university, by the way). The matching law may therefore prove useful in evaluating the skill level of basketball players.

You may have noticed that this type of matching suggests that basketball shots are reinforced on a VI schedule, which contradicts the typical notion that shot-making in such activities is reinforced on a VR schedule (with rate of reinforcement largely dependent on the number of shots attempted). The authors of this study, however, suggest that basketball shots may in fact be reinforced on a combination VR-VI schedule, with reinforcement dependent both on the number of shots attempted (the VR component) and on defensive lapses by the opposition that occur at unpredictable points in time (the VI component).

doing so initiates a slight delay of, say, 2 seconds during which no response will be effective in producing a reinforcer, even if a reinforcer happens to be available at that time. It is as though, when the pigeon switches from one key to another, the first peck on the new key is simply a statement of intent that says "I now want to try this key," following which there is a 2-second delay before any peck can actually earn a reinforcer. This delay feature is called a *changeover delay* or *COD*. Without a COD, a pigeon will simply alternate pecks back and forth on each key, catching each reinforcer as soon as it becomes available. Only when a slight cost for switching is added to the situation does the pigeon spend more time on the richer alternative.

The COD can be thought of as the experimental equivalent of having to travel a certain distance between food patches. If two food patches are extremely close together (say, each patch is separated by only a narrow stream), then undermatching is likely to occur. The animal will simply move back and forth from one side to another, looking for prey, even if one side is generally a much richer area in which to hunt. If, however, the two patches are more widely separated (say, the stream is somewhat broad), then the animal is more likely to match the amount of time it spends on one side of the stream to the number of prey that it obtains on that side. It will spend proportionately more time on the rich side of the stream, and less time on the poor side of the stream.

A second deviation from matching is called overmatching. **In *overmatching*, the proportion of responses on the richer versus poorer alternative is more different than would be predicted by matching** (to remember this, think of *over*matching as *more* different). For example, if the matching law predicts that the proportion of responses should be .67 on the richer schedule and .33 on the poorer schedule, but we instead find proportions of .80 and .20 respectively, then overmatching has occurred. There is more of a difference in responding between the richer and poorer schedules than would be predicted by matching.

Overmatching can occur when the cost of moving from one alternative to another is very high. For example, Baum (1974) found that overmatching occurred when a pigeon had to walk around a partition and climb across a wooden hurdle to switch from one response key to another. The pigeon switched less often and spent more time on the richer alternative than the matching law would predict. Similarly, a predator that has to cross a mountain ridge to move from one food patch to another might make the trip only infrequently and spend considerably more time in the richer food patch than predicted by matching.

1. When the difference in the proportion of responding on richer versus poorer alternatives is greater than would be predicted by matching, we say that _____ has occurred.

2. When the difference in the proportion of responding on richer versus poorer alternatives is less than would be predicted by matching, we say that _____ has occurred.

3. In experimental studies of matching, the act of switching from one alternative to another results in a c_____ d_____: a short period of time that must pass before any response can produce a reinforcer.

4. This experimental procedure seems analogous to foraging situations in which an animal has to t_____ a certain d_____ from one food patch to another.

5. In general, food patches that are separated by a very great distance will produce _____ matching, while food patches that are separated by a very short distance will produce _____ matching.

QUICK QUIZ

The final deviation from matching is called bias. ***Bias from matching* occurs when one alternative attracts a higher proportion of responses than would be predicted by matching, regardless of whether that alternative is the richer or poorer alternative.** For example, suppose that our two schedules are VI 30-sec and VI 60-sec, and that we alternate which schedule is associated with the red key versus the green key. The matching law predicts that the proportion of responses on the red key should be .67 when the richer VI 30-sec schedule is presented on it, and .33 when the poorer VI 60-sec schedule is presented on it. But if the proportions instead turned out to be .77 when the VI 30-sec schedule is presented on it and .43 when the VI 60-sec schedule is presented on it, then bias has occurred (see Table 10.1). The pigeon is emitting 10% more responses on the red key than predicted by matching, both when it is the richer alternative and when it is the poorer alternative. (Of course, this also means that the pigeon is emitting 10% fewer responses on the green key.) In a sense, the pigeon seems to like red more than green so it expends extra effort on the red key over and above the amount of responding dictated by the schedule of reinforcement. Similarly, in conversation with a group of individuals, Erin might spend additional time directing her conversation toward Jason whom she finds very attractive. For example, on one day, he provides 72% of the reinforcers during a conversation, but she nevertheless looks at him 84% of the time; on another day, he provides only 23% of the reinforcers, but she nevertheless looks at him 36% of the time. In each case, she looks at him more than would be predicted by matching. His attractiveness is an additional factor, over and above the amount of social reinforcement he offers, that influences how much she looks at him.

Bias can be a precise way to measure preference. For example, on a concurrent VI 60-sec VI 60-sec schedule, the pigeon should respond equally on the two alternatives. But what if each alternative leads to a different reinforcer, say, wheat on one side and buckwheat on the other? Under these circumstances, the extent to which the pigeon biases its responding toward the schedule leading to wheat indicates the extent of the pigeon's preference for wheat. In fact, Miller (1976) carried out just such an experiment and found that pigeons preferred wheat over buckwheat by a ratio of about 1.4 to 1.0. If

TABLE 10.1 Hypothetical results indicating bias from matching. More responses are emitted on the red key, both when it is the richer alternative (VI 30-sec) and when it is the poorer alternative (VI 60-sec), than would be predicted by matching. (Of course, this also means that fewer responses are emitted on the green key than would be predicted by matching.)

Condition A (richer schedule on red key):	Predicted	Obtained
Red Key: VI 30-sec	.67	.77
Green Key: VI 60-sec	.33	.23
Condition B (poorer schedule on red key):		
Red Key: VI 60-sec	.33	.43
Green Key: VI 30-sec	.67	.57

we think of key pecks as equivalent to how much money pigeons would be willing to spend for one alternative versus the other, then the pigeons were willing to spend $1.40 on a bag of wheat compared to only $1.00 for a bag of buckwheat. (How much they would be willing to spend on Coke versus Pepsi has not, to our knowledge, yet been determined.) Bias in matching can therefore be used to indicate degree of preference for different reinforcers.

In summary, undermatching occurs when the difference in responding between the richer and poorer schedules is less than predicted by matching, overmatching occurs when the difference in responding between the richer and poorer schedules is more than predicted by matching, and bias occurs when one alternative receives more responses than predicted by matching regardless of whether it is the richer or poorer schedule. Each of these deviations has been incorporated into more complex versions of the matching law (Baum, 1974).

As with the phenomenon of behavioral contrast (discussed in Chapter 8), the matching law reminds us that operant behavior should often be viewed in context. The amount of behavior directed toward an alternative is a function not only of the amount of reinforcement available on that alternative but also the amount of reinforcement available on other alternatives. This notion has important implications for everyday behavior. For example, although a child might spend little time reading, this does not mean that reading is not a reinforcing activity for that child. If other highly reinforcing activities, such as computer games and television, happen to be simultaneously available, reading may be losing out simply because it provides less reinforcement (especially immediate reinforcement) than those other activities. Thus, a simple but effective way to motivate the child to read might be to limit the amount of time those other activities are available. In the absence of such alternatives, the child might naturally gravitate toward reading as a source of reinforcement.

1. When preference is shown for a particular alternative, irrespective of the amount of reinforcement obtained from that alternative, we say that the organism has a b_____ for that alternative.

2. Food patches that differ in the type of prey found within them may produce the type of deviation from matching known as _____.

QUICK QUIZ

Matching and Melioration

The matching law describes how behavior is distributed across various alternatives in a choice situation. It does not, however, provide an explanation for why this pattern of distribution occurs. You might think that it occurs simply because it somehow maximizes one's overall level of reinforcement, a proposition known as *maximization (or optimization) theory* (e.g., Rachlin, 1978). An alternative explanation, however, is called melioration theory (to meliorate means to make better). **According to *melioration theory*, the**

distribution of behavior in a choice situation shifts toward those alternatives that have higher value regardless of the effect on the overall amount of reinforcement (Herrnstein, 1990). For example, suppose that when a pigeon is *first* confronted with a concurrent VI 30-sec VI 60-sec schedule, it emits an *equal* number of responses on both alternatives. The responses emitted on the VI 30-sec schedule will result in twice as many reinforcers as those emitted on the VI 60-sec schedule. Thus, in terms of benefits (reinforcers obtained) versus costs (responses made), the VI 30-sec schedule will have a much higher value than the VI 60-sec schedule, because the bird will have obtained twice as many reinforcers on that schedule for the same amount of work. This will make the VI 30-sec schedule a very attractive alternative to the pigeon, with the result that the pigeon will be tempted in subsequent sessions to shift more and more of its behavior in that direction. This shifting, however, will cease at the point of matching, because that is the point at which the two alternatives have about equal value. The pigeon will still be earning twice as many reinforcers on the VI 30-sec schedule, but in doing so it will be expending twice as many responses on that alternative. Thus, the cost of each alternative (in responses made) will now match the benefits obtained from that alternative (in reinforcers earned). Melioration in this situation is thus a sort of leveling-out process, in which behavior shifts until the two alternatives have about equal value in terms of their costs versus benefits.

At this point, you might be thinking that melioration is rather trivial. Why would an animal or person not shift behavior toward the richer alternative? The problem is that this tendency to move toward the richer alternative can sometimes result in a substantial reduction in the total amount of reinforcement obtained. There are three ways in which this can occur.

First, an alternative may not require as much responding as one is distributing toward it in order to obtain all of the available reinforcers. Consider, for example, a pigeon that is presented with a concurrent VR 100 VI 30-sec schedule (note that the first alternative is a VR schedule). On the VR 100 alternative, 100 responses on average will result in a reinforcer, while on the VI 30-sec alternative, the first response after an average interval of 30 seconds will result in a reinforcer. What is the pigeon's best strategy in this situation?

The best strategy is for the pigeon to spend most of its time on the VR schedule, in which the number of reinforcers obtained is directly tied to the number of responses made, and then briefly switch to the VI alternative about every 30 seconds or so to pick up any reinforcer that might have become available on that alternative. This strategy will maximize the amount of reinforcement obtained. In reality, pigeons tend to match the amount of time spent on the VI schedule to the number of reinforcers earned on that schedule, thereby spending more time on the VI schedule and less time on the VR schedule than they should (Herrnstein & Heyman, 1979). Thus, if a pigeon happens to obtain 60% of its reinforcers from the VI 30-sec schedule, it will spend 60% of its time responding on the VI 30-sec schedule and only 40% of its time responding on the VR 100 schedule—a distribution of behavior that greatly reduces the overall amount of reinforcement obtained during the session. Hence, the pigeon's tendency to match (meliorate) has the effect of producing an overall level of reinforcement that is suboptimal.

In similar fashion, Henry, a salesman with a large manufacturing company, might spend too much time courting clients who are relatively easy sells (in reality, he only needs to call on such clients once a month to make a sale), and too little time courting retailers who are relatively difficult sells (who need to be intensively courted before a sale can be made). If Henry shifted some of his time away from the easy clients and toward the difficult clients, he might experience almost no loss of business from the former and a substantial gain in business from the latter. Unfortunately, the rich schedule of reinforcement provided by the easy clients is very attractive to him, with the result that he spends too much time with his easy clients and too little time with his difficult clients.

As another example, consider the manner in which many students distribute study time between the courses they are taking. Students often spend the most time studying the course that is most enjoyable, and the least time studying the course that is least enjoyable. Yet, the least enjoyable course is probably the one on which students should spend the most time studying. The result is that they spend the least time studying those courses that require the most work.

1. According to m_____ theory, the distribution of behavior in a choice situation shifts toward that alternative that has a (lower/higher) _____ value. This shifting will cease at the point where the two outcomes are (approximately equal/maximally different) _____ in terms of costs versus benefits.

2. A rat faced with a concurrent VR 60 VI 80-sec schedule will spend more time on the _____ schedule than it needs to in order to pick up all of the available reinforcers on that schedule. This result is consistent with m_____ theory but contradicts what is known as max_____ (or opt_____) theory.

3. Shona spends a lot of time cleaning her apartment, which she quite enjoys, and little time studying, which she does not enjoy. Chances are that this distribution of behavior, which results from the tendency to m_____, (will/will not) _____ maximize the amount of reinforcement in her life.

QUICK QUIZ

A second problem with melioration is that overindulgence in a highly reinforcing alternative can often result in long-term habituation to that alternative, thus reducing its value as a reinforcer. Suppose for example that you suddenly become so rich that you can eat as much as you want of whatever you want. Prior to becoming rich, you rarely ate lobster, which you absolutely loved. Now, with your newfound wealth, you begin eating lobster almost every day. The problem is that if you eat lobster this frequently, you will likely become habituated to it, such that, although still enjoyable, it is no longer the heavenly treat that it once was. For this reason, many people fondly remember those times in their lives when they had limited resources and had to struggle a bit to get by. The overall amount of reinforcement they experienced at that time, when highly valued items such as lobster could be experienced in only small quantities and truly enjoyed, may have actually been much greater than it is now.

This same process can be a contributing factor to the development of substance abuse. If drinking in a bar is a highly enjoyable activity, you might begin shifting more and more of your behavior in that direction. Eventually, you will be spending so much time in the bar that the overall amount of reinforcement in your life is substantially reduced—both because drinking is no longer as enjoyable as when you drank less frequently, and because you are now in the bar so much that you are missing out on reinforcers from other non-alcohol-related activities. You may in fact be fully aware that your alcohol-oriented life is not very satisfying (in fact, such awareness is one of the defining characteristics of an addiction), yet find it very difficult to break free and reject the pleasure of heading to the bar for another evening of positive reinforcement.

Many of the above examples can also be seen as instances of a *third, more general problem, which is that melioration is often the result of behavior being too strongly governed by immediate consequences as opposed to delayed consequences.* The immediate reinforcement available from studying more enjoyable courses tempts one away from working on less enjoyable courses and maximizing one's overall grade point average at the end of the term (a delayed reinforcer). And the immediate reinforcement available from going to the bar each evening tempts one away from moderating one's drinking and eventually establishing a more healthy and satisfying lifestyle (a delayed reinforcer). The difficulties that arise from the strong preference for immediate reinforcers over delayed reinforcers are described more fully in the following section.

QUICK QUIZ

1. One problem with melioration is that this tendency may result in (over-/under-) _____ indulgence of a favored reinforcer with the result that we may experience long-term h_____ to it. This means that our enjoyment of life may be greatest when we (do/do not) _____ have all that we want of highly valued items.

2. Another problem is that melioration can result in too much time being spent on those alternatives that provide relatively i_____ reinforcement and not enough time on those that provide d_____ reinforcement.

ADVICE FOR THE LOVELORN

Dear Dr. Dee,

My boyfriend spends almost all his time with me, which I find depressing. I try to tell him that I need some breathing space, but he seems to think that if I truly loved him, I would want to be with him always. What is your opinion on this?

Smothered

Dear Smo,

Sounds as if your love relationship may have fallen prey to the damaging effects of melioration. Although some people believe that being in love with someone means wanting to be with that person always, the reality is that too much togetherness can result in a severe case of habituation. Add to this the possibility that the two individuals involved are also spending much less time interacting with other people, and it could well be that the overall amount of reinforcement in their lives is actually less than it was before they met. This suggests that some relationships might improve if the couple spent a bit less time together and worked a bit harder at maintaining other sources of social reinforcement (given that this does not become a cheap excuse for having an affair!). So, behaviorally speaking, I agree with you.

Behaviorally yours,

Self-Control

In our discussion of melioration, we noted that people often engage in suboptimal patterns of behavior. Moreover, although people realize that these patterns are suboptimal, they seem unable to change them. They decide to quit smoking, but do not persist more than a day; they are determined to go for a run each morning, but cannot get out of bed to do so; they resolve to study each evening, but spend most evenings either watching television or socializing. In short, they know what to do, but they do not do it. To use the common vernacular, they lack self-control.

Why people have such difficulty controlling their own behavior has long been a matter of conjecture. Plato maintained that people engage in actions that are not in their best interest because of a lack of education, and that once they realize that it is to their benefit to behave appropriately, they will do so. Aristotle disagreed, however, noting that individuals often behave in ways that they clearly recognize as counterproductive. Many people, at least in this culture, would probably agree with Aristotle. They would probably also contend that self-control seems to require a certain mental faculty called willpower. A person who behaves wisely and resists temptations is said to have a lot of willpower, while a person who behaves poorly and yields to temptations is said to have little willpower. But is the concept of willpower, as used in this manner, really an explanation? Or is it one of those false explanations based on circular reasoning?

> *"Sam quit smoking. He must have a lot of willpower."*
> "How do you know he has a lot of willpower?"
> *"Well, he quit smoking, didn't he?"*

The term willpower, used in this way, merely describes what Sam did—that he was able to quit smoking. It does not explain why he was able to quit smoking. For this reason, telling someone that they need to use more willpower to quit smoking is usually a pointless exercise. They would love to use more willpower—if only someone would tell them what it is and where to get it.

In the remainder of this chapter, we discuss some behavioral approaches to self-control. These approaches generally reject the concept of willpower and instead focus on the relationship between behavior and its outcomes. We begin with Skinner's rudimentary analysis of self-control.

Skinner on Self-Control

Skinner (1953) viewed self-control not as an issue of willpower, but as an issue involving conflicting outcomes. For example, drinking alcohol can lead to both positive outcomes (e.g., increased confidence and feelings of relaxation) and negative outcomes (e.g., a hangover along with that idiotic tattoo you found on your arm the next morning). Skinner also proposed that managing this conflict involves two types of responses: a *controlling response* that serves to alter the frequency of a *controlled response*. Suppose, for example, that to control the amount of money you spend, you leave most of your money at home when heading out one evening. The act of leaving money at home is the controlling response, while the amount you subsequently spend is the controlled response. By emitting the one response, you affect the other.

Skinner (1953) listed several types of controlling responses, some of which are described below.

Physical Restraint. With this type of controlling response, you physically manipulate the environment to prevent the occurrence of some problem behavior. Leaving money at home so as to restrict the amount you spend during an evening out is one example; loaning your television set to a friend for the remainder of the semester so that you will be more likely to study than watch television is another.

Depriving and Satiating. Another tactic for controlling your behavior is to deprive or satiate yourself, thereby altering the extent to which a certain event can act as a reinforcer. For example, you might make the most of an invitation to an expensive dinner by skipping lunch, thereby ensuring that you will be very hungry at dinnertime. Conversely, if you are attempting to diet, you might do well to shop for groceries immediately *after* a meal. If you are satiated, as opposed to hungry, during your shopping trip, you will be less tempted to purchase fattening items such as ice cream and potato chips.

Doing Something Else. To prevent yourself from engaging in certain behaviors, it is sometimes helpful to perform an alternate behavior. Thus, people who are trying to quit smoking often find it helpful to chew gum, and people who are trying to diet often find it helpful to sip sugar-free sodas. A person might also try to prevent a certain emotional response by deliberately cultivating an opposite emotion. For example, someone growing up in a dangerous and frightening neighborhood might suppress his feelings of fear by acting angry, hateful, or coldly indifferent.

Self-Reinforcement and Self-Punishment. A self-control tactic that might seem obvious from a behavioral standpoint is to simply reinforce your own behavior. Although Skinner suggested that this might work, he also noted a certain difficulty with it. In the typical operant conditioning paradigm, the reinforcer is delivered only when the appropriate response is emitted. The rat must press the lever to receive food, the child must clean his room to receive a cookie, and the student must study and perform well on an exam to receive a high mark. In the case of self-reinforcement, however, this contingency is much weaker. You might promise yourself that you will have a pizza after completing 3 hours of studying, but what is to stop you from *not* studying and having the pizza anyway? To use Martin and Pear's (1999) terminology, what is to stop you from "short-circuiting" the contingency and immediately consuming the reward without performing the intended behavior?

A similar problem exists with the use of self-punishment. You might promise yourself that you will do 20 push-ups following each cigarette smoked, but what is to stop you from smoking a cigarette anyway and not bothering with the push-ups? Note too that if you do perform the push-ups, it might punish not only the act of smoking, but also the act of carrying through on your promise to punish yourself. As a result, you will be less likely to do the push-ups the next time you have a smoke. In fact, research has shown that people who attempt to use self-punishment often fail to deliver the consequences to themselves (Worthington, 1979).

cathy®   by Cathy Guisewite

Thus, some behaviorists believe that self-reinforcement and self-punishment do not function in the same manner as normal reinforcement and punishment (Catania, 1975). Rachlin (1974), for example, has proposed that self-reinforcement might simply make the completion of an intended behavior more *salient*, thereby enhancing its value as a secondary reinforcer. For example, eating a pizza after 3 hours of studying might simply be the equivalent of setting off fireworks and sounding the trumpets for a job well done. There is also some evidence that self-delivered consequences are more effective when the person perceives that other people are aware of the contingency, suggesting that the social consequences for attaining or not attaining the intended goal is often an important aspect of so-called *self*-reinforcement or *self*-punishment procedures (Hayes et al., 1985).

Despite these concerns, Bandura (1976) and others maintain that self-delivered consequences can function in much the same manner as externally delivered consequences, given that the individual has been properly socialized to adhere to self-set standards and to feel guilty for violating such standards. It is also the case that many people do make use of self-reinforcement and self-punishment procedures to try to control their behavior. Heffernan and Richards (1981), for example, found that 75% of students who had successfully improved their study habits reported using self-reinforcement. Conversely, Gary Player, the senior golfer, is a staunch believer in the value of self-punishment for maintaining a disciplined lifestyle—such as by forcing himself to do an extra 200 sit-ups (over and above the normal 800!) after a game in which he has let himself become irritable (Kossoff, 1999). Self-delivered contingencies are therefore a recommended component of many self-management programs (Watson & Tharp, 1997).

QUICK QUIZ

1. Behavioral approaches largely (accept/reject) _____ the concept of willpower as an explanation for self-control.

2. Skinner analyzed self-control from the perspective of a _____ response that alters the frequency of a subsequent response that is known as the _____ response.

3. Suppose you post a reminder on your refrigerator about a long-distance phone call you should make this weekend. Posting the reminder is the _____ response, while making the call on the weekend is the _____ response.

4. Folding your arms to keep from chewing your nails is an example of the use of p_____ r_____ to control your behavior.

5. To increase or decrease the extent to which an event can act as a reinforcer for your behavior, you can use the tactics of d_____ or s_____ yourself on that event.

6. A problem with the use of self-reinforcement is that we may be tempted to consume the _____ without engaging in the behavior. This problem is known as s_____-c_____.

7. This can also be a problem in the use of s_____-p_____, in which case we may engage in the behavior and not p_____ ourselves.

8. Some people believe that self-reinforcement is really a way of making the completion of a behavior (more/less) _____ salient, thereby enhancing its value as a s_____ reinforcer.

9. There is also some evidence that self-reinforcement is more effective when others (know/do not know) _____ about the contingency that we have arranged for ourselves.

10. Bandura believes that self-reinforcement and self-punishment can work for people who are likely to feel g_____ if they violate standards that they have set for themselves.

Self-Control as a Temporal Issue

While Skinner recognized that self-control issues involve choice between conflicting outcomes, others have emphasized that a critical aspect of this conflict is that one is choosing between outcomes that differ in the extent to which they are immediate versus delayed (e.g., Rachlin, 1974). As noted earlier, immediate consequences are generally more powerful than delayed consequences, a fact that can readily lead to suboptimal choices. Take, for example, a student who can either go out for the evening and have a good time (which is a relatively immediate or "smaller sooner reward") or study in the hopes of achieving an excellent grade (which is a relatively delayed or "larger later reward"). In a straight choice between having a fun evening and an excellent grade, she would clearly choose the excellent grade. But since the fun evening is immediately available and hence powerful, she will be sorely tempted to indulge herself in an evening's entertainment. Similarly, a pigeon who must choose between pecking a green key that leads to an immediate 2 seconds of access to grain (a smaller sooner reward) or pecking a red key that leads to a 10-second delay followed by 6 seconds of access to grain (a larger later reward) will strongly prefer the small, immediate reward. Thus, *from a temporal perspective, lack of self-control arises from the fact that our behavior is more heavily influenced by immediate consequences as opposed to delayed consequences.*

Self-control can also involve choice between a smaller sooner punisher and a larger later punisher, only in this instance it is selection of the smaller sooner alternative that is most beneficial. In deciding whether to go to the dentist, for example, we choose between enduring a small amount of discomfort in the near future (from minor dental treatment) and risking a large amount of discomfort in the distant future (from an infected tooth). Unfortunately, the prospect of experiencing discomfort in the near future (from a visit to the dentist) might exert such strong control over our behavior that we avoid going to the dentist, with the result that we suffer much greater discomfort later on. Likewise, a rat given a choice between accepting a small shock immediately or receiving a strong shock following a 10-second delay might choose the latter over the former, with the result that it experiences considerably more shock than it had to.

Of course, in many self-control situations, the full set of controlling consequences is a bit more complicated than a simple choice between two rewards or two punishers. Choosing not to smoke, for example, leads to both a smaller sooner punisher in the form of withdrawal symptoms and a larger later reward in the form of improved health, while continuing to smoke leads to a smaller sooner reward in the form of a nicotine high and a larger later punisher in the form of deteriorating health. Note too that later consequences are usually less certain than the "sooner" consequences. There is no guarantee that you will become sick and die an early death if you continue to smoke (though you would be foolish to chance it), nor is there any guarantee that you will become radiantly healthy if you quit smoking (you might, after all, catch some disease that is not related to smoking). You can, however, be pretty certain that your next cigarette will be enjoyable, and that if you quit smoking, you will soon experience withdrawal symptoms. Thus, delayed consequences often present a sort of double whammy: Their value is weakened both by the fact that they are delayed and by the fact that they are less certain. Given this combination of factors, it is easy to understand how delayed consequences sometimes have such weak effects on behavior (see Table 10.2).

Self-control issues therefore often involve a rather complex set of contingencies that vary in the extent to which they are immediate versus delayed and rewarding versus punishing (Brigham, 1978). To investigate this issue, however, researchers have typically focused on relatively simple choices, most

TABLE 10.2 Immediate and delayed consequences for the alternatives of quitting smoking versus continuing to smoke.

	IMMEDIATE CONSEQUENCE (CERTAIN)	DELAYED CONSEQUENCE (UNCERTAIN)
Quitting smoking	Withdrawal symptoms	Improvement in health
Continuing to smoke	Nicotine high	Deterioration in health

commonly a choice between a smaller sooner reward and a larger later reward. The task of choosing between such alternatives is known as a *delay of gratification* task, because the person or animal must forgo the smaller sooner reward (i.e., they have to "delay gratification") to obtain the larger later reward. Thus, in such tasks, **self-control consists of preference for a larger later reward over a smaller sooner reward,** while the opposite of self-control, known as **impulsiveness, consists of preference for a smaller sooner reward over a larger later reward.**

---

1. From a temporal perspective, self-control problems arise from the extent to which we are (more/less) _____ heavily influenced by delayed consequences.

2. Self-control is shown by choice of a (smaller sooner/larger later) _____ reward over a _____ reward. It can also be shown by choice of a (smaller sooner/larger later) _____ punisher over a _____ punisher.

3. With respect to choice between rewards, the opposite of self-control is called i_____, which is demonstrated by choice of a (smaller sooner/larger later) _____ reward over a _____ reward.

4. An additional problem in self-control situations is that the delayed consequences tend to be (more/less) _____ certain than the immediate consequences.

5. Outline the full set of consequences involved in choosing between dieting and not dieting:

	Immediate	*Delayed*
Dieting		
Not dieting		

The Ainslie–Rachlin Model of Self-Control

The Ainslie–Rachlin model of self-control focuses on the fact that preference between smaller sooner and larger later rewards can shift over time (Ainslie, 1975; Rachlin, 1974). For example, have you ever promised yourself in the morning that you would study all afternoon, only to find yourself spending the afternoon socializing with friends? In the morning, you clearly preferred studying over socializing that afternoon, but when the afternoon actually arrived, you preferred socializing over studying. In other words, you experienced a reversal of preference as time passed and the small sooner reward (socializing) became imminent. The Ainslie–Rachlin model provides an explanation for this reversal of preference and suggests ways to minimize its occurrence and facilitate attainment of the larger later reward.

The Ainslie–Rachlin model is based on the assumption that the value of a reward is a "hyperbolic" function of its delay. What this means is that the delay curve for a reward—which describes the relationship between reward value and time delay—is upwardly scalloped (similar to an FI scallop) with decreasing delays producing larger and larger increments in value. Simply put, the value of a reward increases more and more sharply as delay decreases and attainment of the reward becomes imminent (see Figure 10.3).

As an example, think about a young child who has been promised a birthday party. When the party is still 3 weeks away, it is likely to be worth very little to him. Three weeks is a long time for a young child, and if you ask him if he would rather have the birthday party in 3 weeks or a chocolate bar right now, he just might take the chocolate bar. In other words, a birthday party at 3 weeks' delay is worth less than one chocolate bar available immediately. A week later, with the birthday party still 2 weeks away, you might find that little has changed and that he would still be willing to trade the birthday party for the chocolate bar. The value of the birthday party at 2 weeks' delay has increased very little, if at all, compared to its value the previous week. When the party is 1 week away, however, you might find that the value of the party has increased significantly and that you would now have to offer him two or three chocolate bars before he would agree to cancel the party. And by the time another week has passed and the day of the birthday party has arrived, he is so

FIGURE 10.3 Graph indicating relationship between reward value and delay. Moving from left to right along the horizontal axis represents passage of time, with reward delivery drawing ever nearer. As delay decreases (reward draws near), reward value increases slowly at first and then more and more sharply as the reward becomes imminent.

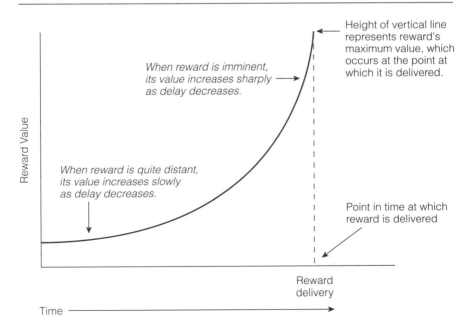

excited that he will reject a year's worth of chocolate bars in order to have that party. The value of the party increased sharply as it became imminent.

Much of the experimental evidence for such upwardly scalloped delay functions is derived from research with rats and pigeons, for whom delays of even a few seconds have significant effects on preference. A hungry pigeon, for example, might show weak preference for a reinforcer that is delayed by 15 seconds, slightly stronger preference for one that is delayed by 10 seconds, moderately stronger preference for one that is delayed by 5 seconds, and very strong preference for one that is available immediately (0 seconds delay). The value of the reward increased only slightly between 15 and 10 seconds, moderately between 10 and 5 seconds, and greatly between 5 and 0 seconds. The delay curve for this pigeon would therefore be relatively flat between 15 and 10 seconds, moderately sloped between 10 and 5 seconds, and steeply sloped between 5 and 0 seconds, which is similar to the delay curve shown in Figure 10.3.

1. The Ainslie–Rachlin model is based on the finding that as a reward becomes imminent, its value increases more and more (slowly/sharply) _____, yielding a "delay curve" (or delay function) that is upwardly sc_____.

2. I offer to give people a thousand dollars. People are told that they will receive the thousand dollars in either 3 months, 2 months, 1 month, or immediately. Between which of the following conditions are we likely to find the largest difference in level of excitement about receiving the money: 3 months versus 2 months, 2 months versus 1 month, or 1 month versus immediately? _____ _____. Between which conditions would we find the second largest difference in level of excitement? _____.

QUICK QUIZ

The manner in which delay functions account for preference reversal is shown in Figure 10.4. At an early point in time, when both rewards are still distant, the larger later reward is clearly preferred. As time passes, however, and the smaller sooner reward becomes imminent, its value increases sharply and comes to outweigh the value of the larger later reward. Thus, the student who, when she wakes up in the morning, decides that she will definitely study that evening is at the far left end of the distribution, where the delay curve for the larger later reward (receiving a high mark) is still higher than that of the smaller sooner reward (going out for an evening of socializing). As evening approaches, however, and the possibility of going out becomes imminent, the delay curve for the latter rises sharply, with the result that the student will be strongly tempted to socialize that evening. By doing so, however, she risks losing the larger later reward of an excellent grade.

Such preference reversals have been demonstrated experimentally with pigeons. Green, Fisher, Perlow, and Sherman (1981) presented pigeons with a choice between two schedules of reinforcement. In one condition, a peck on the red key resulted in 2-sec access to grain following a 20-sec delay (the smaller sooner reward), while a peck on the green key resulted in 6-sec access

FIGURE 10.4 Graph indicating relative values of a smaller sooner reward (SSR) and a larger later reward (LLR) as time passes. At an early point in time, before the SSR becomes imminent, its value is less than the value of the LLR. As time passes, however, and the SSR becomes imminent, its value increases sharply and comes to outweigh the value of the LLR.

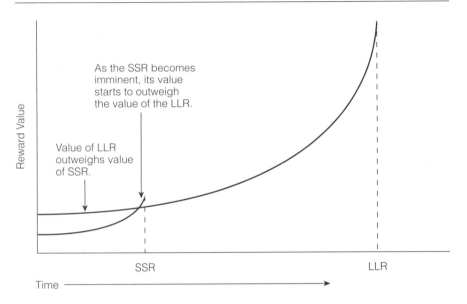

to grain following a 24-sec delay (the larger later reward). In this circumstance, the pigeons strongly preferred the larger later reward, selecting it on over 80% of the trials. In another condition, a peck on the red key resulted in 2-sec access to grain following a 2-sec delay, while a peck on the green key resulted in 6-sec access to grain following a 6-sec delay. This condition is equivalent to the first condition in that the larger later reward occurs 4 seconds later than the smaller sooner reward, but different in that both alternatives are now much closer. Under this circumstance, the pigeons strongly preferred the smaller sooner reward, which was almost immediately available. Thus, just as the Ainslie–Rachlin model predicts, when the smaller sooner reward was imminent, its value outweighed the value of the larger later reward. When both the smaller sooner reward and the larger later reward were some distance away, the pigeons strongly preferred the larger later reward. As the delay values changed, the pigeons displayed a reversal of preference between the two alternatives.

Human subjects making hypothetical choices have also demonstrated preference reversals. In one study by Ainslie and Haendel (1983), most participants said that they would prefer to receive a $100 certified check that can be immediately cashed to a $200 certified check that can be cashed in 2 years. However, when the delays for both alternatives were increased by 6 years—

a $100 check that can be cashed in 6 years versus a $200 check that can be cashed in 8 years—subjects preferred the $200 alternative. Thus, with both alternatives quite distant, the larger later reward was preferred; at shorter delays, the smaller sooner alternative, which was now immediately available, was preferred.

1. Confronted by a choice between one food pellet available in 10 seconds and two food pellets available in 15 seconds, a rat would likely choose the (former/latter) _____. But if 9 seconds are allowed to pass before the rat can make a choice, then it will likely choose the (former/latter) _____.

2. In the above example, as the (smaller sooner/larger later) _____ reward becomes imminent, its value comes to outweigh the value of the (smaller sooner/larger later) _____ reward.

QUICK QUIZ

Given that this type of preference reversal occurs, the question arises as to whether anything can be done about it. Two alternatives suggest themselves: changing the shape of the delay function for the larger later reward and making a commitment response.

Changing the Shape of the Delay Function for the Larger Later Reward
The basic reason why preference reversal occurs is that the larger later reward quickly loses its value with increasing delay, that is, its delay curve is deeply scalloped. If the delay curve were instead less deeply scalloped—meaning that the value of the larger later reward did not decline so drastically as a function of delay—then it would stand a better chance of outweighing any temptations that crop up along the way. This type of situation is illustrated in Figure 10.5.

Herrnstein (1981) has noted that several variables can affect the shape of a delay function. Biological factors are one such variable. For example, *some species are obviously more impulsive than others.* Delays of only a few seconds make a huge difference for rats and pigeons; they make little or no difference for humans, whose behavior is often directed toward rewards that will be delivered several hours, days, or even years in the future. Thus, delay functions for humans are generally less deeply scalloped than they are for other animals.

Biological differences among individuals within a species might also affect the shape of delay functions. People with antisocial personality disorder, which may have a strong genetic basis, are generally very impulsive (Kaplan, Sadock, & Grebb, 1994). Such individuals presumably have deeply scalloped delay functions. Less extreme differences exist among normal individuals in the population, such that some people may have an inborn temperament that predisposes them toward displaying the necessary patience to achieve long-term outcomes, while others have a temperament that predisposes them toward being rather impulsive.

Older children and adults generally have less deeply scalloped delay gradients than young children. As children grow older, they become progressively less impulsive and more resistant to temptations. Thus, while young children find it

FIGURE 10.5 Graph indicating relative values of a smaller sooner reward (SSR) and a larger later reward (LLR) in which the delay function for the LLR is less deeply scalloped (somewhat flatter). Under such conditions, the value of the LLR will remain higher than the value of the SSR even as the SSR becomes imminent.

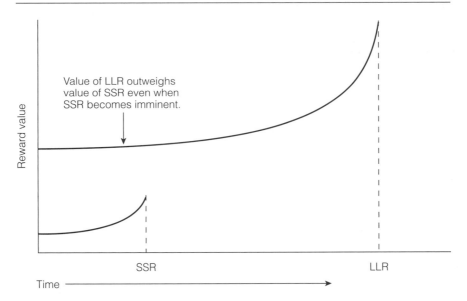

difficult to resist having a cookie before dinner, most adults are quite capable of doing so (well, at least more often than when they were kids). In fact, an increased ability to resist temptation and pursue long-term goals is considered a hallmark of maturity. This change might partially result from biological changes as we grow older; experience, however, also plays a role.

Thus, *another variable that affects the shape of delay functions is repeated experience with responding for delayed rewards.* As a child grows older, caretakers require children to display more and more patience—such as by forcing them to wait until after dinner to have a dessert—thereby gradually shaping their ability to delay gratification. Interestingly, in a scene from Skinner's (1948) novel *Walden II*, which depicts a utopian community designed around behavioral principles, children are described as waiting in front of their meals for a short period of time before eating. With successive meals, the waiting period was gradually lengthened. Although such a procedure might sound frightfully authoritarian, it is probably not much different from what most parents carry out in a less formal manner as they expect their children to gradually display more and more patience as they grow older.

In fact, the efficacy of Skinner's approach has been demonstrated experimentally (Mazur & Logue, 1978). Pigeons were presented with a choice between pecking one key and receiving a large food reward and pecking another key and receiving a small food reward. Initially, both rewards were immediately available, and the pigeons naturally showed a consistent preference for the large reward. The large reward was then gradually delayed for longer and longer periods of time. The result was that the pigeons continued to respond for the large reward even at delays that would normally have resulted in preference for the smaller, immediate reward. In essence, the experimenters had gradually shaped the pigeons to delay gratification beyond what would normally have been found.

In a similar experiment with children, Newman and Kanfer (1976) had first-grade children wait a certain amount of time to receive candy. Across several trials, the children received the candy either at the same delay (0 seconds or 60 seconds), gradually increasing delays (starting with 0 seconds and slowly building to 60 seconds), or gradually decreasing delays (starting with 60 seconds and gradually decreasing to 0 seconds). Following this experience, the children were exposed to a "resistance to temptation" task in which the longer they waited, the more candy they received. Relative to children in the other two groups, children exposed to the gradually increasing delays displayed much greater resistance to temptation.

The availability of other sources of reinforcement may be yet another factor that influences the delay functions. Many people find that they are more impulsive during periods characterized by a lack of overall reinforcement. Thus, Kimberly experiences a strong urge to resume smoking after she loses her job, and Jack begins drinking heavily after his girlfriend leaves him. Under depressing or stressful circumstances, long-term goals seem to lose their relevance, and immediate temptations become quite powerful. This suggests that, in order to maximize the possibility of resisting temptations, it helps if one's environment contains a plentiful supply of reinforcement. A student attempting to study for long periods of time in a dingy, cramped corner of the basement will likely find it extremely difficult to persist. Far better, as Skinner (1987) noted, to arrange a study environment that is both pleasant and comfortable. Good lighting, a comfortable chair, and a well-organized desk (to eliminate the frustration of being unable to find things)—perhaps accompanied by some pleasant music in the background and/or a cup of coffee or tea to sip on—will enable the act of studying to compete more effectively with such temptations as watching television or playing a computer game. Self-reinforcement procedures may also play a role here in that they ensure that the person intermittently engages in some pleasant activities while attempting to complete a difficult task, for example by watching a half hour of television following every two hours of studying.[1]

Finally, as noted in our discussion of behavior chains (Chapter 7), *we can more easily maintain responding for a distant goal by setting up an explicit series of subgoals.* The successful completion of each subgoal provides a salient form of secondary reinforcement that helps maintain progress toward a larger later reward. Additionally, because the secondary reinforcement from the completion of a subgoal is relatively immediate, it can compete more effectively with

---

[1] See Epstein (1997) for an engaging description of the many ways in which Skinner used behavioral principles to enhance self-control and remain academically productive well into his senior years.

any temptations that crop up along the way. Note, however, that the subgoals should be relatively precise. Completing a vaguely worded goal such as "work on my term paper tonight" is likely to be considerably less reinforcing than completing the more explicit goal of "finish a comprehensive outline of my term paper tonight." The latter is a clearer indicator of progress and will therefore serve as a stronger reinforcer.

1. One strategy for increasing self-control is to make the delay function (or delay curve) for the larger later reward (more/less) _____ deeply scalloped.

2. The delay functions for a pigeon will likely be (more/less) _____ deeply scalloped than those for a human.

3. The delay functions for a 6-year-old child will likely be (more/less) _____ deeply scalloped than those for a 15-year-old.

4. Exposure to gradually increasing delays seems to make the delay function (more/less) _____ deeply scalloped.

5. A person is likely to be (more/less) _____ impulsive in a pleasant environment as opposed to an unpleasant environment.

6. From the perspective of the Ainslie–Rachlin model, the setting up and attainment of a subgoal related to a delayed reward serves to (raise/lower) _____ the delay function for that reward, making it (more/less) _____ deeply scalloped.

Making a Commitment Response Raising the delay function for larger later rewards (making it less deeply scalloped) is perhaps the ideal answer to problems of self-control. It seems unlikely, however, that this tactic will always be successful. For a person who smokes, the immediate reinforcement to be derived from having a cigarette (both positive reinforcement in the form of a nicotine high and negative reinforcement in the form of eliminating or avoiding withdrawal symptoms) is likely to be a powerful temptation. In such circumstances, the exercise of self-control might be facilitated through the use of a "commitment response" (Rachlin, 1974, 1991). A *commitment response* **is an action carried out at an early point in time that serves to either eliminate or reduce the value of an upcoming temptation.**

As an example of a commitment response, consider a student who, in the morning, decides that she definitely needs to study that evening. At this early point in time, the value of studying to ensure a good mark outweighs the value of alternate activities, such as going out with friends or watching television. Through experience, however, the student has learned that these early-morning preferences mean little when evening rolls around and more immediate reinforcement from other activities becomes available. To ensure that she studies tonight, she knows that she has to somehow eliminate ahead of time the various temptations that will arise. Thus, that morning, she gives her younger brother $20 and instructs him to keep it if she fails to study that eve-

ning. By making this monetary commitment, she has essentially locked herself into studying. As illustrated in Figure 10.6, the aversive consequence that
would result from not studying (her obnoxious brother having a good time at
her expense) has so reduced the value of any alternate activity that it no longer
effectively competes with the value of studying and the larger later reward of
obtaining a good mark.

Behavioral contracts, in which a person arranges to attain certain rewards
for resisting temptation or receive certain punishers for yielding to temptation, essentially operate on this principle. The contract is arranged at an early
point in time prior to encountering the temptation. The contingencies outlined in the contract serve to reduce the attractiveness of the tempting alternative. Of course, in some circumstances, it might even be possible to completely eliminate the tempting alternative. A student who is spending too
much time playing computer games rather than studying could solve the
problem by simply wiping the game off his hard drive and giving the software
disk to a friend for the rest of the semester, thereby eliminating the option of
playing the game on his computer.

Although the use of a commitment strategy might be seen as one that requires a certain amount of intelligence and foresight, experiments have shown
that even pigeons can learn to make commitment responses. Rachlin and

FIGURE 10.6 Effect of a commitment strategy on preference between a smaller
sooner reward (SSR) and a larger later reward (LLR). The commitment response needs
to be made before the smaller sooner reward becomes imminent. It will be effective
to the extent that it reduces the value of the SSR, even when it is imminent, to below the value of the LLR.

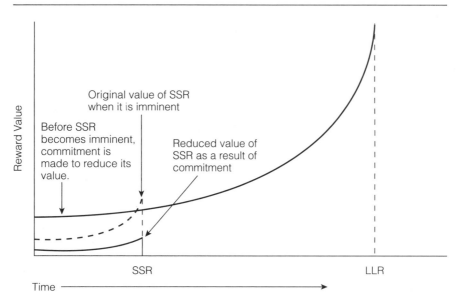

Green (1972) presented pigeons with a choice between a smaller sooner food reward and larger later food reward. The pigeons invariably chose the smaller sooner reward over the larger later reward. The pigeons were then given the option, several seconds prior to being presented with this choice, of pecking another key that would eliminate the smaller sooner reward as an alternative and would leave only the larger later reward to be chosen. Many of the pigeons selected this option, thereby essentially removing the temptation ahead of time. The pigeons did the equivalent of giving away the computer game in the morning so that, when evening came around, they would be more likely to study since playing the game was no longer an option.

1. A _____ response is designed to either eliminate or reduce the value of an upcoming temptation.

2. Such a response is most likely to be carried out at an (early/later) _____ point in time when the temptation is quite (near/distant) _____.

3. Gary would love to go running each evening but always feels so tired after work that he just plumps down in his favorite chair when he gets home and has a glass of wine. If Gary wishes to make a commitment to go running, such as arranging to go running with a neighbor, he is most likely to make this commitment (the day before/immediately before) _____ the run is supposed to take place.

Cognitive Factors in Self-Control

Researchers have also studied the role of cognitive processes in self-control. Most of these investigations have been carried out with young children using a delay of gratification task. In a typical version of this task, a child is led into a room that contains two items (such as pretzels and marshmallows), one of which is clearly preferred. The child is told that he or she can attain the preferred item by simply waiting for the experimenter to return. If the child wishes, however, the experimenter can be summoned by sounding a signal, at which point the child attains only the smaller, nonpreferred item. The question of interest is what sorts of strategies children use to wait out the delay period and obtain the larger reward (Mischel, 1966, 1974).

Researchers who conducted such studies quickly noted that the extent to which children avoided attending to a reward had a significant effect on their resistance to temptation. For example, one strategy employed by many children was to simply avert their eyes from the promised rewards or cover their eyes with their hands. Many children also adopted Skinner's tactic of doing something else, such as talking or singing to themselves or inventing games. Children were also better able to wait out the delay period when the rewards were not present as opposed to when they were present. Thus, resistance to temptation was greatly enhanced by not attending to the tempting reward. Later research revealed that the manner in which children thought about the rewards also made a difference. Children who were instructed to focus on the abstract properties of the rewards, such as viewing pretzels as tiny logs, did better than children who viewed the rewards in a concrete manner. Note that all of these strategies are quite different from what one might suppose should happen from a "positive thinking" perspective, which usually recommends that one should keep one's attention firmly fixed on the desired outcome. In these studies, children who focused on the desired outcome, and conceptualized it as a desired outcome, generally became impulsive and were unable to wait long enough to receive the larger later reward. (See Mischel, 1966, 1974, for comprehensive reviews of this research.)

An interesting aspect of this research is the follow-up evaluations conducted on children who participated in some of the earliest studies (Shoda, Mischel, & Peake, 1990). These children were, on average, 4 years old in the original studies and 17 years old at follow-up. The children who, in the original study, had devised tactics that enabled them to wait for the preferred reward were, many years later, more "cognitively and socially competent"— meaning that they could cope well with frustrations, were academically proficient, and got along well with their peers. This suggests that one's ability to devise appropriate tactics to delay gratification is a basic skill that can enhance many areas of one's life.

1. Children who are (most/least) _____ successful at a delay of gratification task generally keep their attention firmly fixed on the desired treat.

2. While waiting for dessert, Housam imagines that the Jell-O looks like wobbly chunks of glass. By contrast, Ruby views the Jell-O as, well, Jell-O. Between the two of them, _____ is less likely to get into trouble by eating the Jell-O before being told that it is okay to do so. This is because delay of gratification can be enhanced by thinking about the desired reward in a_____ rather than c_____ terms.

QUICK QUIZ

SUMMARY

On a concurrent schedule of reinforcement, the subject responds on two or more independent schedules of reinforcement that are simultaneously available. Choice behavior in such situations often obeys the matching law, which predicts that the proportion of responses emitted on an alternative will match the proportion of reinforcers received on that alternative. The matching law has also been shown to have real-world applicability, ranging from predicting communication patterns in humans to foraging behavior in animals.

Researchers have also discovered certain deviations from matching. In undermatching, the difference in proportion of responses on the richer versus poorer schedules is less than predicted by matching. In overmatching, the difference in proportion of responses on the richer versus poorer schedules is greater than predicted by matching. Bias from matching occurs when one response alternative receives more responses than predicted by matching, both when it is the poorer alternative and when it is the richer alternative.

According to melioration theory, matching results from the subject's tendency to shift behavior toward a better paying alternative. This tendency can sometimes reduce the overall amount of reinforcement. For example, more behavior may be directed to a better paying alternative than is needed to obtain the available reinforcers. Furthermore, overindulgence in a highly reinforcing alternative can result in long-term habituation to that alternative such that it is no longer as enjoyable as it once was. Melioration also results in a tendency to be overly attracted to immediate reinforcers as opposed to delayed reinforcers.

Skinner viewed self-control as involving a choice between conflicting outcomes. He believed that self-control is facilitated by emitting a controlling response that then alters the probability of a controlled response. Specific techniques of self-control include physical self-restraint, self-deprivation or self-satiation, and self-reinforcement and self-punishment. A major problem with the latter is that one can easily short-circuit such self-directed consequences.

Others have noted that self-control involves a choice between immediate outcomes, which are relatively powerful, and delayed outcomes, which are relatively weak. From this perspective, self-control can be defined as choosing a larger later reward over a smaller sooner reward, while impulsiveness can be defined as choosing a smaller sooner reward over a larger later reward.

The Ainslie–Rachlin model of self-control is based on the assumption that the delay function for a reward is often deeply scalloped, such that its value increases sharply as it becomes imminent. This explains why preference for larger later rewards and smaller sooner rewards tends to shift over time. When both rewards are far away, the value of the larger later reward outweighs the value of the smaller sooner reward. As the smaller sooner reward becomes imminent, however, its value rises sharply, possibly exceeding the value of the larger later reward at that point in time.

Thus, one means for facilitating self-control is raising the delay function for the larger later reward so that its value remains fairly high even at long delays. Factors that may affect the shape of a delay function include biological variables (including differences between species and between individuals within a species), age, experience with responding for delayed rewards, the presence of other sources of reinforcement, and the attainment of subgoals relating to the larger later alternative. Another means for facilitating self-control is by making a commitment to the larger later reward at an early point in time, before the smaller sooner reward becomes imminent. A commitment response is a response that serves to reduce the value of the smaller sooner reward so that its value remains below the value of the larger later reward.

Research has shown that children who are good at resisting temptation in a delay of gratification task are those who strive to distract themselves from the tempting reward. As well, children are better able to resist temptation when they think of the reward in terms of its abstract rather than concrete properties. Follow-up research has revealed that children who are successful in such delay of gratification tasks are, in later years, more academically and socially competent.

STUDY QUESTIONS

1. What is a concurrent schedule? Diagram an example of a concurrent schedule as might be used in an operant conditioning experiment with pigeons.
2. Define the matching law.
3. State the matching law as an equation, and define each of its terms.
4. Using the matching equation, show what the matching law predicts concerning the distribution of behavior displayed on a Concurrent VI 20-sec VI 60-sec schedule of reinforcement.
5. What is a changeover delay (COD)? In what sense is a COD similar to a foraging situation with animals?
6. What is overmatching? Give an example of overmatching as might be found in the foraging behavior of pied wagtails (which were mentioned in the chapter).
7. What is undermatching? Give an example of undermatching as might be found in the foraging behavior of pied wagtails.
8. What is bias from matching? Give an example of bias as might be found in the foraging behavior of pied wagtails.
9. Describe melioration theory.
10. Briefly describe three ways in which the tendency to meliorate can reduce overall level of reinforcement.
11. Describe the major difficulty with the use of self-reinforcement and self-punishment.
12. With the help of a graph, describe the general effect of delay on reward value.
13. With the help of a graph, describe how the Ainslie–Rachlin model accounts for preference reversal between a smaller sooner and a larger later reward.
14. List two ways in which biology may affect the shape of a delay function. What is the relationship between age and the shape of a delay function?
15. What type of experience has been shown to decrease impulsiveness in both pigeons and children? What is the relationship of other sources of reinforcement to self-control?
16. With the help of a graph, describe how a commitment response serves to facilitate self-control.
17. Describe the various strategies children use to facilitate success in a delay of gratification task.

CONCEPT REVIEW

bias from matching. A deviation from matching in which one alternative attracts a higher proportion of responses than would be predicted by matching, regardless of whether that alternative is the richer or poorer alternative.

commitment response. An action carried out at an early point in time that serves to either eliminate or reduce the value of an upcoming temptation.

concurrent schedule of reinforcement. A complex schedule that consists of the simultaneous presentation of two or more independent schedules, each of which leads to a reinforcer.

impulsiveness. With respect to choice between two rewards, preference for a smaller sooner reward over a larger later reward.

matching law. The principle that the proportion of responses emitted on a particular schedule matches the proportion of reinforcers obtained on that schedule.

melioration theory. A theory of matching that holds that the distribution of behavior in a choice situation shifts toward those alternatives that have higher value regardless of the effect on overall amount of reinforcement.

overmatching. A deviation from matching in which the proportion of responses on the richer alternative versus poorer alternative is more different than would be predicted by matching.

self-control. With respect to choice between two rewards, preference for a larger later reward over a smaller sooner reward.

undermatching. A deviation from matching in which the proportion of responses on the richer alternative versus poorer alternative is less different than would be predicted by matching.

CHAPTER TEST

12. According to the _____ law, if 25% of reinforcers are obtained on one of two simultaneously available schedules, then _____ of responses are likely to be emitted on that schedule.

6. The Ainslie–Rachlin model is based on the assumption that the value of a reward increases more and more sharply as delay _____ and attainment of the reward becomes _____.

17. The matching law predicts that on a Concurrent VI 15-sec VI 60-sec schedule, 80% of responses should be emitted on the VI 15-sec schedule and 20% on the VI 60-sec schedule. In reality, you obtain 65% on the VI 15-sec schedule and 35% on the VI 60-sec schedule. This is an example of _____matching.

9. A _____ schedule of reinforcement consists of the simultaneous presentation of two or more independent schedules, each of which leads to a _____.

13. The _____ law holds that the _____ of responses emitted on a particular schedule matches the _____ of reinforcers obtained on that schedule.

31. Hoa sometimes feels well and sometimes feels sick. If feeling healthy is a form of reinforcement, we would expect Hoa to be most impulsive when she is feeling (healthy/sick) _____.

18. The matching law predicts that on a Concurrent VI 10-sec VI 30-sec schedule, 25% of responses should be emitted on the VI 30-sec schedule and 75% on the VI 10-sec schedule. In reality, you obtain 15% on the VI 30-sec schedule and 85% on the VI 10-sec schedule. This is an example of _____ matching.

3. From a temporal perspective, lack of self-control arises from the fact that our behavior is more heavily influenced by _____ consequences as opposed to _____ consequences.

20. When the cost of switching between schedules is quite high, then _____ matching is likely to occur. When the cost of switching is extremely low, then _____ matching is likely to occur.

30. Exposure to rewards that are presented at gradually increasing delays is likely to result in a(n) (increase/decrease) _____ in impulsiveness, which also means that the reward delay curve for these individuals has become (more/less) _____ deeply scalloped.

1. You always eat a full meal before going shopping so that you will not be tempted (through hunger) to buy those chocolate cookies you are addicted to. From the perspective of self-control, Skinner would refer to the act of eating the meal as the _____ response and the subsequent decreased tendency to buy cookies as the _____ response.

27. In general, melioration is often the result of behavior being too strongly governed by _____ consequences as opposed to _____ consequences.

10. Given a choice between a VR 140 schedule and a VR 40 schedule of reinforcement, a rat is likely to show (exclusive/partial) _____ preference for the _____ schedule.

23. According to _____ theory, the distribution of behavior in a choice situation shifts toward those alternatives that have _____ value regardless of the effect on the overall amount of reinforcement.

14. Given a choice between a VI 40-sec schedule and a VI 20-sec schedule, a rat is likely to emit _____ % of its responses to the VI 40-sec alternative.

5. From a behavioral perspective, self-control consists of preference for a _____ reward over a _____ reward, while the opposite of self-control, known as _____, consists of preference for a _____ reward over a _____ reward.

26. As soon as Mario retired, he moved to Florida and went for walks on the beach everyday. Unfortunately, although going for walks continued to be his most enjoyable activity, it soon became less enjoyable than it used to be. This appears to be an example of how the tendency to _____ can result in long-term _____.

33. A commitment response is most likely to be made at a(n) (early/later) _____ point in time before the (smaller sooner/larger later) _____ reward becomes imminent.

16. As Sal and his wife converse with the neighbor one evening, Sal is three times more responsive to the neighbor's comments than his wife is. Research evidence suggests that the neighbor should direct his conversation toward Sal, as opposed to his wife, (three times as often/exclusively) _____.

28. In general, humans have a (more/less) _____ deeply scalloped delay function than chickens. As well, a person who is very impulsive is likely to have a (more/less) _____ deeply scalloped delay function than a person who is very patient.

7. In keeping with the Ainslie–Rachlin model of self-control, I am most likely to choose $50 over $100 when the choice is between (A) $50 now versus $100 a year from now, or (B) $50 a year from now versus $100 two years from now. The answer is alternative _____, which means that I tend to become impulsive when the smaller sooner reward is (imminent/delayed) _____.

11. According to the matching law, the proportion of _____ emitted on a certain schedule will roughly equal the proportion of _____ obtained on that schedule.

4. To the extent that Romano decides to get up early to study for that math test next week, as opposed to lying in bed for an extra hour, he is displaying self-_____. To the extent that he chooses to lie in bed, he is displaying _____.

19. As Sal and his wife converse with the neighbor one day, Sal is three times more responsive to the neighbor's comments than his wife is. The neighbor, however, looks at Sal's wife about as often as he looks at Sal. During the next day's conversation, Sal's wife is three times more responsive to the neighbor's comments than Sal is. This time the neighbor looks at Sal's wife five times as often as he looks at Sal. This appears to be an example of the deviation from matching known as _____, which also suggests that the neighbor finds Sal's wife _____.

32. Maria announces to her parents that she is going to study all weekend, knowing that they will severely chastise her if she does not live up to her promise. Given that Maria hates being chastised by her parents, her announcement can be seen as a _____ response that will lower the value of any alternate activity that might interfere with studying during the weekend.

21. You tend to shop at two favorite clothing stores, Madison's Fine Fashions and Mike's Grubbies. Over time, you have learned that Mike's is twice as

likely to have something in stock that you wish to buy. If the two stores are side by side, then you are likely to visit Mike's (twice/equally) _____ as often as Madison's. This is an example of _____ matching.

8. According to the Ainslie–Rachlin model, one way to enhance self-control would be to raise the delay curve for the (smaller sooner/larger later) _____ reward.

24. On a Concurrent VR 50 VI 10-sec schedule, a pigeon is likely to _____ the number of responses emitted on each schedule to the number of reinforcers obtained. By doing so, it (will/will not) _____ maximize the amount of reinforcement it obtains during the session. Such results support the _____ theory of matching.

2. You decide to do your housework each evening at 7:00 P.M., and then reward yourself with 1 hour of playing your favorite computer game. A major problem with this kind of self-reinforcement procedure is that you might _____. This problem is known as _____.

25. Professor Huynh spends a lot of time reading articles, which she enjoys, but little time in the lab doing research, which she does not enjoy. Insofar as she needs to do research to maintain her position at the university, this appears to be an example of how _____ can lead to suboptimal patterns of behavior.

34. Owen finds himself alone in the kitchen with the birthday cake that his mother just made. He is sorely tempted to steal a taste of that maple icing, but he knows that this could get him into trouble if he tries it. To enhance his self-control in this circumstance, which of the following strategies would be worth trying: (A) concentrate on how good the cake will taste if he waits until dinner, (B) ignore the cake and look elsewhere in the room, (C) imagine how the maple icing looks like a lava field, (D) either B or C. The answer is _____.

15. Given a choice between a VI 60-sec schedule and a VI 20-sec schedule, a pigeon is likely to emit _____ of its responses to the VI 20-sec alternative.

22. You tend to shop at two favorite clothing stores, Madison's Fine Fashions and Mike's Grubbies. Over time, you have learned that Mike's is twice as likely to have something in stock that you wish to buy. If the two stores are separated by a long and difficult drive, then you are likely to demonstrate _____ matching in your visits to Mike's versus Madison's.

29. In general, as people grow from childhood into adulthood, their delay curves will likely become (more/less) _____ deeply scalloped.

ANSWERS TO CHAPTER TEST

1. controlling; controlled
2. play the game and not do the house-work; short-circuiting
3. immediate; delayed
4. control; impulsiveness
5. larger later; smaller sooner; impulsiveness; smaller sooner; larger later
6. decreases; imminent
7. A; imminent
8. larger later
9. concurrent; reinforcer
10. exclusive; VR 40
11. responses; reinforcers
12. matching; 25%
13. matching; proportion; proportion
14. 33%
15. 75%
16. three times as often

17. under
18. over
19. bias; attractive
20. over; under
21. equally; under
22. over
23. melioration; higher
24. match; will not; melioration
25. melioration
26. meliorate; habituation
27. immediate; delayed
28. less; more
29. less
30. decrease; less
31. sick
32. commitment
33. early; smaller sooner
34. D

CHAPTER 11

Biological Dispositions in Learning

CHAPTER OUTLINE

Ken was worried about his girlfriend, Chantal, who had lost a lot of weight in recent months. As one of his friends noted, she was starting to look like a "hockey stick with hair." Nevertheless, Chantal maintained that she was still overweight and needed to lose a few more pounds. Ken had heard that anorexia is characterized by a distorted body image, in which people deny how thin they are. He wondered if Chantal was suffering from this type of distortion. He had also heard that anorexia often results from growing up in an overcontrolling family—though on the surface, it seemed like her family was pretty nice.

Other than his concerns about her weight, Ken thought Chantal was terrific. He particularly loved the fact that she shared his enthusiasm for long-distance running. In fact, she was more addicted to running than he was.

By this time, you probably realize that the basic principles of conditioning have a surprising degree of generality and are applicable to a wide range of species and behaviors. But you may also recall how, at certain points in this text, we have noted some limitations in this regard. For example, people more readily learn to be afraid of events that have some type of evolutionary association with danger, such as snakes and spiders, than they do of modern-day events, such as cars and electrical outlets. It is possible then that we have inherited a biological tendency to learn certain types of fears more readily than others. In this chapter, we further explore the role of biological preparedness in conditioning, as well as the manner in which such preparedness seems to produce an overlap between processes of classical conditioning and operant conditioning.

Preparedness and Conditioning

Preparedness in Classical Conditioning

As mentioned above, fear conditioning is one form of classical conditioning in which preparedness seems to play an important role. Another is *taste aversion conditioning:* **a form of classical conditioning in which a food item that has been paired with gastrointestinal illness becomes a conditioned aversive stimulus.** Simply put, an animal that becomes sick after ingesting a food item associates the food with the illness and subsequently finds it distasteful.

Conditioned taste aversions are quite common. In one survey of undergraduate students, 65% reported developing a taste aversion at some point in their lives (Logue, Ophir, & Strauss, 1981). Interestingly (and perhaps not surprisingly), many of these aversions involved an alcoholic drink of some sort. Most taste aversions are quite rational in that the person believes that the food item was actually the cause of the illness. In some cases, however, the person knows that the food was not the cause of the illness and that the illness was instead caused by some other factor (such as the flu) with which the food was only coincidentally associated. Nevertheless, the person still finds the food item highly aversive—a convincing testament to the strength of this type of conditioning.

In a typical experiment on taste aversion conditioning, rats are first given some type of preferred food or drink to ingest, such as sweet-tasting (saccharin-flavored) water. The animal is then made to feel sick, either by injecting a nausea-inducing drug directly into the gut or through exposure to X-ray irradiation. After the rat recovers, it is given a choice of either sweet water or normal water. Although a rat typically prefers sweet water over normal water, it now strongly prefers the normal water. This indicates that the sweet water has become an aversive CS through its association with illness. This procedure can be diagrammed as follows:

Sweet water: X-ray irradiation → *Nausea*
  NS   US   UR
Sweet water → *Nausea* (as indicated by avoidance of the sweet water)
  CS   CR

Taste aversion conditioning is in several ways similar to other forms of classical conditioning, involving many of the same processes (Schafe & Bernstein, 1996). For example, *stimulus generalization* often occurs in that food items that taste similar to the aversive item are also perceived as aversive. For example, a conditioned aversion to one type of fish might generalize to other types of fish. A conditioned taste aversion can also be *extinguished* if the aversive food item is repeatedly ingested without further illness. *Overshadowing* can occur in that we are more likely to develop an aversion to a stronger tasting food item, such as onions, than a milder tasting item, such as potatoes, that was consumed at the same meal. And the presence of a food item that already has aversive associations can *block* the development of aversive associations to other food items.

Of particular importance in taste aversion conditioning is the phenomenon of *latent inhibition.* We are more likely to associate a relatively novel item, such as an unusual liqueur, with sickness than a more familiar item, such as beer (Kalat, 1974). Latent inhibition helps account for why it is often difficult to poison a rat. When a rat encounters a novel food item, such as rat bait, it will eat only a small amount of the item before moving on to other, more familiar items.[1] If the rat later becomes ill, it will associate the illness with the novel item rather than with any of the familiar items. The rat also has a high probability of recovering from the illness because it will have eaten only a small amount of the poisoned item.

---

[1] This tendency to be wary of new food items, which is also present in humans and is especially strong in children, is known as *dietary neophobia.*

1. After he recovered from a bad case of the flu, Robbie could not bring himself to eat oatmeal, which he had tried to eat during his illness. In all likelihood, Robbie has developed a t_____ a_____ to the oatmeal.

2. Robbie now dislikes other types of porridge as well, which appears to be an example of s_____ g_____.

3. Robbie's aversion to porridge would likely e_____ if he repeatedly ate it without experiencing any further illness.

4. According to the o_____ effect, the strongest-tasting item in a meal is most likely to become associated with a subsequent illness. As well, a food item that was previously associated with illness will b_____ the development of aversive associations to other items in a meal.

5. In keeping with the process of l_____ i_____, Robbie would have been less likely to develop a taste aversion to oatmeal porridge if he had frequently eaten oatmeal prior to his illness.

Although taste aversion conditioning is in many ways similar to other forms of classical conditioning, there are also some major differences. These include:

1. *The formation of associations over long delays.* In most classical conditioning procedures, the NS and US must occur in close temporal proximity, separated by no more than a few seconds. By contrast, taste aversions can develop when food items are consumed several hours before the sickness develops. For example, Etscorn and Stephens (1973) found that rats could develop taste aversions to flavored water that had been ingested up to 24 hours prior to injection of an illness-inducing drug. The ability to associate food with illness after lengthy periods of time is highly adaptive in that poisonous substances often have a delayed effect. If animals were unable to form such delayed associations, they would be at great risk of repeatedly consuming a poisonous food item and eventually perishing.

2. *One-trial conditioning.* Strong conditioned taste aversions can usually be achieved with only a single pairing of food with illness, particularly when the food item is novel (Riley & Clarke, 1977). One-trial conditioning sometimes occurs in other forms of conditioning, especially fear conditioning, but not as consistently as it does in taste aversion conditioning. As with the ability to form associations over long delays, one-trial conditioning of taste aversions is highly adaptive insofar as it minimizes the possibility of a repeat, possibly fatal, experience with a poisonous substance.

3. *Specificity of associations.* When you feel nauseous following a meal, do you associate the nausea with the television show you are watching (even though, given the quality of some programs these days, that might seem appropriate), or with the meal? Fortunately for the broadcast networks, you are more likely to associate the nausea with the meal. Similarly, the rat that receives an injection of a nausea-inducing drug several hours

after drinking a sweet water solution does not associate the illness with the injection; it instead associates the illness with the sweet water. In other words, there seems to be a strong, inherited tendency to associate a gastrointestinal illness with food or drink rather than with any other kind of item (Garcia & Koelling, 1966). The ease with which particular stimuli can be associated together is sometimes referred to as **belongingness: an innate tendency to readily associate certain types of events with each other.**

An excellent example of the role of belongingness in taste aversion conditioning was provided by Garcia and Koelling (1966) in their initial demonstration of this type of conditioning. In this experiment, the rats initially drank sweet water that was paired with a light and a noise—a compound stimulus that can be described as "bright, noisy, sweet water." After consuming the water, some of the rats received a slight foot shock that elicited a fear reaction, while other rats received a dose of X-ray irradiation that made them nauseous. Finally, all of the rats were given a choice between two water bottles, one of which contained only "bright, noisy" water (i.e., regular water associated with a light and a noise) and the other of which contained only sweet water. Can you guess the results?

The rats that had been made nauseous by the X-ray irradiation avoided the sweet water and drank the bright, noisy water, which is consistent with the basic notion that nausea is more readily associated with taste than with other kinds of stimuli.

Bright, noisy, sweet water: X-ray irradiation → *Nausea*
           NS   **US**   **UR**
Sweet water → *Nausea*
      CS   **CR**
Bright, noisy water → **No nausea**
          NS   —

But what about the rats that received a foot shock? It turns out that they avoided the bright, noisy water but not the sweet water. In other words, they developed a fear of the noise and lights associated with the water, but not the taste, and were quite willing to drink the sweet water.

Bright, noisy, sweet water: Foot shock → *Fear*
           NS   **US**   **UR**
Bright, noisy water → *Fear*
          CS   **CR**
Sweet water → **No fear**
      NS   —

Thus, not only do rats have a predisposition to readily associate nausea with taste, they also have a predisposition to associate tactually painful events with visual and auditory stimuli. This makes sense from an evolutionary perspective in that tactual pain is more likely to result from something "out

And Furthermore

Conditioned Food Preferences

Just as conditioning processes sometimes make foods aversive, such processes can also make foods more appetitive. For example, a powerful way to increase our preference for a disliked food is to mix it with some food item or sweetener that we strongly prefer. This may be how some people grow to like black coffee: They first drink it with cream and sugar and then gradually eliminate the extra ingredients as the taste of the coffee itself becomes pleasurable. Similarly, in one study, college students developed increased preference for broccoli or cauliflower after eating it a few times with sugar (Capaldi, 1996). Unfortunately, few parents use such a method to improve their children's eating habits, possibly because they perceive sugar to be unhealthy and do not realize that the sugar can later be withdrawn (Casey & Rozin, 1989). Instead, parents often try to entice their children to eat a disliked food by offering dessert as a reward—a strategy that easily backfires in that the contrast between the disliked food and the subsequent dessert might result in the former becoming even more disliked. (See Capaldi, 1996, for other ways in which food preferences can be conditioned.)

there" that a rat can see and hear, while nausea is more likely to result from something a rat ingests and can be tasted. Thus, for the rat to evolve in such a way that it can readily make such associations will likely facilitate its survival.

Further evidence for the role of biological dispositions in taste aversion conditioning is the fact that there are between-species differences in the types of stimuli that can be associated. In one experiment, both quail and rats drank dark blue, sour-tasting water prior to being made ill (Wilcoxon, Dragoin, & Kral, 1971). The animals were then given a choice between dark blue water and sour-tasting water. As expected, the rats naturally avoided the sour-tasting water and strongly preferred the dark blue water. They associated the taste of the water with the nausea. The quail, however, were more likely to avoid the dark blue water than the sour-tasting water. This suggests that quail, which are daytime feeders and rely heavily on vision for identifying food, are more disposed to associate the visual aspects of food with nausea than the taste aspects. Rats, however, being nighttime feeders, rely more heavily on taste (and smell) than vision and are therefore generally disposed to associate the taste (and smell) aspects of food with nausea. (This is not to say that rats cannot learn to associate the visual aspects of food with nausea. They can, but additional conditioning trials are required to form such associations.)

It should be noted that research on taste aversion conditioning has some practical implications. For example, cancer patients sometimes develop aversions to food items that have been inadvertently associated with the nausea resulting from chemotherapy (Bernstein, 1991). Insofar as cancer patients often suffer from severe weight loss anyway, the development of taste aversions that lead to avoidance of certain food items could be serious. Fortunately, research has suggested ways to minimize this problem. One way is to serve meals that consist of highly familiar foods. In keeping with the latent inhibition effect, such familiar foods will be less likely to become associated with nausea. Along the same lines, one can have the patient ingest a highly novel, yet trivial, food item just prior to a chemotherapy session. This novel item will then be associated with the nausea, preventing the development of taste aversions to other, more essential food items. For example, in one study, children about to undergo chemotherapy were given coconut- or root beer–flavored candies following a regular meal. Compared to children who had not been given these candies, they later developed fewer aversions to their regular food items (Broberg & Bernstein, 1987).

QUICK QUIZ

1. Distinctive features of taste aversion conditioning, compared to other types of classical conditioning, include the fact that the associations can be formed over (short/long) _____ delays, typically require (one/several) _____ pairing(s) of the NS and US, and (are/are not) _____ specific to certain types of stimuli.

2. In the classic experiment by Garcia and Koelling (1966), the rats that had been made ill avoided the (sweet/bright, noisy) _____ water, while the rats that had been shocked avoided the _____ water.

3. In the experiment on taste aversions in quail and rats, the rats avoided the (blue/sour) _____ water, while the quail avoided the _____ water.

4. To counter the possibility that chemotherapy-induced nausea will result in the development of taste aversions, patients should be fed meals that consist mostly of highly (familiar/unfamiliar) _____ foods. As well, just prior to the chemotherapy session, they can be given some trivial type of (familiar/unfamiliar) _____ food item, which will essentially "soak up" most of the aversive associations.

Preparedness in Operant Conditioning

Biological preparedness also seems to play a role in some forms of operant conditioning. For example, Stevenson-Hinde (1973) found that the sound of recorded chaffinch songs (chaffinches are a type of bird) was an effective reinforcer for training chaffinches to perch in a certain spot, but not for training them to key peck. Conversely, food was an effective reinforcer for training them to key peck but not for training them to perch in a certain spot. Chaffinches seem to be biologically prepared to associate perching in a certain spot with the consequence of hearing songs, and to associate pecking with the consequence of obtaining food.

In a similar manner, rats will more readily learn to press a lever to obtain food pellets than to avoid shock (Bolles, 1970). But they readily learn to freeze or run to avoid shock. Once more, the explanation for these differences may reside in the animals' evolutionary history. Rats have evolved dexterous forepaws that are often used for eating; thus, pressing a lever for food is not far removed from the type of food-gathering behavior they display in the natural environment. However, avoiding painful events is, for a rat, more naturally related to the responses of freezing or running than it is to manipulating objects with its forepaws.

Biological dispositions for certain types of avoidance responses have also been found in pigeons. Bedford and Anger (cited in Bolles, 1979) found that pigeons will quickly learn to fly from one perch to another to avoid shock, but they will not learn to peck a response key to avoid shock. As with rats, the typical manner in which pigeons flee danger provides an explanation: Flying is the usual way in which a pigeon escapes danger, while pecking is not. Thus, pigeons, like rats, seem predisposed to learn certain types of avoidance responses more readily than others.

You may have noted from the preceding examples that preparedness seems to play a particularly strong role in avoidance behavior. This has led Bolles (1970, 1979) to propose that some avoidance responses are actually not operants (in the sense of being controlled by their consequences) but are instead elicited behaviors (that are controlled by the stimuli that precede them). More specifically, he contends that aversive stimulation elicits a species-specific defense reaction (SSDR), which in the natural environment is often effective in countering danger. For this reason, a rat easily learns to run or freeze to avoid painful stimulation, simply because running and freezing are behaviors that are naturally *elicited* in dangerous situations. Indeed, a rat's tendency to freeze is so strong that it will sometimes freeze even when doing so *results* in shock rather than avoids shock. (Humans too have a strong tendency to freeze when feeling threatened, even when it is counterproductive to do so, such as when giving a speech to a large audience or when being ordered about by a gunman.)

QUICK QUIZ

1. Chaffinches easily learn to associate (perching/pecking) _____ with the consequence of hearing a song, and _____ with the consequence of obtaining food.

2. Rats are biologically prepared to learn to avoid a painful stimulus by (lever pressing/running) _____, while pigeons are biologically prepared to learn to avoid a painful stimulus by (pecking/flying) _____.

3. According to Bolles, these types of avoidance responses are _____-_____ defense reactions that are naturally e_____ by the aversive stimulus.

Operant-Respondent Interactions

Bolles's concept of the SSDR is one example of the manner in which it is sometimes difficult to distinguish between operant behaviors and respondent (or elicited) behaviors. In this section, we discuss two further examples of the overlap between operants and respondents: instinctive drift and sign tracking.

Instinctive Drift

It was once assumed that an animal could be trained to perform just about any behavior it was physically capable of performing. Indeed, examining the remarkable array of behaviors that animals can be trained to display, this assumption does not seem all that unreasonable. There are, however, limits to such training, as two of Skinner's students discovered in the course of training animals for show business.

Marian and Keller Breland were former students of Skinner's who decided to put their knowledge of operant conditioning to commercial use. They established a business training animals to perform unusual behaviors for television commercials and movies. In this endeavor, they were usually quite successful. Occasionally, however, they encountered some rather interesting limitations in what certain animals could be taught (Breland & Breland, 1961). For example, they once attempted to train a pig to deposit a wooden coin in a piggy bank. Using processes of shaping and chaining, the training initially proceeded quite smoothly. As time passed, however, a strange thing began to happen. The pig no longer simply deposited the coin in the bank, but started tossing the coin in the air and then rooting at it on the ground. Eventually, the tossing and rooting became so frequent that the coin never made its way to the bank. The Brelands also attempted to use a raccoon for this trick, but here too they ran into difficulties. As training progressed, the raccoon began rubbing the coin back and forth in its paws rather than dropping it into the bank. This stereotyped action sequence eventually became so dominant that this attempt too had to be abandoned.

With both the pig and the raccoon, it seemed that a naturally occurring, food-related fixed action pattern had gradually emerged to interfere with the operant behavior that was being shaped. This fixed action pattern functioned like a conditioned reflex, with the coin that was associated with the food being treated as though it were food. In the case of the pig, this meant that the coin was subjected to the type of rooting behavior pigs often display when feeding. In the case of the raccoon, the coin was repeatedly rubbed and washed in the way raccoons normally rub and wash their food (often shellfish). In both cases, the coin seemed to become a CS that elicited a fixed action pattern that was related to feeding.

Thus, in the case of the pig, the Brelands intended this:

Coin: *Deposit coin in bank* $\rightarrow$ Food
S^D R S^R

which is an operant conditioning procedure. Initially, this worked quite well, but as the coin became more and more strongly associated with food, what instead happened was this:

Coin: Food $\rightarrow$ *Rooting*
NS   US   UR
Coin $\rightarrow$ *Rooting*
CS   CR

which is a classical conditioning procedure. And as the classically conditioned response increased in strength, it eventually overrode the operantly conditioned response of depositing the coin in the bank. Thus, in *instinctive drift,* **a genetically based fixed action pattern gradually emerges and displaces the behavior that is being operantly conditioned.**

1. In the phenomenon known as i_____ d_____, a genetically based f_____ a_____ pattern gradually emerges and displaces the behavior being shaped.

2. In the experiment with the raccoon, the coin became a (CS/S^D) _____ that elicited a (R/CR/UR) _____ of washing and rubbing.

Sign Tracking

Pavlov once reported that one of his dogs, during a classical conditioning experiment, approached a light that had signaled the delivery of food and licked it (Pavlov, 1941). It seemed as though the light not only signaled food but had also acquired some of its appetitive properties. Little attention was paid to this finding, however, until recently. This phenomenon is now known as sign tracking.

In *sign tracking,* **an organism approaches a stimulus that signals the presentation of an appetitive event** (Tomie, Brooks, & Zito, 1989). The approach behavior seems very much like an operant behavior since it appears to

FIGURE 11.1 Experimental setting for a sign tracking experiment. The dog first learns to sit on the mat to receive food. A light is then presented prior to each food delivery.

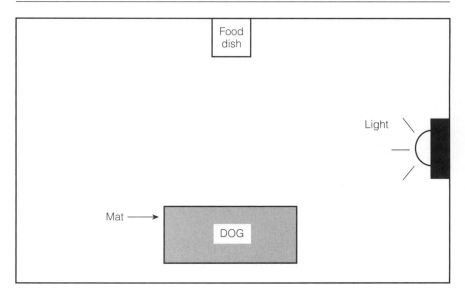

ADVICE FOR THE LOVELORN

Dear Dr. Dee,

My old girlfriend, to whom I was very attached, recently moved away. I am now trying to get over her, but I still find myself going to our favorite restaurant, our favorite beach, and so on. Why do I torture myself like this?

What-a Bird-brain

Dear Bird-brain,

Think of your behavior as similar to sign tracking. Your girlfriend was a powerful appetitive stimulus, with the result that you now approach stimuli that have been strongly associated with her. In fact (and somewhat in keeping with your signature), researchers have found similar behavior patterns in Japanese quail. Burns and Domjan (1996) found that if they lowered a block of wood into a chamber just prior to opening a door that allowed access to a female quail, male quail had a strong tendency to approach and stand near the block of wood rather than near the door. The block of wood had become a CS that elicited what was essentially a sexual sign tracking response. In similar fashion, we may have a tendency to approach settings that are strongly associated with a person with whom we have had an intimate relationship. In any event, your "bird-brained" tendency to approach these settings should eventually extinguish.

Behaviorally yours,

Dr. Dee

be quite goal-directed, yet the procedure that produces it is more closely akin to classical conditioning. Thus, sign tracking is yet another way in which classical and operant conditioning appear to overlap.

Take, for example, a hungry dog that has been trained to sit on a mat to receive food presented in a dish at the far side of the room. Suppose too that a light is presented just before the food, such that this light becomes a cue for food delivery (see Figure 11.1). A couple of things are liable to happen because of this arrangement. One is that the dog will probably start salivating whenever the light is presented. Through classical conditioning, the light will have become a CS for the conditioned response of salivation. But that is not all that will happen. Logically, when the light appears (which is a signal for food delivery), the dog should immediately walk over to the food dish and wait for the food. What happens instead is that the dog *walks over to the light* and starts displaying food-related behaviors toward it, such as licking it or even barking at it as though soliciting food from it. These behaviors are of course entirely unnecessary and have no effect on whether the food will appear. It seems as though the light has become so strongly associated with food that it is now a CS that elicits innate food-related behavior patterns (see Jenkins, Barrera, Ireland, & Woodside, 1978, for a description of a very similar experiment.)

Sign tracking has also been found in pigeons, and in fact it helps to account for the ease with which pigeons learn to peck a response key for food. Brown and Jenkins (1968) presented pigeons with a key light for 8 seconds followed by the *noncontingent* delivery of food. Although the pigeons did not have to peck the key to obtain the food, they soon began doing so anyway. It was as though the pigeons automatically pecked the key, presumably because it was associated with food. The pecking therefore seemed to be an elicited response, with the key light functioning as a CS through its association with food:

Key light: Food → *Peck*
  NS   US   UR
Key light → *Peck*
  CS   CR

This procedure is known as *autoshaping* because it is an automatic way to quickly establish key pecking in a pigeon. Rather than trying to deliberately shape the behavior, the researcher merely has to put the pigeon in the chamber, program the equipment to present light and food in the appropriate order, and presto, within an hour or so, out pops a key-pecking pigeon. Once the pecking response has been established this way, the food can then be made *contingent* upon pecking (i.e., food appears only when the key has been pecked), at which point the pecking begins functioning as an operant:

Key light: *Peck* → **Food**
  S^D   R   S^R

Thus, a behavior that starts off as an elicited behavior (controlled by the stimulus that precedes it) becomes transformed into an operant behavior (controlled by its consequence). In other words, the pigeon initially pecks the key because the key light predicts the free delivery of food; later, it pecks the key because it has to do so in order to obtain food.

Autoshaping is one type of classical conditioning that fits well with Pavlov's stimulus-substitution theory (discussed in Chapter 5). Because of its association with food, the key light appears to become a substitute for food, with the bird attempting to consume it. Further evidence for this stimulus-substitution interpretation comes from an experiment that compared autoshaped key pecks toward a key light signaling water delivery versus a key light signaling food delivery (Jenkins & Moore, 1973). As can be seen in Figure 11.2, when the bird pecked a key associated with water, it did so with its eyes open and its beak almost closed—the standard manner in which pigeons drink water. But when the bird pecked a key associated with food delivery, it did so with its eyes closed and its beak open, which is the standard manner in which a pigeon pecks at food. (The eyes are closed possibly because, in the natural environ-

FIGURE 11.2 Differences in autoshaped key pecks for water versus food. The peck on the left was made toward a key light that signaled the delivery of water; the peck on right was made toward a key light that signaled the delivery of food. (From Lieberman, 2000.)

ment, pecking at food sometimes results in dust or pebbles being thrown upward.) In other words, it seemed as though the bird was attempting to drink the key that was associated with water and eat the key that was associated with food.

Autoshaping procedures have powerful effects on behavior. For example, pigeons will peck a key associated with food even when doing so *prevents* the delivery of food (Williams & Williams, 1969). In other words, although the contingency requires that the pigeons must refrain from pecking to actually obtain the food (they should simply wait for the food when the key light appears), they will nevertheless compulsively peck at the key. The key light exerts such strong control over the behavior that it essentially overrides the negative punishment (loss of food) associated with pecking. This phenomenon, in which sign tracking persists despite the resultant loss of a reinforcer, is known as *negative automaintenance.*

QUICK QUIZ

1. In s_____ t_____, an organism approaches a stimulus that signals the availability of food. In such circumstances, the stimulus is best defined as a(n) (CS/US/S^D) _____, while the approach behavior is best defined as a(n) (CR/UR/operant) _____.

2. In auto_____, a pigeon will begin to peck a lit response key that is presented for 8 seconds prior to the nonc_____ delivery of food. The peck in this situation appears to be functioning as a(n) (reflex/operant) _____. Later, when a peck is required in order for the food to be delivered, the peck becomes a(n) _____.

3. In n_____ autom_____, pigeons will peck a lit response key that signals food delivery even when the act of pecking (prevents/ facilitates) _____ the delivery of food.

And Furthermore

The CAM Model of Drug Addiction

Sign tracking is a prime example of the strong impact antecedent stimuli can sometimes have on behavior. This effect is particularly strong when the cue that signals the presentation of food is combined with the response *manipulandum* (the apparatus the animal manipulates or responds upon). It is for this reason that autoshaping so readily occurs in pigeons—the response key is both the means of responding and the source of the light that signals food delivery. The combination has such a powerful effect that the pigeon pecks the key quite compulsively, even when pecking prevents the delivery of food.

Thus, when cue and manipulandum are combined (a combination that has been abbreviated as CAM), the cue can exert especially strong control over behavior (Tomie, 1995). This same principle can apply to circumstances involving standard contingencies of reinforcement. For example, rats display higher rates of lever pressing on VI schedules when the S^D signaling food availability is somehow combined with the lever (e.g., a lighted lever is used to signal food availability) than when the S^D is separate from the lever (e.g., the light is located on the wall above the lever). Close contiguity between cue and manipulandum seems to strengthen the occurrence of operant responding.

Tomie (1995) has speculated that CAM may be an important factor in the development of drug addictions. The instruments associated with drug use—for example, syringes and sniffers—are both the means (manipulandum) by which the drug is delivered and strong signals (cues) for drug use. Tomie has hypothesized that this CAM combination may encourage the development of uncontrollable urges to take the drug. Evidence for this includes the fact that drug users who use a single means of drug administration (e.g., injection only) appear to develop more severe addictions than drug users who use multiple means of administration (e.g., oral ingestion, sniffing, and injection). The single means of administration is a stronger cue for drug use because it is the only cue, and it therefore contributes to a stronger tendency to become addicted to the drug.

In a similar manner, the CAM model predicts more severe addiction when drug-taking instruments are used solely for drug administration, again because those instruments are more strongly associated with drug use. For example, if alcohol is always drunk from special glasses as opposed to regular water glasses, these special glasses will become especially strong cues for alcohol consumption and should result in a higher probability of excessive drinking. This might account for the higher incidence of *uncontrollable* alcohol consumption in Ireland as opposed to Italy, even though Italians consume significantly higher amounts of alcohol. Italians typically consume alcohol at regular meals from regular water glasses, while the Irish consume alcohol from special glasses in pubs that are specifically devoted to alcohol consumption. The stimuli associated with alcohol ingestion are therefore much more distinct in Ireland than they are in Italy, thereby possibly generating a stronger addiction to alcohol. Thus, what appears to be a purely cultural difference in alcohol use might actually reflect some basic principles of conditioning (Levin, 1990).

Adjunctive Behavior

Instinctive drift and sign tracking represent two types of anomalous (unexpected) behavior patterns that can develop during an operant conditioning procedure. Yet another type of anomaly is adjunctive behavior. *Adjunctive behavior* **is an excessive pattern of behavior that emerges as a by-product of an intermittent schedule of reinforcement for some other behavior.** In other words, as one behavior is being strengthened through intermittent reinforcement, another quite different behavior emerges as a side effect of that procedure. Adjunctive behavior is sometimes referred to as *schedule-induced behavior*, and the two terms will be used interchangeably in this discussion.

Basic Procedure and Defining Characteristics

Falk (1961) was the first person to systematically investigate adjunctive behavior in animals. He found that when rats were trained to lever press for food on an intermittent schedule of reinforcement, they also began drinking excessive amounts of water. During a 3-hour session, the rats drank almost three-and-a-half times the amount they would normally drink in an entire day. (To get a handle on this, imagine that a person who typically drinks 8 glasses of water a day instead drinks 28 glasses of water in a 3-hour period!) In fact, some of the rats drank up to half their body weight in water. These numbers are all the more remarkable in that the rats were food deprived, not water deprived, and food deprivation typically produces a decrease, not an increase, in water intake. This behavior pattern—called *schedule-induced polydipsia* (polydipsia means "excessive thirst")—developed quite rapidly, usually beginning in the first session and becoming firmly established by the second session.

Studies of adjunctive behavior typically employ FI or FT schedules of reinforcement (Falk, 1971). On such schedules, the delivery of each reinforcer is followed by a short period of time during which another reinforcer is not available. It is during such *inter-reinforcement intervals* that adjunctive behavior occurs. For example, when schedule-induced polydipsia is generated by exposure to an FI schedule of food reinforcement, the rat usually drinks during the post-reinforcement pause that is typical of such schedules. Thus, a short period of time during which there is a low probability or zero probability of reinforcement seems to be a critical factor in the development of adjunctive behavior.

Researchers soon discovered that schedule-induced polydipsia could be generated in other species, including mice, pigeons, and chimpanzees. They also discovered that it was possible to generate other types of adjunctive behaviors, such as chewing on wood shavings, licking at an air stream (presumably because of the sensory stimulation it provides), and aggression. In the latter case, it was found that pigeons that were exposed to an FI or FT schedule of food delivery soon began attacking a nearby target pigeon—or, more commonly, a picture or stuffed model of a pigeon—following each re-inforcer (e.g., Flory & Ellis, 1973). Unlike extinction-induced aggression, which often grows weaker over time, this type of schedule-induced aggression tends to remain strong and persistent. (See Falk, 1971, 1977; Staddon, 1977, for overviews of the findings on adjunctive behavior.)

Researchers also found that adjunctive behavior could be generated using reinforcers other than food delivery. For example, rats were found to eat ex-cessive amounts of food (that is, they engaged in schedule-induced eating) when exposed to an intermittent schedule of electrical stimulation to the plea-sure centers in the brain (Wilson & Cantor, 1987). Thus, rather than using food as a reinforcer to produce some other type of adjunctive behavior, these researchers used electrical stimulation of the pleasure centers as a reinforcer to produce an adjunctive pattern of eating. Interestingly, these rats gained considerable weight as a result of their compulsive tendency to snack between reinforcers, suggesting that schedule-induced eating may play a role in the de-velopment of obesity.

QUICK QUIZ

1. Adjunctive behavior is an excessive pattern of behavior that emerges as a _____ of an _____ schedule of reinforce-ment for (that behavior/a different behavior) _____.

2. Adjunctive behavior is also referred to as s_____-_____ behavior.

3. An excessive pattern of drinking that is produced by exposure to an intermittent schedule of food reinforcement is called s_____-_____ p_____.

4. Studies of adjunctive behavior typically use (FI/VI) _____ or (FT/VT) _____ schedules of food reinforcement. This is because adjunctive behavior tends to oc-cur during a period of time in which there is a (high/low) _____ probability of reinforcement.

According to Falk (1971, 1977), adjunctive behavior has several distin-guishing features. These include the following:

1. As previously noted, *adjunctive behavior typically occurs in the period imme-diately following consumption of an intermittent reinforcer.* For example, in schedule-induced polydipsia, the rat will quickly eat each food pellet as soon as it is delivered and then immediately move over to the drinking tube for a quick bout of drinking. The start of the interval between food pellets therefore tends to be dominated by drinking. The end of the in-terval, however, as the next pellet becomes imminent, tends to be domi-nated by food-related behaviors, such as lever pressing for the food (Stad-don, 1977).

2. *Adjunctive behavior is affected by the level of deprivation for the scheduled rein-forcer.* More specifically, the greater the level of deprivation for the rein-forcer, the stronger the adjunctive behavior that emerges as a by-product.

For example, with schedule-induced polydipsia, greater food deprivation not only produces a higher rate of lever pressing for food pellets, it also produces a higher rate of drinking between food pellets.

3. *Adjunctive behaviors can function as reinforcers for other behaviors.* This is in keeping with the Premack principle, which holds that high-probability behaviors can often serve as effective reinforcers for low-probability behaviors. Thus, with schedule-induced polydipsia, the rat will not only press a lever to obtain access to food pellets, but, during the interval between food pellets, it will also press a lever to gain access to water so that it can engage in adjunctive drinking.

4. *There is an optimal interval between reinforcers for the development of adjunctive behavior.* For example, rats will engage in little drinking with an inter-reinforcement interval of 5 seconds between food pellets, progressively more drinking as the interval is lengthened to 180 seconds, and then less drinking as the interval is lengthened beyond that. At an inter-reinforcement interval of 300 seconds, one again finds little drinking. The optimal inter-reinforcement intervals for other types of adjunctive behaviors tend to be similar, often in the range of 1 to 3 minutes.

1. Adjunctive behavior tends to occur (just prior to/just following) _____ the delivery of a reinforcer.

2. As the deprivation level for the scheduled reinforcer increases, the strength of the adjunctive behavior associated with it tends to (increase/decrease) _____.

3. The opportunity to engage in an adjunctive behavior can serve as a (reinforcer/punisher) _____ for some other behavior. This is in keeping with the P_____ principle.

4. The optimal inter-reinforcement interval for the production of adjunctive behavior is often in the range of (a few seconds/a few minutes/several minutes) _____.

QUICK QUIZ

Adjunctive Behavior in Humans

The preceding discussion probably has you wondering about the extent to which adjunctive behaviors occur in humans. Experiments with humans have produced adjunctive-type behavior patterns that are similar, though not as extreme, as those found in animals. For example, Doyle and Samson (1988) found that human subjects exposed to FI schedules of monetary reinforcement for game playing also displayed an increased tendency to drink water following each reinforcer. Similar to schedule-induced polydipsia in animals, the length of the interval between reinforcers was an important variable, with nearly twice as much drinking occurring on an FI 90-sec schedule as on an FI 30-sec schedule.

On a more anecdotal level, Falk (1977) notes that a diverse range of human behaviors, ranging from nail-biting and talkativeness to snacking and coffee drinking, are commonly associated with periods of enforced waiting. Falk (1998) also notes that drug and alcohol abuse is frequently found in environments that provide sparse levels of economic and social reinforcement, suggesting that adjunctive processes might be yet another factor that contributes to the development of drug and alcohol abuse. This is supported by the fact that schedule-induced polydipsia has been used to induce rats to drink excessive amounts of water containing alcohol or other drugs. Schedule-induced polydipsia can thus be used as a means of creating an animal analogue of drug and alcohol abuse (Falk, 1993).

Direct evidence for adjunctive drug use in humans has also been obtained. Cherek (1982) found high rates of cigarette smoking when monetary payment for button pushing was presented on an FI 120-sec schedule as opposed to FI 30-sec, 60-sec, or 240-sec schedules. And Doyle and Samson (1988) found high rates of beer sipping when monetary payment for playing a game was presented on an FI 90-sec schedule as opposed to an FI 30-sec schedule. In both cases, the drug-related behavior (smoking or beer sipping) was most likely to occur during the period immediately following delivery of the monetary reinforcer, which is consistent with the notion that it was functioning as an adjunctive behavior. Studies such as these support the notion that adjunctive processes may play a significant role in the development of substance abuse in humans. Especially in the early phases of an addiction, adjunctive processes may encourage an individual to frequently consume an addictive substance, with the result that the person eventually becomes addicted to it (Falk, 1998).

1. Evidence that humans engage in adjunctive behavior includes the fact that studies of adjunctive-type behavior patterns in human subjects usually (find/do not find) _____ an optimal time interval between reinforcers for producing such behaviors.

2. Certain behavior patterns in humans, such as smoking and nail-biting, are often associated with periods of (extreme activity/enforced waiting) _____ _____, which (agrees with/contradicts) _____ the notion that these may be adjunctive behaviors.

3. It has also been noted that alcohol and drug abuse is most likely to develop in environments in which economic and social reinforcers are (frequently/infrequently) _____ available, which (agrees with/contradicts) _____ the notion that these may be adjunctive behaviors.

4. Adjunctive processes may play a particularly important role in the development of an addiction during the (early/later) _____ stages of the addiction.

Adjunctive Behavior as Displacement Activity

Why would a tendency to develop adjunctive behaviors ever have evolved? What purpose do such activities serve, especially given how self-destructive they sometimes are? For example, it requires a considerable amount of energy for a rat to process and excrete the huge amounts of water ingested during a session of schedule-induced polydipsia. And drug and alcohol abuse is decidedly counterproductive for both rats and humans.

In this regard, Falk (1977) has proposed that adjunctive behaviors represent a type of *displacement activity:* **an apparently irrelevant activity sometimes displayed by animals when confronted by conflict or thwarted from attaining a goal.** For example, a bird that is unable to reach an insect hidden between some rocks might begin pecking at some nearby twigs. This behavior seems completely unrelated to the goal of capturing the insect, which led early investigators to propose that displacement activities like this serve simply as a means of releasing pent-up energy (Tinbergen, 1951).

In contrast to this energy release model, Falk (1977) proposes that displacement activities serve two purposes. First, they provide for a more diversified range of behaviors in a particular setting, and a diverse range of behavior is often beneficial. Consider, for example, a bird that has a tendency to peck at twigs while waiting for an insect to emerge from its hiding place. By doing so, the bird may uncover another source of food or may even stumble upon using a twig as a tool for rooting out the insect. In fact, some species of birds do use twigs to root out insects—an evolved pattern of behavior that may have begun as a displacement activity. In similar fashion, an employee who grows restless and busies herself with some paperwork while waiting for an important phone call is apt to be a more productive employee than one who simply stares at the phone until the phone call arrives.

A second benefit of displacement activities is that they help the animal remain in a situation where a significant reinforcer might eventually become available. Periods of little or no reinforcement can be aversive—as any student knows when buckling down to study a boring subject matter—and anything that can alleviate the aversiveness of these intervals will heighten the probability of attaining a delayed reinforcer. Thus, pecking the ground gives the bird "something to do" while waiting for an insect to emerge from its hiding place, just as whittling a stick allows a hunter to patiently wait for a moose, and munching on licorice enables a student to sit still and study patiently throughout a study session.

Adjunctive behavior can therefore be seen as a natural tendency to do something else while waiting for a reinforcer. To the extent that it enhances the individual's ability to wait out the delay period, it thus constitutes a sort of built-in self-control device. This is a paradoxical notion in that adjunctive behaviors, such as smoking and drinking, are usually the kinds of behaviors that are viewed as indicating a *lack of self-control* (Tomie, 1996). But this depends on the specific consequence to which one is referring. Smoking is an impulsive behavior in terms of providing short-term pleasure at the risk of undermining one's long-term health, but it can also enhance self-control in terms of helping an individual work long hours so as to obtain a promotion. It is for this reason that students often find it particularly difficult to quit smoking during the academic year. Quitting smoking not only results in the temporary onset of withdrawal symptoms, it also undermines the student's ability to

And Furthermore

Extreme Polydipsia: Not Just a "Rat Thing"

Schedule-induced polydipsia is a bizarre behavior pattern, with rats ingesting enormous amounts of water in a short period of time. Experimental studies of schedule-induced drinking in humans have typically produced much lower rates of drinking, suggesting that rats and humans are quite different in their susceptibility to polydipsia (Klein, 1996). But extreme polydipsia does sometimes occur in humans. In fact, as a psychiatric label, the term polydipsia refers to a rare condition in which patients drink incessantly—so much so that they sometimes die from the disruption of electrolytes in their bodies. Although there are no doubt major differences between this psychiatric form of polydipsia in humans and schedule-induced polydipsia in rats, there might also be some similarities. If nothing else, schedule-induced polydipsia, and other adjunctive behaviors, are compulsive-type patterns of behavior and might therefore provide insight into the behavioral and neurological processes that maintain compulsive behaviors in humans. Psychiatrists have therefore shown considerable interest in schedule-induced polydipsia, in sorting out the neurological processes that underlie it and in determining the effects of psychiatric drugs on alleviating it (Wallace & Singer, 1976). Research on adjunctive behavior could therefore have implications for furthering our understanding and treatment of some serious psychiatric conditions in humans.

study for long periods of time.[2] Congruent with this notion, it has been shown that people who successfully overcome an addiction (such as alcoholism) are more likely to seek out a replacement for the addictive activity (such as coffee drinking) than those who are not successful in overcoming their addiction (Brown, Stetson, & Beatty, 1989). The moral of the story is that adjunctive behaviors sometimes serve a purpose, and we might do well to acknowledge that purpose and find other ways to fulfill it.

QUICK QUIZ

1. According to Falk (1977), adjunctive behavior may be a type of d_____ activity, which is an irrelevant activity displayed by animals when confronted by c_____ or when they are (able/unable) _____ to achieve a goal.

2. One benefit of such activities is that it often useful to engage in (just one type/a diverse range) _____ of behavior(s) in a situation.

---

[2] As Freud once complained, if he could not smoke, then he could not work. Interestingly, Freud was famous for his ability to work long hours, which is often attributed to his "self-discipline." Yet, this self-discipline seems to have been at least partially dependent on the availability of an adjunctive activity in the form of smoking. Unfortunately, his 20-cigars-a-day habit resulted in cancer of the jaw, from which he eventually died (Gay, 1988).

3. The second benefit derived from such activities is that they may facilitate (moving away from/remaining near) _____ a potential reinforcer.

4. To the extent that adjunctive activities facilitate waiting for, or working toward, a(n)(immediate/delayed) _____ reinforcer, such activities may (facilitate/impede) _____ efforts at self-control.

Activity Anorexia

One type of behavior that can be generated as an adjunctive behavior is wheel running. When exposed to an intermittent schedule of food reinforcement for lever pressing, rats will run in a wheel for several seconds during the interval between reinforcers (Levitsky & Collier, 1968). A related type of procedure, however, produces even more extreme running. Known as *activity anorexia*, it has some important implications for people who are undertaking a diet and exercise program to lose weight.[3]

Basic Procedure and Defining Characteristics

The procedure for creating activity anorexia is as follows: If rats are allowed to access food for only a single 1.5-hour feeding period each day, and if they have access to a running wheel during the 22.5-hour interval between meals, they will begin to spend increasing amounts of time running during that interval. Not only that, the more they run, the less they eat, and the less they eat, the more they run. In other words, a sort of negative feedback cycle develops in which the two behavioral tendencies, increased running and decreased eating, reciprocally strengthen each other. Within a week or so, the rats are running enormous distances—up to 20,000 revolutions of the wheel per day (equivalent to about 12 miles!)—and eating nothing. If the process is allowed to continue (for humane reasons, the experiment is usually terminated prior to this), the rats will become completely emaciated and die (e.g., Routtenberg & Kuznesof, 1967).

Thus, *activity anorexia* **is an abnormally high level of activity and low level of food intake generated by exposure to a restricted schedule of feeding** (Epling & Pierce, 1991). It is important to note that rats that are given restricted access to food, but with *no* wheel available, do just fine—they easily ingest enough food during the 1.5-hour meal period to maintain body weight. As well, rats that have access to a wheel, but without food restriction,

---

[3] Activity anorexia is considered by some researchers to be a type of adjunctive or schedule-induced behavior (e.g., Falk, 1994), and by other researchers to be a separate class of behaviors involving distinctly different processes (e.g., Beneke, Schulte, & Vander Tuig, 1995). For purposes of this discussion, we will adopt the latter position.

also do just fine—they display only moderate levels of running and no tendency toward self-starvation. It is the combination of food restriction and the opportunity to run that is so devastating.

1. The basic procedure for the development of _____ _____ in rats is the presentation of (one/several) _____ meal period(s) each day along with access to a running wheel during the (meal/between-meal) _____ period.

2. Thus, _____ _____ is an abnormally (low/high) _____ level of _____ and a (low/high) _____ level of food intake generated by exposure to a r_____ schedule of feeding.

Comparisons with Anorexia Nervosa

Activity anorexia was first investigated by Routtenberg and Kuznesof (1967). Two other researchers, Epling and Pierce (e.g., 1988), later noted its similarity to *anorexia nervosa* in humans. Anorexia nervosa is a psychiatric disorder in which patients refuse to eat adequate amounts of food and as a result lose extreme amounts of weight. People with this disorder often require hospitalization, and of those who do become hospitalized, over 10% eventually die from the disorder or from complications associated with it (such as from a disruption of the body's electrolyte balance; *DSM-IV*, 1994).

Epling and Pierce (1991) contend that there are several similarities between activity anorexia in rats and anorexia nervosa in humans. For example, just as activity anorexia in rats can be precipitated by imposing a restricted schedule of feeding, so too anorexia nervosa in humans usually begins when the person deliberately undertakes a diet to lose weight. Even more significant is the fact that anorexia in humans, as with anorexia in rats, is often accompanied by very high levels of activity (Davis, Katzman, & Kirsh, 1999; Katz, 1996). This may consist of a deliberate exercise program designed to facilitate weight loss, or it may be displayed as a severe sort of restlessness. Although clinicians have typically regarded such high activity as a secondary characteristic of the disorder (e.g., Bruch, 1978), Epling and Pierce suggest that it is more fundamental than that. Thus, as with activity anorexia in rats, many cases of anorexia nervosa in humans might result from the combined effects of a stringent diet and high activity levels.

The importance of high activity in the development of anorexia nervosa is supported by several lines of evidence. First, even in nonanorexic humans, a sudden increase in activity is usually followed by a decrease in food intake, and a decrease in food intake is usually followed by an increase in activity (Epling & Pierce, 1996a). Second, individuals who engage in high levels of activity appear to be at high risk for becoming anorexic. For example, ballet dancers, who are under constant pressure to remain thin and are extremely active, show a higher incidence of the disorder than fashion models who are under pressure only to remain thin (Garner & Garfinkel, 1980). Likewise, a surprising number of athletes develop symptoms of anorexia (Katz, 1986; Wheeler, 1996) or an "overtraining syndrome" that bears many similarities to anorexia (Yates, 1996).

In addition to high activity levels, there are other interesting parallels between anorexia in rats and humans. For example, just as anorexia nervosa in humans is more common among adolescents (*DSM-IV*, 1994), activity anorexia is more easily induced in adolescent rats than older rats (Woods & Routtenberg, 1971). Another possible similarity concerns the manner in which anorexics approach food. Although human anorexics eat little, they nevertheless remain quite interested in food (Bruch, 1978). For example, they often enjoy preparing food for others. As well, when they do eat, they often spend considerable time arranging the food on their plates, cutting it into pieces, and slowly savoring each bite. Anecdotal evidence suggests that anorexic rats might sometimes behave similarly (D. P. Boer, 2000, personal communication). Although the rats eat little or no food during each meal period, they do spend considerable time shredding the food with their teeth and spitting it out. And if allowed to do so, they will carry food with them when they are allowed to reenter the wheel following the meal period. In other words, like humans, rats seem to remain quite interested in food, even if they are not eating it.

Thus, activity anorexia in rats appears to be a rather close analogue of anorexia nervosa in humans. As with most analogues, however, the similarity is less than perfect. For example, the anorexic rat is physically restricted from accessing food except during the meal period, while the anorexic human is on a self-imposed diet with food still freely available. Epling and Pierce (1991) argue, however, that the free availability of food may be more apparent than real. Just as the researcher physically restricts the rat's supply of food, so too societal pressures to become thin may psychologically restrict a person's access to food. Women of course are more commonly subjected to such pressures; thus, it is not surprising that anorexia is more commonly diagnosed in women than it is in men (although medical biases toward viewing thin women as anorexic and thin males as, well, just thin, probably also play a role).

A more substantial difference between humans and rats is that anorexia in humans is often accompanied by bulimia: a tendency to binge eat and then purge oneself by vomiting or taking laxatives. In fact, psychiatrists distinguish between two types of anorexia: the *restricting type*, which is characterized by simple food restriction, and the *binge-eating/purging type*, in which dieting is combined with episodes of binging and purging (*DSM-IV*, 1994). Of course, anorexic rats do not binge and purge; indeed, it would be difficult for them to do so as rats are physically incapable of vomiting. Thus, activity anorexia in rats is most relevant to the restricting type of anorexia in humans. And, in fact, the restricting type of anorexia is the type that is most strongly associated with high activity levels (Katz, 1996).

1. As with the development of activity anorexia in rats, most instances of human anorexia begin with the person undertaking a d_____. As well, human anorexics tend to display (high/low) _____ levels of activity.

2. A sharp increase in activity is usually associated with a (decrease/increase) _____ in food intake, which in turn can result in a(n) (decrease/increase) _____ in activity.

3. Anecdotal evidence suggests that, as with human anorexics, anorexic rats are often quite (interested/uninterested) _____ in food.

4. Similar to anorexia nervosa in humans, activity anorexia in rats is more easily induced in (adolescent/adult) _____ rats.

5. Activity anorexia in rats is most similar to the r_____ type of anorexia in humans rather than the b_____-p_____ type of anorexia.

Underlying Mechanisms

Given the self-destructive nature of activity anorexia, what are the mechanisms that underlie it? On a neurophysiological level, the processes involved are probably complex, involving several classes of hormones and neurotransmitters (Epling & Pierce, 1996b). Evidence, however, suggests that endorphins may play a particularly important role. Endorphins are a class of morphine-like substances in the brain that have been implicated in pain reduction. They have also been implicated in the feeling of pleasure that sometimes accompanies prolonged exercise, which is commonly known as "runner's high" (Wheeler, 1996). Significantly, drugs that block the effect of endorphins will temporarily lower the rate of wheel running in food-deprived rats (Boer, Epling, Pierce, & Russell, 1990).

Such evidence suggests that both activity anorexia in rats and anorexia nervosa in humans might be maintained by what is essentially an addiction to an endorphin high (Marrazzi & Luby, 1986). In support of this notion, anorexic patients often report that the experience of anorexia is quite similar to a drug-induced high. To quote three patients: "[O]ne feels intoxicated, literally how I think alcoholism works" (Bruch, 1978, p. 73); "being hungry has the same effect as a drug, and you feel outside your body" (p. 118); and perhaps most disturbing, "I enjoy having this disease and I want it" (p. 2).

From an evolutionary perspective, Epling and Pierce (1988, 1991) have suggested that a tendency toward activity anorexia might have survival value. An animal that becomes highly active when food supplies are scarce is more likely to travel great distances and encounter new food supplies. Under extreme circumstances, the animal might even do well to ignore small amounts of food encountered along the way—the gathering of which could be costly in terms of time and energy spent relative to the amount of energy gained—and cease traveling only when an adequate food supply has been reached. In support of this notion, research has shown that activity anorexia can be halted by suddenly providing access to a continuous supply of food (Epling & Pierce, 1991). Confronted with a plentiful food source, the rats cease running and begin eating.

QUICK QUIZ

1. Endorphins are a class of morphine-like substances in the brain that are associated with p_____ reduction.

2. Congruent with the possibility that endorphins may be involved in activity anorexia, endorphins have been implicated in the feeling of p_____ that is sometimes experienced following prolonged exercise.

3. This suggests that both activity anorexia in rats and anorexia nervosa in humans may be maintained by an _____ high.

4. From an evolutionary perspective, increased activity in response to decreased food intake could (interfere with/facilitate) _____ contacting a new food supply.

5. This evolutionary perspective is supported by the fact that the activity anorexia cycle can be broken by suddenly providing (intermittent/continuous) _____ access to food.

Clinical Implications

The activity anorexia model has several clinical implications. From a treatment perspective, the model suggests that behavioral treatments for anorexia nervosa should focus as much on establishing normal patterns of activity as they do on establishing normal patterns of eating. As well, research into the biochemistry underlying this phenomenon could facilitate the development of drugs for treating anorexia. For example, it may be possible to develop long-lasting endorphin blockers that will effectively reduce the feelings of pleasure that help maintain the anorexic process.

The activity anorexia model also has implications for prevention. First and foremost, people should be warned that combining a stringent exercise program with severe dieting places them at risk for the development of this disorder. The model thus calls into question those disciplines that traditionally combine dieting with intense activity. As already noted, one such discipline is ballet; another is amateur wrestling. Wrestlers are traditionally expected to lose several pounds prior to competition so as to compete in the lightest weight category possible. Many of the physical and psychological changes that accompany this process are similar to those found in anorexia nervosa,

And Furthermore

The Healthy Side of the Diet-Activity Connection

We have so far discussed the negative aspect of the connection between food restriction and activity. There is also a positive side to this connection. Boer (1989) found that by adjusting the *amount of food* eaten by the rats, as opposed to the *length of the meal period,* he could precisely control the amount of wheel running. For example, rats that were given 15 grams of food once per day developed the typical activity anorexia cycle (see also Morse et al., 1995), while rats that were given 18 grams of food displayed only a moderate level of running (5–6 miles per day), with no tendency toward self-starvation. These rats were also quite healthy. Interestingly, the same effect was found using rats that had a genetic predisposition toward obesity (Russell et al., 1989). Raised on a regime of diet and exercise, these "genetically fat" rats remained incredibly lean and fit—an impressive demonstration of the healthy effects of a healthy lifestyle, even in subjects whose genetics are working against them.

It is also worth repeating that, as noted in Chapter 2, calorie restriction is at present the most reliable means known for slowing the aging process, at least in nonhuman animals (Weindruch, 1996). Lest the reader imagine, however, that this might be a good excuse for eating like an anorexic and quickly losing a lot of weight, the health-enhancing effects of low-calorie diets demand regular meals composed of highly nutritious foods—a far cry from the "two carrots and a cookie" diet of many anorexics.

indicating that these athletes are at risk for developing symptoms of the disorder (Symbaluk, 1996).

The activity anorexia model also suggests that people who are dieting should eat several small meals per day as opposed to a single large meal, insofar as rats do not become anorexic when the 1.5-hour meal period is broken up into several shorter meal periods (Epling & Pierce, 1991). As well, people who are attempting to increase their exercise levels should do so slowly, since rats that become anorexic experience the greatest reduction in food intake following a sharp increase in activity (Epling & Pierce, 1996b). (Interestingly, it is also the sharp increase in activity that has been shown to be most clearly associated with appetite suppression in humans.) And finally, dieters should ensure that their meals are well balanced in terms of nutritional composition. Research has shown that activity anorexia is more easily induced in rats that are on a low-protein diet as opposed to a normal diet (Beneke & Vander Tuig, 1996).

Of course, further research is needed to confirm the usefulness of these suggestions for preventing anorexia nervosa in humans. What is clear, however, is that a combination of severe dieting and exercise can have serious consequences and should not be undertaken lightly.

1. The activity anorexia model suggests that therapists should focus as much on establishing normal a_____ levels as they presently do on establishing normal eating patterns.

2. Specific suggestions (derived from activity anorexia research) for minimizing the risk of anorexia in humans include eating (several/one) _____ meal(s) per day, increasing exercise levels (rapidly/slowly) _____, and eating a diet that is (imbalanced/well balanced) _____.

SUMMARY

Animals appear to be biologically prepared to learn some things more readily than others. For example, in taste aversion conditioning, a food item that has been paired with nausea quickly becomes conditioned as an aversive CS. This type of conditioning is similar to other forms of classical conditioning in that processes such as stimulus generalization, extinction, and overshadowing can be found. It differs from other forms of classical conditioning in that strong associations can be formed over long delays and require only a single conditioning trial. As well, the nausea is specifically associated with a food item rather than some other stimulus.

Examples of preparedness in operant conditioning include the ease with which food can be used to reinforce pecking but not perching in chaffinches, while the sound of a chaffinche song can be used to reinforce perching but not pecking. As well, rats more easily learn to run or freeze to escape shock than to press a lever. The latter example suggests that many escape behaviors may be species-specific defense reactions that are elicited by the aversive stimulus.

Instinctive drift is a genetically based fixed action pattern that gradually emerges to displace a behavior that is being operantly conditioned. Sign tracking is a tendency to approach (and perhaps make contact with) a stimulus that signals the presentation of an appetitive event. In both cases, the behavior superficially appears to be a goal-directed operant behavior, yet the procedures that produce it suggest that it is actually an elicited (or respondent) behavior.

Adjunctive behavior, also known as schedule-induced behavior, is an excessive pattern of behavior that emerges as a by-product of an intermittent schedule of reinforcement. In schedule-induced polydipsia, for example, rats drink extreme amounts of water during the interval between food reinforcers that are delivered on an FI or FT schedule. Adjunctive behavior typically occurs in the period immediately following the delivery of the scheduled reinforcer, varies directly with the level of deprivation for the scheduled reinforcer, can function as a reinforcer for another behavior, and is most likely to occur when the inter-reinforcement interval is a few minutes in length. Examples of possible adjunctive behaviors in humans consist of smoking cigarettes, drinking alcohol, and using drugs. Adjunctive behavior may be a type of displacement activity, the function of which is to ensure a diverse range of activities in a setting and to facilitate waiting for a delayed reinforcer.

Activity anorexia is a pattern of excessive activity and low food intake in animals that results from exposure to a restricted food supply. It bears many similarities to certain forms of anorexia nervosa in humans, which is characterized by severe dieting and high activity levels. Evidence suggests that both activity anorexia in animals and anorexia nervosa in humans may be maintained by an endorphin high that accompanies the process. From an evolutionary perspective, a tendency toward activity anorexia might induce an animal to travel long distances, thereby increasing the likelihood of encountering a new food supply. Clinical implications that have grown out of this research include the possibility of developing long-lasting endorphin blockers that could break the anorexic cycle. These findings also suggest that people should be cautious about combining a stringent diet with severe exercise.

STUDY QUESTIONS

1. Define taste aversion conditioning.
2. Outline three ways in which taste aversion conditioning differs from most other forms of classical conditioning.
3. Describe (or diagram) the results of the experiment by Garcia and Koelling (1966) that illustrates the role of biological preparedness in classical conditioning.
4. Describe two examples of the role of preparedness in operant conditioning.
5. Describe Bolles's concept of species-specific defense reactions, and what it implies with respect to the nature of avoidance behavior.
6. What is instinctive drift? Describe (or diagram) one of the Brelands' examples of instinctive drift.
7. What is sign tracking? Describe the experimental example of sign tracking in dogs.
8. Describe autoshaping in pigeons and the procedure used to produce it.
9. Describe the research result that seems particularly supportive of a stimulus-substitution interpretation of autoshaping.
10. Describe the phenomenon of negative automaintenance.
11. Define adjunctive behavior. What other term is used to refer to this class of behaviors?
12. What is schedule-induced polydipsia, and what is the typical procedure for inducing it in rats?
13. List four characteristics of adjunctive behaviors.
14. Provide at least two examples of evidence supporting the notion that adjunctive behaviors occur in humans.
15. What are displacement activities? What are two benefits that may be derived from such activities?
16. Define activity anorexia. What is the basic procedure for inducing this behavior pattern?

17. List some of the similarities between activity anorexia in rats and anorexia nervosa in humans.
18. What type of chemical substance in the brain seems to play a role in the development of anorexia? Briefly describe Epling and Pierce's evolutionary explanation for the occurrence of activity anorexia.
19. List two implications for treatment and four implications for prevention that have grown out of activity anorexia research.

CONCEPT REVIEW

activity anorexia. An abnormally high level of activity and low level of food intake generated by exposure to a restricted schedule of feeding.

adjunctive behavior. An excessive pattern of behavior that emerges as a by-product of an intermittent schedule of reinforcement for some other behavior.

belongingness. An innate tendency to easily associate certain types of events with each other.

displacement activity. An apparently irrelevant activity sometimes displayed by animals when confronted by conflict or thwarted from attaining a goal.

instinctive drift. A genetically based fixed action pattern that gradually emerges and displaces the behavior that is being operantly conditioned.

sign tracking. A type of elicited behavior in which an organism approaches a stimulus that signals the presentation of an appetitive event.

taste aversion conditioning. A form of classical conditioning in which a food item that has been paired with gastrointestinal illness becomes a conditioned aversive stimulus.

CHAPTER TEST

9. To prevent the development of anorexia nervosa, humans who are dieting might do well to eat (several small/one large) _____ meal(s) per day. And if they are exercising, they should increase the level of exercise (quickly/slowly) _____.

20. Taste aversion conditioning differs from other forms of conditioning in that associations can be formed over _____ delays, and in (many/a single) _____ trial(s).

2. According to the phenomenon of negative _____, a pigeon will compulsively peck at a key light that precedes the delivery of food even though the key peck _____ the delivery of food.

28. Displacement activities, including certain types of adjunctive behaviors, may serve as a type of self-_____ device in that they facilitate the act of waiting for a _____ reinforcer.

11. In general, a pigeon that is (more/less) _____ food deprived will display a greater tendency to engage in schedule-induced aggression.

 1. When a key light is presented just prior to the noncontingent delivery of food, the pigeon will begin pecking at the key. This phenomenon is known as _____.

24. When a pig is reinforced for carrying a napkin from one table to another, it eventually starts dropping it and rooting at it on the ground. This is an example of a phenomenon known as _____ in which a _____ pattern gradually emerges and replaces the operant behavior that one is attempting to condition.

 4. An excessive pattern of behavior that emerges as a by-product of an intermittent schedule of reinforcement for some other behavior is called _____ behavior.

12. In schedule-induced polydipsia, a rat likely (will/will not) _____ learn to press a lever to gain access to a (drinking tube/running wheel) _____ during the interval between food pellets.

19. Angie became sick to her stomach when she and her new boyfriend, Gerald, were on their way home after dining at an exotic restaurant. Fortunately for (Gerald/the restaurant) _____, Angie is most likely to form an aversion to (Gerald/the food) _____.

26. A _____ activity is a (highly relevant/seemingly irrelevant) _____ activity sometimes displayed by animals when confronted by conflict or blocked from attaining a goal.

16. Following a turkey dinner in which, for the first time, Paul also tasted some caviar, he became quite nauseous. As a result, he may acquire a conditioned _____, most likely to the (turkey/caviar) _____.

31. Activity anorexia is more easily induced among relatively (young/old) _____ rats, which is (similar to/different from) _____ the pattern found with human anorexics.

 8. Whenever a person combines a stringent exercise program with a severe diet, they may be at risk for developing symptoms of _____.

13. For the development of adjunctive behaviors, the optimal interval between the delivery of reinforcers is often about (3/6/9) ___ minute(s).

22. My canary likes the sound of my whistling. Research suggests that my whistling will be a more effective reinforcer if I am attempting to shape the bird to (perch in a certain spot/peck at the floor) _____.

29. An abnormally high level of activity and low level of food intake generated by restricted access to food is called _____.

 6. From an evolutionary perspective, a tendency toward activity anorexia could (increase/decrease) _____ the likelihood of the animal encountering a new food supply. Indirect evidence for this includes the fact that the activity anorexia cycle can often be (stopped/greatly enhanced) _____ by suddenly presenting the animal with a continuous supply of food.

18. When Selma was eating oatmeal porridge one morning, she broke a tooth on a small pebble that accidentally had been mixed in with it. The next morning, after she ate some bran flakes, she became terribly ill. If she develops aversions as a result of these experiences, chances are that they will be an aversion to the (look/taste) _____ of oatmeal and the _____ of bran flakes.

10. Adjunctive behavior tends to develop when a behavior is being reinforced on a _____ or _____ schedule of reinforcement. Also, adjunctive behavior is most likely to occur in the interval immediately (following/preceding) _____ the presentation of each reinforcer.

23. When a rat is shocked it easily learns to run to the other side of the chamber to escape. According to Bolles, this is because the running is actually a(n) (operant/respondent) _____ that is (elicited/negatively reinforced) _____ by the (application/removal) _____ of shock.

7. The activity anorexia model suggests that behavioral treatments for anorexia nervosa should focus as much on establishing normal patterns of _____ as they do on establishing normal patterns of eating.

14. The tendency for many people to smoke while waiting in traffic can be viewed as an example of an _____ behavior in humans.

3. Adjunctive behavior is also known as _____ behavior.

27. One advantage of displacement activities is that they allow for a more (diverse/focused) _____ pattern of behavior, which is often advantageous.

21. An innate tendency to more readily associate certain types of events with each other is a type of preparedness that is known as _____.

17. Taste aversion conditioning most readily occurs to (familiar/unfamiliar) _____ food items, as well as to the (strongest/mildest) _____ tasting item in the meal. The latter can be seen as an example of the _____ effect in classical conditioning.

5. A class of brain chemicals that may play a particularly important role in the development of anorexia in both rats and humans is _____. Evidence for this includes the fact that people suffering from anorexia often report that the feeling that accompanies the disorder is quite (unpleasant/pleasant) _____.

25. A behavior pattern in which an organism approaches a stimulus that signals the presentation of an appetitive event is known as _____.

30. As with the development of anorexia in rats, many cases of anorexia in humans might be the result of the combined effects of _____ restriction and high _____ levels.

15. Despite getting a shock when he plugged in his toaster one day, Antonio feels only slight anxiety when using it. On the other hand, he is deathly afraid of spiders, ever since one jumped on him when he tried to swat it. The difference in the ease with which Antonio learned to fear these two events seems to be an illustration of the effect of _____ on conditioning.

ANSWERS TO CHAPTER TEST

1. autoshaping
2. automaintenance; prevents
3. schedule-induced
4. adjunctive
5. endorphins; pleasant
6. increase; stopped
7. activity
8. anorexia nervosa
9. several small; slowly
10. FT; FI; following
11. more
12. will; drinking tube
13. 3
14. adjunctive
15. preparedness
16. taste aversion; caviar
17. unfamiliar; strongest; overshadowing
18. look; taste
19. Gerald; the food
20. long; a single
21. belongingness
22. perch in a certain spot
23. respondent; elicited; application
24. instinctive drift; fixed action
25. sign tracking
26. displacement; seemingly irrelevant
27. diverse
28. control; delayed
29. activity anorexia
30. food; activity
31. young; similar to

CHAPTER 12

Observational Learning, Language, and Rule-Governed Behavior

CHAPTER OUTLINE

"I don't care what *Dr. Dee* says!" Gina shouted in exasperation when Steve again pronounced judgment on some aspect of their relationship. "I am starting to wish you had never enrolled in that stupid course. Why don't you just listen to what I am saying rather than acting like 'Mr. Behaviorist' all the time!"

Much of this text has been concerned with basic processes of conditioning in which new patterns of behavior are acquired through direct exposure to the relevant events. Janna fears dogs because she was once bitten by a dog, and Kyle goes to a particular restaurant because in the past he received good food there. However, not all behavior patterns are acquired this directly. Some people acquire a fear of dogs without ever being attacked by a dog, or they eagerly head off to a restaurant despite never having been there before. Such behaviors have somehow been acquired in the absence of any direct exposure to the relevant events.

In this chapter, we focus upon processes that allow us to acquire new behavior patterns through indirect means. We begin with observational learning (a process that was touched upon in previous chapters), which plays a strong role in human learning but which is also found in animals. We then discuss language, which enables us to transmit and receive large amounts of information. Although language has traditionally been considered a uniquely human form of behavior, research on language training in animals is, according to some, now challenging that view. Finally, we outline the manner in which we use language to generate rules (or instructions), and we discuss the effectiveness and drawbacks of rules in modifying behavior.

Observational Learning

Do you remember your first day of school? If so, you probably remember being a little afraid and unsure about what to do when you first arrived— where to stand, who to talk to, even where to go to the bathroom. After a while, though, it all became much clearer because you could watch what other people did and follow them. This type of learning is called *observational learning*.

In *observational learning*, **a behavior is modeled—performed—for an observer, who gains information from that behavior and can then use the information to modify his or her own behavior** (Baldwin & Baldwin, 1998). The model may perform the behavior specifically for the purpose of teaching others how to perform it—for example, by giving tennis lessons— or the model may not even be aware that his or her behavior is being observed. Either way, modeling can have a powerful influence on others. There is considerable evidence that people can improve their performance on many tasks, including sports, simply by *watching* others perform (e.g., Blandin, Lhuisset, & Proteau, 1999; Shea, Wright, Wulf, & Whitacre, 2000). Of course, you are

FIGURE 12.1 Young children learn many behaviors through observation. (Unfortunately for parents, this particular behavior pattern occurs much less readily when children reach their teens.)

unlikely to become an Olympic athlete by watching the Olympic Games on television, but observational learning can help you learn a new sport or improve your abilities at an old one.

Often, we pick up new behaviors without even being aware that our behavior has been influenced. For example, we may see television commercials filled with attractive people modeling new—and even undesirable—behaviors, like smoking. This subtle form of social modeling can strongly affect our behavior when we find ourselves in a similar situation. Observational learning is based on social processes, and because humans are innately social beings, we can quickly acquire new behavior patterns in this way (Bandura, 1986).

How does observational learning work? Both classical and operant processes are involved. First, let us discuss the classical conditioning processes underlying observational learning.

In Classical Conditioning

Although it may not be obvious at first glance, observational learning, like other forms of learning, has a classical conditioning component. The difference is that the stimuli involved are usually *emotional* in nature. That is one of the reasons why observational learning is so effective. For example, imagine a young child walking into a day care center. She sees other children laughing and smiling, playing with a new toy. The smiles and laughter of the other children act as CSs for the observer. Those CSs can elicit conditioned responses in the observer, making her feel similar emotions. Such emotions are called *vicarious emotional responses,* **which are classically conditioned emotional responses that result from seeing those emotional responses exhibited by others.**

Smiles and other social cues, like frowns, tears, and blushes, are strong CSs because they have been conditioned in most of us right from birth. Smiles are usually associated with events that are pleasurable—such as when a smiling mother feeds a baby—and therefore quickly become conditioned to elicit pleasurable emotions. Thus, in diagram form:

> **Smiles in others: Pleasurable events** → *Pleasant emotions (in oneself)*
>   **NS**   **US**   **UR**
> **Smiles in others** → *Pleasant emotions*
>   **CS**   **CR**

Frowns, on the other hand, are often associated with unpleasant or awkward situations, and so they can serve as CSs for unpleasant emotions:

> **Frowns in others: Unpleasant events** → *Unpleasant emotions (in oneself)*
>   **NS**   **US**   **UR**
> **Frowns in others** → *Unpleasant emotions*
>   **CS**   **CR**

Likewise, fearful looks are often associated with frightening events and therefore come to serve as CSs for the emotion of fear:

> **Look of fear in others: Frightening event** → *Fear (in oneself)*
>   **NS**   **US**   **UR**
> **Look of fear in others** → *Fear*
>   **CS**   **CR**

We thus react fearfully when we see others looking fearful because that look has in the past been associated with frightening events. (Additionally, as noted in Chapter 5, we might also have a genetic predisposition to react fearfully when we see a look of fear in others, which would enhance this type of conditioning.)

Once acquired, vicarious emotional responses can then motivate new behavior patterns in observers (e.g., Eisenberg, McCreath, & Ahn, 1988; Gold, Fultz, Burke, & Prisco, 1992). After watching the happy children playing with the toy, the observing child may be eager to play with the toy herself. And once we have seen someone else react fearfully to a snake, we are likely to go out of our way to avoid any encounter with a snake (Mineka & Cook, 1993).

As noted in Chapter 4, many advertisers use emotional conditioning to influence our view of their products. When we see a television family reunited by a long-distance telephone call, with tears of joy flowing freely, the vicarious emotions elicited by the joyful tears of the models can cause us to associate the phone company with that emotion. Thus, the phone company becomes a positive CS, and the likelihood of our subscribing to their service increases.

1. In observational learning, the person performing a behavior is the _____ ; the person watching the behavior is the _____ .

2. Observational learning involves both _____ al and _____ nt conditioning.

3. From a classical conditioning perspective, smiles, giggles and laughs are _____ Ss that can elicit v_____ e_____ r_____ in observers.

4. David watches a television infomercial about a new product guaranteed to promote weight loss. The audience members are smiling, laughing, and enthusiastic in their praise for the product. Later, David decides that he will buy the product, even though he initially viewed it with skepticism. David's buying decision is probably motivated by _____ responses that he acquired through exposure to the infomercial.

In Operant Conditioning

Classical conditioning processes underlie many of the emotional responses involved in observational learning. Operant conditioning, on the other hand, underlies how a model's behavior is translated into the behavior of an observer. It is important to distinguish here between *acquisition* and *performance* of a behavior. You may have watched your parents driving a car for years, and you may have acquired most of the basic information needed to drive the car—how to start it, how to shift gears, how to use the signal lights, and so on. However, until you reached legal driving age, you were not permitted to translate that acquired knowledge into driving performance.

Acquisition Acquisition of information in an observational learning setting requires that the observer pay attention to the behavior of the model. After all, you cannot learn from someone unless you actually watch what they do. So, what makes us attend to a model?

First, we are very sensitive to the *consequences of a model's behavior*. If a model's behavior achieves a desirable goal—in other words, if it is reinforced—an observer is more likely to attend to the behavior. For example, if you see a television commercial featuring a husband receiving lavish praise and affection for sending flowers to his wife, you are likely to learn that sending flowers can result in positive consequences. This also works if an observer sees a model *escape* aversive consequences by performing a behavior (e.g., Hygge, 1978). If you see a husband avoid a fight with his wife by sending her flowers, you are likely to remember that, as well.

A second factor that influences attention is whether the *observers* are explicitly reinforced for attending to a model (e.g., Pepperberg & Sherman,

2000). In fact, teaching is often based on this principle. Teachers demonstrate desired behaviors—something as basic as reading or as complex as writing a college essay—and reinforce their students for attending to their demonstrations. The reinforcement for paying attention might be immediate, in the form of verbal praise, or delayed, in the form of good grades or gold stars. Teachers, whether in a classroom or on a football field, also use many techniques for drawing attention to their behaviors, including prompting ("Look here. See what I'm doing?") and physical modeling ("Hold the football like this, with one hand behind the other"). Teachers then provide verbal reinforcers when students respond appropriately ("Good!"). Reinforcing observer attention in these ways can greatly increase the amount of knowledge that an observer can acquire from a model.

A third determinant of whether we attend to a model depends on whether the behavior being modeled is something that *the observer can actually understand and duplicate*. For example, if a model plays "Chopsticks" on the piano, even a musically inexperienced observer may be able to pick up the tune quickly and, with appropriate help, play it herself. However, if a model plays a complex Beethoven sonata, the observer may give up all hope of ever being able to learn to play the piano. If you play computer video games, you have probably felt this as well. Watching expert players in a video arcade is a humbling experience and may keep observers from trying the games themselves. Modeling only works when observers have the skills necessary to perform the behavior.

Finally, the *personal characteristics* of a model can strongly influence our acquisition of knowledge. We are much more likely to attend to models who resemble us—if they are roughly the same age, dress similarly, and have similar interests (e.g., Bussey & Bandura, 1984; Dowling, 1984). We also attend to models whom we respect or admire. This explains the use of celebrities in advertising campaigns. The idea is that you will pay attention when you see your favorite movie/music/sports star engaging in a particular behavior (usually involving a particular product).

Of course, you can acquire information about a behavior without ever translating that information into performance. Television exposes viewers to thousands of hours of violent scenes, yet only a very small number of people ever "act out" those violent behaviors. How we move from knowledge to performance is the topic of the next section.

QUICK QUIZ

1. In observational learning, _____ conditioning results in the acquisition of vicarious emotional responses, and _____ conditioning results in translation of a model's behavior to the behavior of an observer.

2. You may watch cooking shows on television and learn how to perform complex culinary feats. Translating that knowledge into a gourmet meal is the difference between a_____ and p_____.

3. The characteristics of a model are important determinants in the acquisition of a behavior. You are more likely to learn from a model whose behavior is (reinforced/punished) _____ and who is (similar/dissimilar) _____ to you.

4. While on vacation, Alex visits a local time-share condominium complex. While there, he is paid $50 to attend a short presentation on the value of condo owner-ship. Although he may not buy a condo, Alex is likely to (attend/disregard) _____ the presentation.

Performance How does observational learning translate into behavior? As you might expect, it involves those familiar processes, reinforcement and pun-ishment (e.g., Carroll & Bandura, 1987). There are two ways that reinforce-ment and punishment work to modify our behavior in modeling situations. First, not only are we more likely to *attend* to a model's behavior if we see the model's behavior reinforced, we are also more likely to *perform* that behavior (e.g., Bandura & McDonald, 1994; Fouts & Click, 1979). For example, when a model is seen using a fragrance that appears to attract members of the opposite sex to her like flies to honey, that increases the likelihood that an observer will want that fragrance herself (assuming she desires the same effect!). If you watch a comedian telling a joke that gets a big laugh, you may want to tell that same joke to your friends. This works the opposite way as well: If a model's behavior is punished, you are *less* likely to perform that behavior. If you see a comedian tell a joke that bombs, you are not likely to repeat it when you get home. And if you see a driver zip past you, only to be caught in a speed trap, you are not likely to drive above the legal speed limit (at least for a few minutes).

The reinforcement or punishment of the model's behavior is one factor in determining whether or not an observer decides to perform that behavior. A second factor is the consequence for the *observer* of performing the modeled behavior. If you tell the same joke that got the comedian a big laugh and your friends love it, then you will continue to tell it; if you tell the joke at home and nobody laughs, then you probably will not tell it again. Thus, the reinforce-ment or punishment of the *observer's* behavior is the ultimate determinant of whether a modeled behavior continues to be performed (e.g., Weiss, Suckow, & Rakestraw, 1999).

A third factor that influences our performance of modeled behaviors is our own reinforcement history for performing such behaviors. Throughout our lives, we learn when it is appropriate to perform modeled behaviors as well as who is an appropriate model. Chances are that behavior modeled after that of teachers, coaches, and parents has been explicitly reinforced, while behavior modeled after that of less exemplary individuals has been explicitly punished ("Don't be like that awful boy next door!"). As well, performance of a modeled behavior can be differentially reinforced in different contexts. The perfor-mance of some modeled behaviors—like smoking or swearing—may be rein-forced in the presence of your close friends but strongly punished in the pres-ence of others (your parents, for example). Thus, over the years, we gradually learn, through our own unique history of reinforcement and punishment, when it is appropriate to perform behaviors that have been modeled by others.

1. Not only are you more likely to a_____ to a model's behavior if you see the model's behavior reinforced, you are also more likely to p_____ that behavior.

2. A second factor that influences whether we will perform a modeled behavior is the c_____ we receive for performing the behavior.

3. A third factor that influences our performance of a modeled behavior is our past r_____ h_____ for performing such behaviors.

4. When you repeat an off-color joke to your friends, they laugh heartily, but when you tell the same jokes to your parents, you are met with frowns. Due to dif_____ reinforcement, you soon learn to tell such jokes only when you are with your friends.

Observational Learning in Animals

While observational learning is clearly an important way that humans learn, scientists have become increasingly interested in whether *animals* can learn by observing each other. There is now extensive evidence that observational learning is an important way that animals gain information about their environment—information about which places contain food (Bailey, Howery, & Boss, 2000; Gibeault & MacDonald, 2000; MacDonald & Agnes, 1999), which potential mating partners are preferable (White & Galef, 1999), and which group members are likely to come to their aid in a fight (e.g., Cheney & Seyfarth, 1986). Much of this research has been done with rats, who have turned out to be very reliant on observational learning. For example, rats learn which foods are safe to eat by watching what *other* rats eat (e.g., Galef, 1996). They also learn how much to eat: Rats that see "demonstrator" rats eating large amounts of a specific food are much more likely to eat large amounts of that food as well (Galef, Whiskin, & Horn, 1999). If you have ever ordered a pizza after seeing a television commercial featuring people munching on a large slice of pepperoni, then you can see that this particular type of modeling holds true for humans as well as rats.

While it is clear that animals learn through observation, there may be important differences between animals and humans in one area of observational learning: imitation. Children who play "Simon Says" are practicing imitation. The idea of the game is to duplicate the movements of the person leading the game. If the leader says, "Simon says, touch your nose," you touch your nose in exactly the same manner. This seems like an easy task; in fact, human children play it all the time. However, if you have ever tried to play this game with your pet dog or cat, you know that animals do not find it such an easy task. In fact, many researchers think that animals are incapable of truly imitating the actions of others.

***True imitation* can be defined as duplicating a novel behavior (or sequence of behaviors) in order to achieve a specific goal** (e.g., Galef, 1988; Tomasello, 1996). In the early 1900s it became quite trendy to study imitation in animals (usually monkeys and apes), and several researchers proclaimed that animals could imitate in the same fashion as humans (e.g., Hobhouse, 1901). However, others (including our old friends Watson, 1908, and Thorndike, 1901) suggested that the evidence for animal imitation was very weak. Now the controversy over whether animals can imitate or not has arisen again, with a wealth of experimental studies looking at the issue.

Most of those studies look at the ability of animals, usually monkeys and apes, to solve novel problems such as obtaining food locked away in a box. In these experiments, animals watch a model perform a complex series of behaviors—perhaps getting a key, opening a lock, pulling a lever, and then using a stick to pull food out of a hole in the side of the box. The observer animal is then given a chance to try to open the box. If the animal can imitate, it should be able to duplicate the actions performed by the model in order to obtain the food. What often happens, though, is that animals do *not* copy the actions of the model exactly—they may pull the lever, for example, but not use the key, or they may turn the box over and shake it to remove the food, rather than using a stick (e.g., Call, 1999; Call & Tomasello, 1995; Nagel, Olguin, & Tomasello, 1993; Whiten, 1998). Results like these lead some researchers to suggest that true imitation is uniquely human (e.g., Tomasello, 1996).

However, there is evidence that at least some animals can learn to imitate, under some circumstances. For example, Russon and Galdikas (1993; 1995) observed orangutans living with humans in a camp designed to reintroduce the animals to the wild. They found that the orangutans regularly copied the complex actions of the humans with whom they interacted, including learning to hang hammocks, build bridges, and use boats. In one instance, an orangutan even learned how to start a fire—something that the researchers did not expect and certainly did not demonstrate on purpose!

The jury, however, is still out on the issue of whether animals can truly imitate. Many apparent examples of imitation can be explained by other, less complex, processes of observational learning. For instance, some behaviors that look like imitation can arise through a simple process called ***stimulus enhancement,*** **which involves directing an animal's attention to a particular place or object** (Thorpe, 1956). If you have ever watched a group of monkeys, you have probably seen this for yourself. Whether in captivity or in the wild, monkeys spend a lot of their time searching for food. If one monkey figures out how to extract something especially tasty, say, sap from a tree trunk, the other monkeys in the group quickly come swinging over to investigate. The other monkeys may then soon figure out how to extract the tree sap. To a casual observer, it may appear that the monkeys learned how to reach the tasty sap by imitating each other, but in fact, they were attracted to the location simply by seeing another animal eating at that spot. Eventually, using trial and error, they figured out how to extract the sap for themselves.

Stimulus enhancement works for humans, too. Imagine that you have never seen a vending machine before, but you then see someone pulling out a bag of potato chips from one. If you are hungry, this might be enough to draw your attention to the machine. You may then spend several minutes reading the instructions, figuring out where to put in your coins, and learning how to open the slot at the bottom to obtain your purchase. You have just benefited from the process of stimulus enhancement. You might have learned faster if you had been able to imitate another person—watching exactly what the person did, and then duplicating it—but stimulus enhancement is often enough to get the desired result.

1. If a young gorilla learns how to gather tasty wild ginger plants by watching his mother forage, we can say that he has demonstrated o_____ learning.

2. Copying a new behavior to achieve a particular result is (imitation/stimulus enhancement) _____; having one's attention drawn to a particular place or thing is (imitation/stimulus enhancement) _____.

3. Jessica has just purchased a new computer and is trying to learn how to use the modem to access the Internet. She asks her friend Jill to show her how to do it. Jill performs a complicated series of clicks and keystrokes, and Jessica watches closely. If Jessica then connects to the Internet on her own using the same actions as Jill, we can be confident that Jessica is able to i_____.

4. Joe has also purchased a new computer and is also trying to access the Internet. He calls up his friend Daryl and asks for help. Daryl directs Joe to a couple of applications, and Joe then plays around with the settings on his own until he figures it out. Joe has demonstrated s_____ e_____.

Language

Since you have managed to make it this far in this book, it is a pretty safe bet that you understand language, and not only *written* language, but *spoken* language and *symbolic* language—like road signs, gestures, and "body language"—as well. Language has often been used as the defining feature of human beings—the thing that makes our species unique. We use language, whether written, spoken, or symbolic, to communicate everything—meaning, motives, feelings, and beliefs. In fact, it is difficult to imagine how humans could exist without language.

If language is so basic to the human condition, you may wonder why we even discuss a topic like language in a textbook on learning. After all, many people believe that language is not learned like other behaviors, but instead that it is largely innate (e.g., Chomsky, 1988; Pinker, 1994). According to this view, humans are born with a "black box" that helps them to quickly acquire language, an ability not shared by other species. However, from an evolutionary viewpoint, humans and animals share many common features, including basic learning processes and cognitive abilities. Perhaps animals *can* use language?

There are, in fact, many examples of animal species that have evolved complex communication systems of their own. One of the best examples is vervet monkeys, small primates that live in Africa. Unfortunately for vervets, they are preyed upon by a wide variety of other species, including snakes, leopards, and eagles, each of which attacks the monkeys in a different way. This means that the monkeys have to be constantly on guard against predators. Because of that, they have evolved a communication system of alarm calls, sounds they make to warn fellow vervets that a predator has been spotted in the area. Alarm calling is not unique to vervets; many other animal species use alarm calls, too. What *is* unique is that vervets have different calls for different predator types, and the different calls elicit different behavioral responses from the rest of the group. Thus, if a vervet monkey spots an eagle flying overhead, she sounds the "eagle" alarm, and they all dive for cover in the dense underbrush of the forest. If one of the monkeys sees a leopard, a different call is given, and the monkeys climb into the nearest tall tree (Seyfarth, Cheney, & Marler, 1980). This communication system (which seems extremely logical to us as language-using humans) is very special, because it illustrates that animals can use arbitrary symbols to symbolically refer to objects that exist in the world. **This ability to use arbitrary symbols, which is called** *reference,* is one of the important features of any language (e.g., Savage-Rumbaugh, 1993). We take reference for granted, since human languages are based upon the idea that a combination of arbitrary sounds can stand for actual objects. For example, if I use the word "apple," you know what I am talking about. And when I learn a new language, like French, I have to learn that the word "pomme" means the same thing as "apple" and that they both refer to the tasty round object found on trees.

In addition to reference, there are other important characteristics that define a communication system as language (e.g., Hockett, 1960). One feature of any language is grammar, which you might remember spending tedious hours learning as a child in school. *Grammar* **is simply a set of rules that control the meaning of a string of words.** For example, if I ask you "Who is that?" you know that the appropriate response to my question is a proper name ("Joe") rather than an object ("Apple") or location ("There"). You know how to answer my question because you understand the rules—the grammar—of the English language. There are a finite number of rules for any language, and once those rules are learned, **an infinite number of expressions can be generated to express novel or creative ideas.** This feature, which is called *productivity,* is yet another important characteristic of language. Related to that is the idea of *situational freedom,* **which means that language can be used in a variety of contexts and is not fixed to a particular situation.** Accordingly, you can discuss things that are not currently present, like the fact that you went to a movie last weekend or that you will soon be going on a vacation.

1. Humans communicate through several forms of language, including wr_____, sp_____, and sym_____.

2. Vervet monkeys give different alarm calls when they see different predators. This illustrates that vervet monkey communication has an important feature of language, called r_____.

3. You are taking a fascinating psychology course in learning and behavior and are learning all sorts of new terms, such as stimulus enhancement. You find yourself using these new words at the dinner table to describe behaviors you have observed that day. You have just illustrated the s_____ fr_____ of language.

4. The fact that you know that "John likes Sarah" means something entirely different than "Sarah likes John" suggests that you know the gr_____ of the English language.

5. Your young nephew asks you to make up a story and tell it to him. Much to his delight, you are able to create a story that portrays him as a prince in a fabulous kingdom. This illustrates the pr_____ aspect of language.

Can Animals "Talk"?

Now that we know a few important characteristics of language (reference, grammar, productivity, and situational freedom), we can go back to our original question: Can animals use language? This question has intrigued people for generations. After all, who has not wished that a pet dog or cat could talk, and wondered what the pet might say if it could? The most comprehensive research programs aimed at this question have attempted to teach animals a human-like language. Unlike Dr. Doolittle, who talked *to* the animals, many researchers have tried to teach the animals to talk to *us*.

The best-known research on language learning in animals involves our closest relatives, the Great Apes, including chimpanzees, gorillas, orangutans, and bonobos (also known as pygmy chimpanzees). The Great Apes share many characteristics in common with humans, from anatomy, blood chemistry, and DNA, all the way to social behavior and cognitive skills (e.g., Begun, 1999). Since chimpanzees in particular are closely related to humans, the early experiments in this area focused on them. The first attempts to teach chimps language were based on the idea that wild chimpanzees did not use language simply because they had no motivation or encouragement to do so. This fits nicely with the *empiricist* approach described in Chapter 1. It was assumed that, with proper training, chimpanzees could learn and use human language. The first researchers, therefore, tried to train chimps to speak by raising infant chimps in a home environment reminiscent of that in which infant children are reared (e.g., Hayes & Hayes, 1951; Kellogg & Kellogg, 1933). This research received considerable public interest, and one of the chimps, named Vicki, became quite a celebrity. However, even though the chimpanzees thrived in the home environment, they never learned to talk. In fact, Vicki only learned to produce four words: cup, up, mama, and papa. Watching old films of Vicki, it is obvious that "speaking" is not something that chimps do naturally. Vicki had to tortuously manipulate her mouth with her hand in order to produce those four short words.

Sign Language Experiments

Language experiments with chimpanzees eventually revealed that, while chimps lacked the vocal apparatus to produce comprehensible speech, they might be capable of producing and understanding other forms of language. Thus, the next approach was to teach chimpanzees a different kind of language, one that relied on gestures instead of spoken words. In the wild, chimpanzees do communicate with each other using gestures—pointing, arm waving, and so on—so it seemed logical to assume that they might be able to learn a language that relied on hand gestures, like American Sign Language (ASL). Sign languages have been used by deaf people for many years, and there are many different such languages. ASL has existed for over 100 years and is commonly used in North America. Contrary to popular belief, sign languages are not simply "finger spelling" of English words. They are complex, rich languages that share all the important features of any language, such as reference and grammar. Each signed "word" can convey different meanings, depending on the inflection, and some words can represent entire phrases. Sign languages are also learned in the same way that spoken languages are learned, through modeling, correction by adults, and learning the rules of grammar.

Experimenters set out to use ASL, which could be readily learned by chimpanzees, in a natural home environment to simulate the way human children learn language. This meant that the chimps were not to be taught by rote memorization or language drills, but in day-to-day activities in a family group. These studies were called *cross-fostering* experiments, because the chimpanzees were raised in human foster homes. The prospect of raising chimps like humans was a daunting one. The researchers had to devote years of their lives to the project, since language acquisition is a long-term effort. The researchers also had to become fluent in ASL and to only use signs, not spoken English, in the presence of their foster "children." The first ASL cross-fostering study was named Project Washoe, after Washoe County in Reno, Nevada. An infant chimp, named Washoe, was raised by two scientists, Beatrix and Allen Gardner (e.g., Gardner & Gardner, 1969). Since Washoe, other chimps have been cross-fostered, to replicate the findings of Project Washoe (and to give Washoe other chimps to "talk" to) (Gardner, Gardner, & Van Cantfort, 1989).

The researchers discovered that the best way to teach apes sign language is to use modeling—demonstrating the sign while performing the action that the sign refers to, such as signing "open" while opening a door. They also used a technique called molding, which involves placing the ape's hands in the correct signing position and associating that position with the object being "talked" about. Using these techniques, most ASL-trained chimps ended up with vocabularies of well over 100 signs. Both these procedures worked better than standard operant conditioning, which paired food reward with correct signing. The researchers found that rewarding each sign with food resulted in very reflexive behavior that was oriented to the food reward. Interestingly, this is similar to the process of undermining intrinsic motivation through extrinsic rewards, which was briefly discussed in Chapter 6. Food rewards seemed to focus the chimps on producing the signs, rather than communicating with the researchers. In any case, Washoe (and other language-trained chimpanzees) often signed spontaneously, even when she was alone, which suggests that the signing behavior was rewarding in and of itself.

Strictly controlled tests of language use were performed with many of the chimpanzees trained in sign language (e.g., Fouts, 1973). All the chimps seemed to pass the test of *reference*, since they could all use the arbitrary ASL signals to refer to objects and could easily categorize novel objects using signs. For example, if Washoe was shown a photo of a kitten that she had never seen before, she immediately applied the (correct) sign for "cat." Whether the ASL-trained chimps exhibited the other features of language—grammar, productivity, and situational freedom—is much less clear. There is some evidence that Washoe did follow the grammatical rules of ASL. She responded to questions such as "What is that?" with, for example, "That apple" rather than simply "Apple." (Gardner & Gardner, 1975). However, there is only anecdotal evidence that Washoe and other language-trained chimps used signs in novel contexts or produced novel signs for unfamiliar objects. Further, ASL is not a rigid language. The syntax (or ordering of words) is relatively loose, so ASL speakers are not required to follow strict sequences of words. It is therefore extremely difficult to systematically assess chimpanzees' use of language when the language is a fluid, gestural language like ASL.

QUICK QUIZ

1. Our closest relatives are chimpanzees, orangutans, and gorillas, known as the G_____ A_____.

2. Early attempts to teach chimpanzees to speak failed miserably, probably because chimps (have/do not have)_____ the v_____ apparatus to produce speech.

3. Studies by the Gardners and others looked at whether chimpanzees could learn a symbolic, gestural language called A_____ S_____ L_____.

4. In c_____-f_____ experiments, apes are raised in human environments.

5. W_____ was the first chimpanzee trained in ASL.

6. Researchers found that mod_____ was the easiest way to teach sign language to the chimpanzees. They also found mol_____ to be an effective method.

7. On the other hand, rewarding correct signs with f_____ tended to produce ref_____-type behavior that was oriented more toward producing signs than communicating with the researchers.

8. Almost all apes that have been trained in ASL can demonstrate r_____, the ability to associate particular signs with particular objects or actions.

Artificial Language Experiments

To get around the difficulties posed by the sign language cross-fostering studies, the next series of experiments designed to determine whether animals could use language were conducted in laboratory situations, with artificially constructed languages. These languages did not consist of spoken words or physical gestures; rather, they consisted of visual symbols, either plastic tokens placed on a magnetic board (Premack, 1971; 1976) or symbols on a computer keyboard (Rumbaugh, 1977; Savage-Rumbaugh, McDonald, Sevcik, Hopkins, & Rubert, 1986). The chimps that participated in these experiments were not raised in human-like environments and did not interact with their caretakers in the same way that Washoe and the other ASL-trained chimps did. They lived in laboratories, and they conversed via the artificial language. A typical sentence in one of these languages—called "Yerkish" after the Yerkes Primate Research Center where it was created—is ? WHAT NAME OF THIS. You may notice that Yerkish grammar is *not* the same as English grammar. The question mark is placed at the beginning of the sentence and there are words missing. Nonetheless, it has its own grammar and is a language. The chimps that learned Yerkish could respond to questions and also ask for objects (e.g., PLEASE MACHINE GIVE BANANA). While this type of language may seem restricted compared to ASL—and indeed is, with much smaller vocabularies, and very rigid grammatical rules—such languages were constructed that way purposefully. The idea was to discover, once and for all, whether chimps could learn and use all the basic features of language. Also, the artificial and highly controlled surroundings made systematic assessment relatively easy. Everything the chimps "said" was displayed and recorded by a computer, so the way the chimps were using language was much clearer than in the ASL studies, which could often be interpreted differently by different observers.

Unfortunately, the artificial language experiments did not give the unequivocal answers that scientists were hoping for. The chimps in these experiments, like the ones in the ASL studies, did appear to use symbols to represent or categorize objects, so they seemed to have the ability to *reference* objects. However, whether the chimps had mastered the artificial *grammar* was less clear. Most of the chimps' sentences were of the form PLEASE MACHINE GIVE "X" (where "X" was usually a preferred food item, like apples, bananas, or M&M candies). It can be argued that learning to produce a sequence of symbols like PLEASE MACHINE GIVE X is not the same as learning the underlying rules governing language production. In fact, pigeons can be readily trained to peck a sequence of four symbols to receive food reward (Terrace, 1985), and very few people would say that those pigeons had learned language. It is clear, though, that the chimps in the artificial language experiments did not have much to talk about except obtaining food, so perhaps this type of study was not a fair test of their language ability after all.

Taking the results of the cross-fostering ASL studies and the artificial language experiments together, it is difficult to draw a firm conclusion. Chimpanzees definitely can learn to use symbols to refer to objects, but they just as definitely do not use those symbols in the same way that adult humans do (Terrace, 1979; Terrace, Petitio, Sanders, & Bever, 1979). But perhaps other animal species might.

1. Studies of animals' ability to use symbolic languages created by researchers in a laboratory setting are known as (artificial/cross-fostering) _____ language experiments.

2. These studies allowed researchers to systematically assess the language abilities of chimpanzees in a (more/less) _____ controlled setting than was the case with the sign language cross-fostering studies.

3. One of the first artificial languages created was called "Yer_____."

4. Results of the artificial language experiments strongly suggest that many of the chimpanzees mastered (reference/grammar) _____, but there is less evidence that they mastered (reference/grammar) _____.

Although the language studies with chimpanzees received the most public attention, other researchers have focused on training other species—ranging from parrots (Pepperberg, 1999) to gorillas (Patterson & Linden, 1981) to dolphins (Herman, Pack, & Morrel-Samuels, 1993)—to use language. That list of species might seem completely random to you, but in fact, animals that have been language-trained share some important features. First, they have relatively large, complex brains, which makes it likely that they have the cognitive capacity to represent concepts. Second, they are usually species that are extremely social. Social species, such as humans, generally evolve more complicated communication abilities simply because they have more neighbors to "talk" to and about. Dolphins are a good example of that, because they have both large brains and a social system in which they regularly interact with members of their own and other species. In fact, although dolphins are far removed from primates in an evolutionary sense, they are often thought of as similar to primates in terms of cognitive abilities. (The alleged "mystical" qualities of dolphin-human interactions that have been reported also added to their cachet as potential language users.)

For almost 20 years, Louis Herman and his colleagues have been training dolphins to use a symbolic language (Roitblat, Herman, & Nachtigall, 1993). These researchers have worked with two dolphins, each trained with a different artificial language. One dolphin, called Akeakamai, has learned a gestural language, similar to ASL. The other dolphin, called Phoenix, has learned a computer-generated language of acoustic signals, similar to Yerkish. Both dolphins "work" on their language training in large tanks at the University of Hawaii (nice work if you can get it!). Although the languages are limited to describing things that the dolphins can see and do underwater, it is clear that the animals have learned a vocabulary of symbols—like ball, pipe, surfboard, spit, fetch, bottom, and so on—that *refer* to objects and actions (Herman & Forestell, 1985; Shyan & Herman, 1987). It is also clear that the dolphins understand rudimentary *grammatical* rules. For example, when given a sentence like FRISBEE FETCH BASKET, Phoenix knows to take the Frisbee and put it in the basket. When the sentence is given in the opposite order—BASKET FETCH FRISBEE—she takes the basket to the Frisbee. Both dolphins also show very accurate performance on novel sentences, using new "words" (e.g., Herman, Kuczaj, & Holder, 1993; Herman, Morrel-Samuels, & Pack, 1990). Interestingly, California sea lions, another sea mammal species, have also learned symbolic gestures and can respond accurately to three-word sentences like those used with the dolphins (Schusterman & Gisiner, 1988).

So, back to our original question: Can animals use language? As you now know, this is not a simple question, and it certainly does not have a simple answer. It depends on how you define language, and whom you ask. Some animal species are clearly capable of learning some aspects of language and of using symbols in a variety of situations. Teaching animals to use language has also expanded the types of questions researchers are asking about the way animals think. Although we may never be able to sit down with a chimpanzee and have a deep discussion about the meaning of life, we have been able to study complex phenomena, like concept discrimination and categorization (Savage-Rumbaugh, Rumbaugh, Smith, & Lawson, 1980), and logical reasoning (Premack & Woodruff, 1978), all of which are very difficult to study without "words" of some kind.

1. Dolphins, gorillas, and parrots are all (social/solitary) _____ species that have relatively (complex/simple) _____ brains, which makes them good candidates for studying language acquisition.

2. Dolphins have been taught to communicate acoustically as well as gesturally, evidence that they may be able to use sym_____ language.

3. Results of the dolphin language experiments suggest that the dolphins mastered the (reference/productivity) _____ aspect of language.

4. BALL FETCH BASKET means the opposite of BASKET FETCH BALL to language-trained dolphins. This suggests that, unlike many of the language-trained chimps, dolphins can understand the rules of a language, or gr_____.

QUICK QUIZ

Rule-Governed Behavior

Although determining whether animals are capable of using language is a complex issue, it is obvious that humans are capable of using language. It is also obvious that our use of language greatly enhances our ability to interact with one another and to adapt to the world around us. A prime example of this is the manner in which language ability allows us to influence each other through the presentation of rules.

And Furthermore

Talking to the Animals

What is it like to "talk" to animals that have been trained to use sign language? Chantek, a famous language-trained orangutan, has worked with researcher Lyn Miles for many years (Miles, 1990, 1994, 1999). Lyn Miles has trained Chantek, with a combination of modeling and explicit reinforcement, to use hundreds of ASL signs. Chantek signs all day long—in fact, he is pretty chatty! On a recent visit, I (Suzanne MacDonald) watched delightedly as Chantek talked about what he wanted for lunch (yogurt, which he eats with a spoon). Eventually, Chantek asked Lyn who I was. She made up a new ASL sign for my name, which Chantek promptly used, inviting me to put a jigsaw puzzle together with him. Although Chantek does not discuss the meaning of life—focusing instead on more practical matters, like food—it is an amazing experience to see him forming his huge, hairy hands into the familiar ASL signs, communicating his moods and desires.

The ultimate "ape communicator," though, has to be Kanzi, who is a bonobo (a species also known as a pygmy chimpanzee). Kanzi lives and works with Sue Savage-Rumbaugh at a special research facility outside of Atlanta (for a detailed description, see Savage-Rumbaugh & Lewin, 1994; Savage-Rumbaugh, Shanker, & Taylor, 1998). Kanzi understands spoken English, but since he cannot actually produce speech, he uses a special computer keyboard to "talk." The various keys represent hundreds of different concepts, ranging from simple food items like blueberries to complex ideas like love. If you are not yet convinced that observational learning works, you will be less skeptical when you hear that Kanzi learned this very sophisticated symbolic language as an infant, simply by watching his mother while she was

Definitions and Characteristics

A *rule* can be defined as a verbal description of a contingency. In other words, it is a statement that tells us that in a certain setting, if we perform a certain behavior, then a certain consequence will follow. Thus, "If you drive through a red light, you will get a ticket"; "If you study hard throughout the semester, you will get a good grade"; and "If you are pleasant to others, they will be pleasant to you" are all examples of rules. Likewise, the course syllabus you receive at the start of a course is a set of rules about what you need to do in order to pass the course, and a guidebook to Paris is a set of rules about how best to find and enjoy the sites of Paris. **Behavior that has been generated through exposure to such rules,** such as doing what the course outline tells you to do or touring Paris in the manner suggested by the guidebook, **is therefore known as *rule-governed behavior*** (Skinner, 1969).

In its purest form, a rule is simply a statement about a contingency; it does not say anything about how we should respond with respect to that contingency. If it does says something about how we should respond, then it can also be called an *instruction* (Mallott, Mallott, & Trojan, 2000). Thus, "If you drive through a red light, you will get a ticket" is simply a rule, while "Don't drive through a red light, or you will get a ticket" (or "Don't drive through a

being trained to use the keyboard. Kanzi is also one chimp for whom there is strong evidence of understanding the rules of grammar.

Kanzi with his trainer, Sue Savage-Rumbaugh.

When I met Kanzi I was very impressed by his obvious grasp of the computer symbols and by his strong desire to communicate with his human visitors. When I left Kanzi for the day, I asked him what he would like me to bring him the next day when I returned. Using his keyboard, he quickly replied, "celery." Naturally, I brought celery with me the next morning. However, I did not go to visit Kanzi right away, stopping off in the lab first to work on a computer program. Soon after, the phone rang in the lab; it was Kanzi's keeper, calling to let me know that Kanzi had been using his keyboard to insist that she call me and ask where his celery was! The keeper, who had not been there the day before, was very apologetic, because she had no idea what Kanzi was "talking" about. Needless to say, I brought Kanzi his celery. And I will never forget the day I got a phone call from an ape.

red light!" in which case the consequence is implied) is an instruction. For the purposes of this discussion, however, we will use the terms rule and instruction interchangeably, given that many of the rules that concern us are offered in the form of instructions. (See Baldwin & Baldwin, 1998, for a further discussion of different types of rules.)

Rules (or instructions) are extremely useful for rapidly establishing appropriate patterns of behavior. As with observational learning, we can learn how to behave effectively in a certain setting prior to any direct experience with the contingencies operating in that setting. We do not have to repeatedly drive through red lights to find out what happens if we do, and we do not have to fail a course repeatedly to figure out how to pass the course. We simply have to follow the rules that we have been given in order to behave effectively in those settings.

To illustrate the effectiveness of using rules to modify behavior, consider the task of teaching a rat to press a lever for food whenever it hears a tone. First, you have to shape the rat to press the lever by reinforcing closer and closer approximations to lever pressing. Then, once lever pressing is well established, you reinforce lever presses that occur only in the presence of a tone and not those that occur in the absence of the tone. Eventually, the rat learns to press the lever only when the tone is sounding. Now consider the task of teaching a person to press a button to earn money whenever a light is turned on (a common task in operant conditioning experiments with humans). All you have to do is sit the person down in front of the panel and provide the following instructions: "Whenever the light is on, you can earn money by pressing this button." Instantly, you have a button-pushing, money-earning human on your hands. What requires several hours of training with a rat requires only a few seconds of instruction with a verbally proficient human.

Learning to follow rules is so beneficial and important that parents spend considerable time training this ability in young children. When Billie, for example, complies with his mother's request to pick up his toys, his mother praises him for doing so. Billie soon learns that people are pleased when he complies with their instructions, and he is therefore more likely to comply in the future. Billie later learns that following instructions can also be useful for completing a task. When, for example, he ignores the instructions that accompany a model airplane kit, he makes a complete mess of things; when he follows the instructions, he produces a great-looking model. Billie therefore learns that good things happen when he follows instructions, as a result of which he acquires a generalized tendency to follow instructions. Of course, if bad things had happened when Billie followed instructions, or if good things happened when he did not follow instructions, he might have instead acquired a generalized tendency not to follow instructions and to be noncompliant. Thus, the extent to which we follow instructions—as well as the specific instructions we choose to follow—is largely dependent on the consequences we have received for following instructions (Baldwin & Baldwin, 1998).

1. A rule (or _____) can be defined as a v_____
d_____ of a c_____.

2. Behavior that is generated through exposure to rules is known as r_____-
g_____ behavior.

3. A rule that includes a statement about how you should behave with respect to a contingency is an i_____.

4. Rules are extremely useful in that they allow us to learn about appropriate patterns of behavior in a setting (with/without) _____ direct exposure to the contingencies operating in that setting.

5. Children learn to follow instructions because they are often (praised/ignored) _____ for following instructions. As well, they learn that following instructions is usually a (good/poor) _____ way to actually accomplish a task.

6. The result is that most children acquire a (generalized/localized) _____ tendency to follow instructions.

7. In general, the extent to which we follow instructions—as well as the specific instructions we choose to follow—is largely dependent on the c_____ we have received for following instructions.

Some Disadvantages of Rule-Governed Behavior

As you can see, rules can be very useful. Unfortunately, they also have their drawbacks. One drawback is that rule-governed behavior is often less efficient than behavior that has been directly shaped by the natural contingencies. Take, for example, the task of playing golf. No matter how many books you read on how to play golf, you will undoubtedly be a poor golfer unless you devote considerable time to actually playing and practicing the game. Instructions can provide us with only a rudimentary knowledge of how to play, and while this may be useful for getting started or for modifying certain aspects of an established game, nothing can replace the actual experience of hitting a golf ball and seeing where it goes (Baldwin & Baldwin, 1998).

A second drawback of rule-governed behavior is that such behavior is sometimes surprisingly insensitive to the actual contingencies of reinforcement operating in a particular setting. This phenomenon has been demonstrated experimentally. For example, when human participants are told that they can earn money by pressing a button, they will indeed begin pressing the button. Their button pressing may not, however, be very efficient given the schedule of reinforcement that is in effect. For instance, on an FI schedule of reinforcement, human subjects often do not display the scalloped pattern of responding that is typical of FI performance in rats and pigeons. Some subjects, for example, respond rapidly throughout the interval, as though continuous, rapid responding is necessary to produce the reinforcer (Lowe, 1979). Focusing only upon the rule they have been given—"Push the button to earn money"—some subjects never slow down enough to realize that such a high rate of response is unnecessary.[1] (See also Bentall, Lowe, & Beasty, 1985; Lowe, Beasty, & Bentall, 1983).

Likewise, a person who is taught to swing a golf club a certain way may persist with that swing for several years despite the fact that it is inappropriate for her build and level of flexibility. Locked into the notion that she must follow the instructions she has been given, her golf game may never evolve to a more effective level. In similar fashion, a veteran businessman who has acquired a set of rules about how best to conduct business may have difficulty modifying his business practices to compete effectively in the new global economy. As the world of business changes, his old rules, highly effective in the old economy, are now an impediment. Thus, although rules are often extremely

---

[1] The first author of this text directly experienced this phenomenon when, as a graduate student, he was conducting just such a button-pushing study. Because each session in the study lasted a couple of hours (and because the task was excruciatingly boring), subjects were given 10-minute breaks at regular intervals throughout each session. One subject, however, began spending almost all of her breaks in the washroom. Asked if she was okay, she explained that she was going to the washroom to run her arm under cold water to reduce the pain. As it turns out, having been told that pushing buttons would produce money, she assumed that faster button pushing produced more money. She therefore pushed the button at a blistering pace throughout each session, so much so that her arm muscles had begun to cramp. In fact, the money was being delivered on various VI schedules of reinforcement, and she could have earned the full amount each session with a quite leisurely rate of response.

FIGURE 12.2   Although golf lessons are a great way to get started in the game, the rules learned are, at best, general pointers that must then be modified through the actual experience of hitting the ball and seeing where it goes.

beneficial, we do well to recognize that they have their limitations and often require modification according to the particular circumstances in which we find ourselves.

QUICK QUIZ

1. One problem with rule-governed behavior is that it is often (less/more) _____ efficient than behavior that has been shaped by the natural c_____.

2. A second problem with rule-governed behavior is that such behavior is sometimes surprisingly i_____ to the actual contingencies of reinforcement in a particular setting.

3. As an example of the above, experimental subjects who are told to press a button to earn money sometimes display a (scalloped pattern/high rate) _____ _____ of responding on an FI schedule of reinforcement, which is (the same as/different from) _____ the type of responding typically shown on such schedules by animals.

ADVICE FOR THE LOVELORN

Dear Dr. Dee,

My boyfriend and I very much enjoy reading your columns. Unfortunately, Steve (my boyfriend) has begun using the ideas in these columns to analyze each and every aspect of our relationship. I know he means well, but it is starting to drive me nuts. Furthermore, I think his conclusions about our relationship are usually dead wrong. What is your opinion on this?

Going Nutty

Dear Going,

At the start of this book, we explicitly warned against taking these columns too seriously. For one thing, the advice given is usually quite speculative; it is not grounded in scientific research, nor is it based on a careful assessment of the relationship being discussed (which, in any case, is just a fictional relationship). Thus, our purpose in presenting these columns was simply to give students a sense of the *potential* ways in which behavioral principles *might* be applicable to some important aspects of human behavior.

It is also important to recognize that each relationship is unique, meaning that there is no guarantee that advice that is appropriate for one relationship is relevant for another relationship. In fact, you can think of such advice as a rule for how to improve your relationship, with the act of following that advice being a form of rule-governed behavior. As we discuss in this chapter, such rules may not accurately reflect the actual contingencies that are in effect, and the person following the rule may become insensitive to the actual contingencies. This may be what has happened in your boyfriend's case. He seems to have concluded that the advice given in these columns is relevant to your own situation, which it might not be.

Tell him to lighten up a bit, pay less attention to what is being said in these advice columns (or, for that matter, anyone else's advice column), and pay more attention to what is going on in your relationship. And if you do need advice, there is often nothing better than some plain old common sense from one's close friends and relatives. After all, these people usually have a better knowledge of the type of person you are and the actual contingencies surrounding your relationship than any advice columnist could ever have.

Behaviorally yours,

Dr. Dee

Personal Rules in Self-Regulation

Although rules have their drawbacks, their advantages greatly outweigh their disadvantages. For this reason, we use rules not only to influence the behavior of others, but also to influence our own behavior. In other words, we often give ourselves instructions as to how we should behave: "I should study in the library rather than at home, because it is much quieter in the library"; "I should work out each day if I want to remain fit and healthy"; "If I am polite to others, they will be polite to me." Such statements can be called *personal rules* (or *self-instructions*), **which can be defined as verbal descriptions of contingencies that we present to ourselves in order to influence our behavior** (Ainslie, 1992).

The use of personal rules to regulate behavior is essentially a form of "Say-Do correspondence." *Say-Do correspondence* **occurs when there is a close match between what we say we are going to do and what we actually do at a later point in time.** If I say that I will go running at 4:00 in the afternoon and then actually go running at that time, my statement of what I intend to do matches the actual behavior that I later perform. As with rule-governed behavior in general, parents play a critical role in the development of this correspondence. If Billie promises that he will put his toys away when he is finished playing with them, and later he does put his toys away, his parents are quite pleased and praise him for carrying through on his promise. But when he does not carry through on his promise, they are annoyed. To the extent that Billie's parents apply these consequences consistently, Billie will likely grow up to display a strong level of Say-Do correspondence. He will become known as a reliable individual who can be trusted to carry through on his promises to others. Not only that, he may concurrently develop an ability to carry through on his promises to himself, which means that he will be able to use such promises as personal rules to guide his own behavior (Guevremont, Osnes, & Stokes, 1986).

Although personal rules can be useful in helping us manage our behavior, not all personal rules are equally effective. Ainslie (1986), for example, has proposed that personal rules are most effective when they establish a "bright boundary" between acceptable and unacceptable patterns of behavior. A bright boundary is a strategic concept that holds that military leaders should make use of clearly specified landmarks, such as rivers, streams, or roads, to mark the limits of their territory. Such boundaries are easier to defend, since they allow one to clearly determine when the enemy has intruded on one's territory. Similarly, in trying to carry through on rules for our own behavior, we are more likely to succeed when the rule specifically sets out the conditions under which it has been obeyed or violated. For example, the statement "I will study today" is so vaguely worded that we are at high risk for delaying the act of studying until it is too late to study. The point at which the rule has been violated is not easily determined until we have, in a sense, been overrun and have lost the battle. By contrast, the statement "I will study from 7:00 P.M. to 9:00 P.M. this evening" is so specific that any violation of the rule—it is now 7:10 P.M. and we are still watching television—will be readily apparent.

The importance of clear, specific rules has been empirically supported. For example, Gollwitzer and Brandstätter (1997) asked college students to name two projects they intended to complete during Christmas break, one of which would be easy to accomplish (e.g., go skating) and the other of which would be difficult to accomplish (e.g., complete an English assignment). Students were also asked if they had made a decision about when and where the activity would be carried out. Following the Christmas break, the same students were asked if they had completed the project. For activities that were easy to implement, about 80% of the students said that they had indeed completed them. With such easy projects, it seemed to make little difference if the students had also decided upon a time and place for implementing them. For difficult projects, however, students who had decided when and where their project would be carried out were significantly more likely to have completed it compared to those who had not made such a decision. Similarly, Sheeran and Orbell (1999) found that participants who specified when and where they would take a vitamin supplement were significantly more consistent in taking the supplement than those who merely intended to take the supplement. (See Gollwitzer, 1999, for a review of such research.)

Thus, the act of specifying when, where, and how a goal is to be accomplished can significantly affect the probability of accomplishing that goal. Gollwitzer (1999) refers to such when-where-and-how statements as *implementation intentions*. However, to be more consistent with Ainslie's (1992) terminology, they can also be called ***personal process rules,*** insofar as they are **personal rules that indicate the specific process by which a task is to be accomplished.** And a possible reason why such rules are effective is that they establish a bright boundary between actions that conform to the rule and those that do not. (See also Gollwitzer, 1999.)

1. A _____ rule is a description of a contingency that we verbalize to ourselves in order to influence our own behavior.

2. A close match between what we say we are going to do and what we actually do at a later point in time is called a _____-_____ c_____.

3. People who have been trained to display a high level of _____-_____ correspondence can more effectively use personal rules (or self-instructions) to influence their behavior.

4. P_____ p_____ rules indicate the specific process by which a task is to be carried out. The formulation of such rules tends to (increase/decrease) _____ the likelihood that the task will be accomplished. Such rules have also been called im_____ in_____.

QUICK QUIZ

And Furthermore

Say-Do Correspondence and Willpower

As noted in the preceding section, the use of personal rules to regulate one's behavior represents a form of Say-Do correspondence. Moreover, to the extent that one displays a strong level of Say-Do correspondence, such personal rules might even function as a type of *commitment* response. As you may recall from Chapter 10, a commitment response is any response made at an early point in time that so reduces the value of a smaller sooner reward that it no longer serves as a temptation when it becomes imminent. One is therefore able to ignore the temptation and carry on working toward a larger later reward. Thus, handing your sister $10 with the understanding that she will only return it if you have completed a certain amount of studying that evening will reduce the value of any non-study activity to a level where you will in fact be quite likely to study (because any activity that interferes with studying will be associated with the loss of $10). Perhaps, however, people who display a very strong level of Say-Do correspondence do not require such artificial consequences to control their behavior; perhaps for them the mere act of promising to do something is by itself a sufficient form of commitment.

To what extent can self-promises serve as a strong form of commitment? Consider the following passage from a letter quoted by William James (1907) in his classic article, "The Energies of Men":

> My device [Prince Pueckler-Muskau writes to his wife] is this: I give my word of honour most solemnly to myself to do or to leave undone this or that. I am of course extremely cautious in the use of this expedient, but when once the word is given, even though I afterwards think I have been precipitate or mistaken, I hold it to be perfectly irrevocable, whatever inconveniences I foresee likely to result. If I were capable of breaking my word after such mature consideration, I should lose all respect for myself—and what man of sense would not prefer death to such an alternative? (p. 16)

The prince describes how, once he has vowed to perform or not perform an activity, he feels duty-bound to carry out this vow. As a result, he is able to use this device to accomplish tasks that would otherwise be very difficult. He is also extremely careful in using this device, recognizing that its potency lies in the fact that he *always* keeps his word in such matters. In other words, a major consequence that motivates adherence to his verbal commitments is that he always keeps these commitments, and to the extent that he does so, they will remain a valuable tool (see also Ainslie, 1992). Note too how the prince pronounces these verbal commitments in a "most solemn" manner, thereby establishing a *bright boundary* between statements of intention that must be fulfilled ("I swear most solemnly that I shall complete this project by the weekend") and more ordinary statements of intention, which do not represent a commitment ("I should really try to complete this project by the weekend").

Another example of the power of verbal commitments can be found in the life of Mohandas K. (Mahatma) Gandhi, the famous statesman who led India to independence and whose philosophy of passive resistance strongly influenced Martin Luther King. Gandhi's

(1927/1957) autobiography reveals that he made frequent use of verbal commitments to control his behavior and that the effectiveness of these commitments lay partly in the fact that breaking a commitment produced within him a tremendous feeling of guilt. At one point, for example, he was severely ill and was strongly urged by his doctors to drink milk (as a needed source of protein). As a committed vegetarian, he refused, maintaining that he would rather die than break his vow never to eat animals products. Only when his advisors pointed out to him that he had probably been thinking of cow's milk when he made his vow and not goat's milk did he acquiesce and drink goat's milk. He recovered from his illness but nevertheless felt considerable guilt over violating the spirit, if not the precise intention, of the vow he had made.

The great Indian statesman Mahatma Gandhi displayed a considerable degree of "Say-Do correspondence" during his illustrious life.

The strength of Gandhi's verbal commitments is also illustrated by the effect of his vow to remain sexually abstinent (despite being married). Prior to making the vow—and believing that it should be possible to practice abstinence without a vow—he had found the task extremely difficult. Making the vow, however, immediately resolved these difficulties. As he later wrote:

> As I look back on the twenty years of the vow, I am filled with pleasure and wonderment. The more or less successful practice of self-control had been going on since 1901. But the freedom and joy that came to me after taking the vow had never been experienced before 1906. Before the vow I had been open to being overcome by temptation at any moment. Now the vow was a sure shield against temptation. (Gandhi, 1927/1957, p. 208)

Gandhi's description indicates that the vow was such a strong form of commitment that it essentially eliminated the temptation to engage in sexual intercourse, thereby removing any sense of conflict.

You may remember how, in our discussion of self-control in Chapter 10, we rejected the concept of willpower as useful, arguing instead that it was often no more than a descriptive term for the fact that a person had in fact been able to resist a temptation. Perhaps, however, the concept of willpower is useful if what it refers to is an individual's ability to make use of a verbal commitment—derived in turn from a history of training in strong Say-Do correspondence—to exert control over his or her behavior. In this sense, some individuals may indeed have a considerable amount of willpower. Thus, as often happens when we examine traditional concepts from a behavioral perspective, the examination results not so much in a rejection of the concept, but in a new and possibly useful way of understanding it.

Finally, are there lessons in this for those of us who wish that we could more often carry through on our own verbal commitments? Although we may not be capable of acquiring

(continued)

And Furthermore (continued)

the same ability as a Gandhi (nor perhaps would many of us even desire such an ability), most of us would probably agree that we are too often lacking in our level of Say-Do correspondence. In this regard, we might do well to close with yet another passage from William James (1890/1983), who wrote often on the concept of will (bracketed comments are ours):

> As a final practical maxim, relative to these habits of the will, we may, then, offer something like this: *Keep the faculty of effort alive in you by a little gratuitous effort every day.* That is, be systematically ascetic or heroic in little unnecessary points, do every day or two something for no other reason than that you would rather not do it [*and because you promised yourself you would do it*], so that when the hour of dire need draws nigh, it may find you not unnerved and untrained to stand the test. Asceticism of this sort is like the insurance which a man pays on his house and goods. The tax does him no good at the time, and possibly may never bring him a return. But if the fire *does* come, his having paid it will be his salvation from ruin. So with the man who has daily inured himself to habits of concentrated attention, energetic volition, and self-denial in unnecessary things. He will stand like a tower when everything rocks around him, and when his softer fellow-mortals are winnowed like chaff in the blast. (p. 130; see also Barrett, 1931, and Assagioli, 1974)

SUMMARY

In observational learning, an observer acquires information by watching a behavior performed by a model. In the classical conditioning aspect of observational learning, the emotional cues exhibited by a model serve as CSs that elicit conditioned responses, called vicarious emotional responses, in an observer. The operant conditioning aspect of observational learning concerns the manner in which a model's behavior is translated into the behavior of an observer. First, the observer must acquire information from the model. Such acquisition depends on the consequences of the model's behavior, the personal characteristics of the model, whether the observer is capable of understanding and duplicating the modeled behavior, and whether the observer is explicitly reinforced for attending to the modeled behavior. Translating acquired knowledge into performance in turn depends on whether the observer's performance of the behavior is reinforced or punished.

Animals also learn by observation. However, unlike humans, many animal species appear to be unable to truly imitate the actions of another individual. Apparent examples of imitation can often be explained as examples of stimulus enhancement, which involves directing an animal's attention to a particular place or object, thereby making it more likely that the animal will approach that place or object.

Defining characteristics of language include reference, grammar, situational freedom, and productivity. Research programs have attempted to teach animals, mostly chimpanzees, a human-like language. The first studies in this area attempted, unsuccessfully, to teach chimpanzees to speak. Later studies focused on teaching them to use gestural (sign) language. The chimps learned to use dozens of signs, although systematic assessment of their abilities was difficult. To obtain more experimental control, later studies were conducted in laboratory situations with artificially constructed languages. The chimpanzees participating in these experiments readily used the symbols to refer to food items and behaviors, but evidence of grammatical ability was again less clear. Other species, most notably dolphins, have also demonstrated that they can learn that symbols can be used to represent and categorize objects and actions. They have also shown some evidence of grammatical ability.

A rule is a verbal description of a contingency, while behavior that is generated as a result of such rules is known as rule-governed behavior. A rule that also includes information about how we should behave in a setting is an instruction. Rules are tremendously adaptive in that they allow us to learn about contingencies without having to directly experience those contingencies. Parents therefore spend considerable effort training their children to follow rules. Children learn that following rules not only leads to praise but also facilitates accomplishing a task.

Rules nevertheless have their drawbacks. First, rule-governed behavior is often less efficient than behavior that has been shaped by actual contingencies. Second, rule-governed behavior is sometimes surprisingly insensitive to the contingencies.

A personal rule (or self-instruction) is a description of a contingency that we verbalize to ourselves in order to influence our own behavior. The use of personal rules to regulate behavior is dependent upon training in Say-Do correspondence, which occurs when there is a close match between what we say we are going to do and what we actually do at a later time. Personal rules tend to be most effective when they are stated in such a way that there is a clear distinction (a bright boundary) between when the rule has been followed and when it has not. In support of this, researchers have shown that specifying personal process rules (or implementation intentions) that indicate the specific manner in which a project is to be carried out increases the likelihood that the project will be accomplished.

STUDY QUESTIONS

1. Define observational learning.
2. Give an example of observational learning. Be sure to clearly differentiate the model from the observer.
3. Define vicarious emotional responses.
4. Diagram how a smile can become a conditioned stimulus for pleasant emotions.
5. Distinguish the roles of classical and operant conditioning in observational learning.

6. List three important features that determine whether an observer will attend to a model's behavior.
7. List three ways in which acquisition of information through observational learning translates into performance of the behavior.
8. Describe two examples of animals learning by observation.
9. Define true imitation. Describe evidence that some animals are capable of imitation.
10. Define stimulus enhancement. How does it differ from true imitation?
11. Use examples to illustrate the difference between stimulus enhancement and true imitation.
12. List four main features of language and provide an example of each.
13. Distinguish between ASL and artificial language studies. What was the reasoning behind each type of study?
14. Provide at least two examples of evidence supporting the notion that animals can use rudimentary language.
15. Define the terms rule and rule-governed behavior. What is the distinction between a pure rule and an instruction?
16. Describe the main advantage of rule-governed behavior over contingency-shaped behavior. What are two disadvantages to rule-governed behavior?
17. What is a personal rule? What is Say-Do correspondence, and how is it related to the effectiveness of personal rules for controlling behavior?
18. What is a personal process rule (or implementation intention)? Why (in terms of bright boundaries) are personal process rules particularly effective?

CONCEPT REVIEW

grammar. The rules that control the meaning of a sequence of language symbols.

observational learning. An observer gains information from a modeled behavior and then can use that information to modify his or her *own* behavior.

personal process rule. A personal rule that indicates the specific process by which a task is to be accomplished. (Also referred to as an *implementation intention.*)

personal rule (or self-instruction). A verbal description of a contingency that we present to ourselves in order to influence our behavior.

productivity. The ability of language users to combine language symbols in new and creative ways.

reference. The ability to associate arbitrary symbols with objects or events.

rule. A verbal description of a contingency.

rule-governed behavior. Behavior that has been generated through exposure to rules.

Say-Do correspondence. A close match between what we say we are going to do and what we actually do at a later point in time.

situational freedom. Language can be used in a variety of contexts and is not fixed in a particular situation.

stimulus enhancement. Directing attention to a particular place or object, making it more likely that the observer will approach that place or object.

true imitation. Duplicating a novel behavior (or sequence of behaviors) in order to achieve a specific goal.

vicarious emotional response. A classically conditioned emotional response that results from seeing that emotional response exhibited by others.

CHAPTER TEST

9. Many animal species, when shown a sequence of actions designed to extract food from a locked box, (do/do not) _____ duplicate the sequence exactly. This suggests that few species exhibit true _____.

22. The name of the first artificial language employed in language-learning studies with apes is _____.

1. Improving your golf game by watching a video of an excellent golf player is a form of _____ learning.

14. Knowing that the phrase "dog bites man" means the opposite of "man bites dog" suggests that you know the _____ of the English language.

20. Artificial language experiments taught (laboratory-constructed/ASL) _____ languages to apes.

19. At the start of each day, Victoria carefully plans out her studying for the day, writing down what she will study as well as when and where she will study. Although she is not always successful in fulfilling these plans, she usually accomplishes most of what she sets out to do. Her success is likely due to the fact that she is making use of personal _____ rules that establish a(n) _____ boundary between acceptable and unacceptable patterns of behavior.

4. If Claire observes her friend David laughing while enjoying a game of table tennis, she is (more/less) _____ likely to try the game herself. If Claire observes David frowning while he struggles over a math problem, she is (more/less) _____ likely to tackle the problem herself.

26. A rule that includes information about how we should respond is called a(n) _____.

32. "I should sit straight while working on the computer if I wish to prevent back problems." This is an example of a(n) _____ rule (or self-_____).

10. If a dog sees another dog eating at a particular location, it is more likely to visit that location later. This is an example of _____.

15. Your ability to discuss plans for an upcoming vacation means that language has the feature of _____.

21. Cross-fostering studies taught (laboratory-constructed/gestural) _____ languages (such as ASL) to apes.

3. The stimuli involved in the classical conditioning aspect of observational learning are often (emotional/rational) _____ in nature.

8. Tina tells herself each day that she will study, but she rarely succeeds in doing so. This illustrates a lack of _____ correspondence, which also means that, in general, she may have difficulty in using _____ rules to control her behavior.

18. American Sign Language is a (spoken/written/symbolic) _____ language.

27. A big advantage of rules is that one (has to/does not have to) _____ directly experience a set of contingencies in order to behave appropriately with respect to those contingencies.

2. Observational learning involves both _____ and _____ conditioning.

12. A belief that language in humans is (innate/learned) _____ also implies that animals may be able to learn and use language.

29. Joel is very noncompliant. Chances are that he has been reinforced for (following/not following) _____ instructions and/or punished for (following/not following) _____ instructions.

11. Directing a person's or animal's attention to an object or place is called _____; duplicating the actions of a model to obtain a goal is called _____.

23. Results of artificial language experiments (do/do not) _____ provide strong support for the notion that most apes can master the rules of grammar.

17. Although chimpanzees cannot (speak/use sign language) _____, they have been taught to successfully (speak/use sign language) _____.

30. When Salima's mom became ill with a neurological disorder, Salima was assigned the task of giving her a daily massage to loosen up her tense muscles. By contrast, Byron has taken several massage workshops. Interestingly, Byron is much less skillful at massage than Salima, which may reflect the fact that _____ behavior is sometimes less efficient than behavior that has been shaped through direct exposure to the natural _____.

6. Rob is a great admirer of his new friend, Mario. If Mario's favorite sport is wrestling, Rob is (more/less) _____ likely to watch wrestling on television.

13. The word "cat" stands for four-legged furry animals that meow. This illustrates the concept of _____.

28. Children are reinforced for following instructions, both by their caretakers and by the fact that instructions can help them accomplish a task. As a result, most children acquire a (generalized/specific) _____ tendency to follow instructions.

7. If a juvenile rat watches its mother eat a novel food, like chocolate chips, the young rat is (more/less) _____ likely to try the chocolate chips.

25. A(n) _____ can be defined as a verbal description of a contingency, while _____ behavior is the behavior that is generated by such verbal descriptions.

31. Kent read somewhere that women are very attracted to a man who acts strong and dominant. In spite of his efforts to appear strong and dominant, he is eventually dumped by every woman he meets. He nevertheless assumes that there must be something wrong with these women and persists in cultivating his heroic image. Kent's problem may reflect the fact that _____ behavior is sometimes surprisingly insensitive to the actual contingencies of reinforcement.

16. Your ability to write a short story for your creative writing class illustrates the _____ characteristic of language.

5. If a model is reinforced for performing a behavior, an observer is (more/less) _____ likely to perform the same behavior; if a model is punished for performing a behavior, an observer is (more/less) _____ likely to perform the same behavior.

24. Results of artificial language experiments suggest that dolphins (can/cannot)_____ master the rules of grammar.

ANSWERS TO CHAPTER TEST

1. observational
2. classical; operant
3. emotional
4. more; less
5. more; less
6. more
7. more
8. imitate
9. do not; imitation
10. stimulus enhancement
11. stimulus enhancement; imitation
12. learned
13. reference
14. grammar
15. situational freedom
16. productivity
17. speak; use sign language
18. symbolic
19. was
20. laboratory-constructed
21. gestural
22. Yerkish
23. do not
24. can
25. rule; rule-governed
26. instruction
27. does not have to
28. generalized
29. not following; following
30. rule-governed; contingencies
31. rule-governed
32. personal; instruction
33. Say-Do; personal
34. process; bright

References

Adams, L. A., & Rickert, V. I. (1989). Reducing bedtime tantrums: Comparison between positive routines and graduated extinction. *Pediatrics, 84,* 585–588.

Ader, R., & Cohen, N. (1975). Behaviorally conditioned immunosuppression. *Psychosomatic Medicine, 37,* 333–340.

Ainslie, G. (1975). Specious reward: A behavioral theory of impulsiveness and impulse control. *Psychological Bulletin, 82,* 463–496.

Ainslie, G. (1986). Beyond microeconomics: Conflict among interests in a multiple self as a determinant of value. In J. Elster (Ed.), *The multiple self.* Cambridge, UK: Cambridge University Press.

Ainslie, G. (1992). *Picoeconomics: The strategic intervention of successive motivational states within the person.* Cambridge, UK: Cambridge University Press.

Ainslie, G., & Haendel, V. (1983). The motives of the will. In E. Gottheil, A. T. McLellan, & K. Druley (Eds.), *Etiologic aspects of alcohol and drug abuse.* Springfield, IL: Charles C. Thomas.

Allison, J. (1983). *Behavioral economics.* New York: Praeger.

Amabile, T. M., Hennessey, B. A., & Grossman, B. S. (1986). Social influences on creativity: The effects of contracted-for reward. *Journal of Personality and Social Psychology, 50,* 14–23.

American Psychiatric Association. (1994). *Diagnostic and statistical manual of mental disorders* (4th ed.). Washington, DC: Author.

Anderson, C. M., Hawkins, R. P., Freeman, K. A., & Scotti, J. R. (2000). Private events: Do they belong in a science of human behavior. *The Behavior Analyst, 23,* 1–10.

Antonitis, J. J. (1951). Response variability in the white rat during conditioning, extinction, and reconditioning. *Journal of Experimental Psychology, 42,* 273–281.

Assagioli, R. (1974). *The act of will.* New York: Penguin.

Axelrod, S., & Apsche, J. (Eds.). (1983). *The effects of punishment on human behavior*. New York: Academic Press.

Axelrod, S., Hall, R. V., Weiss, L., & Rohrer, S. (1974). Use of self-imposed contingencies to reduce the frequency of smoking behavior. In M. J. Mahoney & C. E. Carlson (Eds.), *Self-control: Power to the person*. Monterey, CA: Brooks/Cole.

Azrin, N. H., & Holz, W. C. (1966). Punishment. In W. K. Honig (Ed.), *Operant behavior: Areas of research and application*. New York: Appleton.

Azrin, N. H., Hutchinson, R. R., & Hake, D. F. (1966). Extinction-induced aggression. *Journal of the Experimental Analysis of Behavior, 9*, 191–204.

Baeninger, R., & Ulm, R. R. (1969). Overcoming the effects of prior punishment on inter-species aggression in the rat. *Journal of Comparative and Physiological Psychology, 69*, 628–635.

Bailey, D. W., Howery, L. D., & Boss, D. L. (2000). Effects of social facilitation for locating feeding sites by cattle in an eight-arm radial maze. *Applied Animal Behaviour Science, 68*, 93–105.

Baker, T. B., & Cannon, D. S. (1979). Taste aversion therapy with alcoholics: Techniques and evidence of a conditioned response. *Behaviour Research and Therapy, 17*, 229–242.

Balderston, J. L. (1924). *A morality play for the leisured class*. New York: Appleton.

Baldwin, J. D., & Baldwin, J. I. (1998). *Behavior principles in everyday life* (3rd ed.). Upper Saddle River, NJ: Prentice Hall.

Bandura, A. (1973). *Aggression: A social learning analysis*. Englewood Cliffs, NJ: Prentice Hall.

Bandura, A. (1975). Effecting change through participant modeling. In J. D. Krumboltz & C. E. Thoresen (Eds.), *Counseling methods*. New York: Holt, Rinehart & Winston.

Bandura, A. (1976). Self-reinforcement: Theoretical and methodological considerations. *Behaviorism, 4*, 135–155.

Bandura, A. (1977). *Social learning theory*. Englewood Cliffs, NJ: Prentice Hall.

Bandura, A. (1986). *Social foundations of thought and action: A social cognitive theory*. Upper Saddle River, NJ: Prentice Hall.

Bandura, A. (1997). *Self-efficacy: The exercise of self-control*. New York: W. H. Freeman.

Bandura, A., Blanchard, E. B., & Ritter, B. (1969). The relative efficacy of desensitization and modeling approaches for inducing behavioral, affective, and attitudinal changes. *Journal of Personality and Social Psychology, 13*, 173–199.

Bandura, A., & McDonald, F. J. (1994). Influence of social reinforcement and the behavior of models in shaping children's moral judgments. In B. Puka (Ed.), *Defining perspectives in moral development. Moral development: A compendium* Vol. 1. New York: Garland Publishing.

Barlow, D. H. (1988). *Anxiety and its disorders: The nature and treatment of anxiety and panic*. New York: Guilford Press.

Barlow, D. H., & Hersen, M. (1984). *Single-case experimental designs: Strategies for studying behavior change* (2nd ed.). New York: Pergamon.

Baron, R. A., & Byrne, D. (1997). *Social psychology* (8th ed.). Boston: Allyn & Bacon.

Barrett, B. (1931). *The strength of will and how to develop it.* New York: R. R. Smith.

Baum, W. M. (1974). On two types of deviation from the matching law: Bias and undermatching. *Journal of the Experimental Analysis of Behavior, 22,* 231–242.

Baum, W. M. (1979). Matching, undermatching, and overmatching in studies of choice. *Journal of the Experimental Analysis of Behavior, 32,* 269–281.

Baum, W. M. (1994). *Understanding behaviorism: Science, behavior, and culture.* New York: HarperCollins.

Begun, D. R. (1999). Hominid family values: Morphological and molecular data on relations among the great apes and humans. In S. T. Parker, R. W. Mitchell, & H. L. Miles (Eds.), *The mentalities of gorillas and orangutans: Comparative perspectives.* Cambridge, UK: Cambridge University Press.

Beneke, W. M., Schulte, S. E., & Vander Tuig, J. G. (1995). An analysis of excessive running in the development of activity anorexia. *Physiology and Behavior, 58,* 451–457.

Beneke, W. M., & Vander Tuig, J. G. (1996). Effects of dietary protein and food restriction on voluntary running of rats living in activity wheels. In W. F. Epling & W. D. Pierce (Eds.), *Activity anorexia: Theory, research, and treatment.* Mahwah, NJ: Erlbaum.

Bentall, R. P., Lowe, C. F., & Beasty, A. (1985). The role of verbal behavior in human learning: II. Developmental differences. *Journal of the Experimental Analysis of Behavior, 43,* 165–180.

Bernstein, I. L. (1991). Aversion conditioning in response to cancer and cancer treatment. *Clinical Psychology Review, 11,* 185–191.

Beumont, P. J. W., Booth, A. L., Abraham, S. F., Griffiths, D. A., & Turner, T. R. (1983). Temporal sequence of symptoms in patients with anorexia nervosa: A preliminary report. In P. L. Darby, P. E. Garfinkel, D. M. Garner, & D. V. Coscina (Eds.), *Anorexia nervosa: Recent developments in research.* New York: Liss.

Billet, E. A., Richter, M. A., & Kennedy, J. L. (1998). Genetics of obsessive-compulsive disorder. In R. P. Swinson, M. M. Antony, S. Rachman, & M. A. Richter (Eds.), *Obsessive-compulsive disorder: Theory, research, and treatment.* New York: Guilford Press.

Bjork, D. W. (1993). *B. F. Skinner: A life.* New York: Basic Books.

Blandin, Y., Lhuisset, L., & Proteau, L. (1999). Cognitive processes underlying observational learning of motor skills. *Quarterly Journal of Experimental Psychology: Human Experimental Psychology, 52A,* 957–979.

Boer, D. P. (1989). Determinants of excessive running in activity-anorexia. Unpublished doctoral dissertation, University of Alberta, Edmonton, Alberta.

Boer, D. P., Epling, W. F., Pierce, W. D., & Russell, J. C. (1990). Suppression of food deprivation-induced high-rate wheel running in rats. *Physiology and Behavior, 48,* 339–342.

Bolles, R. C. (1970). Species-specific defense reactions and avoidance learning. *Psychological Review, 77,* 32–48.

Bolles, R. C. (1979). *Learning theory* (2nd ed.). New York: Holt, Rinehart and Winston.

Bootzin, R. R., Epstein, D., & Wood, J. M. (1991). Stimulus control instructions. In P. J. Hauri (Ed.), *Case studies in insomnia.* New York: Plenum Press.

Bovbjerg, D. H., Redd, W. H., Maier, L. A., Holland, J. C., Lesko L. M., Niedzwiecki, D., Rubin, S. C., & Hakes, T. B. (1990). Anticipatory immune suppression and nausea in women receiving cyclic chemotherapy for ovarian cancer. *Journal of Consulting and Clinical Psychology, 58,* 153–157.

Braun, B. G. (1980). Hypnosis for multiple personalities. In H. J. Wain (Ed.), *Clinical hypnosis in medicine.* Chicago: Yearbook Medical.

Bregman, E. O. (1934). An attempt to modify the emotional attitudes of infants by the conditioned response technique. *Journal of Genetic Psychology, 45,* 169–198.

Breland, K., & Breland, M. (1961). The misbehavior of organisms. *American Psychologist, 16,* 681–684.

Brethower, D. M., & Reynolds, G. S. (1962). A facilitative effect of punishment on unpunished responding. *Journal of the Experimental Analysis of Behavior, 5,* 191–199.

Brigham, T. A. (1978). Self-control. In A. C. Catania & T. A. Brigham (Eds.), *Handbook of Applied Behavior Analysis.* New York: Irvington.

Broberg, D. J., & Bernstein, I. L. (1987). Candy as a scapegoat in the prevention of food aversions in children receiving chemotherapy. *Cancer, 60,* 2344–2347.

Brown, P. L., & Jenkins, H. M. (1968). Autoshaping of the pigeon's key-peck. *Journal of the Experimental Analysis of Behavior, 11,* 1–8.

Brown, S. A., Stetson, B. A., & Beatty, P. A. (1989). Cognitive and behavioral features of adolescent coping in high-risk drinking situations. *Addictive Behaviors, 14,* 43–52.

Bruch, H. (1978). *The golden cage: The enigma of anorexia nervosa.* Cambridge, MA: Harvard University Press.

Buckley, K. W. (1989). *Mechanical man: John Broadus Watson and the beginnings of behaviorism.* New York: Guilford Press.

Bullock, D. H., & Smith, W. C. (1953). An effect of repeated conditioning-extinction upon operant strength. *Journal of Experimental Psychology, 46,* 349–352.

Burns, M., & Domjan, M. (1996). Sign tracking versus goal tracking in the sexual conditioning of male Japanese quail (*Coturnix japonica*). *Journal of Experimental Psychology: Animal Behavior Processes, 22,* 297–306.

Buske-Kirschbaum, A., Kirschbaum, C., Stierle, H., Jabaij, L., & Hellhammer, D. (1994). Conditioned manipulation of natural killer (NK) cells in humans using a discriminative learning protocol. *Biological Psychology, 38,* 143–155.

Bussey, K., & Bandura, A. (1984). Influence of gender constancy and social power on sex-linked modeling. *Journal of Personality and Social Psychology, 47*, 1292–1302.

Byrne, D., & Clore, G. L. (1970). A reinforcement model of evaluative responses. *Personality: An International Journal, 1*, 103–128.

Call, J. (1999). Levels of imitation and cognitive mechanisms in orangutans. In S. T. Parker, R. W. Mitchell, & H. L. Miles (Eds.), *The mentalities of gorillas and orangutans: Comparative perspectives*. Cambridge, UK: Cambridge University Press.

Call, J., & Tomasello, M. (1995). The use of social information in the problem-solving of orangutans (*Pongo pygmaeus*) and human children (*Homo sapiens*). *Journal of Comparative Psychology, 109*, 308–320.

Cameron, J. (in press). Negative effects of reward on intrinsic motivation—A limited phenomenon: Comment on Deci, Koestner, and Ryan (2001). *Review of Educational Research*.

Cameron, J., & Pierce, W. D. (1994). Reinforcement, reward, and intrinsic motivation: A meta-analysis. *Review of Educational Research, 64*, 363–423.

Capaldi, E. D. (1996). Conditioned food preferences. In E. D. Capaldi (Ed.), *Why we eat what we eat: The psychology of eating*. Washington, DC: American Psychological Association.

Capaldi, E. J. (1966). Partial reinforcement: A hypothesis of sequential effects. *Psychological Review, 73*, 459–477.

Capaldi, E. J., Miller, D. J., & Alptekin, S. (1989). Multiple-food-unit-incentive effect: Nonconservation of weight of food reward by rats. *Journal of Experimental Psychology: Animal Behavior Processes, 15*, 75–80.

Carroll, W. R., & Bandura, A. (1987). Translating cognition into action: The role of visual guidance in observational learning. *Journal of Motor Behavior, 19*, 385–398.

Casey, R., & Rozin, P. (1989). Changing children's food preferences: Parent opinions. *Appetite, 12*, 171–182.

Catania, A. C. (1975). The myth of self-reinforcement. *Behaviorism, 3*, 192–199.

Catania, A. C. (1988). The operant behaviorism of B. F. Skinner. In A. C. Catania & S. Harnad (Eds.), *The selection of behavior: The operant behaviorism of B. F. Skinner: Comments and consequences*. New York: Cambridge University Press.

Chance, P. (1994). *Learning and behavior* (3rd ed.). Pacific Grove, CA: Brooks/Cole.

Cheney, D. L., & Seyfarth, R. M. (1986). The recognition of social alliances by vervet monkeys. *Animal Behavior, 34*, 1722–1731.

Cherek, D. R. (1982). Schedule-induced cigarette self-administration. *Pharmacology, Biochemistry, and Behavior, 17*, 523–527.

Chomsky, N. (1988). *Language and problems of knowledge*. Cambridge, MA: MIT Press.

Cialdini, R. B. (1993). *Influence: Science and practice* (3rd ed.). New York: HarperCollins.

Clark, H. B., Rowbury, T., Baer, A. M., & Baer, D. M. (1973). Timeout as a punishing stimulus in continuous and intermittent schedules. *Journal of Applied Behavior Analysis, 6,* 443–455.

Clark, L. A., Watson, D., & Mineka, S. (1994). Temperament, personality, and the mood and anxiety disorders. *Journal of Abnormal Psychology, 103,* 103–116.

Conger, R., & Killeen, P. (1974). Use of concurrent operants in small group research. *Pacific Sociological Review, 17,* 399–416.

Cook, M., & Mineka, S. (1989). Observational conditioning of fear to fear-relevant versus fear-irrelevant stimuli in rhesus monkeys. *Journal of Abnormal Psychology, 98,* 448–459.

Craig, G. J., Kermis, M. D., & Digdon, N. L. (1998). *Children today* (Canadian ed.). Scarborough, Canada: Prentice Hall.

Crespi, L. P. (1942). Quantitative variation of incentive and performance in the white rat. *American Journal of Psychology, 55,* 467–517.

Danaher, B. G. (1977). Rapid smoking and self-control in the modification of smoking behavior. *Journal of Consulting and Clinical Psychology, 45,* 1068–1075.

Davey, G. C. L. (1992). Classical conditioning and the acquisition of human fears and phobias: A review and synthesis of the literature. *Advances in Behaviour Research and Therapy, 14,* 29–66.

Davis, C., Katzman, D. K., & Kirsh, C. (1999). Compulsive physical activity in adolescents with anorexia nervosa: A psychobehavioral spiral of pathology. *Journal of Nervous and Mental Disease, 187,* 336–342.

Deci, E. L., & Ryan, R. M. (1985). *Intrinsic motivation and self-determination in human behavior.* New York: Plenum Press.

Deci, E. L., Koestner, R., & Ryan, R. M. (in press). Extrinsic rewards and intrinsic motivation: Reconsidered once again. *Review of Educational Research.*

Delk, J. L. (1980). High-risk sports as indirect self-destructive behavior. In N. L. Farberow (Ed.), *The many faces of suicide: Indirect self-destructive behavior.* New York: McGraw-Hill.

Dinsmoor, J. A. (1954). Punishment: I. The avoidance hypothesis. *Psychological Review, 61,* 34–46.

Domjan, M. (1998). *The principles of learning and behavior* (4th ed.). Pacific Grove, CA: Brooks/Cole.

Dowling, J. E. (1984). Modeling effectiveness as a function of learner-model similarity and the learner's attitude toward women. *Dissertation Abstracts International, 45*(1-A), 121.

Doyle, T. F., & Samson, H. H. (1988). Adjunctive alcohol drinking in humans. *Physiology and Behavior, 44,* 775–779.

Dweck, C. S., & Reppucci, N. D. (1973). Learned helplessness and reinforcement responsibility in children. *Journal of Personality & Social Psychology, 25,* 109–116.

Eisenberg, N., McCreath, H., & Ahn, R. (1988). Vicarious emotional responsiveness and prosocial behavior: Their interrelations in young children. *Personality and Social Psychology Bulletin, 14,* 298–311.

Eisenberger, R. (1992). Learned industriousness. *Psychological Review, 99,* 248–267.

Eisenberger, R., Carlson, J., Guile, M., & Shapiro, N. (1979). Transfer of effort across behaviors. *Learning and Motivation, 10,* 178–197.

Eisenberger, R., Masterson, F. A., & McDermitt, M. (1982). Effects of task variety on generalized effort. *Journal of Educational Psychology, 74,* 499–505.

Ellis, N. R. (1962). Amount of reward and operant behavior in mental defectives. *American Journal of Mental Deficiency, 66,* 595–599.

Epling, W. F., & Pierce, W. D. (1988). Activity-based anorexia: A biobehavioral perspective. *International Journal of Eating Disorders, 7,* 475–485.

Epling, W. F., & Pierce, W. D. (1991). *Solving the anorexia puzzle: A scientific approach.* Toronto, Canada: Hogrefe & Huber.

Epling, W. F., & Pierce, W. D. (1996a). An overview of activity anorexia. In W. F. Epling & W. D. Pierce (Eds.), *Activity anorexia: Theory, research, and treatment.* Mahwah, NJ: Erlbaum.

Epstein, R. (1985). Extinction-induced resurgence: Preliminary investigations and possible applications. *Psychological Record, 35,* 143–153.

Epstein, R. (1997). Skinner as self-manager. *Journal of Applied Behavior Analysis, 30,* 545–568.

Epstein, S. M. (1967). Toward a unified theory of anxiety. In B. A. Maher (Ed.), *Progress in experimental personality research* (Vol. 4). New York: Academic Press.

Ericsson, K. A., & Charness, N. (1994). Expert performance: Its structure and acquisition. *American Psychologist, 49,* 725–747.

Ericsson, K. A., Krampe, R. Th., & Tesch-Römer, C. (1993). The role of deliberate practice in the acquisition of expert performance. *Psychological Review, 100,* 363–406.

Esterson, A. (1993). *Seductive mirage: An exploration of the work of Sigmund Freud.* Chicago: Open Court.

Estes, W. K., & Skinner, B. F. (1941). Some quantitative properties of anxiety. *Journal of Experimental Psychology, 29,* 390–400.

Etscorn, F., & Stephens, R. (1973). Establishment of conditioned taste aversions with a 24-hour CS-US interval. *Physiological Psychology, 1,* 251–259.

Exton, M. S., von Auer, A. K., Buske-Kirschbaum, A., Stockhorst, U., Gobel, U., & Schedlowski, M. (2000). Pavlovian conditioning of immune function: Animal investigation and the challenge of human application. *Behavioural Brain Research, 110,* 129–141.

Eysenck, H. J. (1957). *The dynamics of anxiety and hysteria: An experimental application of modern learning theory to psychiatry.* London: Routledge & Kegan Paul.

Eysenck, H. J. (1967). *The biological basis of personality.* Springfield, IL: Charles C. Thomas.

Eysenck, H. J. (1968). A theory of the incubation of anxiety/fear response. *Behaviour Research and Therapy, 6,* 63–65.

Eysenck, H. J. (1976). The learning theory model of neurosis—A new approach. *Behaviour Research and Therapy, 14,* 251–267.

Falk, J. L. (1961). Production of polydipsia in normal rats by an intermittent food schedule. *Science, 133*, 195–196.

Falk, J. L. (1971). The nature and determinants of adjunctive behavior. *Physiology and Behavior, 6*, 577–588.

Falk, J. L. (1977). The origin and functions of adjunctive behavior. *Animal Learning and Behavior, 5*, 325–335.

Falk, J. L. (1993). Schedule-induced drug self-administration. In F. van Haaren (Ed.), *Methods in behavioral pharmacology.* Amsterdam: Elsevier.

Falk, J. L. (1998). Drug abuse as an adjunctive behavior. *Drug and Alcohol Dependence, 52*, 91–98.

Falk, J. L. (1994). Schedule-induced behavior occurs in humans: A reply to Overskeid. *Psychological Record, 44*, 45–62.

Fanselow, M. S., DeCola, J. P., & Young, S. L. (1993). Mechanisms responsible for reduced contextual conditioning with massed unsignaled unconditional stimuli. *Journal of Experimental Psychology: Animal Behavior Processes, 19*, 121–137.

Ferguson, E., & Cassaday, H. J. (1999). The gulf war and illness by association. *British Journal of Psychology, 90*, 459–475.

Ferster, C. B., & Skinner, B. F. (1957). *Schedules of reinforcement.* New York: Appleton-Century-Crofts.

Flory, R. K., & Ellis, B. B. (1973). Schedule-induced aggression against a slide-image target. *Bulletin of the Psychonomic Society, 2*, 287–290.

Foa, E. B., Franklin, M. E., & Kozak, M. J. (1998). Psychosocial treatments for obsessive-compulsive disorder: Literature review. In R. P. Swinson, M. M. Antony, S. Rachman, & M. A. Richter (Eds.), *Obsessive-compulsive disorder: Theory, research, and treatment.* New York: Guilford Press.

Foa, E. B., Zinbarg, R., & Rothbaum, B. O. (1992). Uncontrollability and unpredictability in post-traumatic stress disorder: An animal model. *Psychological Bulletin, 112*, 218–238.

Fouts, G. R., & Click, M. (1979). Effects of live and TV models on observational learning in introverted and extroverted children. *Perceptual and Motor Skills, 48*, 863–867.

Fouts, R. S. (1973). Acquisition and testing of gestural signs in four young chimpanzees. *Science, 180*, 978–980.

Fox, L. (1962). Effecting the use of efficient study habits. *Journal of Mathematics, 1*, 75–86.

Franks, C. M. (1963). Behavior therapy, the principles of conditioning and the treatment of the alcoholic. *Quarterly Journal of Studies on Alcohol, 24*, 511–529.

Furomoto, L. (1971). Extinction in the pigeon after continuous reinforcement: Effects of number of reinforced responses. *Psychological Reports, 28*, 331–338.

Galef, B. G., Jr. (1988). Imitation in animals: History, definition and interpretation of data from the psychological laboratory. In T. R. Zentall & B. G. Galef, Jr. (Eds.), *Social learning: Psychological and biological perspectives.* Hillsdale, NJ: Erlbaum.

Galef, B. G., Jr. (1996). Social influences on food preferences and feeding behaviors of vertebrates. In E. D. Capaldi (Ed.), *Why we eat what we eat: The psychology of eating.* Washington, DC: American Psychological Association.

Galef, B. G., Jr., Whiskin, E. E., & Horn, C. S. (1999). What observer rats don't learn about foods from demonstrator rats. *Animal Learning and Behavior, 27,* 316–322.

Gandhi, M. K. (1957). *An autobiography: The story of my experiments with truth.* Boston: Beacon Press. (Original work published 1927)

Garcia, J., & Koelling, R. A. (1966). Relation of cue to consequence in avoidance learning. *Psychonomic Science, 4,* 123–124.

Gardner, H. (1993). *Multiple intelligences: The theory in practice.* New York: Basic Books.

Gardner, R. A., & Gardner, B. T. (1969). Teaching sign language to a chimpanzee. *Science, 165,* 664–672.

Gardner, R. A., & Gardner, B. T. (1975). Evidence for sentence constituents in the early utterances of child and chimpanzee. *Journal of Experimental Psychology: General, 104,* 244–267.

Gardner, R. A., Gardner, B. T., & Van Cantfort, T. E. (1989). *Teaching sign language to chimpanzees.* New York: State University of New York Press.

Garner, D. M., & Garfinkel, P. E. (1980). Socio-cultural factors in the development of anorexia nervosa. *Psychological Medicine, 10,* 647–656.

Gay, P. (1988). *Freud: A life for our time.* New York: Norton.

Gibeault, S., & MacDonald, S. E. (2000). Spatial memory and foraging competition in captive western lowland gorillas (*Gorilla gorilla gorilla*). *Primates, 4,* 147–160.

Gleaves, D. H. (1996). The sociocognitive model of dissociative identity disorder: A reexamination of the evidence. *Psychological Bulletin, 120,* 42–59.

Gold, S. R., Fultz, J., Burke, C. H., & Prisco, A. G. (1992). Vicarious emotional responses of macho college males. *Journal of Interpersonal Violence, 7,* 165–174.

Gollwitzer, P. M. (1999). Implementation intentions: Strong effects of simple plans. *American Psychologist, 54,* 493–503.

Gollwitzer, P. M., & Brandstätter, V. (1997). Implementation intentions and effective goal pursuit. *Journal of Personality and Social Psychology, 73,* 186–199.

Goodall, J. (1990). *Through a window: My thirty years with the chimpanzees of Gombe.* Boston: Houghton Mifflin.

Gottman, J. (1994). *Why marriages succeed or fail: And how you can make yours last.* New York: Simon & Schuster.

Gray, J. (1999). Ivan Petrovich Pavlov and the conditioned reflex. *Brain Research Bulletin, 50,* 433.

Green, L., Fisher, E. B., Perlow, S., & Sherman, L. (1981). Preference reversal and self control: Choice as a function of reward amount and delay. *Behaviour Analysis Letters, 1,* 43–51.

Guevremont, D. C., Osnes, P. G., & Stokes, T. F. (1986). Preparation for effective self-regulation: The development of generalized verbal control. *Journal of Applied Behavior Analysis, 19,* 99–104.

Guthrie, E. R. (1952). *The psychology of learning* (Rev. ed.). New York: Harper & Row. (Original work published 1935)

Hagopian, L. P., Fisher, W. W., & Legacy, S. M. (1994). Schedule effects of noncontingent reinforcement on attention-maintained destructive behavior in identical quadruplets. *Journal of Applied Behavior Analysis, 27,* 317–325.

Hall, G. C. N., Shondrick, D. D., & Hirschman, R. (1993). Conceptually derived treatments for sexual aggressors. *Professional Psychology: Research and Practice, 24,* 62–69.

Hanson, H. M. (1959). Effects of discrimination training on stimulus generalization. *Journal of Experimental Psychology, 58,* 321–334.

Harackiewicz, J. M., Manderlink, G., & Sansone, C. (1984). Rewarding pinball wizardry: Effects of evaluation and cue value on intrinsic interest. *Journal of Personality and Social Psychology, 47,* 287–300.

Harlow, H. F., Harlow, M. K., & Meyer, D. R. (1950). Learning motivated by a manipulative drive. *Journal of Experimental Psychology, 40,* 228–234.

Haupt, E. J., Van Kirk, M. J., & Terraciano, T. (1975). An inexpensive fading procedure to decrease errors and increase retention of number facts. In E. Ramp & G. Semb (Eds.), *Behavior analysis: Areas of research and application.* Englewood Cliffs, NJ: Prentice Hall.

Hayes, K. J., & Hayes, C. (1951). The intellectual development of a home-raised chimpanzee. *Proceedings of the American Philosophical Society, 95,* 105–109.

Hayes, S. C., Rosenfarb, I., Wulfert, E., Munt, E. D., Korn, Z., & Zettle, R. D. (1985). Self-reinforcement effects: An artifact of social standard setting? *Journal of Applied Behavior Analysis, 18,* 201–214.

Heffernan, T., & Richards, C. S. (1981). Self-control of study behavior: Identification and evaluation of natural methods. *Journal of Counseling Psychology, 28,* 361–364.

Hergenhahn, B. R. (1988). *An introduction to theories of learning* (3rd ed.). Englewood Cliffs, NJ: Prentice Hall.

Herman, J. L. (1992). *Trauma and recovery.* New York: Basic Books.

Herman, L. M., & Forestell, P. H. (1985). Reporting presence or absence of named objects by a language-trained dolphin. *Neuroscience and Biobehavioral Reviews, 9,* 667–681.

Herman, L. M., Kuczaj, S. A., & Holder, M. D. (1993). Responses to anomalous gestural sequences by a language-trained dolphin: Evidence for processing of semantic relations and syntactic information. *Journal of Experimental Psychology: General, 122,* 184–194.

Herman, L. M., Morrel-Samuels, P., & Pack, A. A. (1990). Bottlenosed dolphin and human recognition of veridical and degraded video displays of an artificial gestural language. *Journal of Experimental Psychology: General, 119,* 215–230.

Herman, L. M., Pack, A. A., & Morrel-Samuels, P. (1993). Representational and conceptual skills of dolphins. In H. L. Roitblat, L. M. Herman, and P. E. Nachtigall (Eds.), *Language and communication: Comparative perspectives.* Hillsdale, NJ: Erlbaum.

Herrnstein, R. J. (1961). Relative and absolute strength of response as a function of frequency of reinforcement. *Journal of the Experimental Analysis of Behavior, 4,* 267–272.

Herrnstein, R. J. (1966). Superstition: A corollary of the principle of operant conditioning. In W. K. Honig (Ed.), *Operant behavior: Areas of research and application.* New York: Appleton-Century-Crofts.

Herrnstein, R. J. (1969). Method and theory in the study of avoidance. *Psychological Review, 76,* 49–69.

Herrnstein, R. J. (1981). Self-control as response strength. In C. M. Bradshaw, E. Szabadi, & C. F. Lowe (Eds.), *Recent developments in the quantification of steady-state operant behavior.* Amsterdam: Elsevier/North Holland Biomedical Press.

Herrnstein, R. J. (1990). Rational choice theory: Necessary but not sufficient. *American Psychologist, 45,* 356–367.

Herrnstein, R. J. (1997). *The matching law: Papers in psychology and economics.* Cambridge, MA: Harvard University Press.

Herrnstein, R. J., & Heyman, G. M. (1979). Is matching compatible with reinforcement maximization on concurrent variable interval, variable ratio? *Journal of the Experimental Analysis of Behavior, 31,* 209–223.

Herrnstein, R. J., & Hineline, P. N. (1966). Negative reinforcement as shock-frequency reduction. *Journal of the Experimental Analysis of Behavior, 9,* 421–430.

Herrnstein, R. J., & Loveland, D. H. (1975). Maximizing and matching on concurrent ratio schedules. *Journal of the Experimental Analysis of Behavior, 24,* 107–116.

Hinson, R. E., & Poulos, C. X. (1981). Sensitization to the behavioral effects of cocaine: Modification by Pavlovian conditioning. *Pharmacology, Biochemistry, and Behavior, 15,* 559–562.

Hobhouse, L. T. (1901). *Mind in evolution.* London: Macmillan.

Hockett, C. D. (1960). The origin of speech. *Scientific American, 203,* 88–96.

Hollis, K. L. (1997). Contemporary research on Pavlovian conditioning: A "new" functional analysis. *American Psychologist, 52,* 956–965.

Hothersall, D. (1984). *History of psychology.* New York: Random House.

Houston, A. (1986). The matching law applies to wagtails foraging in the wild. *Journal of the Experimental Analysis of Behavior, 45,* 15–18.

Hull, C. L. (1932). The goal gradient hypothesis and maze learning. *Psychological Review, 39,* 25–43.

Hull, C. L. (1934). The rat's speed-of-locomotion gradient in the approach to food. *Journal of Comparative Psychology, 17,* 393–422.

Hull, C. L. (1943). *Principles of behavior.* New York: Appleton-Century-Crofts.

Hygee, S. (1978). The observer's acquaintance with the model's stimulus in vicarious classical conditioning. *Scandinavian Journal of Psychology, 19,* 231–239.

Jacobson, E. (1938). *Progressive relaxation* (2nd ed.). Chicago: University of Chicago Press.

James, W. (1907). The energies of men. *The Philosophical Review, 16*, 1–20.

James, W. (1983). *The principles of psychology*. Cambridge, MA: Harvard University Press. (Original work published 1890)

Jenkins, H. M., Barrera, F. J., Ireland, C., & Woodside, B. (1978). Signal-centered action patterns of dogs in appetitive classical conditioning. *Learning and Motivation, 9*, 272–296.

Jenkins, H. M., & Moore, B. R. (1973). The form of the autoshaped response with food or water reinforcers. *Journal of the Experimental Analysis of Behavior, 20*, 163–181.

Jones, M. C. (1924). The elimination of children's fears. *Journal of Experimental Psychology, 7*, 382–390.

Kalat, J. W. (1974). Taste salience depends on novelty, not concentration, in taste-aversion learning in the rat. *Journal of Comparative and Physiological Psychology, 86*, 47–50.

Kamin, L. J. (1969). Predictability, surprise, attention and conditioning. In B. A. Campbell & R. M. Church (Eds.), *Punishment and aversive behavior*. New York: Appleton-Century-Crofts.

Kaplan, H. I., Sadock, B. J., & Grebb, J. A. (1994). *Kaplan and Sadock's synopsis of psychiatry* (7th ed.). Baltimore: Williams and Wilkins.

Katcher, A. H., Solomon, R. L., Turner, L. H., LoLordo, V. M., Overmier, J. B., & Rescorla, R. A. (1969). Heart-rate and blood pressure responses to signaled and unsignaled shocks: Effects of cardiac sympathectomy. *Journal of Comparative and Physiological Psychology, 68*, 163–174.

Katz, J. L. (1986). Long-distance running, anorexia nervosa, and bulimia: A report of two cases. *Comprehensive Psychiatry, 27*, 74–78.

Katz, J. L. (1996). Clinical observations on the physical activity of anorexia nervosa. In W. F. Epling & W. D. Pierce (Eds.), *Activity anorexia: Theory, research, and treatment*. Mahwah, NJ: Erlbaum.

Kawamura, S. (1963). The process of sub-cultural propagation among Japanese macaques. In C. H. Southwick (Ed.), *Primate social behavior*. New York: Van Nostrand.

Kazdin, A. E. (1994). *Behavior modification in applied settings* (5th ed.). Pacific Grove, CA: Brooks/Cole.

Keith-Lucas, T., & Guttman, N. (1975). Robust single-trial delayed backward conditioning. *Journal of Comparative and Physiological Psychology, 88*, 468–476.

Kelleher, R. T., & Fry, W. (1962). Stimulus functions in chained fixed-interval schedules. *Journal of the Experimental Analysis of Behavior, 5*, 167–173.

Kellogg, W. N., & Kellogg, L. A. (1933). *The ape and the child*. New York: McGraw-Hill.

Kimble, G. A. (1961). *Hilgard and Marquis' conditioning and learning* (Rev. ed.). New York: Appleton-Century-Crofts.

Kimble, G. A. (1967). *Foundations of conditioning and learning*. New York: Appleton-Century-Crofts.

Klein, S. B. (1996). *Learning: Principles and applications* (3rd ed.). New York: McGraw-Hill.

Kleinke, C. L., Meeker, G. B., & Staneske, R. A. (1986). Preference for opening lines: Comparing ratings by men and women. *Sex Roles, 15,* 585–600.

Klinger, E. (1975). Consequences of commitment to and disengagement from incentives. *Psychological Review, 82,* 1–25.

Klinger, E., Barta, S. G., & Kemble, E. D. (1974). Cyclic activity changes during extinction in rats: A potential model for depression. *Animal Learning and Behavior, 2,* 313–316.

Kluft, R. P. (1998). The argument for the reality of delayed recall of trauma. In P. S. Appelbaum, L. A. Uyehara, & M. R. Elin (Eds.), *Trauma and memory: Clinical and legal controversies.* New York: Oxford University Press.

Kohlenberg, R. J. (1973). Behavioristic approach to multiple personality: A case study. *Behavior Therapy, 4,* 137–140.

Kohlenberg, R. J., & Tsai, M. (1991). *Functional analytic psychotherapy: Creating intense and curative therapeutic relationships.* New York: Plenum Press.

Kohler, W. (1939). Simple structural function in the chimpanzee and the chicken. In W. D. Ellis (Ed.), *A course book of gestalt psychology.* New York: Harcourt Brace. (Original work published 1918)

Kohn, A. (1993). *Punished by rewards.* Boston: Houghton Mifflin.

Kossoff, M. J. (1999, March/April). Gary Player: Swinging hard on life's course. *Psychology Today, 32,* 58–61, 78, 82.

Lakein, A. (1973). *How to get control of your time and your life.* New York: New American Library.

Lang, W. J., Ross, P., & Glover, A. (1967). Conditional responses induced by hypotensive drugs. *European Journal of Pharmacology, 2,* 169–174.

Lepper, M. R., Green, D., & Nisbett, R. E. (1973). Undermining children's intrinsic interest with extrinsic reward: A test of the "overjustification" hypothesis. *Journal of Personality and Social Psychology, 28,* 129–137.

Lerman, D. C., & Iwata, B. A. (1996). Developing a technology for the use of operant extinction in clinical settings: An examination of basic and applied research. *Journal of Applied Behavior Analysis, 29,* 345–382.

Levin, J. D. (1990). *Alcoholism: A bio-psycho-social approach.* New York: Hemisphere Publishing Corporation.

Levis, D. J. (1989). The case for a return to a two factor theory of avoidance: The failure of non-fear interpretations. In S. B. Klein & R. R. Mowrer (Eds.), *Contemporary learning theories: Pavlovian conditioning and the status of learning theory.* Hillsdale, NJ: Erlbaum.

Levis, D. J. (1995). Decoding traumatic memory: Implosive theory of psychopathology. In W. O'Donohue & L. Krasner (Eds.), *Theories of behavior therapy: Exploring behavior change.* Washington, DC: American Psychological Association.

Levis, D. J., & Boyd, T. L. (1979). Symptom maintenance: An infrahuman analysis and extension of the conservation of anxiety principle. *Journal of Abnormal Psychology, 88,* 107–120.

Levitsky, D., & Collier, G. (1968). Schedule-induced wheel running. *Physiology and Behavior, 3,* 571–573.

Lewes, G. H. (1965). *The life of Goethe.* New York: Frederick Ungar.

Lewinsohn, P. M. (1974). A behavioral approach to depression. In R. J. Friedman & M. M. Katz (Eds.), *The psychology of depression: Contemporary theory and research*. New York: Winston/Wiley.

Lichstein, K. L., & Riedel, B. W. (1994). Behavioral assessment and treatment of insomnia: A review with an emphasis on clinical application. *Behavior Therapy, 25*, 659–688.

Lichtenstein, E., & Glasgow, R. E. (1977). Rapid smoking: Side effects and safeguards. *Journal of Consulting and Clinical Psychology, 45*, 815–821.

Lieberman, D. A. (2000). *Learning: Behavior and cognition* (3rd ed.). Belmont, CA: Wadsworth.

Lilienfeld, S. O., Kirsch, I., Sarbin, T. R., Lynn, S. J., Chaves, J. F., Ganaway, G. K., & Powell, R. A. (1999). Dissociative identity disorder and the sociocognitive model: Recalling the lessons of the past. *Psychological Bulletin, 125*, 507–523.

Linnoila, M., Stapleton, J. M., Lister, R., Guthrie, S., & Eckhardt, M. (1986). Effects of alcohol on accident risk. *Pathologist, 40*, 36–41.

Loftus, E. F. (1993). The reality of repressed memories. *American Psychologist, 48*, 518–537.

Logue, A. W., Ophir, I., & Strauss, K. E. (1981). The acquisition of taste aversions in humans. *Behaviour Research and Therapy, 19*, 319–333.

Lowe, C. F. (1979). Determinants of human operant behavior. In M. D. Zeller & P. Harzem (Eds.), *Reinforcement and the organization of behavior*. New York: John Wiley.

Lowe, C. F., Beasty, A., & Bentall, R. P. (1983). The role of verbal behavior in human learning: Infant performance on fixed-interval schedules. *Journal of the Experimental Analysis of Behavior, 39*, 157–164.

Lubow, R. E., & Gewirtz, J. C. (1995). Latent inhibition in humans: Data, theory, and implications for schizophrenia. *Psychological Bulletin, 117*, 87–103.

MacDonald, S. E., & Agnes, M. (1999). Orangutan (*Pongo pygmaeus*) spatial memory and foraging strategies. *Journal of Comparative Psychology, 113*, 213–217.

Mackintosh, N. J. (1975). A theory of attention: Variations in the associability of stimuli with reinforcement. *Psychological Review, 82*, 276–298.

Maier, S. F., Jackson, R. L., & Tomie, A. (1987). Potentiation, overshadowing, and prior exposure to inescapable shock. *Journal of Experimental Psychology: Animal Behavior Processes, 13*, 260–270.

Malott, R. W., Malott, M. E., & Trojan, E. A. (2000). *Elementary principles of behavior* (4th ed.). Upper Saddle River, NJ: Prentice Hall.

Marks, I. M. (1969). *Fears and phobias*. New York: Academic Press.

Marlatt, G. A., & Gordon, J. R. (Eds.). (1985). *Relapse prevention: Maintenance strategies in addictive behavior change*. New York: Guilford.

Marrazzi, M. A., & Luby, E. D. (1986). An auto-addiction opioid model of chronic anorexia nervosa. *International Journal of Eating Disorders, 5*, 191–208.

Marsh, G., & Johnson, R. (1968). Discrimination reversal following learning without "errors." *Psychonomic Science, 10,* 261–262.

Martin, G., & Pear, J. (1999). *Behavior modification: What it is and how to do it* (6th ed.). Upper Saddle River, NJ: Prentice Hall.

Maslow, A. H. (1971). *The farther reaches of human nature.* New York: Viking Press.

Masserman, J. H. (1943). *Behavior and neurosis: An experimental psychoanalytic approach to psychobiologic principles.* Chicago: University of Chicago Press.

Masters, J. C., Burish, T. G., Hollon, S. D., & Rimm, D. C. (1987). *Behavior therapy: Techniques and empirical findings* (3rd ed.). New York: Harcourt Brace Jovanovich.

Mazur, J. E., & Logue, A. W. (1978). Choice in a self-control paradigm: Effects of a fading procedure. *Journal of the Experimental Analysis of Behavior, 30,* 11–17.

McCusker, C. G., & Brown, K. (1990). Alcohol-predictive cues enhance tolerance to and precipitate "craving" for alcohol in social drinkers. *Journal of Studies on Alcohol, 51,* 494–499.

Miles, H. L. W. (1990). The cognitive foundations for reference in a signing orangutan. In S. T. Parker & K. R. Gibson (Eds.), *"Language" and intelligence in monkeys and apes.* Cambridge, UK: Cambridge University Press.

Miles, H. L. W. (1994). ME CHANTEK: The development of self-awareness in a signing orangutan. In S. T. Parker, R. W. Mitchell, & M. L. Boccia (Eds.), *Self-awareness in animals and humans: Developmental perspectives.* Cambridge, UK: Cambridge University Press.

Miles, H. L. W. (1999). Symbolic communication with and by great apes. In S. T. Parker, R. W. Mitchell, & H. L. Miles (Eds.), *The mentalities of gorillas and orangutans: Comparative perspectives.* Cambridge, UK: Cambridge University Press.

Miller, H. L. (1976). Matching-based hedonic scaling in the pigeon. *Journal of the Experimental Analysis of Behavior, 26,* 335–347.

Miller, L. K. (1997). *Principles of everyday behavior analysis* (3rd ed.). Pacific Grove, CA: Brooks/Cole.

Miller, N. E. (1960). Learning resistance to pain and fear: Effects of overlearning, exposure, and rewarded exposure in context. *Journal of Experimental Psychology, 60,* 137–145.

Miller, N. E., & Dollard, J. (1941). *Social learning and imitation.* New Haven, CT: Yale University Press.

Miltenberger, R. G. (1997). *Behavior modification: Principles and procedures.* Pacific Grove, CA: Brooks/Cole.

Mindell, J. A. (1999). Empirically supported treatments in pediatric psychology: Bedtime refusal and night wakings in young children. *Journal of Pediatric Psychology, 24,* 465–481.

Mineka, S. (1985). Animal models of anxiety-based disorder: Their usefulness and limitations. In A. H. Tuma & J. Maser (Eds.), *Anxiety and the anxiety disorders.* Hillsdale, NJ: Erlbaum.

Mineka, S. (1987). A primate model of phobic fears. In H. Eysenck & I. Martin (Eds.), *Theoretical foundations of behavior therapy*. New York: Plenum Press.

Mineka, S., & Cook, M. (1993). Mechanisms involved in the observational conditioning of fear. *Journal of Experimental Psychology: General, 122,* 23–38.

Mineka, S., Gunnar, M., & Champoux, M. (1986). Control and early socio-emotional development: Infant rhesus monkeys reared in controllable versus uncontrollable environments. *Child Development, 57,* 1241–1256.

Mischel, W. (1966). Theory and research on the antecedents of self-imposed delay of reward. In B. A. Maher (Ed.), *Progress in experimental personality research* (Vol. 3). New York: Academic Press.

Mischel, W. (1974). Processes in delay of gratification. In L. Berkowitz (Ed.), *Advances in experimental social psychology* (Vol. 7). New York: Academic Press.

Monte, C. F. (1999). *Beneath the mask: An introduction to theories of personality* (6th ed.). New York: Harcourt Brace.

Morgan, C. L. (1894). *An introduction to comparative psychology*. London: W. Scott.

Morse, A. D., Russell, J. C., Hunt, T. W., Wood, G. O., Epling, W. F., & Pierce, W. D. (1995). Diurnal variation of intensive running in food-deprived rats. *Canadian Journal of Physiology and Pharmacology, 73,* 1519–1523.

Mowrer, O. H. (1947). On the dual nature of learning: A reinterpretation of "conditioning" and "problem-solving." *Harvard Educational Review, 17,* 102–150.

Mowrer, O. H. (1960). *Learning theory and behavior*. New York: Wiley.

Mowrer, O. H., & Jones, H. (1945). Habit strength as a result of the pattern of reinforcement. *Journal of Experimental Psychology, 35,* 293–311.

Mukerjee, M. (1997, February). Trends in animal research. *Scientific American, 272,* 86–93. New York: Harper & Row.

Nagel, K., Olguin, K., & Tomasello, M. (1993). Processes of social learning in the tool use of chimpanzees (*Pan troglodytes*) and human children (*Homo sapiens*). *Journal of Comparative Psychology, 107,* 174–186.

Newman, A., & Kanfer, F. H. (1976). Delay of gratification in children: The effects of training under fixed, decreasing and increasing delay of reward. *Journal of Experimental Child Psychology, 21,* 12–24.

Newman, L. S., & Baumeister, R. F. (1996). Toward an explanation of the UFO abduction phenomenon: Hypnotic elaboration, extraterrestrial sado-masochism, and spurious memories. *Psychological Inquiry, 7,* 99–126.

Newsom, C., Favell, J., & Rincover, A. (1983). The side effects of punishment. In S. Axelrod & J. Apsche (Eds.), *The effects of punishment on human behavior*. New York: Academic Press.

O'Brien, R. M., Figlerski, R. W., Howard, S. R., & Caggiano, J. (1981, August). The effects of multi-year, guaranteed contracts on the performance of pitchers in major league baseball. Paper presented at the annual meeting of the American Psychological Association, Los Angeles, CA.

Obrist, P. A., Sutterer, J. R., & Howard, J. L. (1972). Preparatory cardiac changes: A psychobiological approach. In A. H. Black & W. F. Prokasy (Eds.), *Classical conditioning II: Current research and theory.* New York: Appleton-Century-Crofts.

Ofshe, R., & Watters, E. (1994). *Making monsters: False memories, psychotherapy, and sexual hysteria.* New York: Scribners.

Öhman, A., Eriksson, A., Fredrikson, M., Hugdahl, K., & Olfsson, S. (1974). Habituation of the electrodermal orienting reaction to potentially phobic and supposedly neutral stimuli in normal human subjects. *Biological Psychology, 2,* 85–93.

Ono, K. (1987). Superstitious behavior in humans. *Journal of the Experimental Analysis of Behavior, 47,* 261–271.

Öst, L. (1989). One-session treatment for specific phobias. *Behaviour Research and Therapy, 27,* 1–7.

Patterson, F. G., & Linden, E. (1981). *The education of Koko.* New York: Holt, Rinehart & Winston.

Pavlov, I. P. (1927). *Conditioned reflexes* (G. V. Anrep, Trans.). London: Oxford University Press.

Pavlov, I. P. (1928). *Lectures on conditioned reflexes.* (W. H. Gantt, Trans.). New York: International Publishers.

Pavlov, I. P. (1941). *Conditioned reflexes and psychiatry.* New York: International Publishers.

Pendergrast, M. (1995). *Victims of memory: Incest accusations and shattered lives.* Hinesburg, VT: Upper Access.

Pepperberg, I. M. (1999). *The Alex studies: Cognitive and communicative abilities of grey parrots.* Cambridge, MA: Harvard University Press.

Pepperberg, I. M., & Sherman, D. (2000). Proposed use of two-part interactive modeling as a means to increase functional skills in children with a variety of disabilities. *Teaching and Learning in Medicine, 12,* 213–220.

Perin, C. T. (1942). Behavior potentiality as a joint function of the amount of training and the degree of hunger at the time of extinction. *Journal of Experimental Psychology, 30,* 93–113.

Phelps, B. J. (2000). Dissociative identity disorder: The relevance of behavior analysis. *Psychological Record, 50,* 235–249.

Pierce, W. D., & Epling, W. F. (1995). *Behavior analysis and learning.* Englewood Cliffs, NJ: Prentice Hall.

Pierce, W. D., & Epling, W. F. (1996). Theoretical developments in activity anorexia. In W. F. Epling & W. D. Pierce (Eds.), *Activity anorexia: Theory, research, and treatment.* Mahwah, NJ: Erlbaum.

Pierce, W. D., & Epling, W. F. (1999). *Behavior analysis and learning* (2nd ed.). Upper Saddle River, NJ: Prentice Hall.

Pinker, S. (1994). *The language instinct: How the mind creates language.* New York: William Morrow.

Pliskoff, S. S. (1963). Rate change effects with equal potential reinforcements during the "warning" stimulus. *Journal of the Experimental Analysis of Behavior, 6,* 557–562.

Poling, A., Nickel, M., & Alling, K. (1990). Free birds aren't fat: Weight gain in captured wild pigeons maintained under laboratory conditions. *Journal of the Experimental Analysis of Behavior, 53,* 423–424.

Powell, R. A., & Boer, D. P. (1994). Did Freud mislead patients to confabulate memories of abuse? *Psychological Reports, 74,* 1283–1298.

Powell, R. A., & Boer, D. P. (1995). Did Freud misinterpret reported memories of sexual abuse as fantasies? *Psychological Reports, 77,* 563–570.

Powell, R. A., & Gee, T. L. (1999). The effects of hypnosis on dissociative identity disorder: A reexamination of the evidence. *Canadian Journal of Psychiatry, 44,* 914–916.

Premack, D. (1965). Reinforcement theory. In D. Levine (Ed.), *Nebraska Symposium on Motivation* (Vol. 13). Lincoln, NE: University of Nebraska Press.

Premack, D. (1971). Catching up with common sense or two sides of a generalization: Reinforcement and punishment. In R. Glaser (Ed.), *The nature of reinforcement.* New York: Academic Press.

Premack, D. (1971). Language in a chimpanzee? *Science, 172,* 808–822.

Premack, D. (1976). *Intelligence in ape and man.* Hillsdale, NJ: Erlbaum.

Premack, D., & Woodruff, G. (1978). Chimpanzee problem-solving: A test for comprehension. *Science, 202,* 532–535.

Pryor, K. (1975). *Lads before the wind: Adventures in porpoise training.* New York: Harper & Row.

Pryor, K. (1999). *Don't shoot the dog: The new art of teaching and training* (Rev. ed.). New York: Bantam Books.

Rachlin, H. (1974). Self-control. *Behaviorism, 2,* 94–107.

Rachlin, H. (1978). A molar theory of reinforcement schedules. *Journal of the Experimental Analysis of Behavior, 30,* 345–360.

Rachlin, H. (1991). *Introduction to modern behaviorism* (3rd ed.). New York: W. H. Freeman.

Rachlin, H., & Baum, W. M. (1972). Effects of alternative reinforcement: Does the source matter? *Journal of the Experimental Analysis of Behavior, 18,* 231–241.

Rachlin, H., & Green, L. (1972). Commitment, choice and self-control. *Journal of the Experimental Analysis of Behavior, 17,* 15–22.

Rachman, S. (1977). The conditioning theory of fear-acquisition: A critical examination. *Behaviour Research and Therapy, 15,* 375–387.

Rachman, S., & Hodgson, R. J. (1968). Experimentally induced "sexual fetishism": Replication and development. *Psychological Record, 18,* 25–27.

Rachman, S., & Hodgson, R. J. (1980). *Obsessions and compulsions.* Englewood Cliffs, NJ: Prentice Hall.

Rathus, S. A., Nevid, J. S., & Fichner-Rathus, L. (2000). *Human sexuality in a world of diversity* (4th ed.). Boston: Allyn & Bacon.

Remington, B., Roberts, P., & Glautier, S. (1997). The effect of drink familiarity on tolerance. *Addictive Behaviors, 22,* 45–53.

Rescorla, R. A., & Wagner, A. R. (1972). A theory of Pavlovian conditioning: Variations in the effectiveness of reinforcement and nonreinforcement. In A. H. Black & W. F. Prokasy (Eds.), *Classical conditioning II: Current research and theory.* New York: Appleton-Century-Crofts.

Reynolds, G. S. (1961). Behavioral contrast. *Journal of the Experimental Analysis of Behavior, 4,* 57–71.

Reynolds, G. S. (1975). *A primer of operant conditioning* (2nd ed.). Glenview, IL: Scott, Foresman.

Rickert, V. I., & Johnson, C. M. (1988). Reducing nocturnal awakening and crying episodes in infants and young children: A comparison between scheduled awakenings and systematic ignoring. *Pediatrics, 81,* 203–212.

Riley, A. L., & Clarke, C. M. (1977). Conditioned taste aversions: A bibliography. In L. M. Barker, M. R. Best, & M. Domjan (Eds.), *Learning mechanisms in food selection.* Waco, TX: Baylor University Press.

Robins, L. N. (1974). A follow-up study of Vietnam veterans' drug use. *Journal of Drug Issues, 4,* 61–63.

Rogers, C. R. (1959). A theory of therapy, personality, and interpersonal relationships, as developed in the client-centered framework. In S. Koch (Ed.), *Psychology: A study of a science* (Vol. 3). New York: McGraw-Hill.

Roitblat, H. L., Herman, L. M., and Nachtigall, P. E. (Eds.) (1993). *Language and communication: Comparative perspectives.* Hillsdale, NJ: Erlbaum.

Ross, C. A. (1997). *Dissociative identity disorder: Diagnosis, clinical features, and treatment of multiple personality* (2nd ed.). New York: John Wiley & Sons.

Ross, C. A., & Norton, G. R. (1989). Effects of hypnosis on the features of multiple personality disorder. *American Journal of Clinical Hypnosis, 32,* 99–106.

Routtenberg, A., & Kuznesof, A. W. (1967). Self-starvation of rats living in activity wheels on a restricted food schedule. *Journal of Comparative and Physiological Psychology, 64,* 414–421.

Rumbaugh, D. M. (Ed.) (1977). *Language learning by a chimpanzee: The LANA project.* San Diego, CA: Academic Press.

Russell, J. C., Amy, R. M., Manickavel, V., Dolphin, P. J., Epling, W. F., Pierce, W. D., & Boer, D. P. (1989). Prevention of myocardial disease in JCR:LA-corpulent rats by running. *Journal of Applied Physiology, 66,* 1649–1655.

Russell, J. C., & Morse, A. D. (1996). The induction and maintenance of hyperactivity during food restriction in rats. In W. F. Epling & W. D. Pierce (Eds.), *Activity anorexia: Theory, research, and treatment.* Mahwah, NJ: Erlbaum.

Russell, M., Dark, K. A., Cummins, R. W., Ellman, G., Callaway, E., & Peeke, H. V. S. (1984). Learned histamine release. *Science, 225,* 733–734.

Russon, A. E., & Galdikas, B. M. F. (1993). Imitation in ex-captive orangutans. *Journal of Comparative Psychology, 107,* 147–161.

Russon, A. E., & Galdikas, B. M. F. (1995). Constraints on great apes' imitation: Model and action selectivity in rehabilitant orangutan (*Pongo pygmaeus*) imitation. *Journal of Comparative Psychology, 109,* 5–17.

Salkovskis, P. M. (1998). Psychological approaches to the understanding of obsessional problems. In R. P. Swinson, M. M. Antony, S. Rachman, & M. A. Richter (Eds.), *Obsessive-compulsive disorder: Theory, research, and treatment.* New York: Guilford Press.

Savage-Rumbaugh, E. S. (1993). Language learnability in man, ape and dolphin. In H. L. Roitblat, L. M. Herman, & P. E. Nachtigall (Eds.), *Language and communication: Comparative perspectives.* Hillsdale, NJ: Erlbaum.

Savage-Rumbaugh, E. S., & Lewin, R. (1994). *Kanzi: The ape at the brink of the human mind.* New York: Wiley & Sons.

Savage-Rumbaugh, E. S., McDonald, K., Sevcik, R. A., Hopkins, W. D., & Rubert, E. (1986). Spontaneous symbol acquisition and communicative use by pygmy chimpanzees (*Pan paniscus*). *Journal of Comparative Psychology, 115,* 211–235.

Savage-Rumbaugh, E. S., Rumbaugh, D. M., Smith, S. T., & Lawson, J. (1980). Reference: The linguistic essential. *Science, 210,* 922–925.

Savage-Rumbaugh, E. S., Shanker, S. G., & Taylor, T. J. (1998). *Apes, language and the human mind.* New York: Oxford University Press.

Schafe, G. E., & Bernstein, I. L. (1996). Taste aversion learning. In E. D. Capaldi (Ed.), *Why we eat what we eat: The psychology of eating.* Washington, DC: American Psychological Association.

Schmidt, R. A., & Bjork, R. A. (1992). New conceptualizations of practice: Common principles in three paradigms suggest new concepts for training. *Psychological Science, 3,* 207–217.

Schreiber, F. R. (1973). *Sybil.* Chicago: Henry Regnery.

Schusterman, R. J., & Gisiner, R. (1988). Artificial language comprehension in dolphins and sea lions: The essential cognitive skills. *Psychological Record, 38,* 311–348.

Seligman, M. E. P. (1971). Phobias and preparedness. *Behavior Therapy, 2,* 307–320.

Seligman, M. E. P. (1975). *Helplessness: On depression, development, and death.* San Francisco: Freeman.

Seligman, M. E. P., & Maier, S. (1967). Failure to escape traumatic shock. *Journal of Experimental Psychology, 74,* 1–9.

Seligman, M. E. P., Rosellini, R. A., & Kozak, M. J. (1975). Learned helplessness in the rat: Time course, immunization, and reversibility. *Journal of Comparative and Physiological Psychology, 88,* 542–547.

Seyfarth, R. M., Cheney, D. L., & Marler, P. (1980). Monkey responses to three different alarm calls: Evidence for predator classification and semantic communication. *Science, 210,* 801–803.

Shea, C. H., Wright, D. L., Wulf, G., & Whitacre, C. (2000). Physical and observational practice afford unique learning opportunities. *Journal of Motor Behavior, 32,* 27–36.

Sheeran, P., & Orbell, S. (1999). Implementation intentions and repeated behaviour: Augmenting the predictive validity of the theory of planned behaviour. *European Journal of Social Psychology, 29*, 349–369.

Shoda, Y., Mischel, W., & Peake, P. K. (1990). Predicting adolescent cognitive and self-regulatory competencies from preschool delay of gratification: Identifying diagnostic conditions. *Developmental Psychology, 26*, 978–986.

Shyan, M. R., & Herman, L. M. (1987). Determinants of recognition of gestural signs in an artificial language by Atlantic bottle-nosed dolphins (*Tursiops truncatus*) and humans (*Homo sapiens*). *Journal of Comparative Psychology, 101*, 112–125.

Sidman, M. (1960). *Tactics of scientific research: Evaluating experimental data in psychology.* New York: Basic Books.

Siegel, S. (1983). Classical conditioning, drug tolerance, and drug dependence. In R. G. Smart, F. B. Glaser, Y. Israel, H. Kalant, R. E. Popham, & W. Schmidt (Eds.), *Research advances in alcohol and drug problems* (Vol. 7). New York: Plenum Press.

Siegel, S. (1984). Pavlovian conditioning and heroin overdose: Reports by overdose victims. *Bulletin of the Psychonomic Society, 22*, 428–430.

Siegel, S. (1989). Pharmacological conditioning and drug effects. In A. J. Goudie & M. W. Emmett-Oglesby (Eds.), *Psychoactive drugs: Tolerance and sensitization.* Clifton, NJ: Humana Press.

Siegel, S., Hinson, R. E., Krank, M. D., & McCully, J. (1982). Heroin "overdose" death: The contribution of drug-associated environmental cues. *Science, 216*, 436–437.

Skinner, B. F. (1938). *The behavior of organisms: An experimental analysis.* Acton, MA: Copley.

Skinner, B. F. (1948a). *Walden II.* New York: Macmillan.

Skinner, B. F. (1948b). "Superstition" in the pigeon. *Journal of Experimental Psychology, 38*, 168–172.

Skinner, B. F. (1950). Are theories of learning necessary? *Psychological Review, 57*, 193–216.

Skinner, B. F. (1953). *Science and human behavior.* New York: Macmillan.

Skinner, B. F. (1956). A case history in scientific method. *American Psychologist, 11*, 221–233.

Skinner, B. F. (1957). *Verbal behavior.* Englewood Cliffs, NJ: Prentice Hall.

Skinner, B. F. (1964). "Man." *Proceedings of the American Philosophical Society, 108*, 482–485.

Skinner, B. F. (1969). *Contingencies of reinforcement: A theoretical analysis.* New York: Appleton-Century-Crofts.

Skinner, B. F. (1971). *Beyond freedom and dignity.* New York: Vintage Books.

Skinner, B. F. (1974). *About behaviorism.* New York: Knopf.

Skinner, B. F. (1983). *A matter of consequences.* New York: Knopf.

Skinner, B. F. (1987). *Upon further reflection.* Englewood Cliffs, NJ: Prentice Hall.

Skinner, B. F. (1989). *Recent issues in the analysis of behavior.* Columbus, OH: Merrill.

Skinner, B. F. (1999). *Cumulative record: Definitive edition.* Acton, MA: Copley.

Skinner, B. F., & Vaughan, M. E. (1983). *Enjoy old age: A program of self-management.* New York: Norton.

Soares, J. J., & Öhman, A. (1993). Backward masking and skin conductance responses after conditioning to nonfeared but fear-relevant stimuli in fearful subjects. *Psychophysiology, 30,* 460–466.

Solomon, R. L. (1980). The opponent-process theory of motivation: The costs of pleasure and the benefits of pain. *American Psychologist, 35,* 691–712.

Solomon, R. L., & Corbit, J. D. (1974). The opponent-process theory of motivation: I. Temporal dynamics of affect. *Psychological Review, 81,* 119–145.

Solomon, R. L., Kamin, L. J., & Wynne, L. C. (1953). Traumatic avoidance learning: The outcomes of several extinction procedures with dogs. *Journal of Abnormal and Social Psychology, 48,* 291–302.

Solomon, R. L., & Wynne, L. C. (1953). Traumatic avoidance learning: Acquisition in normal dogs. *Psychological Monographs, 67* (4, Whole No. 354).

Solomon, R. L., & Wynne, L. C. (1954). Traumatic avoidance learning: The principles of anxiety conservation and partial irreversibility. *Psychological Review, 61,* 353–385.

Spanos, N. P. (1994). Multiple identity enactments and multiple personality disorder: A sociocognitive perspective. *Psychological Bulletin, 116,* 143–165.

Spanos, N. P. (1996). *Multiple identities & false memories: A sociocognitive perspective.* Washington, DC: American Psychological Association.

Spence, K. W. (1937). The differential response in animals to stimuli varying within a single dimension. *Psychological Review, 44,* 430–444.

Spiegler, M. D., & Guevremont, D. C. (1998). *Contemporary behavior therapy* (3rd ed.). Pacific Grove, CA: Brooks/Cole.

Staddon, J. E. R. (1977). Schedule-induced behavior. In W. K. Honig & J. E. R. Staddon (Eds.), *Handbook of operant behavior.* Englewood Cliffs, NJ: Prentice Hall.

Staddon, J. E. R., & Simmelhag, V. L. (1971). The "superstition" experiment: A reexamination of its implications for the principles of adaptive behavior. *Psychological Review, 78,* 3–43.

Stampfl, T. G. (1987). Theoretical implications of the neurotic paradox as a problem in behavior theory: An experimental resolution. *Behavior Analyst, 10,* 161–173.

Steketee, G., & Foa, E. B. (1985). Obsessive-compulsive disorder. In D. H. Barlow (Ed.), *Clinical handbook of psychological disorders: A step-by-step treatment manual.* New York: Guilford Press.

Stevenson-Hinde, J. (1973). Constraints on reinforcement. In R. A. Hinde & J. Stevenson-Hinde (Eds.), *Constraints on learning.* New York: Academic Press.

Symbaluk, D. G. (1996). The effects of food restriction and training on male athletes. In W. F. Epling & W. D. Pierce (Eds.), *Activity anorexia: Theory, research, and treatment*. Mahwah, NJ: Erlbaum.

Tacitus (Trans. 1956). *Annals of imperial Rome* (M. Grant, Trans.). New York: Penguin.

Task Force on Promotion and Dissemination of Psychological Procedures. (1995). Training in and dissemination of empirically-validated psychological treatments. Report and recommendations. *The Clinical Psychologist, 48*, 3–24.

Terrace, H. S. (1963a). Discrimination learning with and without "errors." *Journal of the Experimental Analysis of Behavior, 6*, 1–27.

Terrace, H. S. (1963b). Errorless transfer of a discrimination across two continua. *Journal of the Experimental Analysis of Behavior, 6*, 223–232.

Terrace, H. S. (1979). *Nim*. New York: Knopf.

Terrace, H. S. (1985). On the nature of animal thinking. *Neuroscience and Biobehavioral Reviews, 9*, 643–652.

Terrace, H. S., Petitio, L. A., Sanders, R. J., & Bever, T. G. (1979). Can an ape create a sentence? *Science, 206*, 891–902.

Thigpen, C. H., & Cleckley, H. M. (1957). *The three faces of Eve*. New York: McGraw-Hill.

Thorndike, E. L. (1898). Animal intelligence: An experimental study of the associative processes in animals. *Psychological Review Monograph Supplement, 2*, 1–109.

Thorndike, E. L. (1901). Mental life of monkeys. *Psychological Review Monograph Supplement, 15*, 442–444.

Thorpe, W. H. (1956). *Learning and instinct in animals*. London: Methuen and Company.

Timberlake, W., & Allison, J. (1974). Response deprivation: An empirical approach to instrumental performance. *Psychological Review, 81*, 146–164.

Tinbergen, N. (1951). *The study of instinct*. Oxford: Clarendon Press.

Tolman, E. C. (1932). Purposive behavior in animals and men. New York: Appleton-Century-Crofts.

Tolman, E. C. (1948). Cognitive maps in rats and men. *Psychological Review, 55*, 189–208.

Tolman, E. C., & Honzik, C. H. (1930). Degrees of hunger, reward and non-reward, and maze learning in rats. *University of California Publications in Psychology, 4*, 241–275.

Tomasello, M. (1996). Do apes ape? In B. G. Galef, Jr. & C. M. Heyes (Eds.), *Social learning in animals: The roots of culture*. New York: Academic Press.

Tomie, A. (1995). CAM: An animal learning model of excessive and compulsive implement-assisted drug-taking in humans. *Clinical Psychology Review, 15*, 145–167.

Tomie, A. (1996). Self-regulation and animal behavior. *Psychological Inquiry, 7*, 83–85.

Tomie, A., Brooks, W., & Zito, B. (1989). Sign-tracking: The search for reward. In S. B. Klein & R. R. Mowrer (Eds.), *Contemporary learning theories: Pavlovian conditioning and the status of traditional learning theory*. Hillsdale, NJ: Erlbaum.

Ulrich, R. E., & Azrin, N. A. (1962). Reflexive fighting in response to aversive stimuli. *Journal of the Experimental Analysis of Behavior, 5,* 511–520.

Valentine, C. W. (1930). The innate bases of fear. *Journal of Genetic Psychology, 37,* 394–420.

Van der Kolk, B. A. (1989). The compulsion to repeat the trauma: Re-enactment, revictimization, and masochism. *Psychiatric Clinics of North America, 12,* 389–411.

Vollmer, T. R., & Bourret, J. (2000). An application of the matching law to evaluate the allocation of two- and three-point shots by college basketball players. *Journal of Applied Behavior Analysis, 33,* 137–150.

Wallace, I., & Pear, J. J. (1977). Self-control techniques of famous novelists. *Journal of Applied Behavior Analysis, 10,* 515–525.

Wallace, M., & Singer, G. (1976). Schedule induced behavior: A review of its generality, determinants and pharmacological data. *Pharmacology, Biochemistry, and Behavior, 5,* 483–90.

Watson, D. L., & Tharp, R. G. (1997). *Self-directed behavior: Self-modification for personal adjustment* (7th ed.). Pacific Grove, CA: Brooks/Cole.

Watson, J. B. (1908). Imitation in monkeys. *Psychological Bulletin, 5,* 169–178.

Watson, J. B. (1913). Psychology as the behaviorist views it. *Psychological Review, 20,* 154–177.

Watson, J. B. (1930). *Behaviorism.* New York: Norton.

Watson, J. B., & Rayner, R. (1920). Conditioned emotional reactions. *Journal of Experimental Child Psychology, 3,* 1–14.

Webster, R. (1995). *Why Freud was wrong: Sin, science and psychoanalysis.* New York: Basic Books.

Weindruch, R. (1996, January). Caloric restriction and aging. *Scientific American, 274,* 46–52.

Weiss, H. M., Suckow, K., & Rakestraw, T. L., Jr. (1999). Influence of modeling on self-set goals: Direct and mediated effects. *Human Performance, 12,* 89–114.

Welker, R. L. (1976). Acquisition of a free-operant-appetitive response in pigeons as a function of prior experience with response-independent food. *Learning and Motivation, 7,* 394–405.

Wheatley, K. L., Welker, R. L., & Miles, R. C. (1977). Acquisition of bar-pressing in rats following experience with response-independent food. *Animal Learning and Behavior, 5,* 236–242.

Wheeler, G. (1996). Exercise, sports, and anorexia. In W. F. Epling & W. D. Pierce (Eds.), *Activity anorexia: Theory, research, and treatment*. Mahwah, NJ: Erlbaum.

White, D. J., & Galef, B. G., Jr. (1999). Social effects on mate choices of male Japanese quail, *Coturnix japonica. Animal Behaviour, 57,* 1005–1012.

Whiten, A. (1998). Imitation of the sequential structure of actions by chimpanzees (*Pan troglodytes*). *Journal of Comparative Psychology, 112,* 270–281.

Wilcoxon, H. C., Dragoin, W. B., & Kral, P. A. (1971). Illness-induced aversions in rat and quail: Relative salience of visual and gustatory cues. *Science, 171,* 826–828.

Williams, B. A. (1981). The following schedule of reinforcement as a fundamental determinant of steady state contrast in multiple schedules. *Journal of the Experimental Analysis of Behavior, 35,* 293–310.

Williams, D. R., & Williams, H. (1969). Automaintenance in the pigeon: Sustained pecking despite contingent nonreinforcement. *Journal of the Experimental Analysis of Behavior, 12,* 511–520.

Wilson, C. (1972). *New pathways in psychology: Maslow and the post-Freudian revolution.* New York: Taplinger.

Wilson, G. T. (1997). Behavior therapy at century close. *Behavior Therapy, 28,* 449–457.

Wilson, J. F., & Cantor, M. B. (1987). An animal model of excessive eating: Schedule-induced hyperphagia in food-satiated rats. *Journal of the Experimental Analysis of Behavior, 47,* 335–346.

Wolfe, J. B., & Kaplon, M. D. (1941). Effect of amount of reward and consummative activity on learning in chickens. *Journal of Comparative Psychology, 31,* 353–361.

Wolpe, J. (1958). *Psychotherapy by reciprocal inhibition.* Stanford, CA: Stanford University Press.

Wolpe, J. (1995). Reciprocal inhibition: Major agent of behavior change. In W. O'Donohue & L. Krasner (Eds.), *Theories of behavior therapy: Exploring behavior change.* Washington, DC: American Psychological Association.

Woods, D. J., & Routtenberg, A. (1971). "Self-starvation" in activity wheels: Developmental and chlorpromazine interactions. *Journal of Comparative and Physiological Psychology, 76,* 84–93.

Worthington, E. L. (1979). Behavioral self-control and the contract problem. *Teaching of Psychology, 6,* 91–94.

Yates, A. (1996). Athletes, eating disorders, and the overtraining syndrome. In W. F. Epling & W. D. Pierce (Eds.), *Activity anorexia: Theory, research, and treatment.* Mahwah, NJ: Erlbaum.

Zeiler, M. D. (1971). Eliminating behavior with reinforcement. *Journal of the Experimental Analysis of Behavior, 16,* 401–405.

Zelman, D. C., Brandon, T. H., Jorenby, D. E., & Baker, T. B. (1992). Measures of affect and nicotine dependence predict differential response to smoking cessation treatments. *Journal of Consulting and Clinical Psychology, 60,* 943–952.

Zuriff, G. E. (1975). Where is the agent in behavior? *Behaviorism, 3,* 1–21.

Index

TO THE OWNER OF THIS BOOK:

We hope that you have found *Introduction to Learning and Behavior* useful. So that this book can be improved in a future edition, would you take the time to complete this sheet and return it? Thank you.

School and address: _____

Department: _____

Instructor's name: _____

1. What I like most about this book is: _____

_____

_____

2. What I like least about this book is: _____

_____

_____

3. My general reaction to this book is: _____

_____

4. The name of the course in which I used this book is: _____

_____

5. Were all of the chapters of the book assigned for you to read? _____

   If not, which ones weren't? _____

6. In the space below, or on a separate sheet of paper, please write specific suggestions for improving this book and anything else you'd care to share about your experience in using the book.

_____

_____

_____

_____

_____

Optional:

Your name: _____ Date: _____

May Wadsworth quote you, either in promotion for *Introduction to Learning and Behavior* or in future publishing ventures?

Yes: _____ No: _____

Sincerely,

Russell A. Powell
Diane G. Symbaluk
Suzanne E. MacDonald

FOLD HERE

- -

BUSINESS REPLY MAIL

FIRST CLASS   PERMIT NO. 358   PACIFIC GROVE,CA

POSTAGE WILL BE PAID BY ADDRESSEE

ATT: *Russ Powell, Diane Symbaluk, Suzanne MacDonald*

Brooks/Cole Publishing Company
511 Forest Lodge Road
Pacific Grove, California 93950-9968

- -

FOLD HERE